Geoffrey Butcher has been a [...]
collector for many years, larg[...]
Glenn Miller's AEF Band duri[...]
founded the Glenn Miller Society, which still flourishes today,
and was the originator and first editor of its magazine *The
Moonlight Serenader*. In 1955 he edited and helped to compile
the first Glenn Miller discography ever published. He has also
written numerous magazine articles, record sleeve notes and
radio scripts, and edited several small magazines. After a spell
as a newspaper reporter he became a Chartered Librarian in
the Civil Service, until his early retirement in 1985. He lives in
south-west London.

GEOFFREY BUTCHER

Next to a Letter from Home

Major Glenn Miller's Wartime Band

FOREWORD BY NAT PECK

'Next to a letter from home, Capt. Miller, your organisation is the greatest morale-builder in the ETO.'

Lt.-Gen. James H. Doolittle
Commanding General
US 8th Air Force
29 July 1944

WARNER BOOKS

A *Warner* Book

First published in Great Britain
by Mainstream Publishing in 1986
Published by Sphere Books Ltd in 1987
This revised edition published by Warner Books in 1994
Reprinted 1995

A CIP catalogue record for this book
is available from the British Library.

ISBN 0 7515 1078 5

Printed in England by Clays Ltd, St Ives plc

Warner Books
A Division of
Little, Brown and Company (UK)
Brettenham House
Lancaster Place
London WC2E 7EN

For
Charlie, Denis, Royal, Nat and Bob
and all the men who made the music

Contents

Foreword

It was a sparkling summer morning in 1943. I had just debarked from the train in New Haven fresh from my military basic training centre in North Carolina. Nearing the immense green on my way to the Old Quadrangle of Yale University where I was to report for duty, the incredible sound and vision of a marching band came into focus. The air was vibrant with rich, surging harmonies, the trumpets ablaze, the tuttie impelled by a new and vital cadence. It was the 'Saint Louis Blues' – the Glenn Miller Band was on parade!

Over forty years have gone by since those heady events but the exhilaration of my miraculous good fortune in being chosen to join this formidable array of instrumentalists and writers, mustered and manipulated by the Olympian Alchemist, remains very alive in my memory. We were to make our mark on big band musical history and embark on a mission of morale-boosting essential to the successful pursuit of the war effort by the Allied Forces in the ETO, with significant effect also on the civilian population of the UK, France and as widely on the Continent as our BBC transmitters would permit.

In view of the tremendous impact the Band made during its tour of duty in the European Theatre within the framework of the great events of World War II and considering the undiminished fame of the now legendary Glenn Miller, it is a wonder that this book was not written long ago.

My first meeting with Geoffrey Butcher took place on 26 March 1979, in a north London clinic where I had been recuperating from a cartilage operation. With subsequent meetings, endless discussions, exchanges of views and hours of taped interviews, it became apparent to me that here at last was the writer this book had been waiting for. The long tenure at his post of Deputy Librarian in the Civil Service had endowed Geoffrey Butcher with precisely the qualities required for this task. Here was primarily a labour of love that had been given impetus all those decades ago when our author was exposed to the first Glenn Miller broadcasts from the UK. It still remained a daunting undertaking, calling for a lucid mind, a patient and persevering spirit, and the will to see the job through to the end. I believe that this has been largely achieved and these years of sustained effort have resulted in a remarkable document that will make fascinating reading to fans and connoisseurs all over the world.

NAT PECK
London, May 1986

Preface

By 1944 Glenn Miller's music was already well known far beyond his native United States, particularly in Great Britain, through his civilian Band's records issued by His Master's Voice and prominent roles in two Hollywood musical films – *Sun Valley Serenade* and *Orchestra Wives*. The Miller musical style had been copied by many British bands since Miller records were first issued in Britain in 1939 and the Band had a reputation as the best dance band of the day at a time when dance bands and singers, the 'popular music' of the time, had a wide following among the adult population, unlike today's 'pop' music which attracts mainly teenage audiences. From the technical point of view the Band was admired throughout the British dance music profession. The Miller music was the latest thing in popular music but owing to a Musicians' Union ban on American bands playing in Great Britain the Glenn Miller Band had never performed in Britain.

But while the two films had presented the Band in first-class photography and, more important, sound, many of their records had been pressed on poor quality wartime shellac – so much so that Miller records in particular had achieved a reputation for indifferent quality. Because of this it is probably fair to say that if Glenn Miller had never brought his new forty-piece all-soldier American Band of the Allied Expeditionary Force to Britain during the last year of the Second World War and if all we had ever had were the civilian Band's records, Miller might not have had the posthumous following he has today.

For those who have grown up in the era of high fidelity microgroove LPS, stereophonic sound, and all the rest, and never known a world where 78 rpm records were all we had, it must be very difficult to realise the impact of the new Captain (later Major) Glenn Miller AEF Band *live* on the radio, after years of listening to the civilian Band on scratchy 78s, when the Band made its first appearance on the BBC Home Service on the evening of Thursday 13 July 1944.

It was a revelation.

In the ensuing months the Band, with its star personalities Ray McKinley, Mel Powell and Johnny Desmond, became a huge success, not only with the GIs it had chiefly come to play for but also with the British servicemen and women and, via the radio every week for over a year, with the British public. In the last year of the War in Europe the Band brought what Major Miller called a 'hunk of home' to the millions of Americans serving in the European Theater of Operations. By radio and in person it became for the American troops one of the 'greatest morale-builders in the ETO' and to this day Major Glenn Miller's AEF Band, whose music did so much to raise the spirits of the GIs, is remembered with affection and gratitude by the soldiers and airmen who were then so far from home.

But it wasn't only the Yanks of the ETO who were to remember the music of the Glenn Miller AEF Band. Millions of civilians and servicemen in Britain and other nations throughout Western Europe have never forgotten it either, for the AEF Band was what 'Miller' meant to most people in Britain in the mid-1940s. In the fifty years since Major Miller was lost these memories have continued to burn brightly and this is all the more remarkable considering that no records of the Band were made available to the public until ten years after it ceased to exist at the end of the War.

Despite the shattering loss of Glenn Miller halfway through its European mission, the Band spent thirteen months in the ETO during which it played to Allied troop audiences totalling one and a quarter million throughout Britain, France and occupied Germany and, by radio, to further untold millions in Western Europe – 956 separate performances, an average of nearly three a day – making musical history while history of another kind was daily being made around it.

This is the story of that Band.

GEOFFREY BUTCHER
London, June 1994

Next to a Letter from Home

Major Glenn Miller's Wartime Band

Introduction

I shall never forget the summer of 1944. Life in rural north-west Essex – part of 'American-occupied England' – was dominated by the constant flow of British and American military traffic on our country roads, while overhead roared American bombers flying from airfields throughout East Anglia en route to attack Hitler's Germany. From our local airfield American Marauder bombers flew almost daily missions to the Continent to soften up the Germans in preparation for the long-awaited Second Front – the Allied invasion of German-occupied Western Europe.

Throughout the spring excitement and expectancy increased everywhere as we realised that the invasion, the big offensive to end the War, would soon be launched. When D-Day finally arrived on 6 June everything else seemed to stop. As the news poured in from the Continent over the BBC, the Allied landing was the only topic of conversation and people stayed tuned to their radios as never before.

Listening to the radio during five years of war had become universal, not only for news and Government announcements but also for entertainment. There were two emergency wartime programmes – the Home Service and the General Forces Programme – and as a means of keeping up morale for Forces and civilians alike their value was undisputed. The radio also provided a link with home for the Forces listening overseas.

Radio entertainment had changed gradually since 1942. With the huge influx of American troops and airmen into Britain the BBC had introduced more and more American programmes to the Home Service and the GFP, not only for the Americans but also to acquaint the British public with their temporary visitors. These programmes, recorded in America, were mainly variety and comedy shows and dance music and jazz, such as the Bob Hope and Jack Benny programmes, *Command Performance* and, for jazz and swing fans, *Jubilee and Down Beat*. While nobody would suggest we didn't want ITMA, *The Brains Trust* and others, many of the new American programmes, became very popular with British listeners.

The biggest boost to all this new radio fare came the day after D-Day when the BBC opened its new Allied Expeditionary Forces Programme for the Allied invasion forces. The Programme could also be heard by the civil population over most of Southern England, including, thankfully, my own part of Essex, and I became a devoted listener. Early in July I heard over the radio about a new American service band that was to broadcast at half past eight one Thursday evening – a band having some connection with the famous American bandleader Glenn Miller whose records were often played on the radio – and I resolved to listen if I could.

Came Thursday, and it was a showery summer evening. Between the showers I was in the garden and missed the beginning of the programme but I tuned in in time to hear Captain Glenn Miller chatting with his namesake Sgt Jimmy Miller, leader of the RAF Dance Orchestra, the Squadronaires, who was a guest on the programme. So this *was* the Miller Band! I listened enthralled to the rest of the broadcast and although I was to hear many more for nearly a year I never forgot the first one.

The next few months were full of excitement with dramatic war news of Allied successes and the scintillating entertainment pouring out of the radio. With victory the following spring the massive armies and air forces disappeared from our lives, the AEF programme closed down and the Glenn Miller Band returned to America and became for us all a memory, but a memory undimmed by time. Eventually, ten years after the War, some records of the Band were issued. The memories we had preserved for so long were not shattered but enhanced, flooding back from those wartime days.

Over the years my interest in and enthusiasm for this music has, if anything, increased and I remain convinced that the 'Glenn Miller AEF Orchestra', as it is known to enthusiasts, was by far the best band of its kind ever assembled. 'Of its kind' is, perhaps, slightly inaccurate as the Band itself was as unique as the music it played, and but for the times which produced it it might never have existed at all, at least not in the form it did. Many memories of the Band are inseparable from the times in which it reached its peak, while the mysterious circumstances of the death of its leader have resulted in an amount of legend and mythology which has become attached to no other bandleader in history.

I always hoped to produce some account of the Band and its activities and this book is the result of almost a lifetime's interest. Fragmentary accounts have appeared in magazines, radio programmes, record album notes, and elsewhere, including some of my own early contributions, as well as in Stephen F. Bedwell's *Glenn Miller Discography and Biography** in which I also had a hand. But no full-length book on Miller appeared until 1974 when George T. Simon's lengthy biography† was published. Simon's book, however, is basically a life of Glenn Miller and although it covers Miller's sojourn in England with his AEF Band, it says little about the Band's music and activities and displays some notable misconceptions and leaves gaps in the story of the Band.

This book, therefore, is complementary to George Simon's – not a rival to it but rather a corrective. It is an attempt to take a broad and comprehensive view of the subject – the historian's, perhaps, rather than the journalist's – as other accounts of the Band have been written from the point of view of Miller and the Band, or of the BBC, or of some individual associated with them. I have tried to put the story in the context of the times and to relate it to the military and broadcasting background of those times, which has never been done before, so that the story can be seen, from contemporary records and original sources, in its true light – a light which, I must confess, has become more apparent to me during the later stages of research for this book.

The work is a gathering together of material from many sources. It is based primarily on contemporary official documents, including British and American radio archives (particularly those of the BBC) and US military records, together with published accounts of the Band's activities, reminiscences of people associated with the Band and published soon after events, and present-day recollections by some of the men who played in the Band which have been specially contributed for this book.

It is an attempt to produce an accurate and authoritative account of the Band rather than repeat the many myths and distortions of the past, with special emphasis on its thirteen months in England and on the Continent of Europe. The great majority of the information has never been published before.

Where inconsistencies between the various sources remain they have been noted and discussed, and in this connection mention must be made of two key documents to which I have had access through the courtesy of the US Air Force Museum: some extracts from the wartime Diary of the Band's Executive Officer, Lt Don

* Glenn Miller Appreciation Society, London, 1955.
† Thomas Crowell, New York, 1974; W. H. Allen, London, 1974.

W. Haynes, and the day-to-day 'Activities, American Band of the Supreme Allied Command [later renamed the American Band of the AEF], 8 July, 1944–13 June, 1945' which was originally kept by one of the Band's radio producers, S/Sgt George Voutsas. Both these documents are transcribed copies, not wartime originals, and must be treated, therefore, with appropriate reservations – besides inconsistencies between them, both documents contain errors and omissions. These occur also in the radio archives.

In order to make the book useful as a work of reference as well as a straightforward story it has been divided into two parts: Part 1, a chronological narrative, and Part 2, a complete day-to-day record of all the Band's activities (broadcasts, concerts, recordings, etc.) in Britain and on the Continent. Appendices list various categories of recordings of the Band, both published and unpublished.

Acknowledgements

As usual with this kind of undertaking, thanks are due to many individuals and organizations for help and advice. First, and foremost, I must express my sincere appreciation to five gentlemen in particular, without any one of whom this book would not have materialized, at least in its present form. In chronological order, they are my good friends Charles H. Gallagher, Founder of Friends of the Eighth, who has given continued and invaluable advice and encouragement and has opened many doors and made many introductions; Denis Cottam, who turned over to me his research materials for a similar project and has co-operated with me ever since; Royal D. Frey, former Curator of the US Air Force Museum, who has given enormous help with information and photographs as well as encouragement and introductions and a special contribution to the book; Nat Peck, fourth trombonist with the Band from 1944 to 1945, who has not only given generously of his time and recollections of playing in the Band and has lent photographs, but who also put me in touch with other former members of the Band now in America who in turn have contributed recollections and information; and Bob Ripley, 'cellist with the Band from 1943 to 1945, who has helped enormously with recollections, documentation and photographs. Also, I shall not forget the charming hospitality of Nat and Mrs Peck who kindly entertained me to tea so that I could meet and chat with another veteran of the Band – violinist Emanuel Wishnow, when he and Mrs Wishnow were visiting London. I was also delighted to accept Nat's kind offer to write a Foreword for the book.

To all the musicians who sent contributions by letter and casette I express my sincere thanks: John Halliburton, Bernie Privin, Carmen Mastren who, sadly, passed away suddenly before he could see the results of what he called 'the longest letter I have ever written', and especially Harry Katzman, who also passed away while the book was in preparation, and Ray McKinley, and not forgetting, of course, Nat Peck, Emanuel Wishnow and Bob Ripley.

To Connie and Gordon Richards of Oakley, near Bedford, I owe a great deal for their help and hospitality, and to their friends William Morris, John and Diane Mills and John Hadley, as well as to Miss Anona Moser, who, as an American Red Cross organizer, ran the ARC Enlisted Mens' Clubs in Bedford and later in Paris during the War.

Thanks are also due to those in the various organizations who have willingly placed their resources at my disposal: Mrs J. Kavanagh, Head of the BBC Written Archives Centre, and her staff; Miss Bell and her staff at the Bedford Record Office; Lt-Col Royal D. Frey (US Air Force (Ret.)) and the staff of the US Air Force Museum at Dayton, Ohio; the National Archives, Washington, DC; and Mrs Alice B. Price at the Department of the Air Force, Washington, DC.

In addition, many other individuals have helped in various ways: in particular my old friend Paul Doye whose willing help, often at short notice, has been invaluable in many ways; the late Sir Adrian Boult, Martin Bowman, Syd Cullington, Philip Farlow, Bob Farren, Mark Greenfield, Michael Highton, Col. Robert F. Isbell (USAF (Ret.)), Mark Jones (Manager, BBC Sound Archives), the late Michael Maine, Malcolm Osborne, Alastair Robertson, Brian Vincent, Lt-Col John H. Woolnough (USAF (Ret.)), and especially Michael J. Lee and Charles D. Verrall, both of whom read the manuscript and made many helpful suggestions. My thanks to you all.

GEOFFREY BUTCHER
London

from *Listen to My Music: an autobiography* by Ted Heath (1957). *New Musical Express* for the extract from 'Thirty Years of Dance Music', by Jack Marshall, in *New Musical Express 1954 Annual* (New Musical Express, London, 1953).

Acknowledgements are also due to the following for the use of illustrations: BBC Hulton Picture Library (photos 9, 10, 11, 12, 13); *Bedfordshire Times* (6, 7, 8); Eighth Air Force Historical Society (16, 25, 26); Royal D. Frey (58); Charles H. Gallagher (24); Louis Lawrence (45); Jack Marshall (18, 19, 20, 28, 29, 30, 31, 32, 34, 35, 43); National Broadcasting Company (2, 5); Malcolm Osborne (36, 37); Nat Peck (46, 47, 49, 50, 52, 54); Press Association (17); Ivor Richman (38, 39, 40, 41, 42); Bob Ripley (51); Trustees of the Imperial War Museum (44); U.S. Air Force Museum (1, 14, 15, 21, 22, 23, 27, 33, 48, 53, 55, 56, 57).

Note on the name of the Band

Although it has come to be known since 1955 as the Glenn Miller Army Air Force Band, mainly because of the RCA Victor album of five records, this name is not really correct: in 1944 there was no such thing as the Army Air Force (there were in fact sixteen Army Air Forces, linked by a Headquarters in Washington) and the Band actually belonged to the Training Command of the Army Air Forces for much of its life, undergoing several changes of name during its existence.

First, within the United States Army Air Forces it was originally designated the 418th Army Air Forces Technical Training Command Band, but in July 1943 the word 'Technical' was dropped following the amalgamation of the Flying Training Command and the Technical Training Command. Later (by the spring of 1944) the Band was re-designated Army Air Forces Band (Special) and within the AAF it kept this official designation until it was disbanded in November 1945.

Second, for its broadcasts and public appearances the Band had several other changes of name. For its early *I Sustain the Wings* broadcasts from 29 May to 3 July 1943, it was introduced as the Band of the Army Air Forces Technical Training Command; from 17 July onwards the word 'Technical' was dropped as explained above. In July 1944, after arriving in England, it was re-named the American Band of the Supreme Allied Command; early in August 1944 its name was changed to the American Band of the Allied Expeditionary Force until its departure from the ETO in August 1945. On resuming its work back in the United States in September 1945 it became on radio and records Major Glenn Miller's Army Air Forces Overseas Orchestra until it was disbanded.

Throughout all these official and 'unofficial' changes of name, however, it was the same band, although the personnel changed slightly from time to time. The term 'Glenn Miller Army Air Force Band', although incorrect, has become a convenient overall name, but in Britain it is remembered principally as the American Band of the AEF.

PART ONE

A Narrative History

CHAPTER ONE

First news of the Band in Great Britain – The origins of the Band in the
USA

'The sounds of war are better forgotten. The whine of the 88, the woosh of the
flak, the death-belch of the burp-gun are all where they should be, quiet in the
calm of approximate peace. But, silent among the faded noises of conflict, lies
one sound which will be remembered with affection by the Yanks of the ETO.
It was a warm sentimental sound that poured out of liberated radios behind
the lines, spilled into youth-manned cockpits homing for the bomber and
fighter bases; it was a sound that made apple-cheeked warriors feel closer to
home. This was the music of Major Glenn Miller's American Band of the
AEF.' (Paul Dudley, *Bomblight Serenade*, 1946).

It wasn't only the Yanks of the ETO who were to remember the music
of Major Glenn Miller's American Band of the Allied Expeditionary
Force. Millions of civilians and members of other nations' armed
forces throughout Western Europe have never forgotten it either. For
them, too, the Band's broadcasts were regular dates with their radios
several times a week, every week, throughout the thirteen months
during which the Band's music was heard over the air from the BBC in
London – so much so that the AEF Band was what Miller meant to
most people in Great Britain in the mid-1940s. In the forty-two years
since Major Miller was lost, these memories have continued to burn
brightly, and it is ironic that the AEF Band is better remembered in
Britain and Europe perhaps than in the United States, where the
American public knew little of the Band apart from one or two radio
programmes a week – for most of its life the Band was not even
playing in America but serving overseas in England and on the
continent of Europe. That it should be so well remembered is all the
more remarkable as no gramophone records of it were made publicly
available until ten years after it had returned to the United States and

shortly thereafter broken up as its members were demobilised and returned to civilian life.

The first news in Britain, amid wartime censorship and shortage of newsprint, that Glenn Miller would be coming over from America with his Army Air Forces Band, was contained in a front-page report in the *Melody Maker* of 24 June 1944 (actually on sale on 22 June). Describing BBC radio plans for broadcasting British and American dance music to the Normandy invasion forces, the report continued '. . . it is said that SHAEF are determined to bring suitable artists over here, of the calibre of Bing Crosby, Tommy Dorsey, etc., to appear with British aces on the same programme. We understand that, as forerunners of this idea, Captain Glenn Miller and a 60-piece outfit are said to be already en route for these shores.'

Owing to wartime security no official public announcement of Captain Miller's coming was made, but the following week the next issue of the *Melody Maker* carried on its front page the headline 'GLENN MILLER HAS ARRIVED HERE' and the accompanying report gave the following news:

As exclusively forecast in the *Melody Maker* last week, Glenn Miller – America's great trombone-bandleader, and now a Captain in the Army – has arrived in England.

He turned up very quietly during the week, and his whereabouts are extremely hush-hush. He is to be followed by his 46-piece Army Band, and they will then play concerts for the US troops and also broadcast in the Allied Expeditionary Forces Programme.

It is greatly to be hoped that it will be possible for the BBC to arrange to broadcast this star bunch to home listeners, particularly as we understand very interesting plans for Glenn Miller's visit here include his fronting a British band on the radio – of the calibre of the RAF's 'Squadronaires'.

Glenn Miller's first public appearance in England was in the audience at the London Palladium, where he was observed to enjoy thoroughly the stage presentation of Geraldo and his Orchestra.

Geraldo made an announcement of his presence from the stage and dedicated the Geraldo version of the Miller version of 'Bugle Call Rag' to the distinguished visitor.

Individuals who will be featured with the Miller Band include ex-bandleader, drummer and vocalist, Sergeant Ray McKinley; Sergeant Mel Powell, former soloist with Benny Goodman, composer of 'Mission To Moscow'; Sergeant Jerry Gray, composer of 'String of Pearls'; and Sergeant Broderick Crawford, one of Hollywood's film stars.

Brass section of the outfit will be composed of men from the bands of Artie Shaw; Charlie Barnett; Benny Goodman; Glenn Miller's old Band; and Ray McKinley's Band.

Swing and dance music fans were overjoyed at this se[r]
news, as were the musicians in the dance music professi
only would a live American 'name' band be playing in [B]
for the first time for eleven years (they had been prevent[ed] ....
coming for public engagements by a dispute between the
musicians' unions of Britain and America which did not end until
1956), but it would be conducted by the greatest American
bandleader of the time. Glenn Miller's civilian dance band had
already become very popular with the public through its HMV
records and prominent roles in two Hollywood musical films, the
latest of which, *Orchestra Wives*, had been shown widely in Britain
only the previous year. Furthermore, the Miller musical style
itself had been copied by nearly every British band since Miller
records had begun to be issued in Britain in 1939.

Glenn Miller was now forty years old and had been a Captain
in the United States Army Air Forces for nearly two years. The
Band he brought to Britain had its origin in an ideal – by
September 1942 the United States had been in the war for over
six months and Glenn Miller felt he could not stay at home while
others were called to the defence of freedom. He wanted to take
his music direct to those in the services, many of whom in happier
times had been the fans who had swept him to fame, and decided
that the best way to do this was to enlist in the services himself.

Before joining the Army he had had a lifetime's experience in
American popular music. He was born in Clarinda, Iowa, on 1
March 1904, and named Alton Glenn Miller, second of four
children. During his childhood the family, usually on hard times,
moved about the Mid-West often, including a stay at Grant City,
Missouri, where he got his first trombone at about the age of ten,
until they finally settled in Fort Morgan, Colorado. Miller seems
to have acquired his interest in music, as well as his strong,
determined character, largely from his mother, who was the main
strength of the family. In 1921 at the age of seventeen he got his
first full-time job as a professional musician in the band of the
then unknown clarinettist Boyd Senter. In January 1923 he
began to study at the University of Colorado, but after only three
terms music got the upper hand; he abandoned his studies for
ever and became a freelance musician travelling widely in various
little-known bands, eventually finding himself in Los Angeles.

It was in Los Angeles in 1924 that Miller, now a serious and
dedicated musician, who had also learned how to arrange music,
got his big break when he was invited to join the band of

drummer Ben Pollack as trombonist and arranger. The Pollack Band was one of the best and most influential bands of the middle and late 1920s and its journeying to Chicago and eventually New York brought the young Miller into contact with the leading bands and musicians of the time. In 1928 he left Pollack so that he could stay in New York to freelance and arrange for the theatre orchestra of Paul Ash, and during the next few years he played and arranged for many notable theatre, dance and jazz bands of the day, including trumpeter Red Nicholas and His Five Pennies. In 1932 he organized a band for singer Smith Ballew and for the next two years arranged for and managed the band as well as playing trombone in it, until in 1934 he joined the new band of the Dorsey Brothers, again as trombonist and arranger.

Miller was now one of the key figures in the New York music scene, not only as a player but also as a skilful and highly paid musical arranger. He had also a thorough knowledge of the business side of the music profession, so it was no surprise when in 1935 he organized a new band for the British bandleader Ray Noble when Noble first went to America. Noble's reputation as the leader of one of Britain's best bands had preceded him but because of the musicians unions' dispute he couldn't take a British band with him. Miller enlisted many of the best musicians in New York for the new Noble band and once again played in it and wrote many of its best arrangements.

The mid-1930s saw the emergence of the big band boom in the USA and the birth of the 'swing era'. Benny Goodman's Band had successfully integrated the jazz styles of the best black bands with the music of the white dance bands to popularize a style known as 'swing'. By 1937 Miller, who had done so much towards the success of other bands, began to think more and more about starting his own band as a means of developing his musical ideas the way he wanted to.

He had already had one shot at leading his own band in 1935 when he organized a small band to make four records. He formed his first full-time band in March 1937 but it was not a complete success and he disbanded it at the end of the year. Three months later he made a fresh start with new musicians and after a year of mixed fortunes the new band finally achieved a sensational breakthrough in the summer of 1939. By the end of that year it had become the most popular and successful band in America – a position maintained until Miller broke it up in September 1942 and volunteered to join the United States Army.

Miller's phenomenal success was due to the unique and original musical style he had evolved for his Band. Miller had a knack of picking musicians and singers who would fit in with his ideas, a keen 'commercial' instinct for what his public wanted, and first-class business acumen. Professionally he was a perfectionist and a hard taskmaster who insisted on incessant and painstaking rehearsal and demanded and got from his musicians high standards of discipline, behaviour and appearance. He was an outstanding organizer and leader who understood perfectly what went to make up success in the dance band business and by 1942 he was at the top of his profession and comparatively wealthy.

It was an age when dance bands were idolized like film stars and their singers and featured soloists were often as well-known as the leaders themselves. The Miller Band produced one hit record after another – 'Little Brown Jug', 'Moonlight Serenade', 'In The Mood', 'Tuxedo Junction', 'Chattanooga Choo Choo', (the first million-selling record for years), 'American Patrol' and many others – and at the height of its popularity it was estimated that one out of every three coins inserted into juke boxes in America went to play a Miller record. It starred in a long-running sponsored radio series for Chesterfield cigarettes and two Hollywood musical films and drew huge attendances wherever it played. Miller also became business manager for several other bandleaders, including trumpeter Charlie Spivak, pianist Claude Thornhill and saxophonist Hall McIntyre, all of whom had played in his bands at various times, and set up his own music publishing company, Mutual Music Inc., in New York City which also published his guide to the Band's musical style – *Glenn Miller's Method of Orchestral Arranging* – in 1943.

In December 1941, the United States was precipitated into the Second World War by the Japanese attack on Pearl Harbor, although for months she had been giving Britain 'all aid short of war'. Selective conscription had already meant that dance bands were beginning to lose key musicians to the Armed Forces, and now that America was in the war this quickly got worse. Industry gradually turned over to full war production, thousands of young men were called into the rapidly expanding services, and Glenn Miller began to consider what he could do to help the war effort.

At thirty-eight he would never have been called up (the upper age limit was thirty-five) but by the summer of 1942 he was convinced that playing in a civilian capacity on the air and to troops in Army camps was not enough. So at the height of his popular, artistic and financial success he volunteered for purely patriotic reasons for the United States Army, twelve days after the Navy had turned him down. He had asked his band to enlist with him as a unit (as some other bands had done) but they declined.

The story of how he broke up his band in September 1942 is well known. To explain his decision to his shattered public he issued a press statement in which he said (in part):

I, like every American, have an obligation to fulfil. That obligation is to lend as much support as I can to winning this war. It is not enough for me to sit back and buy bonds . . . I sincerely feel that I owe a debt of gratitude to my country . . . I am sure that no matter what my career or livelihood would have been, the mere fact that I have had the privilege of exercising the rights to live and work as a free man puts me in the same position as every man in uniform, for it was the freedom and the democratic way of life we have that enabled me to make the strides in the right direction.

And so, '. . . like a Pied Piper in reverse, he followed the kids to war'.*

He reported for duty with the Army Specialist Corps at the Seventh Service Compound Headquarters at Omaha, Nebraska, on 7 October 1942, and after two months' basic officer training at Fort Mead, Maryland, received a temporary wartime commission as a Captain with effect from 23 November. Shortly afterwards his services were requisitioned by the Army Air Forces,† and early in 1943, after a few weeks at Maxwell Field, Alabama, he was posted to the AAF Technical Training Command Headquarters at Knollwood Field, North Carolina, and became Director of Bands Training for the Technical Training Command. He was full of new ideas for modernizing military music and forming service bands to entertain the masses of new recruits pouring into the Air Forces with his kind of music. As America's most popular and successful bandleader he reckoned he knew what kind of music the young men and women in the services wanted and how he could provide it. Alas, he found the authorities unreceptive to his ideas, and military red tape irksome, and growing more and more frustrated he began to wish

* Paul Dudley, 'Bomblight Serenade'.
† The US Air Force did not become a separate service like the RAF until 1947.

he had stayed at home. Nevertheless, one contemporary report credited him with forming no fewer than forty-nine bands for service at Technical Training Command stations throughout the country. All this time what he really wanted to do was to form his own new band within the Air Forces and after several months at Knollwood Field his chance came.

By the spring of 1943 Captain Miller was stationed at Atlantic City, New Jersey, where a number of AAF basic training units were located, although his official headquarters was still at Knollwood Field. Through these basic training units came thousands of recruits from the eastern states including many musicians from the New York area, and in forming his new orchestra he was able to have the pick of musicians then coming into the Service as well as those already in the Army and the Army Air Forces. He was on the look-out for former professional dance band and jazz players wherever they were stationed, especially men who had played in his own pre-war Band, and whenever he heard of such men he had the authority to requistion them for transfer to Atlantic City for his new orchestra. In this he was greatly helped by a sympathetic Major-General Walter R. Weaver, at that time Commanding General of the Technical Training Command, and backed by the General's authority he proceeded to gather together the finest collection of musicians then in uniform, which became the 418th Army Air Forces Technical Training Command Band.

Eventually, he managed to obtain three of his pre-war musicians and his chief arranger who all became key men in his new orchestra. From an Air Forces unit in Florida came trumpeter Sergeant Reuben 'Zeke' Zarchy who had spent several periods in the Captain's pre-war Band and had also played in other leading bands including those of Tommy Dorsey, Bob Crosby, Benny Goodman and Artie Shaw. He became the new orchestra's lead trumpet. Another from the pre-war Miller Band was bassist Corporal Herman 'Trigger' Alpert, who had been called up from the Miller Band as early as the summer of 1941 and for whom the Captain now reputedly exchanged ten other musicians! The third from the pre-war Band was trombonist Corporal Jimmy Priddy whom Captain Miller appointed lead trombone: Miller was now devoting himself to conducting. He also kept in touch with many of his pre-war musicians still in civilian life and when their turn came to be drafted he offered to arrange for them to be posted to his unit if they wished. Some of them declined and some joined other branches of the service or the Navy, but he did get his pre-war arranger Jerry Gray – perhaps his greatest capture of all.

Besides the men from Captain Miller's pre-war Band many of the other musicians called to Atlantic City had also become household names in other leading bands in peacetime. Tenor saxophone player Corporal Michael 'Peanuts' Hucko had been a well-known jazz soloist in the Will Bradley/Ray McKinley Band among others; brilliant young pianist Corporal Mel Powell had been a star player and arranger in the Benny Goodman Band and Sextet, and in addition to filling the piano chair in the new Miller orchestra he also became one of its arrangers; alto saxophonist Sergeant 'Hank' Freeman, who became the leader of the new orchestra's saxophone section, had held the same job in the Artie Shaw Band; trumpeter Sergeant 'Whitey' Thomas, transferred from the artillery, had played briefly in the early Miller Band in 1938; and baritone saxophonist Private First Class 'Chuck' Gentry had been anchor man of the Benny Goodman saxophones.

One of the most important men in the new orchestra had been a name bandleader himself before being drafted in February 1943 – veteran big band drummer Corporal Ray McKinley. He and Miller had been friends since the mid-1930s and Captain Miller had invited Ray McKinley to get in touch with him if he were drafted. McKinley in turn told Captain Miller about four of *his* former musicians who were then in uniform – trumpeter Jack Steele, trombonist Jim Harwood, pianist Lou Stein and arranger Perry Burgett – and they, too, were transferred to the new Miller orchestra.

Ray McKinley was also responsible for getting one of the orchestra's best jazz soloists – 'Peanuts' Hucko. 'Peanuts had drawn an early draft number,' recalls Ray McKinley, 'and had been stationed at Fort Drum in upper New York State for a very long time. It was so dull musically that he decided to practise many hours a day on the clarinet, an instrument he was deficient on when he went into the Army. He called me one day at New Haven and asked me if I could get him into the Band. I had known him in the band that Will Bradley and I had had. He was a great tenor saxophone player – one of the best. He played just like Eddie Miller – beautiful – and he had complete control of the instrument, but we'd fired him from that band because he couldn't play clarinet well enough. So I went to Glenn and told him about Peanuts, and a couple of weeks later Peanuts called again and said, "I'm joining the Band – I'll be there on Sunday". I told him that we were playing a dance for the officers that Sunday night and if he got there soon enough to bring his horn and sit in – it was just a little six-piece group. So he did and that was the first time I'd heard him play clarinet since we let him go from the Bradley Band. I was so amazed I nearly fell out of my seat! Anyway, he came into the band and he became *the* clarinet player, both for all the solos and the lead clarinet in the famous Miller voicings.'

Some of the men joined the orchestra virtually direct from civilian life, or at least straight after basic training. One was guitarist Carmen Mastren who had played in Tommy Dorsey's Band and in Joe Marsala's jazz band and had then become a New York studio musician: 'Before I was drafted,' he recalled, 'I had many offers to get into other branches of the service by enlisting, also the Merchant Marines which were based in Brooklyn. I was very busy working at the time so I thought I would wait until I was called; at that time I was working at CBS with Walter Gross. That show went off the air just in time for me to have a couple of days to get ready to leave. Through a friend of mine I had a requisition signed by General Weaver which would get you into an Air Force band. Miller had charge of all the music and had the cream of the crop to pick from. Most of the musicians were happy just to get in and be able to play in a band. I went to Camp Upton and did what I was supposed to do, like KP and other uninteresting details. Getting up when you are used to going to bed is not an easy chore. They had a little theatre called the Opera House and they put on shows to sort of cheer up the boys – those first few days can be very depressing. The officer in charge found out I was there and asked me if I would like to play in the band. He said he would try to keep me there for some time but I told him when my orders came through with the requisition he wouldn't be able to stop them, but he made me send for my guitar which was being held by the maker, the Epiphone Co. Even though Upton was about an hour away by train they shipped it to me properly packed. Anyway, I played there for about three months. The orders came through for me to go to Atlantic City for training. Most of the musicians went to that base, that is the ones Glenn picked for his Band. I completed my basic training and prob- ably could have gotten away with some of it but chose to go through with it thinking it might come in handy at some future date.

'I had known Glenn for some time before, since I was with Tommy Dorsey and my brother Al was with Glenn [in the pre-war Miller Band]. I recorded some sides with his Band in 1937. I was happy to hear I was going to New Haven because I knew Glenn was forming his Band there. In fact, I had charge of the roster and the men going on that shipment. Jerry Gray was with us but the name Graziano didn't mean much to me at the time, but it was one of the last batches to go to New Haven.'

However, not all the new men were established stars. Some were young unknowns who had heard on the grapevine about Captain Miller's new orchestra and wrote to him hoping to be able to join it, or came to his notice through intermediaries. One was an eighteen-year-old trombonist from Iowa, John Halliburton:

'I was working in Miami, Florida, with the Clyde Lucas Orchestra (a fine band, if not well known, from California) just prior to my entry into the Air Force. Clyde, who was a trombone player, was told that I intended to join Art Mooney's AAF Band in Miami Beach upon my induction. He told me that he was a good friend of Glenn Miller's and suggested that, perhaps if he sent Miller a wire, he could help me get with "one of Miller's Air Force Bands". The wire was sent and answered immediately. Much to my surprise, being an 18-year-old from Iowa, I'd cleared the first hurdle. After induction and a short nine-day training period, I found myself in New Haven at Yale University playing in the Miller Band.'

But Captain Miller already wanted to develop his music beyond the conventional brass, reed and rhythm sounds of the dance band and he also began to recruit a number of classical string players who before getting into uniform had belonged to leading American symphony orchestras and New York radio orchestras; one had even been a symphony conductor. This was a startling innovation as Miller had never used strings in his pre-war civilian Band, although ever since his early days as an arranger he had been interested in the string possibilities in popular orchestration. As leader of his new string section he secured a former violinist from the NBC Symphony Orchestra in New York, Corporal George Ockner.

Miller's Atlantic City base, however, was only a staging post as far as the new orchestra was concerned and once he had selected the men he wanted from the large numbers who reported there this hand-picked, star-studded orchestra gradually assembled at the Army Air Forces Technical School at Yale University, New Haven, Connecticut, about eighty miles north-east of New York City. New men were arriving all the time, eventually travelling direct to Yale, and among them was Sergeant Harry Katzman, an ex-Juillard graduate and violin prize winner, who before the War had had many years in leading New York radio orchestras.

'I was stationed in the Air Force at Boca Raton, Florida,' he recalled. 'I was the director of a symphony orchestra and a large dance band (17 or 18 men), and I also had a small dance band, about six or seven men, and all really superb players – most of them came down from New York. I got arrangements from New York through the people I used to work with, like Mark Warnow, Leo Reisman and Al Goodman, who sent down arrangements to help the orchestra to get something to play instead of the regular stocks. I enlisted in the Army in, I think, late August 1942 and brought a lot of men from New York City who were on the staff in the studios and the musical comedy field, also in the symphonic field. I was there of course until I was shipped up to Miller. One of the men in the band was Zeke Zarchy, a first-class trumpet player of course. About January or February, 1943, suddenly orders came in for Zeke Zarchy to be shipped. We had all heard about the band being formed by Glenn Miller and we suspected that as long as he was going up there he was going to be with Miller. So he left about January I think it was, to Atlantic City – I don't think Miller had got to Yale at that time. Anyway, about April 1943 I was conducting a dance for the soldiers at the USO and one of the corporals came up to me and said, "Hey, you're getting shipped tomorrow". I couldn't believe it because here I was with the big orchestra, the dance band and the small dance band, and I thought it was just an ugly rumour. But when I came home that night one of the trombone players, Jack Lacey, who used to work with Kostelanetz and who lived off the post as I did, came over to the house about ten or eleven o'clock and said, "Hey, you know you're getting shipped tomorrow". Well, of course we had to be at the base at six or seven o'clock in the morning and when I came in the Captain called me in and said, "You know, you have to leave today. We're going to try to do everything we can to stop it." I said, "Where the hell am I going?" He said, "Well, your orders will be there, we can't say anything about that." There was another violinist there, Nat Kaproff, who was also on the same orders as I was to go up to

Yale. Now this was in April and by that time I think the Band had moved up to Yale.

'Well, of course, I had my wife there and we lived off the post. I had a beautiful little home right on the ocean about ten miles from the base, but I started packing that morning and I think we left that afternoon. We went by train up to New Haven. Although no-one told us where we were going we had pretty good suspicions where we were going – we were going to Yale and that's where Miller was. There wouldn't be anything else. There was another band up at Start Field, near West Point, but we were going to New Haven.

'We got off the train and there was nobody to meet us. I called the base there to find out where the Glenn Miller Band was and I finally got Zeke Zarchy on the phone. I said, "Zeke, we're down here at the railway station and we don't know where the hell we're going. Besides, we're freezing – we didn't have enough time, or even have enough sense, to dress in woollen uniforms. We have got our summer tans on". So he said, "Well, we'll send a car down to pick you up". About fifteen or twenty minutes later the car came and I think it was Zeke picked us up. We went right up to the quarters at Lake Place – a big brownstone house with three or four floors – and as we got out of the car there was the Band coming back from Retreat and they had stopped right in front of Lake Place. They were still playing so we just waited outside and Zeke said that Miller would be there in a few minutes and he wanted me to meet him. When the Band stopped the trumpet player that stopped in front of me (I didn't know who he was at that time) was George Ockner and he was blowing clams – awful! But he was smiling and blowing between smiles I guess. After the Band was through with Retreat we went into the orderly room and a few minutes later Miller came in. I guess through the grapevine and through Zeke Zarchy and some of the men he probably knew about me. I didn't know one person there when I came – evidently a great many of them had heard of me, because I was fairly well established in New York at that time, but I knew nothing about anyone there. I had never seen any of the boys that were there. There were about twenty-five in the Band on the Retreat. There were a few strings that didn't go on the Retreat – didn't play well enough, I guess.

'I was really hacked about coming to New Haven because I was a VIP in the music department; I was leader of all the groups there; I was living in this wonderful climate in Florida – the real tropics. I had come up to New Haven – it was snowing and miserably cold at that time. I had left my wife in Florida because she didn't have enough time to get things ready. We had a car and later, of course, she drove up. I was not in a very good mood. I did not give a damn about playing with Miller at that time. I might have shown some kind of unhappiness, although he never remarked about it. He asked me what I did there. I told him I conducted the orchestra there, and I had made arrangements for strings and also for vocal backgrounds. A warrant officer's wife was a singer and she used to sing arias – they didn't have the orchestrations so I would just make up an orchestration from the vocal copy, having played all these things on the *Telephone Hour* for a year or two.

'As a matter of fact, Miller sort of felt that I was unhappy. He called me in one day and said, "You seem a little bit unhappy". I said "Well, yes, I am. I was very happy where I was". He said, "Well, you'll be making a mistake if you go back there because while you think it's going to last for ever there eventually it will be broken up. I think you'd be wise to stay here." (In the meantime, they had sent up a Colonel from Florida to speak to Miller and I guess that's the reason I was called in. They wanted to know if they could possibly get me back there because everything fell apart after I left.) So he said, "Why don't you talk it over with your wife and if you want to go back I'll arrange the transfer. I'd like for you to stay here and I'd like to have you in the Band." I came home that night and I told my wife the situation and she said, "Never change anything in the Army. Let the Army tell you what to do then you have no regrets in case anything goes wrong." And so the next day when I came to rehearsal in the morning I went over to Glenn and I said, "Captain, I'm staying. My wife wants me not to make any change". He said, "Well, I'm glad you made that decision".

'When I got there, George Ockner was the concert-master. They had already had rehearsals. They had maybe nine or ten strings, eight or nine French horns. The arrangers were Jerry Gray, Danny Gool (who arranged for Hollywood pictures), Will Hudson (who had been making stock arrangements for the song publishing companies in New York), and there was Perry Burgett who was a very good arranger. Of the strings who were there already I remember there was George Ockner, Henry Brynan, – at least ten or twelve.

'I asked George, "How the hell did I get up there?" He said,

23

"Well, you know, Miller would ask Zeke if there were any good guys where he came from and so he mentioned you and Kaproff." He added "You don't know me but I know of you in New York and I've heard a lot about you".'

In its early days the new Miller Band was mainly employed in parade ground duties, where it joined with the post band (the normal military band of about thirty musicians established at most military posts of any importance), with the violinists playing drums, cymbals or sometimes trumpets. It also played for the cadets at mealtimes in the mess halls, sometimes conducted by Ray McKinley, and at dances for officers and enlisted men. With a line-up of four trumpets, four trombones, five saxophones, four rhythm and, later, about a dozen strings and a French horn, a live Glenn Miller Band was once again producing that well-loved and far-from-forgotten music* after a break of several months since the civilian Band had broken up the previous September. Consisting as it did of many of the best musicians in the Service, the Band eventually reached a standard that few civilian bandleaders of the time could equal, and within the Service some other officers were decidedly disgruntled that Captain Miller was able to corner the best musicians in the Air Forces. The musicians themselves – including the jazzmen, some of whom didn't particularly like the Miller style of music – were glad to be playing in a band, especially such a highly professional unit, instead of being posted to a combat unit or wasting away at some routine Army job. Many of them considered it an honour to have been chosen by the greatest bandleader of the day, although as trombonist Nat Peck points out some of the jazzmen would have liked to be playing more of 'One O'Clock Jump' and a bit less of 'In The Mood'.

Within a few weeks, however, the Band was to reach an audience far beyond the confines of Yale University.

---

* Despite the demise of the civilian Band its music was still kept before the public by stockpiled records being issued by RCA Victor and the Band was still coming high in popularity polls after it had ceased to exist.

CHAPTER TWO

I Sustain the Wings – Swinging Sousa – Enlargement of the Miller Band

After the United States entered the war the Army Air Forces set up a special radio production unit at Santa Anna, California, with Captain Eddie Dunstedter (or Dunstan) as musical director, which broadcast several programmes a week to publicize the war exploits of the rapidly expanding AAF and to encourage voluntary recruitment, in the same way that the weekly *Army Hour* had been doing for the Army on Sunday afternoons. The Armed Services appreciated the value of radio as a powerful propaganda and morale-boosting medium in wartime (radio hadn't existed as a mass medium in the First World War) and in the spring of 1943 the AAF set up a second radio unit to broadcast in the Eastern United States. It was based at the AAF Technical School at Yale University and the newly renamed 'Army Air Forces Technical Training Command Orchestra under the direction of Captain Glenn Miller' – with the addition of writers, actors and producers – became part of AAFTTC Radio Production Unit No. 2. The Commanding Officer in charge of production was a Major Francis C. Healey.

On Saturday 29 May, the Unit began broadcasting its new weekly programme *I Sustain the Wings* direct from Yale to the New England area over the Columbia Broadcasting System via Station WEEI in Boston, Mass., from 6.15 to 6.45. After six weeks of trial runs from Woolsey Hall at Yale (except for 26 June when it was broadcast from the TTC School at Pawling, NY), the programme was transferred to New York City and at five minutes past two on Saturday 17 July *I Sustain the Wings* made its debut over the CBS coast-to-coast network, after its scheduled debut the previous Saturday had been cancelled at the last minute. The first network broadcast consisted of 'In The Mood'; 'Dearly Beloved' sung by Corporal Tony Martin and the Glee Club; a dramatized story of a B-17 shot down in the New Guinea jungle; a medley of 'Old Black Joe', 'As Time Goes By' sung by Corporal Tony Martin, 'I've Got Sixpence' sung by Private Artie Malvin, 'Rhapsody In Blue'; and 'The Army Air Corps Song'.

On the air the Band was now called The Army Air Forces Training Command Orchestra,* although within the Service it was still the 418th AAFTC Band. The first network broadcast received widespread praise, including a telegram to Captain Glenn Miller from the Commanding General of the Training Command, General Yount, no less, who had heard the broadcast at AAFTC Headquarters at Fort Worth, Texas: 'Broadcast on 17 July most excellent and believe you have wonderful orchestra. Suggest elimination of General Yount's name at end of program. Congratulations . . . Yount.'

I Sustain the Wings (from the AAF Training Command motto 'Sustineo Alas') was basically an AAF public relations and recruiting exercise. Cut to twenty-five minutes each week, it featured the music of the Miller Band with a five- or ten-minute dramatic interlude in the middle of each programme. These interludes were imaginatively written and convincingly acted playlets portraying the work of various branches of the Training Command and incidents from AAF combat operations with realistic sound effects and background music by the Miller Band. Many of the sketches were based on the experiences of servicemen from various war zones while others presented the exploits of the mythical 'Johnny, the kid next door' who had joined up. The programmes also included plugs for the AAF and the Air WACS (Women's Army Corps) to boost recruitment.

At the time of the transfer to the CBS network the personnel of the Miller Band was:

Trumpets:	Staff Sergeant Zeke Zarchy, Private First Class Steve Steck (jazz soloist) (ex-Benny Goodman), Private First Class Jack Steele (jazz soloist), Sergeant Whitey Thomas (ex-Isham Jones and Tommy Reynolds);
Trombones:	Corporal Jimmy Priddy, Private First Class Jim Harwood, Private First Class John Halliburton, Private Larry Hall;

* This change of name was because in July 1943 the Technical Training Command and the Flying Training Command were amalgamated to form the Training Command of the AAF. The former Commanding General of the Flying Training Command, Major General Barton K. Yount, became Commanding General of the new combined Command.

Saxophones:	Sergeant Hank Freeman, Corporal Peanuts Hucko (jazz tenor sax and clarinet soloist) (ex-Bob Chester, Charlie Spivak and Bradley/McKinley), Private Vince Carbone (tenor sax soloist) (ex-Teddy Powell), Private Jack Ferrier (alto sax) (ex-Woody Herman and Bob Crosby), Private First Class Chuck Gentry (baritone sax) (ex-Jimmy Dorsey, Harry James and Benny Goodman);
Rhythm:	Corporal Mel Powell (piano), Private Carmen Mastren (guitar), Corporal Trigger Alpert (bass), Corporal Ray McKinley (drums);
Strings:	ten, led by Corporal George Ockner, and including Sergeant Harry Katzman, Corporal Nate Kaproff (violins), Corporal Dave Schwartz, Corporal Stan Harris (violas), Corporal Bob Ripley ('cello); also probably Corporal Eugene Bergen and Corporal Dick Motylinski (violins) and two others.

The Band's regular singers were Corporal Tony Martin, who before the War had already become a star of radio, records and Hollywood movies, Private Bob Houston, who had previously sung with Johnny Long's Band, and Private Artie Malvin, plus a seven-man Glee Club (male chorus) consisting of Warrant Officer Robert Boucher, Corporal Tony Martin, Private Johnny Carisi, Private Artie Malvin, Private Bob Carroll, Private Bob Houston and a Sergeant Reid. The musical arrangers were headed by Private Jerry Gray, with Corporal Mel Powell, Private Danny Gool (ex-Hollywood), Private First Class Perry Burgett and Private First Class Will Hudson (former bandleader and song writer, also arranger for many other bands, notably Jimmy Lunceford). Another ex-Lunceford arranger, Roger Segure, also spent a short time with the Band and later in the radio series they were joined by Private Ralph Wilkinson, who had arranged for Andre Kostelanetz, Mark Warnow, Raymond Paige and others, and Sergeant Norman Leyden who had been leading the 28th AAF Band at Seymour Johnson Field at Goldsborough, North Carolina. Captain Miller compèred the musical parts of the programmes as well as some of the dramatic sketches and the radio director was Sergeant George Voutsas, formerly with NBC.

Among the actors and announcers were Corporal Broderick Crawford, already well known as a leading Hollywood 'tough guy' before enlisting – one of his military duties was teaching ju-jitsu; Private Damian O'Flynn, a Hollywood supporting actor who later appeared in a small part in the film *The Glenn Miller Story* in 1953; and Lieutenant Donald Briggs. Some of the men in the Band occasionally played small parts too. The programme's signature tune, also called 'I Sustain the Wings', was composed by Glenn Miller and his old friend and pre-war pianist 'Chummy' MacGregor, with words by one of the programme's script writers Sergeant Sol Meyer, an ex-Hollywood writer.

The series was broadcast live every Saturday, later moving to the National Broadcasting Company network. When the Miller Band left the programme to go overseas in June 1944 another band took their place until they re-joined the programme after their return to the USA in August 1945.

Throughout the spring and summer of 1943 musicians continued to arrive at New Haven from other bases to be tried out for the radio orchestra or the post band; those who were not selected were posted away to other AAF bands. At one stage, Captain Miller was said to have a hundred musicians under his command. 'I felt sorry for some of the people who came,' recalls Harry Katzman, 'an endless number coming in day after day and sitting in with the sections, and they wanted to stay with the Band. I think they realized they had never played in such an organization before, except, maybe, just a few of us, and it was pitiful to see some of the arrangers and violinists and 'cellists and brass and everything leave after they had been there two or three days. George Ockner would have the string players sit in and would give Miller the lowdown on how they played. Sometimes George would ask a few of the other guys in the section or he'd ask me, "How's he doing?" and we'd give him an opinion and he'd give it to Miller – the same way Hank Freeman would probably tell Miller how the saxes were doing, or Jimmy Priddy with the trombones, or Zeke Zarchy with the rest of the brass. It was heartbreaking, and even at that time I wished I was one of the guys who would leave and go back to Florida, but as it turned out it was a very good thing I didn't.'

In early June Miller began to expand his string section by the addition of the first of two 'cellists: twenty-year-old Corporal Bob Ripley, a former Cleveland Orchestra player. 'I first heard of the Miller Band early in 1943,' recalls Bob Ripley, 'while I was playing in an Air Corps band in St Petersburg, Florida, where four of us from the Cleveland Orchestra had gone to join up. The others were violinists Eugene Bergen and Dick Motylinski and viola player Stanley Harris. Besides playing in the orchestra at St Petersburg we also played together in a string quartet and this comprised our military service. Around May of 1943 one of the fellows went home on furlough to New Haven where he met Captain Glenn Miller who was looking for string players. Glenn asked him about other members of the orchestra down there in Florida, especially about the string players – he knew that there was a group of us there from the Cleveland Orchestra – and he asked if we were really classical musicians, or, as he put it, "longhairs", making a sweeping gesture of his hand across his hair. Of course, the term "longhairs" in those days meant classical musicians, and the fellow assured him that, yes, we were genuine "longhairs" and we had been in symphony orchestras, and made the same gesture across his hair. Of course, we didn't know what to make of this, whether it meant anything or not, and we were inclined to be sceptical, naturally. In May or June I went home on furlough to New Hampshire, and when I came back the fellows said, "Hey, Ripley, you're going to New Haven to the Miller Band." I thought they were kidding – I couldn't believe such a thing could be happening to me, but sure enough a few days later off I went to New Haven to join the outfit. Stanley Harris went with me and that broke up the string quartet of Cleveland players which we had there. I was the first 'cellist to join – Morris Bialkin came in a while later.

'As soon as we got to New Haven we started lobbying for having our two violin colleagues to come into the Band – we found that Glenn was still recruiting string players and we told him that they were fine players and that he ought to have them so he got them and they arrived quite quickly after we did. He had a list of all the players in all the bands in the Air Corps throughout the country and he had free rein to requisition anybody he needed for the Band in New Haven. He had a great deal of power in this respect, as I discovered after I joined the Band and found that he was still recruiting string players. Another violinist I knew of was Freddy Ostrovsky – we had become very close friends in the summer before as students at the Berkshire Music Center and we had kept in touch with each other. By that time (1943) Freddy was in the Infantry in Louisiana and I knew it would mean a lot to him if he could get into the Miller outfit and it would be great for both of us. I spoke to Glenn about him, and Glenn said, "Go ahead, tell the officer and have him sent up here". So I wrote to Freddy and told him that Miller wanted him, and I told the officer – a Lieutenant Alexander, I think his name was – in our office that Glenn wanted this man and told him the outfit Freddy was with. Alexander told me a little later, "We can't get him until they release him down there". In the meantime, Freddy had written to me and said, "They won't let me go down here until you request me formally from up there", so it was a typical military "Catch 22"! Of course, Dick and Eugene were in the Air Corps and it was easier to get them transferred, but Freddy was in the Infantry so we had to cross lines from the Air Corps to the Infantry and this apparently caused problems. So I went to Glenn and told him this, and he took a piece of paper and scribbled down something and said, "Give this to the Lieutenant." I looked at it and it said, "Order Private First Class Ostrovsky to report to 418th Band at Yale, New Haven, immediately. Signed Yount.' Now Yount was the Commanding General of the entire Training Command of the Air Forces, and that was the kind of power Glenn had – he could sign a General's name to a telegram. So I gave this to Alexander and he sent it off as a telegram from General Yount, and Freddy was there within a couple of days. They went right out and pulled him off manoeuvres and he came up caked with mud and a few days' growth of beard and all shabby and he looked like a typical genuine sad sack. But there he was with his fiddle and his barracks bag standing in our Orderly Room when I walked in – it was a pretty happy Freddy, and myself, too!

'My first impressions of Glenn Miller were – well, I had been awed by him anyway as a kid. He was my idol as a bandleader when I was at high school, and when they told me I was to join the Miller Band I thought it was too good to be true. I didn't see him when I first arrived. The arrangers would rehearse the Band first and he would come in later in the week to polish things up. There I was, in my first week in the Band sitting there playing away, and in walked Glenn Miller and, oh boy! My heart just skipped a few beats and I got kind of nervous and scared. He looked around and saw that there was a 'cellist there, I guess, and he came over to me and said, "Double the bass in this spot". They were the first words he spoke to me.

'I was very impressed with the whole Band there. Of course, they were very professional – obviously they were the top players in their field. It was all new to me, working with fellows in the jazz field and it impressed me that they just didn't miss – when they went for high notes they hit 'em! In our band in Florida the brass players were pretty good – we had a dance band there and they were o.k., but they'd miss things now and then. But these guys were the tops, the best ones, and it was really a very thrilling thing to hear these guys play. After all, it was the Glenn Miller Band.

'My impressions of Glenn changed as time went on, and as I got acquainted with the fellows in the Band and heard them talk about

Glenn and Tommy Dorsey and Benny Goodman and others that they had played with I found out that their impressions of Glenn were not as lofty as mine had been. Compared to conductors that we had been used to in symphony orchestras Glenn Miller was a heck of a nice guy, but to his colleagues in the jazz field he was the Toscanini of their business – he was a tyrant, he was hard, ruthless and all the rest of the adjectives you'd think would be applied to a stern symphony conductor. He certainly didn't seem that way to us string players, although as we went along you could see what they meant – he was strict; he wanted things his way; he was *the* boss and what he said *went*. The thing about the Band was that Glenn wanted to feature the *Band* – that was the thing that made the Band famous, the *Band sound*, and that's what he wanted to have and preserve, so he didn't like the players to take real loud choruses. When they'd have a chorus to play and improvise he always kept them under clamps a little bit and never really let them go the way they wanted and they sort of resented this, but it was because of his feeling that the *Band* was the thing that made him do this. That's what the fellows didn't like too much about being in the Glenn Miller Band – they thought they had more freedom with other bandleaders, but of course in the Army there wasn't much choice.

'We were pretty well off being with Glenn Miller and Miller knew this too. He would not allow furloughs for the Band and there was a good deal of grumbling about this because we were entitled to a certain amount of time off – before we went overseas we were supposed to have two weeks or something off every year. He was talking about this one day and he said, "Furloughs – if you want a furlough I'll put you in an outfit where you'll get a furlough but you'll be up to your arse in mud, too". That was his attitude about it. He figured we were pretty well off as we were, and there was no answer to that – that just ended it. There was no complaining about furloughs after that because it was true – you just couldn't do better.

'I remember when we were in New York, rehearsing and playing our shows at the Vanderbilt Theatre every weekend, a lot of servicemen would come up to Glenn and ask him for help in getting out of the outfits they were in and getting into a band. He helped a lot of musicians to get into bands who were stuck in infantry outfits or other combat organizations and were losing their musical abilities. He did a great deal of good like that for musicians along the way – he was very willing and anxious to help musicians wherever he could through the war.'

Another new arrival at Yale in the summer of 1943 was an eighteen-year-old New York trombonist. Not long out of high school, he had started his professional career playing in two lesser-known bands – first, trumpeter Lee Castle's, and then Richard Himber's – when his call-up approached. Having heard that Glenn Miller was forming a band at New Haven he volunteered for the Army Air Forces without waiting to be drafted and wrote to Miller asking whether he might be considered for his Band after enlisting. His name was Nat Peck. 'I did my basic training at Greensborough, North Carolina,' he recalls. 'When I was in Greensborough, Phil Cogliano was doing his basic there, and there were a couple of other musicians there as well that I met, but I only met them when we both received our orders to go to New Haven. We didn't travel on the train up to New Haven together. I was given the job of escorting two Japanese aliens for internment in New York, and having delivered these prisoners I continued my trip to New Haven in a great state of elation because I knew the Glenn Miller Band was stationed there and the letter I had written had produced the hoped-for result. So my orders could only mean I was to join the Band.

'I arrived at New Haven on a beautiful late summer morning and I intended to walk to Yale University from the train station. The Band was stationed in a part of the University building called the Old Quadrangle and that's where most of the fellows were billeted. My arrival in New Haven coincided with the morning parade and my direction took me towards the green where this parade took place every morning. I couldn't believe my ears when I saw and heard this incredible military band playing the usual Army repertoire marches but in the most astounding jazzed-up arrangements that had the Air Force cadets marching with a zest and enthusiasm that I'd never seen before. I just couldn't believe my ears – it sounded just fantastic. Some of the tunes they played were "St Louis Blues" and some of the John Philip Sousa tunes that had these incredible trumpet high register passages and so on. It was really unbelievable – I just couldn't believe what I was getting into. I finally got the courage to report in to Sergeant Sanderson, who was the chap who used to look after the administrative details in the Band – he later came overseas with us. He assigned me a room in the Quadrangle. We all had private quarters, would you believe – everybody had their own little room and it was an unheard-of luxury for a soldier.

'I reported with trepidation for duty the next day, knowing not a soul in the Band but aware of the fact that very many big-time musicians were part of this organization – guys like Zeke Zarchy, Ray McKinley, Trigger Alpert, people who were household names in the United States. I was kind of scared and nervous and I was immediately assigned for parade ground duties with the military band. These parade ground duties took place in the morning and the retreat parade in the afternoon. Now this military band was composed of the members of the Glenn Miller orchestra and the post band as well. Both bands were all under the same administration and some of the post band were chosen to work with the Glenn Miller dance orchestra – that is, the Glenn Miller big band with strings. Now the post band, of which I was member to start with, also had a dance band of sorts – excellent musicians, of course – but its primary function was a staging post for those fortunate enough to be chosen for the Glenn Miller orchestra, and besides the military parades we were scheduled to do the rest of the time was spent in practice, rehearsals, and we used to play for the mess hall luncheons for the Air Force cadets. It was a busy schedule. They kept us going, and of course for me it was an incredible experience because I really was – well, along with Gene Steck I think I must have been the youngest kid in the Band. Gene, myself and then, later on, a little fiddle player from Poland I think, called Freddy Ostrovsky, who joined the Band – we were the three kids of the Band. Everybody else was a little bit older so obviously I was thrilled at being in this fantastic set-up and I enjoyed it thoroughly.

'I became very friendly almost immediately with Addison Collins, Jr., the French horn player who took me under his wing, and with Johnny Halliburton. George Simon at that time was part of the post band – he used to play a bit of drums in the military band from time to time – and he and I got quite friendly too. Everybody was extremely friendly – they really were a great bunch of guys right from the very beginning.'

Ever since joining the Service, one of Captain Miller's favourite ambitions had been to 'moderize' Army marching music by giving it a jazz beat – jazz and marching music had always had much in common – not only the military marches themselves but also having special marching arrangements made of famous jazz classics and popular tunes of the day which would, he felt, put new life into parade ground music and appeal much more to the men who had to march to it. As soon as his Band became established at Yale, Captain Miller put his ideas into practice and soon the marching of the Air Cadets was transformed by spine-tingling arrangements not only of Sousa's hallowed classics but also special marching versions of 'St Louis Blues' (arranged by Private Jerry Gray, and based on an original idea of Corporal Ray McKinley), 'Blues In The Night' and 'Jersey Bounce'.

As the highspot of all this, Miller, ever the showman, unveiled a novel idea for military parades before a huge public audience in the Yale Bowl. On Wednesday afternoon, 28 July, 30,000 people attended a Bond Rally there in aid of the new US Navy aircraft carrier, the USS *Shangri-La**, during which the Air Cadets performed in a retreat ceremony accompanied by the 418th AAFTC Band. As the Band marched out on to the field two Army jeeps drove slowly along in the middle of the Band and mounted on a platform on one of them were drummer Corporal Ray McKinley and bassist Corporal Trigger Alpert, and on the other Private Frank Ippolito at the drums and another bassist, all providing a swinging beat for 'St Louis Blues March' which had the huge audience on its feet. As the Band counter-marched the jeeps turned in neat little circles and caught up with the Band again. Nearly two and a quarter million dollars were raised by the sale of war savings bonds at the Yale rally.

Within the Service, however, Captain Miller's swinging the Army marches provoked furious opposition from the regular bandmasters which at one stage became a big public controversy. *Time* magazine quoted Captain Miller as saying, 'There hasn't been a successful army band in the country, and if someone doesn't get after band music and streamline it army music will become extinct in another couple of years. We've got to keep pace with the soldiers. They want up-to-date music. Why, there's no question about it – anybody can improve on Sousa'.† These were fighting words and *Time* continued: 'Old guard army musicians creaked with suppressed fury. One old Sousaphile, Bandmaster

* The USS *Shangri-La* was launched at Norfolk, Virginia, in February 1944 and saw action in the Pacific in 1945.
† 6 September 1943. One example of a Miller version of a Sousa march survives on a nowadays very rare record: 'El Capitan' on a V-Disc 91, labelled as Music for Marching Men, by the 418th AAFTC Band; it has been re-issued on a British long-playing record (*see* page 402).

Edwin Franco Goldman, most famous of present-day US concert bandleaders, rose to denounce this outrage. Said he, 'Personally, I think it's a disgrace! There isn't an excuse for it. Perhaps they think they can add more dash and appeal. But no-one can improve on a Sousa march . . . My God!'

Captain Miller retorted that he had been misquoted, but *Time* did not publish any correction, though another blast from Edwin Franco Goldman did appear in the magazine, and the Band continued with its unique marching music. The jeep band was seen briefly in a March of Time documentary film entitled *Upbeat In Music* and to this day a version of Miller's 'St Louis Blues March' is played by American military bands.

'The platforms on which the drummer and a full set of drums were placed on the jeeps,' explains Ray McKinley, 'were designed and built to fit on the rear of a jeep by myself and Bill Mather, an Englishman who ran the best drum shop in New York at that time – mostly by Mather.' Incidentally, 'Blues In The Night March' came later than 'St Louis Blues March', as did 'Jersey Bounce'. Neither was nearly as good as 'St Louis Blues March' and were hardly ever played except by brass and drums only while marching to and from the retreat ceremony. Another arrangement played at the Yale Bowl was a shortened version of 'The Anvil Chorus'. This was the one that was the bone of contention in the famous argument between Glenn and the Commandant of Cadets, with the Commanding Officer, Colonel Arnett, acting as referee:

Commandant: 'Sousa's marches were good enough for our troops in the last war.'

Glenn: 'Tell me, Major, are we still flying the planes we flew in that war?'

Captain Miller didn't march with the marching band himself. On parade the band was led by an Army drum major, Sergeant Harold ('Doc') Winters. Not all the string players took part either – some had other duties, such as guitarist Carmen Mastren who was on the copying staff and therefore was excused marching. 'Others had to do what they could,' recalls Bob Ripley. 'They carried drums, they beat cymbals. Stanley Harris had done a bit of brass playing so he carried a baritone horn and the first day he came out with that thing to march in the band Glenn saw him and said, "What the —— is that!" I had had some lessons on the drums when I was a kid, enough for me to play the drum beats, so I carried a drum and I actually played the beats but others just carried the drums and beat what they could. Gene Bergen, who was quite diminutive, had to carry those great big cymbals and he used to complain how they hurt his wrist and it was hard for him to play the violin after carrying those heavy cymbals around the marching field. The soldiers who had to march to this music really liked it. It was lots of fun for us, too.'

Inevitably, perhaps, Captain Glenn Miller was not too popular with some of the other officers at New Haven. Ray McKinley recalls: 'It seemed like there was a certain clique up there that disliked Glenn, first because he had gotten a commission right away and hadn't gone through any Army training that *they* knew of. Also, there were certain officers there – like the guy who called Glenn up for playing "St Louis Blues March" and those things on parade or to and from the green for retreat, and so on – who wanted the old Sousa marches. Thank goodness the CO, Colonel Arnett, didn't agree with that faction. He agreed with Glenn, but he was kind of in the middle and he could only go so far. This clique resented this and they tried to think up things for the Band to do apart from music. What could be better than to think of something that all soldiers do, and in this instance it was to take 'em out to a rifle range and teach them to shoot. Well, all of a sudden a little Major whose clothes were so tight that the guy couldn't get his hands in his pockets showed up there. I think he had a nervous breakdown after this – you'll see why. He took us out in the trucks to a rifle range where the cadets were doing some rifle shooting and he wanted to know if any of us had had any arms training. I had, and I started giving some of the guys in the Band a little of the "manual of arms" – I think there were one or two others who did, too. It soon became evident that not only was no-one familiar with firearms but at least a goodly proportion of the Band, about twenty-five per per cent, were scared of them. So this Major gave up on the manual of arms when he saw how they were being handled and started to explain how a rifle worked. Then he broke the Band up into three groups and sent two groups down to the trench below the targets for target marking and kept the other group back at the firing point. This group was given live ammunition and told to shoot at the targets. Well, you should have seen it! These guys were spraying bullets all over the hillside up there – they weren't getting anywhere near the targets. If they'd been firing at elephants no-one would have hit any of 'em!

'Down in the trench below the targets a regular army sergeant was in charge – a twenty-year man, a real tough talker, and he was telling these guys how to mark the targets using small discs on the end of long rods. All of a sudden, Lou Stein, who's a little bit of an imp anyway, got an idea. It was a very long trench and while the Sergeant was down at the far end of it with one group and the Band was shooting, Louis started ringing up these shots as "bullseyes". They weren't hitting bulls – they weren't even hitting the hill behind it, but they thought they were because the markers would go up showing bullseyes. Louis had Steve Steck and a couple of the other guys ringing these bullseyes up and the guys back there shooting were saying, "Hey, look at that, I'm doing good!" When the Sergeant saw what was going on he ran up and started cussing Louis out, and the group he had just left at the other end got the idea and they started ringing up bullseyes, and the first thing you know all those monkeys back there shooting were hitting bullseyes.

'This Sergeant was going nuts, yelling at all these guys in the pits to cut out this nonsense – this was serious stuff. They were saying, "Yes, sir", and the minute he'd leave and run down the other end they'd start all over again. Finally, this poor little Major who was in charge of all this called everybody back and he stood 'em up and said, "Attention", and they all snapped more or less to attention. He just stood there looking at them and, honestly, I never saw anybody look so frustrated. This was the first time we saw him, and the last time. He just gave up on that unit – the orchestra – he gave up completely. It was just like something out of MASH.'

On 11 September Corporal Tony Martin made his last broadcast with the Band on *I Sustain the Wings* before leaving for Officer Candidate School. After several weeks his place was taken by Private First Class Johnny Desmond, who had sung with Bob Crosby's and Gene Krupa's Bands before the war and was then stationed with the AAF at Enid, Oklahoma, from where he had written to Miller asking to be considered for the Band. He first broadcast on *I Sustain the Wings* on 16 October singing 'How Sweet You Are' and 'Blue Rain', and quickly became one of the Band's stars, remaining with it until it was demobilized in November 1945.

The *I Sustain the Wings* radio series soon became established as a major weekly event and on 18 September it was transferred from CBS to the National Broadcasting Company (NBC), then the biggest of the four networks, again coast-to-coast, and it stayed there for the rest of the series. The Band travelled to New York for the broadcasts every Friday, rehearsed for the broadcasts on Saturday mornings and played two thirty-minute live broadcasts from the Vanderbilt Theatre on West 48th Street – one in the late afternoon to the Eastern USA and another five hours later to the West Coast, returning to New Haven on the Sunday. The men had Mondays off and during the week their time was spent at practice and rehearsals and playing in the marching band. They were glad of the trips to New York where they were able to keep in touch with the music scene and with former colleagues still in civilian orchestras, and after the broadcasts the jazz musicians could visit the city's jazz clubs and listen to all the interesting new music on Fifty-Second Street where Charlie Parker and Miles Davis were first becoming known.

In addition to *I Sustain the Wings* and other Government-sponsored broadcasts the Band played in public for war savings drives (the 'Bond Rallies') including concerts at Indianapolis, Rochester (NY), Buffalo (NY), St Louis and Chicago. At many of the Bond Rallies Hollywood stars also appeared, including Bob Hope, Rita Hayworth, Jimmy Durante, Bing Crosby and Dinah Shore; Major La Guardia once appeared with the Band. At a WAC recruiting rally in Providence, Rhode Island, Johnny Desmond's singing literally stopped the show. The Band also entertained troops, including those in hospital.

The Band also made dozens of radio transcription recordings for the Overseas Branch of the Office of War Information* for supplying to foreign radio stations as part of the American Government's propaganda activities, and for the Armed Forces Radio Service* under the aegis of the War Department for broadcasting on American forces radio stations in those parts of the world where American forces were operating, as well as some of the famous V-Discs* which were issued free by all the American Armed Forces exclusively to American servicemen and their canteens. No records at all, however, were made for issue to the public owing to a recording ban imposed by the American Federation of Musicians which lasted from 1 August 1942 until November 1944.

By November 1943, Captain Miller was relieved of his responsibilities for other AAF bands and was able to devote all his time to his own Band, now renamed the 'Army Air Forces Band (Special)' although on the air it was still introduced as the Army Air Forces Training Command Band, and the radio series and

* *See* pages 389–93.

recordings. With more punch and beat than the pre-war civilian Miller Band had ever achieved, exciting jazz solos by the featured jazz stars and the new string section the Band reached unprecedented standards for a popular orchestra. 'It took three or four months for the Band to get the precision it was famous for,' remembers Harry Katzman. 'In New York, all the studio musicians would come in for the rehearsals and they were all absolutely flabbergasted. They said this was absolutely the greatest musical organization they had ever heard. I remember after one broadcast I went over to Captain Miller and I said, "Do you know, Captain Miller, this is the greatest musical organization I have ever played with" (and I had worked as a sideman in New York playing in the same orchestras as Benny Goodman, Tommy Dorsey, Jimmy Dorsey and Artie Shaw). He was very pleased, and I think, at that time, he said, "Aren't you glad you didn't leave and go back to Florida?" and I said, "Yes, I'm damn glad". Of course, I wasn't too crazy about going overseas – I thought I would be staying in Florida for the duration of the war. As a matter of fact he was right because about four or five months after I did get to New Haven they broke up the whole organization down in Florida.

'Our usual routine in New Haven was rehearsal in the morning and in the afternoon, and the way Miller rehearsed was very painstaking. Of course, it's great when you don't have to pay a nickel to the musicians for rehearsal – you had all the time you wanted. There was one time when we spent the whole day, morning and afternoon, on just the "Rhapsody In Blue" – they had an arrangement of the middle part. They tried it with different nuances or different players. Now the original fill-ins in the "Rhapsody In Blue" were done by Peanuts, and he did them just so beautifully, but somehow or other when the final thing came down it was Vince Carbone, who was not in the class with Peanuts as a tenor man, but somehow this was what Miller wanted – that particular one-note style of filling in. But it would just take time, back and forth, and different nuances here and there, until when he got through with it it sounded absolutely magnificent.

'When the arrangers brought in the arrangements there were some very, very good ones. Miller got the best that he could – Jerry Gray was fantastic, and Ralph Wilkinson, whom I knew in civilian life, was a first-class arranger; Norman Leyden was a marvellous arranger, too; Perry Burgett was excellent. Miller had never used any strings in his civilian Band, but he did an arrangement, I think, of "Moonlight Serenade" – I thought at the time it was very good, a little bit flowery, maybe a little too many notes in it, too much movement. Later he found out the way to use the strings as a background, a sustained background against the saxes or the trumpet solos or the full orchestra. Someone would bring in an arrangement and we'd play it over and it sounded pretty damn good, but he would go over it with the arranger, or they would meet afterwards, and he would just tell them what he wanted and you would never recognize the arrangement after he had fixed it up or given his suggestions as to what he wanted, what instruments he wanted. A case in point is "Holiday For Strings". When the original things came in it was completely different from the final version that you probably know, but he suggested certain things and what happened was that Ralph Wilkinson did the introduction and when he got through with it it sounded entirely different from the original version; Jerry Gray did the bulk of the arrangement when it went into a rhythm. The pizzicato passage was just taken from the David Rose original, but the final dance part turned out to be entirely different from when we heard it for the first time. Every arrangement was that way – it would take time, we had five or six hours a day.

'I felt that Miller was really an extraordinary musician with immaculate taste and a wonderful idea of how music should really sound. For a man who had never used strings in his civilian band he used them so much better than anyone else has ever done even to this day. Generally he used the strings as a cushion to soften the sounds of the brass – the sound was really extraordinary. When we were recording or rehearsing in London all the English musicians were just eating it up, and I think we had a terrific influence on the English dance musicians.

'I think all the other musicians in the Band respected him just as much as I did because they saw what he did to an arrangement. He never did anything cheap. He would take no matter what arrangement came in – it might sound terrific. He always improved on it and you would never imagine how he would think of such things. He was innately a very musical person – he had complete control of the Band and we were never in any doubt about his beat. We knew exactly when to start, and one of the remarkable things about him – and I've seen many other well-known conductors fail to do this on a television show

– is that on those introductions from one number to another he would be able to talk and make the retard and keep that orchestra together, which is a very difficult thing. But he was just a natural musician, with immaculate taste. I think if he had gone into the classical field he would have been just the same way, but he found, of course, his medium and it was original, and that's what he went with. I think he was a musical genius and I had the greatest respect for him as a musician, and as a man too. I think everybody felt the same way. The men had learnt to realize that here was an extraordinary musician. Miller was great for organization – he was in control.

'He originally had the idea of using four horns. A lot of horn players came and sat in – even Carl Swanson, one of the violinists, sat in at one time.'

Eventually Captain Miller kept only one French horn player in the orchestra – Corporal Addison S. Collins, Jr.

Gradually, the Band attained what was to be its permanent size and instrumentation and by the beginning of 1944 it consisted of five trumpets, four trombones, six saxophones, four rhythm, one French Horn, fifteen violins, three violas and two 'cellos. The saxophone section was increased to six by the addition of Corporal Freddy Guerra (alto sax). Trumpet player Private First Class Steve Steck moved over to join the new five-man vocal group, The Crew Chiefs, which made its first appearance on the air on 28 August as a quartet called the Tail End Charlies, became a quintet on 9 October and gradually replaced the Glee Club. The trumpet section was brought up to five by the addition of nineteen-year-old Corporal Bobby Nichols, who had been the trumpet soloist in Vaughn Monroe's Band, and Corporal Bernie Privin, a veteran jazz soloist from the bands of Artie Shaw, Charlie Barnet and Benny Goodman. Bernie Privin was still enduring the miseries of basic training at the vast training camp at Greensborough when he received his orders to report to New Haven 'This was a Godsend,' he recalls, 'not only because I wanted to be associated with a good band but prior to being called to New Haven I was very uncomfortable doing KP in Greensborough as well as not playing my horn.' He became the main jazz trumpet soloist in the Band.

Later Corporal Bob Carroll from the Glee Club became an extra solo singer but compared to Private First Class Johnny Desmond he was seldom featured although, before the war, he had sung with the Charlie Barnet and Jimmy Dorsey Bands.

When the Miller Band left for overseas he transferred to another AAF orchestra.

Early in January a string of promotions came through – Private Jerry Gray, Private First Class Johnny Desmond, Corporal Ray McKinley, Corporal Peanuts Hucko, Corporal George Ockner and Corporal Mel Powell all became Sergeants, and during the following months more stripes were handed out.

One of the last to join the string section was violinist Sergeant Emanuel Wishnow, then in his early thirties. Before being drafted he had been a teacher on the music faculty at the University of Nebraska since 1933, and had had a varied career which had included radio, theatre and concert work. 'Miller requisitioned me while I was stationed at Las Vegas, New Mexico. Some of the players already in the Miller group evidently recommended me – they wanted to fill out the string section. I drove by car from Las Vegas to New Haven in the winter time, and when I saw Miller at Yale he said, "I know you're a violinist and if you prefer to play the violin that's perfectly all right, but what I'm really trying to do is fill out my viola section – I have three violas but I want four and I understand you play the viola". I said, "Well, I don't have an instrument." He said, "We'll get you an instrument, a GI one, and then maybe you can pick up a better instrument on your own." So there was no ducking out! Within a day or two I had a Government issue – not a very good instrument but it was workable. Then I was loaned an instrument by a friend of mine in Hartford. At that time we had no idea we were going overseas, but later on when we got to Chicago on the Bond Tour, I saw an old friend whom I had known for many years – he was one of the biggest and best violin dealers in Chicago and had helped to arrange for my violin studies – and told him I was playing a borrowed viola. He said, "Let me give you a nice new Italian instrument." I said, "Well, look, I may not bring it back – we don't know where we might be going." He said, "Well, never mind," and gave me a viola which I played for the entire time we were overseas. When we got back to the States I took the viola back to Chicago and from playing a lot outdoors, as we did, the weather had ruined the varnish. It was a new instrument and I was ashamed to give it back to him, so I said to him, "Let me pay to have it re-varnished". He replied, "Absolutely not. This thing's got a history now. I'll never part with it!"'

As finally constituted the string section, totalling twenty-one, was one of the finest collections of string players to be found at that time, and in a popular orchestra at that. Of course, had it not been for the war most of them would never have been playing in what was, after all, really a very superior type of dance orchestra, and it may well be that there will never be such a collection again. The section was a mixture of 'commercial' players from radio orchestras and symphony players from orchestras such as the Boston Symphony and the Cleveland Orchestra, although some of the symphony players had earlier worked in radio or theatre orchestras. Emanuel Wishnow points out: 'Their background before that time could very well have been commercial, playing a lot of things because your jobs would be variegated – one day you'd be playing film music, or recording dates, for example, then in a ballet orchestra which is different music entirely, and then finally ending up in the Cleveland or Boston. So the strings' background wasn't all that pure. Their experiences had been varied and therefore their attitudes weren't crystallized, and I don't think any of them looked down on playing in a "dance band". They just took things as they came.

'Although I was an academic, I had been somewhat "polluted" from early days! I had played theatres, too, and pop music but not really as what we used to call a dance musician – I didn't have much experience at that. After a while, playing in the Miller Band palled on me, but the interesting thing was on Friday mornings when we'd get the new arrangements. The arrangers were very clever, but we'd watch Miller tearing their arrangements apart. I remember it was uncanny how he was able to say, "Well, O.K., let's cut from B to D – at D brass muted – at F pizzicato strings; at G leave it out, no strings at all, and then maybe put it up an octave. All right, start from the top". And that's the way those corrections were made and nine times out of ten that's how the arrangements stayed.

'Of course, he had good people on the arranging staff – Jerry Gray, Norman Leyden, Ralph Wilkinson – good as they come. He left Ralph's stuff pretty much alone.

'Miller used the string section a little differently than other people had been using it. He said, "They're going to sound like a string section should." And it was used as another section as opposed to reinforcing the other sections. I think sometimes he was a little diffident about the strings – he'd never had experience with strings and he used to ask George occasionally. Of course, he was not a classical conductor, but his instincts for rhythm and timing were good enough for him to do what he needed to do. I think he may have had a few lessons in conducting techniques.

'We had a very nice string section and the boys wanted to play things like Tchaikovsky's "Serenade" or some Delius pieces, but Miller said, "That stuff doesn't send me". He was interested in the orchestration possibilities in the works of composers like Ravel, Delius and Sibelius for use in the Band's popular repertoire rather than straightforward performances of the classical works themselves, and he got a lot from them.

'We did some half-hour string programmes of pops and standards on our own over the Yankee Network (about thirteen or fourteen stations in New England – New Hampshire, Vermont, Rhode Island, Maine, and so on), some with vocals by Johnny Desmond. The arrangers for those programmes were Dave Herman, who had done 'society' work as we used to call it (ballrooms, dinner music, and so on) and knew the popular repertoire, and I think Norman Leyden and George Ockner did some. It was a very good programme.'

'We enjoyed those weekly programmes,' recalls Bob Ripley. 'They were called *Strings With Wings* and it was a nice opportunity for us to play a little more than we did in the full dance band. We also had Trigger Alpert on the bass with us and in this case he played with the bow and he enjoyed doing that – it gave him a chance to play something a little different. Jerry Gray conducted it most of the time, but Glenn would take a turn at it once in a while and he would experiment with the different string effects that you can get – pizzicato, playing with mutes, play things up an octave, down an octave, and tremolo (which he called "gillerando") and dynamics.

'I remember he was talking about the Band after rehearsal one day at New Haven and said, "You know, you can always tell a Glenn Miller Band from any other 'cause we play with dynamics, we don't always play loud all the time. When the music goes up we play loud and when it goes down we play soft." Well, that was a pretty simplistic approach to dynamics but at least he did try to do something like that and it was true that the Band did have a character and dynamic range that other bands just didn't bother to use.

'As to Glenn's attitude about the strings and the combination of using strings in the dance band he had an idea that the pop and classical elements could be combined into a synthesis that would make an attractive kind of presentation and he tried to do this in some of the arrangements. He would have the arrangers write the introductions, for instance, in a symphonic, classical style, and

44

then go on to the dance element. For instance, "Pistol Packing Mama" started with a real grandiose, serious sounding thing and then all of a sudden it broke into this country and western type thing with Carmen Mastren singing the song. It was a good thought that he had to bring people together more, and the two different elements to show people who thought they liked only classical that there were things about pop music they could enjoy and also the other way around – people who listened only to jazz and dance bands to show them that there were things in the classical field that they could enjoy also.'

Popular and successful as the new Miller Band was, this safe and comparatively 'cushy' military assignment wasn't exactly what Captain Miller had in mind when he volunteered to help the war effort, and as the months passed he became anxious to take the Band overseas to play to the troops on active service (Artie Shaw's Navy Band had already made an arduous and highly successful tour of the South Pacific war zones). However, the AAF refused to let them go: the work they were doing was considered too important for them to be released, and, after all the trouble of setting up the radio unit, if the Band went overseas another radio unit would have to be set up all over again. Besides, all available shipping space was desperately needed for combat troops and war supplies and the AAF didn't want to draw criticism from politicians for allocating vital shipping space to what they thought of as a 'jazz band' (!) when it was badly needed for the war fronts. So Miller's pleas were in vain and the Band continued with its broadcasts and savings drives through the winter and into the spring of 1944.

CHAPTER THREE

The call from SHAEF – The Band's departure for overseas

Serving with the Radio Unit as producer and script writer in 1944 was Technical Sergeant Paul Dudley. He had joined the writing team of *I Sustain the Wings* in November 1943 as an Air Forces Private. A friend of Captain Miller from pre-war days, he had already become a noted radio producer and writer and his peacetime programmes had included the Coca Cola *Spotlight Band* series six nights a week, one of the most prestigious dance music programmes during the war years. One Saturday morning in the spring of 1944 another radio producer whom Dudley had known in civilian life came to the Vanderbilt Theatre in New York to listen to a rehearsal of *I Sustain the Wings*. He was Colonel Edward M. Kirby of the US Army, then serving as Radio Chief of the Public Relations Division of the War Department in Washington, who before the war had been Director of Radio Station WSM in Nashville, Tennessee, and Public Relations head of the National Association of Broadcasters. Kirby, a senior and influential officer, was about to return to England to be attached on broadcasting duties to the staff of General Eisenhower's Supreme Headquarters Allied Expeditionary Force (SHAEF) where the long-awaited Allied invasion of German-occupied Europe was in an advanced stage of preparation. He was keenly interested to hear from Dudley about Captain Miller's desire to take the Band overseas and was highly impressed by the scintillating music he heard. Before leaving for London he met Captain Miller in Washington and discussed Miller's ideas for taking the Band overseas.

By the middle of May Kirby was established in London with

SHAEF which was in the process of negotiating with the BBC to set up a new radio service for the Allied invasion armies now poised, several million strong, in the southern half of England. Colonel Kirby was involved in the later stages of these negotiations, providing him with the opportunity to help realize Captain Miller's long-held desire for overseas service. He lost no time in suggesting that the Miller Band should be transferred to England to broadcast in the new service.

SHAEF decided that it wanted the Miller Band, and at that stage of the war its supra-national requirements had over-riding priority over all other military needs. The agreement between SHAEF and the BBC for the new radio service, The Allied Expeditionary Forces Programme, was signed on 23 May, and the very next day a radio signal went out from the headquarters of the US Army in Europe (on behalf of SHAEF) to the War Department in Washington requesting the urgent transfer of the Miller Band to the European Theatre of Operations (ETO). Classified 'Secret' and 'Priority', 'from Eisenhower to Marshall and Arnold' (General George C. Marshall, Chief of Staff, US Army, and Lieutenant-General H. H. Arnold, Commanding General, US Army Air Forces), the formal request for the Miller Band was set out as follows:

With the co-operation of BBC, there is to be established by SHAEF, a radio service for all troops of the Allied Expeditionary Force. This is expected to be a potent instrument for maintenance of troop morale and disseminating orientation material to them.

For this purpose we require a musical organization similar to the 2001 AAF Base Unit (Radio production), commanded by Captain Glenn Miller. No such organization exists in ETO, nor can one be improvised in the time available.

Request that Captain Miller's unit be shipped to this Theater for permanent assignment. The unit should be added to Theater Troop Basis. As strength of requested unit is 4 officers and 63 enlisted men request that you delete 3 regular bands from troop basis and credit extra 20 bodies to our Adjutant General Troop Basis.

Personnel for this unit should be selected for technical proficiency and should be given security clearance.

Further request that Captain Miller and Technical Sergeant Paul Dudley, ASN 32987492, be shipped by air with class 2 priority, in advance of unit, reporting on arrival to SHAEF. Request remainder of unit be shipped as soon as possible, with listing of urgent on priority list. Benefit to be gained from this unit is sufficiently important to warrant backlogging other units that are set up to sail.

D-Day was only twelve days away.

Once the SHAEF request was received in Washington things moved quickly. Messages flowed back and forth settling the military technicalities of the Band's overseas posting, while in the War Department General Arnold (under whose control the Band was at that time) had agreed by 27 May to release it for transfer to the ETO. On 30 May orders were issued for the Band to prepare for overseas shipment. On the same day a message went from the War Department to the Army in the ETO that the Band would be ready to sail by 15 June (subsequently postponed to the 19th). They finally sailed from New York Harbor on 21 June – only 28 days after the original request from London was received in Washington.

To achieve this rapid transfer – SHAEF had testified that the Band's posting was 'vital to the war effort' – the Band was shipped to England as a 'casual detachment' (as they were not organized at that time on the usual basis for Army and AAF Bands) and activated as a Band on arrival in the ETO and the military ends were still being tied up when the the Band was halfway across the Atlantic! As suggested in the original request from London, three regular bands were deleted from the ETO Troop Basis of the AAF to compensate for the posting of the Miller Band to Europe, so strained were the military resources at the time. Looking back over the years now, one wonders where the Army Air Forces thought they might find other groups to compensate for the unique and highly professional Miller Band, but of course the military minds were only concerned with numbers!

The Band did its *I Sustain the Wings* broadcasts on Saturday, 3 June, from New York as usual, and early the following week set off on a war savings tour known as the War Bond Caravan in aid of the Fifth War Loan Drive. It had been planned that its weekly programmes would be broadcast from various locations on the tour but that was barely under way when it was cut short and the Band made its last *I Sustain the Wings* broadcast from the Servicemen's Center in Chicago on Saturday 10 June. Understandably, as it was a military unit, no public explanation of the Band's withdrawal from the radio series was given (although rumours had appeared in the American press), but at the end of the broadcast Captain Miller said 'so long' and announced that another band* would take their place the following week.

* The Band of Radio Production Unit No. 1 from Santa Ana, California, then conducted by Sergeant Harry Bluestone (who had played in the band on the first

'When we got to St Louis,' recalls Emanuel Wishnow, 'I knew the next stop was Chicago. They had told us we were going overseas and we had had no leave. I left the tour without any permission to see my father in Lincoln, Nebraska. I couldn't get a train and I was finally on the way up to the airport and I saw Miller. He said, "Where do you think you're going?" I said, "I'm going home." He said, "You're nuts. You don't have any orders. I can't do anything for you." I said, "Well, I'll just have to take a chance." So, technically, I was AWOL – I had no orders, so I was ducking the MPS.

'I saw my father, and I got a midnight train to Lincoln – the Rock Island was still running. I had a reservation. I got to Chicago in time and Miller said, "Just make sure you're on the stand on time for rehearsal."

'We were staying at the Sherman Hotel and Veronica Lake and Walter Pidgeon were in the war bond show in Chicago. After the last *I Sustain the Wings* broadcast we had to catch a train and we were already late. Somebody brought us some sandwiches and stuff, and then the Mayor of Chicago held up all the traffic on Michigan Avenue and they took us tearing down the Avenue in our GI trucks. I don't think the traffic has been stopped that way since! A few days later we were in Camp Kilmer.'

Paul Whiteman replaced them on the War Bond Caravan and the Band returned to New Haven to prepare for their departure for England, including a long series of medical inoculations so familiar to all servicemen bound for overseas.

Among the men in the Band, feelings about the trip varied somewhat: while many of the younger jazz musicians were keen to go some of the older men were not so enthusiastic. 'After all, we were doing all right in the States,' says Emanuel Wishnow who originally came from London and still had relatives in England. 'I thought we'd be touring, making money for Uncle Sam, or whatever, and then out, but it didn't work out that way. I'd only been in the Band maybe two months, and then bang, we were going overseas already – it was a bit of a shock. My first thought was that I'd see my relatives. Many of the men said, we've got bad ears, we've got bad eyes, and so on, but I remember Miller called us up and said, "You know a lot of you have been declared unfit for overseas duty but I've had that waived – you're all going

Glenn Miller records ever made back in 1935). Captain Miller's closing announcement was included on a special sales promotion record released by RCA Victor in the USA in 1955 (for details of this record *see* page 396).

no matter what they said on your service records!" Miller wanted desperately to go over – he was the only one who really did.'

'Glenn worked for a long time to persuade the powers-that-be to let the Band go overseas,' recalls Bob Ripley. 'He thought that we weren't doing our part for the war effort unless we were right up there as close to the front as possible playing for the guys who were really doing the dirty work, so he worked very hard to have the Band go overseas. I remember once in the train going from New York back to Yale after a broadcast we were sitting around talking about the possibility of going across and Glenn said, "Boy, you know, I bet if we do ever go over we'll have a *ball*." Well, he found out that it was not such a ball once he got over there, and he had anything but a good time.'

Miller was concerned to ensure that the musicians got on well together and that not only was every man who was to make the trip at the peak of his musical proficiency but also that they were free from worries, so that they could face up to whatever trials might lie ahead without affecting the Band's musical standards. If any of the musicians were to drop out during the trip it would be difficult to obtain replacements of the high standard that Captain Miller required. Accordingly, when the overseas trip became a certainty two personnel changes had been made in the Band: baritone saxophonist Chuck Gentry, whose wife was ill, was released on compassionate grounds and his place was taken by Private First Class Mannie Thaler from the post band, and trombonist Jim Harwood, who suffered from ill-health, was replaced by Private First Class Nat Peck. To Nat Peck this was a 'bolt from the blue'. 'I was sitting in the Band's day room at New Haven one day,' he recalls, 'chewing the fat with Sergeant Sanderson the administrative NCO when the phone rang. It was Lieutenant Don Haynes congratulating me on being chosen to replace Jim Harwood who would not be going overseas. Until then I had no idea that Jim Harwood would not be going and I was amazed at this incredible stroke of luck, especially as I felt that other trombonists there had better claims to be in the Miller Band than I had.' Harry Katzman, however, said: 'Nat, of course, made it right away. I felt that of all the trombonists he was by far the best trombone player there, as far as I was concerned anyway.'

By early June Miller had selected from those under his command the men he wished to take overseas (see pages 76–8), and papers sent on 15 June from the Headquarters of the 3510th AAF

Base Unit (Technical School), Yale University, to which the Band was attached, to the Special Services Division of the AAF in Washington in preparation for the transfer overseas gave the composition of the Unit as 2 Officers (Captain Miller and 2nd Lieutenant Don W. Haynes, the Unit's Executive Officer – he had been Miller's band manager in civilian life and the two men had become close friends) and a 62-man Band* consisting of 2 Master Sergeants, 4 Technical Sergeants, 9 Staff Sergeants, 16 Sergeants, 19 Corporals and 12 Privates First Class. Most of the musicians took their own instruments instead of Army ones, some of which were quite valuable, especially the classical players' stringed instruments. There were also two bulky music libraries (the full orchestra's and Sergeant Ray McKinley's) to be taken, as well as music stands and a large collection of instrument spare parts and repair equipment, enormous stocks of manuscript paper and a spare set of drums.

All personnel had completed basic training and all were physically fit for overseas duty except for four with incomplete dentures. Their withdrawal would have reduced the Band's musical efficiency so the Army granted a special clearance for them to make the trip. As a technicality the Band was briefly transferred from the Training Command to the First Army Air Force (which was based in the north-eastern States) as no unit could go straight from the Training Command to an overseas posting. Approval for the movement of the Band to the ETO in its current state of readiness was given by General Joseph T. McNarney, Deputy Chief of Staff, US Army, on 14 June† and five days later, at 8.30 am on Monday 19 June, 61 enlisted men under Lieutenant Haynes left New Haven by train for Camp Kilmer, New Jersey, where they arrived at 3 o'clock in the afternoon.

For the next two days they were confined to camp. No telephone calls were allowed, and although they were able to write letters they could not disclose their whereabouts and of course their letters were censored. Lectures, films and more inoculations filled the two days and new, warmer uniforms were issued to the men.

At last, at 11.15 pm on the evening of 21 June they boarded a

* Not all the 62 enlisted men were musicians: the total included arrangers, announcers, producers and administrative personnel. The Band totalled 40 (*see* pages 76–8).

† Confirmed in writing on the 16th. On the 14th the Band were detached from the 2001st AAF Base Unit and became Casual Detachment 8245-MM (Band); they were activated as a Band on arrival in the ETO.

train at the camp's railway station and an hour later arrived in Jersey City. In sweltering heat, wearing steel helmets and greatcoats, loaded down with packs and barracks bags as well as their instruments and with their rifles slung over their shoulders, they marched to a pier on the Hudson River.

After coffee and doughnuts on the pier provided by the American Red Cross a ferry took them up the Hudson towards a huge ocean liner moored opposite Pier 90. Lieutenant Haynes' orders merely stated that the Band was to proceed to the ETO 'via NY 8245' and still lugging all their gear they climbed a stairway equivalent to five flights of stairs up the side of the immense ship towering above them. As they crossed the gangplank at the head of the stairs they discovered the identity of the vast ship they were boarding: 'NY 8245' was the British liner *Queen Elizabeth*.* As they stumbled on deck it was 1.15 in the morning.

Harry Katzman recalls their departure: 'It was supposed to be very secret, but actually I think there were over fifteen thousand people on that ship and as our turn came to board a band started playing "In The Mood" which tipped everyone off that the Glenn Miller Band was going overseas. The walk was very long – about a mile and a half, walking with that damned pack on our back – and when I got up on our deck and took off the straps there was nothing but blood on my shoulders; they had just cut in from the heavy stuff that we were carrying. I didn't even care if they sank that ship that night, we were so exhausted.'

'We had to carry all our gear to the top deck,' said Carmen Mastren, 'and I never wore the helmet till that day. We always wore the helmet liner. I was so tired I just fell into a bunk with everything on and woke up miles at sea. I had a headache for three days from that helmet.'

At five past eight next morning NY 8245 cast off and as tugs took the ship slowly out into the Hudson River all eyes were fixed on that familiar New York skyline – as it gradually receded everybody wondered when they would see it again and what might lie in store for them in the far-off ETO.

Captain Glenn Miller and Sergeant Paul Dudley, meanwhile, had left New Haven on 18 June and flown to England on the 21st

* The *Queen Elizabeth* was still under construction at Clydebank when the war began: when it was finished it (and the *Queen Mary*) was used as a troopship (minus the luxury) throughout the war. It did not make its civilian maiden voyage till 1946.

with orders to report to SHAEF in London. They took living quarters at the Mount Royal Hotel in Bryanston Street, near Marble Arch, which they retained throughout their sojourn in London. The Band was to be stationed in London from where they were to broadcast regularly in the Allied Expeditionary Forces Programme of the BBC which had been on the air all day, every day, since the day after D-Day. BBC planners had been expecting them for some time: as early as 13 June an internal memo from the Programme's Director had noted, *inter alia*, that 'Captain Glenn Miller and his band are said to be arriving about 1 July'.* Had it not been for the AEF Programme – and Colonel Kirby acting as go-between – they might never have come to Britain at all.

* Director, AEFP, to Acting Controller (Overseas Service) BBC, 13/6/44 (BBC Written Archives Centre R34/184/1).

CHAPTER FOUR

The Allied Expeditionary Forces Programme of the BBC – The arrival of the Miller Band in London – The Band's move to Bedford

The AEF Programme was General Eisenhower's idea. It had been set up in great secrecy by the BBC at the express personal request of General Eisenhower, Supreme Commander of the Allied Expeditionary Force. Some months before D-Day, during the planning for the invasion of Europe early in 1944, he informed the SHAEF Command that, as part of his policy of integration of all the forces under his command (British, American and Canadian), he wanted a special radio service for the troops who would be invading the Continent and for as long as the fighting in the West continued. The troops (including the naval and air forces) of the AEF numbered several million men of the three nationalities and a few from other Allied nations, and the new service would be a vital means of maintaining their morale, team spirit and sense of unity which would be so essential to the military success of the invasion and the hard fighting which would follow – possibly for many months. The service, to start when the invasion started, would provide troops with news, information and entertainment specially suited to their needs and interests, and would also be available to General Eisenhower for passing on instructions to them when necessary. Supreme Headquarters were anxious for the BBC co-operation: it already had a high reputation for its technical expertise and professional broadcasting skill and, moreover, it could provide a suitable transmitter. SHAEF wanted the service broadcast on the medium wave between certain hours of the day with a range of approximately three hundred miles from London and South Devon. The area of coverage could not be specified precisely owing to military security, although a top secret map of the proposed area of reception gave a privileged few a good idea of the actual landing areas selected for the forthcoming invasion!

Secret preliminary discussions between Major-General Ray W. Barker (US Army), head of SHAEF G-1 Division (Personnel), on behalf of General Eisenhower, and the BBC began at the end of March 1944. By early May, however, the BBC decided that it wanted nothing to do with what had become known inside the Corporation as 'the SHAEF programme'. But General Eisenhower, with Churchill's backing, persisted and under pressure from the Minister of Information, Brendan Bracken, and a warning that if they refused to run the programme SHAEF would do it themselves, the BBC acquiesced. SHAEF got what it wanted, although control and direction was to lie with the BBC. The programme was to be on completely integrated lines, like the SHAEF Command itself, and broadcast a mixture of the best of all three nations' resources. Music, variety and news would be the main ingredients – 50 per cent American, 35 per cent British and 15 per cent Canadian, the proportions of the three armies in the Allied Expeditionary Force. It was to be for the invasion forces only and not to be advertised or directed at the home (British) audience, and no public announcement about it was to be allowed until 6 pm on D-Day itself.

Once the agreement to run the AEF Programme had been signed on behalf of SHAEF by Lieutenant-General Walter Bedell Smith, General Eisenhower's Chief of Staff and General Barker's immediate superior, and for the BBC by the Director General W. J. Haley, on 23 May, the BBC lost no time in setting it up and the same day Haley appointed Maurice Gorham, at that time Acting Assistant Controller of the BBC Overseas Services, as director of the Programme. Although a bit of a 'rebel' Gorham was a BBC career man and had previously been in charge of the North American Service, including a spell in the USA. For advice and liaison with the BBC SHAEF appointed as its Director of Broadcasting Services Colonel Ed Kirby, who had worked with Gorham in the past and Kirby, in turn, secured Lieutenant-Colonel David Niven as Associate Director. Before becoming a Hollywood movie idol, Niven had been a regular British Army Officer and returned home at the outbreak of war to join up, seeing service as a Commando Officer. Later he did staff work at the War Office. Appearances in the wartime British films *The First Of The Few*, with Leslie Howard, and *The Way Ahead*, as well as his work as a BBC broadcaster kept him in the public eye. However, his work with the AEF Programme was quite unknown to the public at the time and Niven himself did not mention it in his autobiography, *The Moon's a Balloon*. But despite unsuccessfully resisting his transfer to SHAEF he seems to have done a very good job and was decorated for it by the Americans at the end of the war.

At Broadcasting House a specially selected staff began the intensive and hectic planning for the Programme. Many of them were former BBC personnel recalled from the Forces, including Captain Franklin Engelman who became Head of Presentation and Chief Announcer, and AC2 Ronnie Waldman, RAF, a producer and announcer. The planners had to set up a completely new service from scratch to meet an approaching deadline the date of which no-one was allowed to know – D-Day itself. They were required to have the Programme ready to go for 17 hours a day at three weeks' notice, but as Maurice Gorham wrote in *Sound and Fury*, 'It could have come at any time after 24 May'. As things turned out it went on the air only 15 days after the 'off' on 23 May. Administratively, the Programme was put under the Overseas Services, where it was known as the Violet Network, and not only was Gorham an extremely successful Director but the whole enterprise turned out to be a first-class example of inter-Allied co-operation from Barker/Kirby/Niven/Gorham downwards, despite backstage friction from time to time.

It was agreed that the American Forces Network, then operating in the UK using low-powered transmitters over localized areas where American troops were concentrated, would provide the American programmes including Armed Forces Radio Service recordings from Hollywood; the BBC would provide the British material mainly but not exclusively from their General Forces Programme, and the London office of the Canadian Broadcasting Corporation would supply Canadian programmes. Announcers from all three countries would alternate on the air. As most of the programmes would be in the form of recordings a small production unit was also set up to make programmes specially for the AEFP under producer Cecil Madden who was brought in as Executive Producer in addition to his existing duties in charge of all entertainment programmes in the Overseas Services. General Eisenhower wanted to approve the actual programme schedules himself.

The BBC provided a transmitter at Start Point, South Devon, to broadcast the AEFP on 285 metres, 1050 kilocycles, medium wave. All the technicians were BBC staff and great care was taken with the engineering side so that the Programme could be picked up by wireless sets used by the troops in the field and in the rest areas. It was to be carefully beamed towards the areas on the Continent where the invasion forces would be operating and it was also arranged that it could be received by Allied forces still in Southern England awaiting their turn to cross the Channel as well as those in UK hospitals, camps, airfields, etc.

Once D-Day arrived the BBC got the go-ahead and the AEF Programme began broadcasting at 05.55 a.m. on Wednesday 7 June, the morning after D-Day. From the start it was a great success with the troops. With news on the hour, it consisted mostly of dance music and jazz, vocal and light music, variety and comedy, sport, and some classical music although less of this than other types. Talks and 'serious' music were deliberately avoided for the most part as a matter of policy, but up-to-the-minute despatches from War Correspondents at the front were broadcast regularly as the troops were cheered up enormously to hear reports of actions in which they had been engaged. It was all carefully selected to suit the special circumstances of the troops many of whom would be listening in crowded, noisy canteens and billets, or even in foxholes or lining up in cookhouses and thus unable to concentrate on the more serious stuff. And all the time it was providing a constant link with home enabling them to hear many of the programmes they would be hearing if they were at home and often at the same time as their families were listening. Wherever troops were gathered – in assembly areas, cookhouses, rest areas and hospitals – their radios were often tuned to the AEFP throughout the day, sometimes with loudspeakers hung from trees or balanced on tanks or lorries. Naval ships in the Channel relayed the programme over their Tannoy systems and aircrews flying home from combat missions tuned in. General Eisenhower listened to it while travelling in his staff car.

Drawing its material as it did from such widespread sources the Programme had the pick of the best entertainment from Britain, Canada and the USA, mostly in recorded transcription form but also in simultaneous live broadcasts from the Home Service and GFP.

Once the AEFP was under way, more and more programmes specially produced by it in London were included in the schedules – eventually up to six hours a day – reflecting the principle of 'integration': not only American announcers introducing British artists and *vice versa*, British singers with American bands, and so on, but also making use of the increasing flow of stars from America, many of whom, like Bing Crosby, were not billed in advance owing to wartime security blackouts.

The AEFP was always keen to obtain live talent as a contrast to the staple diet of 'canned' entertainment and Colonel Kirby, for instance, who saw his job as not just policy but 'service . . . and originating suggestions'* 'had from the first talked of bringing over American star talent from Hollywood'. The AEFP policy was that 'this imported talent should be built into joint shows by using British guest artists, announcers and scriptwriters'.†

Thus, it was to fit into this overall plan for inter-Allied co-operation and 'integration' in radio entertainment that Captain Glenn Miller and his Army Air Forces Band came to England at the end of June, 1944.

Captain Miller and Sergeant Paul Dudley found London a stark contrast to the New York they had left behind. Ruined buildings were everywhere and many bombed sites had been converted into emergency brick-built 'static water tanks' for fighting air raid fires, and important buildings were sandbagged. The city was full of troops of all Allied nationalities on leave as well as those stationed at military headquarters all over London. Shops were drab and sparsely stocked and most of their windows were boarded up with small panes of glass in the middle to minimise flying glass in air raids. Practically everything was rationed and there was a five shillings limit on the price of restaurant meals which in any case were usually austere. Many West End hotels and blocks of flats were requisitioned to accommodate military personnel and walking down Piccadilly, for instance, one was confronted with khaki washing hanging from windows of formerly exclusive blocks! Military vehicles outnumbered civilian and traffic drove on the other side of the road! At night there was the blackout. Worse of all, a few days earlier the new German pilotless aircraft – the V-1 flying bombs, nicknamed 'doodlebugs' – had begun to drop all over the city and south-east England with increasing frequency (up to about a

* From Minutes of Meeting at Broadcasting House, 14 June 1944 (BBC WAC R34/184/1).

† From Memorandum from Maurice Gorham to Acting Controller (Overseas Service) 13 June 1944 (BBC WAC R34/184/1). An interesting account of his experiences in setting up and running the AEF Programme is given by Maurice Gorham in his book *Sound and Fury*, (P. Marshall, London, 1948); Professor Asa Briggs also describes briefly the origins and conduct of the Programme in *The War of Words* (History of Broadcasting in the United Kingdom, Vol. III, OUP, London, 1970).

hundred a day at the height of the attacks) and Miller found himself sleeping in a bomb shelter deep underneath Broadcasting House which was covered in camouflage paint, scarred by bombs and fortified till it looked like a military blockhouse. After a week in the bomb-blasted city, Miller concluded that 'London was rotten to the core – they ought to tear the whole thing down and start over again'.

The Band arrived at Gourock on the Clyde on 28 June after a six-day voyage. Although by that time the U-Boat war had been largely won and the U-Boat menace considerably reduced their voyage had not been without hazard and incident. The two *Queens* never sailed in convoy or with escorts as their speed was enough to outstrip any pursuing enemy vessel so the liner was on its own once it got out into the Atlantic. Nevertheless, it maintained radio silence and changed course regularly to confuse enemy radar. Several days out a pack of U-Boats were detected but the liner's tactics successfully avoided them. For the first few days, with the ship heading in the general direction of the Azores, the sea was calm and the weather warm but as it turned north-east and approached the British Isles storms blew up and the sea became so rough that several of the Band were laid low by seasickness.

'The ship was divided into three sections – red, white and blue,' recalls Bob Ripley, 'and we were in the red section on the Main Deck. You weren't allowed to leave your section because you could get lost in that ship it was so huge. They served two meals a day, which I think was standard procedure on troop ships, and the Mess Hall just had a constant line of troops all day.'

'It was most certainly not a luxury cruise,' says Nat Peck. 'The ship had been gutted to accommodate many times the normal number of passengers since its transformation as a troop carrier and contained rows of berths layered four or five deep with minimum spacing to permit access – just within limits for breathing and avoiding claustrophobia. We shared these quarters with other troops but despite crowding and discomfort flareups between members of the Band were of little consequence and griping was minimal. One of the main problems was catering for the great number of troops on board – something like 15,000. The food queue was interminable. Having finished breakfast we immediately got back on the queue for the next meal. Some of us solved this problem simply by getting provisions of chocolate bars from the ship's PX that served to replace breakfast, lunch and dinner. Occasionally we would give impromptu concerts, much appreciated by the troops. They were more like jam sessions, really, but they did serve to keep us in playing shape. The remaining leisure was spent on the sun deck trying to spot that submarine, and, of course, the traditional immense dice games, commonly known as crap games, where fortunes were made and lost. Broderick Crawford kept us amused with his Hemingway- ish stories straight from the ship commander's table and reports on the war's progress. The landing at Gourock after six days at sea was much welcomed. We were delighted by the picturesque hilly greenery – the views were fine and the weather splendid, and Captain Miller was there to greet us.'

Carmen Mastren also recalled that it was not too smooth a trip; however, there were compensations: 'We met some very nice chaps from an artillery outfit who cleaned our rifles for us and when the inspecting officer came round he couldn't believe this was a bunch of musicians. Little did he know who did the work.'

As an officer Lieutenant Haynes was spared the worst horrors of life aboard a troopship. He shared a stateroom with eleven other Air Force Officers – newly trained pilots, navigators and bombardiers headed for bases in England and bombing missions over Germany. On the seventh day he was awakened at 3.30 am for a Unit Commanders meeting where, after warnings not to disclose to anyone ashore how they got there, they were given instructions for disembarkation and shortly afterwards the ship dropped anchor at Gourock.

At 11.30 that morning, 28 June, Lieutenant Haynes was called over the ship's PA system to report to the Captain's cabin and, as he entered, there to welcome him grinning broadly was Captain Miller who had flown up from London the previous day. Looking tired after nights in the shelters in London, he accompanied Lieutenant Haynes down to the Band's quarters and in a serious mood told them about the day and night attacks on the capital by the flying bombs.

The Band disembarked mid-afternoon and after a short train journey they had several hours in Glasgow for sightseeing and their first taste of the local beer. At 10 pm they boarded a troop train for the overnight journey to London and at first, in the long light evenings (it was Double British Summer Time), the men were impressed by the beautiful British countryside they were travelling through. Later, as darkness fell, the train was blacked-out and some managed a few hours sleep.

At Euston at seven o'clock the next morning it was clear that Miller's warnings about the dangers of the flying bombs had been accurate. As they trooped out of the station the sirens went and hardly had their ominous notes faded away when the drone of a flying bomb grew steadily louder. While people ran for shelter in all directions the Band stood under an archway at the station entrance and as they peered skyward the bomb flew overhead. Almost at once its engine cut out. Seconds later a huge explosion shook the area and they could see a cloud of smoke not far away. It was a grim welcome.

Soon afterwards, US Army trucks and a staff car took the Band to its London billet in a requisitioned block of flats in Sloane Court, Chelsea, off Lower Sloane Street. Two of the men, however, Sergeant Broderick Crawford and Corporal Julie Zifferblatt, had stayed behind in Glasgow until the Band's equipment could be unloaded from the *Queen Elizabeth* and they could bring it to London. It was another week before they caught up with the Band.

Unprepared as they were for such an abrupt transition from the bright lights and safety of America the men found themselves in an unexpectedly hazardous situation. They were, after all, professional musicians, albeit in uniform, who had never heard a shot fired in anger, not experienced troops accustomed to being under fire. The dangers were obvious – one flying bomb on their billet could wipe out a unique and highly professional unit which could not be replaced. At best it could adversely affect their musical performances, at any rate until they got used, as Londoners had, to the noisy and dangerous existence. Miller felt a personal responsibility for this all-star outfit, some of whom were personal friends from civilian life, which he had put together and eventually contrived to bring to London and he had already resolved to lose no time in getting them away to a safer place. The military authorities, too, were worried that a flying bomb might make a direct hit on a studio during a live broadcast – there were not enough security (underground) studios for all broadcasting needs at the time – and thus reveal to the Germans that they had the correct range for attacking London at the very time when Allied deception measures were being put into operation.

While the Band settled into its new quarters, Miller, Haynes and Paul Dudley went by staff car to SHAEF headquarters at Bushey Park, near Teddington, Middlesex, to meet Colonel David Niven and a SHAEF transport officer who, at Miller's request, was already trying to obtain transport to move the Band out of London. As the Band had been sent to London in the first place to fulfil a regular broadcasting commitment – a posting arranged before the flying bomb attacks had started on 13 June – any move would have to be to somewhere where broadcasting facilities comparable to those in London were available and which were out of range of the flying bombs.

After lunch, twice interrupted by air raid warnings, Niven took them to Bedford, which had become an important wartime centre of BBC broadcasting, to see whether studios and accommodation could be made available. They looked first at a single-storey building on the western outskirts of the town, just off Ford End Road: this was Co-Partners Hall, taken over by the BBC from the local gas company in 1941, and decided that, with some special modifications, it could be used by the Band for broadcasting. Then they crossed the town to the American Red Cross Officers Club, a prefabricated building at the corner of Kimbolton Road and Goldington Road (the site is now a car park) where they arranged accommodation for Miller and Haynes as well as quarters for the Band at 42–44 Ashburnham Road,* two large detached houses which had been taken over as a dormitory annex to the ARC Enlisted Mens Club round the corner in Bromham Road, near Bedford Station. After dinner at the Officers Club they returned to London, with Captain Miller greatly relieved that the Band could be relocated out of London. The only remaining problem was transport to get them there.

They arrived back in London as dusk was falling (about 11.15 Double British Summer Time at that time of the year) and as they were on their way to spend the night in the BBC deep shelter, where Captain Miller had slept every night since his arrival in London eight days earlier, an air raid warning sounded and not far off a flying bomb passed over. As they watched, its motor cut out and seconds later a tremendous explosion lit up the sky. Lieutenant Haynes noted, at the end of his first day in London, 'The past seventeen hours were eventful to say the least'.

Haynes and Miller awoke at 6.30 the next morning to the strains of a string quartet and realized that they had been sleeping on the other side of the wall of an underground security studio. Despite only five hours sleep, they got up, walked to the Mount Royal and after a shower, a shave and a somewhat makeshift snack, they went by taxi to Sloane Court to see how the Band had fared during its first night in London. As they got out of

* Now occupied by local offices of the Ministry of Agriculture and the Department of Environment.

the taxi they saw about a dozen of the men coming along the street carrying blankets and instrument cases which they had used as pillows: all but four of the Band had spent the night in a shelter near the Billet. Sergeants Dudley, Zarchy and Desmond and Corporal Cochrane couldn't stand the stuffy atmosphere of the shelter and had returned to their quarters where the continuous droning of the doodlebugs overhead had given them a sleepless night. 'The bombs were coming over thick and furiously,' recalls Nat Peck, 'and sleep was impossible. I was pretty damn scared about the whole depressing business. The air raid shelter became a home away from home where I was able to meditate on the peaceful campus and quadrangle of Yale University where the most dangerous assignment would be the daily retreat parade with Sergeant Ray McKinley directly behind me giving me a bad time. Obviously I am not too proud of my uninhibited cowardice at this time, but the war in Europe was something that one read about in the newspapers back in the States and although we were all very aware of how much suffering had been endured during the bombing of the principal cities during the Battle of Britain through the medium of newsreel and cinema and so on, by the time we were preparing for the crossing that period of the war was over and we expected that England would be quite safe.'

'I can't tell you how impressed I was during our stay in England,' says John Halliburton, 'by the casual bravery shown by the civilians, what with bombs going off all over the place. They erased any fears one might have had by example.'

Naturally, Captain Miller was more determined than ever to get the Band out of London as soon as possible. He and Haynes drove to SHAEF on Friday the 30th, and after telephone calls to a dozen or more US air bases they finally secured two buses to move the entire unit to Bedford two days later, and by mid-afternoon SHAEF had given official approval for the move. Back in London, they called at Sloane Court to give the Band the good news and then once more slept underground at the BBC where several flying bombs landed so close to the building that the concrete floor shook beneath their beds.

Next morning (Saturday) Captain Miller and Lieutenant Haynes called again at Sloane Court to see how the Band had got through the night and found that *all* of them had spent the night in the shelter. But business was pressing now and Captain Miller was anxious to start the work they had come to do, so with Lieutenant Haynes and Sergeant Dudley he spent the whole day at SHAEF with Colonels Kirby and Niven working out broadcasting schedules for the Band. That evening, after dinner with Colonel Kirby and Teddy Gower, the BBC balance engineer who had been allocated full-time to the Band for their broadcasts, Colonel Kirby took Miller and Haynes down to an Underground station where the sight of hundreds of Londoners sleeping on the platforms made a deep impression on them. Once again they spent this, their last night in London for the time being, sleeping under Broadcasting House, interrupted at intervals by flying bombs exploding nearby.

On Sunday 2 July, Captain Miller and Lieutenant Haynes were up at seven and took a taxi to Sloane Court, to find the buses already there and the men loading their kit. They had had another night of flying bombs, one of which had come down only three blocks from their shelter, and they could hardly wait to get out of London. They left Chelsea at 10 am and as they drove into Bedford about noon and made their way to Ashburnham Road the sun came out which cheered everyone up as like most Americans they thought the sun rarely shone in England! What cheered them up even more of course was the knowledge that there would be no more flying bombs. From now on, the only aircraft noise they would hear would be the daily drone of US Eighth Air Force and RAF planes en route to bomb Germany almost round the clock from the many American and British airfields surrounding Bedford. Subsequent events only a few hours later were to show tragically that they had not left London a moment too soon.

CHAPTER FIVE

The BBC in Bedford – A flying bomb on Sloane Court – Three bands of the Supreme Allied Command – The Band's first BBC broadcast

The seeds of the Miller Band's move to Bedford had been sown some three or four years earlier, though quite unknown of course to the Band themselves who were then far away in the still-neutral United States and not yet even in uniform. But why Bedford?

At the outbreak of war in 1939, in accordance with meticulously prepared plans, many BBC departments had been evacuated overnight from London to various places in the provinces, several of them to Bristol, so that regular broadcasting could continue uninterrupted by German air raids. But as the war progressed, air raids spread to many provincial cities and Bristol suffered considerable damage. Eventually, some of the BBC units had had to leave Bristol, among them the Music Department and the BBC Symphony Orchestra and its conductor Sir Adrian Boult, who had moved to the comparative safety of Bedford from where they had been able to broadcast regularly since September 1941. Bedford had been chosen because the BBC needed a town not too far from London and on a main railway line, capable of billeting about 500 staff and artists. It also needed the use of four or five halls of convenient size and suitable acoustics, and somewhere which had access to main telephone trunk lines.

The BBC moved in in July 1941 and by 1944 had developed several groups of studios, including the main hall of the Corn Exchange in St Paul's Square and the Co-Partners Hall, and many Bedford people were able to attend broadcasts, especially from the Corn Exchange which was used for the latter part of the

1944 Promenade Concerts after the London Proms were abandoned on 29 June owing to the flying bomb danger to the Royal Albert Hall. Programmes performed in the Bedford studios were fed to London by landline and broadcast via Broadcasting House.

The Corn Exchange also housed a Forces canteen in the extensive basement rooms which had been set up for the Bedford Council by Alderman J. Canvin in Jauary 1940 and the main hall was often used for concerts for the Forces and sometimes for the civilian public. Besides the Army and RAF personnel in and around Bedford, including the regular intake of new recruits at nearby RAF Cardington, there had been a large influx of American servicemen and women into the area as the US Eighth Air Force airfields sprang up around Bedford from 1942 onwards and by 1944 there were numerous American Red Cross Clubs in Bedford for the Americans, including a large one for enlisted men in Bromham Road (the building is now a petrol station).

Bedford, therefore, was the ideal, safe place to send the Miller Band and it remained there until it went to France in December 1944.

Bedford was also within easy reach of many of the Eighth Air Force airfields in eastern England to which Captain Miller intended taking the Band to play concerts for the airmen, and during that time they made many trips to airfields and military bases by road and by air, usually flying from the nearby RAF airfield at Twinwood Farm or the Flying Fortress base at Thurleigh.

After settling into its new quarters on Sunday afternoon, 2 July, the Band had its first good night's sleep since arriving in Britain. The following morning Miller and Haynes called at the Band's billet and finding the men still asleep left a message for Sergeant Sanderson, the administrative NCO, to get them into fatigue dress and over to Co-Partners Hall at 12 noon to clean it up and prepare it for broadcasting. They reported on schedule and got to work and, after BBC engineers had put in extra wiring, by the end of the week it was ready for use. Harry Katzman suggested the hall should be christened '8H' after the big studio at Radio City in New York from where many of the men had broadcast before the war, and the name stuck.

The Co-Partners Hall was a rather insignificant-looking, single-storey brick building belonging to the local gas company. Before being taken over by the BBC it was the firm's social club and had got its name because the company had a profit-sharing scheme with its staff. It was partly surrounded by open space, mostly allotments, grass and a tennis court, and was overshadowed by the gas works. It seemed an unlikely place to produce the latest American swing music and jazz by professional musicians from the heart of the sophisticated American music world in New York City and it became known among the Band as 'the shack in the field'.

'It was a little, dingy, miserable place that we all loved,' recalls Nat Peck, 'mainly because it was out of London and away from the bombs. It was an informal set-up where we could relax and do our work without interruption.'

Sometimes between broadcasts and rehearsals some of the men played soft-ball on the grass outside. It was here, too, that they discovered fish and chips: on the corner of Lawrence Street, which leads down to Co-Partners Hall from Ford End Road, there was a fish and chip shop, which is there to this day, where Captain Miller also joined the hungry queue!

The Band was given exclusive use of Co-Partners Hall for broadcasting and rehearsals and it was from there that all the *Swing Shift*, *Uptown Hall* and *Strings With Wings* broadcasts were made. It was too small to accommodate a studio audience as well as the performers, but some of the broadcasts by the full Band were also made from there later on when the Corn Exchange was not available. Live broadcasts were fed to London by landline and transmitted over the air via Broadcasting House and from time to time pre-recordings by the various bands were also made in London over the landline from Co-Partners Hall.

'The sound in Co-Partners Hall was terrible,' recalls Carmen Mastren, 'until we took our shelter halves and tied them to the ceiling. We had a big band and had to try to absorb some of the sound. It worked out fine and as you know some mighty fine sounds came from that studio.'

On Wednesday morning, 5 July, Haynes obtained a weapons carrier, similar to a British Army 15-cwt lorry, and a driver from a nearby AAF Service Command Base (probably at Milton Ernest Hall) and went to London to pick up the Band's mail from SHAEF's London headquarters. During lunch with a SHAEF transport officer, who was organizing a staff car for Captain Miller and a licence for Lieutenant Haynes to drive it,* the transport officer

---

* Officers were not normally allowed to drive military vehicles on duty but a severe shortage of drivers made it necessary for Haynes to do so. They were allocated a British Wolseley car and two British buses, which were frequently in the motor pool because of breakdowns, and two GI drivers.

casually mentioned that a flying bomb had dropped on Sloane Court at eight o'clock on Monday morning – the day after the Band had moved out to Bedford! After lunch, Haynes' curiosity got the better of him and before returning to Bedford he instructed the driver to go via Sloane Court, little dreaming that within the hour he himself would have a narrow escape in a flying bomb 'incident'.

They arrived to find the area roped off and the Band's former billet a shambles. The bomb had apparently dropped in the roadway outside the building and just behind an Army truck, killing 25 US Military Police in the truck. Seventy other victims had been dug out of the surrounding ruins. While they were looking at the rubble the sirens went and as they ran for cover a flying bomb passed not more than three hundred feet overhead, its engine cut out and it dived to earth. As Haynes and his driver hurled themselves to the ground the bomb went off with a deafening roar and when they got to their feet and brushed the dust from their uniforms the clouds of dust and smoke from the explosion had almost turned day into night. They ran towards the scene of the explosion and helped to lift the injured on to stretchers until ambulances arrived. Miller's insistence on moving out of London had been amply justified and he confided to Haynes that he had had an intuition about Sloane Court.

'When Miller decided he wanted us to move to Bedford on the Sunday (2 July)', recalls Bob Ripley, 'the Motor Pool said, "We don't work on Sunday". Miller replied "We're moving on Sunday", and he had enough authority and power to force the issue. He made them move us on the Sunday and it was our good fortune that he did. We went back to Sloane Court later – the end of the block where we had been living had not been demolished but the windows were all out and the door was knocked off and who knows what might have happened. We might have been walking to breakfast at the time the bomb fell, as we did every day early in the morning and we might have gotten it that way, or the jolt of the blast might have injured some of us. There's no way of telling, but we had to agree that it was very fortunate that Miller had insisted that we move on Sunday and not wait another day. Miller saved our lives.'

Two days after his narrow escape at Sloane Court, Haynes again drove to London, this time with Miller and Dudley, for discussions at SHAEF with Colonel Kirby and Colonel Niven about the Band's AEFP radio schedule and personal appearances in the London area. Waiting for them at SHAEF were the two men they had left behind in Glasgow, Sergeant Broderick Crawford and Corporal Julie Zifferblatt with the Band's equipment. While they were having lunch in a London restaurant the sirens went and it was Crawford's and Zifferblat's turn to experience their first flying bomb which exploded several blocks away.

At SHAEF that morning Miller, Haynes and Dudley were told that in future the Band would be known as 'The American Band of the Supreme Allied Command' for broadcasts and personal appearances. This change of name reflected its new military connection. On arriving in England it was attached to the Headquarters Command at SHAEF, although it was still an Army Air Forces unit (the AAF had ensured this when arranging its transfer to the ETO) and within the Service it still retained the official designation Army Air Forces Band (Special) which it had had in America. It remained an AAF unit throughout its overseas posting. The Band – 2 officers and 62 enlisted men – kept its identity as a small independent unit with Captain Glenn Miller as Commanding Officer, Lieutenant Haynes as Executive Officer and Master Sergeant Zeke Zarchy as senior non-commissioned officer. Miller was responsible, through Colonel Kirby (Director of Broadcasting Services. SHAEF) to General Barker. The SHAEF Broadcasting Service worked from offices at 80 Portland Place, conveniently close to Broadcasting House, which also housed the headquarters of the British operations of the American Forces Network, commanded by Major John S. (Johnny) Hayes – all three organizations worked closely together in the AEF Programme. Captain Miller and Sergeant Dudley were given an office on the fifth floor of the Langham Hotel opposite Broadcasting House, then and until recently a BBC office block.

General Barker, a former artillery Colonel, had been posted to England soon after America entered the war and helped to plan the Allied landings in North Africa in 1942 and then the D-Day invasion of Europe. In the spring of 1944 he was appointed SHAEF G-1 and an Assistant Chief of Staff to General Bedell Smith, in command of the Personnel Division of SHAEF where among his many responsibilities were radio broadcasting to the troops of the Allied Expeditionary Force and relations with the BBC with whom he had negotiated the setting up of the AEF Programme. Maurice Gorham remembered him as 'a formidable character' although warm-hearted underneath who eventually became a fervent admirer of the BBC. Certainly, he must have been something of a diplomat as it fell to him to smooth over various crises in SHAEF's relations with the BBC. After Miller's disappearance he took a personal interest in the Band and it was probably due to him as much as anyone that the Band continued to function instead of being broken up or sent back to the United States. Captain Miller's position in the military hierarchy (Miller – Kirby – Barker – Smith – Eisenhower) was only four steps away from the Supreme Commander himself and he and the Band had personal associations with General Eisenhower and his staff on various occasions.

The Band had come to England specifically to broadcast regularly in the AEF Programme for as long as it lasted and personal appearances to the troops had to be fitted in between broadcasting commitments. Civilian engagements were not allowed, although several charity performances were given while the Band was in England and, latterly, in France. Their military duties consisted of morale-boosting broadcasts and concerts for the troops and there were no parade ground duties. Together with rehearsals and travelling they were soon to find it a very full schedule.

However, back in June, before the Band had left the United States, the BBC had decreed that 'Glenn Millar [sic] should not be allowed to become the single "house band" of the AEFP'.*

This meant that, true to the spirit of 'integration' as laid down for the AEFP, as it was also for the SHAEF Command, British and Canadian bands had to be found to take their allotted places in the radio schedules and provide between them roughly the same amount of air time as the American Band to satisfy the proportions of 50 per cent American programmes, 35 per cent British and 15 per cent Canadian already laid down. The British provided the Army Radio Orchestra conducted by RSM George Melachrino and specially augmented to about fifty musicians as the British Band of the Supreme Allied Command, and the Canadians their Royal Canadian Artillery Band, directed by Warrant Officer Reg Newman, as a temporary Canadian Band until the 'new' Canadian Band conducted by Captain Robert Farnon arrived from Canada and began broadcasting in September 1944. Early in August all three Bands were renamed

* From a Memo from the Acting Controller (Overseas Service) to Director, AEFP, 19/6/44 (the same day the Band left New Haven for Camp Kilmer) (BBC WAC R34/184/1).

the American (etc.) Band of the Allied Expeditionary Force and they kept these titles until the end of the AEF Programme in July 1945 when they went their separate ways.

The American Band was the first of the three 'house bands' to broadcast on the AEF Programme and in a remarkably short time its daily broadcasting schedule, including programmes by three smaller bands drawn from the full personnel (*see* page 78), was worked out and slotted into the programme's timetable. Less than two weeks after its arrival in England its programmes were all printed in advance in the new special AEF edition of the *Radio Times* distributed free to the troops every week.

Once the Band's music arrived in Bedford with Sergeant Crawford and Corporal Zifferblatt on Friday 7 July, they could begin rehearsals for their new broadcasts. The Band's first engagement in the ETO, however, was on Saturday evening, 8 July, when Sergeant Ray McKinley led a small group from the Band at an officers' dance at the Eighth Air Force Service Command HQ at Milton Ernest Hall, about five miles north of Bedford. Then, on Saturday morning, 9 July, the whole Band assembled in the Corn Exchange for a rehearsal for their first broadcast due from 7.15 to 8 pm that evening, live on the AEF Programme. A small group of interested BBC staff gathered to listen to the rehearsal, such was the reputation that had preceded Glenn Miller. It was a revelation to them – his dedication, attention to detail and the standard of perfection he constantly sought far exceeded anything they had seen and heard from 'dance band' leaders in the past, particularly to get the sound and balance he wanted.

The broadcast that evening was a 'big' occasion with many high-ranking American officers in the large audience (the Corn Exchange could accommodate about 750 for a broadcast). Colonel Kirby, Colonel Niven and Maurice Gorham travelled from London and they were joined in the front row by senior officers from Milton Ernest Hall. The broadcast was not just the first in the Band's regular series but a special extra programme presented as a welcome from the AEFP and the forces in the ETO to their new 'visitors' the Miller Band. True to the spirit of integration the BBC brought in two of the leading British singers of the day – Dorothy Carless and Bruce Trent – as guest artists together with Movietone Newsreel's commentator Leslie Mitchell, as host and joint compere with Captain Miller.

The script today seems embarrassingly corny and naïve, even allowing for the atmosphere of the time and the excitement of the occasion. But the music was the thing. Nothing like it had ever been heard in the Corn Exchange, and for forty-five minutes this memorable, and evocative music, which many of the American servicemen in the hall and over the air recalled only too well from hearing the Band back in the States, poured out what Glenn Miller called 'a hunk of home'. It is not difficult to imagine their reactions.

The programme opened with the familiar Glenn Miller signature tune, 'Moonlight Serenade', with strings added to the Miller saxophone sound, and it was followed by a new tune which Leslie Mitchell announced was to be the Band's new theme music for their AEFP broadcasts – 'The Flaming Sword Of Liberation',* composed by Captain Miller. There is no trace, however, that the Band ever played this tune after that night, as all their subsequent broadcasts opened and closed with 'Moonlight Serenade'! The rest of the programme was a thrilling parade of many of the Band's best-loved numbers from 'In The Mood' to 'What Do You Do In The Infantry'. Dorothy Carless sang 'Begin the Beguine' and Bruce Trent sang one of the biggest hit songs of the day 'I Couldn't Sleep A Wink Last Night'. The programme ended with what seems to have been the last performance of 'The Flaming Sword Of Liberation'.

Recalling the programme some years later, Maurice Gorham wrote:

I remember the night he had his first broadcast and I went down to Bedford for the occasion. There were six of us in a big American Army car: an American Colonel [probably Colonel Kirby], two Sergeants (one of them Broderick Crawford, afterwards famous on the films), David Niven, a driver and me.

We dined at an American officers' mess about twenty miles the other side of Bedford, in a fake Elizabethan manor-house that our hosts thought was genuine. The food was American and better than you could get anywhere else in England in 1944; the whiskey was genuine Bourbon, but the conversation was so fatuous that Niven and I were driven nearly frantic. Then we drove back to the Corn Exchange at Bedford, which was packed with American uniforms; all the top brass in Britain seemed to be there.

I went up to the control box to see how the serious side of the business was going on and ran into a balance-and-control man I knew, so before the broadcast we nipped out to have a quick pint in the pub round the corner

* An allusion to the flaming sword in the official SHAEF emblem which all SHAEF personnel, including the Miller Band, wore on their left sleeves and which was painted on the Band's music stands and on Sergeant Ray McKinley's bass drum, although by the first broadcast there hadn't been time to paint them on yet.

and for ten minutes I felt human again. I got back to the box just in time to hear David Niven introduce me from the stage. He had been put up there without any warning to introduce all the personalities present. You never saw such a fuss before a broadcast went on the air.

It was a first-rate broadcast when it came. His Band had plenty . . . soloists like Ray McKinley the crazy drummer, Mel Powell, Gerry [*sic*] Gray, and those glorious strings. Glenn worked them hard, too. He never spared himself or them.*

* *Irish Times*, 28 January 1961. Gorham later explained that 'Glenn Miller was not present at the dinner party where I described the conversation as fatuous. (There was a smaller party in his billet after the show.)'

CHAPTER SIX

Relations with the BBC – The personnel of the Band and the bands-within-the-Band – The American Dance Band (*The Swing Shift*) – The Swing Sextet (*The Uptown Hall*) – The Strings with Wings – Sergeant Johnny Desmond – The Band's radio schedule – The British public hear the Band for the first time – A disagreement with the BBC – The first airfield concert: Thurleigh

There is no doubt that throughout SHAEF and the BBC Captain Glenn Miller and the Band were regarded as a splendid acquisition. Maurice Gorham described it later as 'a real achievement [by Colonel Kirby] and a great asset to the Programme, though it led to plenty of trouble and to Glenn's own tragic death in the end'.* They were also determined to make the best possible use of the Band and the heavy broadcasting schedule (almost daily) which it fulfilled throughout its thirteen months in England and Europe had complete priority over all its other work, for broadcasts could reach a much vaster audience than any number of concerts to a few thousand servicemen, valuable morale boosters though these personal appearances were.

Much has been written and talked about the relations (sometimes less than harmonious) between Miller and the BBC. A lot of this seems to have been due to misunderstandings on both sides. When Miller first came to London he thought he was coming over to run a radio service, not simply to fit into one with programmes by his Band. Perhaps this was not surprising, considering the wording of the original request from the US Army in England for the Band to be sent over from America – no doubt carefully composed (reportedly by Colonel Kirby) so as to ensure that the request was not refused. Soon after Miller's arrival Franklin Engelman went to see him at the Mount Royal Hotel where he put the BBC's plans for broadcasts by the Band.

* *Sound and Fury.*

74

Although at first hostile to the integration of his Band into the AEFP Miller eventually agreed – indeed he could really do little else now that he was in England.

Friction also arose over the Band's personal appearances at American air bases lest they should interfere with the AEFP broadcast schedule, and later over Miller's repeated attempts to take the Band to France to play to the combat troops, 'the ones who are slugging it out for all of us', as he put it. But the BBC was only protecting its assets, and the broadcasts *were* the primary reason for bringing the Band to England. Eventually, Miller became convinced, wrongly, that everyone was working against him and making life as difficult as possible. The BBC tried hard to give him everything he asked for, although some felt that, like many Americans posted to Britain from a land of plenty, he never really appreciated the difficulties, and particularly the severe shortages of practically everything in a country in its fifth year of war. Once misunderstandings were removed, and the two nationalities understood each other's attitudes and methods better, things ran more smoothly.

The Band began its regular schedule of daily AEFP broadcasts on Monday 10 July, but not all the programmes were by the full Band. Once in England, Miller realized that with such a heavy broadcasting schedule it would soon run out of material, or be forced into constant repetition, for it was a major undertaking to keep up a regular flow of new arrangements for the full 40-piece orchestra. Nevertheless, it is remarkable how little repetition there was during the six months the Band was broadcasting from England, although this changed somewhat when it went to the Continent. So plans were worked out for several smaller bands to be drawn from the full personnel to broadcast on their own playing different kinds of music, thus making the Band an all-round musical organization able to provide a wide range of music from Goodman-type jazz trio and quartet, small band swing and Dixieland by a sextet, the whole field of big-band swing and dance music (not just the Miller style) by the band without the strings, popular singers with orchestral accompaniment and the full orchestra with strings, to light and classical music by the string section on its own.

These smaller 'bands-within-the-band' were another innovation for a Glenn Miller band, as the civilian Band had never had a small group as had many other big-name bands in the USA and even the AAF Band itself had not had them back in America. But in England their assignment was a different one and the needs of the AEF Programme made a wider range of activity inevitable. The British and Canadian Bands also provided smaller bands for separate broadcasts, as all three Bands covered a similar musical spectrum.

The basic performing instrumentation of the full forty-piece Band normally consisted of five trumpets, four trombones (plus Captain Glenn Miller joining in on some numbers) six saxophones, twenty strings, French horn and four rhythm. The personnel was as follows:

Trumpets: Master Sergeant Zeke Zarchy (lead, and occasional solos)
Sergeant Bernie Priven (most of the jazz solos)
Sergeant Bobby Nichols (occasional solos)
Sergeant Whitey Thomas
Private First Class Jack Steele

Trombones: Staff Sergeant Jimmy Priddy (lead)
Sergeant John Halliburton
Private First Class Larry Hall
Private First Class Nat Peck

Saxophones: Staff Sergeant Hank Freeman (lead alto, clarinet; alto solos)
Sergeant Peanuts Hucko (lead clarinet in the 'Miller-style' saxophone sound, alto, tenor; featured clarinet solos, occasional tenor solos)
Sergeant Vince Carbone (tenor, clarinet; tenor solos)
Corporal Jack Ferrier (tenor, clarinet; tenor solos)
Corporal Freddy Guerra (alto, clarinet)
Private First Class Mannie Thaler (baritone, alto, bass clarinet; occasional baritone solos)

French horn: Corporal Addison Collins, Jr.

Violins: Staff Sergeant George Ockner (1st violin and concert-master) (leader)
Staff Sergeant Harry Katzman (deputy leader)
Staff Sergeant Carl Swanson
Sergeant Dave Herman
Sergeant Dave Sackson
Corporal Eugene Bergen
Corporal Phil Cogliano
Corporal Earl Cornwell

	Corporal Milton Edelson
	Corporal Nathan Kaproff
	Corporal Ernest Kardos
	Corporal Richard Motylinski
	Private First Class Joseph Kowalewski
	Private First Class Freddy Ostrovsky
Violas:	Sergeant Dave Schwartz
	Sergeant Emanuel Wishnow
	Corporal Henry Brynan
	Corporal Stanley Harris
Cellos:	Corporal Morris Bialkin
	Corporal Bob Ripley
Rhythm:	Staff Sergeant Mel Powell (piano)
	Sergeant Carmen Mastren (guitar)
	Staff Sergeant Trigger Alpert (bass)
	Technical Sergeant Ray McKinley (drums)
Reliefs:	Private First Class Jack Rusin (piano)
	Corporal Joe Shulman (bass)
	Private First Class Frank Ippolito (drums)

Singers:	Sergeant Johnny Desmond
	Sergeant Steve Steck, Jr.
	Corporal Murray Kane
	Corporal Artie Malvin (also relief soloist for Sergeant Johnny Desmond)
	Private First Class James Lynne Allison
	Private First Class Gene Steck

The Crew Chiefs singing group

	Technical Sergeant Ray McKinley (novelty and 'personality' songs)
Arrangers:	Technical Sergeant Jerry Gray (chief arranger)
	Master Sergeant Norman Leyden
	Staff Sergeant Ralph Wilkinson
Copyist:	Sergeant Jimmy Jackson
Producer and Scriptwriter:	Technical Sergeant Paul Dudley
Radio Director:	Staff Sergeant George Voutsas
Scriptwriter:	Sergeant Harry Hartwick
Announcers:	Sergeant Broderick Crawford*
	Corporal Paul Dubov

* On 12 July, Sergeant Broderick Crawford was detached from the Band and returned to London where he was used as an announcer on other AEFP programmes, notably *Mark Up The Map* (the daily summary of the latest military

Instrument
Mechanics: Corporal 'Julie' Zifferblatt
                Private First Class Vito Pascucci
Administration: Technical Sergeant Jack Sanderson
                Private First Class Tommy Cochrane

Apart from Miller, most of the Band, being of compulsory military service age, were under thirty. The oldest at thirty-four was Sergeant Ray McKinley, Carmen Mastren was thirty, Zeke Zarchy twenty-nine, Jerry Gray and Trigger Alpert twenty-eight, Peanuts Hucko twenty-six, Bernie Privin twenty-five, Johnny Desmond twenty-three, Mel Powell twenty-one and Joe Shulman twenty, while Bobby Nichols and Nat Peck were only nineteen.

Having had the pick of musicians in the AAF, as well as those coming in from time to time, when forming this large orchestra back in the States, Miller had assembled a judicious mixture of musical veterans and promising but lesser-known men – famous jazz stars, top-class dance band musicians and classical string players.* It was a band full of first-class talent which would have been an impossible dream in civilian life. Now all this talent was organized into three smaller bands as well as continuing to play together in broadcasts and concerts.

The smaller bands were: The American Dance Band (the brass, saxes and rhythm), directed by Technical Sergeant Ray McKinley; The Swing Sextet, led by Staff Sergeant Mel Powell; and the Strings With Wings (the full string section), conducted by Staff Sergeant George Ockner.

---

situation on the Continent), as well as entertainment programmes. As Captain Miller and Sergeant Ray McKinley compèred their own programmes, and Corporal Paul Dubov did most of the rest, there wasn't enough left for Sergeant Crawford to do, although he rejoined the Band on the Continent in May 1945 and compèred most of the remaining programmes by the full AEF Band and some *Swing Shifts*.

* When playing to the GIS in England Captain Miller often lightheartedly introduced members of the orchestra to the audience and mentioned their pre-war musical connections, saying that the string players had come from leading American symphony orchestras including 'the New York Philharmonic, The Boston and Cleveland Orchestras, and Stokowsky's little group down in Philadelphia'! In fact, none of them had actually been members of the Philadelphia Orchestra – Bob Ripley thinks this was just one of Miller's little jokes.

In addition, singer Sergeant Johnny Desmond was to have his own programme once a week, accompanied by the full orchestra conducted by Captain Glenn Miller; and Private First Class Jack Rusin, the relief pianist, played a solo quarter of an hour once a week. They all came together for a weekly half hour broadcast as the American Band of the Supreme Allied Command under Captain Miller.

The American Dance Band, whose half hour broadcasts were called *The Swing Shift*, played, as their name suggests, a repertoire of big band swing music. The programmes were a mixture of new arrangements, some of the instrumental hits of the pre-war civilian Miller Band, and some from other bands, especially Ray McKinley's own pre-war band, featuring his matey and humorous singing. Current hit songs and standards were sung by Sergeant Johnny Desmond and the Crew Chiefs. Most of the *Swing Shift* broadcasts also included a number by a trio of piano (Sergeant Mel Powell), clarinet (Sergeant Peanuts Hucko) and drums (Sergeant Ray McKinley) – known eventually as the Boogie Woogie Trio – or a quartet with bass added. All this was served up with a musical flavour of its own.

The Band was the approximate equivalent of the pre-war Miller Band and from time to time – surprisingly for a mainly swing band – it turned out some beautiful examples of the well-known civilian Miller sweet style of arrangements such as 'Stardust' and the accompaniments to Johnny Desmond's songs. The *Swing Shift* was broadcast twice a week (with recorded repeats from 21 November onwards) throughout their thirteen months in the ETO.

The Band's signature tune was a catchy and swinging little song written by McKinley and originally called 'The Git Along Song' (although it was listed in the radio archives as 'Song and Dance'!) in which he outlined the tunes to be played in the programme with an ingenious new lyric each time. After the war he recorded it with his own Band as 'Howdy Friends (The ETO Curtain Call)' and used it throughout the rest of his career.

'We all needed a theme song,' explains Ray McKinley. 'I didn't have a theme song. I had these Johnny Mercer-like verses I'd been singing in the States in the Mess Hall at Yale, but we didn't have any music for it – we were just faking it. I'd sing it and the band would just jazz it up and fake a little two-bar ending and that would be it – we didn't have any written music. In England, all the arrangers were busy writing a lot of new stuff, and the copyists were all busy, and the only person who was free to write this little thing of mine who was an arranger was Glenn. It was a very simple little song, an eight-bar bluesy strain, with several changes in it – harmonic changes – and I told him I'd like to have that to be my theme. So he had me sing it to him again and he said, "OK, we're going to need an introduction". He sat down and sketched out the arrangement – he had to work with a piano, by the way. I think he did it in concert, which means he didn't transpose the altos to E flat, the trumpets to B flat – he let the copyists do that. He did write the introduction, and I sang the figures I wanted the brass to play, and he put that down, otherwise that's all there was to it. And then we wrote a last chorus, a sort of ride-out, and then we wrote the coda. We did all this in about an hour or something like that, and he wrote it. In other words, he was the arranger with just a little help from me – not much, suggestions and things I sang to him that I wanted. He did this arrangement – the last arrangement Glenn Miller as an arranger ever did.'

Several recordings of the *Swing Shift* have been issued on long-playing records in recent years (*see* pages 399–409).

The Swing Sextet was a small jazz band with a most unusual instrumentation for the time, consisting of clarinet and tenor saxophone (Peanuts Hucko), bass clarinet (Mannie Thaler), French horn (Addison Collins Jr.) trombone (Nat Peck), bass (Trigger Alpert, or sometimes Joe Shulman), drums (Ray McKinley, or sometimes Frank Ippolito) and led by Mel Powell at the piano. The Sextet's music was mostly improvised solo work with opening and closing ensemble choruses, but they did sometimes use written arrangements such as Dizzy Gillespie's 'Night In Tunisia' arranged by Addison Collins who was a 'modern jazz' enthusiast; Carmen Mastren also made several arrangements for the Sextet, and Mel Powell composed numerous numbers for its programmes. Most of the solos were by Powell who, as leader, was featured in nearly every tune, Peanuts Hucko (usually on clarinet but sometimes on tenor saxophone) and occasionally by trombonist Nat Peck. Other musicians from the full Band sometimes broadcast as guest artists with the Sextet, notably Bernie Privin and on these occasions the Sextet produced some rousing Dixieland jazz sparked by Privin's Armstrong-style trumpet playing. Most of the broadcasts also included a song by Johnny Desmond and the Crew Chiefs and there were several guest appearances by British singer Beryl Davis and Dinah Shore.

The first two broadcasts by the Sextet were called *Something For The Boys* but after that they became *The Uptown Hall* and were presented as a jazz club for those who liked sophisticated but swinging small band jazz, 'soft but solid' as the compère used to say, although there was never any studio audience in the programme (at least, not an audible one). Their signature tune was written by Mel Powell, with a little help from Glenn Miller (*see* page 82). At first it didn't have a title but later Ray McKinley wrote a lyric for it and added another melodic strain and the song became famous as 'My Guy's Come Back'. It was published in London in February 1945 by the Peter Maurice Music Co. Ltd., and many famous artists recorded it, including Benny Goodman's Band and Ted Heath, and today it is still widely remembered as a musical reminder of the last months of the war. When the Swing Sextet played it as *The Uptown Hall* signature tune Mel Powell played on an upright piano with a special attachment which made many listeners think it was a harpsichord.

The Sextet broadcast fifteen-minute programmes from the Co-Partners Hall three our four evenings a week, but the series came to an end in February 1945, once the BBC had used up a stock of pre-recordings the Band had made before leaving for France.

For Nat Peck, a nineteen-year-old unknown among a group of leading jazz players, being chosen for the Sextet was a slightly unnerving experience! 'It was an awkward situation', he declares; 'because according to grades and ratings and things like that it should have been either Jimmy Priddy or Johnny Halliburton or Larry Hall, all of whom had higher ratings than I had, but Mel Powell took a particular liking to me for some odd reason and I was chosen to do it. I felt a little embarrassed about it because I knew that feelings were going to be hurt by that, because I was really jumping a grade there, but it was a musical decision and Miller didn't object. Jimmy got over it quickly enough, and Larry wasn't the sort of person to be upset by anything like that, and Johnny Halliburton was my very good friend and he wasn't going to be jealous either. The reason I was picked, I think, is that I was the only one in that trombone section who had any sort of experience in playing jazz. Jimmy was definitely not a jazz musician – he was a very, very sure and solid first trombone player, but he couldn't play the blues and I could. Mind you, at the time I was very nervous about it – I didn't know Mel that well. Mel was a very distant sort of a personality – not that he was unkind, or anything like that, but he was already very big-time – he had played with Benny Goodman – and I used to sit in *The Uptown Hall* band a little worried about things and he misinterpreted my attitude. He thought that I was putting him down, or being critical about what was going on in the band, when, to tell you the truth, I was more scared than anything else. He discovered that, though, soon enough and we ended up really very, very good friends.

'I remember when we went to the studio in Bedford where we started *The Uptown Hall*. We gathered together at the Co-Partners Hall, this little band – we were all sitting around and we had to figure out things. What were we going to do? So Mel and Glenn Miller put their heads together and they both co-composed the theme and we tried it on the spot and it seemed to work well and that was it – it was put together like that. The broadcasts were always a very relaxed informal affair where Mel would be sitting at the piano and we'd be sitting in the studio and Mel would dictate what was to be played, how we were going to play it, and so on. We never had anything written down, no such thing! We'd all bring pencils with us and make notes.

'Mel had a completely free hand. The only time that Miller ever turned up was on the first rehearsal where they composed "My Guy's Come Back" together. Probably it wasn't from lack of interest, but he listened to the broadcasts and he found them eminently satisfactory and decided not to intervene in any way and Mel was completely free to do as he wanted. If he wanted extra musicians like Bernie Privin he just had them. It's marvellous being a soldier – you can do whatever you like. You don't have to worry about musicians unions, you don't have to worry about overtime or budgets, you can do whatever you please. I did a rapid calculation – you know, the activity was really incredible, the work we did for the BBC during the war. A quick bit of arithmetic proved to me that if I were paid union scale for the eight months or so that we were in England recording for the BBC I could have retired at the end of the war for the rest of my life on that money, not taking into account today's inflation.'

The Swing Sextet can probably claim a small place in musical history: it may well have been the first band to play 'How High The Moon' on a BBC radio programme in England. The tune came from an obscure 1940 American stage show, *Two For The Show*, which was not produced in London until after the war. In those days theatre music could not be broadcast before the show from which it came was produced on the London stage, but this rule seemed to be waived, or ignored, by American forces broadcasters. As Maurice Gorham put it, 'If anybody complained of breach of copyright they just said, "Sue Uncle Sam".' The Sextet often broadcast 'How High The Moon', although curiously the full AEF Band never broadcast its arrangements of two songs from another American musical, *Oklahoma*, which didn't open in London until 1947, although first staged on Broadway in 1943; perhaps because of its Home Service broadcasts it was too much in the public eye. 'How High The Moon' later became one of the favourite tunes of the modern jazz musicians.

A number of recordings of the Swing Sextet have been issued in recent years (*see* pages 399–411). However, some records labelled as 'Glenn Miller's Uptown Hall Gang' recorded in Paris in 1945 and issued originally in France and later in Britain by Esquire records were not by the original broadcasting sextet but were made when some of the AEF Band musicians played in the Jazz Club Français with some French jazz musicians (*see* page 237). The original *Uptown Hall* broadcasts remain one of the fondest broadcasting memories of the time.

The Strings With Wings consisted of the complete twenty-piece string section of the Band and was conducted by Concertmaster George Ockner. It broadcast quarter-hour programmes of light classical pieces and popular evergreens in the slow restful style nowadays known as 'mood music', with frequent violin solos by George Ockner. Its signature tune was a strings-only arrangement of 'I Sustain the Wings' and they were on the air twice a week. At first their broadcasts also included announcer Corporal Paul Dubov reading topical wartime poems, some written by one of the Band's script writers Sergeant Harry Hartwick, but these were soon dropped. Normally, there were no songs in the programmes, but in the summer of 1945 Johnny Desmond sang on some of the broadcasts after his own series had ended.

Many of the arrangements for the Strings With Wings were written by the players themselves, including Harry Katzman, who recalled: 'Miller asked me if I would make some arrangements for them and I asked just particularly what he wanted and he said, "Well, just anything you think would be good for the strings". The first arrangement I did was the "Londonderry Air" and then "The Flight of The Bumble Bee" as a solo for George Ockner which he played marvellously well. I think I did at least ten or twelve arrangements in the United States and maybe four or five in England. Those I made in the USA were "Clair de Lune" by Debussy, "The Maid With The Flaxen Hair" by Debussy, the "Pavanne" by Ravel, "The New World Symphony" (the second movement, known popularly as "Going Home"). "Mood Indigo" was one of the first things that I did for the strings and Miller liked that very much and we played it on a number of broadcasts. There were many others, mostly the classical things, which is what he actually wanted. George Ockner did "I'm In The Mood For Love", and "Clouds" by Debussy, and I also did "The Sunken Cathedral" by Debussy ["La Cathédrale Engloutie"] and I remember that the boys who copied it put "The Cathedral Is Sunk" which struck me as quite funny – it really was sunk, I guess. It wasn't one of the better things, but it seemed that Miller had an affinity for Debussy and Ravel.

'Another violinist, Gene Bergen, did a very excellent arrangement of "Annie Laurie", and Dave Herman did, oh maybe a dozen arrangements of pop tunes and they were almost always the same because he always had a running figure going through them all the time – we used to call them the snake arrangements. We had quite a good library. Jerry Gray did "Serenade In Blue" and one Jerome Kern tune that I just can't think of, Norman Leyden did "Indian Summer" by Victor Herbert, and "Stardust". Ralph Wilkinson did "Sweet and Low" – he seemed to have the best feel for strings of all the arrangers. His writing was really first class and I think were the best of all the string arrangements. We made up our own minds what we were going to do – no-one was really telling us, "make an arrangement of this, or that", but we really covered all the pop tunes of the day besides the very well-known classical pieces.'

In recent years several recordings of the Strings With Wings have been issued publicly (*see* pages 399–408).

Johnny Desmond was obviously more than just another dance band singer and soon became recognized as one of the best male Sinatra-type crooners of the day, though with more 'body' in his voice and a very sensitive style and immaculate phrasing. Indeed, he became known as the GI Sinatra, and at that time he was probably a better singer than Sinatra himself. With his dark good looks and smooth baritone voice he quickly became a great favourite with service and civilian audiences alike – particularly the girls.

He was given his own fifteen-minute programme once a week accompanied by the full orchestra conducted by Captain Miller, or sometimes by Sergeant Norman Leyden. The first programme was called *Sergeant Johnny Desmond Sings*, some *A Soldier And A Song*, others just *Sergeant Johnny Desmond*. (*A Soldier And A Song* later featured another GI singer, Corporal Jack Powers.) His signature tune was "Time On My Hands" and each programme consisted of two songs, an instrumental by the Band and another Desmond song. Like *The Uptown Hall* series, however, the Johnny Desmond programmes were discontinued early in 1945. When recordings of the AEF Band were issued at long last in 1955 it was apparent that he had indeed been one of the big stars of the Band.

The Band's schedule on the AEFP was ten broadcasts a week – a total of three hours, fifteen minutes, on the air, including Jack Rusin's solo piano appearance on Thursdays in the daily series *Keyboard Contrasts* and later in *Piano Parade* on Saturday mornings. Many of the musicians played on practically all the broadcasts. The rhythm section were on all but the 'Strings With Wings', although the relief bassist and drummer, Joe Shulman and Frank Ippolito, sometimes deputised for Trigger Alpert and Ray McKinley in the Swing Sextet broadcasts. For guitarist Carmen Mastren, however, there was no relief, although he didn't play in *The Uptown Hall* programmes.

At first, all the broadcasts were made from Bedford and with rare exceptions all of them were live. This was deliberate BBC/SHAEF policy. The Miller unit's programmes were only pre-recorded where this was unavoidable in order to fit in with some other type of engagement required by the military authorities, but even then the BBC, although reluctant, preferred to alter slightly the time of the broadcasts rather than pre-record them.

The first week's programmes, all live from Bedford, were as follows:

Mon. 10 July
7.45–8 pm *Strings With Wings* (announcer Corporal Paul Dubov; commère Lieutenant Charmian Sansom (Canadian Women's Army Corps)
Tues. 11 July
4.30–5 pm *The Swing Shift* (The American Dance Band) (announcer, Corporal Paul Dubov; commère, Lieutenant Charmian Sansom)

6.15–6.30 pm *Something For The Boys* (The Swing Sextet) (announcer Corporal Paul Dubov; commère, Lieutenant Charmian Sansom)
Wed. 12 July
6.15–6.30 pm *Something For The Boys* (The Swing Sextet) (announcer, Corporal Paul Dubov; compère Geoffrey Peck (BBC))
7.45–8 pm *Strings With Wings* (announcer, Corporal Paul Dubov; compère Geoffrey Peck)
Thurs. 13 July
8.30–9 pm *American Band of the Supreme Allied Command* (compère Captain Glenn Miller, introduced by Jean Metcalf)
Fri. 14 July
9.35–10 am *The Swing Shift* (The American Dance Band) (announcer, Corporal Paul Dubov, commère, Jean Metcalf)
6.15–6.30 pm *The Uptown Hall* (The Swing Sextet) (announcer, Corporal Paul Dubov; compère Lieutenant Don Haynes*)
Sat. 15 July
6.15–6.30 pm *The Uptown Hall* (The Swing Sextet) (announcer Corporal Paul Dubov, commère, Andrea Troubridge (BBC))
Sun. 16 July
12.45–1 pm *Sergeant Johnny Desmond Sings* (announcer, Corporal Paul Dubov; commère, Margaret Hubble)

The only programme given a recorded repeat was the Thursday evening broadcast by the American Band of the Supreme Allied Command: this was at 11 am the following morning in the daily series *Morning After*. Not until November were the *Swing Shift* programmes repeated; none of the other programmes were repeated regularly.

The first week's schedule continued with minor variations until a new one was introduced on 13 November. After the first few weeks the 'integrated' announcers disappeared and the full Band programmes were compèred by Glenn Miller, the *Swing Shift* by Ray McKinley, and the others by Paul Dubov. Miller had previously worked with regular announcers, even in civilian days, and no doubt felt that this worked better than having different announcers from programme to programme. In any case, the Band had its own announcer, Paul Dubov, and the BBC accents sounded a little out of place!

The Miller unit functioned as a separate little radio production unit with its own Programme Director, Sergeant Paul Dudley, and its own producers and writers, Sergeant George Voutsas and

---

* Possibly a misprint in the radio archives, although the Activities listing also gives Haynes as MC and Sergeant Paul Dudley, not Dubov, as announcer.

Sergeant Harry Hartwick, supplying their regular programmes to the AEFP schedule.

The Thursday programmes by the full Band came at first from the Corn Exchange, while the smaller bands broadcast from the Co-Partners Hall. After a few weeks, its programmes were transferred to the Co-Partners Hall, which was too small to accommodate an audience, probably because the Corn Exchange was needed for the Promenade Concerts. From 10 August the full Band broadcasts were made from the BBC's Paris Cinema studio in Lower Regent Street on alternate Thursdays when the Band travelled to London to broadcast in *The American Eagle in Britain* series and from 14 September practically all the full Band programmes were broadcast from the Queensberry All-Services Club in London.

In pursuit of the policy of integration the Thursday evening programmes by the full Band also included guest artists, usually leading British girl singers. Producer Cecil Madden suggested several singers to Miller and they broadcast with the Band over the first four months: Vera Lynn, and Sergeant Jimmy Miller, Anne Shelton, Sam Browne, Paula Green, Doreen Villiers, Gloria Brent and Pat Kirkwood. Some, including Dorothy Carless and Paula Green, also sang with the Band at airfield concerts.

Unfortunately, Glenn Miller didn't specially want any British guest stars, as Franklin Engelman later recalled:

He was quite a surprise to us in the AEF Programme . . . a popular bandleader who looked anything but. Tall, lean, sardonic-looking in his rimless glasses, he was more like a university professor in a Captain's uniform. But he talked like a hard-boiled showman. He knew to a fraction what went to make up his success. He knew what made him tick. His ideas were cut and dried before he set foot in England. It took us some time to realize that. . . . I told Glenn we could let him have the top British stars to broadcast with his Band – and we were some time finding out that he didn't want them. He had a complete entertainment unit and a set of formats for all his shows. What he really wanted was to be given studios, technicians and air time and left to get on with it. In fact, he was pretty sarcastic about some of our attempts to be useful.*.

The format of the broadcasts by the full Band differed fundamentally from those they had made back in America.

* Spoken contributions to 'Close-up of Glenn Miller and the American Band of the AEF' (BBC documentary radio programme, 8 June 1953).

Whereas *I Sustain The Wings* had been a public relations and recruiting programme, on the AEFP their programmes were first and foremost morale-boosters for the troops and so consisted entirely of music. Gone were the propaganda and the recruiting plugs, to be replaced by Miller addressing his announcements directly to the troops, plugging the 'all-Allied team' and emphasising Allied unity.

Of course, the Band's broadcasts were heard mainly by the invasion forces on the Continent and in Southern England. So far as the British public was concerned, only those whose radios could pick up the AEF Programme and had discovered the programmes were on had been able to hear them, although reception varied according to the time of day and sometimes was subject to fading, especially in the evenings. But all this was about to change.

Unexpectedly, the first Thursday evening broadcast was put out simultaneously in the Home Service, not the GFP which was then the light entertainment service, replacing the programme billed in the *Radio Times* called *Sitting On The Fence*, a satirical review with music based on the popular humorous column by Nathaniel Gubbins in the *Daily Express* and the *Sunday Express*.

In those days, dance bands and singers, the 'popular music' of the time, had a wide following among the adult population in general, unlike today's 'pop' music which attracts mainly teenage audiences. Glenn Miller, or at least his music, was already well-known to the British public from his pre-war civilian Band's records: about fifty 78s had been issued in Britain during the previous five years, mainly on HMV. The Miller Band had also been seen in two Hollywood musicals, *Sun Valley Serenade* and *Orchestra Wives*. Musically, the civilian Band had long been considered the best dance band in the world for technical proficiency, precision and original and beautiful arrangements. Jazz and swing fans, however, mostly thought it corny and unswinging. The latest Glenn Miller record to be issued in Britain had been 'Ciribiribin' and 'My Isle of Golden Dreams' both commercial numbers of which the *Melody Maker* critic said: '. . . precision and tone colours are still the last word. Vibratoless playing just about perfection in balance . . . langourous, spineless, boring'* although 'Rhapsody In Blue' issued a few months earlier had drawn rapturous praise from the same critic. The Miller style,

* *Melody Maker*, 10 June 1944.

sweet and swing, was similarly well-known because many British bands had adopted it and played some of the best Miller arrangements copied from records. Indeed Joe Loss had become known as 'Britain's Glenn Miller' having taken the Miller hit 'In The Mood' as his signature tune, and from a technical point of view the Miller Band was admired throughout the British dance music profession. In short the Miller civilian music was the latest thing in popular music in 1944.

On the other hand, the Army Air Forces Band was virtually unknown in Britain before it arrived. It had been heard once or twice in radio programmes from the USA, including the first edition of a new weekly Anglo-American programme called *Transatlantic Spotlight* on 1 January 1944, and on 5 May in the weekly American programme *Command Performance* playing 'What Do You Do In The Infantry' and 'Pistol Packing Mama'. Doubtless a few enthusiasts and musicians had also been able to pick them up via shortwave broadcasts from the United States. The Band had also been seen briefly in an eighteen-minute 'March of Time' film called *Upbeat In Music*, in which they marched in the Yale Bowl playing a rousing 'Blues In The Night March' with the rhythm section mounted on a jeep. These occasional glimpses apart, the public knew little or nothing of the Band.

The impact of the new Glenn Miller Army Air Forces Band live on the radio then, after years of the civilian Band on scratchy 78s, at 8.30 pm on the evening of 13 July 1944, was nothing less than a revelation. This is how the *Melody Maker*'s Laurie Henshaw reported it:

GLENN MILLER ON THE AIR

It's happened. Adolph, on behalf of swing fans, take a bow! You've violated a few treaties since the early 'thirties, but you won't be razzed for ripping this barrier aside.

In 1934, in retaliation for a long-standing AFM edict, the Ministry of Labour placed an embargo against the engagement of American orchestras in this country. And it's taken a major war to tear this ban apart.

But now it's happened, and British bandleaders' preserves, guarded from foreign encroachment for the past decade, have been gaily trampled upon, but I bet the selfsame British leaders will be the first to stampede to shake the hand of a man whom they've been copying since the Glenn Miller tone colour and 'In The Mood' became famous.

Why don't the papers tell us these things? Miller should have been given the headlines; the doodle-bugs could have taken second place.

The only indication readers had that a major air offensive was about to start was the bland announcement that at 8.30 on Thursday evening (13 July) the American Band, Supreme Allied Command, would broadcast. Thinking this was a field day for Sousa, I nearly missed the airing; and how many 'MM' readers did the same? The announcement wasn't even in the 'Radio Times', which told us that we were going to hear the ill-fated and short-lived 'Sitting On a Fence'.

The great Glenn was introduced by 20-year old BBC commère Jean Metcalf, and proved to have a most pleasing voice and microphone manner – all this and a Captaincy, too. Jazz has definitely grown out of the musical ranks.

Miller announced that Sgt. Ray McKinley would kick the tunes rolling with a drum intro to 'American Patrol'.

MEL POWELL TOPS

Ray hit out, and the rest of the personnel, including such well-known names as Mel Powell (ex-Goodman piano), Zeke Zarchy (ex-Goodman trumpet), Carmen Mastren (ex-Tommy Dorsey guitar), and Bobby Nichols (ex-Vaughn Monroe trumpet) rocked into the first number.

Twenty-year-old Mel Powell took the first solo spot, and 20,000 British jazz pianists dropped in their tracks. Powell tolled the death-knell to the esteem of a lot of self-opinionated young men.

An interesting trumpet solo by Zeke Zarchy was also featured in this number.

Jean announced that Miller had brought over a special arrangement of Gershwin's 'Summertime'. Although played in more commercial vein, this was good. Twenty fiddles bolstered up the background harmonies, and Miller should know there are twenty since he hired them. To me they sounded full enough to be the string section of the London Symphony Orchestra.

A comedy swing number followed entitled 'Juke Box Saturday Night', wherein the boys chanted a rhyme about Harry James (the trumpet even did the James chorus of 'Ciribiribin', and it was a grand burlesque), and a vocal team did a playful skit on the Ink Spots, even to the stock guitar intro, and the phony tenor voicing of the arch demon of the coloured quartet.

Dorothy Carless sang next and made a good job of 'I Couldn't Sleep A Wink Last Night'.

TRENT FLOWS

A blues followed with the Basic English title 'It Must Be Jelly 'Cos Jam Don't Shake Like That'.* The number rode all right, with thrilling solo spots by tenor and trumpet, and the rhythm section merged like mad.

* The civilian Miller Band's record of this hadn't yet been issued in Britain – GB.

Bruce Trent then sang 'Without A Song' and has certainly improved since he's been 'Student Prince-ing' round the country. But whether his thick sort of voice is right against the Miller bunch – ah, that's another story.

Finally, Dave Rose's 'Holiday For Strings' was dressed up in a new setting by arranger Sgt Jerry Gray. Miller's symphony section plucked their pizzicato passages most precisely, and the full sax and brass sections did some smooth things on their own account.

Thus ended a half hour's broadcast. And the Captain himself announced that he'll be back next Thursday. The radio remains switched on for a week: we won't nearly miss him a second time.

Whether Miller's broadcasts are continued depends on his Army commitments, and also, maybe, to listeners' reactions. We don't have to be assured that 'MM' readers will do their part to see that the BBC finds out what's wanted!

Ray Sonin [Editor of the *Melody Maker*] *adds*: Henshaw has reported the airing quite accurately, and the general effect was one of superb musicianship and teamwork.

Mel Powell was undoubtedly the solo man of the broadcast, but Zeke Zarchy's trumpet didn't impress me personally, nor would I say the band was always up to the terrifically high wax standard associated with Miller.

Two things stood out a mile from this broadcast and explain the difference between crack US and crack home grown bands. America has arrangers of genius and section leaders who can really inspire their teams.

Did I hear you say that America also had the musicians and the leaders? Perhaps you're right.*

The programme was also transmitted live to the USA via shortwave and broadcast there on the Blue Network (at that time owned by NBC).

From the start the Band was a huge success, not only among the GIs and the British servicemen and women but also, as the weeks went by with the British fans and the public. But in one particular quarter the Band was less than an instant hit – within the BBC itself.

Sometime on Thursday 13 July,† Haynes received a telephone call at Bedford from Maurice Gorham in London, summoning him and Miller to Broadcasting House the next morning for an important meeting with him at 11 o'clock sharp. Arriving promptly at 11 am they were amazed to learn that the Miller orchestral

* *Melody Maker*, 22 July 1944.

† Haynes' diary does not record the time he received the call, but in view of Gorham's complaint and his references to reception it was probably after the 8.30 pm broadcast on the 13th.

dynamics did not meet with the approval of the BBC who contended that all the music should be played at the same volume! This was, apparently, the BBC's theory of 'constant modulation' (shades of *Music While You Work* and the Palm Court), a theory applied presumably to popular music and not to the classical repertoire. According to Lieutenant Haynes, Gorham was accompanied by five other BBC men and first complimented Miller and the Band on the marvellous programme of the past week. Then he said that the Corporation had been receiving complaints from listeners that during quiet passages in the Band's music and with reception being fainter on the fringes of the reception area many people had thought the BBC had gone off the air. Using a long pointer to indicate on a map on the wall the reception area of the broadcasts he insisted Miller should keep the volume constant!

Miller and Haynes looked at each other in disbelief. Miller asked Gorham to repeat what he'd said, which Gorham did. Barely able to restrain his temper, Miller rose to his feet, looked Gorham straight in the eye and raising his voice perceptibly pointed out that certain contrasts in his music were for a definite purpose, the soldiers he had come to play for liked it that way and he could not alter his arrangements to suit the BBC. He suggested that since the Band had come to England to broadcast to the troops of the Allied Expeditionary Force the BBC should stick to the AEFP for the Band's future broadcasts and cancel any further transmissions over the home wavelengths. With that he and Haynes abruptly walked out of the meeting.

Here was a fine kettle of fish. The Band had come on a mission to bring Anglo-American relations closer together, yet within a week a heated disagreement had erupted with the monopolistic and monolithic BBC telling the leading bandleader of the day and the originator of some of the most artistic popular music ever heard how his music should sound! But it continued to sound the way its creator intended.*

Despite Miller's suggestion the weekly programmes by the full Band went out simultaneously in the Home Service until 10 August, by which time they were billed regularly in the *Radio Times*. After this they ceased, but starting on 29 July the General Forces Programme began recorded repeats of the Thursday pro-

* Some years after the War Maurice Gorham said he couldn't remember any such discussion with Captain Glenn Miller (in private correspondence with Mr M. E. Highton, of Sunderland, England).

grammes at 2 pm on Saturday afternoons (from 18 November onwards it was the Friday programmes or sometimes the Tuesday ones). These GFP repeats continued till July 1945, although their time varied and from 11 March 1945, they were transferred to Sundays at 12.30 (1.30 from 18 April onwards).

The discontinuance of the Home Service broadcasts caused some controversy, and has been hotly debated since, with the BBC usually being condemned for depriving British listeners of their only chance of hearing the Band. The late Franklin Engelman once told the author that he thought the BBC had been very unfairly blamed over the issue, as he understood that the request to take the Band off the Home Service had come from General Eisenhower: there had been a spate of serious crime by American servicemen (usually deserters) and he didn't want the British public to think that the Americans were just a 'jazz-happy bunch of gangsters'. Be that as it may, the broadcasts were originally put out in the Home Service to fill the gap left by the abandonment of the series *Sitting on the Fence* and were discontinued when the new Home Service series *Songs From The Shows* began on 17 August. It seems likely that the Home Service relays of the Miller Band were only meant to fill the gap till *Songs From The Shows* began. The British public were not being deprived of the Band as the GFP repeats had already started and continued almost uninterrupted for the next twelve months.

After the meeting with Maurice Gorham, Captain Miller and Lieutenant Haynes returned to Bedford in the afternoon. After the scheduled 6.15 pm broadcast by Mel Powell's Swing Sextet, the whole Band played the first of their many celebrated airfield concerts for the GIs. This was at Thurleigh USAAF base a few miles north of Bedford, the home of the veteran 306th Heavy Bombardment Group and their Flying Fortresses – the group which had made the first Eighth Air Force raid on Germany itself and which eventually clocked up the longest combat record in the Eighth Air Force.

That night, at Thurleigh Heavy Bombardment Base, . . . the American Band of the AEF mounted a makeshift stage inside a giant steel hangar. 3,500 men of the Eighth Air Force sat on the dirt floor, on the wings of planes and on the lofty beams overhead. As the opening theme 'Moonlight Serenade' pumped the psychological life blood of American music back into those youthful, homesick hearts Captain Miller walked out on to the stage and an eerie yell of welcome swelled from the audience: a happy cry, yet filled with the weird wildness of a torrential spill of suddenly released frustrations. Colonel Kirby, whose efforts had transported the Band to the ETO, stood proudly listening at the far end of the hangar. After the show, Glenn walked straight to him to say, 'Colonel, making all the money in the music business could never have made me feel this rich'.*

* Paul Dudley, *Bomblight Serenade*.

CHAPTER SEVEN

The Band's repertoire and musical style – The arrangers and soloists – The airfield concerts

The Band rapidly became the sensation of the day among the British dance music profession and, via their broadcasts, the British public. Bandleaders and musicians would wangle their way by any means they could into its rehearsals and broadcasts in Bedford and London and turned up en masse to the Band's first public concert in London on 27 July, while the *Melody Maker* (the 'Bible' or perhaps the *Tatler* of the music business) assiduously reported its activities almost week by week.

Glenn Miller, the architect of this musical phenomenon, became the idol of the hour and hardened musicians jostled to shake him by the hand, while on the airfields he was constantly mobbed by hordes of GIs. British civilians, however, saw very little of the Band and had to be content with hearing them on the air. No gramophone records of the Band were available, apart from V-Discs issued direct to the American troops.

Even apart from the twenty-piece string section and French horn, the Band was large by the standards of the day – nine brass, six saxophones and four rhythm, compared to the more usual seven or eight brass and four or five saxophones. But what distinguished the AEF Band, quite apart from its size, was the quality of its music, showing plainly that there was far more to Miller's music than 'In The Mood' and 'Moonlight Serenade'. Here was a band with, at its best, the beat of Basie and Goodman, a brass section packing more punch than almost any other before or since, a saxophone section with some of the familiar and well-loved Miller sounds as well as new and beautiful voicings, and the full-bodied, soaring and sometimes dainty strings, enormously enhanced with violas and 'cellos alongside violins, alternately taking the lead or filling the orchestrations with imaginative touches. Miller had succeeded in welding together the apparently disparate elements of the Andre Kostelanetz/David Rose light orchestra, the swinging Goodman/Miller dance music and the Basie rhythm into a musically satisfying whole, in many ways a cross section of the popular music of the time and a high point in the big band era before the changes soon to be brought about by 'modern jazz' and bebop had begun to be felt on the big band scene.

It was also, perhaps, up to the 1950s, the most successful attempt at combining classical music and jazz ('symphony and swing', in the contemporary phrase, a combination which had defeated so many bandleaders from Paul Whiteman onwards), due perhaps to Miller's musical background rooted in jazz rather than the light or classical fields. As an attempt at introducing classical sounds into popular dance music the Band's music was unsurpassed – what further directions his music might have taken had its development not been cut short by Miller's untimely death can only be guessed at, although from what is known of his post-war plans it seems certain that it would have continued along the paths he had taken in the Army. Fortunately for him, his activities in what he called his musical workshop were not hampered by commercial considerations as they would have been in civilian life – no salary bills, no advertising agencies dictating musical policies, no worries about audiences, no unions and no risk of losing musicians, who couldn't leave even if they wanted to! From his earliest days as a bandleader he had said he didn't want the best jazz band in the world, but a good *all-round* band, and making the most of his wonderful opportunities he produced the dream band of popular music.

Despite its military status and Miller's musical innovations, the Band was unmistakably a Glenn Miller Band, a direct and logical development from his pre-war civilian band. Apart from the strings and French horn, the greatest single improvement over the earlier band was, perhaps the wonderful all-star rhythm section, four of the best rhythm men in the USA. In place of the sometimes stolid beat of the civilian band they produced a lift and a drive that carried all before it, providing a swinging foundation for the Band's jazz soloists as well as the entire ensemble, and thus propelled by one of the finest rhythm sections any band ever had the entire orchestra played with such precision, tone, technique, attack and swing as seemed to prove beyond argument the almost universally-accepted view that American bands were far superior to any band in Britain. Perhaps Nat Peck sums it up best: 'That Band played with such conviction!'

Naturally, Miller brought into the Band many of the best items from his civilian repertoire, mainly the famous instrumental hits such as 'American Patrol', 'Tuxedo Junction', 'Song Of The Volga Boatmen', 'Caribbean Clipper', 'The Anvil Chorus' and of course 'In The Mood'. Conspicuous by their absence, however, were the civilian Band's sweet-style hits including 'At Last', 'I Know Why' and 'Perfidia', although some of its arrangements were re-scored with the addition of strings, including 'Rhapsody In Blue' and 'Serenade In Blue'. But musically speaking it was clear that the pure civilian style had been left behind and even the famous Miller sound exemplified in 'Moonlight Serenade' was heard only occasionally from the AEF Band.

Most of its repertoire was new, both new arrangements of established music and compositions written since the civilian band broke up. In many ways, despite the Band's exciting swing music, the cream of its output was Jerry Gray's special concert arrangements with a jazz beat for the full orchestra including strings of 'Stardust', 'Smoke Gets In Your Eyes', 'Body And Soul', 'Holiday For Strings', then a comparatively new composition by David Rose which he had popularized only in 1942, and, later, 'The Red Cavalry March', 'Oranges And Lemons' and 'The Trolley Song', for which Jerry Gray will always be remembered. Other outstanding arrangements which included the strings were the slow, soulful orchestrations of blues tunes like 'Farewell Blues', 'Wabash Blues' and the 'old' and 'blue' tunes in the Band's memorable medleys,* while some of the numbers which went with the greatest swing were the topical wartime novelty and patriotic songs like 'The Victory Polka', 'There Are Yanks' and 'There'll Be A Hot Time In The Town Of Berlin', usually with the strings and all the singers. But whatever the Band played it was always with a swing and a spirit seldom achieved by a band of that size, whether it was the driving swing of the big band instrumentals or restrained and subtle as in the orchestral arrangements. Although jazz as

* The medleys of 'something old, something new, something borrowed, something blue' were carried over from the civilian Band where they had originated as a means of getting as many songs as possible into fifteen-minute broadcasts; in the AEF Band they were dedicated to the servicemen's mothers, wives, sisters and sweethearts.

such was not a feature of the Band's music, except in the Swing Sextet and to a lesser extent in *The Swing Shift*, the best of its spirit and influence was always present, whether it was the rousing swing of 'The Anvil Chorus' or 'Flying Home' or the gentle beat and melodic simplicity of 'Stardust' and 'The Way You Look Tonight'.

In one respect, in particular, the Band was very fortunate – the popular songs of the day. This was a vintage period and many of the biggest hits of the time – 'I'll Be Seeing You', 'Goodnight Wherever You Are', 'I'll Walk Alone', for instance – naturally had a special poignancy and appeal because of the long family separations imposed by the war, and strangely enough these slow sentimental ballads had wide popularity among the troops who were away from home for long periods and not knowing when they might see their loved ones again. These songs, beautifully sung by Johnny Desmond with wonderfully sympathetic orchestral accompaniments were regular features of all the Band's performances.

As was the way with a Miller band the Band as a whole was the star of the show, and such a band with its large and diverse instrumentation is heavily dependent on its musical arrangers. As with the civilian Band, much of the credit for the AEF Band's success belonged to their chief arranger Jerry Gray, Miller's right-hand man, who besides many of the Band's concert arrangements also continued to write big band swing arrangements such as 'Great Day' and compose new ones including 'Jeep Jockey Jump' and, in France, 'Passage Interdit'. The two other principal arrangers were Norman Leyden, whose work included orchestral accompaniments for Johnny Desmond songs, and Ralph Wilkinson who not only made arrangements for the full Band with strings but also for the Strings With Wings. 'For me,' recalls Nat Peck, 'Jerry Gray was the musical genius of that Band, a sort of *éminence grise*. Norman Leyden was a very important arranger and I used to admire his work immensely. He was a marvellous person, really charming. And then, maybe lesser known, was Ralph Wilkinson, and I must say that of all the people writing for that Band Ralph was really the innovator. He was the man who was ahead of his time with the string writing – this is my opinion. Jerry was a dance band arranger and he came up with a lot of very interesting things, but as far as the string writing was concerned I felt that Ralph made a more important contribution than Norman Leyden in his contemporary vision of how to write for strings.'

The jazz stars were Mel Powell, Ray McKinley, Peanuts Hucko and Bernie Privin. Mel Powell was one of the latest sensations in the jazz world with a sparkling technique and great virtuosity in the Teddy Wilson/Earl Hines stride tradition as well as a sensitive touch in the more classical type works such as his own Debussy-style composition 'Pears on Velvet'. He was featured more than any other soloist. Ray McKinley was a veteran from the late 'twenties, equally at home playing and singing in big bands or small groups and is widely considered one of the best jazz drummers. His big feature was a spectacular solo in 'The Anvil Chorus' and although his drum solos were comparatively rare his breaks and fill-ins were rhythmic masterpieces and his all-round drive and infectious swing were largely responsible for the Band's unfailing beat. He was also an important leader, compère and breezy singer of light-hearted novelty songs like 'The GI Jive', as well as an extremely ingenious lyric writer.

The other soloists were not quite of the same magnitude, although well up in the 'second division'. By far the best in the saxophone section was Peanuts Hucko with an outstanding Goodman clarinet tone and technique in 'Mission To Moscow' and his special feature 'Stealing Apples'. He also played the occasional tenor and alto saxophone solo, but most of the tenor solos were by the Vido Musso-sounding Vince Carbone or less often by the smoother-toned Jack Ferrier, neither of whom had been widely known as jazzmen in civilian bands. The rarely heard alto solos were usually by Hank Freeman.

Trumpet solos were usually taken by Bernie Privin who played with an excellent tone and technique remarkably similar to Louis Armstrong. One of his special features was a brilliant imperson-ation of Armstrong in 'I Can't Give You Anything But Love, Baby'. Some were by Bobby Nichols, who did the Harry James impersonation in 'Juke Box Saturday Night'. Occasionally Zeke Zarchy also played solos, but although a brilliant section leader he wasn't primarily a jazz player.

There were no recognized trombone soloists, but the up-and-coming Nat Peck was sometimes heard in *The Swing Shift* and *The Uptown Hall*. 'There was very little in the big band repertoire for trombone solos,' Nat Peck recalls, 'but Ray McKinley brought along some Fletcher Henderson arrangements that had been written originally for Benny Goodman's Band and it was in the Ray McKinley Band that I used to get to play jazz solos, but it was a very rare thing for a trombone player to get a shot at a solo in that

Band.' By that time, Glenn Miller had given up playing regularly and was only conducting, although he sometimes joined in the ensembles of tunes like 'In The Mood'.

Besides the Miller classics the Band also played swing numbers from the repertoires of other American bands of the day, especially Benny Goodman's and the pre-war Will Bradley/Ray McKinley Band which featured Ray McKinley songs, with occasional items from Harry James, Charlie Barnet and others. Miller's philosophy was primarily to bring to the American troops the kind of music they had known back home and of which, for the most part, they were starved in England, apart from the radio. Basically he sought to supply what his audience wanted and at one stage he angrily took exception to a critic in the American musical magazine *Metronome* who was serving in the US Army in England and who accused him of pursuing a reactionary and out-dated musical policy and not being progressive enough in view of the resources (jazz musicians) at his disposal, saying '. . . we didn't come here to set any fashion in music or to create any new swing styles – we came merely to bring a much-needed touch of home to some lads who have been here a couple of years. . .'. But despite his modest denials, he did set a style with his AEF Band – his crowning achievement and one of which he was very proud, and it was soon only too clear that his ideas met with the overwhelming approval of the services audiences the Band went out to play for at airfields and bases all over Britain.

The US Army Air Forces first became established in Britain in 1942, and by 1944 both the Eighth Air Force – the heavy bombers carrying out the long-range strategic daylight bombing of Germany – and the Ninth Air Force – medium bombers engaged in tactical missions over Western Europe in support of the Normandy invasion and subsequent battles – were operating almost daily from bases in England. The Eighth Air Force was distributed over about seventy airfields and supporting installations mostly in Suffolk, Norfolk, Cambridgeshire and Bedfordshire, while the Ninth Air Force flew from airfields further south, mostly in Essex, Kent and Hampshire.

These airfields were sited out in the countryside; most were remote and off the beaten track, although some of them were adjacent to villages and one was on the outskirts of Norwich. Most of them were temporary wartime airfields with few substantial buildings and the personnel lived in Nissen huts or even tents, although a few, like Bassinbourn, Hertfordshire, were permanent pre-war RAF aerodromes leased to the Americans for the duration of the war. With an average of 3,000 men at each airfield they were virtually small townships, with their own clubs, theatres, cinemas, sports facilities and canteens, isolated and in some ways small worlds of their own, their personnel far from home and often homesick. None of them knew when they would see their homes again, and many of the flyers rated their chances of survival as very low. One bomber pilot recalled:

Most of us had an awful time in England. Sore throats and one cold after another. Never warm enough, food fit for Germans, fog, lumpy-damp beds and warm beer. You had to stand up on the trains or ride your bike if you wanted a little freedom. If that wasn't enough, the money system was a crime, there wasn't any food in the restaurants, the pubs ran out of grog before you could get to the bar, and you needed ration stamps to buy anything. Top that all off with the fact that we had to get up at all hours to fight a horrible war every few days and you can see that England wasn't a lot of fun.

All that has changed in retrospect. We see that period now as the most remarkable time in our lives. Most of us have not since been challenged like we were then. Many of us cannot remember more exciting times. We lived through an experience unique in the history of aerial warfare. We were part of the greatest air force ever assembled by any country. We fought in a cruel environment, under conditions that were next to impossible. We were a part of history. At that time we thought it would never end – now we wonder if it really happened.*

Naturally they welcomed visits by entertainers of all kinds – variety shows, bands and singers, especially visiting artists from back home in the USA. Many of the leading popular stars of the day, both American and British, toured the bases with shows which for a time at least took the GIs' minds off the grimmer sides of wartime life. General Eisenhower himself later testified† to the great value of entertainment and recreational activities towards maintaining the troops' morale, especially the combat troops'.

Once they became settled at Bedford Captain Miller lost no time in adding his and the Band's own contributions to the entertainment at the airfields and bases, and he put Lieutenant

* From the introduction to *The Eighth Air Force Album* by Lieutenant-Colonel John H. Woolnough [Captain Woolnough in 1944] (8th AF News, Hollywood, Fla., 1978).
† *Crusade in Europe*, by General Dwight D. Eisenhower (Doubleday, New York, 1948; Heinemann, London, 1948).

Haynes in charge of organizing the schedule of these personal appearances. During the summer the Band did several concerts a week, sometimes playing at two airfields in one day, travelling in Army trucks or motor coaches, and sometimes in USAAF transport planes or combat bombers, usually flying from nearby RAF Twinwood Farm or the Eighth Air Force Flying Fortress base at Thurleigh, just north of Bedford, and eventually clocking up about 500 hours flying time before they left the ETO. These flights, however, could sometimes be very unpleasant for some of the men in the Band: Jack Steele and Nat Peck had a lot of trouble flying in the unpressurized planes. 'The noise and vibration in those airplanes was tremendous – just awesome,' recalls Bob Ripley, 'the whole plane shaking from the engines. There was no sound- deadening or padding in the empty planes – there were hardly any seats in them, even.'

For the men in the Band, these airfield visits were their closest contact with the war and the men who fought the enemy; they were sometimes significant for another reason – the food there was often better than their routine Army rations. Inevitably, however, one airfield began to look very much like another – the Band went in, played their music and left, although at some they stayed overnight.

The concerts normally lasted about an hour and were usually played in huge aircraft hangars on makeshift stages built from packing cases, or on the long trailers used for transporting dismantled aircraft by road and, sometimes when the weather was fine, out in the open air. On some of these appearances the Band put on a show on its own; at others it played as part of an organized programme, especially at airfield 'parties' to celebrate the completion by the unit of a hundred or two hundred bombing missions against the enemy. Then the entire base would be 'stood down' for at least twenty-four hours, with no combat missions, and not surprisingly some of these parties, to which large numbers of British women and girls were invited, got pretty wild and lasted well into the early hours. 'It was a mad thing at the British bases,' recalls Harry Katzman. 'I never saw so much enthusiasm. It was incredible – it was really hysteria because they'd never heard a band like that. They just flocked to the concerts, and of course it made the orchestra feel good, too, because they were *so* enthusiastic – absolutely incredible. We flew in B-17s or Liberators and sometimes in B-26s which were a smaller plane, and sometimes we flew in transport planes which were marked with stripes and on the side of them was marked "Condemned for Combat". This didn't make us feel too good, but we had the feeling that they wouldn't be flying us in dangerous planes – unless they might have been dangerous for combat but not for us.'

Other musicians agree about the airfield concerts. 'They got such a kick out of our Band,' said Carmen Mastren, 'that you couldn't help feeling good about it regardless of how hard we worked.' Johnny Halliburton says: 'They were a thrill, since our reception was always excellent. While we played many bases and hospitals (sometimes three a day) and worked hard, we were aware that many times the audience had waited hours for our arrival.'

Nat Peck remembers one particularly wild airfield party: 'We were celebrating a 50th or 100th Mission in an airfield somewhere, where, under the influence of too much booze which I couldn't hold when I was 19 years old, I remember taking a siphon of soda water and spurting Miller right in the face. He looked at me in amazement because up to then my attitude had been simply one of extreme respect and military formality. There, of course, I was drunk (say the truth!) but he didn't say anything, and I never got punished for it or reprimanded. He might have been a little bit under the weather as well! I think he rather liked me – he must have!'

Ray McKinley recalls one particularly scary incident while the Band was flying to play at one of the airfields: 'After we'd played a lot of the bases around Bedford we went over to Northern Ireland, which was the longest flight we'd undertaken. It took, probably a couple of hours. We were in either a Liberator or a Fortress. Anyway, they stuck me and all the drums and Trigger Alpert and his bass fiddle in the bomb bay and we were there all alone – the other guys were up in the plane, but we were in the bomb bay with a board spread across the "floor". Well, we didn't know – we thought that underneath the floor would be some steel, or whatever, that closes when the bombs are encased and opens when the bombs drop, but we were wondering all during the trip why we kept bouncing around so much. The plane would hit a little air pocket and we'd bounce, and so on – what's going on? Well, that's normal, I suppose. So finally we got to this base and the youngster who's flying this plane – I don't know if he qualified, he was probably trying to get flight pay for flying once a month (one of those Special Service guys) – he pushed a button to open the bomb bays and instead they closed! In other words, Trigger and I had been sitting on a piece of half-inch plywood through the whole trip, you see, and the bomb bay was open the entire trip. The piece of plywood was between us and . . .

'The amusing thing was, there was a crew chief on that plane who was a Latin of some kind – a Mexican or Puerto Rican, or whatever – and, boy, the chewing-out he gave the pilot (who was a Captain) would have done credit to Patton! Well, when Trigger found out he just turned green, and I probably changed hues myself. The drums were heavy, the bass fiddle wasn't very heavy but the drums were, especially the traps case was a pretty heavy thing, about seventy or eighty pounds. Add my 170 to it – bomp bomp, it could have split the plywood and there we'd go. That would have been the end of it.'

British singers sometimes appeared with the Band at these airfield concerts, including Dorothy Carless and Paula Green, while at the Rougham 200 Mission party in September Dinah Shore sang with the Band for over an hour.

Usually, the whole Band played at the airfields, though sometimes the strings did not, when they had live Strings With Wings broadcasts scheduled. Some of the photographs in this book capture vividly these occasions, as did the 'Chattanooga Choo Choo' scene in the film *The Glenn Miller Story*. Recalling these concerts, the late Paul Dudley once told me that playing in the huge metal hangars gave the music a wonderful sound. Dudley himself gave a graphic glimpse of the concerts and their effect when writing about the Band's appearance at Thurleigh (*see* page 93).

At this time, Glenn Miller was at the peak of his popularity, and to have perhaps the biggest attraction in the entertainment business playing specially for them, free of charge, was a big thing for the American troops. Once again, the GIs' old favourites from back home swung out in the flesh instead of from records or the radio – 'In The Mood', 'Tuxedo Junction', 'American Patrol', 'Down The Road A-Piece' and the rest – music they had heard 'live' at the Glen Island Casino, perhaps, or the Meadowbrook, or the Hollywood Palladium, or in their own home town during a one-night stand by the pre-war civilian Miller Band. They loved it, and took the Band to their hearts – the more so as the Band were serving, like themselves, in the AAF. The roars of applause which always greeted the Band were ample testimony to the first-class morale-boosting job it was doing, bringing what Captain Miller called 'a hunk of home'. Here at last the ideal for which he had first enlisted was coming true.

CHAPTER EIGHT

Milton Ernest and Melchbourne Park – The Royal visit to Bedford
– Wattisham-Hitcham and Newbury – *The American Eagle in Britain*
– The Plaza concert – Polebrook – 'Pinetree' (High Wycombe) –
Variety Bandbox

The Band quickly settled down in Bedford, although for some time
the men were too busy to have much time to appreciate it. 'We
loved Bedford,' says Nat Peck. 'The town was beautiful and we
had pretty good digs at the Red Cross. There was an interesting
night life in Bedford, believe it or not, during the war!' Emanuel
Wishnow says, 'I remember at the Red Cross billet there was a guy
in the morning who used to serve us tea and biscuits – he would say
"Biscuits, please?" – he'd always give you two, never three or one,
always two. I remember that guy well – it was his tone of voice.'

'The Red Cross billet was very plush for the Army in wartime,'
recalls Bob Ripley. 'We didn't have to do anything – our rooms
were cleaned for us by Red Cross people, linen was changed twice a
week, we had fresh towels all the time. We didn't have to stand
reveille, or account for any of our doings as long as we were where
we were supposed to be at the appointed time, which was for
rehearsals and concerts and getting on buses to travel or on trucks.
It was pretty much like civilian living, except that there were
obvious wartime restrictions which everybody had to face.'

When the men did have spare time they spent it as most soldiers
would – in the Red Cross Club in Bromham Road (which was run
by an American lady, Miss Anona Moser, who became very friendly
with the musicians), in the cinemas and pubs, and in card and dice
games.

When the Band was first transferred to Bedford – in the words of
its movement orders, 'to carry out the instructions of the Supreme
Commander' – the men were given a special Army allowance and
'found' their own food, including fish and chips near the Co-

Partners Hall. But before long the unit was attached for day-to-day administrative purposes such as meals, medical attention, and so on to the Eighth Air Force Service Command Headquarters at Milton Ernest Hall, a large Victorian mansion in the heart of the countryside near the village of Milton Ernest some five miles north of Bedford, where an extensive hutted camp had been built in the grounds. However, the Band remained officially part of the Headquarters Command at SHAEF. For most of its stay in Bedford the Band was taken out to Milton Ernest Hall in trucks for their meals in between broadcasts and rehearsals at Co-Partners Hall.

'I remember sitting there one day having lunch or dinner,' recalls Nat Peck, 'and looking out of the window we saw a plane – it was a B-17? – badly battered. It had obviously had problems over Germany and it crashed right in front of our eyes.'

In command there was Brig.-General Donald R. Goodrich, Commanding General of the Eighth Air Force Service Command. His Executive Officer was Lieutenant-Colonel Norman F. Baessell who became friendly with Miller and Haynes and was very helpful to the Miller unit. In return, Miller thought it would be a gesture of gratitude for the Band to play a concert for the Hall's personnel and on a sunny Sunday afternoon (16 July) the Band played on the lawn at the back of the mansion for an audience of about 3,500 officers and enlisted men from the Hall and other bases in the area.

Next day the second week's broadcasts commenced according to plan, and the Thursday evening programme by the full Band from the Corn Exchange produced another memorable broadcast with guest singers Vera Lynn and Sergeant Jimmy Miller, leader of the RAF Dance Orchestra, the Squadronaires, who were by far the most popular British services dance band of the time and frequent AEFP broadcasters. Captain Franklin Engelman, who had travelled from London, opened the programme by introducing Captain Glenn Miller who thanked the British people for the welcome they had given the Band. Jimmy Miller, who was also one of the singers with the Squadronaires, sang 'This Is A Lovely Way To Spend An Evening' and Vera Lynn's contribution was another big hit of the day 'Besame Mucho'. The finale of the programme was a rousing performance of 'The Anvil Chorus' with an exciting drum feature by Ray McKinley.

According to Lieutenant Haynes the Band spent the next morning pre-recording programmes for the AEFP although no trace of any recordings on this day remain in the radio archives and none are mentioned in the Activities list. The regular *Uptown Hall* programme went out on schedule at 6.15 and according to the radio archives and the Activities list it was a live broadcast. Possibly it was pre-recorded, for later in the day the Band went in their buses to play a concert at a nearby Eighth Force base. According to Lieutenant Haynes the concert was at a B-24 base at Melchbourne Park, whereas the Activities list gives the location as an unnamed ordnance depot and Bob Ripley noted it as being at Melchbourne Ordnance Depot. There was indeed an Ordnance Depot at Melchbourne Park, about 12 miles north of Bedford, while 2½ miles to the north-west of the Park was the airfield of the 305th Bomb Group* at Chelveston, flying B-17s, not B-24s as noted by Haynes. Haynes records the concert as taking place at a bomber base with the band playing on a platform erected alongside a hangar as there wasn't a hangar large enough for an indoor concert but in fact the band played on a long trailer outside the big house at Melchbourne Park. Haynes notes the weather as cool, cloudy and damp and says the concert began shortly after the last plane had landed from a bombing mission over Germany. After the concert the band stayed for dinner and returned to Bedford about 10 pm.

Sunday 23 July, besides being filled with rehearsing, broadcasting Johnny Desmond's weekly programme at lunchtime, and recording, was a red letter day for some of the Band and especially for Haynes and Harry Katzman. That afternoon, Her Majesty Queen Elizabeth (now the Queen Mother) came to Bedford for an informal visit to the American Red Cross Clubs, and by the time she arrived, large crowds had gathered and the streets were decked with flags.

She went first to the ARC Officers Club in Goldington Road, where Miller and Haynes were billeted, and chatted to many of the officers in the Club. By chance, Haynes happened to be at the Club at the time and he was presented to her by her sister-in-law, Mrs Bowes-Lyon, one of the organizers of the Club whom Haynes had met on his first visit to Bedford with Colonel Niven and Captain Miller.

Haynes had spent the morning at Co-Partners Hall and after lunching on fish and chips, at the nearby fish shop, he returned to the Officers Club to write up some reports for SHAEF. As he entered he was met by Mrs Bowes-Lyon who took him into the Club's dining room where the Queen and her party were talking to a

* Commonly used abbreviation for Bombardment Group.

group of officers. The Queen shook his hand and complimented him on the morale-raising work that Miller and the Band were doing, adding that the Princesses Elizabeth and Margaret Rose were great fans of the Band and listened to their broadcasts. Thanking her and bowing slightly, Haynes backed away amid the flashes of Press photographers' cameras and was surrounded by reporters wanting to know what the Queen had said. He was deeply impressed by her sincerity and gracious manner, and on returning to '8H' several hours later he told Captain Miller and the Band about his royal encounter.

The Queen then went on to the Enlisted Mens Club in Bromham Road, and in the course of a long and detailed report of the Royal visit the *Bedfordshire Times* (28 July 1944) described the events there:

Nearly two hours before the Queen was due to visit the Enlisted Mens Club in Bromham Road, townspeople, mostly women and children, began to surge round the Club's premises. By the time Her Majesty arrived a huge crowd had gathered, and there was a spontaneous burst of applause as she stepped from her car.

Conversation in the Club ceased when the Queen appeared at the entrance, and everyone stood to attention while the National Anthem was played by 25 members of Captain Glenn Miller's US Army Band – the American Band of Supreme Allied Command.

Immediately afterwards officials of the club were presented to Her Majesty.

As the Queen passed slowly round the main hall she showed a lively interest in all she saw, and during her stay of three-quarters of an hour at the club she took many opportunities to speak with American Servicemen, club officials, canteen staff and porters.

For a few minutes the Queen paused to hear the band playing Grieg's delightful melody, 'The Last Spring', and afterwards the leader of the band, Sergeant Harry Katzman, of New York, was introduced to her.

At the end of her visit, the Queen, with characteristic grace and charm, waved farewell to everyone in the club, and she walked to her car through cheering crowds.

Harry Katzman remembered: 'That was a curious thing that happened. Someone told me that the Captain wanted to see me. He called me "Katzie", and he said, "Katzie, take the strings over to the Red Cross Club. I think the Queen is coming this afternoon – play some music for her". I got all the strings together, and I think Carmen Mastren was also there – one of his arrangements was "Someone To Watch Over Me" by Gershwin (he did a couple of arrangements for Strings With Wings). We set up in the Red Cross Club, and figured, well, she'll go by and we'll play, maybe, "Sweet And Low" or some English music that she would recognize – we had an arrangement of "Drink To Me Only With Thine Eyes". Now, I am sure that if Miller had thought about it he would have gone down himself but perhaps he figured it wasn't too important or it was possible that he had some other military commitment or to meet with somebody or something to do with the orchestra. At any rate, we went down to the Red Cross Club and we had a big book of arrangements – we must have had at least thirty or forty arrangements, and of course we had played them on our broadcasts from Yale and also in England. We had been playing about ten or fifteen minutes and then the Queen came in with her entourage and of course the photographers were busy snapping pictures. She came up to me and I didn't know what the hell to do, but I made a sort of half bow as respect to the Queen and she told me, "You know, the Princesses listen to your music on the wireless all the time!" I also wore glasses and I'm sure she thought I was Glenn Miller. Of course, everybody in the orchestra was smiling – here was this Jewish Sergeant from New York meeting the Queen and all these debutantes here who spend thousands of dollars for dresses to go up and bow before the Queen, and here I was talking to her and it struck them as very funny. We talked maybe another few words and I thanked her very much and she went on. There were pictures taken of her talking with me, or me talking with her or else just letting her do the talking (which I did of course, and just said thank you), but I could never get a picture of that event at all. I asked Miller, Haynes and Dudley if I could get a picture because I would have liked to send it home, but I never could get a picture. But I think it was a boo-boo on the part of Miller, because I'm sure if he'd gone the pictures would have been released and it would have been great publicity, whereas with me it didn't mean a damned thing. But everyone was saying, "Hey, look at Katzman, he met the Queen, he met the Queen!" and all that.'

Meanwhile the rest of the Band had been rehearsing at Co-Partners Hall for the following Thursday evening's broadcast with guest singer Anne Shelton, and the programme was pre-recorded at 8.30 that evening. At the time the programme would normally be broadcast live from Bedford the Band was scheduled to be in London. After the recording, the Band with Anne Shelton played a two-hour concert for servicemen at the Corn Exchange.

The next week was to be the Band's busiest so far with four concerts and two trips to London to be fitted in between their usual broadcasts and some pre-recordings.

More and more requests for airfield concerts were coming in and on Monday 24 July, the Band (without the strings who stayed behind for their regular Monday evening *Strings With Wings* broadcast) played at the Eighth Air Force base known as Wattisham-Hitcham, situated between the villages of Wattisham and Great Bricett in West Suffolk, nine miles north-west of Ipswich. Wattisham was the home of the 479th Fighter Group and their P-38 Lightnings and the adjoining Hitcham base was the 4th Strategic Air Depot (maintenance and repairs).

The Band flew from Twinwood Farm in six B-17s almost wing tip to wing tip for the sixty-odd miles to Wattisham-Hitcham. This was the largest base they had played so far and an audience of over 10,000 assembled for the open-air concert. After dinner at the base – with the best food since their arrival in Britain, noted Haynes – they were flown back to Twinwood Farm an hour before dark.

Next day, the Band played at Newbury, for airborne troops. According to Haynes this concert took place at an Air Transport base but according to the Activities list it was in Newbury Corn Exchange (local residents also remember a concert by the Band at the Corn Exchange). The 6.15 *Uptown Hall* broadcast for that evening had been pre-recorded the previous Saturday and shortly before noon the Band piled into three C-47s (Dakotas) with the names 'Skylark', 'Patches' and 'Patsy Ann' painted on their fuselages for the flight to Newbury. After playing to an audience of over 4,000 troops the Band stayed for dinner. Bad weather prevented it returning to Twinwood Farm that night and while Miller, Haynes and Dudley drove to London by staff car and stayed at the Mount Royal the Band stayed in Reading and returned to Bedford by bus next morning. Because of this *The Swing Shift* broadcast on the Tuesday evening was cancelled and replaced by gramophone records; such cancellations, however, were rare. On Wednesday morning, the 26th, Miller, Haynes and Dudley had more meetings with Colonel Kirby and Major Stearns at SHAEF and returned to Bedford in the afternoon.

Throughout SHAEF, the BBC and the American forces Miller and the Band were widely regarded as celebrities and increasingly they found themselves making guest appearances on radio and at special occasions connected with the war effort. Within the next four days the Band was the star attraction on four very different engagements: a broadcast to the USA in *The American Eagle In Britain*, a public charity concert at the premiere of the new Bing Crosby film *Going My Way*, an open air concert at Eighth Air Force Headquarters, and a special broadcast in the regular weekly BBC programme *Variety Bandbox*.

On 27 July, the entire unit travelled to London. Its first engagement was a guest appearance in Cecil Madden's long-running programme *The American Eagle In Britain*, produced jointly by the BBC and the American Red Cross for the BBC's North American Service. It had been recorded in London practically every week since Thanksgiving Day 1940 and by 1944 the recordings were being re-broadcast on about 150 stations in the USA, mostly on the Mutual Network. It was designed to foster Anglo-American relations by letting the American public hear at first hand how their servicemen were faring in far-off Britain. Originally, the only Americans on active service in Britain had been those flying in the three American Eagle Squadrons (all volunteers) of the RAF,* but after the United States entered the war in December 1941 American forces gathered rapidly in Britain and by 1944 American servicemen were brought to the microphone every week to send greetings back home. There were also interviews with wounded men in hospitals in Britain and on the Continent, as well as music and entertainment, and most of the programme was recorded in the American Red Cross Club, called 'Rainbow Corner' (a converted Lyons tea shop at the Piccadilly end of Shaftesbury Avenue) in an underground room known as 'Dunkers' Den' from the GI habit of 'dunking' their doughnuts in coffee. As well as producing the shows Cecil Madden also acted as MC and on 27 July, Glenn Miller, Ray McKinley and the American Dance Band made the first of several appearances in the programme. They set a new attendance record and in the following two months they played in the programme four more times.

Later that day the Band crossed Piccadilly Circus to play in their first public concert in Britain, on what was to be a memorable occasion for the fans and musicians who were able to get tickets. The concert had been announced two weeks earlier and it was a sell-out, more than fulfilling expectations. The *Melody Maker* reported the concert with a banner headline 'Glenn Miller's Super London Show':

* The Eagle Squadrons were quietly transferred to the US Eighth Air Force in 1942.

The real spirit of the great pre-war get-togethers in the musical profession was manifested last Thursday (27 July) when Glenn Miller and the American Band of the Supreme Command made their first – and probably only – public appearance in London.

Occasion was a super-gala premiere of Bing Crosby's new Paramount film, *Going My Way* at the Plaza, Piccadilly Circus, W., in aid of the London Stage Door Canteen, and every musician and bandleader who could possibly get time off paid a large sum of money for a seat – and thoroughly enjoyed himself. Nearly £4,000 was raised for the venture for a very worthy cause.

The foyer of the Plaza before and after the event reminded one of the Palladium way back in 1933, when Duke Ellington was here.

I spotted Harry Roy, Mantovani, Max Bacon, Chappie d'Amato, Eric Winstone, Mrs Tawny Nielson, Victor Feldman, Johnny Claes, Tommy Bromley, Harry Latham, Robin Richmond, Jimmy Skidmore, George Shearing, Art Thompson, Maestro Mario, Gordon Crier, Hearne Lewis, Frank Weir, Don Barrigo, Kenny Baker, Alan and Gloria Kane . . . well, that's enough to be going on with.

Sufficient to say that everybody who is anybody in our business defied the doodle bugs and came along to see the great Miller.

And he certainly *is* a great Miller. His band, some 46 pieces, is a magnificently competent organization. Everything about its playing is clean and artistic; the men understand the full meaning of light and shade, and the whole 46 of them can 'whisper' as artistically as they can play fortissimo. And the arrangements – but you've heard the band on the air, so you'll know what they're like.

Not, mind you, that all this is any revelation; we have gone well past the days when we gaped at such bands and wondered how on earth the American aces did it; now we know they do, and we are even sufficiently familiar with their brand of genius to be able to criticize it.

But let's start from the beginning. For the benefit of those readers who couldn't get along, this is what happened.

MCKINLEY SCORES

The curtain rose to disclose a khaki-clad band consisting of five trumpets, four trombones (Captain Glenn bringing them up to five for certain numbers), six saxes, guitar, piano, bass, drums, French horn, twenty violins and six vocalists.

After the signature tune we had 'In The Mood' – you may know the tune! – in which the brass section had us completely enthralled and the saxes left us in two minds as their phrasing was, occasionally, corny.

But even more corny, to our way of thinking, was the peculiar antics of the trombones, who pointed their instruments in various well-drilled directions – two up, two down, facing one another with the slides crossing, and so on. Pretty to watch – but it was just as pretty in 1924.

However, that is possibly carping, for the band then presented a varied swing programme, consisting of 'Juke Box Saturday Night' (with some amusing impressions of Harry James and the Ink Spots, plus the super blend of voices at which America excels); the Jerry Gray arrangement of 'Holiday For Strings', with a superb string section coming into its own; Johnny Desmond singing 'Poinciana' and 'GI Jive'.

The last-named deserves a new paragraph because it introduced to the audience one of the most breezy and relaxed personalities it has ever been our good fortune to see on the stage – the drummer-vocalist-ex-bandleader Sergeant Ray McKinley.

There is nothing exuberant about this cheery gent. He merely sings, does a few antics and conducts the band for the number, but his manner is so infectiously cheerful, he is so completely at ease and he has such a personal charm that the audience rose to him.

He was most ably assisted by perky, gum-chewing Sergeant Trigger Alpert, who combined swell comedy with great bass playing.

Glenn Miller who had left the stage clear for Ray and Trigger to do their stuff, then returned to lead the band in their famous version of the 'Anvil Chorus', which featured McKinley again – this time at the drums. It was a delightful exhibition of happy-go-lucky tub-thumping beautifully controlled and showy only in parts.

Well, that was the half-hour programme, and it was all too short. We could have done with a lot more, and the audience expressed its appreciation in full-throated fashion.

You will notice that I haven't so far said much about Glenn Miller himself. This is because I can't quite make up my mind about him. He announces the items most competently but quite coldly, and his demeanour on the stage is austere.

He didn't seem to share at all in the tremendous enthusiasm his show created, and remained so unmoved as to suggest that he was not the least bit surprised or pleased at the ovation.

He wasn't the bowing, smiling bandleader at all; he was more like a military automaton with a job of work to do.

NO MEL OR CARMEN

The programme had obviously been selected for an audience of fans rather than for an audience of bandleaders and musicians, and it was a great disappointment to find pianist Mel Powell thrust so far in the background that he was inaudible throughout.

We in England know Mel's work well and would like to have heard him featured; we also know guitarist Carmen Mastren, but neither of them was given a solo.

And while criticizing, we thought the ensemble tone of the saxes was pretty 'windy', although a swell lead alto deserves high praise.

Yes, it was a great show and a great band, and John J. Davis, who organized it for the Stage Door Canteen, deserves the profession's thanks for a memorable affair.

Greatest tribute to Miller and his boys is that so many of the musicians in the audience trooped out after his show and didn't stay for the premiere of Bing Crosby's film *Going My Way*.

Nothing, not even Bing, could follow a band like this! R. S.*

After the concert the Manager of the Plaza told Haynes that the Band's standing ovation had surpassed anything he had seen for an orchestra playing popular music. Later that evening the Band returned to Bedford as no-one wanted to stay in London with the doodle-bugs.

The next morning was spent rehearsing and pre-recording a programme by the Swing Sextet and a Sergeant Johnny Desmond programme with the full Band conducted by Norman Leyden. After a late lunch, four B-17 Flying Fortresses took the Band from Twinwood Farm to the 351st Bomb Group base at Polebrook, Northants, about twenty miles north of Bedford, the airfield where Major Clarke Gable, the Hollywood film star, had been stationed. The Band waited for the B-17 crews who had just returned from a mission over Germany to get over to the hangar and then played a concert to more than 5,000 officers and GIs, before returning to Bedford.

After the regular live *Swing Shift* broadcast on 29 July, the Band travelled in buses to High Wycombe, for a special appearance at the Eighth Air Force Headquarters (codenamed 'Pinetree') at Wycombe Abbey, the famous girls' public school, which had been taken over by the RAF early in the war and subsequently 'lent' to the USAAF. Miller and Haynes went in a Jeep because their staff car was in the Motor Pool for repairs.

The Band played outdoors, using a crash truck parked in front of a school building as a stage with the GIs seated on the grass. The concert was in support of the American War Savings campaign with many high ranking Eighth Air Force officers in the audience, including Lieutenant-General James H. Doolittle (Commanding General of the Eighth Air Force) and Brig.-General Orville A. Anderson (a distant relation of Captain Glenn Miller). Army film crews were there to film it. This is the film (part silent, part sound) from which extracts have been seen on television in recent years, and in some sequences Glenn Miller can be heard introducing the Band and individual musicians. Also on the soundtrack are snatches of 'In The Mood', 'Stardust', 'I'll Be Seeing You' and

* *Melody Maker* 5 August 1944. 'R. S.' was Editor Ray Sonin.

'What Do You Do In The Infantry', while in the silent footage one of the tunes being played is obviously 'Juke Box Saturday Night'. The film contains many interesting shots of the Band as well as Miller queueing to buy war bonds.

After the concert, General Doolittle climbed up on the crash truck, shook Miller's hand and said, over the microphone, 'Next to a letter from home, Captain Miller, your organization is the greatest morale-builder in the ETO'.*

Later, while the Band returned to Bedford, Captain Miller and Lieutenant Haynes were taken by staff car to General Doolittle's quarters for dinner. They stayed overnight, after talking with General Anderson until the early hours with the General explaining the seriousness of the air war over Germany. At seven the next morning they were awakened by an orderly with tomato juice and hot coffee and after breakfast they were taken back to 'Pinetree' where, after being vouched for personally by Generals Doolittle and Anderson, they were taken on a guided tour of the Headquarters nerve centre from which the entire Eighth Air Force operations were controlled – an underground bunker with top security known as the Mole's Hole, which is still there to this day – with Miller and Haynes sworn to secrecy as to what they saw.

After their visit to the Mole's Hole, Miller and Haynes returned to Bedford where they and the Band faced another hectic day. Johnny Desmond's broadcast at 12.45 had been pre-recorded two days earlier and after lunch the entire unit went in their buses and staff car to London for its fourth guest appearance in four days – a pre-recording of *Variety Bandbox*, one of the BBC's General Forces programmes, which was also broadcast simultaneously in the AEF Programme.

Variety Bandbox was a weekly one-hour programme of top class music and variety which had been on the air since December 1942 – a sort of British equivalent to the American series *Command Performance*, and was one of the BBC's most important variety programmes. Produced by Stephen Williams and the indefatigable Cecil Madden, it was intended primarily for the Forces and presented a different selection of singers, comedians and bands each week. It was a variety show with a more modern approach than the traditional *Music Hall* and *Palace of Varieties*, the

---

* This statement was erroneously attributed to General Eisenhower by Universal International Pictures in their publicity for *The Glenn Miller Story* in 1954, no doubt for greater dramatic effect.

long-established highspots of Saturday evening listening. It was pre-recorded every Sunday evening at the huge Queensberry All-Services Club (*see* page 134) in Old Compton Street, Soho, before Forces audiences of 4,000 or so and broadcast in the GFP the following Tuesday afternoon from two to three and repeated on Sunday evenings from six to seven. The Tuesday transmissions were put out simultaneously in the AEF Programme, although the Sunday repeats were not. The edition featuring the Miller Band on 30 July was broadcast on Tuesday 1 August and Sunday 6 August.

The Miller Band was the star attraction and made up about half the programme. The resident band was John Blore and his Dance Orchestra, who usually played on the raised pit platform, but for the AEF Band's appearance the whole of the large stage was used for the first time to accommodate both bands. After John Blore's Band had played the programme's signature tune, 'I Love To Sing', commère Margaret Lockwood, the film star, introduced Miller and the Band to a rapturous welcome and after 'Moonlight Serenade' they played 'In The Mood', 'Stardust' and 'Poinciana'. The other acts were the Scottish comedian Peter Sinclair, singer Bertha Wilmott, the show's semi-resident cockney comedian Hal Monte and the xylophone virtuoso Teddy Brown. The AEF Band rounded off the show with 'American Patrol', 'Time Alone Will Tell' and 'Holiday For Strings'. As the finale, the two bands, the other artists and the audience joined together in 'Let's Have Another One'! Unfortunately, this was the Band's only appearance in *Variety Bandbox*, though not its last at the Queensberry Club.

Despite the capacity audience there was still a queue of over a thousand servicemen and women waiting outside in the street in the hope of getting in, and ignoring the efforts of the police to persuade them to disperse because of the danger from the flying bombs. Hearing this Miller decided to put on a second show that evening and received a terrific ovation. Through this gesture Miller became firm friends with the manager of the Queensberry Club, John Harding, and before he left that night he promised Harding that he would try and do a show at the Club every week even though it would mean travelling in from Bedford. In due course, the Band did play regular concerts at the Club every Thursday evening during which they also did their weekly broadcast in the AEF Programme, and eventually played there twice a week.

After the second concert the Band returned to Bedford, and Miller and Haynes stayed overnight at the Mount Royal Hotel.

CHAPTER NINE

Abbots Ripton and Kimbolton – Dinah Shore – SHAEF (Forward) –
Halesworth and Boxted – Cirencester – SHAEF (Main) – A public
concert at Bedford – On tour to Northern Ireland, Warton and
Burtonwood – Bentley Priory – Steeple Morden and Attlebridge

Throughout the ensuing weeks the Band's heavy schedule of
broadcasts (usually live) and airfield and many other personal
appearances continued: in August the Band played eighty-nine
separate jobs, including thirty-five concerts at the bases and camps,
some of them in Northern Ireland.

On Monday morning, 31 July, Captain Miller and Lieutenant
Haynes drove from the Mount Royal out to SHAEF to attend to
something of great importance to all servicemen away from home – to
collect the Band's pay and letters from home, returning to Bedford
after lunch. That night Sergeant Ray McKinley and the Band,
without the strings (who stayed behind in Bedford for their Monday
evening broadcast), played at the Eighth Air Force airfield at Abbots
Ripton, Huntingdonshire, about four miles north of Huntingdon.
The Abbots Ripton base was a repair and maintenance installation
(the 2nd Strategic Air Depot) and had been built adjoining the
bomber base just outside the village of Alconbury: the entire base is
still in use by the US Air Force today. The Band drove the twenty-odd
miles from Bedford in their buses and staff car and played in a huge
hangar to an audience of 7,000 with many of the GIs watching from
vantage points up in the framework of the hangar or sitting on the
wings of B-17s parked around the hangar. After dinner at the base the
Band were back in Bedford by eleven.

On Wednesday 2 August, the Band (again without the strings),
this time under Captain Glenn Miller, went by road to the Flying
Fortress base of the 379th Bomb Group at Kimbolton, about ten
miles north-east of Bedford, and the Band was joined by British
singer Dorothy Carless.

Thursday 3 August was another red-letter day, for both the Band and radio listeners. To Bedford, escorted by General Barker, General Goodrich, Colonel Kirby and Colonel Niven, came America's number one girl singer of the time, Dinah Shore. She had arrived in England several days previously for a two-month USO tour of troop shows and had come to Bedford to broadcast as guest singer in the Band's regular Thursday airing.

Dinah Shore had been heard often on the AEF Programme in recorded programmes from America ever since the AEFP had started, not only in her own weekly programme and as the singing hostess in *Showtime* but also in frequent appearances in other regular series such as *Command Performance*, *Mail Call* and *GI Journal*, and singing on the *Paul Whiteman Programme* every week. Indeed, at one time she had been heard in three different programmes in the same evening. She had also been in several Hollywood musicals, and now at the height of her popularity she was to the GIs what Vera Lynn was to the British troops. Dinah was an appealing personality and was extremely popular wherever she went.

In the broadcast that evening, she sang two of the top hits of the day, 'Long Ago And Far Away' and 'I'll Be Seeing You', replacing British singer Beryl Davis who had been billed in the *Radio Times* but who subsequently broadcast with the Band two weeks later.

Dinah Shore was a more jazz-orientated singer than many popular vocalists, and had become well known with an American radio show called *The Chamber Music Society of Lower Basin Street*. After the broadcast she pre-recorded several songs with Mel Powell's Swing Sextet which were included in *Uptown Hall* broadcasts during the next couple of weeks. After touring Allied-occupied areas of Normandy, Dinah was back in London in September where she again sang with the Band in their legendary but elusive recordings for HMV (*see* page 152).

Almost every day in the Band's hectic schedule was becoming notable for one reason or another. Friday 4 August was no exception. A SHAEF Staff Officer, Major Stearns, had arranged with Haynes for the Band to play another base concert on the 4th but for security reasons declined to tell Haynes much about it. That afternoon the Major sent three C-53 transport planes to pick up the Band at Twinwood Farm and it was not until they were airborne that the men discovered they were heading for General Eisenhower's advance headquarters – SHAEF (Forward) (codenamed 'Sharpener'), a mainly tented camp near Portsmouth.

The planes landed on an airstrip on Thorney Island and the Band was taken in trucks and cars through eight miles of densely wooded countryside. The roads were hidden from the air by wiring the tops of trees together and the whole area was heavily guarded by US Military Police.

The Band set up in the open under camouflage netting covered with foilage, while an audience of about a thousand SHAEF personnel gathered together to listen. After General Eisenhower and his staff were seated in the front row the Band played for an hour to tremendous applause. When the concert was over General Eisenhower walked up to Captain Glenn Miller and congratulated him on the morale-boosting job the Band was doing and thanked him for bringing the Band down to play at his headquarters. Major Stearns told Haynes that General Eisenhower himself had asked for the Band after he had heard several of their broadcasts.

The Band was taken back to the airstrip and as they were loading their equipment on to the plane a C-14 landed nearby and out stepped a smartly dressed German General recently captured in Normandy. As the Band watched he was surrounded by six MPs and marched off to a waiting staff car and quickly driven away. The Band arrived back at Twinwood Farm as darkness fell.

'When we played for Eisenhower,' recalls Carmen Mastren, 'I think our music was way over his head, but he seemed to enjoy it. I later read somewhere that his favourite tune was "Home On The Range" and songs like that. A far cry from what we did.'

'The feeling I recall,' says John Halliburton, 'would be similar to the common response of most soldiers when seeing their leaders in wartime – that is, a feeling of comfort and identification, a desire to please (in this case, to play and look well), pride in the common cause, and a strange feeling of pity for someone with such an awesome responsibility.'

'The concert didn't go too well,' recalls Bob Ripley. 'We were all kind of nervous about playing for Eisenhower – the Band was nervous, Glenn was nervous, and there were some misses here and there and Glenn was pretty glum afterwards. On the way back he said, "Well, boys. I guess we'll go home on a banana boat." The big question was always, when would we go home? That was always at the back of our minds – when would we go home?'

On Sunday 6 August, the Band played for the first time at two airfields on the same day – one being arranged while they were on the way to the other.

It had been arranged for the Band to play that evening at the P-47 Thunderbolt fighter base of the 56th Fighter Group of the Eighth Air Force known as Boxted, near the village of Langham, Essex, about six miles north of Colchester. The 56th was commanded by Colonel Hubert Zemke, one of the outstanding Eighth Air Force fighter aces of the war, and was known as 'The Wolfpack'; only a couple of weeks previously another of its legendary aces, Lieutenant-Colonel Frances Gabreski, who held the record of twenty-eight enemy aircraft destroyed in combat, had been shot down and taken prisoner in Germany.

In the morning Harry Katzman took a small group from the string section to play at morning service at the chapel at Milton Ernest Hall, and Johnny Desmond's *Soldier and a Song* went out on the AEF Programme as usual. After lunch the Band climbed into two of the 489th Bomb Group's Liberator bombers at Twinwood Farm for the flight to Boxted, and while awaiting take-off one of the pilots asked Miller when the Band would play at their base at Halesworth near which they would be flying on their way to Boxted. Haynes suggested the pilot telephone his CO from the control tower at Twinwood Farm, get his approval for a concert that afternoon, and then get the base Special Services Officer to prepare a hangar and announce over the PA system that the Miller Band would be at the base within the hour. By the time it landed forty minutes later a crowd of several thousand had gathered and soon the strains of 'Moonlight Serenade' floated through the hangar bringing the sounds of home to another four thousand lonely GIs – what Haynes called 'the fastest deal yet'. The Band received the usual tremendous ovation and after the concert the base commander announced that they had a special treat for the Band – ice cream, a wartime rarity and the first they had seen since leaving the States. Some of the mechanics at the base had improvised an ice cream machine from equipment meant for other purposes, and after consuming large quantities of a luxury not many bases could offer the Band got back into the Liberators and resumed their flight to Boxted.

An hour later at Boxted the pattern was repeated. After the concert, and dinner in the Officers Mess followed by a programme of combat films in the base cinema, Captain Miller and Lieutenant Haynes were flown back to Twinwood Farm in a Fairchild aircraft by another of the 56th Group's fighter aces Lieutenant-Colonel

Dave Schilling, Group Executive Officer of the 56th, while the Band flew back in the Liberators.

Next day the Band headed west to Gloucestershire to play at American military hospitals in the Cirencester area. Three C-53s picked them up at Twinwood Farm after lunch and flew them to an RAF aerodrome at South Cerney, near Cirencester, but the strings stayed in Bedford for their Monday evening broadcast. According to the Activities list the Band under Glenn Miller played two concerts at a General Hospital at Cirencester – one in the afternoon to 3,500 personnel and another in the evening to 4,000. During this trip Miller split the Band into several units which played in the wards and he went round the wards talking to the wounded men, signing autographs and cheering them up. After dinner at an RAF mess the Band flew back to Twinwood in the dark. The pilots lost their way but eventually got their bearings and landed safely.

Local residents claim to remember the Band playing at Cheltenham Town Hall and the Queen's Hotel, as well as in Cirencester Park and the American military hospital at Ullenwood (a large country seat, perhaps the hospital referred to in the Activities list). The Band could hardly have fitted in all the Cheltenham concerts on the same trip as the hospital visits, so they may have visited the area more than once; however, no mention of the Band playing at Cheltenham appears anywhere in the Activities list.

On 9 August, the Band travelled by road to SHAEF (Main) (codenamed 'Widewing') at Bushey Park for a concert, for several thousand SHAEF headquarters personnel on the lawn in front of the HQ building; it was here at this concert that the coloured photograph of the band was taken which appears on the cover of this book.

The Band was in London on the 10th for another appearance in *The American Eagle in Britain* at Rainbow Corner, and that evening the regular weekly broadcast was played in the BBC's Paris Cinema studio in Lower Regent Street with British singer Paula Green making the first of her two guest appearances with the Band. After the broadcast, the Band stayed on in the Paris Cinema to record a special programme for the National Broadcasters' Association Convention in the USA in which Colonel Kirby and Sergeant Broderick Crawford also took part.

Next day, Friday 11 August, the Band played their first public concert for the people of Bedford in the Corn Exchange from 8.30

till 10 pm. Some weeks previously, when the Band was at the Corn Exchange for one of their broadcasts over the AEF Programme, Alderman Canvin, who ran the Forces Canteen at the Corn Exchange had asked Captain Miller whether the Band could play a public concert there for charity. Miller agreed, and eventually the concert was arranged for the evening of the 11th in aid of the Borough Entertainment Committee for the Forces. The money raised was to be used to provide Christmas entertainment for the Forces in the town and ironically when the time came to use it in this way Glenn Miller himself had just been reported 'missing'.

On Saturday 12 August, after a day of broadcasting and recording, Sergeant Mel Powell and a seven-man group flew in an ATC plane to Grove, Berkshire, to play for a dance, probably at the Ninth Air Force Service Command Headquarters, thus ending another busy week but with even more to come.

The Band's next trip was to take them away from Bedford for three days – a military version of a tour of one-night stands!

After lunch on 13 August, the Band took off in two C-47s from Twinwood Farm, leaving the string section behind, and an hour and a half later landed at the vast USAAF maintenance depot (the 3rd Base Air Depot) at Langford Lodge, a large country estate near the village of Crumlin, fifteen miles from Belfast. They were taken in trucks to Belfast to play an afternoon concert at an American Red Cross Club (formerly the Plaza Ballroom). Back at Langford Lodge they played another concert in the base theatre, flying out immediately afterwards to another huge maintenance base at Warton, near Blackpool (the First Base Air Depot), where they spent the night.

Next day the Band played to no less than 10,000 personnel of the Warton base in bright sunshine. That evening they had a few hours off and went into Blackpool to see the sights – including a character called Blackpool Mary!

The following morning the Band took off once more, this time in two B-24 Liberators bound for the 2nd Base Air Depot at Burtonwood, near Liverpool, arriving in time for lunch. Here again they played two concerts – one to 8,000 personnel in the afternoon and another to 9,000 in the evening. Lieutenant Haynes in his diary for that day refers to only one concert in the largest hangar they had yet seen, playing on an improvised bandstand which the GIs had built up for them with crates containing aircraft parts worth over fifty million dollars! The Band's reception here was even more tumultuous than usual as the base hadn't had as many shows as others further south and before leaving they were taken on a tour of the vast depot. After supper the Band flew back in the two Liberators, got lost in the dark again and landed at Thurleigh before flying on to Twinwood Farm.

On Wednesday 16 August a frightening incident occurred involving Miller and Haynes which, in the light of what was to happen a few months later, might be considered ominous and which certainly did not endear Miller to flying. So far, the Band's continuous and far-ranging air travel had been free of alarm. On Wednesday 16 August, the Band was scheduled to play at a military hospital at Bentley Priory, Stanmore (Middlesex). The Band went by road but Miller and Haynes went by air. As their plane was about to land at Hendon aerodrome red flares suddenly shot up around them as a signal not to land and the pilot, by that time barely a hundred feet off the ground, managed to pull the plane up so that they could go round again. A B-17 had been taking off and although they had been given permission to land, had they not been warned off they would have landed in front of or right on top of the bomber. Somewhere, someone got his lines crossed and as Haynes noted, 'just about scared the pants off us!'

Meanwhile the Band was set up on a lawn in front of the hospital building but no sooner had it got into 'In The Mood' than a flying bomb approached. The Band kept on playing although Miller quietened it down so that everyone could hear if the motor cut out, but it passed over and out of sight. Afterwards Miller and Haynes returned to Bedford by staff car!

The incident with the flying bomb was later portrayed realistically in the film *The Glenn Miller Story* in 1953, although some dramatic licence was employed in having the flying bomb actually explode nearby during 'In The Mood' – with the Band never missing a beat!

In the midst of all this hectic activity Captain Miller was promoted to Major on 8 August, receiving his majority on Thursday the 17th. After the weekly broadcast that evening with British singer Beryl Davis as guest singer the Band gave its new Major a promotion party in the Bromham Road Red Cross Club that lasted, according to Haynes 'till the wee small hours'.

About this time* the Band was re-named for radio broadcasts and personal appearance The American Band of the AEF as were its British and Canadian counterparts.

* Between 3 and 10 August; Paul Dudley once said that this change of name was made at the suggestion of General Eisenhower.

According to local residents, the Band played in public at various places in the Norwich area on August 17, 18 or 19, but no mention of any such performances appears in the Activities list, nor in the local papers at the time.

Friday the 18th was another very full day indeed. The morning was spent pre-recording *Uptown Hall* and *Swing Shift* programmes in the Co-Partners Hall for broadcasting the next day as the Band was scheduled to leave in the afternoon on a trip which would keep it from Bedford overnight again.

They flew first to the P-51 Mustang base of the 355th Fighter Group of the Eighth Air Force at Steeple Morden, Cambridgeshire, about fifteen miles south-east of Bedford, near Royston. Then they were taken to the Attlebridge airfield in Norfolk, where the 466th Bomb Group flying B-24 Liberators was stationed.

The Band left Bedford after lunch and drove to Twinwood Farm where three B-24 Liberators from Attlebridge were expected to pick them up for the flight to Steeple Morden, but as they reached the airfield six Liberators were coming in to land. Everyone it seemed wanted to fly the Glenn Miller Band so, although only three planes were needed six were picked for the job. One of them was the Group's Assembly plane, painted in vivid red zig zag stripes. Much to Miller's anxiety the six Liberators flew in close formation to Steeple Morden where the Band played to an enthusiastic 5,000-strong audience in a hangar. After the concert, followed by the best dinner they had had in a long time, it turned out that they were at Steeple Morden on the day of a spectacular incident in Eighth Air Force operations. Shortly before the Band arrived the fighters had just returned from a mission escorting heavy bombers attacking German airfields in France in support of the Allied armies pounding the Germans west of the Seine. During the return flight one of the fighters piloted by Captain Bert Marshall had been shot down in a field near Soissons, France. The pilot wasn't injured and another pilot in the same Squadron, Second Lieutenant Royce Priest, actually landed his fighter in the field and while other fighters shot up approaching German troops both men squeezed into Priest's cockpit and successfully flew back to Steeple Morden. Both men were at the concert and by the time Major Miller and Lieutenant Haynes made it to the bar in the Officers Club after dinner a party for the hero of the story, Second Lieutenant Priest, was well under way and when they left to fly on to Attlebridge the two fliers were still 'hugging one another and crying in their beer'!

At Attlebridge that evening an enormous audience of 10,000 crammed into a hangar. Serving at Attlebridge as a pilot in a

Liberator lead crew was twenty-one-year-old Captain John H. Woolnough and thirty-one years later he recalled the day the Miller Band came to Attlebridge:

The next highlight [in his service career, which had included bombing missions to Germany, occupied France, and in support of the D-Day landings] was when Glenn Miller came to the post. He had the biggest Band ever and that sound was something in that hangar! I mean, people were nuts – it was just out of this world! And then to see him later in the Club and talk to him was, personally, you know – Cloud Nine! It was the highlight of the whole war. It made my war. So I got the picture with Glenn . . . and the reason I was able to get it was I had taught photography at photo school and knew the Sergeant that ran the photo lab . . . I went up to him and said, 'How about a picture?' And then he takes the picture of Glenn Miller and me and the Chaplain, and he hands me the camera and says, 'OK you take one of me'. So I took a picture of him and Glenn Miller, so I not only got in a picture, but I was honoured to be able to take a picture of him, you see. [In the most unusual studio ever! – Interviewer] Yeah, in the latrine!

Glenn said OK – I went up to him and said, 'Hey, my twin brother is a big fan of yours' (I was a big fan, too, but I don't know if that was important). 'He is in Hawaii and I'd sure like to send him a picture of you and I together' – you know, the big sad story! He was the nicest guy – Glenn just said, 'Well OK as long as it's in private where nobody can see us because otherwise they'll mob me just like they did the other day'. So I said, 'Well, there's the Club office'. He said OK. So we go down there and the door's locked. Oh boy! We stand there for a minute, and the only place left was the latrine. He says, OK, so we go into the latrine – Glenn Miller, and the Chaplain, and the photographer and myself. So we get in there and suddenly discover that a WAC has followed us in – a Lieutenant (either a nurse or a WAC, I'm not sure which) but she was a female either First or Second Lieutenant – kind of a short, frumpy thing, and she screamed 'Oh!' threw her hands in the air and went flying out! . . . She was *really* embarrassed, and she went out and Glenn had a big smile on his face and he says, 'That's the first time I've been rid of her all day. She's trying to get me to audition some Corporal friend of hers, some GI from the hospital or some place, that sang pretty good, and she's been after me all day long'. So we had a big laugh. We got kind of close to him, because of that – he was a real human man, you know. And then we lined him up . . . and he put his arm around me . . . having Glenn Miller's arm around me and my arm around him – old buddy buddy, you know! That was a *real* highlight.*

* Edited extract from private tape recording: quoted by courtesy of Lieutenant-Colonel John H. Woolnough (ret.) and Charles H. Gallagher.

The Band stayed overnight at Attlebridge. Bad weather next day prevented flying back to Twinwood so they went by road. Paul Dudley's promotion to Warrant Officer had come through so that evening saw another promotion party. Mel Powell, however, took a small group to the 56th Fighter Group based at Boxted to play for an officers' dance.

On Sunday, apart from a rehearsal, the Band had the rest of the day off – the first in six weeks of ceaseless broadcasting, recording, rehearsals, concerts and travelling. Everyone took it easy. Some went to London, and some just hit the sack.

CHAPTER TEN

Podington and Framlingham – Wendling and Knettishall – Twinwood Farm – Concerts at Plymouth for the US Navy – Bing Crosby – Tibbenham and Thorpe Abbotts – *Atlantic Spotlight* – The Queensberry Club and the Feldman Swing Club

For the next few days there were no personal appearances and the Band was engaged in its regular broadcasts, interspersed with pre-recordings for use on the AEF Programme over the next few days when it would be away playing at US air and naval bases.

On 23 August, the Band left Bedford to play at two more airfields which would keep the men away overnight and which once again would bring Miller and Haynes into contact with the grimmer realities of the air war over Germany.

In the morning the Band pre-recorded a Johnny Desmond programme and then after lunch the entire Band including the string section drove to the airfield of the 92nd Bomb Group at Podington, a former RAF aerodrome in wooded countryside about ten miles north-west of Bedford. It played that afternoon in the open air on crash trucks drawn up on a hardstand area known as 'the slab' which the GIs had laid down for games, to an enthusiastic crowd of several thousand (the largest crowd in the history of the base). After the concert and the thanks of the Group Commander Colonel William H. Reid, six B-17 Flying Fortresses from the 390th Bomb Group at Framlingham, East Suffolk, picked up the Band and flew them to their base near the village of Parham (the name by which the base was sometimes known).

At Framlingham the base was holding a massive party to celebrate 100 missions over enemy territory, many local girls had been invited and there were large quantities of food and drink. The Band played for a dance in a large hangar decorated with greenery to a huge crowd of 6,000 servicemen and guests, and afterwards the CO gave a party for the Band in the Officers Club. The CO also invited Miller and Haynes to attend a briefing for the next day's mission, so at 2.30 am after only two hours sleep, they were awakened and taken to the briefing room where coffee and doughnuts helped to revive them as they sat down among the aircrews. The briefing lasted an hour and a half and Miller and Haynes were deeply impressed by the detailed information painstakingly given to the crews by the weather and bombing officers and the detailed answers given when it was the crews' turn for questions. The announcement of the target – oil installations in the Reich – was greeted by groans from the aircrews: it was a tough one and the Group had lost several planes on previous missions there. After the briefing, as the crews went out in the early dawn to board their B-17s, Miller and Haynes walked back to their billet in silence thinking of how many of the crews might never come back.

In the morning after breakfast the Band was flown back to Thurleigh, and driven to Bedford. The weekly full Band broadcast that evening from the Co-Partners Hall included one of Geraldo's singers, sixteen-year-old Doreen Villiers, as guest singer, as well as the first airing of a song written by Glenn Miller and Artie Malvin, one of the Crew Chief's singing group, 'I'm Heading For California'. Miller was not noted as a composer of popular songs, although in addition to his famous theme 'Moonlight Serenade' he had written a few instrumental tunes for his pre-war Band, but this song (which doubtless summed up his and most GIs' feelings at the time) was later repeated in several of the Band's broadcasts and after the war was recorded by the re-formed Miller Orchestra under Tex Beneke in 1946.

On 25 August, after pre-recording a *Swing Shift* in the morning, the Band was off again in five B-24s to play for the 392nd Bomb Group at Wendling, Norfolk, and the 388th Bomb Group at Knettishall, West Suffolk, about six miles south-east of Thetford. After dinner at Knettishall the Band played to 7,000 in a hangar so cold that some of the musicians, including Miller, played with their gloves on. After breakfast next morning, the Band were flown back to Twinwood Farm in three B-17s, one of which, piloted by an officer named Richard D. Richard, had been christened 'Moonlight Serenader' and had the name painted on the side of the fuselage.*

* Many bombers were unofficially given names by their crews and had these names and often pictures of glamorous girls painted on the fuselage: these paintings are now celebrated as 'nose art'. Other musical names given to bombers included 'In The Mood', 'Jersey Bounce', 'Stardust', 'Sunrise Serenade', 'Frenesi' and 'I'll Be Around'.

The early Miller AAFTC Band in the Yale Bowl, summer 1943. Among the singers seated on the left is Tony Martin (with legs crossed).

'I Sustain the Wings': left to right, Maj. Francis Healey, Sgt George Voutas, Capt. Glenn Miller, Lt Don Briggs, Pte Jerry Gray.

George Ockner conducting the string section, spring 1944: left to right, front row, Addison Collins, Harry Katzman, Ernie Kardos, Gene Bergen; second row, Phil Cogliano, Dave Sackson, Nathan Kaproff, Joseph Kowalewski, Alfred Alwurm; third row, probably Dave Herman (behind guitar), Milton Edelson, Freddy Ostrovsky, Dick Motylinski, Carl Swanson; fourth row, Stanley Harris, Dave Schwartz, Henry Brynan, Emanuel Wishnow; back row, Bob Ripley (in shadow), Morris Bialkin. Guitarist Carmen Mastren is on the left.

The Band in New York for an 'I Sustain The Wings' broadcast, spring 1944, conducted by Jerry Gray; the group round the central microphone includes Broderick Crawford (right) and Johnny Desmond.

Ray McKinley beats out a solo to the obvious delight of trumpeters Bobby Nichols and Bernie Privin.

Lt-Col. David Niven, Associate Director SHAEF Broadcasting Services, at the Band's first broadcast in the Corn Exchange, Bedford, 9 July 1944.

Capt. Glenn Miller at the Band's first broadcast over the BBC's AEF Programme from the Corn Exchange, Bedford, 9 July 1944.

VIP front row at the Band's first broadcast, 9 July 1944: left to right, Col. Niven, Lt-Col. Norman F. Baessell, Col. Edward M. Kirby, Col. Heffley (Chief of Staff to General Goodrich at Milton Ernest Hall), unknown, unknown, 2nd Lt Don W. Haynes, Sgt Broderick Crawford; General Goodrich is next to Col. Niven at the extreme left of the picture.

Announcers Jean Metcalf (of the BBC) and Paul Dubov introducing the Band's broadcast from the Corn Exchange, Bedford, 13 July 1944, while Capt. Glenn Miller conducts the Band.

The saxophone section: left to right, Peanuts Hucko, Hank Freeman, Vince Carbone, Freddy Guerra, Mannie Thaler; the other tenor player Jack Ferrier is hidden behind Peanuts Hucko. This picture was taken at the Corn Exchange broadcast on 13 July 1944.

Trumpeter Bernie Privin spreading joy all around at the Band's broadcast from the Corn Exchange, Bedford, 13 July 1944.

Mel Powell, during a broadcast from the Corn Exchange, Bedford, 13 July 1944.

Bob Ripley (left) and Morris Bialkin, during a broadcast from the Corn Exchange, Bedford, 13 July 1944.

Left to right, Don Haynes, Joe Loss, Vera Lynn, Glenn Miller, unknown 8th Air Force officer, perhaps at Thurleigh airfield on 20 July 1944.

Glenn Miller (third from right) and Don Haynes (fourth from right) with a group of officers, possibly taken when the Band played at the Wattisham-Hitcham Airfield on 24 July 1944. Second from right is Lt-Col. Norman F. Baessell.

Capt. Glenn Miller talking to Adj. Harold H. Gourley and surrounded by GIs at Wattisham-Hitcham airfield, 24 July 1944.

Capt. Glenn Miller and Tech. Sgt Paul Dudley, seen here at the Plaza Cinema, London, 27 July 1944.

Ray McKinley signing autographs after the Plaza concert.

Mel Powell with British pianist George Shearing after the Plaza concert.

Zeke Zarchy chatting to Belgian trumpet star Johnny Claes and friend after the Plaza concert.

Capt. Glenn Miller introducing Peanuts Hucko to the audience at the Kimbolton bomber base on 2 Aug. 1944.

A typical airfield scene with the Band playing to GIs crammed together on the floor, on the wing of a plane and clinging to the hangar frame at Halesworth bomber base, 6 Aug. 1944.

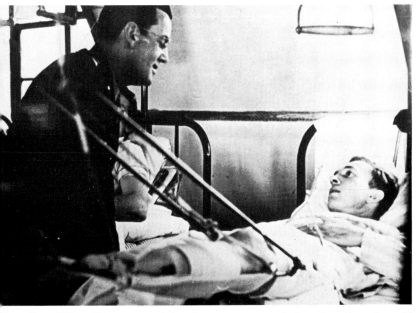

Capt. Glenn Miller talking to a wounded serviceman, an opportunity he took as often as he could when the Band played at military hospitals.

The Band playing at Warton supply base, 14 Aug. 1944.

Maj. Glenn Miller and Capt. John H. Woolnough at Attlebridge bomber base, 18 Aug. 1944, photographed by Sgt Russell Clements.

Maj. Glenn Miller and Sgt Russell Clements at Attlebridge, photographed by Capt. John H. Woolnough.

The Band playing at an open-air concert at Podington bomber airfield, 23 Aug. 1944.

Four of the Miller Band's jazzmen at the Feldman Swing Club, London, probably 3 Sept. 1944:
left to right (in uniform), Carmen Mastren, Ray McKinley, Peanuts Hucko, Mel Powell.

The Band had no live broadcasts on the 26th – the 9.35 am *Swing Shift* had been pre-recorded the previous day to cover its absence overnight at Knettishall, and the 6.15 *Uptown Hall* broadcast was replaced by repeating the recording broadcast on 29 July. In the evening Haynes took Zeke Zarchy and a small jazz group to play at a dance at the fighter base at Steeple Morden where the Band had played a week earlier. On the way back to Bedford they got lost, eventually arriving back at 7 am on Sunday morning.

That Sunday afternoon, in beautiful sunshine, the Band played on crash trucks in the open air at Twinwood Farm for the RAF personnel numbering over a thousand, in return for all the times they had used the airfield to fly off to concerts at other bases. Twinwood Farm was a satellite field of RAF Cranfield, about ten miles to the south-west: Cranfield and Twinwood Farm were the base of No. 15 Operational Training Unit of RAF Fighter Command, used for night fighter training and flying mostly Beaufighters and Mosquitoes. They had also helped to train USAAF night fighter crews (known as 'Cousin training') and the fields were used a great deal by both the Americans and the RAF.

Still there was no let-up for the Band. They were off again on 28 August, this time to play for the US Navy in south-west England. The whole trip was bedevilled by bad weather – they were delayed leaving and afterwards were stranded at Plymouth.

They were due to be picked up at Twinwood Farm at 10.30 am but because of the weather the planes didn't arrive till noon. The Band finally took off after lunch and flew to an RAF landing strip known as Harrowbeer on the edge of the Dartmoor village of Yelverton. From there they were driven in US Navy trucks and buses across the moor to the Royal Naval College at Manadon, near Plymouth. Here the Band without the strings played to hospital patients in a large hall, then went on to the Navy's nearby Shafter's Field for a concert to nearly a thousand 'Seabees' (Construction Battalion personnel). Meanwhile the string section played two concerts on their own – one at Shafter's Field and one in the early evening at Manadon. The Band was billeted at Queen Anne's Barracks and after dinner the entire Band including the strings played a concert at the Odeon Cinema in Plymouth for American and British troops.

Although they were due to leave Plymouth the next morning the weather was so foggy and damp that they had to stay there throughout Tuesday and Tuesday night. However, they lived well on Navy rations, with steak for breakfast, lunch and dinner! They also saw something of badly bombed Plymouth – the City centre was almost completely destroyed – and Miller and Haynes were taken on a tour of Plymouth Harbour in a motor launch by the CO of the naval base.

By Wednesday morning the weather had cleared enough for the Band to fly back to Bedford. When they landed at Twinwood Farm who should be there to meet them as they got off the planes but the Old Groaner himself, Bing Crosby.

Bing Crosby was the latest American star to come to Europe in what the *Melody Maker* called the 'entertainment invasion' – the increasing flow of famous entertainers sent over by the USO -Camp Shows organization in Hollywood, the American equivalent of ENSA, to entertain the Allied forces in the ETO. It had arranged Dinah Shore's visit earlier in August and as the Second Front became firmly established and the fighting moved eastwards from Normandy more and more stars were going over to the Continent to perform in the rest areas behind the lines and in some cases almost in the combat areas – at one place Spike Jones and his City Slickers actually came under German fire.

The 'entertainment invasion' reached its peak with the arrival of Bing Crosby, then at the top of his show business career – unquestionably the greatest popular star of the time, perhaps of any time. He arrived quietly in London on Saturday 26 August. He had never previously appeared in Britain and even his USO tour was meant strictly for the Forces, but once the news that he was in London got around it caused a sensation and during the next few days there were some spectacular scenes in the West End as the public got wind of his whereabouts during a whirlwind tour of broadcasts and stage shows for the Forces.

On Sunday evening, 27 August, to a tumultuous reception from the packed audience in the Queensberry Club he was the surprise guest star in that week's edition of *Variety Bandbox*, introduced by Tommy Handley and accompanied by the Miller Band's pianist Jack Rusin, who had come down to London with Warrant Officer Paul Dudley while the Band was playing at Twinwood Farm. A long and moving account of the broadcast appeared in the *Melody Maker* of 2 September 1944, written by its editor Ray Sonin, which gives some idea of the esteem in which Crosby was held at the time, and after the broadcast there followed the oft-related occasion when Bing sang from the window of Kettner's Restaurant in Romilly Street to a large crowd in the street below. As darkness fell and the crowd shone torches on him, he sang no less than nine songs before they at last quietly dispersed, much to the relief of the police and the air raid wardens!

On the 29th, Bing went to Bedford, expecting to make some recordings with the Miller Band, and while waiting for them to return from Plymouth he recorded some songs with Jack Rusin for *Keyboard Contrasts*, the solo programme which Rusin broadcast every Thursday or Saturday. Once the Band got back on Wednesday, Bing recorded a fifteen-minute programme in which he sang four songs with the Band and which was broadcast the following Sunday as *Bing Crosby Sings*, in place of the Johnny Desmond programme. He also recorded songs which were used in later broadcasts by the *Swing Shift* and the full AEF Band.

Bing Crosby was greatly impressed by the Band and Haynes noted an incident during a break in the proceedings while he, Miller and Crosby were sitting chatting. Miller and Crosby had been friends for years and Glenn admired Bing Crosby's colourful hand-painted tie, which was in marked contrast to his drab khaki one, the only kind he had been able to wear for the last two years. Bing offered to swop, and taking off his tie he borrowed Haynes' fountain pen and wrote on it 'Glenn Miller AAF Band – the greatest thing since the invention of cup mutes', signed it 'Bing' and passed it over to Miller who, however, kept his tie on!

Later, Bing, Major Miller and Lieutenant Haynes drove to London, where Bing broadcast from the BBC's Paris Cinema in Lower Regent Street as guest singer in the weekly programme by RSM George Melachrino and the British Band of the AEF. After the broadcast they went round to Kettner's Restaurant for dinner where, once again, a crowd outside got wind of Bing Crosby's presence, so again he went out on to the balcony and sang 'Pennies From Heaven'. After a great cheer the crowd quietly dispersed.

There was another *American Eagle* recording next day at Rainbow Corner. Miller, Crosby, Haynes and Dudley went to dinner at Grosvenor House in Park Lane (where the American Army had a Junior Officers Mess) and then it was back to the Paris for the Band's regular Thursday evening broadcast with a surprise guest star – none other than Bing (he wasn't billed in the *Radio Times*), surprisingly without an audience. He sang all the songs in the programme, replacing Johnny Desmond, and in one, 'Swinging On A Star' was accompanied by Mel Powell and the Swing Sextet. The finale of the programme was Jerry Gray's classic arrangement of 'Poinciana', and earlier, at rehearsal, the free and easy Bing had come up against the perfectionist bandleader who was wont to rehearse everything repeatedly to get it exactly right. The two men had been great friends since the early 1930s, but after running through 'Poinciana' Miller wasn't satisfied and wanted to go through it again. Bing refused, saying 'What, and make all those boys tired? Glenn, dear boy, just wave your baton and I promise I'll come in.'* Needless to say, with Crosby the complete professional it was 'all right on the night'.

'When Miller arrived at rehearsal,' recalls Bernie Privin, 'he called the Band to attention and told us to take our seats, whereupon Crosby reminded Miller that it was a 'freebie' and with a wave of his hand a waiter appeared with a table on wheels on which there were about six bottles of booze. Bing said for us to come over and have a taste before we did the rehearsal and the programme, which was a complete success.'

'I don't think Miller approved of that too much,' says Nat Peck. 'I mean, he didn't mind the odd drink after the job but we were very strict about not boozing during working hours. Of course, Bing didn't worry too much about military discipline, or anything like that, and Miller liked him so much that he finally didn't raise any objections to that bit of boozing at the Paris Cinema!

'Bing was an absolutely incredible person – we all loved him immediately. He was really one of the boys and it was an unforgettable afternoon. He proved himself to be such a professional. Subsequently I've worked with him in recording studios in London and things hadn't changed – he was still an incredible professional.' A recording of Bing Crosby's broadcast with the Band was issued on an LP in America in 1983 (*see* page 405).

After the broadcast Bing went round the corner into Piccadilly, where police were holding back excited crowds on both sides of the road, for the opening night of the Stage Door Canteen for the Forces. Here, again accompanied by Jack Rusin, he sang to a jam-packed audience of Allied Servicemen and women. Fred Astaire, who had arrived in London earlier that day, did an impromptu song and dance. Recordings of Bing taken during the opening night's show were broadcast in the AEF Programme the following evening replacing the usual *Uptown Hall* programme at 6.15.

When Bing Crosby moved over to France early the following

* As related in *Bing: the Authorised Biography*, by Charles Thompson (W. H. Allen, London, 1975).

week with what he called 'his little troupe' of entertainers to sing to the troops behind the lines, Miller 'lent' him Jack Rusin as accompanist, but owing to the rapidly changing military situation and consequent transport difficulties Rusin never caught up with Bing.

The day after its broadcast with Bing Crosby, the Band was off on its travels again. They flew out from Twinwood Farm after lunch in three B-24 Liberators from the Eighth Air Force airfield of the 445th Bomb Group at Tibbenham (also known as Tivetshall), Norfolk, about fifteen miles south-west of Norwich where it played an afternoon concert in another very cold hangar to about 3,000 personnel of the base. Then, off again, this time in trucks to the B-17 base of the 100th Bomb Group at Thorpe Abbotts, about five miles east of Diss. The 100th was known in the Eighth Air Force as 'The Bloody Hundredth' owing to their high casualty rate on some of their missions. After dinner at the base the Band played to another 3,000 in a hangar and stayed overnight. Next morning, as the planes were weathered in, the Band was taken in a bus, a weapons carrier and a staff car to London for another notable broadcast, as the star attraction in *Atlantic Spotlight*, followed by a show at the Queensberry Club.

The Band's broadcast in *Atlantic Spotlight* on Saturday 2 September, was another landmark in its service in the ETO. Its appearance in the programme was announced in advance in the *Radio Times*, as a live broadcast not only to the British public and the listeners to the AEF Programme, but, via shortwave* back home to America as well.

Atlantic Spotlight was a joint production by the BBC in London and NBC in New York and was heard live in both countries simultaneously. It was broadcast in Britain on the General Forces Programme and the AEF Programme on Saturdays from 6.30 to 7 pm, with a recorded repeat next day. Glenn Miller and the Army Air Forces Band had broadcast from New York in its very first edition on 1 January 1944 (*see* page 89). Like *Variety Bandbox*, it featured different bands and singers each week.

The Band's participation in *Atlantic Spotlight* was notable in more ways than one, for it included a reunion over the air between Major Miller in London and his pre-war vocal group the Modernaires with Paula Kelly in New York, and, in another link-up from Atlantic City, Marion Hutton. Also in the New York end of

* There were no direct broadcasting lines across the Atlantic in those days.

the programme were Roy Fox and the NBC 'Spotlight' orchestra and compère Herb Sheldon. The compère in London was AC2 Ronnie Waldman, the AEFP announcer and producer.

The first part of the programme came from New York and consisted of music by Roy Fox and songs by the Modernaires. Then from London Ronnie Waldman introduced Glenn Miller and the AEF Band who kicked off with 'Flying Home'. Johnny Desmond sang 'I'll Be Seeing You', then Miller, coming over loud and clear from London, renewed acquaintance with his old singing stars Marion Hutton and the Modernaires and they all combined in a historic three-way performance of 'Juke Box Saturday Night'. After that Miller sent greetings to 'all the Pollys, Kays, Joys, Helens, Marges, Nancies and Connies . . .', the wives of Haynes, Broderick Crawford, Paul Dudley, and other members of the Band, and after expressing the hope that they would all be home soon the Band signed off with 'In The Mood'.

After *Atlantic Spotlight* the Band went to the Queensberry Club to play for the Forces there – not for a broadcast but to entertain the nightly audience of Allied troops.

The Queensberry All-Services Club had been opened in 1942 in the large former Casino Theatre* in Old Compton Street. It was sponsored by a group of wealthy sporting and entertainment celebrities, presided over by the Marquis of Queensberry who took an active part in running it and sometimes introduced acts from the stage himself. The Manager of the Club was John Harding, and besides providing films and stage shows for the troops in the huge theatre, presenting top-class professional artists and bands, the Club also provided meals, a 'wash and brush up' and dancing downstairs. Soon after its establishment, its potential as a regular broadcasting venue for the BBC was recognized by imaginative producers, especially as it could supply large and enthusiastic audiences, and, after some initial objection from BBC chiefs, permanent microphones and control cubicles were set up and connected to Broadcasting House. By 1944 some of the best light entertainment broadcasts were coming from the Club.

The AEF Band had first played there for the *Variety Bandbox* recording in July, and its return performance was reported once again by that devoted chronicler of their activities, the *Melody Maker*'s Jack Marshall:

* After the war it was known as the London Casino and later became the home of Cinerama for several years. It has now reverted to its original name – the Prince Edward Theatre.

The men and women of the Services who go in their thousands to the London Queensberry Services Club, that famous Soho institution for the rest and entertainment – with a capital 'E' – of the Forces, have certainly been having their fill of exciting Transatlantic musical fare lately.

Apart from the almost legendary Bing – whose visit there has been recorded by our Editor, Ray Sonin, in an article which most of us will remember for a long time – and Spike Jones' capers there (reported by Laurie Henshaw on page 3), last Saturday (September 2) the 'customers' were thrilled by a visit from Major Glenn Miller and his Band, and next Saturday (9th) the very fine Artie Shaw Naval Band (directed and led by saxist-celebrity Sam Donohue [sic]) is scheduled to play at the Queensberry.

Through the courtesy of the Queensberry's energetic and popular secretary-manager, Mr John Harding, I spent one of my most memorable evenings listening to the Glenn Miller Band last Saturday (writes Jack Marshall).

It is difficult, in mere words, to convey just the precision, perfect musicianship, versatility, and all-round remarkable finesse of this wonderful band.

The main difference between last Saturday night's show, before thousands of Service people at the Queensberry, and the recent Glenn Miller concert at the London Plaza Cinema is that on Saturday the band was so entirely *relaxed*. Its good-humoured abandon and lack of starchiness was a treat, and although the musicianship didn't suffer in any way, the result was a pleasant intimacy between musicians and audience that introduced a warmth into the proceedings rather lacking at the earlier London concert aforementioned.

There was still a lot of unnecessary showmanship; the 'physical jerks' of the trombones is one example of this. On the other hand, there was a glorious little bit during 'In The Mood', where the massive string section, having sat tacit throughout the piece, suddenly played exactly one note, and then mopped their brows with great vigour and in complete exhaustion. It was a most amusing bit of by-play.

It is impossible, in the space available, to go, number by number, through the whole show (I could write a page about the band's rendering of 'Holiday for Strings' alone) or to mention each individual in the band who distinguished himself in the course of a programme which included some beautifully played, serious moments in addition to the exhilarating swing numbers.

One of the highspots, definitely, was the wonderful bit of fast-moving by-play way out in front, by Ray McKinley and 'Trigger' Alpert, on drum and bass respectively. This took place during that part of the show when Major Miller hands over the whole band to Ray McKinley for a short spell (as was done during the Plaza show).

Others who distinguished themselves particularly, apart from the impeccable vocalism of Johnny Desmond, and the fine singing of the vocal quartette, the Crew Chiefs, was the young red-headed trumpet star whom they call 'Red' Nichols The Second. Gosh, can that boy go to Town!

There was another big spot in the show for a quartette containing Mel Powell (piano); 'Trigger' Alpert (bass); Ray McKinley (drums); and 'Peanuts' Hucko (clarinet); also a solo spot for Mel Powell, in which it is no exaggeration to say that he played the most tasteful piano ever heard in Town (yes, I know this will cause cries of rage from all sorts of people, but that's my opinion and I stick to it).

But there it is – I could go on all night raving about the show; but with space as it is you'll have to take my word for it that it was one of the best things ever.

I was lucky enough to have a few words with Major Miller himself afterwards. They say he is 'big-time' and reserved. Don't you believe it. He was charming to the nth degree and as friendly and cordial as anyone could wish.

And please don't forget, all of you, that since 8 August he has been Major, not Captain, Miller.

After last Saturday's show it won't be too much if they make him a Field-Marshal . . .!

Did I say I had the thrill of a lifetime on Saturday night? Well, in a way I definitely did; but even in my wildest dreams I hardly expected to follow it up with such a jazz fan's night out as I enjoyed at the Feldman Club the following night, when a party of the Miller musicians, with Mel Powell, Ray McKinley, Carmen Mastren, 'Peanuts' Hucko, and trumpet star Jack Steele came down to enjoy an evening of English swing.

After listening with interest to the resident band – with Carlo Krahmer (drums); Dick Katz and Ralph Sharon (sharing piano); Billy Amstell (clarry and tenor); Arthur Mouncey (trumpet); Jimmy Skidmore (tenor); and Bert Howard (bass) – the Miller boys were obviously getting nicely in the groove, and before long Mel Powell, Ray McKinley, Carmen Mastren and 'Peanuts' Hucko were persuaded to come up on the stand and go to town.

And what a session they played! It was quiet, relaxed: no loud stuff at all. Mel Powell is the quietest pianist we have heard for a long time, just as he is one of the greatest anywhere.

Despite playing so much with the big band, Ray McKinley is equally at home in a small combo, and his drumming on this occasion was not a scrap too loud. Carmen Mastren played quiet guitar, once or twice taking a single-string solo that got the fans gasping. In 'Peanuts' Hucko we have a tenor sax and clarry ace whose technique and style are downright amazing.

After playing for about half an hour, during which the fans simply wouldn't let them leave the stand, the four boys at last finished off what was undoubtedly one of the greatest jam sessions ever heard in this country.

At the finish they were thanked by '*MM*' record critic Edgar Jackson, and by famous Geraldo guitarist Ivor Mairants, who welcomed the boys on behalf of the British musicians, and wistfully remarked that it had needed such a major event as a world war to bring this great aggregation of talent across the Atlantic.

After this, the Miller boys – plus their trumpet man, Jack Steele – jammed in with some of the resident band, including Arthur Mouncey, Jimmy Skidmore, etc., while Tommy Bromley – who was among the big concourse of London musicians present on this historic night – took over the bass.

The atmosphere became more and more explosive, and Mouncey was in particularly great form – but the excitement still had not quite reached its peak.

To bring this wonderful evening to a close, the youthful drum wonder, 10-year old Victor Feldman, was brought in to play a number on the drums.

The scene that followed beggars description. Most amazing part of it was the astonishment apparent in the American boys after hearing the young drum wizard do his stuff.

Mel Powell literally stopped playing to stare round open-mouthed at the unexpected phenomenon; Ray McKinley was obviously so impressed that he just didn't know what to do about it.

After it was all over and the tremendous ovation which followed had at last died down and the hand-shaking and autograph-hunting was over, we had a brand new spectacle to watch – the Glenn Miller boys lining up to ask Victor Feldman for *his* autograph!

As for Victor, he finished the evening with his book full of new autographs – and what nice ones! Mel Powell wrote: 'To Victor – you've been responsible for the most delightful musical experience I've ever enjoyed. I'll always feel honoured to play on the same stand with you – Respectfully, Mel Powell.'

Ray McKinley wrote: 'To Victor – aged 10 – who ranks already in the first thirty. You could not miss if you tried.'

Carmen Mastren wrote: 'To Victor – one of the finest drummers I've ever heard. Keep it up and you'll kill them all . . .'

Finally, 'Peanuts' Hucko wrote: 'You've got it, and don't forget you're in my band . . .'.

A real credit to our British drum genius, Unquestionably, if this kiddy were in America he would be a world-beater.*

Although Jack Marshall was able to have a chat with Glenn

* *Melody Maker* 9 September 1944.

Miller that Saturday evening, his experiences with him were not always so successful. For several years during the war Jack worked as compère at the Feldman Swing Club in Oxford Street and he recalled:

Major Glenn Miller came to the Club several times. I remember how he came striding in late one evening and asked if Victor Feldman had played yet. 'Yes', I told him, 'Victor has been on'.

'Then I see no possible reason for remaining', he said stiffly, and strode out before I had time to assure him that Victor could easily be persuaded to go on a second time.

Glenn . . . was about the most temperamental person you could expect to meet. All who were able flocked to the London Casino, where Glenn and his Orchestra . . . played for the Forces on certain nights of the week in 1944.

The impact of the Miller music on London's musical world was the most exciting thing that had happened in at least ten years. The profession devoured the music avidly, and after many years of musical attrition, fairly worshipped at the Miller shrine.

While feeling this spirit of exaltation to the full, I was stymied in my personal relations by the extremely unpredictable temperament of the great GM himself, and as I was constantly striving to obtain pictures of his outfit, this attitude could be very trying.

I once struggled, jampacked in a stuffy guard's van, all the way to Bedford, as a result of Glenn's personal invitation – only to find when I got there that the temperamental American was in a great rage, and 'didn't want to know' about anything.*

In his report of the concert at the Queensberry Club Jack Marshall referred to the one note played by the strings during 'In The Mood'. Harry Katzman explained how he and George Ockner dreamed up this bit of fun: 'As you know, after the theme the first number we played on our personal appearances throughout the United States, England and Europe was always "In The Mood". Now, here we were, twenty strings sitting on the stage and the saxes and the brass and the rhythm were going at it full swing and everybody was screaming – as soon as that thing started everybody used to yell. But we sat there with our instruments on our laps like a bunch of dummies. I don't know when we got this idea, whether it was just the last part of our stay in the United States or whether it was in England – I can't

* From *Thirty Years of Dance Music*, by Jack Marshall (in *New Musical Express 1954 Annual*, London, 1953).

remember. But I was talking to George and I said, "You know, we look like a bunch of dummies up there – we sit there, and after the Band plays 'In The Mood' they all stand up and we sit there like a bunch of dumb-bells". I suggested that just before the piece ends, where the trombones have that low A flat pedal tone we all stand up and play that one note. We weren't going to tell anybody about it as far as I remember (or maybe we did, I'm not sure) but certainly Miller didn't know anything about it. But George Ockner improved on it and said, "After we play that one note we'll all take our handkerchiefs out – and be sure everybody's got a white handkerchief – and just wipe our brows". I forget where it was that we first did it but certainly Miller was not aware of it and when we came to that part in "In The Mood" – and of course the trombones were very soft on that note so it made no difference – all the strings, including the 'cellos, stood up to play that low A flat. We knew the arrangement so well, having played it hundreds of times, and we waited and waited and George told us just when to stand up only just a bar before so it would be sudden, and we stood up like a bunch of soldiers of course. When we played that note and Miller saw us standing up like that he was so surprised, and when we took out our handkerchiefs and you could see all that white with everybody wiping his brow the soldiers in the audience went crazy – it was one of the funniest things they had ever heard. You could see Miller's frown change to a big smile and he applauded the strings! After that it was in, and every time we played "In The Mood" we all knew that we had to stand up and it went right through the war – we never played "In The Mood" where the strings didn't stand up and then wipe their brows with the white handkerchiefs and it was always a terrific laugh.'

The Band returned to Bedford late on the Saturday night, and Sunday was a day off – only the second day off since it had begun operations early in July! On the Sunday evening some of the men turned up at the Feldman Swing Club in London and took part in the session described by Jack Marshall on pages 136–7.

Remarkable though it may seem, throughout this hectic period of eight weeks – from Sunday 9 July to Sunday 3 September – with broadcasts almost every day, pre-recordings for future use, frequent airfield concerts, the trips to Northern Ireland and Plymouth, journeys to London for the *American Eagle* broadcasts, the Plaza concert, *Variety Bandbox* and *Atlantic Spotlight*, all but twenty-four of the scheduled eighty broadcasts were live and only eight were cancelled. In addition to performances and rehearsals there was the constant travelling, often not in the best or most comfortable conditions or the best of weather. By any standards it was an impressive record – a major contribution to the AEF Programme and an incalculable morale-boosting job to the men on the airfields and in the hospitals.

Plenty more was yet to come!

CHAPTER ELEVEN

Plans to go to France – The 'Miller Memorandum' on pre-recording – Horham, Leicester and Hardwick – 'The Wishing Well' – Rougham

These were heady days for everyone. In addition to the tumultuous receptions accorded the Band wherever it played, the war was going well. The Allied breakout from Normandy began in early August, Paris was liberated on the 25th, and the British and American Armies began their spectacular pursuit of the fleeing remnants of the Wehrmacht across Northern France and Belgium. The Allied invasion of southern France on 15 August quickly linked up with the Armies in the north and pressed on towards the German border and the Siegfried Line. The Germans were on the run and it really began to look as if the war might be over by Christmas and the troops (and the AEF Band) going home sooner than they had expected.

During August, there was much discussion in SHAEF and the BBC of various ways of getting the Band to France to play for the fighting troops as near the front line as possible, and the AEF *Radio Times* actually announced that the Band might be going over to France. This was exactly what Miller really wanted, although the discussions were in the wider context of getting more original programme material of all kinds from France for inclusion in the AEF Programme – not only entertainment but also on-the-spot war news, interviews and service activities. Material of this kind had been coming in to the Programme in small amounts for some time – Franklin Engelman and David Niven had been to France soon after D-Day recording messages from the troops in the field for broadcasting from London, in addition to the recorded despatches from the war correspondents. But now that the fighting had moved beyond Paris the Programme organizers wanted more permanent arrangements. The entertainment material they hoped to obtain would include, for example, British and American artists entertaining service audiences while on trips arranged by ENSA, the USO and the military authorities, as well as regular quarter and half-hour programmes by bands specially sent out to make radio programmes, in which the AEFP policy of having British artists with American bands and vice versa, could be continued. As far as the Miller Band was concerned, Colonel Kirby (no doubt with prompting from Miller) was anxious to establish it in France as soon as practicable, with or without guest artists, and suggested that the Band should alternate between England and France, pre-recording programmes during their periods in England for use on the AEF Programme while they were away. But the Programme planners were against this. They wanted live broadcasts and they also felt that the constant coming and going would lose the advantage of having the Band in France at all.

The big snag to all these plans was the lack of reliable technical facilities across the Channel. The retreating Germans had destroyed many studios and transmitters in Paris and the pre-war landlines to London were not yet restored. Recording on the spot would be necessary with the recordings flown back to London and (if satisfactory) broadcast at the first available opportunity. Even bringing recordings from France to London for use in the Programme was liable to delay, or even non-arrival, as military air transport (there were, of course, no civilian communications) was all reserved for essential military supplies and personnel. Certainly, *regular* programmes from France were out of the question at that time, and as the maintenance of regular broadcasts by the AEF Bands and others was essential, the transfer of the Miller Band to France was clearly impracticable for the time being. In any case, they were already doing a first-class job in Bedford and on their visits to airfields and bases around Britain.

Despite the great success and popularity of the Band, the exciting progress of the Allied liberation of Western Europe and the crushing defeats inflicted on the Germans in France, behind the scenes of the AEF Programme all was not sweetness and light. Following the initial disagreement with Maurice Gorham after only a week of broadcasting Glenn Miller was becoming steadily more frustrated by the BBC's preference for live broadcasts, whereas *he* wanted to pre-record them as much as possible and leave more time for playing at airfields, camps and hospitals. During the first four weeks' broadcasting, out of forty scheduled programmes only eight were pre-recorded. Early in August, Miller – never one to compromise if he could avoid it – felt these frustrations and restrictions had become intolerable and he put his views in writing to his military superiors in what now appears a rather peevish and hastily composed memorandum:

ARMY AIR FORCES BAND (SPECIAL)

HEADQUARTERS COMMAND, SHAEF. APO 757, US ARMY

Subject: Broadcast Recording

8 August 1944

1. Information available to the AAF Band indicates that the British Broadcasting Corporation refuses to record programmes in advance of scheduled broadcast time.

2. This refusal precludes the playing of British and American Posts, Camps and Stations by personnel of the AAF Band.

3. It is the opinion, based on past co-operation shown, that the BBC is not only unconcerned with providing facilities which will make time available to the AAF Band to play British and American Posts, Camps and Stations, but is arbitrarily making it difficult for the AAF Band to play other than 'live' broadcasts with the hopes that higher authorities will discontinue broadcasting by the AAF Band, thus removing a serious threat to the BBC's lackadaisical and ineffective broadcast methods.

4. It is urgently recommended that necessary steps be taken, immediately, to set up SHAEF controlled transmitters in England and France so that the officers and enlisted men of the Allied Expeditionary Forces may be the recipients of expert broadcasting efforts, and that they may have the pleasure of hearing and seeing as many 'live' programs at Posts, Stations and Camps as is humanly possible.

5. Proof of the BBC's position as to a whole-hearted effort to promote inter-allied relations and to provide recreation and entertainment is evidenced by the fact that the AEFP transmitter is screened in southern England so as to prevent any competition with regular scheduled BBC broadcasts.

6. Many of the Allied soldiers are evacuated or on furlough from active duty on the Continent and, as a result of this transmitter screening by the BBC, are unable to 'tune in' AEF Programmes.

7. It is the opinion of the CO of the AAF Band that BBC is more interested in maintaining its political 'status quo' and antiquated type broadcasts, than in servicing the ultimate consumer, the personnel the AEF programs were designed to serve, namely GI Joe and Tommy Atkins and their counterparts with the various Allied nations.

Alton Glenn Miller

*Major AC Commanding**

* In *Star Spangled Radio*, by Edward M. Kirby and Jack W. Harris. (Ziff-Davis, Chicago, 1948.)

Of course, this could have been a put-up job between Kirby and Miller, or at least presented with the former's active encouragement. But regarding Miller's complaints about pre-recording programmes, besides the eight pre-recordings actually broadcast before his memorandum, a number of other pro-grammes had also been pre-recorded by then and were broadcast shortly afterwards. Indeed, pre-recording continued during the next few days and weeks – some were actually made on the date of his memorandum. However, considering the great popularity of the Band and Miller's aim to provide live entertainment to the GIS, his anxiety to do more and more concerts was understandable. On the other hand, the vast majority of the output of the AEF Programme consisted of recordings of one kind or another and equally understandable was the BBC's desire to put out as many live broadcasts as possible with their immediacy and topicality in contrast to the almost constant flow of recorded programmes. The dissension rumbled on, although during the next couple of months the proportion of pre-recorded broadcasts by the Band did increase until early in October SHAEF ordered that all the Band's broadcasts should be live unless there were exceptional reasons for pre-recording them. From then until the Band went to France in December practically all their broadcasts were live.

As for Miller's assertion that the AEF Programme was screened from southern England (and Maurice Gorham stated in passing in his memoirs that 'we screened it from Britain as far as we could'), what screening there was was not very effective, for it was well-known at the time that large numbers of the British public in Southern England listened to it regularly, as I did myself in north-west Essex. Indeed, Gorham himself admitted later that 'our AEF Programme, too, was a first choice for jazz fans. The music publishers, in dealing out plug money, had a saying that AEFP was all that mattered south of the Trent.'*

By early September, the rapid advance of the Allied Armies north-eastwards into France and Belgium meant that they were getting beyond the range of the AEFP transmitter. So on Tuesday 5 September, the Programme was transferred to 514 metres, 583kc, and it remained on this wavelength until it closed down in July 1945. Ray McKinley had to alter the phrase 'tune in to

* *Sound and Fury.*

144

medium 285' in his closing theme song of the *Swing Shift* programmes to 'tune in to medium 514', which he did most successfully.

At the same time a behind-the-scenes tug of war was going on between SHAEF and the BBC. According to a colourful account by Colonel Kirby in *Star Spangled Radio* SHAEF contended that Continental reception of the AEF Programme was unreliable and wanted to remove the Programme from the BBC and set it up independently using the only transmitter in newly-liberated Paris that had not been destroyed by the retreating Germans. The BBC insisted that the Programme *could* be heard and fiercely resisted the breakaway. A top-level row ensued, but despite Kirby's partisan account the fact remained that the BBC had reached a binding agreement (signed on its behalf by no less than the Director General) to run the Programme for SHAEF at the direct request of General Eisenhower and at the insistence of the British Prime Minister and the Cabinet. This was high-level politics and any rupture could damage Anglo-American relations at a crucial stage of the war. For his part Maurice Gorham was always conscious of strong American pressures inside SHAEF and in turn much influence from AFN: 'ETOUSA had not wanted the AEF Programme; they had wanted to give their troops AFN, and all through its history ETOUSA thought that our programme was all the better the more it sounded like AFN. Luckily, Johnny Hayes, who was in command of AFN, was an old acquaintance of mine and too business-like to be unco-operative, but I felt that at all times I had to have my eyes very wide open in dealing with AFN.'*

The row rumbled on, but the BBC kept the AEF Programme. Besides changing the wavelength, it put it on short wave later on, and in due course both the British and American Armies put mobile transmitters in the field to relay the Programme to the forward troops. AEFP offices were set up in Paris and Brussels to organize programmes from the Continent. Early in October, Colonel Kirby returned to the USA at the end of his posting to SHAEF.

Of course, none of this reached the listeners, and the Programme continued in its bright and breezy style pouring out its all-star fare to the troops of the AEF.

Sound and Fury.

At Bedford the American Band of the AEF spent the first week of September pre-recording programmes by its various smaller bands (including several by the Swing Sextet with British singer Beryl Davis), interspersed with all the regular scheduled broadcasts. The Thursday evening broadcast by the full Band was made from Co-Partners Hall with Gloria Brent as guest star. This programme ended with the first performance of a Jerry Gray arrangement of the new British song 'All's Well, Madamoiselle'.

There were no airfield concerts that week until Sunday evening, 10 September, but here an element of mystery creeps into the story. According to Haynes' diary and the Activities list the Band played on the 10th at the 200 Mission Party of the 95th Bomb Group at their Flying Fortress base at Horham, three miles east of Eye in East Suffolk. However, according to the published history of the 388th Bomb Group the Band – or perhaps some of it – played at its base at Knettishall, West Suffolk, for *their* 200 Mission Party that evening! The Band had played previously at Knettishall on 25 August, although no mention of this appears in the 388th Bomb Group history. The evidence for the Knettishall 'date' on 10 September seems undeniable but equally so does that for Horham, especially as Bob Ripley, too, noted the location that evening as Horham and there is a photograph of Major Miller supposedly taken there. At any rate, it seems that the Band were flown to Horham that Sunday afternoon where, after watching a baseball game and having dinner, they played to over 6,000 personnel. Later they were flown back to Bedford, but the pilots lost their way and had to land at RAF Cranfield, taking off later for Twinwood Farm where they landed in the dark.

The two airfields, Horham and Knettishall were only about fourteen miles apart as the crow flies, though rather more by road. The answer to the mystery of the two dates may be that while the Band played at Horham a small unit played at Knettishall, where the printed programmes specially produced for their party announced four bands for their various dances: Don Marino, the Flying Yanks and the Gremlins (both of which were notable Eighth Air Force dance bands) and 'Glenn Miller Unit'. No mention of anyone from the Miller Band playing at Knettishall that night appears in the Activities list, and enquiries to clear up the question have so far proved unsuccessful.

Next day, after pre-recording *Uptown Hall* and *Swing Shift* programmes in the morning the Band set off by road once more, this time to Leicester, in their own buses and staff car, for a concert to 4,000 men of the US 82nd Airborne Division in the De Montford Hall. The paratroops were due to jump behind enemy lines shortly afterwards, according to Haynes (in fact they dropped over Nijmegen, Holland, the following Sunday as part of the Arnhem operation) and Miller extended the concert to an hour and a half to roars of applause from the soldiers. Later, an appreciative letter from the unit's CO was received at SHAEF praising the marvellous job the Band had done in relaxing the keyed-up troops.

On Tuesday, the 12th, the Band flew to Hardwick, about 12 miles south of Norwich, to play at the 93rd Bomb Group base. Four B-24 Liberators from the base picked up the Band at Twinwood Farm in mid-afternoon and after dinner at the base the Band played for about 5,000 personnel in what Haynes called an 'air-conditioned hangar – open at both ends'. It was so cold that once again some of the musicians, including Glenn Miller, played with their gloves on. After the concert Haynes met up with some of the officers he had come over with on the *Queen Elizabeth*. The Band stayed overnight at Hardwick and next morning were flown back to Bedford in four B-24s, but ground fog delayed their landing at Thurleigh for nearly an hour; eventually three got down while the fourth diverted to Podington from whence the base CO provided a bus to take the musicians back to Bedford.

Their next trip was to London on Thursday the 14th, for another *American Eagle* recording at Rainbow Corner. During their performance one of Britain's leading dance band drummers, Maurice Burman, played a number with the Band; the MM's Jack Marshall was there:

. . . here is a helluva gesture from one drummer to another. Listen . . . when the section of the Miller outfit which Ray McKinley leads was playing a session at London's Rainbow Corner Club the other day (one of the sessions which, as most of you know, is broadcast to the American stations) Ray introduced popular London drum-man Maurice Burman with a little speech somewhat as follows: 'And now, ladies and gentlemen, we are glad to welcome the drummer from Geraldo's Orchestra, the most famous English dance band. He is Maurice Burman, who is going to play a number with us.'

Maurice says it was one of the thrills of a lifetime to sit in with the McKinley boys. Everything really was grand. Only one fly in the ointment, and that a very tiny one – they didn't play 'Soft Shoe Shuffle'!*

* *Melody Maker*, 23 September 1944.

That evening, the weekly broadcast by the full Band came from the Queensberry Club for the first time, with Paula Green making her second appearance with the Band on the air. From then onwards practically all the regular broadcasts by the Band were made from the Club until it went to France in December.

There is some doubt about the activities of Major Miller the next day, Friday 15 September. According to the radio archives he recorded an interview for the BBC. However, according to Haynes, Miller was ill that day suffering from sinus trouble and feverish headaches which were so bad that he stayed at Bedford and the Band played an airfield concert at Rougham without him. There seems little doubt that we must accept Haynes' account, and that therefore the date given by the BBC for the interview is wrong. The programme in which the interview was featured – *Here's Wishing You Well Again* – was pre-recorded on the 15th at the BBC's Monseigneur studio (later a cinema) near Marble Arch, and the interview was probably a previously recorded insert into the programme, perhaps recorded on the 14th when Miller was in London for the Queensberry broadcast. From Haynes' account, Miller could hardly have been in a fit state to record such an interview on the 15th and a recording of it reveals no sign of illness.

Miller was interviewed by Vernon Harris, a BBC script writer and producer who later became producer of the BBC *Scrapbook* programmes and a noted film script writer. *Here's Wishing You Well Again* was a weekly British variety programme for Forces in hospital, with singers and light orchestras such as Mantovani and actors in sketches and was introduced by Marjorie Anderson.

Each week the programme had a short request feature called 'The Wishing Well' in which Vernon Harris talked with celebrities requested by servicemen. The three British soldiers whose request brought Miller to the microphone were serving in, of all places, East Africa – presumably they had heard the AEF Band in the Saturday recorded repeats on the GFP which went overseas as well as to the British home audience. The producers had written to Cecil Madden, who passed on the request to Colonel Kirby, asking whether Major Miller would take part and perhaps play a trombone solo. He agreed to be interviewed but firmly declined to play a solo, and the interview lasted about two and a half minutes. Besides Miller, Vernon Harris also introduced BBC Variety Orchestra conductor Charles Shadwell and Sadlers Wells opera singer Joan Cross in 'The Wishing Well' that day. There was no Miller music in the programme and no-one else from the Band took part. Miller's appearance was not billed in the *Radio Times* but 'Wishing Well' celebrities never were so that the feature could retain its topicality and surprise element. The programme was actually broadcast the following week on Thursday 21 September, from 6.15 to 7 pm in the GFP and the AEF Programme.

The existence of a recording of the interview only became generally known in 1955 when RCA Victor obtained the recording from the BBC in rather curious circumstances. Earlier in 1955 when Victor was collecting together the recordings for their Miller Air Force Band album, I had been instrumental, following correspondence with David Mackay, Attorney to the Miller Estate in New York, in arranging for the BBC to send to Victor for possible inclusion in the album copies of the only broadcast recordings they had preserved in their archives after the war. While these recordings were being copied in London the recording of the interview was discovered by accident and was sent to Victor in New York with the AEF Band recordings. Although the interview was included on a Victor sales promotion record* in 1955, the AEF Band recordings have never been issued to this day.

The Band left Bedford after lunch on Friday 15 September in trucks for what must have been a cold and uncomfortable journey on the sixty-odd miles to Rougham, leaving Glenn Miller behind at Bedford. It was heading for the B-17 base of the 94th Bomb Group at Rougham airfield, barely two miles east of Bury St Edmunds (the name by which the airfield was sometimes known) to play yet another 200 Mission Party where a big celebration had been arranged as well as one of the best stage setups that the Band had encountered. Ray McKinley and Jerry Gray shared the conducting and during the concert the Band was joined by one of the GIs' favourite singers – Dinah Shore, back in England after singing to the troops over in France.

One of the GIs based at Rougham, Cedric Crink, noted his impressions of the party:

15th of September of course was the big party in honor of the 200th. Colonel Dougher had a cocktail party for all the COs of the various

---

* The record (a 7-inch 45 rpm disc) was used to promote the sale of the Army Air Force Band album and is now very rare. However, the interview was also included on a more recent LP (*see* page 404).

organizations. Dinner was everything you could possibly ask for. They built a tremendous stage in Hangar One at three levels and Major Glenn Miller's Band was there. He was not there because some general had detained him in London. Ray McKinley his drummer took over as leader, and the string section had some eighteen violins, and many of the original Glenn Miller men from the States were in it. In the middle of the show Dinah Shore came out and sang – what a homely, skinny gal she is, carrot-coloured hair, buck teeth, but boy, how she can sing. The fellows loved her, she loved them. She sang for better than an hour and the whole show lasted more than two hours. There were seven hundred women guests from all over England. The officers left after the Miller floor show to go to the Officers Club for their dance, and the enlisted men stayed in the hangar to dance to Glenn Miller. Things finally wound up about 2.30 in the morning.*

After the festivities the Band stayed at Rougham overnight and next morning it was taken in buses direct to London where it was re-joined by Glenn Miller, now recovered, for what has become, perhaps, the most publicized event in the whole of its six months' stay in England and the one which in the years since has caused more speculation and curiosity than almost anything else it did – its HMV recording session with Dinah Shore.

* Courtesy of Charles H. Gallagher.

CHAPTER TWELVE

The recording session with Dinah Shore – The Feldman Swing Club – The broadcast with the US Navy Band – North Witham, Grantham, Oxford and Mount Farm – A protest against the BBC – Great Ashfield, Nuthampstead and Kingscliffe – RSM George Melachrino broadcasts with the Band

One of the reasons the AEF Band was virtually unknown in Britain when it arrived in June 1944 was because no commercial gramophone records of it had been issued. Starting on 1 August 1942, the American Federation of Musicians (the American musicians' trade union) had forbidden its members to make any commercial records, and the AFM ban was not lifted until early 1944 for some recording companies and not until November 1944 for others including RCA Victor, the company for whom Glenn Miller had recorded with his civilian band before joining the Army. So for the entire period the AEF Band had been playing in America no recordings other than radio transcriptions were allowed, although in 1943 the union had given special permission for some of its members to make recordings for V-Discs (special records for servicemen) provided they were not used for commercial purposes, and many famous bands and orchestras did in fact make V-Discs for the troops.

Captain Glenn Miller and the Army Air Forces Band also made some V-Discs in America, but as the V-Discs were issued directly to the troops few civilians (especially in Britain) had ever heard of them, much less possessed any. So the AEF Band became known to the British public solely through their broadcasts, which once performed were gone for ever: in the days before tape, few people owned home recording machines. It was virtually impossible for civilians to obtain permanent souvenirs of the Band in the shape of records – although, like everything else in wartime, from nylons to Lucky Strike cigarettes, a little of what people want filters through somehow, and a few V-Discs did turn up now and again.

It was hardly surprising, therefore, that when it was announced that the AEF Band had made some commercial recordings in London, well publicized by the musical press, great interest was aroused – especially as it was also announced that the records were to be issued the following month!

The recording session took place at the HMV studios in Abbey Road, St John's Wood, London, on Saturday afternoon, 16 September, the day after the Band had played at the Rougham airfield. Not only was the Band making records, but it was joined by no less than Dinah Shore, who was about to go back to America.

The *Melody Maker* made the recordings front page news with a banner headline and a large photograph of the whole Band playing in the studio:

MILLER AND SHORE RECORD HERE

Recording history was made in London last Saturday (16th), when Major Glenn Miller and the American Band of the AEF with Dinah Shore, recorded four titles for the HMV label at the Gramophone Company's studios at Abbey Road, Hampstead, NW.

The session – which took place before a small, specially invited audience of professional notabilities – was unique on two counts.

First, when Major Glenn Miller's present band ultimately returns to America, it will disband. These British records, therefore, will be the only means of perpetuating an orchestra which – apart from the magnificent work it has done for the Allied troops – has been a real musical eye-opener to the profession in this country.

It was specially formed for Army purposes, and is not, of course, the same band with which Glenn Miller has recorded in the States.

Secondly, this session was the first occasion that Dinah Shore and Glenn Miller have recorded together. In the States she is usually accompanied by Paul Laval and his Lower Basin Street outfits.

Credit for this double-handed recording scoop goes to enterprising EMI recording manager Walter Moody, who conceived the idea over six weeks ago and successfully brought it to fruition, overcoming countless difficulties and headaches in the process.

Titles recorded were 'Stardust' and 'All I Do Is Dream Of You' by Dinah Shore, with really beautiful backing by the Miller Band; and 'Farewell Blues' and a new American tune, 'I've Got A Heart Filled With Love', by the Orchestra.

In the last-named title the vocal chorus was sung by Johnny Desmond, accompanied by the Crew Chiefs.

This unique session – which lasted for over four hours – gave us an opportunity to witness the painstaking thoroughness and terrific attention to detail of American musicians and artistes, and very impressive it was too.

The results were well worth all the trouble, and for impeccability of musicianship and originality of scoring these records will rank high in this year's list of best discs.

The *Melody Maker* is informed that the HMV Company is aiming to bring the records out in their October list, and another interesting point about them is that proceeds will be devoted to British and American Army charities.*

Elsewhere in the same issue, Editor Ray Sonin described the recording session:

Last Saturday's HMV recording session with Dinah Shore and Major Glenn Miller was a real eye-opener to me (*writes Ray Sonin*).

For sheer musical efficiency and austere control over a band, the Major takes some beating.

Conducting with, in turn, his hands, a cigarette and a pencil, he dominated the proceedings with quite military dignity, only unbending beneath the charm of Dinah Shore, who has only to come into any gathering to make everybody her slave.

That girl is really the tops! She's much smaller than you would imagine, and she clumped her way into the studio, dressed in dark-green betrousered uniform of the USO-Camp Shows, set off, incredibly by a large pair of brown boots!

Proudly she told us that she had swapped them with a little US paratrooper in France, and she seemed almost childishly pleased with them.

As the top vocal star of the States, she could be forgiven if she were a little big-time, but Dinah doesn't know the meaning of that word.

She is friendly, charming, and a really grand trouper. The way she sang her two numbers over and over again without complaint, taking any criticisms Glenn Miller had to offer with a co-operative smile, congratulating the arrangers and treating everybody in the studio as her buddies, was a treat to behold.

She dashed off after the recording to broadcast 'psychological songs' in German, French and Danish to the German troops – and, on the following day, she returned to the States leaving everyone here who has met her candidates for the presidency of her fan club!

Personal Note. – Dinah Shore's intimates call her 'Tinker'.

It was interesting to note the importance of arrangers in the American scheme of things.

Every note was listened to in the recording-box by Sergeant Jerry

* *Melody Maker*, 23 September 1944.

Gray, who came out and discussed the performance with Miller after each run-through. By the way, Jerry first came to fame with his arrangement of 'Begin The Beguine' for Artie Shaw; that shows you what kind of arranger he is.

And the leader's own attention to the tiniest subtleties of phrasing, the minutest details of tone and volume, was most illuminating. When he told the boys what he wanted, they did it with good grace and as well as they knew how; when he pointed out that someone had played a wrong note, that someone didn't immediately start to argue and say it was the chap next to him – as I have heard happen on home-grown sessions.

When you hear the records you will realize that all the time and trouble these Americans devote to their performances are amply justified.

It was a great experience to watch the aces at work, and the little bunch of people invited to act as audience by recording manager Wally Moony, whose brainwave this was, had a thrilling afternoon.

Greatest tribute to Glenn Miller and Dinah Shore is if I told you how many professional figures in the audience requested me to arrange for them to be photographed with the two stars . . . but that's another story.

All this was sensational news! Miller and Shore fans could hardly wait for the October records. But October came and the records did not – likewise, November – and December. What had gone wrong?

On 23 December the *Melody Maker* printed a brief explanation by one of their record reviewers:

What's happened to those records which Dinah Shore made with Glenn Miller's Ork for HMV over three months ago – the first ever made by these artists in this country – which we were told would be issued on October 1 last?

If this question has been worrying you like it has me, you may care to know that the hold-up is because the sides have to be approved by America before they may be released here, so goodness knows when they will come out.

Prophetic words!

After that, silence. To this day the records have never been issued. Enquiries over the years have usually drawn some vague response such as that the records were made for the American military authorities and were not for public issue. At one time, around the late 1940s it was rumoured that the masters had been sunk during the war while crossing the Atlantic. Among Glenn Miller enthusiasts and record collectors the records (or the lack of them!) became something of a *cause célèbre*, but enquiries at the record company drew a blank. The original *Melody Maker* report, however, had been correct – it *was* proposed to issue them and to devote the proceeds to forces charities.

The idea for the recordings had originated early in August 1944, while Dinah Shore was in the ETO and she was eager to make them before returning to the USA as it would be the only opportunity she would have to record with the AEF Band. The records would be made and sold through the normal commercial channels – in this case HMV, who were the British outlet for RCA Victor. Profits would go to British and American service charities, and it was estimated by SHAEF that these might amount to several hundred thousand dollars. General Barker approved the idea in principle, and after negotiations between Colonel Kirby and the Gramophone Company (HMV) the company made a formal offer to SHAEF to pay it a specified sum of money for the services of the artistes involved and to divide the proceeds of the sale of the records throughout the world on a percentage profit-sharing basis between the Company and service charities nominated by SHAEF.

Approval of the War Department in Washington was needed, and of the USO-Camp Shows in Hollywood in respect of Dinah Shore (she was touring the ETO under the auspices of the USO), but time was short. War Department and USO approval was sought as a matter of urgency.

There had been precedents for such arrangements in recordings by Irving Berlin's all-soldier stage show *This Is The Army* and by the New York production of the AAF show *Winged Victory*, both of which had made records for charity. And so, apparently anticipating permission, the Miller/Shore records were made on 16 September – the day before Dinah Shore went back to America.

One week later, USO-Camp Shows, ETO, replied to the Gramophone Company's offer: the policy of the Hollywood Victory Committee (who provided the stars for the Camp Show tours) was that the stars' services were not to be made available for any commercial enterprise, but that if the Gramophone Company were willing to donate all profits from the records to service charities approval for the project would probably be given. This was passed on by SHAEF to the Gramophone Company, and they were invited to make a new proposal. What the Company's reply might have been can only be guessed at, for by this time General Barker had changed his mind and by the middle of November it was amicably agreed by all concerned that the project would be abandoned and the company formally withdrew their original offer, agreed not to issue the recordings and undertook to destroy the matrices they had made.

So ended what would have been the coup of the day – a superb recording collaboration by the leading girl singer of the time, a spectacular scheme under which it was planned to record other artists as well, including Bing Crosby. But at least some records were made, and who knows – one day, something may filter through.

After the recording session the AEF Band stayed on in the studio to record music for a Special Services film, then returned to Bedford, and Miller decided to give the unit four days off. There were enough pre-recorded programmes in hand to keep the radio schedule going and Haynes moved several personal appearances back to the following week. Some of the band stayed in London on the Saturday night and several of them visited the Feldman Swing Club again on the Sunday evening. After listening to the resident band, led by drummer Carlo Krahmer, Peanuts Hucko and Jack Steele were invited to the bandstand and joined in with British musicians Ralph Sharon (piano), Bert Howard (bass) and Maurice Burman (drums) for an impromptu jam session which received a terrific ovation from the packed audience. Later, Johnny Desmond was persuaded up to the microphone to sing – Mel Powell played piano for him and the little accompanying band included the ten-year-old British drum sensation Victor Feldman, who had also performed earlier at the Club. The *Melody Maker* called it 'one of the most thrilling nights on record'.

Days off were a rarity for the Band. During its four-day break from 17 to 20 September, several of the men persuaded Haynes to go with them on a visit to Stratford-on-Avon, stopping off for a look round Warwick Castle on the way. Another day, Haynes did an exhausting tour of famous London landmarks. Some of the Band were keen racegoers, and Harry Katzman vividly remembered visits to English racecourses: 'One time Jerry Gray and I had a day off and we went to the race track because Jerry and I both liked to go to the races – we had gone to the races in civilian life when we had a day off in New York. Mel Powell also liked to go to the races. We went to Newmarket and it was the St Leger. We really hiked and got rides in jeeps and a fire truck and way out in the country a horse and wagon – there was a shortage of petrol at that time. We finally made it to Newmarket and we didn't have a very successful day, actually. We didn't have the winners in the big race and I think I probably lost about fifteen or twenty dollars (about four or five pounds) and I think Jerry lost about forty or fifty pounds – he was a heavy better. On the way back we got on a train and wound up at Cambridge. We had a good time and we had a lot of laughs on the way.

'On another occasion Jack Hylton gave a dinner for the Band and we went to a very good restaurant which I can't remember (*see* page 185). Then we played a medley of his arrangements which, of course, sounded a little bit out-dated to us at that time, but he was very warm to us and we enjoyed the evening very much, and that was when I found out that he had his own stable of horses. Miller introduced him to Jerry and me and we talked about his horses, and he said, "If you want to come out to the track I have two of my horses running tomorrow". I'll never forget the names – one was Sangro and the other was Covenant. So everybody thought, well he's got a sure thing, so the next day Miller let me off the rehearsal and everybody gave me some money – I think Jerry Gray gave me fifty dollars, five pounds on each horse, and I think Miller gave me twenty dollars to bet on a horse. Everybody was giving two dollars or one dollar and there was a pool and I wrote all the things down and I met Jack Hylton. He told me where his office was and his wife was there and so we went to Windsor. What struck me at the track at Windsor was that the infield had nothing but anti-aircraft guns – it was a very eerie feeling. I don't know how many pounds I bet, but it must have been close to four hundred or five hundred dollars, which meant that I must have bet about two hundred or two hundred and fifty dollars on each of these two horses of Jack Hylton's. He was very nice to me – he took me to eat in the club house with his wife and it was very good food compared to what I'd been getting in Bedford. Well, the first one Sangro went off at 13 to 1 – it was the very first race. When I went up to the window the teller looked at me and I put down fifty or seventy-five pounds on Sangro at 13 to 1 and he must have thought there's some guy who must be in the black market! Sangro lost, and so did Covenant, and the only winner I had was some horse that paid 8 to 1 so I didn't do too badly – I bet about ten dollars a piece on each horse myself. Both horses lost, and when I got back (they drove me to London to get the train) I got in a terrific bomb raid and it was pitch dark and I couldn't find where I was. Everything was blacked out and I was walking along trying to get to the subway to get to the railroad station and someone grabbed my arm – I thought it must be Herman Goering! Anyway, it was a hooker and she wanted to know if I'd like to have a party tonight. I said, "Just get me to the Tube and I'll give you ten shillings" (it was about two dollars at that time), and so she directed me to the Tube and I ran down that Tube so fast because you could hear the buzz bombs coming over! That's one of the reasons I never stayed in London.

'We used to go and play at the Queensberry Club twice a week even when the buzz bombs were flying. They released the restrictions slightly and some of the fellows used to stay overnight in London at a certain barracks. Miller and Haynes and Dudley never came back to Bedford, and Ray McKinley and Mel Powell always stayed in London, but I didn't want to take any chances of being some place where I shouldn't be and I got on the truck back with, I think, the majority of the fellows who went back to the barracks. The Queensberry Club was absolutely packed every time we played there – we did play there once during a bomb raid and the lights momentarily went out inside the Club.

'Everyone in the unit got on well, and there were no fights. I was rooming with George Ockner, Morris Bialkin and Dave Schwartz. George was a wonderful violinist and a wonderful guy. Gene Bergen was a very nice guy and excellent violinist, although not very free with his money; Dick Motylinski was a notorious eater – never had to wash his plate; Earl Cornwell was a very nice guy, very close to everybody; Joe Kowalewski was nicknamed "Cow Cow" because no Sergeant could pronounce his name; Nate Kaproff was quiet, well behaved, never in any trouble; Carl Swanson was a wonderful guy – so young, he died after the war; Freddy Ostrovsky was also very young, only nineteen or twenty; Milton Edelson, who was also a booker in civilian life known as Al Milton, was known as the agent – he always had angles; Phil Cogliano was very nice, very friendly; Stan Harris was a little guy, a ladies' man; Harry Brynan was a wonderful, friendly guy, so was Manny Wishnow; Morris Bialkin was known as the ear – always looking for rumours.

'Trigger Alpert, who had been a great favourite of Miller's, always had a smile; Mel Powell, a great arranger, was really a loner, sitting out the war; we rarely saw Ray McKinley, except at rehearsals and broadcasts; Frank Ippolito was a very nice guy; Jack Rusin was always scared, a big worrier; Carmen Mastren was tremendously talented – a funny guy, nick-named "Quonk" – a terrific guitarist; Peanuts Hucko never worried – he was nicknamed "Lum De Do"* and he and Mel Powell, I think, were the two outstanding talents in the Band; Freddy Guerra was a very nice guy; Mannie Thaler never worried – everybody liked him; everybody loved Whitey Thomas, and everybody liked Johnny Desmond.'

Other musicians agree. 'As a group, the Band was a tight-knit and friendly bunch,' says John Halliburton. 'All of us are friends to this day. Considering the different ages, personalities and backgrounds the group had very few minor misunderstandings.'

Carmen Mastren said, 'I think the relationships between the musicians in our orchestra were great considering we saw each other day and night and that can sometimes cause dissensions, but all in all I think there were good feelings in the Band. In every band I can think of there are certain guys that hang out with each other and this Band wasn't any different from the rest. This Band mixed pretty well – we even had the string players swinging!'

One of the 'swinging string players', Emanuel Wishnow, feels the same way: 'For people who lived together twenty-four hours a day I think we got along pretty well, because you get to know people better than you expected, maybe more than you wanted to. There were arguments – you expect that – hot, quick, but usually over in a day. One of the great melting pots, the great mixers, is the Army anyway, regardless of us being a musical organization, so we learned to expect anything.

'Most of the string players chugged around all day – Nate Kaproff was with me and also Dave Sackson, Henry Brynan and Gene Bergen, and George Ockner a little.'

Off-duty friendships naturally sprang up. The string players, some of whom had known each other in civilian life, tended to associate among themselves, and groups which formed among the dance band players included Nat Peck, John Halliburton and Addison Collins; Johnny Desmond and Freddy Guerra; and Ray McKinley, Jack Steele and Peanuts Hucko. Some of course went their own way.

Relations between Miller and the men in the Band were conditioned to some extent by their military status, at least on duty, although some of the musicians including Ray McKinley, Jerry Gray and Zeke Zarchy, were old friends of the Major from pre-war days.

* A tune called 'Lum De Do' was featured by the quartet (Mel Powell, Ray McKinley, Peanuts Hucko and Trigger Alpert) on some of the *Uptown Hall* broadcasts.

'We all, of course, called him Captain, or later Major,' said Harry Katzman. 'I think that was just our military training – as enlisted men we were taught to respect an officer. Our relationship with him was friendly but not really informal. He liked to play bridge occasionally and I was one of the few who could play – I think Jimmy Jackson was about the only other bridge player, and maybe Norman Leyden played a little bridge. I also played a very good game of tennis – I was the champ there and I used to play tennis with him. I was on his baseball team – we used to throw the football around, too.'

'I always found Major Miller to be an excellent officer and leader,' says John Halliburton, 'and basically a friend. He was usually informal and friendly, but of course had to maintain a certain military stance in many situations. Considering it was a war situation, and that our activities were always in the spotlight, I believe he was more than considerate of our well-being and individual feelings.'

'Glenn wasn't strictly military and he got along with most of the band,' recalled Carmen Mastren. 'Remember he was a perfectionist and it certainly showed in that organization. Until he was reported missing, we didn't see too much of Haynes and Dudley. Haynes would just pass on orders and Paul was busy writing and putting things together. We got to know them better when they were put in charge and got along well with both.'

Emanuel Wishnow says, 'Miller and I had a little empathy going, actually, because, when I first got in you see, Miller was a graduate of the University of Colorado and I was from a neighbouring State – Nebraska – and the only one of the group who was from his area of the woods. He was very cordial and, I felt, a little diffident to me because I was an academic from the faculty. We got along pleasantly. He was very warm – occasionally he had his lapses. He was a bit curt and withdrawn as a personality – he was not an open person to start with. On his good days a quick smile was about all you ever got out of him. I'm not really an analyst, but I would guess he was basically shy. If he hadn't been such a public figure he had the makings of a recluse – someone who would get away on his own and never bother anybody; absolutely alone most of the time – strange. I had played under some conductors who you could label SOB very easily – lots of them – but he wasn't that type. He could be curt, he could be non-communicative, he could be monosyllabic, but he never hurt anybody that I *know* of. He'd just avoid people if he didn't agree with them.'

While the Band was at Bedford some of the men would set up dice and poker games at the Co-Partners Hall, usually on Friday nights. Sometimes Glenn Miller would come in and play dice with the men.

'Miller was an incredible gambler,' recalls Nat Peck, 'because he had a lot of money and we were restricted. He used to come in and take all our money away and say with a wide smile, "This'll keep you all out of trouble!" He would invariably win. It was very frustrating!'

'I don't think Miller ever insulted anyone, or got angry,' said Harry Katzman. 'If he did momentarily about a difference or phrasing or interpretation he would immediately smile or tell a joke, or pass it off. There was one time that he called us in and sort of chewed up the Band. I think it was something he regretted very much later. It wasn't a good thing to say. A few of the guys were goofing off. They would be coming in a little bit late to the rehearsals, they would be playing poker till four or five o'clock in the morning, and by the time they came to rehearsal – it was nine o'clock in the morning – they were pretty dead and had been falling asleep. So he called in the whole Band. It struck me as so damn corny and so cheap, and I think what he should have actually said was just, "Hey, guys, you're goofing off and it's got to stop now". It was embarrassing, and most of the fellows of course didn't have any black marks. I think it was the only thing I saw him do that was not up to his taste and character. George Ockner had told me that he was having a pain in his kidney and wasn't feeling well.'

Ray McKinley also remembers that day: 'The guys were beginning to bellyache and bitch about things – you know, everything from food to working too hard, to this and that. It was quite a bit different from what they had been used to back in the States, especially the guys who had achieved what you might call star status, so they didn't like it too much. Now Mel was a very intelligent boy, but he was complaining about everything and not co-operating insofar as he got by with it as a Sergeant, which wasn't much, but it was still a source of irritation to Glenn to hear these things secondhand. So a lot of it had been going on, some of them had been late, they'd been goofing off or weren't playing their best, or talking on the bandstand when they shouldn't have been while the music was going on, and so forth. So he just had enough of it and finally he called us all together one morning and he had us stand up one at a time and told us just what he thought of how we were doing our job. Of course, he called me first and the only thing he had to criticize about me was the fact that Bernie Privin and I would exchange a few words while the fiddles were playing – Bernie sat on my left and Trigger on my right –

and that annoyed Glenn. It was only small talk – didn't mean a thing. We weren't bellyaching too much, just talking, which he could hear and he didn't like anything at all unprofessional, no distraction. A brass player could miss notes if he went after them honestly, but if he neglected to pick up the right mute – say you were a trumpet player and it says right on the music a harmon instead of a cup mute or a straight mute, and you pick up the wrong mute when you knew better and stuck that in your horn and you played – boy, that kind of inefficiency just annoyed him out of all proportion. Oh he'd chew that guy up for a little thing like that. He'd come back and say, "Don't ever do that again", and he'd mean it. So this was the same way – "That's all, Sergeant", and I sat down. Then he started warming up, and finally he got to Mel Powell. Oh, Mel sat there and stared at the floor, and Glenn really cussed him out with some four-letter words. In fact, I understand that Teddy Gower, our British engineer, is supposed to have been in the control room and opened the channels down to London and this whole thing was heard down there. A lot of us heard later that to talk to enlisted men like that was forbidden in the British Army and had he been a British officer he could have been demoted or reprimanded or something for talking that way to the men. After he got everybody told off he went on to say, "A lot of you are bitching about having no money. Hell," he says, "I've got money – if you need money come to me." And then he softened up – he just got it off his chest, but he really laid it to some of them.

'Mel was pretty much that way before we went overseas. He hated the Army – he just wasn't cut out to be a soldier of any kind. He hated regimentation, he was a free soul. He had some guys around him that he talked into thinking like he did too. Up in New Haven Glenn called him in and told him we wasn't carrying his weight. He knew he was a good arranger, but he hadn't arranged anything like he had for Benny, like "Mission to Moscow" the famous one he did for Benny Goodman. So Glenn said, "Now, come on, you could be over there getting shot at – let's get on the ball", words to that effect. So we didn't see Mel for a while, I don't know how long, and he finally turned up with this composition which featured the piano – himself – a great thing (Mel was only nineteen years old) called "Pearls on Velvet". Glenn named it – he had a weakness for pearls, I guess. Had to call it something, and right away it became one of our big production numbers. It was quite a thing. After we'd played it for the first time the whole Band stood up and applauded him.'

Bob Ripley still remembers the incident which sparked off Major Miller's reprimands to the Band: 'Each of us had duties to perform outside of actual playing in the Band – I helped in the library – and someone was always in charge of the music when we would arrive to play anywhere and had to see to it that the music was taken off the buses or trucks and got to its destination properly. On one trip we went on the sergeant in charge of the music didn't do this and the music was left out on an airstrip and could have been run over by a plane at any time. It was discovered finally, and brought along to the stand but Miller was furious at this and decided he would call the whole Band together and see whether or not everybody was doing his job properly. He dressed down this sergeant and said that if it were not for his wife back home he would bust him down to a private, but for her sake he would keep his rank. But he let him know he was very unhappy with the whole thing and then he asked each one of us in turn what we were doing for the organization besides merely playing our instruments, and that was a pretty black day.'

The AEF Band resumed activities on Thursday 21 September, when it travelled to London to play its regular broadcast from the Queensberry Club. This was the legendary occasion when instead of the usual British singer or visiting American star the guests were the complete United States Navy Dance Band, directed by Musician 1st Class Sam Donahue. This band had been formed in the US Navy in America in 1942 and was originally led by Chief Petty Officer Artie Shaw, and under him it had made a lengthy tour of American bases in the South Pacific, becoming to servicemen in that theatre what the American Band of the AEF was to the Americans in the ETO. On its return to the USA late in 1943, Artie Shaw and several of the musicians, including drummer Dave Tough and trumpeter Max Kaminsky, had been invalided out of the Navy and tenor saxophonist Sam Donahue stepped out front to take over the leadership. Abandoning the Artie Shaw library, the Band was posted to Britain in April 1944 and stationed at Exeter in the area where some US Navy bases had been set up for the duration of the war, and it eventually made many radio broadcasts from London in the AEF Programme until its return to the United States in 1945.

It was a full seventeen-piece dance band of the highest professional standard playing powerful and exciting swing music and with many well-known musicians in its ranks, including one of Glenn Miller's pre-war trumpet stars, John Best. In the dance and swing music field it was a band to be reckoned with and in the opinion of many enthusiasts it ran a very close second to Glenn Miller's AEF Band. Now, the two bands played side by side in the same programme and the result was an evening's music which those who heard it will never forget. The *Melody Maker* carried a long report:

Another exciting manifestation of the American 'invasion' serial, which I have been reporting with such gusto for the last few weeks (*writes Jack Marshall*), took place last Thursday (21st).

The splendid co-operation of the US authorities enabled the Queensberry All-Service Club to feature not only the greatest dance band coup over staged in London, but one of the most exciting aggregations of celebrated musicians ever lined up anywhere at one and the same time.

And these words, my boys, are absolutely no exaggeration. It definitely *was* one of the grandest aggregations ever – nothing less than the full GLENN MILLER ork, plus the ARTIE SHAW Naval Band – led by Sam Donahue – both together, on the vast Queensberry Club stage.

Certainly a big chapter of London's dance band history was made that night, whilst the AEF Programme could claim a really stupendous broadcast.

Passing thought: The funny part of all this is that whilst the efforts of the greatest bookers, theatrical and radio impresarios, etc., have never succeeded in getting together such a dazzling dance band attraction as this (possibly even in the States), this war's insistent – and very proper – demand for only the very best in Services entertainment made it possible, not for any smartly dressed audience of the *élite* who alone would be able to pay for such star-spangled attractions in normal times, but for the ordinary boys and girls of the Services, Privates Smith, Jones, Brown and Robinson, here in London.

First thing on the programme, the whole thing is explained and the various groups of musicians introduced by Major Glenn Miller, who makes us feel at home, and even essays an occasional wisecrack, without relaxing one iota of that stern, militaristic manner which so many of us have now come to know so well.

The Major introduced the sections and the various corner-men in his own combination, reminding us that 'Hank' Freeman, leader of the saxes, used to be a shining light with Artie Shaw, that guitarist Carmen Mastren was with Tommy Dorsey before drafting; that Mel Powell was a gifted composer as well as a great pianist; Ray McKinley a famous leader back home, etc.

Coming to the Naval outfit Glenn Miller paid a warm tribute to 'his old musical friend' Sam Donahue, praising the Naval Band's extensive travels, in the far Pacific, etc., in their heavy year and a half's itinerary of Services entertainment half-way round the world, 'which', said Glenn Miller generously, 'completely puts our own record to shame.' And in this fine band, we were reminded, was one of the old Miller corner-men, trumpet ace John Best.

The Major raises his baton, and there is great expectancy in the air as this battle of the bands – and the giants – gets into stride.

Yes, in a sense it was a big band battle – but you couldn't say that either contestant won it; the combatants were so very differently equipped. The Miller outfit's 'heavy artillery' – *i.e.*, the massive string section, French horn, etc. – made it an entirely different setup from the Navy Band, with its more or less conventional dance band instrumentation.

If Glenn Miller intended to place the issue beyond all doubt at the outset by 'slaying' us with that exquisite arrangement of 'Stardust' he certainly succeeded, so far as this critic is concerned, anyway. I defy anyone, even perhaps those not musically gifted at all, not to be completely bowled over by that incredibly beautiful bit of wizardly scoring from the band's 'staff' arranger, Sergeant Jerry Gray, and by its interpretation in the hands of this remarkable bunch of players.

Yes, and Miller went on 'slaying' us, too, one number after another, throughout this memorable broadcast. When he had exhausted all the degrees of style, versatility, exquisite tone colour, and sheer staggering technique, in which his boys specialize, he went on a different tack and brought Johnny Desmond to the microphone – and Johnny 'slayed' us all, too.

The Naval Band, who played as if they might have been just a trifle nervous in their first number, 'Convoy', soon warmed up and were getting in some great work also, the whole of their efforts dominated by their wonderful brass team and by the superb tenor-sax tooting of Sam Donahue himself.

For the final number both outfits combined together in a rendering of 'One O'Clock Jump', and that glorious swell of sound made by the combined brass teams is something I shall always remember.

Afterwards, Mr J. Harding brought the Marquis of Queensberry himself to the microphone, and in a short speech the Marquis warmly thanked Glenn Miller and Sam Donahue and their bands for a wonderful evening's entertainment.

Among the several London musical celebrities who somehow managed to be present on this great occasion were Victor Silvester, Joe Loss, Wally Moody, etc.*

Friday and Saturday, the 22nd and 23rd, were taken up with the usual broadcasts and some pre-recordings by the smaller bands

* *Melody Maker*, 30 September 1944.

and Johnny Desmond. On Sunday afternoon, the 24th, the Band travelled in their buses to North Witham, about ten miles south of Grantham, to play an afternoon concert in a hangar to 2,500 airborne troops and then on to Grantham to play a public charity concert from 3 to 4 pm at the State Cinema in aid of the town's 'Thank you' fund for the forces. Crowds gathered outside the cinema several hours before the concert was due to begin, and 'House full' signs went up soon after the doors opened. The concert was relayed over loudspeakers to more than a thousand people outside who were unable to get in.

Next day the Band played two more concerts for the Americans. They left Bedford in their own buses and drove to Oxford to play for the patients and staff of the 91st General Hospital. Despite a cold day the Band played on the lawn in front of the hospital to the great delight of the wounded troops, recent casualties of the fighting on the Continent. Then, into the buses again and on to the 7th Photographic Reconnaissance Group of the Eighth Air Force based at the RAF airfield at Mount Farm, about five miles south-east of Oxford, where another audience of over 3,000 cheered the Band to the echo. Afterwards the Band piled into the buses once more for the ride back to Bedford but on the way they got lost in the dark and it was midnight before they were back at Ashburnham Road.

'This was kind of a standard thing,' recalls Bob Ripley. 'We often got lost going to these places on buses, and I had maps – wonderful maps. You have marvellous maps in England, with every little bridge and house and everything indicated on them. I would follow the routes with the maps and usually I was the one who had to tell the driver how to go.'

The rest of the week was spent on the regular live broadcasts and some pre-recordings. On Thursday, the 28th, the Band travelled to London for the last of their *American Eagle* recordings at Rainbow Corner and the usual Thursday evening broadcast from the Queensberry Club, with musical comedy singer Pat Kirkwood as guest. This appearance by the Band was notable for another reason.

For some weeks there had been resentment among the dance music profession and the fans at what they considered to be the BBC's restricting and unfeeling attitude in not broadcasting some of the best of the AEFP programmes to home listeners via the Home Service or the GFP. That very day the *Melody Maker* had published a front-page protest castigating the BBC for 'cold-shouldering' AEFP stars including Bing Crosby, Spike Jones and his City Slickers and above all the American Band of the AEF. The *Melody Maker* also claimed that the forthcoming GFP schedules for Saturday 14 October had dropped the usual recorded repeat of that week's broadcast by the AEF Band and that this meant the BBC considered 'Glenn Miller's music not suitable for the British public'.

At the Queensberry Club a group of famous British bandleaders gathered on the stage before the broadcast to pay a public tribute to Major Miller and the AEF Band. The *Melody Maker* again gave the affair front page treatment under the heading in large type 'British Leaders Pay Tribute to Glenn Miller as Protest Against BBC.'

As a protest against the attitude of the BBC in stigmatizing the music of Major Glenn Miller and the American Band of the AEF as 'unsuitable for the British public', leading British bandleaders paid him a graceful and spontaneous compliment before his weekly broadcast on the AEF Programme last Thursday (28th).

Before an audience of 3,000 members of the Forces of all nations at the London Queensberry All-Services Club, they came on to the stage to express in glowing terms their appreciation of Major Glenn Miller's work for the troops and their admiration for the brilliant quality of his music.

Tommy Trinder introduced the bandleaders, and got a great laugh when he suggested that the BBC was not broadcasting Glenn Miller's music to listeners at home because it made 'British bands sound so shabby'.

He then called up Jack Hylton, who paid sincere compliments to Glenn Miller and the men of his orchestra, and then announced to the audience that the BBC had said that the Miller music was not suitable for the British public.

This was greeted with cries of 'Oh!' and Jack went on to say:

'I am sure somebody has made a mistake. As far as I am concerned – and I speak for every dance music fan in this country – I could hear him on the air every day' – an opinion that was received with roars of appreciation from the audience.

Similar speeches were made by Harry Roy, Geraldo, Maurice Winnick, Victor Sylvester, RSM George Melachrino, and Lieutenant Ben Oakley [conductor of the Band of the 28th Group, Pioneer Corps. – GB].

Geraldo made a particularly happy speech, referring to himself as 'the leader of one of those "shabby" bands that Tommy Trinder mentioned' and said how honoured the dance music profession was to welcome so great an orchestra as that of Major Glenn Miller.

167

Background of this unique tribute is that Miller's Band is no longer heard on the Home Service, and is shortly coming off the General Forces Programme. This means that it will only be heard on the AEF wavelength, which is quite unobtainable in most parts of Britain.

Representing as this orchestra does the finest in dance music, the BBC, in suggesting that it is 'not suitable for the British public', is casting a slur not only on these great American musicians, but on the whole profession to which they belong. It was in order to challenge this that the bandleaders made this spontaneous and very well-deserved gesture.

It also showed Major Miller and his boys that the hidebound opinions of the BBC moguls are not shared by the musical profession here.

There has been a quick repercussion to the 'MM' revelations last week of the way that the BBC cold-shoulders the brilliant American stars who perform on the AEF network, by not allowing their programmes to be heard by the British public on the Home or General Forces wavelengths.

The Spike Jones Half-Hour – a programme that was specifically mentioned as a case in point – is now at last to be heard on the Home Service. You will have to wait until 17 November (8 to 8.30pm) to hear it, but at least that's a step in the right direction.

Now we would like to know when we may hear some of the 'forgotten' Bing Crosby broadcasts; the Glenn Miller-Sam Donohue 'band-battle'; and a few of those brilliant *Uptown Hall* sessions which Mel Powell and a group of the Miller boys broadcast regularly on the AEF.*

However, the evening at the Queensberry also had its lighter side:

There was an amusing sequel to the tribute to Glenn Miller at the Queensberry Club . . .

After noted British bandleaders had come on the stage to express their admiration of the great work and playing of the Major and his orchestra, Tommy Trinder decided that the occasion was getting too serious, so he immediately set about organizing a 'jam session'.

In a trice, he had Jack Hylton sitting down at the piano, and borrowed violins for Maurice Winnick and George Melachrino and a clarinet for Harry Roy. Appointing Victor Sylvester as leader, he then used all his wiles to persuade Geraldo to sing the vocal chorus, but in this ambitious suggestion he was not successful!

* *Melody Maker*, 7 October 1944.

Well, in response to vociferous shouts from the huge audience, the number selected for this epic combination was 'Bless 'Em All!' which was duly rendered.

The conducting of Victor Sylvester kept it all in strict temp – but we certainly needed a Jerry Gray arrangement to do justice to the instrumental genius of the combatants.

It was all good fun – even if it wasn't good music!

And speaking of arrangements reminds me that a few days before the occasion chronicled above, Mr John Harding, Queensberry Club manager, announcing to a packed audience that these events were going to take place, said:

'We shall have a big party of British bandleaders here that night, so I have asked Major Glenn Miller to play some of his arrangements *at dictation speed*!'*

Echoes of the protest appeared in national and provincial newspapers, including a column in the *Sunday Chronicle* and *Sunday Referee* under the name of Lord Queensberry himself:

I am relieved that Glenn Miller, who is probably America's greatest band leader, is to continue to broadcast to British listeners.

Last week a story went about that the BBC were cutting his broadcasts on the ground that they were 'not acceptable' to British audiences.

Nothing could be further from the truth.

Nobody would suggest that Lady Cunard, the fairy godmother of British opera, had a bias towards dance and against serious music. She told me that she considered his band one of the finest she had ever heard.

After Glenn Miller's show at my club last week, a party of Britain's big names from the dance band world were introduced from the stage to a crowded house by Tommy Trinder.

Among them were Jack Hylton, Victor Silvester, Geraldo, Harry Roy, Maurice Winnick, and George Melachrino.

They paid tribute to Major Glenn Miller, as he now is, and expressed their resentment at the BBC's 'decision'.

Fortunately, the 'decision' has proved to be a myth and you will be able to hear this fine combination of America's swing stars on the General Forces Programme next Saturday at 1 pm.

Glen [*sic*] Miller, himself a quiet spoken young man, took the story admirably. 'I am not interested in the debate,' he told me.

'My job is to carry out orders, as any man in uniform must do. My job is to play to the men and women of the Allied Forces, and that is what I'm doing.'

Melody Maker, 7 October 1944.

The recorded repeats of the American Band of the AEF continued uninterrupted in the GFP on Saturday afternoons – and, incidentally, they were billed in the *Radio Times* without a break throughout this period, which suggests that, since the *Radio Times* had to be printed in advance, there was never any intention of discontinuing the GFP repeats. On the other hand, the publicity may have been useful because more and more AEFP programmes were re-broadcast in the home wavelengths from time to time.

The next airfield concert was on Sunday afternoon, 1 October, when once again the full Band faced another sixty-mile road journey to Great Ashfield, about eight miles north-east of Bury St Edmunds. This time it was bound for the B-17 base at the 385th Bomb Group close to the village of Great Ashfield and about three miles north of Elmswell, the name by which the base was sometimes known. Major Miller did not go with the Band, but it played for the Group's 200th Mission Party, with General Doolittle among the guests, what Haynes called 'a rousing group and they blew the lid off.' Nevertheless, next morning, without any sleep it was off on a mission to bomb an aircraft factory at Kassel, Germany, returning to base without any losses.

While at Great Ashfield, the Band took part in a fifteen-minute broadcast relayed by the BBC back to the USA in honour of the Group's 200 missions.

Next afternoon the Band went by road to the 398th Bomb Group base at Nuthampstead, Herts, about five miles south-west of Royston, again without Glenn Miller. Here it played a 3.30 pm concert in another 'air cooled' hangar, with Ray McKinley conducting.

But it was well into autumn and the cold, wet weather (early October that year was one of the wettest for years) was making airfield appearances increasingly uncomfortable and the cold weather affected the instruments. The Band played one more, however, on Tuesday 3 October, when they drove the forty miles to Kingscliffe, Northants, about twelve miles west of Peterborough, to play a concert at the P-51 Mustang base of the 20th Fighter Group of the Eighth Air Force, and this time Miller did go with the Band.

From then on the Band concentrated on its radio broadcasts and trips to London to broadcast from the Queensberry Club, although a few dance dates by small groups from the Band were played at military clubs in the Bedford area. In any case, airfield concerts would be difficult to fit into its schedule in future following the SHAEF order early in October that all its broadcasts should be live and not pre-recorded.

In the next Thursday evening broadcast by the full Band from the Queensberry Club the guest singer was the conductor of the British Band of the AEF, RSM George Melachrino, one of the British bandleaders who had joined in the protest against the BBC the previous Thursday. As usual, the *Melody Maker* was there:

It was a real treat, and very appropriate also, to have RSM George Melachrino (leader of the British Band of the AEF) as guest artist with Major Glenn Miller's American Band of the AEF on the latter's air show last Thursday (6th) [actually, the 5th], when the broadcast again took place at the Queensberry All-Services Club in London. Original idea was for George to sing one number with the Band on the broadcast, which he did, and very well, too. However, during that half-hour before the red light flicks on to announce that the Band is on the air, during which time Major Miller usually introduces the various 'cornermen' in his band (usually with some pretty incredible wisecracks, too!), he also introduced George Melachrino.

Said the Major: 'Besides singing, George is also a bit of a multi-instrumentalist; he plays clarinet, violin, etc., and I'm going to suggest that he plays them now' – and in spite of George's protests, he was handed a clarinet by 'Peanuts' Hucko, and made to play a chorus, after which he borrowed a violin from a member of the string section and played a slow, tasteful version of 'Amor Amor', which tickled the audience no end in its tuneful simplicity.

Main feature of this particular Miller airing, by the way, was the playing of the new super Sergeant Jerry Gray arrangement of 'Great Day'.

Containing some pretty intricate scoring, this masterpiece took a lot of rehearsal, and the boys didn't seem quite at home with it, even when they played it over in that half-hour before the broadcast commenced.

However, as seems to be the case with everything from the Miller outfit, when it went out over the air, a little later, it sounded perfect.*

Half-way through the programme a flying bomb flew over the Club, and Major Miller quietened the Band until it had passed over and the audience knew it was not going to come down through the roof.

A recording of part of the 5 October broadcast has been preserved in the sound archives of the BBC – the first twelve minutes or so, comprising the opening announcements and

* *Melody Maker*, 14 October 1944.

signature tune 'Moonlight Serenade', 'Great Day', 'Goodnight Neighbour' sung by George Melachrino accompanied by the full orchestra, and 'String Of Pearls'. This is almost the only recorded fragment of the ninety-eight broadcasts the Band made during its thirteen months on the AEF Programme which the BBC troubled to save, although every one was recorded either from live transmissions or as pre-recordings. Thus, what could have been a valuable historical collection (even if only part of it was kept) was lost to posterity through lack of interest by those responsible at the time, for these recordings were destroyed as a deliberate policy after the AEFP closed down (as, of course, were recordings by many other artists). One *Uptown Hall* programme, one *Strings With Wings* programme, which included a Sergeant Johnny Desmond song, and part of a *Swing Shift* programme were also preserved (*see* page 413).

CHAPTER THIRTEEN

Major Miller summoned to Paris – Colonel Kirby returns to
America – Jack Hylton conducts the Band – The Jazz Jamboree
and the Feldman Swing Club – A mysterious cancellation – ABSIE
and *Music for the Wehrmacht* – Major Miller's premonitions – Sir
Adrian Boult conducts the Strings with Wings

One day, about the end of September or early October,
Lieutenant Haynes received a telephone call at Bedford from
Colonel Kirby telling him that Major Miller was to report to
headquarters (presumably SHAEF (Rear) at Bushey Park) first
thing next morning and the Colonel said it was important. So
Miller and Haynes drove to London in the staff car and had
dinner with Colonel Kirby who had no idea why Major Miller
was to report to SHAEF. They stayed at the Mount Royal overnight and next morning, on arrival at headquarters, Miller discovered that he had been ordered to report immediately to
Lieutenant General Walter Bedell Smith, Chief of Staff to General Eisenhower, at SHAEF (Main) which had just moved to
Versailles, near Paris.

Orders were issued for him to fly to Paris via the 'SHAEF
Shuttle', the regular military plane flights run by the Air Transport Command of the USAAF from Bovingdon Airfield, near
Hemel Hempstead, to France for SHAEF VIPs: all non-combatant
flights out of the UK had to go via Bovingdon for customs and
security clearance.

Haynes saw him off and then drove back to Bedford. In his
diary Haynes did not record the exact date of Miller's visit to
Paris,* but Kirby left the ETO to return to Washington on 6
October, so Miller's visit to Paris was probably some time between the broadcasts of 28 September and 5 October, both of
which he conducted – this would account for his non-appearance

* It appears in the Diary a little out of sequence and may have been a later
addition.

at Great Ashfield and Nuthampstead (which, curiously, Haynes omitted to mention) though he was back in time to go with the Band to Kingscliffe on the 3rd. According to Haynes, Major Miller was away for four days. On his return, he telephoned Haynes from London and Haynes drove down to take him back to Bedford. On the way back Major Miller told him what had happened when he reported to General Bedell Smith.

Before seeing the General, Major Miller had talked to General Barker and his Executive Officer, Major May, but neither of them knew why General Bedell Smith had sent for him. Eventually, after waiting with mixed feelings for about ten minutes in an outer office, the General's WAC secretary ushered him in. With the best military bearing he could muster, he marched in to the General's office where the General sat at his desk studying some papers. After what seemed an eternity, General Bedell Smith looked up, Major Miller saluted and the General responded with a formal move of his hand and a brief 'Sit down, Major'.

Bedell Smith, known as 'Beetle', had been General Eisenhower's Chief of Staff since the Mediterranean campaigns of 1942 and he was a stern and dedicated military man, also, apparently, a man of few words. Major Miller told Haynes later that his encounter with the General must have been the fastest interview on record, for hardly had he taken a seat when the General asked him how he would like to take over the US Army Band (the 'number one' band in the entire US Army) to which Miller replied that he wouldn't like that. The General asked him why not, and Miller, also on occasion a man of few words, said that they didn't play his kind of music! That was enough for the General and Major Miller was dismissed abruptly from the room less than a minute after he went in.

This curious episode apparently came about because some of the Army top brass evidently felt that the US Army Band, then in the ETO, had not been doing too well compared with the bands of the other Allies. The Band was a special interest of General Marshall, US Army Chief of Staff, back in Washington, who was said to be unhappy about the Band's current performances and was determined that it should be brought up to scratch. Someone in Washington told him about a Major Miller over in England who led a band which was the talk of the ETO and if anyone could revitalize the Army Band he could. General Marshall passed on the idea to General Bedell Smith, Bedell Smith located Major Miller and summoned him to Paris. In view of Major Miller's unhappy experiences with Army bandmasters at Yale it was probably just as well that he declined the offer, though the idea of the 100-piece Army Band playing 'St Louis Blues March', or, who knows, 'In the Mood March' is one to be wondered at. Major Miller was to hear no more about it.

On 6 October, Colonel Ed Kirby gave up his post as Director of Broadcasting Services, SHAEF, on being recalled to Washington for a special assignment in the Pacific. His appointment at SHAEF had already been extended once at the request of General Barker and his energetic and devoted work had been a significant contribution to the success of the AEF Programme. Before leaving the ETO, however, he wrote, at General Barker's request, a report on the AEFP – a provocative and controversial memorandum which he circulated without permission not only among SHAEF officers but to the BBC as well. This was hardly likely to improve relations between SHAEF and the BBC and not unnaturally the BBC took instant and deep offence at Kirby's views, concluding that his memo was official SHAEF policy. It led to a top-level crisis in relations between SHAEF and the BBC and another behind-the-scenes threat to inter-Allied unity. General Barker ordered Kirby to recall all copies of his memo and explain in writing that it did not represent SHAEF policy. While the General poured oil on troubled waters, Colonel Kirby unfortunately left the ETO under a cloud.

Kirby was succeeded by the logical man for the job – his former number two, Lieutenant-Colonel David Niven, with the title of Director of Troop Broadcasting, SHAEF, while Niven's place as Deputy Director was taken by Major Johnny Hayes, the head of AFN, who had worked closely with the AEFP since its inception. They continued in these posts till the AEFP closed down in July 1945.

The Hollywood actor thus became the bandleader's Commanding Officer, and there survives in the radio archives a copy of orders from Colonel Niven to Major Miller dated 5 October, concerning the future of the AEF Programme and the employment and activities of the AEF Band. In impersonal military language, the document recognized the valuable work done by the Band. It went on to consider how its contributon to the AEFP could be increased and called for early discussions between the Band's producers Warrant Officer Dudley and Sergeant Voutsas (after prior consultation with Major Miller) and Cecil Madden for making greater use of the Band's potential, and their ideas for new programmes. It also requested Major Miller to contact Maurice Gorham as soon as possible to 'discuss freely any points that have arisen so far'. It went on to say that the proposed transfer of the Band to Paris had been turned down by General Barker for the time being, but it would be reconsidered when technical facilities were available to guarantee the Band's regular broadcasting from the Continent. However, a limited tour of duty in France was a possibility and Miller was asked for details of what part of his unit he would want to take to France bearing in mind that serious transport difficulties existed there. Next, Miller was authorized to continue with personal appearances by the Band at military camps, etc., provided they did not interfere with the radio schedule and that he kept the SHAEF Broadcasting Office informed of all such arrangements. It was emphasized, however, that the broadcasts had complete priority at all times, and any other commitments were subject to the overall SHAEF policy. Pre-recording of broadcasts was to be avoided in future and live broadcasts were to be treated as assigned military duty, although some flexibility of programming might be possible if Miller wished to do some special appearance. Lastly, the return of the unit to London was not contemplated at present.*

No direct connection of these orders with Major Miller's memorandum of 8 August is evident from the radio archives (which are somewhat fragmentary) and it is impossible to say how far up the military hierarchy his memo progressed (if at all), or whether it ever reached the BBC. However, in view of the relations between the two partners in the AEF Programme, the conclusion seems inescapable that the orders of 5 October were in some measure a means of letting Major Miller know 'where he stood'. All things considered, it was hardly likely to improve his temper or his views on the BBC and the restraints to which he felt subjected.

From this point onwards, practically all the broadcasts by the AEF Band and its smaller bands were made live – with the curious exception of the 9.30 am *Swing Shifts* on Saturdays which continued to be pre-recorded until they were transferred to Saturday

---

* There had been some consideration of bringing the Band back to London permanently during September, as the doodle-bug bombardment began to decline; however, soon a more deadly menace than the doodle-bug materialized – German V-2 rockets began to descend all over the same areas that had been hit by the doodle-bugs so the Band were obviously better off in Bedford.

afternoons at 3 o'clock from 14 November onwards when once again they went out live.

On Thursday 12 October, the Band travelled to London for its regular Thursday evening broadcast, and this time the guest artist was the former British bandleader-turned-theatrical-agent Jack Hylton, another of the bandleaders who protested against the BBC at the Queensberry Club two weeks earlier. The *Melody Maker* reported on the broadcast:

A fine gesture towards the further cementing of Anglo-American musical relationships took place last Thursday (12 October), when our own Jack Hylton was honoured by being asked to conduct Major Glenn Miller's Orchestra during the outfit's AEF Programme broadcast from the London Queensberry All-Services Club.

Jack conducted a famous old arrangement which had been resurrected for the occasion – the evergreen number recorded so successfully by the Hylton outfit about twelve years ago, 'She Shall Have Music'.

Introducing Jack Hylton, Major Glenn Miller remarked that he was a famous bandleader of an earlier general who had now 'gone respectable' and become a great theatrical impresario.

Jack said: 'Aren't you afraid you'll find me a bit rusty and dusty, Glenn?' But the Major waved aside such protests, saying, 'Ladies and gentlemen, Jack's back. Here is Jack Hylton' – and Jack duly conducted the evergreen arrangement with great success.

After the show Major Glenn Miller remarked that at the rehearsal he had seen Jack Hylton conducting with a drumstick.

He and his boys couldn't allow such a state of affairs, and accordingly, as a spontaneous gesture, he and the members of his orchestra had purchased a fine baton which had previously been used by many famous conductors of the Covent Garden Opera.

The baton was duly presented to Jack by Major Glenn Miller amidst deafening applause.

This Thursday's show at the Queensberry by the Miller Band was full of the usual good things.

During the half-hour's 'warming-up' period before the broadcast the Miller Band featured popular Ray McKinley at the mike in 'Is She Is Or Is She Ain't My Baby?' [*sic*] and later gave pianist Mel Powell a chance to shine by playing a first-class rendering of the 'Warsaw Concerto'.

Mel shone again in the actual broadcast, when his own 'Mission to Moscow' was played, which Mel both composed and arranged, and in which he also featured some very tasteful piano.

No other very special highspots in this programme, except that vocalist Johnny Desmond 'slayed 'em' – as usual!*

* *Melody Maker*, 21 October 1944.

Three days later came one of the best-remembered events of the AEF Band's stay in Britain – their surprise appearance at the 6th annual Jazz Jamboree concert at the now-demolished Stoll Theatre in Kingsway, London, on Sunday afternoon 15 October. This was only the Band's second (and last) public performance for a civilian audience in the capital – the first had been at the Plaza Cinema back in July.

The Jazz Jamboree, organized by the Musicians' Social and Benevolent Council, was the highspot of the British dance music year when a dozen or so of the leading dance and jazz bands of the day performed in aid of the Musicians Union Benevolent Fund, and the demand for tickets was always so great that only people who applied on the first day they were available stood any chance of getting them. Indeed, the entire 'house' could have been sold out several times over, and this continued to be the case when after the war the Jamboree was transferred to the larger Gaumont State Cinema at Kilburn.

The 1944 Jazz Jamboree was first announced in the *Melody Maker* of 16 September, and the following week's issue said that no more applications for tickets could be accepted as already three times as many applications had been received as there were tickets available – and this when only six of the final total of twelve bands appearing had been announced. Each succeeding issue of the *Melody Maker* (the only medium of publicity for the Jamboree) announced additional bands which had agreed to appear. Finally, the issue of 14 October (on sale on the 12th, only three days before the Jamboree, carried the exciting and unexpected news that Major Glenn Miller and the American Band of the AEF would play at the Jamboree.

This was a tremendous scoop for the organizers, as the AEF Band were not normally allowed to play civilian engagements, except for charity and they only appeared at very few of these – two in London, one in Bedford and one in Grantham. The Committee of the MU Benevolent Council had been looking for something special as top of the bill, and the appearance of the AEF Band had been brought about by Ted Heath who was at that time on the organizing committee for the Jamboree. He had managed to get in to a few sessions by the AEF Band at Bedford and had become friendly with Miller. Ted Heath went to see him at the Mount Royal to explain about the Jamboree and ask Miller if he and the Band would play there. The *Melody Maker* gave the news on its front page:

A very charming demonstration of the comradeship existing between British and American dance musicians lies behind the news that Major Glenn Miller and the American Band of the AEF are to play at Sunday's Jazz Jamboree at the Stoll Theatre, Kingsway, London.

This last-minute 'scoop' was conceived and carried through by famous Geraldo trombonist Ted Heath, on behalf of the MSBC who told the *Melody Maker*:

'I thought it would be a grand gesture if a famous American band could appear at the Jamboree, so I approached Major Glenn Miller and found him most helpful. When I was going to tell him what the Jamboree was in aid of and all about it, he stopped me with a smile and said "You don't have to tell us about the Jazz Jamboree: we read the *Melody Maker* you know!"

'He and his boys were only too willing to co-operate in this worthy show for British musicians, and the US Army officials to whom I was referred were just as helpful, sympathetic and encouraging.

'So now everything is fixed, and Major Miller and the Band will give a half-hour show.'

This enterprising bit of work by Ted Heath sets the seal on what promises to be a grand day for the fans.*

However, as Ted Heath recalled in later years in his autobiography, he was not as confident as the *Melody Maker* report had indicated:

I was on the council of the Musicians' Social and Benevolent Council and attended a meeting to discuss the composition of the Jazz Jamboree, our annual charity concert. Various bands were suggested and there were counter-suggestions. I was preparing to toss in the biggest counter-suggestion of all, but like a child who drops a rock in a pool, I was a bit afraid of the splash it would cause. Vanity prompted me to do it.

I found myself saying: 'Why don't we get the Glenn Miller Band?'

There was a hush and all eyes swivelled in my direction.

'*You* know him,' said someone. 'You think he'd agree?'

My reply came straight from a swollen ego. 'I think he could be persuaded . . .'.

By who else than by me? When I left the meeting I didn't feel so pleased with myself. I'd taken on something and no mistake. I had no idea whether Miller would be staying in this country *until* the Jamboree, let alone whether he would be willing to attend. And, even if he were prepared to help us, there were such things as army schedules. The one

* *Melody Maker*, 14 October 1944.

thing I knew, thanks to that nose of mine, [Ted was nicknamed by a fellow musician as Reuter because of his 'nose for news of musical doings'] was that Miller was staying at the Mount Royal Hotel. I went to see him.

He listened politely and, to my immeasurable relief, he said he would see what he could do. Wires would have to be pulled . . . you know how red tape could be . . . but this was a British charity . . . Anglo-American relations . . . he'd do his best.

We all felt that this assurance was good enough. The musical press was told that the Glenn Miller Orchestra was expected, the only snag being that no one knew what time the band would arrive, least of all me.

I can remember that Sunday at the Stoll Theatre very clearly. The anxiety etched itself into my mind. Every few moments I came out of the stage door and gazed up and down Kingsway, looking for some hopeful sign of Miller's arrival. When my time came to play with the Geraldo band, I was a mass of nerves. Would Miller let me down? In my mind it was a personal arrangement between him and myself, with my prestige at stake.

After coming off-stage, I went out to keep my vigil at the stage door. Other members of the committee came and stood with me and hope was dwindling. Reproach was on every face that I saw.

When my faith had ebbed, a convoy of lorries turned into the top of Kingsway. Was it? Could it be? It was! I had expected a single coach, but the Americans did things in style. Miller had brought not only his band, but also his rostrums from Bedford *and* a fatigue party to set them up.

Miller was very brisk and unemotional. There was enough emotion on my side to serve us both.

'How long do you want us to play?' he asked.

I could barely speak for excitement. 'A quarter of an hour,' I managed to blurt out.

As the first sounds of Miller's signature tune, 'Moonlight Serenade', seeped through the heavy curtains to the crowd, a cheer broke out, People slapped my back and hard-boiled musicians ran to the side of the stage like fans.

We all listened and applauded. The Miller band was on there for an hour. At the end, Glenn made a short speech of thanks. Then they were off, packed away in minutes by the fatigue party. I watched them drive up Kingsway. There had been none of the chit-chat of social exchange that I'd hoped for, but if Miller had come and gone, he'd left me with a little glory.

Later, I was to meet him again, back-stage at the London Casino (then called the Queensberry Club), for the last time. We talked of many things, trombone playing, orchestrations, and my aspirations as a bandleader. He was most encouraging and interested, having been a trombone player himself, and he told me that, on his return from the Continent, before he went back to America, he would give me his trombone as a memento, and suggested that it might help if he sent me some of his arrangements when he returned to the USA. Then he wished me luck as a bandleader. It was with very deep regret that, a few days later, I heard the news that he was missing. Not only was this tragedy a great loss to the dance music world, but also a personal loss to every musician who had the honour to meet him and know him.*

As to the Jamboree itself, the *Melody Maker* devoted a long and detailed report to the four-hour concert under the front page banner headline THE BEST JAZZ JAMBOREE EVER! Not unnaturally, most space was given to the British bands in the programme comprising as they did the cream of the British bands of the time, but the Miller contribution was far from neglected especially as one of the highspots of the entire afternoon occurred during the AEF Band's part of the concert:

The seal was set on a very fine programme of dance bands by the personal apearance of Major Glenn Miller and the American Band of the AEF, and their friendly co-operation was very nicely referred to by Major Miller when, in introducing his band, he said:

'We are only too glad to show a little gesture in appreciation of the treatment we have received here from musicians all over the country. In fact, I'll go so far as to say that no group has done more to make our stay pleasant over here than the musicians.'

And he paid another tribute to this country by having ten-year-old drum genius Victor Feldman play a number with a section of his orchestra – the greatest honour yet conferred on this amazing child.

After going through the programme band by band, Ray Sonin, Editor of the *Melody Maker*, wrote:

. . . the reception accorded to this band [the *Melody Maker* all-star poll winners band, directed by George Chisholm] seemed to me to be as much possible noise as the packed house could make – but I was wrong, for it made even more noise in giving Major Glenn Miller and his Orchestra one of the most terrific ovations I have ever heard.

What is there new that can be said about this band? It played for half an hour with that brilliant musicianship to which we have become accustomed, and the Major himself was in sparkling form – dignified as ever but obviously thoroughly enjoying himself.

* *Listen To My Music: an autobiography*, by Ted Heath (Frederick Muller, London, 1957).

He then told us that he had arrived too late to hear Victor Feldman, but that all his boys had been raving to him about the child.

He therefore brought Vic on to the stage so that he could have an opportunity of hearing him, and he seated himself in the string section watching with keen interest while Ray McKinley fixed up his drums so that the diminutive percussionist could be comfortable.

Accompanied by 'Peanuts' Hucko on clarinet, Mel Powel on piano, Carmen Mastren on guitar, and Trigger Alpert on bass, the ten-year-old wizard crashed into an impromptu version of 'Sweet Georgia Brown', with the whole Miller band looking on in wonderment.

It says much for the amazing confidence of this child that he was not at all nervous or flustered in this ordeal. He played like the little wonder that he is, and when he had finished, Major Miller and his band were the first to burst into spontaneous applause.

Major Miller walked to the microphone, shaking his head as if he couldn't believe what he had just seen. In a voice that was really awed, he said: *'That's the greatest I've ever heard'* – and he meant it.

It was a wonderful tribute to a little British artist.*

That evening, visiting celebrities at the Feldman Swing Club included not only some of the men from the AEF Band but Major Glenn Miller as well:

It was a natural follow-up to this year's record, super-super Jazz Jamboree that the event should be followed by one of the most bumper nights of all time at the Feldman Club (100, Oxford Street, W1).

At the head of the big list of distinguished visitors on this great night, the Club was honoured by the presence of Major Glenn Miller.

Major Miller, who had been frankly astounded by the prowess of ten-year-old Victor Feldman at the Jazz Jamboree, was no doubt given further food for thought when the young drum genius played a brilliant session with two of the famous Miller stalwarts, Sergeant Mel Powell (piano) and Sergeant 'Peanuts' Hucko (clarinet).

Just before the close of the evening's hectic jamming, Major Miller came to the microphone and expressed his pleasure at visiting a spot where the jazz atmosphere was kept so gloriously alive, and said how pleased and surprised he was to find the jazz tradition going so strong in Britain and to find that the type of music 'for which we have plugged so much back home' was so strongly established over here. He also warmly praised the various musicians who had contributed to the evening's success.*

* *Melody Maker*, 21 October 1944.

The following Thursday 19 October, the Band performed its usual broadcast from the Queensberry Club. However, here another little mystery crops up, for there was no broadcast that night (it was replaced by gramophone records), yet the Band did play at the Queensberry and a programme was recorded at the usual broadcast time with Geraldo vocalist seventeen-year-old Sally Douglas as guest star, and the recording was broadcast next morning in *Morning After*, and the regular GFP repeat the following Saturday afternoon. Why there was no broadcast on Thursday evening remains a mystery: a note in the radio archives merely states 'broadcast cancelled owing to emergency' – perhaps a fault at the transmitter.

During the next few weeks, the broadcast schedule continued as usual. The guest singer on the 26th was Anne Shelton, making her second broadcast appearance with the Band when she sang 'Spring Will Be A Little Late This Year'. She was the last British singer to broadcast with the Band – thereafter Miller dispensed with guest singers altogether.

At the end of October the Band began a new series of broadcasts with a difference – not for the AEF Programme nor to the Allied audience at all, but propaganda broadcasts beamed at the German Army. These were for broadcasting over the American Broadcasting Station in Europe (ABSIE) operated from London by the Overseas Branch of the Office of War Information. This was the civilian propaganda outlet for the American Government, although OWI work in the ETO had by now become integrated into the SHAEF Command as its Psychological Warfare Division.

The ABSIE station had first gone on the air on 30 April 1944, as part of the Allied preparations for the invasion of Europe, with technical assistance from the BBC and working from underground studios in the Gaumont British building in Wardour Street, Soho. Broadcasting in almost every European language, the station broadcast news, talks and music. News and talks were most important as they were the means of sending out the Allied 'message' to Occupied Europe and waging psychological warfare on the Germans. The broadcasts were directed originally to the people of the occupied countries to prepare them for the forthcoming Allied liberation; then after D-Day to foreign workers in Germany urging them to sabotage the German war effort, and later, as the liberation of Europe progressed, to the German people and the German Armed Forces urging them to surrender.

Post-war research revealed that, despite intensive German jamming of the station's several wavelengths, the broadcasts successfully reached their audiences, especially the Germans. Many American and Allied statesmen and public figures broadcast over ABSIE, including some European monarchs in exile in England, as well as American journalists, radio correspondents and servicemen – anyone who could project the Allied cause was roped in, including refugees from the Occupied countries.

Entertainment, too, played a vital role in these broadcasts, and ABSIE's 'pride and joy' (to quote *Time* magazine) was its music programmes, and among American stars who broadcast were Bing Crosby and Dinah Shore, introducing their songs and putting over 'the message' by reading from phonetic German scripts.

In October, Glenn Miller and the AEF Band were asked to do a programme for German troops and on Monday 30 October, the whole Band travelled to the Abbey Road studios of HMV to record a typical half hour programme of their music interspersed with messages to the Germans. Miller read his announcements partly in English and partly in halting, phonetic German, much to the amusement of his colleagues, assisted by a German-speaking girl announcer known in the programme as Ilse. The scripts plugged the Allied cause and better international understanding after the war; the music was from the Band's normal repertoire and the programme consisted of 'Moonlight Serenade', 'In The Mood', 'Stardust', 'Song Of The Volga Boatmen', 'Long Ago And Far Away' (sung in German by Johnny Desmond), 'Is You Is Or Is You Ain't My Baby' (sung in English by Ray McKinley) and 'Great Day'.

The recording was a great success, and the Band subsequently returned to Abbey Road to record seven more over the next four Mondays. The programmes were broadcast every Wednesday in ABSIE's *Music For The Wehrmacht* from 8 November onwards.

In February 1952, two ten-inch LPS appeared on the record market in New York containing extracts from several of the *Wehrmacht* programmes with some of the announcements and opening and closing themes (*see* page 394). They were entitled *An AFN Presentation – Major Glenn Miller and the AEF Orchestra*, although of course the original wartime broadcasts had nothing at all to do with AFN. Following court action by the Glenn Miller Estate in New York City these records were held to have been issued illegally and were suppressed and copies are now extremely rare. However, in more recent years extracts from the programmes have also been issued on other LPS. (*See* pages 399–410.)

Over the next few weeks the Band's live broadcast schedule continued as usual. After their broadcast from the Queensberry Club on Thursday 2 November, the Marquis of Queensberry gave a dinner for Major Miller and the Band at Kettner's Restaurant in Soho as a gesture of appreciation for their performances at the Club. A special four-page printed menu was produced for the occasion and among celebrities listed on the cover as attending were Jack Hylton, John Harding and the First Lord of the Admiralty A. V. Alexander; others present (according to Lieutenant Haynes) were Tommy Trinder, Morton Downey (the American tenor who had come to the ETO on a US tour) and an (unnamed) niece of Winston Churchill. The menu also listed every member of the Band and carried a tribute to the Band which noted that during its ten visits to the Club 30,000 men and women of HM and Allied Fighting Forces had been its guests.

After dinner, Jack Hylton took Miller and Haynes back to his flat for drinks, where they were soon joined by some of Jack's friends, including A. V. Alexander. As the night wore on and the drinks flowed free, the First Lord sat at the piano and played and sang some saucy songs and to Miller's and Haynes' surprise began telling them figures of the damage and casualties inflicted on London by the flying bombs, and (according to Haynes), even more amazingly the existence of the atomic bomb and its possible consequences. Miller and Haynes spent what was left of the night in London and after working at SHAEF for most of the following day returned to Bedford on Saturday.

There, they spent Saturday evening playing poker at the Officers Club at Milton Ernest Hall till the early hours. During the game Miller was on a losing streak – unusual for him – and on the drive back to Bedford afterwards he was in a very subdued mood and began talking to Haynes as he had never talked before, saying that for a long time he had a strong feeling that one of the flying bombs had his name on it and he would never see his wife and adopted son again. Although he had never known Miller to be superstitious, Haynes had noticed that Miller had become jumpy and always in a hurry as though he hadn't enough time to do all the things he wanted to do; he had also lost weight (which was not surprising, considering their hectic life and his sinus trouble and unfamiliar and erratic food) so that his made-to-measure uniform from Saks on Fifth Avenue no longer fitted him like it used to.

From the start of the Miller unit's radio work at Bedford in July, the string section, conducted by George Ockner, had been providing their two programmes a week, one of the few regular light and classical series on the AEFP. Amid the greater publicity for jazz and dance bands in general the strings had been comparatively out of the limelight, although the high quality of their music had been recognized both on the air and in person. There had also grown up much mutual appreciation between them and the players in the BBC Symphony Orchestra and they sometimes attended each others' rehearsals, while Sir Adrian Boult was always very good in providing the Miller men with tickets to the Symphony Orchestra broadcasts. 'We used to have free time in the evenings in Bedford,' recalls Bib Ripley, 'and the BBC Symphony Orchestra would play up at the boys school (Bedford School) a little distance from where we were billeted at the Red Cross. It was a lovely evening walk – we'd go up around 6.30 or so. I think the broadcasts were at 7 o'clock and lasted for only an hour, and we used to go up there almost every day to hear the BBC Orchestra play their broadcasts.

'Sir Henry Wood did a few of them and it was really very nice to be able to go up there and listen to the BBC Symphony. Sir Henry Wood, who was really the top conductor of the BBC at the time, did no more than a couple of the concerts and I remember one evening after one of his concerts we went down to talk to the musicians in the Orchestra while Sir Henry was still there and a lady from the Orchestra came up to him and asked him for his autograph. He said, "Well, are you a member of the Orchestra?", which was an interesting indication that he had so little to do with it that he didn't even really know who was in the Orchestra! [Sir Henry Wood was a guest conductor at the time and died on 19 August 1944].

'We also heard Yehudi Menuhin play the premiere (or, at least, the English premiere) of the Bartok violin concerto at the Corn Exchange with the BBC Symphony Orchestra [20 September]. We heard them rehearse it and perform it, and I was amazed at the sight reading ability of the Orchestra. My gosh, they played that thing at rehearsal as though they had already been playing it many times – it was remarkable.'

In October, Major Miller invited Sir Adrian Boult to conduct the Strings With Wings on one of their broadcasts. Sir Adrian accepted, and the programme went out live on Monday 6 November, at their regular time of 7.15 to 7.30 pm from the BBC's Maida Vale studios after the Band's second ABSIE recording session at nearby HMV.

The programme consisted of Elgar's 'Serenade For Strings', Debussy's Nocturne 'Clouds' and 'Annie Laurie'. The following review appeared soon afterwards in the *Melody Maker*:

I wonder if Ralph Hill (*writes Stanley Nelson*) happened to be listening to the string section, of the Glenn Miller Orchestra recently when it was conducted by Sir Adrian Boult in a short programme on the AEF wavelength.

If he was, he must have regretted his criticism in the *MM* that this body of players lacks tone.

This, in my view, was a most impressive broadcast, and not the least impressive thing about it was the playing of a beautiful arrangement of Debussy's 'Nuages', one of his 'Orchestral Nocturnes'.

This is the work of Sergeant George Ockner, the leader of the String Section, and was specially selected by Sir Adrian Boult.

Essentially a work for woodwind, Sergeant Ockner has made a clever job of stimulating woodwind tone and filling in with the strings at his disposal, and the lovely impressionism of the French composer loses, in my view, very little indeed.

The short programme ended with another splendid and rather contrapuntal treatment of 'Annie Laurie' by another member of the Orchestra.*

A few years after the war, in a BBC documentary radio programme, Sir Adrian Boult recalled the broadcast:

I was conducting the BBC Symphony Orchestra, and our headquarters were at Bedford, so I saw quite a lot of the Miller Band. I often dropped in on their rehearsals – they used the Corn Exchange as we did. I found it fascinating to watch Glenn Miller at work. He was a thorough craftsman – he knew just what he wanted from his band and how to get it, and he didn't mind how hard he worked himself or them. Of course it was the string section which interested me most. Twenty players, all from famous orchestras (there were even some who had played with me in America). I always enjoyed their programmes *Strings With Wings* – though I wished they could have been playing better stuff. Glenn Miller asked me if I would like to conduct *Strings With Wings*

* *Melody Maker*, 2 December 1944.

myself. I was delighted to, and I still remember that little programme we did in November 1944.

We played, amongst other things, an arrangement for strings of the beautiful 'Clouds' Nocturne of Debussy. It was arranged by a member of the band, Mr George Ockner, who very kindly gave me a copy of his arrangement. Some idea of the friendliness and permanence of these strings can be derived from the fact that when the writing had been subdivided to any considerable extent, leaving a group of soloists each playing a particular line, their names are inserted in the score – George, Harry, Ernie and Gene on the violin, Dave and Stan on the viola line were the most prominent.

We certainly missed them when they left Bedford.*

Harry Katzman remembered this broadcast: 'I have to say that Adrian Boult is one of the best conductors that I have ever played with – he was such a gentleman and it was just so easy to play with him – you could just get every nuance and it was so simple. I remember we did the Elgar "Serenade For Strings", and then one of the things we played was George Ockner's arrangement of "Clouds" by Debussy. Everybody in the orchestra was just flabbergasted how pleasant and musically honest this man was when he conducted, and you never had any question of his beat – you knew where everything was at one time and he worked so easily. One of the most pleasant experiences of my musical career.'

Viola player Emanuel Wishnow also remembers this programme with affection: 'Boult was very fascinated by the arrangement we played of "Clouds" because the original had an English horn solo in it and we found out that by having one viola play it with a mute on the strings near the bridge (it was played by Dave Schwartz) it sounded very much like an English horn, and Boult was knocked out! It sounded terrific – I enjoyed that broadcast very much, and he did too. Of course, it made a pleasant change to play under a symphony conductor again because we had hardly any opportunity to do so, although later we did play under Kostelanetz in Paris.'

A sad little footnote to this collaboration exists in a file in the radio archives: at a programme meeting at Broadcasting House, Colonel Niven was asked by Maurice Gorham to ask Major Miller not to make direct approaches to BBC personnel to take

* Spoken contribution to 'Close-up of Glenn Miller and the American Band of the AEF', 8 June 1953.

part in his programmes as in the case of Sir Adrian Boult but to go through the routine channels.

Another projected classical collaboration at about this time did not materialize, however. Violinist Yehudi Menuhin came to the ETO from America to play for the Allied forces and it was reported in the *Melody Maker* of 30 September that he was to play at the Queensberry Club the following week accompanied by the Strings With Wings. He broadcast live with Sir Adrian Boult and the BBC Symphony Orchestra on 20 September, went over to play to troops on the Continent, and then went to Bedford on 27 October to play with the Symphony Orchestra again, but had to return to America immediately afterwards.

There was another ABSIE recording session by the AEF Band on Monday 13 November, in the HMV studios. In the programme Artie Malvin sang 'Where Or When' instead of Johnny Desmond: it is not clear why this substitution was necessary, unless Desmond was saving his voice for his own AEFP programme which was broadcast live at 7 pm that evening for the first time in his new regular Monday spot (from the BBC's nearby Maida Vale studio). At a later ABSIE session the Band was joined by Hollywood singing star Irene Manning who had come to England on a USO tour (she was to be seen in the new musical film *Hollywood Canteen* then showing in British cinemas and had previously starred with James Cagney in *Yankee Doodle Dandy* among others). Miss Manning sang several songs in German with the Band for the *Wehrmacht*.

During November illness hit several members of the Band: Johnny Desmond missed some AEF Band and the *Swing Shift* broadcasts between 16 and 24 November because of influenza and Artie Malvin took his place but he was back on the air with *Swing Shift* on the 25th; Mannie Thaler was also ill on the 16th and the usual *Uptown Hall* that evening was replaced by a pre-recording; and on Saturday, the 18th, it was Mel Powell's turn so the *Uptown Hall* was cancelled altogether and replaced by records of classical music.

CHAPTER FOURTEEN

A new radio schedule – The Beverley Sisters – Major Miller called to Paris again – The Band to play in Paris for six weeks – *Visiting Hour* – Eight weeks' broadcasts pre-recorded – 'Carnival of Music' – The Band's last broadcast in England

On Monday 13 November, the AEF Band and its smaller bands began a revised weekly broadcasting schedule in the AEF Programme. Although no direct evidence remains in the radio archives to connect the new schedule with Colonel Niven's orders of 5 October to Major Miller, it does seem likely that there was some connection between the two. Certainly there had been some discussion and exchange of ideas between the BBC, SHAEF and Miller during this period, for one interesting and intriguing paper does survive: a memorandum dated 21 October 1944, from Maurice Gorham to Major Hayes (Colonel Niven's second in command) giving Gorham's reaction to nine suggestions from Glenn Miller for new programme series. Unfortunately, Major Miller's nine suggestions do not survive, and from Gorham's brief comments it is not possible to deduce exactly what they were, but of the nine three were rejected outright by Gorham, two he considered impracticable, one of doubtful value, one dull, and only two were given qualified approval. Two of those rejected seem to have been connected with football results and for programmes featuring particular instrumentalists in the Band. The two which received qualified approval seem to have been very similar, if not practically the same: one was for a second weekly programme by the full Band, and the other apparently for some type of programme built around Major Miller's name and personal popularity – hitherto the full Band programme had always been billed and introduced as 'The American Band of the AEF, under the direction of Major Glenn Miller' rather than giving the primary billing to Major Miller himself, as was also the case with the other two AEF Bands. Gorham's comments concerning these two suggestions are interesting:

(1) I'll buy it, if Major Miller thinks from his own experience that the best show he can offer would be identical in format with the present Thursday night show, which is repeated on Friday mornings. (Major Miller is proposing to discontinue the use of British singers in his Thursday shows, so the two shows will be even more identical.) This would probably be best placed on Sundays at 12.30, substituting for the present Johnny Desmond quarter-hour which employs the full band.

(8) This I believe arose from Major Miller's belief that AEFP is not making sufficient use of his personal popularity, which in turn arises from my literal interpretation of his original request that his name should not be featured as his was a Service band and he didn't want to be thought to be seeking personal publicity. I should be glad to schedule this programme once weekly but not every night.

You will notice that of these nine suggestions, only four are for regular series by Major Miller or his band. This seems to me to reflect his own uncertainty over his real function here, which I hope to clear up in our forthcoming talk.*

A programme planning meeting was scheduled for 23 October, at which the suggestions and Gorham's comments were to be discussed. No minutes of such a meeting remain, but from the new schedule introduced on 13 November, it seems that the two suggestions described above were combined into one, for the only new programme series to go on the air was a second weekly programme on Friday evenings by the full Band entitled *Moonlight Serenade*, which was introduced on the air as 'Music by the Moonlight Serenader – Major Glenn Miller, presenting the American Band of the AEF . . .'. The Thursday programmes by the full Band were moved to the same time on Tuesdays, and the rest of the new schedule merely consisted of moving some of the existing programmes to new days and times and leaving the rest where they were! The full Band's recorded repeat in *Morning After* was moved from Friday to Wednesday (a repeat of the Tuesday programme) but the Friday *Moonlight Serenade* was not usually repeated at all. From 21 November onwards the *Swing Shift* programmes by Ray McKinley and the American Dance Band on Thursdays and Saturdays were repeated in the new *Return Engagement* series at 7.30 am on Tuesdays and Fridays respectively. (This new series also included on other days of the

* BBC WAC R34/183/1.

191

week repeats of the Canada Dance Band, the British Army Radio Orchestra, and *Top Ten* among others.) As before, the other small bands' programmes were not repeated at all. This new AEFP schedule for the Miller unit programmes continued until early in 1945 when once again it was reorganized from 12 February onwards. The recorded repeats by the full Band in the GFP on Saturday afternoons were not affected by the AEFP changes, although sometimes the Tuesday programme and sometimes the Friday programme was used in this spot.

The following table compares the two schedules:

Day	Old Schedule	New Schedule
Mon	7.15pm Strings With Wings	7.00pm Sgt Johnny Desmond
		7.15pm Strings With Wings
Tues	6.30pm Swing Shift	8.30pm American Band of AEF
Wed	6.15pm Uptown Hall	6.15pm Uptown Hall
	7.45pm Strings With Wings	7.45pm Strings With Wings
Thur	8.30pm American Band of AEF	7.30pm Swing Shift
		9.15pm Uptown Hall
Fri	6.15pm Uptown Hall	8.30pm Moonlight Serenade
		(American Band of AEF).
Sat	11.45am Piano Parade	11.45am Piano Parade
	(Pfc Jack Rusin)	(Pfc Jack Rusin)
	3.00pm Swing Shift	3.00pm Swing Shift
	6.15pm Uptown Hall	6.15pm Uptown Hall
Sun	12.45pm Sgt Johnny Desmond	

By this time the AEF programme was producing an increasing number of its own programmes (totalling about six hours a day) in addition to taking recorded programmes from other BBC services, AFN and the Canadian Broadcasting Corporation. Besides the more prestigious productions such as *Top Ten* and *AEF Special* and the programmes by the three Bands of the AEF, there were several more modest series, some of fifteen minutes each like *AEF Extra*, and some of these provided promising newcomers with their first broadcasts. Thus, three young typists from Northampton turned up at Bedford one day hoping to get on the air – the singing Beverley Sisters. They came to the notice of Glenn Miller, who, after giving them advice on their singing, sent them to AEFP production chief Cecil Madden in London. As a result they made their first BBC broadcast in *AEF Extra* (live) on Monday afternoon, 13 November, singing 'It's Love, Love, Love' and 'The Banks of The Wabash', accompanied by Carmen Mastren.

'I sure remember the Beverley Sisters,' said Carmen Mastren. 'They were three cute little girls who came to Bedford and I got to know them, and they said they had a chance to do a broadcast for the BBC and asked if I would play for them. I told them to arrange it when we were in London and I asked Trigger to do it with me and we played for them. They were very grateful and we had correspondence for a long time. I was so happy to hear they had a hit record. I saw them in New York when I was at NBC and they appeared on our morning show with Skitch Henerson and I must say they gave me a lot of credit.'

On Wednesday morning, 15 November, Major Miller again took the 'SHAEF Shuttle' to Paris, having been summoned by General Barker to report to him at SHAEF (Main) headquarters at Versailles. This time, however, Miller's visit was to be more successful than when he had reported to General Bedell Smith six weeks earlier.

Now that the fighting front had become relatively stabilized along the German frontier and in Southern Holland, following the unsuccessful airborne landings at Arnhem, although heavy fighting continued on many sectors, Paris was about to become a leave centre for Allied (principally American) combat troops. The military authorities were anxious to arrange as much high-quality star entertainment for troops on leave in the French capital as possible, and Miller was at last able to persuade General Barker that he should be allowed to take the AEF Band to Paris to play for troops on a regular basis, or at least for some weeks.

Miller spent three days in Paris and after obtaining General Barker's approval for the Band's transfer he lost no time in finding out what facilities would be available there for broadcasting and concert appearances. A number of theatres and clubs had been requisitioned by the military authorities and on the advice of the AEFP's Paris office he approached Basil Dean, the Director of ENSA, who was also in Paris. Dean promised Miller the use of the Marigny Theatre (at that time under ENSA's control for troop shows) for the Band's rehearsals and AEFP recordings: BBC equipment had already been installed there, and the AEFP Band would be able to use the theatre on most days of the week up till 6 pm, after which time it would be needed for ENSA shows. However, the Marigny was rather small for a band the size of the AEF Band, and would need extra equipment, so Major Miller also secured the promise of recording facilities under the control of

SHAEF Public Relations Division to record up to a maximum of four hours a week. He also arranged for concert appearances at the Olympia Theatre and the Palais de Glace (in peacetime an ice rink)* to be organized by the Special Services Section of the Seine Base, US Army, and which would not interfere with the recording of programmes for the AEFP.

On the 17th, he drew up a report to General Barker on what he had been able to organize, complete with a weekly timetable showing proposed locations and times for the Band's activities, and the next day he flew back to England. General Barker sent a formal request to Maurice Gorham for the transfer of the Band to Paris, provided it would not interfere with their radio schedule on the AEF Programme, which then totalled three hours forty-five minutes live broadcasting each week.

At first the BBC were opposed to the transfer, arguing that the severe shortages of equipment and, especially, engineers on the Continent made it impracticable. Although the landline from Paris to London had by then been restored, it was under the control of SHAEF Signals personnel and its use by the AEFP could not be guaranteed, except perhaps at night between 2200 hours and 0600 next morning – during most of which time the AEF Programme was off the air. Any use by the AEFP would have to be booked in advance, and would depend on the military situation, which meant that it might be taken back by the military at a moment's notice, even in the middle of a programme or a recording. Thus its use by the BBC would be uncertain and perhaps limited, and the BBC was not prepared to deprive itself of all other material from the Continent in order to ensure regular recordings by the AEF Band. So, both live and recorded use of the landline by the AEF Band was out. This left the possibility of using recordings made in Paris, but because of the uncertain flying conditions at the time (recordings would have to be sent to England by military transport plane) the arrival of recordings at the BBC in London in time for quality checks and then broadcasting at scheduled times could not be guaranteed. Miller's proposed work schedule, therefore, would have to be abandoned.

On 21 November, Miller and Haynes attended a long meeting at Broadcasting House with Maurice Gorham and Major Hayes (deputizing for Colonel Niven, who was away in France doing valuable

* The Olympia Theatre (one of the largest in Paris) and the Palais de Glace were among several theatres and clubs which had been requisitioned by the military authorities for entertaining troops.

field research into reception and audience reaction to the AEF Programme) to discuss what to do next. Privately, Major Hayes shared the BBC's doubts about the practicability of the Band operating from Paris, but in view of General Barker's official request for the Band something would have to be worked out.

The transfer of the AEF Band would obviously have no advantages for the BBC, who were already well served by the Band's broadcasts in England. However, Gorham went on record as saying that it fully appreciated General Barker's reasons for wanting the Band in Paris, and was willing to do whatever it could as long as the Band's broadcasts were not lost to the AEF Programme. What General Barker's reasons were for wanting the Band in Paris are not recorded, but they were probably connected with a US Army ban at the time on civilian entertainers from America performing in Paris following complaints from troops near the front lines that all the shows were in Paris. To make matters worse, British artists were appearing in ENSA shows in Paris, as were French stars such as Maurice Chevalier (who had been in France throughout the Occupation), and General Barker was no doubt anxious to secure American entertainment for American troops who made up the vast majority of Allied servicemen in Paris.

Miller suggested an alternative arrangement, whereby he would take fifty-one members of his unit to Paris for periods of six weeks and before going they would pre-record enough programmes to keep the AEFP schedule going while they were away, including travelling time. This was exactly the plan proposed by Miller and Colonel Kirby the previous August, and rejected by the BBC. Now, in the face of the request from General Barker, the BBC had no alternative but to agree – pre-recordings and all. At last, Major Miller had got what he wanted.

Next day, a telephone conference between Gorham, Hayes and Miller in London and General Barker in Versailles was fixed up and the revised proposal was put to the General. He accepted the plan and expressed his gratification that his request could be met without affecting the Band's services to the AEF Programme. He was asked to send a formal SHAEF request for the six weeks visit, and Gorham explained that despite the six weeks pre-recordings the BBC still hoped to get some programmes by the Band from France and suggested that SHAEF also ask for the BBC's balance engineer Teddy Gower to go with the Band to Paris. Gower had worked on all the Band's broadcasts so far and the BBC was anxious that the quality of any output from France should be maintained. At that time the AEFP still had only one engineer on the Continent who was already fully employed, not necessarily just in Paris.

It was finally agreed that the Band would record thirty hours of programmes – i.e., six weeks' (sixty-six programmes: twelve and a half hours) programmes, plus reserve recordings, between 27 November and 15 December, in addition to keeping up their regular live schedule during this period, and be ready to move to the Continent on or after 16 December. SHAEF would be responsible for the Band's transportation, billeting, etc., and Haynes would go to Paris as soon as possible to arrange the details with General Barker's Executive Officer, Major May. Only one visit of six weeks was agreed: by the end of that time the technical resources might exist in Paris to enable the Band to stay there and yet maintain their contribution to the AEF Programme. If not, they would return to England and record more. Teddy Gower would go with the Band as a civilian technician with officer status.

The plan would involve an exceptional amount of recording in a very short period and the BBC feared that they would not have enough blank recording discs for the job. However, Miller was nothing if not resourceful, and he and Haynes managed to secure enough discs from AFN and ABSIE (where an old friend of the Major's, Oliver Nichol, came to the rescue) which combined with those the BBC could spare from its strained resources would be enough to finish the job.

The only loss to the AEF Programme by the Band's absence in Paris would be that some of the programmes to be pre-recorded by the full Band would be without an audience (as they would probably have to be recorded in the Co-Partners Hall at Bedford), although as the Band was to continue with most of its Tuesday and Friday appearances at the Queensberry Club one wonders why all the full Band programmes couldn't have been recorded there. Gorham thought, however, that the lack of an audience in some programmes would be offset if broadcasts from Paris with audiences of combat troops could be obtained and perhaps used instead of some of the pre-recordings.

One programme he was particularly anxious to obtain while the Band was in Paris was a Christmas Day special, when he hoped to get the use of the landline for a special live concert in a troop theatre. He had received a request from the Home Service programme planners who wanted a contribution from the AEF Programme to be included in the Home schedules on Christmas Day: the idea was for such a programme to be offered to the American networks and to Canada via shortwave, so that they could join the troops in their Christmas listening and the AEFP could say to the troops, 'the folks at home now join us', thus providing a Christmas link between the soldiers overseas and their families at home. At Gorham's request, Miller promised to consider it as a prior commitment and the programme was eventually incorporated into *The AEF Christmas Show* on Christmas night – although, in the event, without Glenn Miller.

Back at Bedford, Miller had already put the proposal to pre-record six weeks' extra programmes as well as keeping up the normal live broadcasting schedule to the musicians and they were told the decision was up to them. Although it would involve them in three or four times their normal amount of playing they agreed unanimously – just to get to Paris! Despite the war and all its shortages and deprivations, Paris still cast its traditional spell.

Besides their broadcasts in the AEF Programme, the Band and its smaller bands were also heard at this period in an American Forces Network series for troops in hospital called *Visiting Hour* on Wednesday afternoons from two o'clock till three. The Band broadcast twice in the series (on 15 and 22 November) each time playing the whole hour. They were probably broadcast live from Bedford, with Jerry Gray conducting the full AEF Band on the 15th. Each programme opened with several numbers by the full Band, followed by two or three by each of the Swing Sextet, the *Strings With Wings* and the American Dance Band, and finished with a full Band medley and a closing instrumental number.

Once the Band's visit to Paris had been finally agreed to on Wednesday 22 November, arrangements for the intensive recording project were put in hand, and the work began on the 25th – two days earlier than originally planned. It was also completed ahead of schedule.

The recordings were made in London as usual over the landline from Bedford, with the Band and the various smaller bands playing in the Co-Partners Hall, although some of the programmes by the full Band were recorded at the Queensberry Club during the Band's regular Tuesday and Friday visits there which continued for most of this period. Altogether, the radio schedule called for a total of sixty-six programmes for the six weeks the Band would be away. They were:

  12 by the full AEF Band
  12 by the American Dance Band (*The Swing Shift*)
  12 by the Strings With Wings
  18 by the Swing Sextet (*The Uptown Hall*)
   6 by Sergeant Johnny Desmond
   6 by Private First Class Jack Rusin (*Piano Playtime*)

In addition, a number of reserve programmes were also recorded, equalling a further two weeks' airtime* and some of these were broadcast as well making a total of 75 actually used on the air. These programmes were recorded over a period of just eighteen days and during this time twenty-seven scheduled live broadcasts were played as well, making a grand total of 115 programmes in eighteen days. It was an intensive and sustained effort which few bands in history have ever had to undertake, averaging eight programmes a day sometimes from early morning till late at night, with no days off and several trips to London as well, and sometimes made worse by the fact that now and again a disc would turn out to be faulty and an entire programme would have to be done all over again.

On the first day (Saturday 25 November) three shows were recorded by the full Band and three by the Strings with Wings; in addition to the recordings were the regular live broadcasts by the American Dance Band at 3 pm and Mel Powell's Swing Sextet at 6.15.

Four Johnny Desmond programmes were recorded on the 26th, but that afternoon Glenn Miller went off to make a brief appearance at a public concert in Bedford's Granada Cinema. The concert was called a 'Carnival of Music' and was organized for Allied servicemen and women by the Special Services Section of the Eighth Air Force Service Command in aid of the Allied Prisoners of War Relief Fund. Judging from photographs of the audience wearing their overcoats it must have been a rather cold day! Comedian Vic Oliver appeared in the show, but most of the programme consisted of music by four Eighth Air Force dance bands – the 'Yanks', the 'Gremlins', the 'Continentals' and the 'Hi-Flyers'. Compère of the show was Lieutenant-Colonel Ben Lyon (the comedian and film star), public relations chief of the Eighth Air Force, and he persuaded Miller to appear at the concert and conduct the combined bands in the finale of 'The

---

* A total of eighty-eight programmes, not 129 as has often been stated elsewhere.

Army Air Corps Song', 'The Star Spangled Banner' and 'God Save The King'.

Haynes, meanwhile had flown over to Paris to arrange with Major May and the Special Service Officers there for billets and concert venues for the Band's visit in December. His stay in Paris was to give him a foretaste of the conditions they would all have to face in the French capital. Although Paris had been liberated from the Germans three months previously conditions were still very far from back to normal. It was effectively 'occupied' by the American Army: their headquarters units were scattered all over the city, they had requisitioned practically all the hotels and American troops and vehicles were everywhere. Almost the only transport for civilians was bicycles. There was little war damage, as the Germans had withdrawn without defending the city. The weather was very cold and there was no heating and no hot water in the Hotel Bellevue, where Haynes was billeted. But he was able to eat well at the SHAEF Officers Mess at the Hotel Crillon where the best French food was being served.

He flew to Paris from Bovingdon on Saturday morning, 25 November, and after lunch with Major May (General Barker's Executive Officer) at SHAEF Headquarters at Versailles, he obtained the necessary military orders to requisition a hotel in Paris for the Band's billet. On the Sunday, after some sightseeing, he went to the US Army Special Services office and met Lieutenant Gene Jerowski, with whom he was to plan a schedule of concerts and hospital appearances by the Band in the Paris area starting on 16 December. That evening and all the next day they worked on the schedule, but they also managed to fit in visits to a show for American troops starring Maurice Chevalier, and the famed Folies Bergère. On Tuesday, the 28th, Haynes looked at about a dozen hotels in his quest for a billet for the Band and finally found one in the Montmartre. On the 29th, Major May approved all his arrangements and next day he delivered the SHAEF billeting order to the hotel – the small, fifty-room Hotel des Olympiades at 22 Square Clignancourt, and arranged for buses and a staff car to be made available for transporting the band while they were in Paris. He was now ready to return to Bedford.

On the morning of the 30th, however, he unexpectedly met Colonel Baessell from Milton Ernest, who was on one of his frequent trips to the French capital, and the Colonel took him on a tour of expensive perfume shops and then to lunch at the exclusive Raphäel Hotel (reserved for Generals and VIPs!). That evening, he again met the Colonel and his pilot, Flight-Officer John R. S. Morgan, and after dining at the Crillon they went to a spectacular show at the Casino de Paris. Next morning, Colonel Baessell took Lieutenant Haynes on another luxurious shopping spree, and lunch at the Raphäel ('nothing but the best', noted Haynes). That afternoon he reported to the Air Transport Command only to find on arrival at Orly Airfield (which had been badly damaged by Allied bombing and not yet repaired) that all flights back to England were grounded by bad weather, so he returned to Paris for the night and flew back to Bovingdon on the first 'SHAEF Shuttle' on Saturday morning. He arrived back at Bedford in the late afternoon and met Major Miller at the Officers Club at Milton Ernest Hall where over a late dinner he gave Miller all the details of the arrangements he had made in Paris. Major Miller seemed satisfied and told Lieutenant Haynes that the Band had been working day and night on the pre-recordings so that the Paris trip could go ahead.

The Band was almost halfway through its marathon pre-recording project. Throughout this period it had also kept up its scheduled live broadcasts with one curious exception – there was no AEF Band broadcast on Tuesday evening, 5 December, although the Band *did* play at the Queensberry Club that night. Perhaps there was a transmitter breakdown. Their half hour on the air was filled by commercial gramophone records, including some by the pre-war Glenn Miller Band. Even more curious is that, although Haynes mentions in his diary 'a three-hour session recording for later broadcasts', no trace of any recordings on that day remain in the radio archives: they may well have been programmes which were subsequently never broadcast as the Activities list for that day also includes two 'Reserve records' by the full Band.

On Friday, the 8th, the Band did not make the usual journey to the Queensberry Club: *Moonlight Serenade* was broadcast that evening from Bedford.

The marathon series of pre-recordings was finally completed on 12 December, three days earlier than originally planned. That day, the full Band went to London for its last show at the Queensberry Club until its return from Paris. As things turned out it was to be its last show ever at the Queensberry Club, and the AEF Band broadcast that evening was the last live broadcast by any of the Miller units before they left for the Continent. It was also the last time that Glenn Miller ever conducted his American Band of the AEF.

It appears from the radio archives that the last pre-recordings of all (both made on Tuesday the 12th) were a *Swing Shift* programme by the American Dance Band (actually broadcast on Thursday the 14th) and an AEF Band *Moonlight Serenade* (broadcast on the 15th).*

It is not clear whether these were played at Bedford or in London, but as the Band went to the Queensberry Club that day it seems likely that the recordings were made there, especially as two extra recordings had already been scheduled at the Queensberry for that afternoon from four o'clock till five after the usual two o'clock rehearsal. According to the radio archives, these recordings were both to be *Swing Shift* programmes, but it is likely that in the event they were the *Swing Shift* and *Moonlight Serenade* referred to above, especially as only one and not two *Swing Shifts* from this date were subsequently broadcast.

The AEF Band broadcast that evening had an unexpected guest star – the American tenor Morton Downey. The finale to the programme was the first broadcast of a new Jerry Gray arrangement, perhaps the most exciting number the AEF Band ever played: an eight-minute version of the well-known Russian traditional song 'The Cossack Patrol', also known as 'Meadowlands' or, as announced by Glenn Miller on this occasion, 'The Red Cavalry March'. From quiet beginnings by muted trumpets, it gradually built up to a rousing swing arrangement for the whole orchestra, including the strings, gently subsiding at the end to the muted trumpets that began the piece as the Cossacks ride off into the distance, while in a novel interlude in the middle Bernie Privin (trumpet) and Peanuts Hucko (clarinet) joined the rhythm section in a little 'jam session' improvising around the theme. The whole thing was a masterpiece of 'orchestral swing' arranging, especially considering how short is the original theme.

The broadcast concluded with the Band's version of 'Stomping At The Savoy' instead of the usual signature tune 'Moonlight Serenade': how ironic that Miller's last broadcast should not sign off with his own theme, so indelibly associated with him.

After the broadcast, the Marquis of Queensberry gave a farewell dinner for the whole Band at Kettner's Restaurant.

---

* Only the AEF Band recording is given in the Activities list, which doesn't say *where* it was recorded.

Later, the Band went back to Bedford but Miller, Haynes and Dudley stayed at the Mount Royal.

They had all had a gruelling two and a half weeks getting the extra eight weeks' programmes in the 'can' in addition to all their regular live broadcasts and were eagerly looking forward to the trip over to Paris. 'One of the few times that Glenn showed any real appreciation and warmth to the Band,' recalls Bob Ripley, 'was when he commended us and thanked us for the hard job we had done getting those extra programmes recorded before we left England. Just as we were getting ready to leave he said he wanted to thank the Band for the way we got through that – he said it was "a good deal". I remember him saying those words – it was "a good deal" – and that was as much as he could say in the way of commendation to the Band. It was one of the few times he seemed human – the other was when he met us in Scotland on the *Queen Elizabeth*. He was very reserved and seemed to find it difficult to warm up and become very close and friendly with almost anybody. I suppose there were a few fellows, perhaps two or three, in the Band with whom he had a more friendly relationship, but he was pretty much his own man – he was the boss, he was the top officer in the organization and he did keep a certain distance from most of us.

'Once he got over to the Continent he wanted to take small groups of musicians as close up to the front as he could get – he wanted to play for the guys that were getting killed, as he put it. So he had a large sound truck fitted out while we were in Bedford with broadcasting equipment with two huge loudspeakers on top of it facing in opposite directions and all set up for microphones, and he was going to take these little units up there and have them play and be broadcast to the guys right up at the front. This was his ultimate sense of what he should be doing for the war effort but of course it never happened because when he was lost there was nobody else who was very interested in doing that sort of thing, so it just died on the vine right there! But it just indicates how serious he was and how deeply he felt about his mission in the war effort. I don't think he would have taken any string players up there – it would just have been small combos of the jazz fellows. None the less, it was an uncomfortable feeling for all of us.'

CHAPTER FIFTEEN

Major Miller flies to Paris and disappears en route – The Band's arrival in Paris – BBC crisis over the Band's broadcasts – The Band's first concert in Paris – Major Miller posted 'missing' – *The AEF Christmas Show* – The Band carries on without Major Miller

In Bedford the Band began to pack up ready to leave for Paris on Saturday the 16th. Not all the Unit was to go, however: only the Band, the singers, Jerry Gray, Paul Dudley and other essential personnel (a total of fifty-one) were scheduled to make the six-week trip, leaving ten* men at Bedford to await the Band's return at the end of January. Eventually, nine enlisted men and one officer remained behind at Bedford (according to the Activities list); the officer was probably Lieutenant Paul Morden, referred to by Haynes later in his Diary.

Maurice Gorham recalled in *Sound and Fury*:

I first became friendly with Glenn over this Paris trip. When SHAEF turned down his Paris project he came back with a new scheme: he would pre-record all his scheduled programmes for the period of his absence, and then if we couldn't get regular lines to Paris by the time the pre-recordings were running out, he would come back.

This seemed to me a workable scheme and I said so, much to his surprise; I think by that time he thought we were all against him, SHAEF, BBC, and AFN. Anyway, we went into it carefully and I said we could work it without losing any of his programmes for the AEFP and we would do our best to get the lines organized so that once he got there he could stay.

He was very grateful to me, ironically enough. As he was leaving my office after we had fixed it all up I said to him, 'Now, Glenn, there's only one more thing. For heaven's sake make sure the boat they put you on is seaworthy. We don't want to lose you all.' He smiled and said, 'You don't have to worry. You'll have the recordings anyway'.

* Sergeant Broderick Crawford had been detached from the unit soon after arriving at Bedford, thus reducing the EM complement to sixty-one.

In view of Major Miller's fate a few days later, Gorham's comment about a seaworthy boat was all the more ironic. But they did not go by boat. However, it was far from the only ironic coincidence associated with the Major's departure – on 4 December he had written to his brother Herb in America, 'By the time you receive this letter we shall be in Paris, barring of course a nose-dive into the Channel.'*

The original plan was for Haynes to go on ahead by the 'SHAEF Shuttle' to Paris from Bovingdon on Wednesday 13 December, and for Miller to follow with the Band on Saturday the 16th in three C-47 planes of the Air Transport Command. Then the plans were changed, first by Miller and then by the weather.

Major Miller decided that he would go on ahead himself, leaving Haynes to take the Band over on Saturday the 16th. Haynes' orders were then cancelled and fresh orders dated 12 December were issued by SHAEF (Rear) to Major Glenn Miller:

1. You will proceed by military aircraft (ATC) on or about 16 December 1944 from present station to SUPREME HQ AEF MAIN on the Continent to carry out the instructions of the AC of S, G-1, SUPREME HQ AEF, and on completion thereof return to present station.
2. Travel on military aircraft is directed. Baggage allowance is limited to sixty five (65) pounds. [The AC of S, G-1, was General Barker.]

Miller, however, was anxious to leave for Paris as soon as possible. On the 13th, he was in London with Haynes and Dudley, but the weather was very bad and all ATC flights from Bovingdon were grounded for the day. Major Miller, hoping to get away next day, and Dudley stayed overnight at the Mount Royal, but Haynes returned to Bedford in the staff car. The fog was so thick in London that bus conductors were walking in front of the buses with torches and Haynes' drive back to Bedford, normally an hour and fifteen minutes run, took four hours. On the Thursday he had lunch in the Officers Club at Milton Ernest Hall with Colonel Baessell who said he was flying to Paris the next day and offered Haynes a lift. When Haynes told Colonel Baessell that Miller was going on ahead instead of him Baessell suggested that Miller fly over with him on the Friday as he knew the ATC planes were still grounded.

* The original letter is on display in the US Air Force Museum at the Wright-Patterson Air Force Base, Dayton, Ohio, USA.

They telephoned Major Miller in London, who confirmed that there were still no flights to Paris and was only too pleased to accept the Colonel's offer of a lift. Haynes drove to London and took Major Miller back to Bedford, but Dudley stayed on at the Mount Royal against Major Miller's advice because of the V-2 rockets then dropping all over the city.

On Friday 15 December the weather in the Bedford area improved a little and shortly after lunch at the Officers Club at Milton Ernest Hall Haynes saw Miller and Baessell off from Twinwood Farm in the now-famous Norseman aircraft piloted by Flight-Officer John Morgan.*

Three days later, after being delayed by bad weather Haynes took the Band over to Paris in the C-47s, to find that Major Miller hadn't arrived.

He never saw him again.

The night before he took off for Paris Major Miller had dinner at the Officers Club at Milton Ernest Hall with Haynes and Colonel Baessell who arranged to telephone Miller early next morning as soon as he had clearance for the flight to Paris. After dinner Miller and Haynes played a few games of poker with the Colonel and two of the many officers they had become friendly with at Milton Ernest Hall – Major Bill Koch and Warrant Officer Neal Earlywine. Then they drove back to the ARC Officers Club in Bedford where Miller hoped to get a good night's sleep before the flight to Paris next day. Back at the ARC Club, however, he wanted to stay up and talk and he and Haynes sat in front of the fire till 3 am discussing their post-war plans and the new Band that Miller intended to form once he was back in civilian life and who he hoped to have in it, including many of the musicians then with him in the AEF Band.

Next morning, Friday the 15th, Haynes was woken by a telephone call from Colonel Baessell at Milton Ernest Hall: the weather was still very bad and he couldn't get clearance for the flight that morning, but the forecast was better for later on and he hoped to take off in the afternoon. He suggested that Haynes and Miller drive out to the Hall and wait for the weather to improve.

After breakfast Miller packed his bag and he and Haynes sat around in the Club for a couple of hours reading the morning papers and then set off in their staff car to Milton Ernest Hall, calling at the

* Ironically, that very night listeners to the AEF Programme heard Major Miller introducing as usual his regular *Moonlight Serenade* – the programme they had recorded three days earlier. By the time of this broadcast, he was almost certainly already dead.

men's billet in Ashburnham Road on the way. At the Hall Colonel Baessell told them he had had a telephone call from the pilot, Flight-Officer Morgan, at Station 595 (the 1st Strategic Air Depot at Troston, near Bury St Edmunds) to say that the weather was improving and he would know shortly after noon if he had got clearance for the flight. During lunch the Colonel had another call from Morgan to say that he had received clearance and would pick them up at Twinwood Farm within an hour.

After lunch the three men set out in the staff car for the airfield. Major Koch and Warrant Officer Earlywine came out to see them off, and after some kidding from Earlywine and Koch to look out for those madamoiselles on the Rue de la Paix Haynes drove them to Twinwood Farm, stopping on the way at General Goodrich's quarters for Colonel Baessell to pay a quick call on the General who was confined to bed after a heart attack and was due to return to the USA the following week. At the airfield they parked the car next to the control tower. The rain had now eased to a steady drizzle but there was still solid cloud at about two hundred feet so they sat in the car to await Morgan's arrival. After an hour there was still no sign of him, so Colonel Baessell got out of the car and went up into the control tower to telephone the airfield Morgan was flying from, returning to tell the others that Morgan had taken off nearly an hour ago in a c-64 Norseman and should be at Twinwood any minute. Major Miller got out of the car and stood looking up at the sky and wiping the drizzle off his glasses with his handkerchief. After a few minutes he was joined by Baessell and Haynes. It was so cold that Haynes walked over to look at the thermometer on the wall of the control tower: it was 34 degrees. The three men wrapped their coat collars tightly round their necks to keep out the chill and the rain, and hardly had Major Miller expressed doubts that Morgan would find the airfield at all, saying 'Haynsie, even the birds are grounded today', than they heard the sound of an approaching plane. Although they couldn't see it they heard it pass over the airfield, turn round and come back, and a few minutes later it was down on the concrete runway.

They drove over towards the plane and Morgan taxied along the runway to meet them. With the motor still running he opened the door, explained that he had run into heavy squalls which made him late and said the weather was supposed to be clearing over the Continent. Colonel Baessell handed up his luggage (which included a case of empty champagne bottles he wanted to exchange for full ones in Paris), Haynes passed Miller's B-4 bag into the plane and the two men climbed aboard, Baessell taking the co-pilot's seat and Miller a bucket seat behind the Colonel with his back to the side of the plane. As Haynes waved goodbye he shouted to Major Miller, 'Happy landings and good luck – I'll see you in Paris tomorrow' and Major Miller replied, 'Thanks Haynsie, we may need it'.* Haynes closed the door and fastened the catch and stepped away from the plane as Morgan revved up and taxied down the runway. In less than a minute the plane rose out of sight – it was 1.45 pm and if all went according to plan it should arrive in Paris in about three hours time.

Early on Saturday morning Haynes and the fifty-one men destined for Paris piled into the Band's buses for the two-hour journey to the ATC base at Bovingdon airfield. It was still cold and raining and all planes were grounded, so in early afternoon they went back to Bedford. On Sunday morning they tried again, but still the planes were grounded and Haynes learnt that nothing had taken off from Bovingdon for the last six days. Again they hung around till noon with coffee and doughnuts, trying to keep warm. Then it was back to Bedford, but this time Haynes arranged that if the weather improved enough next day the three C-47s would fly to Twinwood Farm and pick up the Band there.

Monday morning, 18 December, was bright and clear and the rain had stopped. At ten o'clock Haynes received a telephone call from the Flight Control Officer at Bovingdon to say that the planes were on their way. As the Band drove in the buses to Twinwood Farm airfield the planes were circling to land. But here another hitch delayed them – Peanuts Hucko discovered he had left his clarinet at the billet so a truck was hastily obtained and he went back to get it. After all the frustrations of the last few days Haynes was furious. 'Haynes could have killed him!' recalled one of the musicians. They finally took off for Paris at half past eleven and after a smooth flight in bright sunshine they landed at Orly airfield at 1.45.

Everyone had expected Miller to be at the airfield to meet them, but there was no sign of him, nor of the buses to take them to their billet at the Hotel des Olympiades which Haynes had

* Paul Dudley later wrote (in *Bomblight Serenade*) 'Lieutenant Haynes heard Glenn ask, "Where are the parachutes?" Then, Baessell's bluff reply, "What the hell, Miller, do you want to live forever?"' (Baessell's favourite expression). Curiously, this famous and oft-quoted exchange does not appear in Haynes' Diary.

arranged for on his visit to Paris three weeks before, despite a coded message from Bovingdon that the Band were on their way. Haynes went off to check at the Transportation Desk, but discovered that Miller's plane had not been logged in* and in the light of this recalled with some concern what he had been told at Bovingdon the day before – that no planes had taken off from there for the last six days, which included Friday the 15th. He telephoned the Transport Officer at the us Army's Seine Base Section who hadn't heard from Miller and therefore hadn't sent the buses to pick them up.

Haynes next telephoned Major May at shaef in Versailles: he hadn't heard from Major Miller either and in fact had been expecting Haynes since Friday the 15th. While Haynes was explaining to May that Miller and Baessell had taken off from Twinwood Farm last Friday, General Barker's voice came on the line and told him to get the men to the billet and then get a car from the Seine Base and get over to shaef as soon as possible; meanwhile he and May would do some checking up.

Haynes returned to the Band, the men unloaded the equipment from the aircraft and went off to the arc for doughnuts and coffee, while Haynes got back on the phone to try and find out what had gone wrong. He tried the Raphäel Hotel and the Ritz Hotel, both of which were requisitioned by the us Army and at both of which Colonel Baessell was well known, then the billeting officer at Seine Base and finally Lieutenant Jerowski at Special Services with whom Haynes had arranged the Band's forthcoming concert schedule. None of them had heard from either Baessell or Miller, and Haynes became convinced that they had not reached Paris, although of course they could have landed somewhere else and in the confusion following the German attack in the Ardennes two days earlier been unable to get to Paris. Still, it was now three days since they were last heard of and no-one in Paris seems to have known they were coming.

After arriving at Orly, the Band had a long and miserable wait in the open. The airfield, which still bore scars from Allied bombing before the Liberation, was a scene of mud and confusion with a background of steadily worsening news of the German advance on the American front in the Ardennes. It was bitterly cold and while Haynes was away on the telephone there was

* Its destination had actually been the atc airfield at Villacoublay, Paris, not Orly.

nowhere for the Band to shelter. 'When we finally landed at Orly,' recalled Harry Katzman, 'we got out of the planes with our stuff and there was just nobody to meet us – nobody there, and we were just bitching like hell. It was cold and every time a damn plane took off the wind would blow, cold as hell. Nothing to drink, nothing to eat, and nowhere to go to the bathroom or anything like that – just right out in the middle of a field. Of course, we had no idea, really, what had happened in the interim, and after about – it seemed like an hour and a half or two hours – there comes Don Haynes, and I don't know whether he didn't get the instructions right or whether he couldn't get the buses to take us to the quarters where we eventually wound up, but we finally got in the buses after all that time. We were just absolutely freezing, it was so cold and windy. It didn't dawn upon us that Miller was lost or anything. We just assumed he was doing something else in Paris with regard to the Band. But when we were in the bus Haynes told everybody to get down in the orderly room downstairs when we arrived at the hotel – "I want everybody there". Of course, we heard about the Battle of the Bulge through some of the people at the airfield. We finally arrived at the Olympiades Hotel – it was in the Montmartre section, not very far from the Sacré Cœur. Then Haynes told us that Miller hadn't been heard from and was presumed to be lost but everybody's looking for him. Of course, it seemed like one of those statements that was not the real truth – if a man is missing for three or four days, now then he's really lost. His conjecture was that there was a possibility that the plane went down and he was taken prisoner, and they hadn't heard anything at all.

'We were also told not to unpack our gear as we might have to go back to England because the Battle of the Bulge had started and the Germans were a hundred and some odd miles – a hundred and ten miles – from Paris. Of course, as one of the fellows said, you can be sure that if anyone is going to get out it will be the big shots that get out first. At any rate, we didn't even notice how cold it was in the hotel. There was no heat, we were hungry and tired – nothing to eat. The Mess Hall was about a mile or so away – a terrible joint. At any rate, we talked about it and the guys said, "Gee, I hope they find him – you think he's lost?" But we knew (as far as *I* felt at that time) that it was the death knell of the organization, that it would never be the same again, and I was proved to be right.'

'When Glenn wasn't there to meet us,' said Carmen Mastren, 'I knew something was wrong. He had gone on ahead to make arrangements for us and I knew he would accomplish what he started out to do.'

While the men dumped their duffle bags in their new quarters and headed for the nearest café (they hadn't had a meal since breakfast) or went sight-seeing on the Metro, Haynes and Dudley got a car from Seine Base and drove out to Versailles and reported to General Barker at about six o'clock. He and Major May had been busy telephoning bases on both sides of the Channel and discovered one significant piece of information: a single-engined aircraft had been logged out over the south coast of England across the Channel in the general direction of Paris but had not been reported as crossing the French coast. Nor had any Allied anti-aircraft guns been in action in the area, thus cutting out the possibility of the plane having been accidentally shot down. While Haynes and Dudley were with him General Barker got through to General Goodrich in England to ask if Baessell was there, for he had been due back at Milton Ernest on Sunday 17 December. Goodrich, obviously annoyed, said that Baessell hadn't returned and he hadn't heard from him, and at Barker's invitation Haynes brought General Goodrich up to date on what had happened. General Goodrich was even more infuriated to learn that Flight-Officer Morgan had taken a single-engined aircraft with no de-icing equipment out over the Channel in such conditions. Nevertheless, he promised to have a search made after daybreak next morning. He thought that the plane must have iced up and gone into the Channel, but it was possible they might have landed at some out of the way spot and been unable to let anyone know. They arranged to speak again next day.

The situation now began to look very serious and as General Barker put the phone down he turned to Haynes and said, 'It looks very bad, Lieutenant, I'm afraid Major Miller has had it.'

After dinner at the SHAEF Officers Mess with General Barker and Major May, Haynes and Dudley drove back to Paris with heavy hearts and were billeted at the Hotel des Etats-Unis, near the Opéra. The two men had been close friends of Major Glenn Miller for some years, especially in the Service, and were beginning to have to come to terms with the fact that they might never see him again. Having your friends and colleagues killed or taken prisoner was common enough in war but it was much less likely in a non-combatant unit and thus much harder to take. After telephoning Sergeant Sanderson at the Hotel des Olympiades to tell him what little they knew and asking him to pass it on to the Band, they turned in, but their first night in Paris was sleepless, such had been the unexpected and depressing turn of events.

With mounting apprehension Haynes spent the next few days in Paris in frequent journeys to SHAEF or waiting for news at the end of a telephone. There was a military curfew in force – at 6 am on the morning of the 16th the German Army had launched a surprise major attack, the Battle of the Bulge, in terrible weather on a thinly held part of the American front in the Ardennes area of Luxembourg, and for nearly a week made extensive and alarming advances against the American First Army. The bad weather prevented the full weight of Allied air power being used against the Germans and the entire Allied position was seriously threatened. To make matters worse German soldiers dressed in American uniforms were reported to be active in Paris. First thing on Tuesday morning, Haynes obtained Class B passes for the Band from the Army which allowed them to be absent from their billet only between 6 am and 11 pm. He also got them Metro tickets, and having been issued with a staff car and a French driver by the Army to use while he was in Paris he set off for Versailles, stopping at the men's billet on the way to hand out their passes and Metro tickets. At SHAEF he found that Major May had already been on the telephone to England three times that morning and the Air Ministry were checking for crashes at RAF airfields. At Major May's request Haynes stayed at SHAEF all day where reports did come in but told them nothing. Back in Paris in the evening Haynes and Dudley met up again with Morton Downey at the Ritz Hotel and, later, with William Randolf Hearst, Jr., war correspondent in the ETO for the Hearst newspapers in America, who when Haynes told him what had happened promised to pass the word round unofficially among the other correspondents in case they could pick up any leads which the military authorities could follow up.

Early next morning (Wednesday the 20th), Haynes again telephoned Major May but there was still no news – indeed, he and General Barker had practically given up hope and said that if no trace of the plane or its occupants were reported that day an official casualty report would have to be made the following morning. This meant that Major Miller's wife Helen would have to be informed that her husband was 'missing', but May promised that she would be told before any announcement was given to the press. In the afternoon Haynes went to the Palais de Glace, where the Army Special Services had arranged for the Band's first concert the next evening, to check up on the p.a. system and the stage set-up and found that it was colder inside the former ice rink than it was in the street outside. Afterwards at the Hotel des Olympiades he worked out with the Band a programme for the concert, with Jerry Gray conducting the first two-thirds and Ray McKinley the last part. In the evening he telephoned Major May once more – there was still no news, but he managed to persuade the Major to postpone the casualty report for one more day in the desperate hope that Miller might turn up.

It was still freezing cold on the 21st and again Haynes and Dudley drove to SHAEF to confer with General Barker and Major May. Still they had heard nothing of Major Miller or his companions or even of any wreckage, and the General said it boiled down to three possibilities: they might have strayed over enemy territory and been shot down or taken prisoner, crashed in a remote place and not yet been found, or gone down in the Channel. Sympathetic as he was, General Barker said that the casualty report *must* be released next morning and promised that he and Major May would see them at the Palais de Glace concert that evening.

When the news of Glenn Miller's disappearance reached the BBC it was more than a personal shock to those who knew him and had worked with him. It presented them with what Maurice Gorham later described as the Programme's 'worst crisis'. There were several reasons for this. First, the BBC was broadcasting the pre-recorded programmes by the AEF Band which were all announced by Major Glenn Miller, and as his disappearance had not yet been publicly announced by SHAEF it would have to continue broadcasting these programmes until SHAEF announced he was missing. After the SHAEF announcement it would still have to broadcast the pre-recorded programmes as scheduled but would have first to remove his voice from the recordings. But it would need to know exactly when to do this otherwise it might reveal he was missing before SHAEF announced it officially. And of course he might still turn up. But looking beyond the immediate future, the BBC had to face the possibility that if Major Miller did not turn up the Band might be sent back to the USA or disbanded and so leave the AEF Programme without one of its three house bands (the one with the largest broadcasting schedule of the three) and nearly four hours a week in the programme schedules to be filled in some other way.

Second, and of more pressing concern, was the forthcoming special Christmas Day broadcast, *The AEF Christmas Show*, due to include a live contribution from the AEF Band for which the BBC had at last obtained the use of the only landline from Paris to London. The line was still under the control of the US Army Signal Corps who were operating it for SHAEF and who were extremely unwilling to allow the BBC to use it at all at that time: the German counter-attack in the Ardennes had caused a serious reversal in the Allied military position and for a time it looked as though the Germans might drive through to Antwerp and the Channel coast. In this acute crisis the line would be needed for constant military communications back to England and the USA. Eventually, thanks to the persistence of the AEFP's chief engineer on the Continent, Major Peter Blair, the US Army finally agreed to the BBC having access to the line on Christmas Day for three specified periods only: 2200 hours to 0100 on the 24th/25th for Midnight Mass, 1330 to 1500 for a contribution to the BBC's annual Christmas round-the-world 'hook-up', and 1800 to 2000 for relaying the AEF Band from the Olympia Theatre. Now that the promise of the landline had ensured that the AEF Band's broadcast could go ahead it had been publicized in advance, but Major Miller's disappearance might mean that the AEF Band would not take part after all. It also presented the BBC and particularly producer AC2 Ronnie Waldman, who was in charge of *The AEF Christmas Show* and would be compèring the London end of it, with a more technical problem. Besides the AEF Band relay from Paris, the British and Canadian Bands would be taking part in the show from the Queensberry Club in London, and the complicated cues and switching instructions already worked out between London, Paris, New York and Toronto would probably have to be revised in the light of Miller's disappearance – but strict military security prevented any alterations being notified to the other countries before he was publicly announced 'missing'. And there were only a few days to go before the broadcast!

The BBC was in a difficult position and this was not made any easier when, as the word got around that Major Miller was not with the Band in Paris and there was still no SHAEF announcement, the BBC was accused of hushing it up. As the days went by and there was still nothing official from SHAEF, the BBC had no alternative but to remain silent, while the well-known voice of Major Glenn Miller continued to be heard over the air several times a week as though nothing had happened.

In Paris the men in the Band, still dazed by the disappearance of their leader and commanding officer, were naturally worried that once it became known that Major Miller was missing their families back home would think the whole Band was lost. Luckily, Carmen Mastren recalled, singer Joy Hodges (who was Dudley's wife and was in Paris on a USO tour) was soon to leave for New York and when she got home she managed to call everyone's family and put their minds at rest. 'The Band took it badly,' said Carmen, 'but we knew we would have to carry on and we just hoped they would let Haynes carry on. We felt sure some real corn ball would be put in charge, but it didn't happen. Special Services could really mess things up.'

Meanwhile, there had already been some talk at SHAEF that if Major Miller was not found the Band might be disbanded and the men re-deployed as stretcher-bearers or ambulance drivers, or even sent to the front as infantrymen. The military situation in the Ardennes was worsening almost by the hour as the bad weather prevented the Allied air forces using their full power right up until Christmas Eve to halt the German breakthrough, and the need for more support personnel was growing greater every day. Also, a serious shortage of infantrymen was intensifying owing to heavy American casualties in the Ardennes battle, and even as the Band arrived in Paris SHAEF was making desperate efforts to comb out every fit man from non-combatant units so that they could be sent to the front. The Band's military value, however, as Nat Peck points out, would have been somewhat limited: 'No-one knew how to load a rifle, let alone fire one. We had a certain amount of basic military training, but it was really a joke.' All the same, Nat himself had earned a marksman's badge back at New Haven.

The Band had spent much of its time since arriving in Paris huddled in its billet trying to keep warm and listening to the radio – including the recordings of its own programmes and hoping for news of their missing leader.

'I remember one night,' says Nat Peck, 'we were sitting in the day room listening to the radio. We were all there and a car backfired in the street and Mel Powell jumped up and said, "Kamarad" with his hands in the air! I don't know whether he was serious, or whether he really meant it, but at the time there was a lot of talk about Germans infiltrating and shooting up American soldiers who were walking around alone in Paris and we were issued instructions *never* to leave the hotel alone – always to be accompanied by somebody, and preferably not to leave at all.'

Despite the passes, however, one of the string players was actually arrested by the Military Police: 'Our MPs caught one of our fiddle players – Stanley Harris – one night,' recalls Ray

McKinley, 'and started asking him questions about who was Li'l Abner's sweetheart, and how many home runs did Babe Ruth hit, and all that stuff, to try and trick him. Well, he didn't know any of that stuff, you see, he told them he was a musician, so they said, "Yeah, he's on the level, all right, let him go. He's an American – he's gotta be." He didn't know about the curfew, either.'

The Band's morale was at its lowest ebb. The weather was freezing cold and so was the hotel, the Army food was terrible, the military situation was serious and getting worse all the time, there was the curfew and the danger of German assassination squads, and it became increasingly likely that Major Miller would never be seen again. One of the Band members has recalled that with Miller gone there seemed to be a certain fragmentation of authority in the unit: while he was there he was *the* boss, nobody contradicted him or went over his head, but once he was gone they seemed to acquire several bosses and this was demoralizing for them and gave rise to more frictions than there had been in the past. Also, without Major Miller they didn't know what their future might be. It was a depressing run-up to Christmas.

The Band's first troop concert in the French capital on the evening of Thursday 21 December, at the Palais de Glace, removed for good any ideas the Army might have had for breaking up the Band: the audience reaction was so overwhelming that the Band's value to the troops' morale was recognized as overriding.

The concert was scheduled for eight o'clock but when the Band arrived an hour before curtain time the Palais was already packed with over 5,000 troops, mainly American combat troops on forty-eight hours leave from the front, with a sprinkling of British personnel – an audience 'as enthusiastic as any we had played for since our arrival in the ETO six months ago' commented Haynes. After the concert, General Barker and Major May went backstage to congratulate the assembled Band on its performance and to assure Haynes that if it could fulfil the concert schedule already arranged they would have his complete support. After he had left, Major May told Haynes that the General had been astounded at the Band's performance and the audience reaction and now that he had seen what they could do, even without their leader, the Band would be allowed to carry on.

At SHAEF next morning May showed Haynes the casualty report they had just received from the Eighth Air Force in England, listing Major Miller missing, but Haynes still could not bring himself to believe that Miller was dead. May took him into General

Barker's office where the General told him (Haynes) that he was now in command of the unit. He also said that he would personally see to Haynes' promotion to First Lieutenant, and that came through a few weeks later. He also asked if there was anything the Band needed, so Haynes told him about the bad food the men were getting. Barker called the Army's Seine Base and the next day the Band were assigned to another Mess Hall where the food was better.

While he was at SHAEF Haynes also discovered that an extra man had been posted to the Band and was waiting at SHAEF to join it – none other than Private First Class Bill Conway, formerly one of the singers in the Modernaires vocal group with the pre-war Glenn Miller Band and occasional guitarist in the Band. Major Miller had put in a request for him back at New Haven but Conway was in the Infantry and the requisition had taken all that time to catch up with him. He had been in the thick of the Ardennes battle where his unit had been surrounded by the Germans for a time before being relieved by American tanks and he had come straight from the front to join the Band. Haynes took him back with him to the Hotel des Olympiades where many of the men already knew him from pre-war days, and they were up half the night swapping experiences.

By the end of the week, when intensive enquiries by the military authorities had failed to find any trace of the missing Norseman aircraft or its three occupants, an announcement about Major Miller could be delayed no longer. An official notification had been sent on Wednesday, 20 December, from the Eighth Air Force Service Command HQ at Milton Ernest Hall to General Barker in Versailles confirming that Major Miller was missing and he and his two companions were listed among many others in the Eighth Air Force casualty report as 'Missing in flight, presumed to be lost'. This meant that Mrs Helen Miller in America would have to be informed that her husband was missing, after which it could be announced to the public.

A copy of the Eighth Air Force casualty list arrived at SHAEF on Friday the 22nd, where by now it was common knowledge that Major Miller was missing. Formal confirmation of the news was sent at once to the Headquarters of the US Army in the ETO with a request that an immediate radio casualty report on Major Glenn Miller be sent to the War Department in Washington and suggesting that in view of the forthcoming Christmas Day broadcast and the publicity already given to it in the United

States the news be released to the press at 1800 hours (ETO time) on 24 December, making sure that Mrs Miller was informed first.

Helen Miller, then living at Tenafly, New Jersey, received the customary telegram from the War Department on the morning of the 23rd, and shortly afterwards had a telephone call from General H. H. Arnold (Commanding General of the Army Air Forces), offering condolences. Meanwhile, in Paris the Deputy Director of the SHAEF Public Relations Division, Colonel R. Ernest Dupuy, was organizing a Press Release (Miller was after all, a famous celebrity, not just a Major in the Army Air Forces) announcing Major Miller's disappearance – a brief factual announcement, making it clear that no members of the Band were on the missing aircraft – ready for issue the next day, Christmas Eve.

At 6 pm (London Time) on Sunday 24 December, the Press Release was given to the newspapers and radio organizations. It read:

Major Alton Glenn Miller, director of the famous United States Army Air Forces Band which had been playing in Paris, is reported missing while on a flight from England to Paris. The plane in which he was a passenger left England on December 15 and no trace of it has been found since its take-off.

Major Miller, one of the outstanding orchestra leaders in the United States, lived at Tenafly, New Jersey, where his wife presently resides.

No members of Major Miller's band were with him on the missing plane.

The BBC's AEF Programme was interrupted just after 6 pm with a news flash announcing Major Miller's disappearance. It was also included in the nine o'clock news on the Home Service, as the last item in the news following details of flying bomb attacks on Northern England the previous night:

Major Glenn Miller, the well-known American band leader is reported. missing; he left England by air for Paris nine days ago. Major Glenn Miller came over from the States earlier this year to direct the American Band of the AEF, which has often been heard playing in the Allied Expeditionary Forces Programme of the BBC.

In Paris, the Army Special Services had suspended the Band's concert schedule for the time being after the Palais de Glace show on the 21st owing to the curfew and the risk of German troops operating in Paris in American uniforms, as had already happened in the Ardennes battle areas.

The Band resumed its schedule on Christmas Eve (Sunday) with a concert at the Olympia Theatre in the afternoon and another in the evening.

Christmas Day was a busy day. Early in the morning the entire unit attended a special Mass for Major Glenn Miller at the Madeleine Church in the centre of Paris, arranged two days earlier by Morton Downey. After the Mass the Band had a 10 am rehearsal at the Olympia Theatre, an afternoon concert and a radio recording, and another concert at the Olympia Theatre in the evening, part of which was the special live Christmas broadcast which Maurice Gorham had asked Major Miller to do back in November.

According to the Activities list the afternoon recording was a Christmas broadcast for the BBC, although it was more likely a line test as no trace of such a recording remains in the radio archives. However, in his diary Haynes describes a special five-minute Christmas greeting recorded by the Band and introduced by Dudley and Haynes, for later broadcast in the USA.

The evening broadcast was the Band's contribution to the AEF Programme's live two-hour *AEF Christmas Show* – it played a half-hour stint from 7 to 7.30 (London Time) and the last item in the show just before 8 pm.

Over that Christmas period some of the regular programmes in the AEF Programme were dropped to make way for special Christmas features and Christmas editions of some of the best shows such as *Command Performance*. But the high spot for many listeners on Christmas Day was *The AEF Christmas Show* from 6 pm to 8, devoted entirely to all three Bands of the AEF – the only time they all broadcast together in the same programme.

The first half-hour went to the Canadian Band, the second to the British Band (conducted by its leader Sergeant Eric Robinson as RSM Melachrino was away on Christmas leave), the third to the American Band conducted by Jerry Gray and compèred by Paul Dudley, and the last half hour was a 'combined round-up' of all three Bands ending with the American Band playing 'Oranges and Lemons'. The Canadian and British Bands' contributions also included popular guest stars, among them Cyril Fletcher, Gwen Catley and Teddy Brown and, as planned, the second hour was also broadcast to British listeners to the Home Service. The Canadian and American Bands were relayed by short-wave to Canada and the USA and broadcast live. The American Band's part in the programme was the first live music programme broadcast from Paris to England since the fall of France in 1940. Producer and compère Ronnie Waldman linked the whole show together on the air and after the trials and tribulations of the previous few days the entire broadcast went like clockwork.

The London end of the broadcast came from the Queensberry All-Services Club where the British and Canadian Bands played to a packed audience of servicemen and women. Manager John Harding later recalled an unexpected incident that evening:

When . . . the dramatic message was received at the Club that Major Glenn Miller was reported missing on a flight to Paris, I witnessed the most spontaneous tribute in my forty years' experience. Unrehearsed and unasked, three thousand uniformed men and women in the audience stood up together in silent sympathy for the loss of one who did so much to provide entertainment when and where it was so badly needed.*

The final 'grand round-up' of *The AEF Christmas Show* was given a recorded repeat in the *Morning After* spot in the AEF Programme on Boxing Day and recorded extracts from the show were broadcast in the General Forces Programme on Thursday afternoon, 28 December.

Throughout the last week of December the regular programmes by all the Miller units were broadcast from London as usual in the AEF Programme, using the pre-recordings made in Bedford, except that on Boxing Day the Tuesday evening programme by the full AEF Band was replaced by a gala production entitled *Ali Sadsack and the Forty Quartermasters – an unbelievable pantomime for the AEF* with an all-star cast of AEFP regulars. The Friday evening broadcast by the AEF Band was a recording made on 25 November, with Major Glenn Miller's voice replaced by an announcer.

By this time, following the SHAEF announcement on Christmas Eve, Major Glenn Miller's disappearance had been widely reported in the press (I first saw it in Socialist pundit Hannen Swaffer's column in the *Daily Herald* of all places) and at the end of the week the *Melody Maker*, which had reported so many of the Band's activities in London, gave the story with a front page headline.

* *Star-Spangled Radio.*

The *AEF Radio Times* also printed its own report, together with a photograph of Major Miller taken in the Corn Exchange at Bedford at the Band's first BBC broadcast.

Over in Paris, the Band – free from broadcasting commitments for the time being owing to the pre-recordings they had made in England – were able to concentrate on personal appearances at troop concerts and military hospitals in the Paris area where they were a great success, although some of the evening concerts were cancelled because of the curfew. Conducting was now shared between Ray McKinley and Jerry Gray, and on Saturday afternoon, 30 December, the Band actually played a concert on the lawn at a military hospital in a temperature of 32 degrees.

Throughout the week Haynes remained in close daily touch with Major May, either by telephone or by driving to SHAEF, but the news of the missing Major Glenn Miller was always the same: 'No news'. On the 28th he spent all day at SHAEF completing detailed reports on Major Miller's disappearance, and while there had the first hint that the Band might not return to England after their six-week visit but might stay in Paris indefinitely. On the 29th he unexpectedly met two officers from Milton Ernest Hall on a visit to Paris who confirmed that there had been no trace so far of the missing Norseman or its occupants.

Meanwhile, the battle in the Ardennes had taken a turn for the better. Since the start of the German offensive on the 16th, very bad weather had prevented the Allied air forces from attacking the Germans in full strength, but on the 23rd the weather broke, the Allied air forces seized their opportunity and by Christmas Day the German advance was stopped, and after further heavy fighting they were back where they started by the end of January. The curfew in Paris was lifted and on 29 December the Band resumed its full concert schedule.

Also by 29 December a welcome transformation had suddenly taken place in the availability of the Paris to London landline: after all the difficulties the BBC had encountered in getting the line for the Christmas Day broadcasts Gorham was told that the AEFP could have the use of lines from Paris* at any time of any day without the danger of interruption by the military authorities during a programme. The Christmas Day programme by the AEF Band had shown that the sound quality of the transmissions was

---

* The BBC got their own line fixed up in December and it was probably this that made them independent of the SHAEF Signals link.

good enough for all AEF Programme purposes, both live broadcasts and recordings, including music. This meant that the special New Year's Eve live programme by the Band which Maurice Gorham had told Major Miller he wanted broadcast live from Paris if the line became available could now go ahead, and so, after the 11 pm news headlines on 31 December, the voice of Paul Dudley came over the air once again introducing a forty-minute programme from the Olympia Theatre packed to capacity with Allied troops.

Although Major Miller was lost, his objective was not. Even without him, the Band was able to carry on just as he would have wanted, bringing to the troops 'a hunk of home'. It was to continue its work for another seven months until the AAF called it back to America in July 1945.

CHAPTER SIXTEEN

New recordings from Paris – The Band's hardships in Paris –
Rumours about Major Miller – Haynes returns to England – A
new radio schedule – The concert at the Opéra – Recordings at the
Jazz Club Français – More changes to the radio schedule – The
Band goes to the south of France – The end of the war

From London the AEF Programme continued the full
broadcasting schedule of all the Miller units without interruption
using the pre-recordings made before the Band left England.
These pre-recordings lasted for nine weeks, until Friday 9
February, which was longer than originally planned when the
Paris trip was first arranged. However, there was one exception
to this – by the middle of January the AEF Programme began
broadcasting new recordings of the full AEF Band made in
London over the line from Paris.

Only seven of the English pre-recordings by the Band were
actually broadcast after Major Miller's disappearance was announced. These pre-recordings were all compèred by Miller
himself and after his disappearance was announced his voice
could no longer be included on the air. This meant that either the
programmes would have to be re-recorded (i.e. copied, or
dubbed) with Major Miller's voice replaced by someone else who
was readily available in London, or the recordings would have to
be played on the air and faded out or cut as Major Miller was due
to speak and his voice replaced by an announcer in the studio, as
seems to have been done with the 2 January broadcast when
Major Miller's voice was replaced by that of AEFP announcer
Sergeant Keith Jamieson. This required split-second timing and
was only second best,* although as this particular programme
had been recorded on 25 November without an audience the

* As all recording was on discs in those days, editing was more difficult than it
is today, using tape.

voice substitution was easier than it would have been if the programme had included applause as some of the pre-recordings probably did.

Starting on 16 January, therefore, the AEF Programme began broadcasting new recordings from Paris and for the next five weeks these alternated with the UK pre-recordings, the last of which was heard on Tuesday, 13 February. The two live relays from Paris on Christmas Day and New Year's Eve had been a complete success and, on 15 January, two programmes by the full AEF Band were recorded in London over the landline from the Olympia Theatre and broadcast on Tuesday, the 16th, and perhaps Friday, the 19th, with the usual repeats of the Tuesday broadcast in *Morning After* and on Saturday in the General Forces Programme.

The fact that the Paris to London landline could now be used for recording new programmes by the Band direct from Paris without risk of interruption from the military completely changed the situation of the Band. It meant that after all it might not be necessary for it to return to England when their six-week visit to Paris was up, at least as far as continuing the radio schedule into 1945 was concerned – it could obviously be continued by means of new recordings from Paris and this was done right up until the end of the AEF Programme in July 1945.* However, throughout this period there were no more live broadcasts by the full AEF Band or any of its smaller groups.

In Paris, the Band's schedule was never as hectic as it had been in England. But although its work load was lighter, the Band had other hardships to contend with – the weather was bitterly cold, with heavy snow at times, heating in their quarters was usually inadequate or even non-existent and often the only way the men could keep warm was to go to bed in their uniforms. Electricity supplies were unreliable and they sometimes played in unheated halls.

'Conditions in the hotel were so bad,' recalled Harry Katzman, 'that for us it wasn't much like living in there because we froze to death. Some of the windows were broken. The room I had, which was on the second floor, had five or six window panes that were

* The programmes were never announced over the air as coming from the Olympia Theatre, or even from Paris, but merely in the familiar wartime phrase 'somewhere on the Continent'. This was deliberate policy of the BBC, which thought it best not to put too much emphasis on Paris for troops who had no hope of ever getting there.

broken. When the rooms were assigned I was Staff Sergeant, so I was on the second floor and the lowest ranking guys on the fourth or fifth floor and their rooms were even colder than mine, although they didn't have the broken windows. The water pipes were frozen, you couldn't brush your teeth. We finally complained to Haynes about it, and it took so long to get coal there that when we did finally get it the guy that ran the hotel sold it on the black market, so we kept on freezing. It was impossible to have a bath, but Bialkin met some Red Cross person who had a room in the Grand Hotel and he fixed up a deal where we could come in there and have a bath while she was at work – she was very nice. You couldn't keep your feet warm at any time. Even the Mess Halls were cold. It happened to be one of the coldest winters that they'd had in Paris in many years.

'When we played at the Olympia Theatre it was, I would say, about thirty-five or forty degrees, and some of the concerts we played it was so damn cold we played in overcoats. As a matter of fact, at one time when George Ockner played the 'Flight Of the Bumble Bee' (which we played at every concert because he played it very well) he put on gloves and played it with his gloves on – a remarkable feat.

'The food, I can tell you, was the *worst* that I have ever had. The first Mess Hall that we had was run by French civilians, and the cups were greasy, and the food. You'd get some kind of stew and some mashed potatoes in gravy, and then some tapioca pudding, and some awful coffee. You'd have your stew and after you'd get it back to your table to eat it the stew would be mixed up with the mashed potatoes and the tapioca pudding. Finally, we couldn't go there any more, and a few of the guys got dysentery, so most of the fellows instead of going there for breakfast or anything went to a bakery across the street from the hotel and they got a loaf of bread and some wine, and that's what they had for breakfast. We finally complained so much to Haynes and Dudley, who had heat where they were (the officers had heat but we were freezing to death), that we finally got a new Mess Hall right across the Seine where the food was fairly good.'

'I was rooming with Gene Steck,' said Carmen Mastren. 'We had a little leak in the sink and it was ice in the morning. We had no heat. We had to go to the hotel where the Red Cross girls were staying and they would lend us the room to take a quick shower. They were very good to us. It was one cold winter!

'Who else but Special Services would have had us playing at the Palais de Glace? Boy, was it cold. I kept thinking my guitar was going to split wide open but it held together. The bus driver got lost going there, a Frenchman at that – how could a GI find it.'

During January, with no broadcasting or recording commitments for most of the month, their schedule consisted of two, sometimes three, concerts a day – one in the afternoon, often at military hospitals for troops wounded in action, and one in the evening. Theatre appearances were usually at the Olympia Theatre, the principal centre for American troops, but they also played at the AEF Club at the Grand Hotel, the American Red Cross Rainbow Corner (located in the Hotel de Paris), the Marignan Theatre, and the Palais de Glace until the intense cold in the former ice rink forced them to discontinue playing there. During a concert at the Palais de Glace on 16 January all the lights went out and the concert continued by the light of hundreds of hand torches directed at the stage by the crowded audience of GIs. On 5 January the Band played to wounded troops in a huge heated tent – a small improvement on their open-air concert on 30 December in a temperature of 32 degrees! But wherever they played their performances were packed out with troops, mostly American* but sometimes with British and other Allied servicemen and women as well, while letters came in from hospital COs praising the Band for the uplifting effect of their music on the spirits of the wounded troops they played for.

When visiting hospitals, the Band usually divided up into various groups so that it could play in as many wards as possible as indeed it had done in hospitals in England and back in the United States. The strings, for instance, would split into two groups and George Ockner would take half and Harry Katzman the other half. Playing for wounded troops, however, could be depressing at times. 'When we went to France and Germany,' recalls Nat Peck, 'we played in hospitals where many were dying. It was a very eerie situation playing the usual Miller repertoire for people who were lying in bed, and there was one place in particular I remember where the Sergeant in charge of the infirmary told us that everybody in that particular ward was going to die, and we were playing for a lot of dying people. It was very depressing, but we were well trained and in show business the show must go on and we did it.

'Of course Paris at that time was the place where all the front-line troops used to come. It was quite impressive to see these big lorries coming straight from the front line in Germany loaded with

---

* Paris was a leave centre for American troops, while British leave centres were in the Brussels area; the comparatively few British troops stationed in Paris were mainly Lines of Communication (signals) personnel.

mud-splattered soldiers. It was an uproarious town because, there again, you were alive today and dead tomorrow in those days, and everybody would really be drunk and carrying on – it was rugged – it was like a pioneer town out West! That's the way it was then, but it was very exciting.

'As far as we were concerned of course, Miller was no longer there and I must report that discipline became very loose, to the extent that most of us even removed insignia that we had – those SHAEF headquarters flashes that we wore. What we sought to achieve was the greatest anonymity possible. We had to wear soldier's suits, of course, but we didn't want anybody to know who we were, where we were, what we were doing, or anything, which meant that outside of the concert schedule that we had we were completely free to roam about, and roam about we did because Paris was a fascinating city and we really had a tremendous time there. But all semblance of military discipline was completely gone by the time we were settled at the Hotel des Olympiades.'

Zeke Zarchy and Ray McKinley tried to instil a little discipline into the unit, but it was eventually agreed that provided the men turned up on time for rehearsals and concerts the rest of the time was their own.

Harry Katzman recalled: 'I used to make up little satires and put them up on the Bulletin Board at the Hotel when we were in Paris – they had to do with the idiosyncracies of certain members of the Band, like Joe Kowalewsky, one of the violinists, who had a phobia for visiting all the graves and monuments of the famous people who were buried in Paris – he was the worrying type; and Dave Herman, a very talented violinist who loved to drink a lot and would sell extra pants to buy booze, although he was never drunk on duty; and Dave Sackson, who was known as the operator – he was always looking for bargains in violin bows and violins and he did come home to the billet one time with a painting on a piece of board full of termites which he said was an original Gauguin.'

Haynes, meanwhile, as the new CO was kept busy and had to make frequent trips to General Barker's headquarters at Versailles to confer with the General and Major May. On one of these visits, on 12 January, he learned of his promotion to First Lieutenant, as from 1 January 1945. He also had some help with the administrative work of the unit. A Lieutenant Paul Morden was posted to the Band from SHAEF in London as Executive

Officer. On 13 January, Haynes put in an application to SHAEF for Warrant Officer Dudley to be commissioned as a Second Lieutenant, although it was several months before Dudley's commission actually came through.

Meantime, a succession of rumours had begun about the fate of Major Miller. On 5 January, as the Band played at the Grand Hotel, an Army captain told Haynes that he had heard over the radio that the Major's body and the wreckage of a plane had been found on the Normandy coast, but Haynes followed it up and found that it was not the missing Norseman. At the end of January there were 'plenty of rumours' that Major Miller had been seen in a German POW camp, but these, too, proved false.

'We soon heard rumours that Glenn was in a hospital in England with his arms and legs amputated and out of his mind,' adds Bob Ripley. 'We heard that he was back in New Jersey with his wife. We heard that he was a prisoner of war in Germany – in fact, somebody said that they got a letter from the States from a mother of a friend of one of the Band members and this friend was a prisoner in Germany and had written to his mother that there was a famous bandleader in his prison camp and after the war we would find out who it was. We all assumed it had to be Glenn, but nothing ever came of that. That was the most tantalizing rumour of all and the one on which we pinned our hopes mostly.' The POW rumours persisted for some time, for Jerry Gray mentioned them in a letter to a friend in Bedford in March 1945.

On 10 January, Haynes returned to his hotel late in the afternoon to find an old acquaintance from Milton Ernest waiting for him – Major Bill Koch. Koch brought him the latest news from Milton Ernest, but said that nothing had been unearthed about Major Miller or his two companions or the missing aircraft.

On 17 January Haynes was called to SHAEF for a conference with General Barker who told him that the Band would not be returning to the United Kingdom but would remain in Paris indefinitely but that he (Haynes) was to return to London on the 19th to attend an Eighth Air Force enquiry into the ill-fated flight of the Norseman, as well as to organize the transfer to Paris of the men of the Miller unit who had been left behind in December.

In London Haynes went to see John Harding at the Queensberry Club. Harding showed him the London papers with their reports of Major Miller's disappearance: military censorship had allowed the publication of only brief details, so Haynes told John Harding and his wife Muriel as much as he could without breaching military security. Haynes stayed at the Mount Royal during his four-day visit to England.

On Saturday, the 20th, Haynes attended the Eighth Air Force court of enquiry in London into the missing aircraft and its occupants – but nothing of the enquiry appears in his diary. Later he telephoned the men in Bedford, and then arranged flights to Paris for them. Next day he went to Bedford to see the men at their billet at Ashburnham Road and told them what he could about Miller's disappearance and what the Band was doing in Paris, and that evening he returned to London.

After another day in London Haynes left for Bovingdon on Tuesday morning, the 23rd, arriving there in the ATC bus at half-past ten. Bad weather delayed the take-off for the Continent until after lunch, but the 'Shuttle' finally took off at 1.40 for what was usually a routine flight of just over two hours to Paris but which turned out to be the opposite. The entire flight was made in fog with visibility nil. Nevertheless, they reached Orly in the normal flying time, but after coming down out of the fog and making two attempts to land the plane turned back towards England eventually landing as dusk was falling at a coastal airstrip near war-shattered Cherbourg. Here, accommodation was so scarce that, after a good dinner at a Transient Officers Mess, the Army billeted the passengers and crew – nineteen officers, including two generals – for the night in an empty house with all the windows blown out and gave them each a canvas bed and three blankets. Haynes shared a large room with a General, two Colonels and a Major and it was so cold that he gave a Polish refugee a packet of cigarettes and a pound note to find them some firewood. Pushing their beds as close to the fire as they could they slept for a few hours, but by 5 am it was so cold that they got up, re-lit the fire and sat around till it was time to go over to the mess for breakfast. A truck took them back to the airstrip at half-past eight and their plane finally got clearance to take off again at 10 o'clock, this time landing safely at Orly an hour and a half later.

Next morning, Haynes went to SHAEF at Versailles to report to General Barker on his trip back to England. That evening the Band played its last performance for the time being at the Palais de Glace, finally defeated by the cold in the huge ice rink. At the end of the week, as the usual Saturday show at the Palais was cancelled, the Band had the weekend off, and Haynes – who frequently came into contact with celebrities of all sorts and nationalities who were in Paris in one connection or another with the war – went with Dudley to a slap-up birthday party on the Saturday evening for William Hearst,

Jr., in a beautiful mansion in the centre of Paris. The host was Air Commodore Ralph Forbes and among the guests were General Carl Spaatz (Commanding General of the United States Strategic Air Forces in Europe), General Orville Anderson and many other senior American officers, as well as film actress Danielle Darrieux and her husband Porfirio Rubirosa. Haynes and Dudley walked back to their hotel at 4 am.

On the Sunday Lieutenant Morden arrived in Paris with eleven men* who had been left at Bedford, and the entire unit was together once again.

On the 30th Lieutenant Haynes had another visitor from Milton Ernest, a Major Ash, for whom Haynes signed a statement as to who was actually on the missing Norseman with Major Glenn Miller when he took off on 15 December. 'There had been some conflicting statements made by the personnel at the Officers Club at Milton Ernest,' noted Haynes 'that there were five on the plane, not three . . . this was because Warrant Officer Earlywine and Major Bill Koch had left the Club with Glenn, Colonel Baessell and myself, right after lunch on 15 December.'

Nearly two months had now passed since Glenn Miller had disappeared without the slightest clue to his fate turning up. Early in February he was honoured by the award of the Bronze Star Medal 'for meritorious service in connection with military operations during the period 9 July 1944 to 15 December 1944' (ETOUSA General Orders No. 14, dated 9 February 1945). The medal was actually presented to his widow, by Colonel F. R. Kerr (Acting Director of the Army Special Services Division) in the Miller office in New York. Later, Haynes, Ray McKinley and Jerry Gray were also awarded the Bronze Star.

On 31 January, Haynes was approached by Lieutenant Jerowski of the Army Special Services, on behalf of the Committee of the Mouvement de Liberation National, for the Band to play at a charity concert at the Théâtre National de l'Opéra in Paris in aid of French war relief funds. He agreed, and the concert was arranged for Sunday evening, 18 February, leaving two and a half weeks to sell the tickets.

The Band had begun new recordings for the AEF Programme every Monday at the Olympia Theatre – usually one in the

* Originally, fifty-one were supposed to go to Paris, leaving ten at Bedford. The eleventh was probably Private First Class Fred Rauls, one of the unit's two GI bus drivers (the other driver stayed in England). At one point in his diary, Haynes notes that twelve men were left at Bedford, here he says eleven. The twelfth could have been the other GI driver.

afternoon and one in the evening during their concerts there. The programmes were still recorded in London, of course, over the direct line from Paris and the recordings were then broadcast from London as the regular Tuesday and Friday programmes by the full Band. By the end of January, the BBC was approaching the end of its stock of English pre-recordings by the smaller bands, and so on 30 January Ray McKinley and the American Dance Band began recording new *Swing Shift* programmes on Tuesdays and Thursdays, and the Strings With Wings recorded two programmes every Friday evening and sometimes on Wednesdays as well. This general pattern of weekly recordings, all made in London over the line from Paris – Monday (and sometimes other days),the full AEF Band, Tuesday and Thursday, the *Swing Shift*, Friday, the Strings With Wings – continued with minor variations over the next few months and the AEF Programme continued to broadcast the recordings of all three bands twice a week until the Programme closed down in July.

On the other hand, when the English pre-recordings of the Swing Sextet (*The Uptown Hall*) and *Sergeant Johnny Desmond Sings* ran out these two series were abandoned and none were recorded from Paris. The last *Uptown Hall* was broadcast from London on Friday 9 February, and the last Johnny Desmond programme on Monday 5 February, although he later sang on some Strings With Wings programmes. In any case, a new 'soldier and a song' was being heard more and more on the AEFP – Corporal Jack Powers, from AFN. Jack Rusin's last appearance in *Piano Parade* was on Saturday 3 February. The weekly AEFP schedule for the AEF Band and its remaining smaller bands thus became as follows from 12 February onwards.

Day	Old Schedule	New Schedule
Mon	7.00pm Sergeant Johnny Desmond	
	7.15pm Strings with Wings	7.15pm Strings With Wings
Tues	8.30pm American Band of AEF	8.30pm American Band of AEF
Wed	6.15pm Uptown Hall	
	7.45pm Strings With Wings	7.45pm Strings With Wings
Thur	7.30pm Swing Shift	7.30pm Swing Shift
	9.15pm Uptown Hall	
Fri	8.30pm Moonlight Serenade	8.30pm Moonlight Serenade (American Band of AEF)
Sat	11.45pm Piano Parade	
	3.00pm Swing Shift	3.00pm Swing Shift
	6.15pm Uptown Hall	

Also, during the early months of 1945 the Home Service broadcast for British listeners some of the recordings of the Swing Sextet and the Strings With Wings and, later on, some recordings of the full AEF Band on Monday afternoons in May. The Saturday Lunchtime recordings of the AEF Band on the GFP also continued every week until they were transferred to the same time on Sundays, from 11 March 1945 onwards.

In Paris, the AEF Band continued its established pattern of concerts at troop theatres and military hospitals within an area of about fifty miles of the capital and with the radio recordings for the AEF Programme, through February, March and April. Compared to its stay in England, however, it was never under such heavy pressure, but it was still a pretty full schedule with engagements of some kind practically every day. The Band was now announced as 'Major Glenn Miller's American Band of the AEF' and its programmes were compèred in bright and breezy style by Paul Dudley who never let the audience forget that it was Glenn Miller's Band it was listening to. Most programmes still had their quota of the big Miller hits ('Miller thrillers', as Dudley called them) such as 'In The Mood', 'A String Of Pearls', 'Chattanooga Choo Choo' and the rest, besides new arrangements of standards and current popular songs sung by Johnny Desmond, and the Miller medleys of 'something old, something new, something borrowed and something blue'. In short, the Band's performances were much as they had been when Major Miller had been in command and it continued to draw huge attendances of servicemen and thunderous and enthusiastic applause wherever it played.

There were those, however, who thought that the Band never sounded quite the same after Major Miller's disappearance. Perhaps it is more realistic to say that it sounded *different* in various subtle ways, rather than better or worse. Harry Katzman, for instance, said: 'It seemed that when that Christmas concert was arranged to show that everybody was still alive except Miller, the Band still had that spark because it was the very first performance we had, or the first performance that was broadcast over the networks to the United States. But after that the Band completely deteriorated in my opinion. I know that Jerry Gray and Ray McKinley were very talented musicians but they weren't Miller. The Band lost its precision and it lost its fire. Miller was a wonderful conductor and there was so much precision on all starts and any retards – everything was done over and over until it was automatic, but when you have a new guy getting up there and giving the beats it's not the same thing. The fellows didn't lie down or anything like that, but the genius in front of the Band was gone and it was never the same. The best, I would say, was only 50 per cent – it didn't have that spark.'

Nat Peck, however, feels that the Band went through various periods of different sorts of playing: 'Just before leaving the United States, the Band was absolutely tops, technically – the precision, the sounds. The intonation was really incredible because Miller was there and the standard of playing was just unbelievable. I remember when I joined the Band I felt so incongruously out of place because of the high standard of playing. But something else happened when we went to Paris – Miller was no longer there and this great genial disciplinarian was no longer in front of the Band to maintain that particular standard. But what happened was that we *gained* something. We may have lost technical excellence, but we gained something. The Band started to really open up, to loosen up, and started to play jazz in a much more convincing, organic way – this at the price of a little bit of precision and so on, but it was finally more satisfying for all of us.

'It was a question of the general atmosphere where we were no longer bound by Miller's precision and discipline – Jerry Gray loosened up, Ray McKinley loosened up, the Band loosened up and consequently we all played better for it. This is my opinion – it might be a very subjective one and I might be completely wrong in what I'm saying, but this is the way I feel about it. If you're talking about precision playing, then yes, Harry's right, but if you're talking about *music* it's a different thing. I felt the Band was playing more music in France than they were in England and certainly more music in France than in the United States. This is my *own* personal opinion – I might be wrong. One has a tendency to be subjective about these things.'

In truth, these are the contrasting viewpoints of the orchestral player and the jazzman.

During this difficult period, Jerry Gray played a major role in keeping the show going – besides conducting the broadcasts and sharing the conducting at concerts with Ray McKinley (they would usually take half a concert each) he was still working on new arrangements. 'Jerry Gray was marvellous,' recalls Nat Peck. 'We all loved Jerry. He took on all these responsibilities with equanimity and did a really fantastic job. He didn't get on anybody's back – he really behaved like a brother to all of us. He was working all the time. He loved the Band and he loved what it stood for and he really didn't intend to let Glenn Miller down – who might have been up there watching! He was very serious about keeping things going the way Miller would have done.'

While the Band was in Paris one unfortunate incident occurred, however, which was not related to the music but was a disciplinary matter. Nat Peck recalls: 'I think Dudley was pretty generally popular with everybody – he was quite a nice chap. But there were some people who didn't care too much for Don Haynes and he proved himself in an unfavourable light later on in Paris with that business that has never really been discussed in public too much but where Mel Powell, Peanuts Hucko and Bernie Privin were brought up on the carpet because they had transmitted letters home through couriers. At that time all mail had to be censored,* and because they had strong feelings about Haynes they obviously wanted to express these feelings to their wives or girl friends or mothers or whatever and they didn't particularly care to have Haynes read them, and so they sent their letters off by friends returning to the USA, but these friends were discovered and the mail was intercepted. There was a meeting in the rehearsal room at the Olympia Theatre where Haynes held forth and then stripped Mel and Peanuts and Bernie Privin of their rank – they were reduced to Privates I think. This obviously caused a great deal of unhappy feelings. I didn't like it at all – I thought it was very unfair.'

Ray McKinley, too, vividly recalls the night when things came to a head up in the rehearsal room, and particularly Peanuts Hucko's involvement: 'You've got to remember that I was instrumental in getting Peanuts with the Band and when we went overseas Peanuts and I became very close – I liked the guy. Once overseas, the bellyaching in the Band started before we left England and a clique developed – I don't mean anything organized, it was just a bunch of guys who criticized Glenn, the Army, the Air Force, the war, and everything else. They all hated it. Peanuts was sort of half in and half out of that little group and sitting around on those long nights when we weren't doing anything and absorbing all this stuff.

'Over in France, Glenn was gone, Haynes was in command and Haynes was not popular, especially with this little group which included Joe Shulman the substitute bass player, Bernie Privin, Mel Powell, and for all I know a couple of other guys in the fiddle section.

* Enlisted men's mail was usually censored by unit Officers, in this case Haynes and Morden.

Will Roland, who after the war became Arthur Godfrey's manager, came over to Paris with the USO and he was around the Band for some time. He knew several of the guys in the Band from before the war. Now Peanuts wanted to write a letter for some reason to his wife which he knew stood a chance of being censored and he didn't want that to happen. So he wrote the letter, 90 per cent of it criticism of Haynes, and gave it to Will to take back to the States and mail to Peanuts' wife. Well, wouldn't you know – as luck would have it they spotchecked Will Roland when he got back to the States, they saw this letter, thought it looked suspicious, they read it and relieved Will of the letter and sent it back to Haynes.

'One night, after a concert at the Olympia Theatre word went around the Band for everybody to go upstairs after the concert. So we went up to one of those rooms where the girls practised their ballet stretches, with the mirrors and handrails all round the walls, and the whole Band sat on the floor and Haynes read this letter to the entire Band. Before he read it he told us who had written it. Peanuts sat through the whole thing just looking at the floor, changing colour every few minutes – talk about insubordination, if this had happened in a regular Army unit they would have put the guy in the stockade. Well, Haynes was infuriated by this, he really was, and they decided right then and there that first of all they were going to stick a rifle in his hand and send him up to an infantry unit, and they meant it. When I say "they" I mean Dudley was in on this, too – he didn't approve of this sort of thing: whatever else he was he was an obedient soldier. Mel was quoted in there, too, but the main culprit in the letter, since it was written by him, was Peanuts.

'I sat there and listened to this and I knew the words in the letter didn't come out of Peanuts' head because he didn't really talk or think in those terms. So I asked if I could make a little talk and I got up and I said just that. I also said that I thought the proposed penalty was too harsh. I went through a whole bunch of stuff about the cold, the lack of food, the schedule we were playing, and this and that. When we got downstairs out on to the street I got Paul Dudley and I said, "Hey, Paul, we *need* this guy – you can't send him to the Infantry", and he said, "No, I don't think he'll do that – what we'll probably do is bust him". Peanuts was a sergeant at the time and had been sending an allowance from his pay back to his wife in the States. They busted him to a buck private and after making the allowance to his wife he wasn't getting any pay at all, not a penny, and we used to help him out. But they kept him on as a plain old private – as low as you can get, not even a private first class.'

On Sunday evening, 18 February, came the charity concert at the Opéra for French war relief. The programme was an outstanding selection of the best and most popular items from the Band's large repertoire – a recording of the concert, if one existed,* would almost comprise the definitive record of the Band's music. The concert was a sell-out and raised several million francs in aid of French POW relief. Jerry Gray conducted the first half and Ray McKinley the second and the Band was a sensational success with the French audience. Two compères announced the tunes, one in French and one in English, with hilarious results when the French announcer tried to explain 'It Must Be Jelly 'Cause Jam Don't Shake Like That'. As far as Haynes was concerned, however, the most important person there was General Barker, for the success of the concert reaffirmed the General's support for the work the Band was doing. Part of the concert was broadcast over the French radio from 9 to 10 pm.

Johnny Desmond was also a big hit with the audience: he had already been nicknamed 'Le Crémaire' by French fans because of his smooth singing style and this was later taken up by *Time* magazine in America when they called him 'The Creamer' in a story about his great popularity not only with the Allied troops but with civilians as well.

Also appearing at the concert was a small group from the Band which by this time was a regular feature of its stage shows and sometimes in broadcasts. This was a jazz trio consisting of Corporal Phil Cogliano (violin) Sergeant Carmen Mastren (guitar) and Sergeant Trigger Alpert (bass) and they played tunes such as 'Lady Be Good' and 'I've Found A New Baby' in the style of the famous Joe Venuti/Eddie Lang partnership of the 'twenties and 'thirties.

'I don't remember exactly how our trio got started,' said Carmen Mastren. 'Phil and I both loved Joe Venuti and Eddie Lang and we used to play some of their solos mostly for our own benefit. Eddie, who was Bing Crosby's guitar player until he

---

* It has been suggested that part of the concert was recorded by the BBC although they do not seem to have broadcast any of it: a BBC disc number quoted in this connection is actually that of a *Swing Shift* recording on 24 April 1945.

passed away in 1933, in my book was responsible for the guitar coming into bands. I was playing banjo and when I heard Eddie I knew I had to make the change. Phil and I played for Stéphane Grappelli in London and I think we got the idea there. They called on us and we went out and played – Phil, myself and Trigger on bass, and we went over pretty big.

'I guess it was sort of a relief from hearing the big band. We kept it in the show and it got a good reception.'

The trio broadcast from time to time in programmes by the AEF Band and the *Swing Shift* and as guests in the *Uptown Hall* as early as September 29th 1944, and they continued to perform at concerts throughout the Band's stay in the ETO.*

After the concert at the Opéra the Band played at several other concerts in addition to their regular schedule at the Olympia and elsewhere, including a jazz festival at the Empire Theatre on 18 April and another charity concert in aid of French POWs at the Salle Pleyel on 27 May to a capacity audience of 3,700. They also played two concerts at SHAEF (Main) at Versailles on 7 March and a concert for British troops at the Hotel Commodore on 14 March.

During March and April the famous American symphony conductor Andre Kostelanetz and his French-born wife Lily Pons, the operatic soprano, came over from America on a USO tour to entertain Allied forces. Among many concerts they gave, both in Paris and at various places near the combat areas in Western Germany, were two shows at the Paris Opera House on 24 and 25 March in which the Strings With Wings took part.

'It was Lily Pons' first visit to France since before the war,' recalls Emanuel Wishnow (she had married Kostelanetz in 1938), 'and I remember her little nieces and nephews came on the stage. There was a great deal of crying and throwing garlands of flowers around each other. We came in with an orchestra that Kostelanetz already had – it wasn't his own, but either he brought it with him or it was assembled over there for him. Anyway, he wanted our string section to make this orchestra up to a full symphony.'

Among other notables in Paris at this time was the celebrated American *avant garde* writer Gertrude Stein, then aged seventy-one, who had lived in Paris since 1902. She and her secretary/

* One tune by the trio, 'Lady Be Good', has been issued on a British LP (*see* page 405)

companion Alice B. Toklas came to one of the AEF Band's concerts and talked with the musicians backstage.

Just as in London some of the jazz men from the AEF Band had visited the Feldman Swing Club and joined in impromptu jazz sessions there with British musicians, so in Paris some of them went to the Jazz Club Français in the Rue de Ranelagh in off-duty periods and sat in with French jazzmen. On several occasions some recordings of the AEF Band musicians were made at the Club which had its own recording equipment.

'We'd go down to this night club,' recalls Ray McKinley, 'and they had a good piano and the worst set of drums you've ever seen in your life! There was a twenty-eight inch bass drum with towels stuffed into it to deaden it – I hadn't seen a set of drums like that since I was a kid. It was just terrible trying the things. Joe Shulman the substitute bass player was the guy who set this up, and we would go down there and just get a little routine on a tune – any tune – and they had some recording apparatus set up through the microphone system back in the control booth across the dance floor, and we'd do two or three takes and they'd take one, and we'd get another tune and routine it more or less the same.

'These recordings were made in the afternoons while the club was empty. We only did it 'cause we needed the money. They gave us forty dollars apiece – translated into Francs that was money! After the war they put the records out on the market – I guess when the records were made they were looking further ahead than we were.'

The musicians who actually took part in the recordings were Mel Powell, Peanuts Hucko, Bernie Privin, Joe Shulman and Ray McKinley, and in one session they were joined by the legendary French guitarist Django Reinhardt who had been in France throughout the German occupation and at one time before the Liberation was reported to have died there. On other sessions guitarist Carmen Mastren joined in.

'We had fun making the records at the Hot Club,' recalled Carmen Mastren. 'I remember the owner putting a lot of cognac on the bar before we started. They seem to think American musicians can't play until they've had a few. I guess you can see me holding the jug in one of the album pictures. I was never much of a drinker, but might have one now and then. I think Joe Shulman arranged the whole thing. Joe had a good command of the language. Mostly head arrangements and we enjoyed it.'

After the war, a total of sixteen tunes by the group from these recording sessions were issued publicly in France on the Jazz Club Français record label on 78 rpm records under the name of 'The Jazz Club Mystery Hot Band', with another four by a trio of Mel Powell, Peanuts Hucko and Ray McKinley, and four piano solos by Mel Powell. Most of the records were also issued in Belgium on the Victory label, and in the late 1940s they were all issued in Britain by the new Esquire company run by former jazz band leader and drummer Carlo Krahmer when for the first time they were labelled as 'Glenn Miller's Uptown Hall Gang' although none of the records were by the original *Uptown Hall* Sextet which had broadcast on the AEF Programme. In recent years all the records have been reissued on long playing records in both France and Britain (*see* page 412).

They remain the only publicly issued records by this particular group of musicians and as such they will always be very interesting collectors' items. But they are not the real *Uptown Hall* Band.

While in France, Johnny Desmond also made some records accompanied by a small French band, but these records are quite rare as they were never issued as widely as the Jazz Club Français ones.

At the beginning of April, the BBC in London brought in one last reorganization of the Band's radio schedule on the AEF Programme – although changes in the schedule did not affect the Band itself, of course, as in Paris it still pre-recorded all its programmes for broadcasting anything up to six weeks later. The new schedule, which began on 2 April, did not call for any additional programmes but merely moved the Strings With Wings and the *Swing Shift* broadcasts to different days and times, although after 9 May the *Swing Shift* was heard only once a week instead of twice. The full AEF Band broadcasts remained at 8.30 pm on Tuesdays and Fridays, with the Tuesday programme repeated on Wednesday mornings in the *Morning After* series. The GFP repeats of the AEF Band also continued at Sunday lunch time from 1.30 to 2 pm instead of 12.30 to 1.00 as previously. The new schedule, therefore, was as follows:

Day	Old Schedule		New Schedule	
Mon	7.15pm	Strings With Wings		
Tues	8.30pm	American Band of AEF	8.30pm	American Band of AEF
Wed			12.45pm	Strings With Wings
	7.45pm	Strings With Wings		
			9.15pm	Swing Shift
Thur	7.30pm	Swing Shift		
Fri	8.30pm	American Band of AEF	8.30pm	American Band of AEF
			9.45pm	Strings With Wings
Sat	3.00pm	Swing Shift	5.00pm	Swing Shift

On Thursday 12 April, President Roosevelt died suddenly, virtually on the eve of Allied victory. This was a severe blow to the Allies, especially to the American troops, and over the next couple of days various alterations were made to the AEF Programme schedules, including the substitution of two *Strings With Wings* recordings run together in place of the *Swing Shift* broadcast on Saturday afternoon, 14 April.

During the spring, some rather more curious alterations to the Band's programmes were also made by the BBC: the song 'Accentuate The Positive', a light-hearted Johnny Mercer novelty song sung by Ray McKinley and the Crew Chiefs with additional topical lyrics written by McKinley and entitled 'The Parable of Normandy', was deleted from several *Swing Shift* recordings and replaced by songs from other recordings, although the song was left in several other *Swing Shifts* as well as an AEF Band programme. Perhaps the words which included the line 'and the Lord said to Winnie and to Franklin D.' offended BBC susceptibilities, although why they should take them out of some programmes and leave them in others remains a mystery.

Ray McKinley, who is a great admirer of Johnny Mercer as a lyric writer, was a gifted lyric writer himself: besides the words to Mel Powell's tune 'My Guy's Come Back' he also wrote the rhyming couplets for the introductory theme to all his *Swing Shift* programmes, with different words for each programme, and he recalls how he came to write 'The Parable of Normandy': 'I swear it didn't take me more than fifteen minutes – just as fast as I could write it. The arrangement was a combined job by Jerry Gray, Artie Malvin and somebody else in the Crew Chiefs, with the fiddles and the deliberate corn in the middle. They asked me to write an extra lyric that I could sing with the Crew Chiefs humming behind me, swinging in the style of the Golden Gate Quartet. It was a funny thing, but I rushed up to the end of it and then I thought to myself,

"I hope D-Day *was* 6 June – I think it was but I'm not sure". I went out to the head of the stairs in the Hotel Olympiades and I yelled out to whoever might be listening, "When was D-Day?" and about half a dozen guys said, "6 June". Thank God, I thought, it's OK – if it had been anything else, the 5th or the 7th, it wouldn't have worked. The last two lines went, "If you accentuate the positive June six; they did and now the Devil's in a hell of a fix".'

By mid-April the weather had become warm and spring-like and the Band was able to play open-air concerts once more at hospitals, setting up the Band platforms on the lawns outside. Then, on 25 April, at the request of the Army Special Services and with the approval of General Barker, the Band was taken in three C-47 transport aircraft from Villacoublay military airfield, near Paris, to Nice on the French Riviera for twelve days. Nice was being used as a rest centre for Army Air Forces personnel, and the Band was to play concerts for the airmen for the first seven days of its visit followed by five days leave for themselves – a real pick-me-up after their cold, depressing winter in Paris. Before leaving Paris it had pre-recorded enough extra radio programmes to keep its AEFP schedule going while it was away, as well as some recordings for the Armed Forces Radio Service on 24 April.

The Band was billeted at the Martinez Hotel in Nice, while Haynes stayed at the high-class Hotel Carlton at Cannes, sharing a suite overlooking the Mediterranean with a SHAEF Lieutenant who had travelled from Paris with the Band. For five francs a day they lived in a suite which in peacetime cost the equivalent of seventy-five dollars. Nice was reserved for enlisted men and Cannes for officers, and each was off-limits to the others as military regulations forbade officers to mix with enlisted men while off duty, but the regulations were waived for a concert by the Band for 2,500 officers and men at the American Red Cross Club at the Casino Theatre at Nice. In between playing concerts in the afternoons and evenings the men spent their off-duty time and their five days leave on the beaches or the tennis courts enjoying a well-earned rest and the Mediterranean sunshine soon gave them a good sun tan. In Paris it was snowing!

By late April there were persistent rumours that the war was over – at first proved false. But the end was near. On 1 May came the news that Hitler had committed suicide in the Berlin bunker and the next day Berlin fell to the Russians. American and

Russian troops had already linked up on the Elbe River in the heart of Germany and British troops raced to the Baltic coast. The thousand-year Reich was rapidly being overrun by Allied troops from all directions. In Cannes, Haynes saw guns being placed on the beach ready to signal the end of the war.

On Sunday afternoon, 6 May, three C-47 transport planes flew into Nice to take the Band back to Paris and by 8.30 that evening they were back in the French capital ready to resume their schedule of concerts and radio recordings the next day.

On Monday, the 7th, Haynes learned at SHAEF that the fighting had stopped at 0241 that morning and that it was to be announced the next day. Tuesday 8 May, was the long-awaited V-E Day and Paris, like the rest of the Allied world, went wild. The Band played at official V-E Day ceremonies at the Palais de Chaillot that afternoon, and another show at the Grand Hotel in the evening. 'Went up on the roof after the show,' wrote Haynes in his diary, 'and watched the French celebrating below in the Place de l'Opéra ... and Paris celebrated for five days ... couldn't get our laundry out of the shops as they just closed up and celebrated ...'.

CHAPTER SEVENTEEN

A concert for the Russians – The AEF Programme to close down –
Last recordings for the AEFP – Glenn Miller Day in the USA –
The Band's tour of Germany – A farewell concert at Frankfurt –
The end of the AEF Programme – The Band goes home – The
Band's last days

Eight days after the end of the war the Band flew from Paris
into Germany for the first time for one of their most distinguished engagements in the ETO which had been arranged by
General Barker – to play at a special VIP luncheon given by
General Omar N. Bradley, Commander of the US Twelfth Army
Group in honour of the eminent Russian General, Marshal
Ivan Koniev, Commander of the First Ukranian Army Group,
and his staff at General Bradley's Headquarters at Bad Wildungen,
a spa town about seventy miles north of Frankfurt.

The Band flew from Orly in three C-47s on Wednesday 16
May, and during the flight were able to look down on the wreck
of the Remagen Bridge where the first Allied crossing of the
Rhine had been made by American troops in April. It landed at
an airfield at Fitzlaur littered with smashed Luftwaffe planes
and was taken in a fleet of Cadillacs to the Hotel Fürstenhof in
Bad Wildungen. A ten-thirty curfew confined the men to the
hotel that night where in the crowded lounge after dinner Mickey
Rooney, then an Army Private First Class, sang and played the
piano.

General Bradley's luncheon next day was given in the
Banqueting Hall of the Hotel Fürstenhof and, besides a large
number of Russian generals, distinguished American Generals
present included Lieutenant-General William H. Simpson
(Commanding General of the US 9th Army) and Lieutenant
General Leonard T. Gerrow (Commanding General of the US
15th Army). 'Everybody was there except Patton,' recalls Ray
McKinley. 'I asked why they didn't invite Patton, and they said

they couldn't trust him – they were afraid he would try to steal the show or embarrass somebody, or get himself into trouble.'*

The Russians arrived just before mid-day, flying in low over the town in two transport planes escorted by six fighters, arriving at the Hotel shortly afterwards in the fleet of Cadillacs that had brought in the AEF Band the day before. General Bradley and his staff welcomed Marshall Koniev and the Russian officers and took them into the hotel lounge for a cocktail reception, where George Ockner and the string section were playing. Haynes was introduced to Marshall Koniev and a little later a Russian officer walked up to Ockner and asked him to 'sving it' so the strings obliged with a bright swingy tune! After half an hour of heavy imbibing, General Bradley led his guests into the large Banqueting Hall where he and Marshall Koniev took their places at the head of an enormous horseshoe-shaped table with Russian and American officers (including Lieutenant Haynes) alternately seated around the table with an American interpreter standing between each Russian and American officer. After an hour and a half of eating and endless toasts, the entertainment programme began.

'The show consisted of four things,' recalls Ray McKinley, 'of which we were the main feature – we were last. Jascha Heifitz played a violin solo – I don't think he had any accompaniment. The next thing was Mickey Rooney who did a pantomime slow motion wrestling match – he had on long underwear or something and he was kind of amusing. Then they had a team of four couples of GI jitterbugs and we played for them. I think we played a little incidental music while Rooney was doing his act. And then after these GI jitterbugs got through we came on and played some things – we didn't do a full two-hour concert, we only did about, I'd say, thirty minutes, maybe forty, but everything was cut. We had to play the Soviet national anthem and Heifitz detected one half note difference in what we had been playing and the way it really is. Oh, that would have made a lot of difference, you know – international relations would have been jeopardized – so he came out and told me about it but I said, "Tell Jerry Gray, he's the arranger". So he had Jerry Gray go around changing this one note on all the parts just about ten minutes before we played. And, of course, we played "The Star Spangled Banner". But, you

* General George S. Patton was Commanding General of the US 3rd Army, one of the four American Armies comprising the 12th Army Group; he was often involved in controversy and held strong anti-Russian views.

know what killed me? We had a big production, a seven-minute arrangement on "The Red Cavalry March" and they wouldn't let us play it. They were afraid that by jazzing it up, which we did, that that would be the wrong thing to do. Before the concert, they were discussing with Haynes and Jerry Gray and myself what we should play and how to cut it down, and so forth, and some major or colonel was there – I think he was the only major there, everybody else was above major and he was in charge. He was one of those typical guys that you meet in big corporations nowadays – you know, passed the buck to everything – you can do this but you shouldn't do that, big smile all the time. No, we didn't do anything that would offend the Russians. So we did the West Point football song. We had an arrangement of "On Brave Old Army Team" and that would give a big kick to Bradley and the US guys who graduated from West Point. I forget, frankly, what tunes we played, but we played four or five big things and the Russians liked it. They applauded vigorously.'

Although Mickey Rooney's comedy routine was rather lost on the Russians owing to the language barrier, the AEF Band were a decided hit, especially with the Russians, music being an 'international language'. By four o'clock it was all over, and after General Bradley had presented Marshall Koniev with the gift of a large white horse the Russians got back into the Cadillacs and were driven away. Tensions relaxed, and General Bradley thanked Haynes several times for bringing the Band and doing such a good job, and two days later wrote a letter to Ray McKinley thanking him for the Band's performance and mentioning particularly the West Point football song!

That evening the Band played in an open-air amphitheatre with a partially-covered stage to 3,000 American troops stationed in the district. In the middle of the concert it began to rain but no-one left and although the concert was slightly shortened everyone got soaked, including the Band.

Next morning the Band was taken in the Cadillacs back to the airfield for the return flight to Paris which took them over Bastogne where the US 101st Airborne Division had been surrounded temporarily by the Germans during the Ardennes battle back in December. By one o'clock they were back in Paris and as they went in to land it started to rain. There were no concerts that day and the Band had the weekend off, resuming their concert schedule on Monday, the 21st.

Soon after V-E Day the BBC in London decided to close down the AEF Programme on Saturday 28 July 1945. When it had been set up in June 1944, the BBC had given an undertaking to General Eisenhower that it would continue to broadcast the Programme for between sixty and ninety days after the end of the war, by which time the Allied Armies would have taken over their prearranged occupation zones of Germany and would each be able to organize their own broadcasting stations in their zones of occupation. The closing of the AEF Programme was timed to coincide with the return of the BBC to peacetime broadcasting in Great Britain.

Lieutenant Haynes heard of the impending end of the Programme from Major May while visiting SHAEF on 19 May (the day after the Band returned from Bad Wildungen). The AEF Programme had been the reason for the Band's posting to England a year earlier and the news of the Programme's close-down meant that their mission to the ETO was virtually at an end and the time was approaching when they would be able to return home to the USA. General Barker complimented Lieutenant Haynes on the Band's performance at the reception for Marshal Koniev and said that General Bradley had telephoned him and told him about the Band's part in the proceedings. But he added that it would be another week before definite news of when they would be sent back to the States could be expected to come through, and the Band continued with their concerts and radio recordings as before.

Early on the morning of 29 May, Haynes heard from Major May that General Barker had approved a plan for the Band to tour the American occupation zone of Germany to play for the US 3rd and 9th Armies for six weeks starting on 11 June, provided they could complete their recordings for the AEF Programme by then – enough to last until the Programme closed down at the end of July. Haynes confirmed that the recordings would be completed in a week's time, and it was agreed that he would go to SHAEF to arrange the details of the tour with Major May. SHAEF had moved by this time from Versailles to Frankfurt, so on Saturday afternoon, 2 June, Haynes left Paris in a B-26 Marauder bomber and was met at Frankfurt airport by Major May who told him that General Barker had left for a weekend away and wouldn't be back till Monday.

That evening Lieutenant Haynes and Major May flew in another B-26 to Venlo, Holland, and on the Sunday were taken on a tour of the northern end of the Siegfried Line before flying in the B-26 back to Frankfurt on Sunday afternoon. On the flight the pilot flew over Cologne from various angles to give them a bird's eye view of the city, nearly all of which was completely destroyed except for the smoke-blackened Cathedral. At times the plane flew so low that the pilot asked those in the nose of the aircraft to look out for telephone wires! In the evening Haynes walked around Frankfurt finding that it too was almost totally destroyed. The only large building still standing was the IG Farbenindustrie headquarters which SHAEF had taken over shortly after the German surrender – a vast, imposing complex of buildings with much marble and ornamental gardens and fountains. Only the main streets of the city had so far had the rubble cleared for motor traffic; in other streets only a narrow path had been cleared down the middle of the street just wide enough for pedestrians to walk along them.

On Monday morning, 4 June, Haynes reported to General Barker and finalized with him and Major May plans for the Band's tour of Germany. General Barker also told him that the Army Air Forces had asked for the Band to be transferred back to the United States, possibly in July or early August, so that, after leave, they could be redeployed to the Pacific theatre. By 3 o'clock he was back at Villacoublay, via a C-47 of the 'SHAEF Shuttle'.

By 29 May, when General Barker had approved their tour of Germany, the Band had already recorded enough radio programmes to last about six weeks ahead, and during the next week it recorded another dozen to take its AEFP schedule right through to the Programme's close-down on 28 July. The last pre-recording was made on the afternoon of Tuesday 5 June, during its last concert at the Olympia Theatre. The recording was a special programme called *The American Band of the AEF Says Farewell* for broadcasting at the end of its schedule and it actually went out over the air on the very night of the AEF Programme on 28 July. This last programme, and several others recorded in May and June, were compèred by Sergeant Broderick Crawford instead of Paul Dudley, who by now was Second Lieutenant Dudley. Crawford had re-joined the Band from London where he had worked on other AEFP programmes since just after the Band arrived in England – in particular, the daily summary of the latest Allied battle lines called *Mark Up The Map* which, now that the fighting had stopped, was no longer needed. At this last concert Mickey Rooney and Bobby Breen, former American boy soprano who had appeared in several Hollywood musicals, were in the GI audience and they were persuaded up on to the stage to take part in the show. In contrast to his performance for the Russians Mickey Rooney was a great success with the American troops. That evening the Band played as usual at the AEF Club.

By now the war had been over for a month but the Allied occupation of Germany and the release of American and British POWs had produced no clues whatever to the fate of Major Glenn Miller. He had now been missing for six months and any prospects there may have been of solving the mystery of his disappearance were fading rapidly.

In the United States his popularity was still as high as ever and 5 June was proclaimed 'Glenn Miller Day' in a nationwide tribute by the entertainment world in support of the Seventh War Loan Drive. The tribute centred on a five-hour radio marathon from New York's Paramount Theater with hook-ups to other cities during the proceedings. Many leading bands and artists of the day took part, some with Miller connections, others not, and at the Paramount Charlie Spivak's Band was joined by Chief Petty Officer Tex Beneke while later in the programme Beneke and Marion Hutton, both from the pre-war Glenn Miller Band, sang with Benny Goodman and his Orchestra, and throughout the evening many tributes were paid to Glenn Miller by singers and musicians expressing hopes for his safe return. It was reported that nearly five million dollars were raised at the Paramount alone.

As a curtain-raiser to the tribute the American magazine *Down Beat*, one of the world's leading dance music and jazz magazines, published special Glenn Miller features and photographs in their 15 May issue, including a long report from Paris on the AEF Band's work there written by American war correspondent First Lieutenant Herb Caen, who had become friendly with Haynes and Dudley. Now one of America's leading newspaper columnists and a lifelong jazz aficionado, his informed and perceptive appreciation of the Miller Band concluded:

Taken all in all the Band is a good thing from every standpoint. I think it satisfies, at times and in its own ways, just about every musical taste represented in the Army over here – which is to say, it pleases everybody, cats [i.e., jazz fans] included. And for these small favors we are duly grateful. Things could have been oh, so much worse.

Wednesday 6 June was a day off for the Band and after its usual Thursday afternoon performance at the Grand Central Red Cross

Club and Friday evening concert at the AEF Club the men spent the next two days preparing for their tour of Germany. They were due to leave Paris on Monday 11 June, but were delayed for two days by bad weather over Germany and eventually took off in three C-47s from Villacoublay after lunch on the 13th, landing at 4.50 at Regensburg, on the banks of the Danube about fifty miles south-east of Nuremburg. They were billeted at the Bishopshofen and that night played the first concert of their tour to 5,000 GIs of the 1137th Engineering Group. Afterwards the Band was entertained to a steak dinner in the Officers Mess. Next day, it played two more concerts in Regensburg in the town's largest theatre, the Half Crown, one in the afternoon and one in the evening, both to capacity audiences of 1,500.

On the morning of the 14th Haynes received a telephone call from Major May telling him to report to General Barker. He requisitioned a small L-5 observation plane and pilot and flew to Frankfurt. He found that the General had received the Band's transfer orders back to the USA. General Barker complimented Haynes on the work the Band had done while attached to SHAEF and told him he was recommending him for the Bronze Star and promotion to Captain.

Haynes stayed overnight at SHAEF and next morning he again saw Major May who told him that a Major Fred Brisson had come over to Paris from Washington to speed up the Band's transfer back home in response to a cable General Barker had sent to the War Department saying that the Band would be available to leave the ETO by 22 July. The AAF certainly seemed anxious to get them back. Brisson was due at Frankfurt next day, so Haynes stayed on for another day at SHAEF, this time at Bad Homburg, near Frankfurt, where General Eisenhower had his quarters. Here he ran into General Bedell Smith's WAC secretary who described to him Major Miller's interview with General Bedell Smith the previous October. He also met General Bradley who thanked him again for the Band's concert for the Russians at Bad Wildungen.

Early next morning (the 16th), Major Brisson, who was the son of the Danish singer Carl Brisson, arrived at SHAEF and at a meeting with him in Lieutenant Kay Summersby's office Haynes settled the details of the Band's transfer back to the United States. In the afternoon Haynes flew back to Paris where he arranged transport for the Band back to the States and then flew back to Frankfurt. On Monday morning he flew in his ob-

248

servation plane back to Regensburg where the Band were over-joyed at the news that they would be going home in just over a month's time.

While he was away the Band had been playing at Army bases in and around Regensburg. On the 22nd it went in trucks to Passau, where it was billeted in a castle high above the town until the 25th when, after five concerts in the area, they returned to Regensburg. On the 30th they flew in two C-47s to Ninth Air Force Headquarters at Erlangen, near Nuremburg, where they played a concert, and next day went to Nuremburg for a concert to no less than 40,000 cheering GIs in one of the former Nazi stadiums. It finally left Regensburg for good on 9 July and for the rest of the tour travelled in trucks or transport planes from base to base, including concerts at Schweinfurt, Bad Neustadt, Bayreuth and Venlo (Holland) among other places and frequently to au-diences even larger than for such stars as Bob Hope who was also touring troop bases at the time.

'Regensburg was the place where the Messerschmidt planes were made,' recalled Harry Katzman. 'That was pretty well smashed up, but the Cathedral seemed to be intact. From there we used to go to the different American bases and play for the soldiers. We used to go out in the morning in trucks, about fifty or sixty miles, and when we got back there was so much rubble and dust (it was just a few weeks after the war was over) that when we got out of the trucks we all had grey hair from the dust.'

'It was pretty grim in Germany at that time, immediately after the war,' says Bob Ripley. 'Everything was all bombed out. We were not allowed to talk to the people – fraternization was a crime – and it was difficult for us to live like that. At first we played shows around Regensburg, usually returning there at night, but I remember we played two shows at Dingolfing and afterwards slept on straw mattresses in a barn – that was pretty rough. We spent several days at Passau – that was a pretty nice place to be, relatively speaking! We also went to Nuremburg in the trucks and as we rode through the city we saw the tremendous destruction – unbelievable. We played to forty thousand troops in a stadium, a smaller annex to the main stadium, where Hitler had addressed Nazi rallies. Our programme there was nearly two hours long and the stage was decorated with coloured cloths from Nazi flags. After the concert we left Nuremburg in the trucks and ate our supper of C-rations along the road, arriving back at Regensburg late at night.

'We also went to Bayreuth along the autobahn and played in the Wagner Theatre. I remember that very well, of course – we saw the special boxes that Hitler had for himself and his crowd to watch the opera, very beautifully appointed with red upholstery and carpeting. Later, we flew to Venlo, in Holland. We took off from Schweinfurt in 13 B-26 aircraft and I remember that trip because the pilot of my plane was buzzing the countryside and that was kind of scarey. But those guys didn't care what they did, of course. We played one show there in the early evening and stayed overnight in a very nice hotel. When we took off again next morning they crowded us into seven B-26s instead of thirteen.

'Near the end of the tour we had a beautiful trip flying over Geneva and the Alps to Chamonix, France, where we played a show and stayed overnight. Next morning we went up a tramway and got a breathtaking view of Mont Blanc and other peaks – the most thrilling part of the entire trip. At the end of the tour we played one show at Frankfurt, where again we saw terrific destruction. At this concert the Band received a citation.

'Altogether, we played 43 shows in 25 different places from 13 June to 21 July.*

'I enjoyed our tour of Germany,' said Carmen Mastren, 'because we had a chance to see what we accomplished in the war. We did meet up with that same artillery outfit we met on the boat coming over from the States and we played softball and spent the night with them drinking Schnapps. It went down easy but would hit you suddenly – like lightning!'

The Band returned to Paris from Chamonix on 18 July, where Haynes learnt that his promotion to Captain had come through so he replaced his Lieutenant's bars with Major Miller's old Captain's bars. The Band's tour of Army bases was virtually over, but there remained one last prestigious farewell concert before it left for home, so on the 20th they left Villacoublay in three C-47s and flew to Kaufbeuren, about fifty miles from Munich, en route to SHAEF at Frankfurt. At Kaufbeuren it played an afternoon concert and then flew on to an airfield at Fürstenfeldbruck, near Munich, for another performance, where the men stayed overnight.

Next morning the Band took off in the C-47s from Fürstenfeldbruck bound for Frankfurt and the big show that evening. Before the concert Captain Haynes called in at Lieutenant Kay Summersby's office to say goodbye and while he was there

* Full details of the Band's itinerary are given on pages 381–7.

General Eisenhower came in and was surprised to see him until Lieutenant Summersby reminded 'Ike' about the concert that evening. The General said that if he hadn't been expecting a visit from some British VIPs he would have been in the front row and would have personally pinned the Bronze Star on Captain Haynes' 'manly chest'! Then he shook hands with Haynes, wished good luck to him and the Band and thanked them for a job well done.

The concert that evening was outdoors at SHAEF* as a big farewell to the ETO and was attended by 10,000 SHAEF personnel. Ray McKinley conducted the Band and MC'd the show. It was its last official performance before going home, everybody let their hair down and in among the more serious musical items there were some light-hearted interludes by various members of the Band. Halfway through the concert, Colonel A. H. Rosenfeld (Acting Commander, Headquarters of United States Forces in the European Theater) came on to the stage and presented to Captain Haynes and the Band a commemorative plaque by special order of General Eisenhower for meritorious service in bringing entertainment to the troops of the Allied Expeditionary Force on the radio and throughout the European Theater. Then Colonel Rosenfeld presented the Bronze Star to Captain Haynes.

Its job was done. The day after the concert the Band flew back to Paris, landing at Villacoublay just after 11.30 am on Sunday 22 July, to begin the long-drawn-out preparations for their return to the USA. The Band was billeted at Camp Prince Albert on the outskirts of Paris near Villacoublay while Haynes and Paul Dudley stayed at the Deux Mondes Hotel.

By Tuesday, the 24th, the Band was ready to go. Before leaving Paris it played one last concert – this time for the 3,000 GIs at the Villacoublay airfield in return for all they had done for the Band while they had been flying in and out of the airfield. Shortly after the concert the Band left Paris for the last time riding in buses past the sights and landmarks which had become so familiar to them all during the last six months to St Lazare Station to catch a ten o'clock train for Le Havre. At 10.54 precisely (!) the train pulled out. They were on their way.

* Strictly speaking, it was no longer SHAEF Headquarters: SHAEF had been formally dissolved at one minute past midnight on 14 July and the British and Canadian personnel had departed to the British Zone of Occupation. The American personnel remained at Frankfurt as the staff of the new Headquarters of the United States Forces in the European Theater (USFET).

They arrived at Le Havre at 6.15 next morning and were taken by buses to a vast tented embarkation camp called Camp Herbert Tareyton, one of three in the area.* Here they spent eleven dull and exasperating days, dry days alternating with rain and mud and the monotony relieved only by the usual inspections and medical examinations. 'There was nothing to do all day,' recalls Bob Ripley. 'I remember very well the frustration and utter boredom of just waiting and waiting to go home, but at least we knew we *were* going home.'

While the Band awaited embarkation at Camp Herbert Tareyton, the AEF Programme came to the end of its 417 days of broadcasting and shortly after 11 pm on Saturday 28 July 1945, the Programme's 'Oranges and Lemons' chimes were heard for the last time. On that last evening the usual programme schedules were abandoned after 9 pm and replaced by special farewell shows featuring many of the bands and artists who had been heard regularly week by week. From 9 pm till 10 there was a live relay from the Queensberry Club where the indefatigable Cecil Madden had excelled himself in gathering together as many stars of the AEF Programme as was possible for a gala variety show *Farewell AEFP*. Then, Canadians who had broadcast in the Programme bade their goodbyes in their own ten-minute spot, and the last full show was the half-hour broadcast 'The American Band of the AEF Says Farewell',† compèred by Broderick Crawford, which had been pre-recorded from Paris on 5 June. It was introduced by a spoken appreciation by Captain Franklin Engleman, who had often worked with the Band, and the programme consisted of the tunes for which the Band had received the most requests from their services audiences during their thirteen months in the ETO – from 'In The Mood' to 'The Anvil Chorus'.

The very last programme on the AEFP was a little fifteen-minute presentation by AC2 Ronnie Waldman, telling the story of 'Oranges and Lemons' and saying goodbye to the Programme's audience of several million servicemen and women of the three Allied Nations. It included a specially compiled montage recording of the signature tunes of nineteen of the most popular

---

* The other two (all three were named after American tobacco companies) were Camp Lucky Strike and Camp Philip Morris.

† Broadcast on the last night instead of the usual Friday spot the previous evening.

progammes on the AEFP, among them 'Moonlight Serenade' – the opening theme of a programme announced by Paul Dudley and recorded on 16 April 1945.

In a recording made at SHAEF in Frankfurt a few days previously, General Eisenhower expressed his appreciation of the work of the AEF Programme and this recording was broadcast twice during the evening of the 28th. The last goodbye was spoken by announcer Margaret Hubble, who had made the first announcement in the AEF Programme on 7 June 1944.

A unique era of international co-operation in radio broadcasting was over, and arguably the best variety and light entertainment radio service the BBC has ever presented would be heard no more. The American shows which had been heard on the AEF Programme would in future only be heard on the American Forces Network stations in Germany – difficult to listen to in Britain. British and Canadian shows were broadcast on the new British Forces Network in the British Zone of Germany, and some were continued on the BBC Overseas Service. Only a handful of the home produced AEF series were carried on in the new Light Programme for British home listeners which began on Sunday 29 July, including one of the best – *Top Ten*. But lost forever to British listeners were the three Bands of the AEF.

AEFP Director, Maurice Gorham, had already become head of the new Light Programme and the AEFP's wavelength was allocated to the West of England Home Service.

General Eisenhower presented a signed testimonial to the BBC for running the Programme and General Barker travelled to London to present it to the Director General, Mr W. J. Haley; after the ceremony it was framed and hung in the Council Chamber at Broadcasting House – today it can be seen on display in the entrance hall. At the same time General Barker conferred American decorations on some of the officers who had worked on the Programme, including the Legion of Merit to Lieutenant-Colonel David Niven and the Bronze Star to Captain Franklin Engelman.

The *Melody Maker*, which had so often reported the activities of the Miller Band as well as many other star-studded shows in the AEF Programme, and had strenuously campaigned for more AEF programmes to be available to British listeners at home, printed its own farewell to the Band on its 4 August front page.

Under the headline 'Farewell To The Glenn Miller Band' it concluded prophetically:

> . . . The visit of the Miller Band, however, will never be forgotten here. Both as an inspiration to our own musicians and as a means of cementing a warm and lasting friendship, the visit of the American boys to these shores has become a treasured memory with us all.

While the Band was kicking its heels at Camp Herbert Tareyton it played a concert for the GIs there on Saturday 28 July, and later that day Haynes was told that it would sail for home on the *Santa Rosa* on 3 August. They had only six days left on European soil – six days of continuing boredom and frustration.

The ship came into Le Havre during the night of 31 July/1 August, and on the 3rd the Band was alerted for embarkation the next day. At last the day the men had long awaited dawned bright and sunny. They boarded the ship at 8.30. Loading of troops and equipment lasted all day until finally the ship cast off at a quarter past six and backed out into the Channel.

The voyage home lasted seven days and was uneventful apart from several patches of rough and foggy weather. Once again they were back to two meals a day but with only about 3,500 troops aboard the ship was a far cry from the *Queen Elizabeth* which had brought them over. The string section gave two concerts during the voyage, one for the officers and the other two days later for the enlisted men.

On the third day out came the momentous news over the ship's PA system that the atomic bomb had been dropped on Hiroshima, and the Allies had given Japan an ultimatum to surrender unconditionally. This meant that the Japanese war might be over before the Band got home and the men might not have to go out to the Pacific Theatre after all. Two days later Russia declared war on Japan, on the 9th the second atomic bomb wiped out Nagasaki, and on the 11th it was announced that the Allied governments were awaiting Japan's surrender.

The Band was nearly home. At 6.35 pm on the 11th they sighted Coney Island and an hour later as the Band played on deck the ship dropped anchor off Staten Island where eighty-seven Japanese captured in Berlin and brought to America on the *Santa Rosa* were put ashore. Early next morning the *Santa Rosa* steamed slowly up the Hudson River past the Statue of Liberty to a chorus of welcome from the sirens and whistles of ships in the harbour and signs hung over the rails saying 'Welcome Home Glenn Miller AAF Band' and 'Miller Band Welcome Home' and the Band played on deck again. It was one year, one month and twenty-one days since it had sailed out of New York Habour en route for the ETO.

The Band disembarked at 10.20 am and was taken to Camp Shanks near Orangeburg, New York State, on the west bank of the Hudson about 10 miles north of New York City. Haynes, meanwhile, took the Band's equipment and library to 1 Park Avenue, New York City, where it was to be based, and then obtained a staff car and driver and went to see his wife Polly and then on to Tenafly to see Mrs Helen Miller. In the afternoon he rejoined the Band at Camp Shanks where that evening there was a homecoming party. Then the Band were given thirty days leave.

In just under fourteen months overseas the Band had played no fewer than 956 separate engagements – 505 broadcasts and 353 personal appearances to audiences totalling one and a quarter million throughout the ETO, an average of nearly three performances a day, a record that few bands in history can have equalled.

After their thirty days leave the men reassembled in September in New York City but did not return to New Haven – instead they were assigned to Headquarters, Army Air Forces, and based for a time at 1 Park Avenue New York City, and on Saturday 29 September, they resumed their broadcasts on *I Sustain The Wings* over NBC. The Band was now known as 'Major Glenn Miller's Army Air Forces Overseas Orchestra' and once again was conducted by Sergeant Jerry Gray.

By this time, however, the Pacific War was also over and under the 'points' system* for servicemen's demobilization some of the men returned to civilian life. A few left as soon as the Band got back to America, including Mel Powell, and there was also a special scheme under which men who had reached the age of thirty-five could apply for early release. Under this scheme Harry Katzman left the Service early in October without actually rejoining the Band at all; Ray McKinley got out in mid-October, Emanuel Wishnow and Henry Brynan in late October, and Don Haynes in November. Most of the musicians, however, being

---

* Servicemen needed a minimum of eighty points, based on length of service and other conditions, in order to become 'separated from service'.

younger than the others, stayed on awaiting their release, the Band continued with *I Sustain the Wings* and after a while was transferred to the AAF's Bolling Field, near Washington DC.

While they were in New York some of the musicians also played in another AAF orchestra – the one directed by Sergeant Harry Bluestone which had replaced the Miller Band on *I Sustain the Wings* back in June 1944 when the Miller Band left for England, although by now it was conducted by Master Sergeant Felix Slatkin (father of the symphony conductor Leonard Slatkin). 'During this period,' says John Halliburton, 'we did many Miller programmes and the brass section also did the Harry Bluestone programme. We were, more or less, New York studio musicians, but we were all anxious to be discharged from the service and begin our civilian lives.'

'The Harry Bluestone Band was also a fine orchestra,' adds Carmen Mastren, 'but played different style arrangements. I enjoyed doing a few shows with them. We went back to Washington because this Band was also breaking up. Most of the guys got out but some of us were shy a couple of points and were going to have to serve about six months more even though we were promised that we would all be discharged. You know how the service is, abide by the rules. I happened to be in the office on the base and one of the enlisted men asked me who we were attached to in Europe. When I told him SHAEF he said we were entitled to a battle star which gave me five points – enough for a discharge.'

But now that the war with Japan was over and demobilization of the United States forces was getting under way, the needs of the AAF that had brought the Band into existence were no longer there and the Band's last broadcast, which was also the last *I Sustain the Wings*, went on the air from Bolling Field on Saturday 17 November 1945, with the earlier dramatized recruiting episodes replaced by compère Sergeant Vernon Wilson urging airmen still in the service to sign on for the peacetime Army Air Forces.

Before this, though, British listeners heard the Band for the last time when it broadcast once again live in *Atlantic Spotlight* on Saturday afternoon, 20 October, from New York City. After playing the programme's usual New York signature tune 'Yankee Doodle Doo' the Band opened the show with 'Oranges and Lemons'. The British artists in the programme were Dorothy Squires, Edric Connor, Wee Georgie Wood and the BBC Dance

Orchestra conducted by Stanley Black. The Miller Band closed the show with Johnny Desmond singing 'Symphony' and the Band's rousing instrumental swinger 'Flying Home'.

'Symphony' was a song the Band had originally heard in Europe although it had not featured it over the air in the ETO. It was originally called 'C'est Fini' and was said to have been written by three Frenchmen in a German POW camp or a concentration camp. Americanized as 'Symphony' with words by veteran songwriter Jack Lawrence, it became quite a big hit and the Miller Band version was a showcase for Johnny Desmond who sang the second chorus in French when the Band recorded it for a V-Disc after it returned to America.

The Band's last public appearance was on the evening of 13 November at the Annual Dinner of the National Press Club at the Statler Hotel in Washington DC, at which the guest of honour was President Harry S. Truman. This event was always a 'big' occasion in the Washington social calendar, packed with celebrities, and in this year of Allied victory the Dinner was no exception, for besides President Truman a host of politicians, including Canadian Prime Minister Mackenzie King, and military leaders attended, among them General Eisenhower and General H. H. Arnold (Commanding General of the Army Air Forces). After the formal dinner and speeches, during which President Truman was presented with a small upright piano by the Club, the AAF Band with Ray McKinley recalled from civilian life, played as the finale in a programme that had also included comedian Joe E. Lewis, Metropolitan Opera tenor Nino Martin, Dorothy Shaw, the Murphy Sisters and Joy Hodges (Mrs Paul Dudley), with Eddie Cantor as MC. A standing ovation for the Band was led by President Truman himself.

'I was delighted to be asked to come back and lead this performance,' recalls Ray McKinley, 'and I remember going down to Washington on a train. The Band showed up and it was snap for us – we'd played these tunes so many times that there was really nothing to it. When the Band was introduced, Eddie Cantor read a eulogy which Paul Dudley had written about Glenn, about how he had volunteered and lost his life, and with that Truman stood up. Of course, when the President stands up everybody stands up, and we went into our thing and did about a half dozen numbers and broke it up. I think we also played for Joy Hodges to sing a couple of songs.

'After it was over, Truman cut out – he had his Secret Service boys and they went out pretty fast. After the concert we were told to stay on the stage and General Arnold brought General Eisenhower up on to the stage to talk to us. He said nice things about us and recalled the concert we did for him in England at SHAEF up in the woods. He kind of shuffled around and looked at the ground – he seemed a little embarrassed in front of musicians. Meanwhile, Arnold was standing there with his chest out about four feet – you know, "These are my boys!" – and grinning broadly.

'Arnold is supposed to have turned to someone there at the table at the conclusion of this concert and said, "Let them out, they've done their share of duty", or words to that effect. They were trying to get out – Haynes and other people wanted them out – so the Band was released as a unit right then – out! That was it. The minute he said that the orders were issued, because you don't delay when Arnold tells you to do something. The guys didn't know it at the time. Some of them were a little worried they might wind up playing on the White House lawn for the rest of their lives! They wanted to get back to their civilian jobs.'

The Band's Pacific trip was cancelled, and in due course the men returned, as they had come, to leading civilian dance and jazz bands, radio orchestras and symphony orchestras all over America. They never played together again, although nineteen of them, most of the Crew Chiefs and arranger Norman Leyden joined the new civilian Glenn Miller Orchestra which Don Haynes organized in New York early in 1946. Brought together by the demands of the greatest war in history, the Army Air Forces Band had carved a place in the memories of millions – not only among their own countrymen and women but throughout Western Europe and, by means of radio, far beyond – at the same time ensuring for the Band a unique niche in the annals of popular music. In doing so, they had played a vital and unforgettable part in the defeat of the worst tyranny which had so far threatened mankind – the finest tribute possible to the Band and its founder and director, the late Major Glenn Miller, who had made the supreme sacrifice in the cause of freedom so far from home in pursuit of the ideal he had set himself.

A legend had passed into history.

CHAPTER EIGHTEEN

A new Glenn Miller Band – The musicians today – What happened to Major Glenn Miller? – The Norseman's last flight – 'Men like Glenn Miller don't just die'

Back in civilian life the men of the Army Air Forces Band lost no time in resuming their civilian careers, although for many their careers were different from what they might have been if Major Glenn Miller had returned from the war and been able to carry out his post-war plans.

While in England Major Miller had made extensive plans for forming a new civilian band after getting out of the Army. He had discussed these plans in detail with Don Haynes – indeed the post-war band had been one of the topics of conversation with Haynes the night before he flew off to Paris in December 1944, and he had asked some of the men in the Army Band to join him when they returned to civilian life.

Miller had also planned to move from New York* which had been his base ever since the late 1920s, and take his family to California (shades of the song he wrote in England, 'I'm Heading For California'!). Before the war he had bought a ranch near the town of Duarte, about fifteen miles from Los Angeles, and named it 'Tuxedo Junction' where he had planned to build a new home and develop his orange groves there; while stationed at Bedford he made a large model of the new house, helped by instrument technician Vito Pascucci and others. He had also offered part of his land at Tuxedo Junction to Don Haynes and the men who would be in the new band so that they, too, could build new homes on a sort of 'Miller campus'. Once the new band was operating, he proposed to concentrate on concerts, theatre and radio work (and, no doubt, television in due course), but was

* He had actually lived just across the State border in Tenafly, New Jersey.

determined to avoid the wearying grind of one night stands. Before leaving for England in June 1944 he had signed a new contract for more film work after the war with 20th Century Fox in Hollywood, the company for which he and his Band had appeared in the highly successful *Sun Valley Serenade* and *Orchestra Wives* and for which he had been scheduled to make a third film with the Band had he not enlisted in the Army.

Besides the new band he had hoped to build up other business activities outside music in addition to the orange growing: he had been promised a distribution agency for Coca Cola which could have paid him very well and had hoped to go into the motel business. Thus he would have combined his musical career with other business interests as well as presumably continuing with his music publishing company Mutual Music Inc. which he had set up in New York before the war. Already comparatively wealthy he might well have become a millionaire, although planning to work only six months a year and taking it easy for the rest of the time!

One of the Army Band musicians whom Major Miller had asked to join him after the war was violinist Harry Katzman: 'I think Miller liked me very much and he wanted me to go with him in civilian life to California – if we ever got there, of course. He wanted me to be the manager or the contractor of the orchestra. If Miller had been alive I would probably have gone with him to California, although I was very well established in New York at that time.'

Not all the musicians Major Miller approached accepted his offer, however – Bernie Privin, for instance, says: 'He asked me to join his band after the war and I gave him a firm but polite NO.'

Many of the men from the Army Air Forces Band, therefore, resumed their professional careers more or less where they had left off three years or so earlier. Mel Powell was recording with his old boss Benny Goodman as early as the end of August 1945, remaining with him for several months; Bernie Privin and Peanuts Hucko both joined the Goodman Band in December. Bassist Trigger Alpert, saxophonist Hank Freeman and guitarist Carmen Mastren became studio musicians in New York: so did Harry Katzman who rejoined the orchestra on the *Bell Telephone Hour* which he had played in before the war. Bassist Joe Shulman joined the new Buddy Rich Band (Buddy's first band) in New York in December.

Ray McKinley, after waiting for the right men to get out of the

Army, formed a new fourteen-piece band in New York in January 1946, recruiting several former AAF Band musicians for it, including Lou Stein, Jim Harwood, Jack Steele and Peanuts Hucko, who left the Goodman Band to join McKinley. Arranger Jerry Gray became a conductor and arranger for radio programmes in New York, later moving to Hollywood, as did Norman Leyden and Ralph Wilkinson. Johnny Desmond began a successful solo career and almost at once signed a recording contract with RCA Victor. Most of the string players returned to the classical field.

Any ideas that the loss of Major Glenn Miller in the war would mean the end of the Glenn Miller music were very quickly dispelled, however. As soon as the musicians were released from the Army Don Haynes lost no time in organizing a new civilian Glenn Miller Orchestra. It was based in New York, not California, and Haynes ran it on behalf of Mrs Miller and the Glenn Miller Estate (which was managed by Major Miller's attorney and close friend David Mackay). Mrs Miller withdrew from the musical scene and moved to California with her two adopted children, Stephen and Jonnie Dee, where she died in 1966.

The new Miller orchestra was based on the plans which Major Miller had discussed with Haynes while they were overseas in England and almost half the men from the AAF Band formed the bulk of the orchestra. It totalled thirty players – the conventional dance band instrumentation of four trumpets, four trombones, five saxophones and four rhythm, plus twelve strings and a French horn – and was presented to the public as the band Glenn Miller would have led if he had returned from the war. Although a little smaller than the AAF Band it was nevertheless a large orchestra by the standards of the time. It was conducted by Glenn Miller's pre-war tenor saxophone star and singer 'Tex' Beneke, who had led a band in the US Navy during the war – the logical man for the job once Ray McKinley had declined.

The ex-AAF Band musicians who joined the new orchestra were trumpeters Bobby Nichols and Whitey Thomas, trombonists Jimmy Priddy, John Halliburton and Nat Peck; saxophonists Vince Carbone, Freddy Guerra and Mannie Thaler; French horn player Addison Collins, Jr. (later known as Junior Collins); violinists Eugene Bergen, Phil Cogliano, Earl Cornwell, Richard Motylinski, Joseph Kowalewski and Fred Ostrovsky; violas Dave Schwartz and Stan Harris; and 'cellist Bob Ripley; a total of nineteen of the complement of thirty in the new orchestra. In addition, four of the five Crew Chiefs joined it: Artie Malvin as solo singer, Steve Steck as one of the trumpet section, and Murray Kane and Gene Steck as part of a reorganized vocal group still called the Crew Chiefs. Arranger Norman Leyden became the principal arranger for the orchestra and Jerry Gray also contributed arrangements from time to time.

It was billed as 'The Glenn Miller Orchestra directed by Tex Beneke'. After some break-in theatre dates in Providence, Rhode Island, the orchestra's 'official' public debut was at the Capitol Theater on Broadway where it opened for a three-week engagement on 24 January. It was a sensational success. It shared the programme with the new Judy Garland film *The Harvey Girls* and in its first week the show took a total of $110,100 – the highest in the history of the Capitol Theater (the previous record was set by Garbo's film *Anna Christie* in 1930). 'We played five shows a day, with an extra one at midnight on Saturdays,' recalls Bob Ripley. 'The Band was on a rising stage and as we appeared playing 'Moonlight Serenade' the voice of our own Murray Kane on the PA system in the theatre would say, "Ladies and gentlemen, the Capitol Theater takes great pride in presenting the Glenn Miller Orchestra" and with those words a tremendous cheer would go up from the audience. The theatre held three or four thousand people, I guess – it was sheer bedlam, an incredibly exciting thing to hear. That happened every day. It was just one of the biggest thrills in one's life to hear that reception five times a day, week after week! It was really quite a thing, and it made you wonder and think how things would have been if Glenn had come back. With the reception we got even without Glenn, just think what it would have been if he'd been with us – he'd have had a tremendous career. People would call out from the audience for Glenn, saying "Where's Glenn?" and it was apparent that a lot of people didn't even know he wasn't with us. They were expecting to see Glenn Miller in those shows, and that was kind of surprising.'

The Miller name and music was still magic at the box office, and besides the vast civilian following for the pre-war Band there were now millions of ex-GIs who had heard the AEF Band in the ETO and were keen to hear the new civilian edition of it. The Band played many of the AEF arrangements as well as favourites from the pre-war Band and in many ways was an ideal combination of the Glenn Miller civilian and AEF Bands. Like the pre-war Band, the new one made many recordings for RCA Victor and for five years touring throughout the USA as the 'official' Glenn Miller Band it was very popular and successful in an age when the big bands were mostly on the decline. The personnel of the Band underwent many changes as most of the original members gave up the life of touring musicians for more settled careers as studio musicians in New York or Hollywood. After three years the string section was dropped and the Band reverted to a conventional seventeen-piece dance band. It ceased to be the 'official' Glenn Miller Band in November 1950 (by arrangement with the Glenn Miller Estate) and leader Beneke continued with the band as his own though it still continued to play many of the famous Glenn Miller tunes. Thenceforth there was no 'official' Glenn Miller Band until June 1956 when the 'New Glenn Miller Orchestra' was launched by the Miller Estate with Ray McKinley as leader, and this Band has continued to this day although Ray McKinley gave up the leadership in 1966.

But the music of Major Glenn Miller's American Band of the AEF has never been re-created with complete fidelity in the post-war years and no formal attempt has ever been made to re-form the Band as it was during the war. Indeed, such a project, at any rate on a permanent basis, would have been almost impossible, even in the 1940s and 1950s, owing to the costs involved in salaries and expenses and conflicting career interests of the people concerned. Later, the declining economics of the dance band business made it even more difficult.

In the immediate post-war years, however, there were a few revivals of the AEF Band's music in the USA. Most notable of these, at least in popularity and staying power, was the Beneke–Miller Orchestra, principally in its early years till 1948. Its AEF arrangements came passably close to the originals despite a rather thin sound due to the Band being smaller than the AEF Band, and at times a comparative lack of power and attack and a rather plodding rhythm section. Secondly, Jerry Gray made several recordings of the AEF Band's music just after the war with a large orchestra containing some former members of the AEF Band, and again many of these came close to the wartime originals, at least as far as the orchestral items with strings were concerned. But Jerry Gray's orchestra was only a recording orchestra, not a permanent one, and by the time he embarked on a career as a dance band leader in 1950 he only assembled a seventeen-piece band without strings and did not set out to re-create the AEF Band.

Perhaps the best re-creation of all came in 1959 when Johnny Desmond recorded twelve of the songs he had sung with the AEF Band, using the same orchestral accompaniments he had had with it, for a long-playing record entitled *Once Upon A Time*. For this he was accompanied by Norman Leyden conducting a thirty-three-piece orchestra including strings which contained some of the men from the AEF Band, and the re-creations for this recording, made in New York for Columbia Records, came remarkably close to the originals, despite some small revisions to the arrangements. This, too, was only a recording project.

Re-creations, however, became superfluous, at least as far as records were concerned, when at long last some recordings by the original Army Air Forces Band were issued publicly for the first time in the USA in 1955, and in 1956 in Great Britain. Here at last we could hear once again, in brilliant high fidelity, the genuine music just as it was heard during the war. Our recollections were not shattered but enhanced.

At the same time it underlined the inescapable fact that the music of Major Glenn Miller's American Band of the AEF was unique – not just any forty musicians playing those arrangements but *those* forty: that brass section with its punch and attack, that swinging rhythm section perhaps impossible to duplicate, those superb strings and that saxophone section (six players, not five); it was Ray McKinley, Mel Powell, Peanuts Hucko, Bernie Privin, Vince Carbone, Trigger Alpert, Johnny Desmond and the Crew Chiefs – but most of all it was the feeling and control of its conductor and creator, Major Glenn Miller. There will never be another band like it.

Today most of the men from the Band are still at the top of their profession playing full time in symphony orchestras, in theatre, radio and recording orchestras, or in dance or jazz bands. Some are retired, or semi-retired, while others have left music altogether. Sadly, some are no longer with us: George Ockner, Joe Shulman, Carl Swanson, Henry Brynan, Stanley Harris, Dick Motylinski, Bobby Nichols, Frank Ippolito, Addison Collins, Jerry Gray, Carmen Mastren, Harry Katzman, John Halliburton, Jimmy Priddy, Lynn Allison, Dave Herman, Murray Kane and Johnny Desmond have all passed on after very successful careers in various musical fields. Paul Dudley died in 1959 after a distinguished career as a radio and television writer including a spell in England in the mid-fifties as writer of the television series *Robin Hood* starring Richard Greene. Don Haynes died in 1971.

At least thirty are still active in music, although a few have given up playing and turned to management or contracting work. Zeke Zarchy, Bernie Privin, Whitey Thomas, Jack Steele, Jimmy Priddy, John Halliburton, Jim Harwood, Hank Freeman, Peanuts Hucko, Jack Ferrier, Freddy Guerra, Chuck Gentry, Ray McKinley, Dave Sackson, Eugene Bergen, Phil Cogliano, Earl Cornwell, Ernie Kardos, Joseph Kowalewsky, Freddy Ostrovsky, Dave Schwartz, Morris Bialkin, and Bob Ripley are still playing regularly – most of them full time and others now and then. Ray McKinley is semi-retired after twenty years as a bandleader followed by various work as a leader, drummer and singer over the years in radio, television, concerts and recordings. Peanuts Hucko is now one of the world's outstanding jazz clarinettists and plays all over the world as a soloist and recording artist. Zeke Zarchy is still one of the leading studio playtes in Los Angeles.

Nat Peck left the Beneke–Miller Band in 1946 to study at the Paris Conservatoire and then settled in Paris and later Berlin until moving to London in 1965 where he became a leading freelance session musician and jazzman in many types of orchestras and dance bands. Today he is an important musicians contractor for films, radio and television in London and abroad, but he has put away his trombone for good.

Bob Ripley returned to the Cleveland Orchestra in 1946 after four months in the Beneke–Miller Band and moved over to the Boston Symphony Orchestra in 1955. He is still there today, along with Freddy Ostrovsky who is one of the first violins. Norman Leyden and Ralph Wilkinson are busy orchestral conductors after years in radio and television. Murray Kane and Artie Malvin wrote and arranged for shows and singers.

Mel Powell, after studying for years under Paul Hindemith at Yale, left jazz altogether and is now Dean of a music college in California. Emanuel Wishnow retired from the University of Nebraska in 1975. Trigger Alpert, Larry Hall and Lynn Allison left music for other careers.

Harry Katzman worked as an orchestral player, concertmaster and contractor in New York until he retired in 1972. He frequently worked with other men from the Band, including his friend George Ockner: 'George Ockner was a wonderful violinist and a wonderful guy. It was ironic that I had a call one time, round about 1968, I guess. I had just come home from doing a record date in the morning and the radio registry called me and said, "Could you come down right away? Someone didn't show up on a record date". The studio was within two or three minutes of where I was and I just walked over and said, "Who didn't show up?" They said, "George didn't show up". Well, that was the time that George had a heart attack in the street coming to this particular date. He had died in the street. When they got him to the hospital he was gone. It was a big blow to me. Dave Schwartz, Morris Bialkin and I played for the funeral. We did the slow movement from one of the Beethoven Trios. It was a very sad thing. I could hardly play, I was just so broken up. Many musicians came to the funeral. It was one of the saddest performances of my life.' Now, Harry too has gone.

What happened to Major Glenn Miller?

His disappearance was so unexpected, and the known details are so sparse, that it has become regarded as one of the major mysteries of flying and is often included in omnibus collections of unsolved aviation stories, often including inaccuracies and misconceptions about Miller's activities.

The original US Army announcement on 24 December 1944, that Major Miller was missing, gave no details at all beyond the fact that his plane had left England on 15 December and had not arrived in Paris as scheduled. It didn't even say that the plane had taken off from the RAF airfield at Twinwood Farm. This lack of information was partly due to wartime military security, but largely because the Army had no information to give as they were as much in the dark as everyone else. To this day, no further statement has ever been issued by the US military authorities beyond confirming on 18 December 1945 that he was presumed dead. Thus, far from subsiding in the public mind, the mystery of his disappearance remains as intriguing as ever, for nothing sustains a mystery more than a lack of information. Glenn Miller has remained a worldwide celebrity and his musical following is as great today as it has ever been, so it is hardly surprising that speculation and conjecture have flourished as well as a desire to discover the truth. And at least if his remains were ever found they could be given a Christian burial.

There has certainly been no lack of speculation, conjecture, rumour and even sensational assertion. Although the theory that Major Miller's plane had gone down in the English Channel had been generally accepted as the likely solution, especially by those most closely concerned with him, even by the end of the war in

May 1945 it was rumoured that he had not crashed in the Channel at all but had been stabbed to death in Paris. Over the years this allegation has reappeared from time to time, usually embroidered as the years go by. Other stories put about in the late 1940s included suggestions that Major Miller was a black marketeer in hiding, and a physical or psychological wreck in an ex-servicemen's home who couldn't face the world.

It was not until late in 1946 that the first authoritative information was published by someone who was involved with Major Miller at the time he disappeared and which added something to the bare facts given two years earlier. The AEF Band's former Programme Director, Paul Dudley, wrote in *Bomblight Serenade*:

The following facts are listed to belie the fictions of the many rumor-happy gossipers who have erroneously reported the details surrounding Major Miller's departure: For those whose carelessly flapping tongues have reported that they witnessed Glenn taking off that day in a twin-engined Douglas C-47, it was actually a single-engine Norseman C-64, an all-metal plane equipped with one-way radio, fixed landing gear and a reputation for treachery in bad weather. For those badly informed 'experts' who claim that Miller was flying without orders, he was proceeding under official order issued by SHAEF (Rear) to travel via Military Aircraft to the Continent on or about December 15. For the hundreds of others whose adventuresome imaginations have claimed that 'they were supposed to have been on the same plane', it was a seven-passenger ship. It was flown by a pilot who had completed a lengthy tour of combat missions, Flight Officer Johnny Morgan. Lieutenant Haynes heard Glenn ask, 'Where are the parachutes?' Then, Baessell's bluff reply, 'What the hell, Miller, do you want to live forever?'

Five years later, Don Haynes gave a more detailed account of Major Miller's disappearance to *Down Beat* magazine for their special Glenn Miller Tribute issue of 27 July 1951 (substantially what is contained in his diary of the time), and at the same time attempted to refute once and for all the rumours surrounding the Major's disappearance.

For some years the reminiscences of Haynes and Dudley remained almost the only published information on Glenn Miller's disappearance and (apart from small details) they have not been invalidated by later research. However, in recent years more information on the AEF Band's career has come to light and new theories have been put forward, by aviation archaeologists among others, concerning Major Miller's last flight.

Although Major Miller and Colonel Baessell boarded the Norseman at the RAF airfield at Twinwood Farm, the USAAF Missing Aircrew Report dated 23 December 1944, concerning the disappearance of the three men, shows that the plane began its flight from the 2nd Strategic Air Depot of the Eighth Air Force at Abbots Ripton which adjoined the Flying Fortress base at Alconbury, about fifteen miles north-east of Twinwood Farm. Abbots Ripton was AAF Station no. 547, but in his diary entry for December 15 Haynes refers to Colonel Baessell speaking by telephone to Flight Officer Morgan at Station 595 which was Troston (the 1st Strategic Air Depot, adjoining the fighter base at Honnington) near Bury St Edmunds. This could have been a slip by Haynes, who sometimes got his distances and sense of direction wrong, unless Morgan took the plane via Troston first for some other purpose: if so, it would have added an extra hundred miles or so to the overall flight. The Missing Aircrew Report also shows that the destination of the Norseman was Bordeaux, with a stop at the AAF airfield at Villacoublay, near Paris.

Doubts have been expressed as to whether the Norseman could have flown as far as Paris non-stop, especially as it doesn't seem to have refuelled at Twinwood. However, the Norseman had a range of 1,150 miles at normal cruising speed and maximum petrol tankage. The overall distance from Abbots Ripton to Paris, on a course flying over Newhaven, Sussex, and Dieppe in Northern France, which was the probable course the flight would have taken, is approximately three hundred miles (or if it went via Troston first, about 400 miles) – well within its range in normal conditions.

But conditions that day were not normal and all Air Transport Command flights from Bovingdon to France were grounded by the weather. There was no 'operational' flying from Twinwood or Cranfield (Twinwood's parent airfield) that day. Over large areas of England there were varying densities of fog with low cloud ceilings and freezing temperatures. However, the idea that the Norseman carrying Major Glenn Miller was the only, or one of the few, aircraft flying that day is very far from the truth. Besides large-scale RAF bomber operations, the Eighth Air Force also mounted two large bombing missions against Germany, although a third mission of approximately 350 B-24 Liberators of the 2nd Air Division based mainly in Norfolk and Suffolk was 'scrubbed', probably because of the deteriorating weather conditions. One of the two successful missions was by the 1st Air Division totalling 334 Flying Fortresses from the area of Huntingdonshire, Cambridgeshire, Bedfordshire and Hertfordshire, and 296 escorting fighters (the other was mounted by the 3rd Air Division from Suffolk and Essex airfields). The bombers took off in hazardous weather conditions to bomb Kassell, although one crashed on take-off at Podington (about seven miles north-west of Twinwood) after aborting rather than climb into low cloud with a faulty airspeed indicator. On return from the mission in the early afternoon the bombers found themselves in serious difficulties owing to low cloud and bad visibility. Two Fortresses from the 306th Bomb Group (Thurleigh) collided in thick cloud near Newbury, one from the 305th Bomb Group at Chelveston (a few miles north of Twinwood) crashed into a radar tower at Daventry, while of the thirty-six Fortresses of the 398th Bomb Group at Nuthampstead, Herts, only three were able to land because conditions were so bad, the rest being diverted to Bassingbourn. All this happened in the very area from which Major Miller's plane took off and would fly over, and although they couldn't possibly have known of the bomber crashes and diversions they knew the ATC flights from Bovingdon were grounded. They were also aware of the overall weather situation – indeed at Twinwood Farm they were right in the middle of it! So why did they take off in such conditions? At the very least it seems to indicate poor judgement by the three men, particularly, perhaps, the pilot, especially as the planes based at Twinwood were grounded for the day. It seems they were anxious to get to Paris and just decided to take a chance.

All the circumstances of their departure seem rather curious. Would one day's delay have mattered very much? For Major Miller there would seem to have been no special urgency – Haynes had already arranged billets for the men in Paris and although the Band was due to fly over on the Saturday its first concert in Paris did not take place till the following Thursday, 21 December (although the delay in getting the Band over to Paris until Monday the 18th may have prevented earlier performances). The Norseman's flight was Colonel Baessell's: Major Miller was only being given a lift and presumably could have chosen to wait another day for better weather. In view of his dislike of flying anyway it seems surprising that with the weather so bad he didn't decide to wait until the Saturday. But he had already been held up for two days and by this time was probably impatient to get away.

In the case of Colonel Baessell, perhaps delay would have

mattered more, since the eventual destination of the plane was Bordeaux, and having reached Paris in the late afternoon he would hardly have flown on to Bordeaux until the Saturday. If he didn't leave England till Saturday it might have meant that he would not get back to Twinwood and Milton Ernest until Monday, and we know from Haynes' diary that General Goodrich was expecting him back on Sunday. So Baessell was probably anxious to get started. Whatever their feelings, they took off from Twinwood at 1.45 pm on a flight which should have taken about three hours. But in all the circumstances it seems hard to account for such a rash decision, the clue to which no doubt lay more with Colonel Baessell than with Major Glenn Miller.

Baessell became very friendly with Haynes and Miller and was helpful to the Band in various ways. One of the Band recalls him as a short stocky man (see photograph 15) with a pronounced Southern accent which he made the most of, very energetic and always in a hurry. According to Haynes, he 'left an indelible impression wherever he went . . . he was loud and boisterous – had more brass than a pet store and enjoyed life to the fullest'. He seems to have made frequent trips to Paris where he was well known at the leading bars and the best hotels in the city. Haynes also noted that on the fatal flight on 15 December Baessell took some empty champagne bottles with him in order to buy a new case of champagne which wasn't possible without returning the empties as bottles were in short supply: this, and Baessell's apparent life-style in wartime, has prompted suggestions – without any evidence – that he was some sort of black market operator. It is certainly intriguing to speculate on the purpose of his flight to Bordeaux that weekend, which might well have been a perfectly legitimate quest for supplies of French wines for the Officers' Club at Milton Ernest.

Flight Officer Morgan, who had flown Baessell over to Paris before, is a somewhat shadowy figure about whom little is known. He was serving with the 35th Depot Repair Squadron at the 2nd Strategic Air Depot at Abbots Ripton where he was a ferry pilot, not, as Haynes and Dudley stated, a former B-24 pilot. His former CO remembers him as something of a loner, while some of those who served with him do not remember him as a particularly outstanding pilot, especially when flying on instruments.

Their route from Twinwood would presumably have taken them almost due south and to the west of London rather than the east (military aircraft were forbidden to fly over the capital), turning south-east in the Windsor area perhaps and heading almost in a straight line for Paris and passing over Newhaven and Dieppe. This was the route normally followed by the 'SHAEF Shuttle' of the ATC flying from Bovingdon. The route east of London might have taken them too close to the German-held positions in the Dunkirk area which had been by-passed and cut off by the Allied advance towards the Low Countries. Haynes refers in his diary to the Channel being ninety miles wide on the route the plane would have taken – this is almost exactly the distance between Newhaven and Dieppe. On the other hand, they may have decided to chance the eastern route which at least would have involved a shorter distance over water.

No trace of the plane after it took off has ever been found but there is a significant reference in Haynes' diary on 18 December to 'one startling fact, that a single motor ship had been charted out of the UK from a southerly point headed over the Channel in the general direction of Paris but was not reported as flying over the French coast'. This is the only concrete clue, albeit slight, to the aircraft's fate that has ever turned up.

There is another curious aspect to the flight which should be noted. At that period of the war, flights from the UK to France by non-combatant military personnel were usually made via the ATC airfield at Bovingdon for purposes of security and customs clearance and changing money into French currency, though perhaps this only applied to SHAEF personnel and not, for instance, to the Eighth Air Force. On the evidence of Haynes' diary for 17 and 18 December no planes had taken off from Bovingdon for Paris 'all last week' which would include Friday the 15th. Evidently the Norseman flew straight on towards Paris without landing at Bovingdon, but to judge from Haynes' comment that 'it had me worried' he must have expected it to land at Bovingdon. And yet a rumour has arisen in recent years that Glenn Miller was seen at Bovingdon on the 15th: confusion with one of Major Miller's earlier visits to Paris in October and November via the 'SHAEF Shuttle' may account for this, however.

There is yet one more curious aspect to Major Miller's disappearance, which also concerns Haynes. Despite the fact that the Band's scheduled flight to Paris on Saturday the 16th was called off and was again called off on the Sunday, nowhere in Haynes' diary is there any indication that he tried to get in touch with Major Miller in Paris to tell him of the delay, yet it seems likely that Miller would be planning to meet them when they arrived. Perhaps Haynes assumed, or was told, that someone at SHAEF would let Miller know of the delay, in which case it is reasonable to suppose that SHAEF would have told Haynes whether or not they had been able to contact Miller in Paris.

On the other hand, at dawn on the morning of Saturday the 16th the heavy German attack on the American front in the Ardennes in Belgium began and the 'Battle of the Bulge' was under way: this was a major crisis for the Allied Command, and all telephone lines to Paris would have been heavily booked for operational traffic thus preventing any other calls. All the same, it seems very odd that Haynes makes no mention whatever of any attempt to notify Major Miller of the Band's delayed departure, especially considering the detailed record of those days contained in the diary.

No wreckage from the plane or its contents ever seems to have come to light, although there have been at least two instances where aircraft wreckage recovered from the bed of the Channel has been said at first to have come from the missing Norseman: in September 1973 it was claimed that some wreckage brought up by a diver off Calais was part of the plane, and in November 1977 similar claims were made for some engine parts caught in a fisherman's net off Newhaven, Sussex. Both claims turned out to be mistaken. Yet another claim to have located the wreckage in the English Channel was made in 1985: this claim has yet to be proved (or disproved).

The fact that no identifiable wreckage has ever been discovered has prompted other suggestions that the aircraft did not go down in the Channel at all but crashed in a remote area of England and still lies undiscovered, perhaps in thick and inaccessible woodland. One theory has connected the Norseman with a crash in the Chiltern Hills on 15 December 1944, in which it is said the aircraft was never found, while another has suggested it may have crashed on the South Downs. In view of the fact that numerous Second World War crashed aircraft have been discovered and excavated, both in Britain and in several countries on the Continent, these theories are not as unlikely as they at first appear. Furthermore, the Chiltern Hills area is more or less under the Norseman's probable flight path, although perhaps a little too far to the west (which might be accounted for if the weather had forced the plane off course). However, there is an inconsistency in the time of the Chiltern crash, which was evidently in the dark, whereas the Norseman took off at a quarter to two in the afternoon and would have flown over the Chilterns shortly afterwards. On the other hand, if the Norseman did come down in England this might explain its failure to go through Bovingdon which clearly worried Haynes at the time.

Perhaps the most sensational claim of all was made in 1984 when a former Royal Air Force navigator said that when his Lancaster bomber was returning as part of a large bomber force from an aborted raid on Germany on the afternoon of 15 December and jettisoned their bombs in the Channel the crew noticed too late that the blast waves from the bombs overturned a Norseman plane far below them and it dived into the sea. However, evidence shows that by the time Miller's plane would have reached the Channel the bombers were back at their bases in Suffolk, so the plane could not have been Miller's.

What of the flight itself and the aircraft involved?

The Norseman was a single-engine high-wing monoplane of metal and wood frame and fabric-covered construction with a fixed undercarriage, about the size of the British Lysander. It had an enclosed cabin with two seats in front for the pilot and co-pilot and eight passenger seats along the sides of the cabin in the rear.

Norseman aeroplanes were originally built by Noorduyn Aviation, Ltd., of Montreal, Canada, and first flew in 1936. They were used with great success by Canadian airlines and transport operators, particularly for rough work in the Canadian North-West. The landing gear wheels could be removed and replaced by floats or skis. In 1942 the plane attracted the attention of the US Army Air Forces and was subsequently built under licence by the Aeronca Company at Middletown, Ohio, and used in considerable numbers by the Army Air Forces during the Second World War when it was designated the UC-64A. In the summer of 1944 the AAF began to use it in Great Britain for transporting passengers and freight between airfields and later between Great Britain and the Continent. It had a maximum cruising speed of 148 mph and a range at normal cruising speed and maximum petrol tankage of 1,150 miles. Its use, therefore, for Colonel Baessell's flight to France would have been quite usual in normal wartime conditions.

Of course, no-one will ever know for certain what happened to the plane that December afternoon, but various possibilities can be seriously considered and among those people best fitted to offer an informed and authoritative assessment of what might have happened are undoubtedly experienced flyers from that period of the Second World War. In 1943–4, Lieutenant Royal D. Frey was serving as a P-38 Lightning fighter pilot with the 55th Fighter Squadron of the 20th Fighter Group of the Eighth Air Force. Although the 20th and two of its Squadrons (the 77th and 79th) were based at Kingscliffe, Northamptonshire, the 55th was based at this time about three miles away at Wittering RAF Station on the Great North Road. Now Lieutenant Colonel Frey, USAF Reserve (Ret.)* of Springfield, Ohio, he suggests what might have been the fate of the now-famous Norseman.

'Firstly, regardless of what some people claim, the UC-64A did not have de-icing equipment on it. For the record, I have in front of me AAF Technical Order No. 01-155CB-1, which was the pilot's flight operating instructions for Army model UC-64A airplanes. This was the Bible for pilots who were going to fly the UC-64A, and no reference is made in this Technical Order anywhere as to de-icing equipment. Had the plane had such equipment it would have been in this TO. The engine did have a carburetor heater to prevent the formation of ice, or to remove ice already formed, which you generally used when you were throttled back and gliding down and you didn't want ice to form inside the carburetor which would have reduced or cut off the fuel flow to the engine. However, under certain humidity and temperature conditions you could encounter carburetor icing while flying straight and level or even climbing.

'Among the instruments, the airplane had a compass of the remote indicating type; later airplanes also had a standby compass of the magnetic type. For flight in inclement weather the plane had a gyro horizon, a directional gyro, and a turn-and-bank indicator, all of which were operated by the engine-driven vacuum pump, and a rate-of-climb gage. It also had an airspeed pitot heater and drain – the electrically-heated type – and the usual complement of instruments such as altimeter, airspeed indicator, engine rpm gage, and manifold pressure (boost).

'The UC-64A also had the SCR-274N radio set in it. This consisted of three receivers and two transmitters. The receivers could be used for voice or code and could be used individually or simultaneously; each had its own set of controls, including tuning

* Prior to his retirement in January 1981 as a civilian employee of the US Civil Service, Colonel Frey had worked for the US Air Force Museum at Wright-Patterson AFB, Ohio, for twenty-one years, the last nine years as its Curator. He has been an avid Miller buff since 1939.

and volume controls and jacks for headsets. The two transmitters were pre-set on two different frequencies, and transmission was possible on either frequency but not both at once. The pilot had the choice of three types of emission on either of the two frequencies – voice, CW (to use the telegraph key for Morse code or a coded message), or tone (to send out a solid tone to Direction Finding Stations on the ground so that they could get a directional bearing on the transmitting airplane). There was also provision for an SCR 595 radio set in case the AAF wished to install them, but UC-64As didn't automatically have them. The 595 was an IFF (Identification Friend or Foe) radio, the one that ground-based radar would pick up so your signal would properly identify you to the friendly radar stations so that the anti-aircraft guns wouldn't fire on you. There was also provision for the storage of an SCR 578 radio set, equipped with a small parachute to permit dropping from an airplane in case of an emergency; it was waterproof and designed to float. I doubt whether the plane being flown by Morgan had one of these sets. I do not ever recall seeing one in England.

'Miller's plane took off at about two in the afternoon in low clouds (at 800 or 1,000 feet) with a mist or light rain coming down and a temperature of 34 degrees, which would have meant that they wouldn't have had to have climbed more than about 1,200 to 1,500 feet before they would have been in the freezing level. This could have meant that as the plane passed through the air moisture could have collected and frozen on its wings and propeller – in fact, all over the plane. This would have had two effects: it would have increased the weight of the aircraft, and it would have tended to disturb the aerofoil, decreasing the lift of the wings. Also, if the propeller blades had collected ice, this would have tended to decrease the efficiency of the propeller.

'There is an idea that some people are kicking around pertaining to the Chiltern Hills, a supposedly desolate area west of London. A number of people have written to me and said, "Well, they're still finding airplanes there". Now let's look at it practically. The airplanes they're digging up all over England are primarily tactical-type high-speed aircraft that were all-metal (such as the Spitfire, P-38, P-47, P-51, and even the Ju 88) and when they hit the ground they were in a steep or vertical dive travelling at 400 or 500 miles an hour. When a high-speed airplane in a high-speed dive hits the ground it fragments – everything fragments, including the human beings in it, and the heavier items such as the machine guns, the engines, the landing gear struts, and the props, this type of thing, tend to go on down into the ground, while some of the lighter, thin-type metal that's broken off may be scattered on top of the ground. Even the slower bombers, such as the B-17, would often bury their engines and bombs if they hit soft earth while in a steep dive. The UC-64A was a relatively light aircraft, fabric-covered, and in my experience, all aircraft that I can ever remember crashing that were fabric-covered and light wing loading like the UC-64A – when they hit the ground they did *not* go in. Maybe the engine and the propeller would be buried a couple or three feet, but everything else would be crushed and fractured. However, the fabric tended to hold it together. The wheels might come off and bounce hundreds of feet; the broken wings might rebound one way and the tail another, but in general the airplane would still be on top of the ground, including the bodies even though they might be mutilated. These two different circumstances could be compared to dropping a ball bearing and a wad of paper into a mud bank.

'Now, one of the flying restrictions on the UC-64A SPECIFICALLY PROHIBITED ANY DIVING SPEED OVER 200 MILES AN HOUR INDICATED AIRSPEED, AND FROM WHAT I KNOW OF THE UC-64A with a maximum diving speed of 200 miles an hour, if it got up to around 280 or 300 miles an hour it probably would have come unglued in the air. I don't think you'd ever get the plane going that fast without it disintegrating before it ever hit the ground.

'I don't think Miller's plane went down in England unless it dove into a river, a lake or a bank of quicksand and was completely swallowed up. If it had crashed on land the airplane would still be on top of the ground with pieces scattered around thirty or forty or fifty feet – a wing here, a rudder there, etc., with the bodies or skeletons or remains such as they might be at this late date. You cannot tell me that in forty-odd years someone would not have stumbled onto that airplane had it been lying on top of the ground – it would have been found by someone out chasing a fox, or looking for a lost dog, or hunting a rabbit, or just out for a hike. Someone would have discovered it by now, as opposed to a World War Two aircraft which crashed at high speed, where pieces on top of the ground would have been picked up by salvage teams at the time of the crash and what went into the ground was forgotten about for 35 years until some of those buffs in England began to look for pieces in the ground that they could recover by digging. You'll never convince me that the UC-

64A went down in England unless it went into a river or a lake somewhere.

'Let's assume the plane crossed out over the coastline headed for France – what could have happened? Well, any number of things *could* have happened. Though extremely improbable, it is ridiculously possible it was hit by a meteor entering the earth's atmosphere; they could have been so low they hit the conning tower of a German submarine; they could have run into a seagull that knocked the engine out – any number of things could have happened to the plane. But let's pick the one that, based on the experience of people who fly (and, I assume you will agree, are probably most capable of guessing to the best degree what happened) is most likely to have happened: the plane headed out over the water in those bad weather conditions and probably iced up, causing any number of things to occur.

'First of all, let's spell out the various situations in which the plane would have had to have entered the water. One would have been an uncontrolled spin; another would have been a glide, dive, or spiral, either under control or out of control; and the third would have been a controlled ditching with Morgan levelling out and holding the plane in the air as long as possible in order to reduce airspeed to a minimum before contact with the water. We can discount the occupants parachuting because Don Haynes personally told me that there were no 'chutes on board.

'Now, let's go back to the pitot heat. The pitot tube on an airplane is what measures airspeed – it's nothing more than a tube that sticks out from the airplane and the ram air being forced into the tube head from the airplane passing through the air creates a pressure that is passed through a line to an instrument that has a needle on it and shows you how fast you're going. If you start to get ice in that pitot tube and you don't have that heater on for some reason – say the heater element isn't working, or the pilot forgets to turn it on, or there's a break in the electrical heater line – the pitot tube head doesn't heat up, ice forms in it, the air pressure to the instrument is affected, and the airspeed registered on the instrument decreases. A pilot flying on instruments always keeps his eyes on that airspeed, along with the gyro compass and his artificial horizon – your artificial horizon shows you whether you're flying level whether you're banking one way or another and also whether you're nose up or nose down. You're flying on instruments, you can't see out and all you've got are your instruments; if your airspeed tends to drop off, subconsciously you'll probably push forward on the stick or control wheel, ever so slowly to pick up your airspeed again. When flying, be it on instruments or not, maintaining a minimum safe airspeed is critical and some pilots would tend to discount the artificial horizon, fearing most of all a stall due to low airspeed and a resulting spin. Now, let's assume that Morgan – for some reason his pitot tube froze up and his airspeed started to drop off – subconsciously began to push forward on his control wheel to regain a safe airspeed. If the airspeed continued to drop off, the more he could have dropped his nose until he was actually in a dive at a high speed while his airspeed indicator read a slow or even "below stalling" speed. If he were only a thousand or twelve hundred feet in the air, it would not have taken very long before his plane would have hit the water. And in rain or fog, with his eyes glued on the instrument panel he would never have even seen the water coming up. I'm not saying that's what happened – I'm just saying that's what *could* have happened. It has happened to others.

'I don't know much about Morgan's past experience, but as a Flight Officer he probably would not have had too much flying experience – if he'd been a very experienced pilot he should have been more than an AAF Flight Officer. I certainly don't think he would have been very experienced on instruments. I don't think there are very many Flight Officers *or* Second Lieutenants in World War Two who had very much instrument experience. I know that *I* didn't, and whenever I had to go on instruments I always liked to keep the airplane fairly straight and level until I got to good weather, be it five minutes or thirty minutes. But let's say Morgan was on instruments and the plane iced up heavily. He then decided he'd better get back to England. He put the aircraft into a fairly steep bank and if he had had very much ice on the airplane it would have been heavier, it would have had a higher wing loading, the aerofoil would have been a little screwed up with ice, and the wing would have had less lift – he could have stalled and gone into an immediate spin and spun in.

'I don't think we'll ever know for certain what happened to that airplane, but I think most people will agree that whatever happened it was so sudden that Morgan had no time to radio. With the radios he had in that airplane he should have been able to reach one coast or the other from the middle of the English Channel – lets say he got half way across, well, he should have been able to transmit and reach both sides. Someone would have heard him had he transmitted, I'm almost certain, because those transmitters would have been on – they would have been set on the ground (he couldn't set them in the air) on standard frequencies that everyone used. In the control towers at various airfields the receivers would have been set to those frequencies, so I'm *certain* that had he transmitted someone would have heard him somewhere up and down the English coast or over in France. But, whatever happened, he didn't have time to radio. If it had been a slow process where he slowly became concerned, such as a gradual loss of engine power, I think he would have gotten on the radio and called someone. You'll never convince me that he sat out there and didn't transmit because he just didn't feel like it. Either something critical (such as a crash) happened to him before he had a chance to transmit, or he got into a situation where he was so damn busy that he couldn't take the time to transmit – and I'm talking about a graveyard spiral, or a spin. Say he was on instruments and he started to turn to come back, or he got into bad weather and it got bumpy, or he got vertigo and the airplane began to drift off on one wing or the other as usually happens if an inexperienced pilot on instruments doesn't maintain his concentration. You've got to concentrate on those instruments constantly, you've got to look at your compass, your airspeed, that artificial horizon, the rate of climb. I'm sure that anyone who's ever flown an airplane and who got into a bind while on instruments will agree with me. When you're fighting that plane to get it back under control, I guarantee you don't take time to call someone on the radio to tell them what's happening because there's not a damn thing they can do for you. Every ounce of concentration, every ounce of energy, and every ounce of prayer goes to getting that plane under control. I think anyone who has ever flown any amount at all will agree that whatever happened to Morgan it didn't give him the time to make a radio call. Again, all this is strictly conjecture, and I'm no expert on it; I'm simply relying on my own personal experience and that of friends with whom I've flown over a period of years.

'Now, let's consider another aspect. Let's say that for some reason Morgan had engine trouble – water in the gasoline line, the carburetor heater didn't work, or the prop ran away, or he simply ran out of gas (he wouldn't have been the first to do this) – let's say they got out over the Channel and the engine quit. If that had happened I would assume Morgan would have made a radio call if he'd had any appreciable altitude. But let's say the engine quit at a fairly low altitude and he was so busy trying to get the plane down that he didn't have a chance to make a radio call. He would have tried to keep the airplane going straight ahead, I would imagine, and would have dropped the nose to keep the airspeed up so he would not have stalled and gone into a spin. Let's say he broke out of the overcast over the Channel and looked down at that cold water and realized he was going to have to ditch. Well, he had a fixed landing gear on that airplane and I'm sure that if he had tried to ditch that plane in the water and it was a choppy sea, the first time one of those wheels hit one of those waves the plane would have flipped on its back. If that had happened, that probably would have taken care of the people inside. But let's say, for the sake of discussion, that he was able to make a safe water landing and the plane had remained right side up and they had gotten out of the airplane into the water. What then? As far as I can recall, Don Haynes never told me they had Mae Wests, much less a life raft on that airplane. So, they got out into that horribly cold water and it's in the middle of winter – in no time at all they're going to be dead. When I was flying combat over there in the winter of 1943–4, we were told that if we went down in the Channel or North Sea with our Mae Wests on, or even if we were able to get into our dinghies, within seven minutes, ten minutes at the most, we would be unconscious and die almost immediately of exposure. You just don't survive in cold water like that. Let's say they did get into the water, with or without dinghies, with or without Mae Wests – it doesn't make a damn bit of difference – they were dressed in only their uniforms, they were not wearing rubberized exposure suits – they get into that water and they're dead in minutes.

'That was on 15 December 1944. It was not until three days later that Don Haynes and the Band got to Paris. Now, Don Haynes told me this himself – it was after they had landed at Paris that he gradually realized that Glenn hadn't sent the trucks to pick them up, and it was a matter of two days after that, while they were checking, before they found out that there was no indication that Miller had arrived in France. So it was five days before they were positive that he hadn't gotten there. By that time there was absolutely no use in searching for survivors. Another thing – the Battle of the Bulge had just popped, there were hundreds of guys being killed and captured every day, and here were three fellows who had disappeared on a flight five days before across a stretch of water in which, had they gone into it, they would have died in a matter of a few minutes. So why in the world would anyone ever launch any kind of a search at that time, with the military situation being what it was? You've got to put it in the context in which it actually took place – they were having airplanes shot down every day, and every time an American bomber was shot down there were ten guys who were dead or captured. In the Battle of the Bulge they were losing fellows faster than they could probably keep track of them, and here was an airplane that had disappeared – a little put-put – flying from England to France with three guys on board: one was a Flight Officer; one was a Lieutenant Colonel ground-pounder, a non-flying officer; and the third was a fellow named Miller, a major who played the trombone. That's cold-blooded, but let's face it, with the war going on like it was and the circumstances under which they disappeared, I don't think anyone could have been expected to send out an air-sea rescue boat to look for them. If they had found anything at all it would have been a corpse floating in the water. But that's the way it goes, tough as it still is to me, a person who has practically worshipped Glenn Miller since I was fifteen years of age.

'I don't know the exact dimensions of the English Channel – about ninety miles across, more than two hundred and fifty miles long, and that's a hell of a lot of water. After five days the top brass found out that the airplane had not reached France – if they had decided to launch a search where would they have conducted it? Generally, when you search for someone you usually know within a few miles his last position, you know where to start. They had an area ninety miles wide and two hundred and fifty miles long – they would not have had any idea where to begin, even if they had assumed Morgan had stayed on course.

'So, to sum up – I don't think they went down in England. I believe they got over the Channel and in all probability went into the water in either a crash or a ditching. Since they left England and apparently didn't get to the Continent, and didn't have unlimited fuel to fly away for ever, they had to have gone down in the water. Based on my own personal experience of flying over there and under the winter conditions that I flew in and they were flying in, I think that if my life depended upon a "best guess" I would have to stick with the "into the Channel" premise as being the most logical.

'Incidentally, I remember the day that Glenn Miller went down very, very, clearly, just like it were yesterday, although I didn't know at the time that he had gone down that day. I was in Stalag Luft I, a German POW Camp at Barth on the Baltic, north of Berlin. It was cold and it was gloomy, with thick cloud above us about a thousand or twelve hundred feet up. It wasn't raining, but it looked like it could at any time and it wouldn't have had to have gotten much colder to have been snow. It was one of those days when you go out and the cold just goes right into your bones. There were twenty of us just lying around in the room – that's all we did in prison camp, we didn't work, we were officers – and suddenly we heard a loud long whistling noise outside like a bomb falling, but there was no explosion. Some of the guys had been in a POW transient camp in Frankfurt about a year before when there had been some bombings by B-17s and B-24s and they thought bombs were coming down on us. They all dived under their beds and I had quite a trip as I was on the top bunk, third high, right by the window. Well, the whistling went on and then got fainter, and when the bombs didn't go off we all began to run outside. We thought it must be an airplane but we didn't know what. It was an Arado 234, the first German jet I'd ever seen. He'd buzzed our prison camp from west to east, levelled out over the camp right across the rooftops and went out east, pulled up into a chandelle and came down on us again right across the camp and up and over the pine forest on the left of the camp and then flew away. I immediately went into the barracks and sat down and made a drawing of that plane, which I still have, and dated it 15 December 1944. That must have been within a matter of an hour or so of the time Miller went down because I remember it was in the early afternoon.

'Of course, at the time we didn't know for quite a while, I think probably a couple of weeks, that Miller had gone down, but when we heard the news that's the time I started going out and hanging on the fence. At that period of the war, all the captured AAF officers were being brought to my camp. I realized that unless Miller was injured and in hospital for recuperation somewhere, he would probably come to my prison camp. We had two orchestras there and they were pretty darned good; with 10,000 Americans, we had guys who had done everything. We had one fellow who had played with Matty Malneck and one who had played trumpet with Jimmy Dorsey (I forget their names). One of the orchestras was called the "Round the Benders" – they said in prison camp that when you flipped your lid, when you went nuts or crazy, you went "round the bend" (a few guys did but not many of us) – so they called the orchestra the "Round the Benders". Every time they'd bring in a new batch of prisoners, oh, maybe every week or ten days, I'd run out and hang on that fence looking for Major Miller, because I thought, wouldn't it be wonderful if he'd been captured and came to our prison camp. We already had the musicians, he could do the arranging and conducting and we could have our own Glenn Miller Orchestra. Really, that's one of the things I looked forward to during that bleak winter of 1944–5, because when the Battle of the Bulge came along we went on starvation rations for about the next four months – about five hundred to eight hundred calories a day. We didn't get enough food to keep the flesh on our bones, and there wasn't very much in life that was pleasant at that time other than the fact that we were still alive, although we didn't know what was going to happen to us. Looking forward to having Glenn Miller there was one of the few highlights of my life at that time, but of course he never showed up, much to my regret.'

The hard truth is that the fate of Major Miller and his two companions will remain a mystery unless and until positive evidence turns up in the shape of identifiable wreckage of the Norseman or human remains with their identity discs intact. Meanwhile, alternative theories to the Channel crash can be neither proved nor disproved, but on such evidence as does exist the balance of probability seems to point to the aircraft going down in the English Channel sometime in the afternoon of 15 December 1944.

Neither Major Glenn Miller nor the Army Air Forces Band are even mentioned in the official history of the Army Air Forces in the Second World War* nor in the memoirs of General Eisenhower or those of his wartime associates such as Captain Harry Butcher, USN, or of Lieutenant Kay Summersby for instance, which seems a little surprising since Major Miller and the Band were attached to SHAEF throughout their service in the ETO and were associated with General Eisenhower and his staff on several occasions.

But at the US Air Force Museum at the Wright-Patterson Air Force Base at Dayton Ohio, there is a permanent exhibition devoted to Major Miller and the Band which includes photographs, documents, items of uniform and equipment and one of

---

* *The Army Air Forces in World War II*, edited by W. F. Craven and J. L. Cate, 7 vols. University of Chicago Press *and* Cambridge University Press, 1948–58.

Major Miller's trombones, and visitors can listen to recordings of the Band.

In England the names of Major Glenn Miller, Lieutenant-Colonel Norman F. Baessell and Flight Officer John R. S. Morgan are listed in the personnel records held at the United States Military Cemetery at Maddingly, Cambridgeshire, and their names appear with 5,122 other US servicemen with no known graves carved on the 'Wall Of The Missing' which was unveiled when the wall and the cemetery itself were dedicated on 16 July 1956.

There are still probably hundreds of people living in the Bedford area with personal memories of Major Glenn Miller and the men in the Band from the time they were stationed there, and to this day a prominent feature of many of the reunions of ex-Eighth Air Force veterans organizations is the music of the Miller Band which did so much to lighten their spirits in the dark days of the Second World War.

As a dance band leader Glenn Miller is as popular now as he was during his lifetime. Records of his Bands – not only his pre-war civilian Band but also his Army Air Forces Band, or, as people in Great Britain remember it, the American Band of the AEF – continue to be issued from time to time, and his continuing popularity, not to mention the sales of his records, still surpasses that of any other bandleader. Over the years dozens of bands in America and other countries have copied the Glenn Miller style and his famous hit records and made it the most imitated band in history. There has been an 'official' Miller Band in the United States ever since the end of the war, except for the period 1951–6, and the present band still tours all over the world playing the old Miller favourites and present-day tunes in the Miller style, usually to large and enthusiastic audiences many of whom were not even born when the original band was in its hey-day. The Glenn Miller Society founded in England in 1950 still flourishes world-wide. The film biography *The Glenn Miller Story* made in 1953 was, despite its historical inaccuracies, one of the most popular films ever made in Hollywood and was one of the biggest money-makers its production company Universal-International ever had. It is still shown on television from time to time and the film has had the almost unprecedented distinction of being reissued for the cinema with its original stereophonic soundtrack restored.

Let the last words lie with Major Glenn Miller's friend and colleague, the late Paul Dudley:

On December 18, 1945, the US Army declared the Major 'officially dead'. But men like Glenn Miller don't just die.

He will live musically for a long, long time. But, more important, the Moonlight Serenader, who was drafted into the Army by his own sense of responsibility, will live forever as a great and good friend in the hearts of the three million Yanks with whom he served overseas. Glenn Miller carried his quality wherever he went. As a civilian, his own personal and musical standards made him America's top band leader. In the Army, it made him the kind of a leader men kept following after he was gone.

Glenn possessed the ability to bless musical perfection as vigorously as he could blast imperfection. Working in a Miller band was always a matter of serious business. But the big, be-spectacled six-footer had a heart of warm mush hiding behind a quick-freeze kisser. I knew that best of all one night with the bombs dropping on London as I tried to elude fear and escape to the peace of sleep. Glenn was in the bed across the blacked-out room and through the dark came his typical, tight-lipped voice paraphrasing the 'hello, little friend' with which bomber pilots greeted their fighter escort in a rendezvous over enemy territory. 'Goodnight, little friend,' said the Major.

I felt reassured and closer to home, just as all the GIs felt when they heard from Glenn Miller, and said, proudly as I say now, 'Goodnight, Big Friend.'*

* *Bomblight Serenade.*

PART TWO

Day-By-Day Chronology

28 June 1944–28 July 1945

Glenn Miller and the Band on the stage of the Queensberry Club, London.

Maj. Glenn Miller with Ray McKinley and Mel Powell in the Co-Partners Hall, prob[ably]
Sept. 1944.

Maj. Glenn Miller and British guest singer Gloria Brent at the Band's broadcast fro[m]
Partners Hall, Bedford, 7 Sept. 1944.

Maj. Glenn Miller conducting the American Band of the AEF in the HMV recording studio in London, 16 Sept. 1944. The rhythm section is just off the picture to the right.

Ray McKinley and Dinah Shore with AAF officers at the Rougham bomber base, 15 Sept. 1944.

Maj. Glenn Miller and Musician 1st Class Sam Donahue, at the Queensberry Club, London, 2 Oct. 1944.

Maj. Glenn Miller at the Queensberry Club with some of the British band leaders who protested against the BBC, 28 Sept. 1944: left to right, R.S.M. George Melachrino, comedian Tommy Trinder, Maj. Miller, Lt Ben Oakley, singer Pat Kirkwood, Harry Roy, Maurice Winnick and Victor Sylvester.

Although giving only a distant view of the Band, this picture shows well how GIs crowded into airfield hangars to hear the Band, as here at the Nuthampstead bomber base on 2 Oct. 1944.

'Enlisted Men's Mess', Nuthampstead, 2 Oct. 1944. The officer standing at the left is Capt
William T. Priestly (601st Squadron Operations Officer) who led his own small band at the base.

The Band playing 'In the Mood' at the Jazz Jamboree, London, 15 Oct. 1944; trumpet soloist i
Bobby Nichols. Watching from the wings is boy drummer Victor Feldman.

The brass section: left to right, front row, Jimmy Priddy, John Halliburton, Nat Peck, Larry Hall; back row, relief drummer Frank Ippolito, Bernie Privin, Whitey Thomas, Zeke Zarchy, Bobby Nichols, Jack Steele, pictured at the Jazz Jamboree in London, 15 Oct. 1944.

'Juke Box Saturday Night' at the Jazz Jamboree, with the Crew Chiefs and Bobby Nichols.

Johnny Desmond, singing with the Band at the Jazz Jamboree in London, 15 Oct. 1944.

The Crew Chiefs vocal group: left to right, Gene Steck, Murray Kane, Lynn Allison, Arti Malvin, Steve Steck, at the Jazz Jamboree in London, 15 Oct. 1944.

Maj. Glenn Miller with Victor Feldman (known as 'Kid Krupa') and drummer/comedian Max Bacon backstage at the Jazz Jamboree. Victor Feldman later became a prominent jazz musician in the USA.

American singer Irene Manning joins Maj. Glenn Miller for a 'Music for the Wehrmacht' broadcast from London, Nov. 1944.

Maj. Glenn Miller with Col. Ben Lyon and musicians from 8th Air Force dance bands at th. Granada Cinema, Bedford, 26 Nov. 1944.

The only known photograph of the Band playing in the Olympia Theatre, Paris; once again Bernie Privin is 'sending' all around him, especially Nat Peck.

roup from the Band outside the Hotel des Olympiades: left to right, Morris Bialkin, Nat Peck,
ke Zarchy, Phil Cogliano, Addison Collins, Dave Herman, Lynn Allison, Paul Dubov; front
w, George Ockner, Harry Katzman, Carmen Mastren, Trigger Alpert.

rs Helen Miller receiving her husband's Bronze Star from Col. F. R. Kerr in New York City,
eb. 1945.

Jack Rusin, Nat Peck, Addison Collins and John Halliburton outside the Palais de Méditerranée, Nice, May 1945.

Whitey Thomas, Zeke Zarchy, Norman Leyden and Nat Peck sunbathing on the roof of the Martinez Hotel, Nice, May 1945.

roup from the Band on the steps of the Opéra, Paris, spring 1945: left to right, front row, athan Kaproff, Joseph Kowalewsky, Gene Bergen, Emanuel Wishnow, Stanley Harris, Henry 'ynan; second row, Dave Sackson, ?Joe Shulman, S/Sgt Emile Mitterman (attached to the .nd, but not a player, in front of Shulman), George Ockner, Dick Motylinski, Bob Ripley, Earl ornwell, Harry Katzman, Freddy Ostrovsky, Carl Swanson, Ernie Kardos; at the back, Morris .alkin.

ernie Privin, Addison Collins and John Halliburton, and, in the background, the castle at .ssau where the Band was billeted.

Jerry Gray conducting an open air concert 'somewhere in Germany', 1945; bassist Trigger Alpert in the foreground.

Bernie Privin shows his feelings for the Führer!

il Cogliano, Carmen Mastren and Trigger Alpert doing their 'Venuti and Lang stuff' at the remberg concert, 1 July 1945.

Ray McKinley and Trigger Alpert 'duet' at Nuremberg, 1 July 1945.

Band's-eye view of the vast GI audience 'somewhere in Germany', 1945.

Part of the Major Glenn Miller Army Air Force Band permanent exhibit in the US Air Fo
Museum at the Wright-Patterson Air Force Base, Dayton, Ohio, USA.

Part 2 lists all known radio broadcasts, concerts and other engagements by the American Band of the AEF and its smaller bands in the ETO, together with other related information. With regard to concerts, however, there may well have been others which are not listed and which are not mentioned in the Band's Activities List: for instance, in addition to those mentioned by Lieutenant Haynes in his diary a number of place names are marked on the pages of a pocket atlas he used which may indicate other locations at which the Band played while they were in Great Britain. These places are Deenethorpe, near Kingscliffe, Grafton Underwood, Glatton, Molesworth, Bassingbourn, Duxford, Debden and Bovingdon; no dates are given against these names (unlike others marked in the atlas and in the list of concerts written in the front of the atlas) but they were all locations of USAAF airfields. Also, in recent years local residents have recalled the Band playing in Norwich and Gloucestershire (in August) and Dorset (in September), although no confirmation of this has turned up in 'official' records on in the local press.

Wednesday 28 June 1944
Band arrived at Gourock, Scotland, in the *Queen Elizabeth*, and left Glasgow at 10.00 pm on overnight troop train journey to London.

Thursday 29 June
Band arrived at Euston Station, London, at 7.00 am and travelled in US Army trucks to their billet at Sloane Court, Chelsea.

Sunday 2 July
Band left Sloane Court at 10.00 am and moved to Bedford.

Saturday 8 July
evening Sergeant Ray McKinley and a small group from the Band played at an Officers dance at 8th Air Force Service Command HQ at Milton Ernest Hall.

Sunday 9 July
19.15 AEFP Broadcast from Corn Exchange, Bedford – AMERICAN BAND OF SUPREME ALLIED COMMAND (45 mins) (live). Guest artists: Dorothy Carless and Bruce Trent; compères Leslie Mitchell and Captain

Glenn Miller; producer Sergeant Paul Dudley. Moonlight Serenade/The Flaming Sword Of Liberation/In The Mood/Stardust/ Begin The Beguine (vocal, Dorothy Carless)/*Medley*: My Buddy, Now I Know (vocal, Sergeant Johnny Desmond), Music Makers, Farewell Blues/The GI Jive (vocal, Sergeant Ray McKinley and the Crew Chiefs)/I Couldn't Sleep A Wink Last Night (vocal, Bruce Trent)/Poinciana (vocal, Sergeant Johnny Desmond and the Crew Chiefs)/What Do You Do In The Infantry (vocal, Sergeant Johnny Desmond and the Crew Chiefs)/The Flaming Sword Of Liberation.

Monday 10 July

19.45 AEFP Broadcast, Bedford – STRINGS WITH WINGS (15 mins). Announcer, Corporal Paul Dubov; commère, Lieutenant Charmian Sansom (CWAC). *Theme*: I Sustain the Wings/I Dream Of Jeannie With The Light Brown Hair/Some Day I'll Find You (featuring Sergeant George Ockner, violin)/Holiday For Strings/*Theme*.

Tuesday 11 July

16.30 AEFP Broadcast, Bedford – AMERICAN DANCE BAND: The Swing Shift(30 mins.) Announcer, Corporal Paul Dubov; commère, Lieutenant Charmian Sansom. *Theme*: Song And Dance (later known as The Git Along Song) (composed by Sergeant Ray McKinley) (vocal, Sergeant Ray McKinley)/I Hear You Screaming/My Buddy/Peggy The Pin-Up Girl (vocal, Sergeant Ray McKinley and the Crew Chiefs)/It Must Be Jelly/Cow Cow Boogie (vocal, Sergeant Ray McKinley)/Going My Way (Vocal, Sergeant Johnny Desmond)/Stealing Apples/*Theme*.

18.15 AEFP Broadcast, Bedford – SWING SEXTET: Something For The Boys (15 mins). Anouncer, Corporal Paul Dubov; commère, Lieutenant Charmian Sansom. *Theme*(a composition by Sergeant Mel Powell, later entitled My Guy's Come Back)/S'Wonderful/I Heard You Cried Last Night (vocal, The Crew Chiefs)/Honeysuckle Rose/Halleluja/*Theme*.

Wednesday 12 July

18.15 AEFP Broadcast, Bedford – SWING SEXTET: Something For The Boys (15 mins). Announcer, Corporal Paul Dubov; compère Geoffrey Peck. *Theme*/Love Is Just Around The Corner/A Lovely Way To Spend An Evening (vocal, The Crew Chiefs)/How High The Moon/I Couldn't Sleep A Wink Last Night (vocal, The Crew Chiefs)/Jubilee/*Theme*.

19.45 AEFP Broadcast, Bedford – STRINGS WITH WINGS (15 mins). Announcer, Corporal Paul Dubov; compère Geoffrey Peck. *Theme*/Annie Laurie/Maid With The Flaxen Hair/Someone To Watch Over Me/*Theme*.

Thursday 13 July

20.30 AEFP and Home Service Broadcast – AMERICAN BAND OF SUPREME ALLIED COMMAND (30 mins). Announcer, Jean Metcalf; compère, Captain Glenn Miller. Guest artists, Dorothy Carless and Bruce

Trent. *Theme*: Moonlight Serenade/American Patrol/Summertime/Juke Box Saturday Night (vocal, The Crew Chiefs)/I Couldn't Sleep A Wink Last Night (vocal, Dorothy Carless)/It Must Be Jelly/Without A Song (vocal, Bruce Trent)/Holiday For Strings/ *Theme*.

This broadcast was also transmitted by shortwave to the Blue Network in the USA.

Friday 14 July

09.35 AEFP Broadcast, Bedford – AMERICAN DANCE BAND:The Swing Shift (25 mins). Announcer, Corporal Paul Dubov; commère, Jean Metcalf. *Theme*/King Porter Stomp/Rhapsody in Blue/Shoo Shoo Baby/(vocal, The Crew Chiefs)/The Music Stopped (vocal, Sergeant Johnny Desmond)/Beat Me Daddy Eight to A Bar (vocal, Sergeant Ray McKinley)/Time Alone Will Tell (vocal, Sergeant Johnny Desmond)/ Snafu Jump *Theme*.

11.00 AEFP Broadcast, London – AMERICAN BAND OF SUPREME ALLIED COMMAND: Morning After (recorded repeat of last night's broadcast).

11.00 Broadcasting House, London – Meeting between Captain Glenn Miller and Maurice Gorham to discuss the Band's music.

18.15 AEFP Broadcast, Bedford – SWING SEXTET: The Uptown Hall (15 mins). Compère, Lieutenant Don Haynes (possibly a misprint in the radio archives). *Theme*/Blue Room/Love Is The Sweetest Thing (vocal, The Crew Chiefs)/What Is This Thing Called Love/Irresistible You (vocal, The Crew Chiefs)/China Boy/*Theme*.

evening: Concert by the full Band at USAAF 8th Air Force bomber base at Thurleigh, Beds.

Saturday 15 July

18.15 AEFP Broadcast, Bedford – SWING SEXTET: The Uptown Hall (15 mins). Announcer, Corporal Paul Dubov; commère, Andrea Troubridge. *Theme*/Rose Room/Where Or When/Don't Be That Way/I Couldn't Sleep A Wink Last Night (vocal, The Crew Chiefs)/ Liza/ *Theme*.

Sunday 16 July

12.45 AEFP Broadcast, Bedford – SERGEANT JOHNNY DESMOND SINGS (15 mins). Announcer, Corporal Paul Dubov; commère, Margaret Hubble. *Theme* (Time On My Hands)/Long Ago And Far Away/Blue Orchids/String Of Pearls (*Band*)/How Sweet You Are/*Theme*.

afternoon: Concert at USAAF 8th Air Force Service Command Headquarters, Milton Ernest Hall, Near Bedford (Attendance 1,600).

From here onwards, in order to save space the following have been omitted: themes (signature tunes), which were always the same; compères, unless they were unusual personalities – the full Band programmes were compèred by Captain Glenn Miller (after his disappearance by Warrant Officer Paul Dudley or Sergeant

Broderick Crawford), the Swing Shift by Sergeant Ray McKinley, the Uptown Hall, the Strings With Wings and Sergeant Johnny Desmond by Corporal Paul Dubov or sometimes by Warrant Officer Dudley; duration of broadcasts – the full Band programmes were always thirty minutes, the Swing Shift thirty minutes unless otherwise stated, the Uptown Hall, Strings With Wings, Sergeant Johnny Desmond and Private First Class Jack Rusin programmes fifteen minutes.

Military ranks have been omitted and the following abbreviations used: CC – The Crew Chiefs, JD – Johnny Desmond, RM – Ray McKinley, V – vocal refrain. Broadcasts were made from the Co-Partners Hall, Bedford, unless otherwise stated. For pre-recorded broadcasts, details of music, singers, etc., are given under date of first broadcast, not under date recorded.

Monday 17 July

19.45 AEFP Broadcast – STRINGS WITH WINGS. All The Things You Are/Serenade in Blue/Trees/Sweet And Low.

Tuesday 18 July

18.15 AEFP Broadcast – SWING SEXTET: The Uptown Hall. Trigger Fantasy (featuring Trigger Alpert, bass)/The Very Thought Of You/ Bugle Call Rag (featuring Peanuts Hucko, tenor saxophone)/A Lovely Way To Spend An Evening V, CC/Flying Home (featuring Mel Powell, piano).

20.05 AEFP Broadcast – AMERICAN DANCE BAND: The Swing Shift (25 minutes) The Eyes And Ears Of The World* /Stardust/GIJive V, RM & CC/Along the Santa Fe Trail V, JD/Irresistible You V, CC/Everybody Loves My Baby.

Wednesday 19 July

18.15 AEFP Broadcast – SWING SEXTET: The Uptown Hall. Blue Skies/ These Foolish Things/How High The Moon/There's A Small Hotel V, CC/Between The Devil and The Deep Blue Sea.

19.45 AEFP Broadcast – STRINGS WITH WINGS. Stairway To The Stars/ Estrellita/Trees/Poem, 'The Soldier' by Rupert Brooke, read by Paul Dubov/Our Waltz.

Thursday 20 July

20.30 AEFP and Home Service Broadcast – AMERICAN BAND OF SUPREME ALLIED COMMAND. Guest artists, Vera Lynn and Sergeant Jimmy Miller (RAF). Compères, Captain Franklin Engleman and Captain Glenn Miller. Caribbean Clipper/A Lovely Way to Spend An Evening V, Jimmy Miller/Put Your Arms Around Me Honey V, CC & BAND *Medley*: Mighty Like A Rose, Amor V, JD, Chattanooga Choo Choo V, RM

* A swing arrangement of the signature tune of the Paramount Newsreel, also known as 'Paramount on Parade'.

& cc, Bye Bye Blues/Besame Mucho, v, Vera Lynn/The Anvil Chorus.

Friday 21 July
11.00   AEFP Broadcast, London – AMERICAN BAND OF SUPREME ALLIED COMMAND: Morning After (recorded repeat of last night's programme).
late afternoon   Concert at 8th Air Force Ordnance Depot at Melchbourne Park, near Bedford.
18.16   AEFP Broadcast – SWING SEXTET: The Uptown Hall, probably pre-recorded, date unknown. Louise/Don't Blame Me/Blow Top/ Goodnight Wherever You Are v, cc/The Earl.
Note – According to Haynes' diary, some pre-recordings were made during the morning and early afternoon: no details survive in the radio archives, but in view of the concert at Melchbourne Park it seems likely that the 18.16 broadcast by the Swing Sextet was pre-recorded.

Saturday 22 July
10.30   AEFP Pre-recording – AMERICAN DANCE BAND: The Swing Shift (25 minutes). Broadcast 1/8/44.
18.15   AEFP Broadcast – SWING SEXTET: The Uptown Hall. S'Wonderful/Where or When/Rose Room/There's A Small Hotel v, cc/Don't Be That Way.
19.30   AEFP Pre-recording – SWING SEXTET: The Uptown Hall. Broadcast 25/7/44.
20.00–01.00   Zeke Zarchy and a small group played at the Officers Club at 8th Air Force Service Command Headquarters at Milton Ernest Hall.

Sunday 23 July
12.45   AEFP Broadcast – SERGEANT JOHNNY DESMOND. Going My Way/ That Old Black Magic/Poinciana.
afternoon   H.M. The Queen visited American Red Cross Clubs in Bedford: Strings With Wings played at the Enlisted Mens Club in Bromham Road (16 men, conducted by Harry Katzman).
2.30   AEFP Pre-recording – AMERICAN BAND OF SUPREME ALLIED COMMAND, with guest artist Anne Shelton. Broadcast 27/7/44.
21.30–23.30   Concert (full Band) for Servicemen at the Corn Exchange, Bedford, with Anne Shelton. (1,200).

Monday 24 July
Late afternoon   Concert (full Band) at 8th Air Force fighter base, Wattisham-Hitcham, West Suffolk.
19.45   AFEP Broadcast – STRINGS WITH WINGS. Largo (Dvořák)/ Dancing In The Dark/Stars In Your Eyes/Poem, 'Beach-Head' by Harry Hartwick/Embraceable You.

Tuesday 25 July

am AEFP Pre-recording – SWING SEXTET:The Uptown Hall Broadcast 29/8/44.

pm Concert at USAAF Air Transport Command base at Newbury, Berks. (according to Haynes); at Newbury Corn Exchange for Eagle Div. of Paratroops (according to Activities List).

18.15 AEFP Broadcast – SWING SEXTET: The Uptown Hall (rec. 22/7/44). Love Is The Sweetest Thing/These Foolish Things/Louise/I Don't Know Why v, CC/Blue Skies.

20.05 AEFP Broadcast – AMERICAN DANCE BAND: The Swing Shift. Broadcast cancelled – Band were unable to get back from Newbury to Bedford; record fill-up instead.

Wednesday 26 July

18.15 AEFP Broadcast – SWING SEXTET: The Uptown Hall. Stomping At The Savoy/Sweet Lorraine/Blow Top/There's A Small Hotel v, CC/Between The Devil And The Deep Blue Sea.

19.45 AEFP Broadcast – STRINGS WITH WINGS. My Heart Stood Still/Claire De Lune/Love Walked In/Poem, 'Embarkation' by Harry Hartwick/You're My Everything/Trees (after closing theme).

Thursday 27 July

15.30 BBC Pre-recording – AMERICAN DANCE BAND: American Eagle In Britain, from the Rainbow Corner (ARC Club), London, for future broadcast in USA.

17.30 Concert at charity premiere of film 'Going My Way', Plaza Cinema, Lower Regent Street, London.
Moonlight Serenade/In The Mood/Juke Box Saturday Night v, CC/Holiday For Strings/Poinciana v, JD & CC/The GI Jive v, RM & CC/The Anvil Chorus.

20.30 AEFP and Home Service Broadcast – AMERICAN BAND OF SUPREME ALLIED COMMAND, with guest artist Anne Shelton. (rec. 23/7/44).
Flying Home/Smoke Gets In Your Eyes/The Victory Polka v, CC & Band/I'll Get By v, Anne Shelton/*Medley*: In The Gloaming, A Fellow On A Furlough v, JD, Stomping At The Savoy, Deep Purple/Time Alone Will Tell v, JD/Song Of The Volga Boatmen.

Friday 28 July

10.00 AEFP Pre-recording – SWING SEXTET: The Uptown Hall. Broadcast 29/7/44 and 26/8/44.

11.01½ AEFP Broadcast, London – AMERICAN BAND OF SUPREME ALLIED COMMAND: Morning After (recorded repeat of last night's broadcast).

14.30 AEFP Pre-recording – SERGEANT JOHNNY DESMOND. Orchestra conducted by Norman Leyden. Broadcast 30/7/44 and 20/8/44.

late pm Concert at 8th Air Force bomber base at Polebrook, Northants.

18.15 AEFP Broadcast – SWING SEXTET: The Uptown Hall, probably recorded, date unknown but possibly this morning. China Boy/The Very Thought Of You/Honeysuckle Rose/Irresistible You v, cc/Hallelujah.

Saturday 29 July

09.35 AEFP Broadcast – AMERICAN DANCE BAND: The Swing Shift (25 minutes). That's What It's All About v, RM/On The Alamo/Watcha Know, Joe v, RM/Time Alone Will Tell v, JD/Everybody Loves My Baby/I'll Get By v, JD/Seven-O-Five/Flying Home.

12.45 AEFP Broadcast – JACK RUSIN: Keyboard Contrasts.

14.01 GFP Broadcast – AMERICAN BAND OF SUPREME ALLIED COMMAND (recorded repeat of last Thursday's broadcast).

pm Concert at 8th Air Force Headquarters, High Wycombe, Bucks.

18.15 AEF Broadcast – SWING SEXTET: The Uptown Hall (recorded 28/7/44). Liza/Sweet Lorraine/Blue Room/I Couldn't Sleep A Wink Last Night v, cc/The Earl.

Sunday 30 July

12.45 AEFP Broadcast – SERGEANT JOHNNY DESMOND (recorded 28/7/44). Now I Know/Star Eyes/Tuxedo Junction (*Band*)/The Music Stopped.

18.00 GFP Pre-recording – AMERICAN BAND OF SUPREME ALLIED COMMAND in Variety Bandbox, from Queensberry All-Services Club, London (broadcast 1/8/44 (GFP and AEFP) and 6/8/44 (GFP)).

evening Concert (full Band) at the Queensberry All-Service Club.

Note: According to Haynes' diary some pre-recordings were made this morning but no details survive in the radio archives, and none are mentioned in the Activities list.

A 'dance unit' from the Band played at a Red Cross Officers Club according to the Activities list, personnel and location unknown.

Monday 31 July

evening Concert (dance band and singers, conducted by Ray McKinley) at 8th Air Force base at Abbots Ripton, Hunts. String Section remained in Bedford.

19.45 AEFP Broadcast – STRINGS WITH WINGS. I'm In The Mood For Love/They Didn't Believe Me/Trees/Poem, 'Beach-head' by Sergeant Harry Hartwick/Our Waltz.

Tuesday 1 August

14.00 GFP and AEFP Broadcast London – Variety Bandbox included the AMERICAN BAND OF SUPREME ALLIED COMMAND (recorded 30/7/44). *Theme* (I Love To Sing) JOHN BLORE ORCHESTRA/AMERICAN BAND: Moonlight Serenade, In The Mood, Stardust, Poinciana v, JD & cc/ PETER SINCLAIR/BERTHA WILLMOTT/HAL MONTY/TEDDY BROWN/

AMERICAN BAND: American Patrol, Time Alone Will Tell v, JD/Holiday For Strings/BOTH BANDS AND ALL ARTISTS: Let's Have Another One.

18.15 AEFP Broadcast – SWING SEXTET: The Uptown Hall. I'll Remember April/Don't Blame Me/On The Sunny Side Of The Street/I'll Be Seeing You v, JD/Rosetta.

20.05 AEFP Broadcast – AMERICAN DANCE BAND: The Swing Shift (25 minutes). Mission to Moscow/Georgia On My Mind/Chattanooga Choo Choo v, RM & CC/Going My Way v, JD/Can't Get Stuff In Your Cuff v, RM/It's Love, Love, Love v, CC/Here We Go Again.

Small dance unit played at opening of Enlisted Mens Dayroom at Milton Ernest Hall (500).

Note: According to Haynes' diary some pre-recordings were made today but no details survive in the radio archives and none are mentioned in the Activities list.

Wednesday 2 August

pm Concert at USAAF 8th Air Force Bomber base at Kimbolton, Hunts. (2,000)

18.15 AEFP Broadcast – SWING SEXTET: The Uptown Hall. Flying Home/Rose Room/You Took Advantage Of Me/Goodnight Wherever You Are v, JD/Louise.

19.45 AEFP Broadcast – STRINGS WITH WINGS (conducted by Jerry Gray) These Foolish Things/Stars In Your Eyes (featuring George Ockner, violin)/Poem, 'V-Day' by Harry Hartwick/Trees/Moonlight Serenade.

'Small Dance unit' directed by Phil Cogliano played at ARC Club, Midland Road, Bedford.

Thursday 3 August

11.00 AEFP Pre-recording – SWING SEXTET: The Uptown Hall. Broadcast 4/8/44.

20.30 AEFP and Home Service Broadcast – AMERICAN BAND OF SUPREME ALLIED COMMAND, Guest artists Dinah Shore and Sam Browne. Sun Valley Jump/Time On My Hands v, Sam Browne/It Must Be Jelly/Long Ago And Far Away v, Dinah Shore/*Medley*: Flow Gently Sweet Afton, Moondreams v, JD & CC, Don't Be That Way, Blue Champagne/I'll Be Seeing You v, Dinah Shore/With My Head In The Clouds v, JD, CC & Band.

21.00 AEFP Pre-recording – SWING SEXTET with Dinah Shore: Night and Day (broadcast 11/8/44 and 18/8/44) Tessa's Torch Song (broadcast 12/8/44) I Couldn't Sleep A Wink Last Night (broadcast 15/8/44) Honeysuckle Rose (broadcast 16/8/44).

'Small dance unit' directed by Phil Cogliano played at ARC Officers Club, Goldington Road, Bedford. (300)

Friday 4 August

10.30 AEFP Pre-recording – AMERICAN DANCE BAND: The Swing Shift (25 minutes). Broadcast 5/8/44.

11.01 AEFP Broadcast – AMERICAN BAND OF SUPREME ALLIED COMMAND: Morning After (recorded repeat of last night's broadcast).

? pm Concert (full Band) at SHAEF (Forward), near Portsmouth (Codenamed 'Sharpener') (850)

18.15 AEFP Broadcast – SWING SEXTET: The Uptown Hall (recorded 3.8.44). Bugle Call Rag/Love Is The Sweetest Thing/Sugar/What A Difference A Day Made v, JD/Don't Be That Way.

Saturday 5 August

09.35 AEFP Broadcast – AMERICAN DANCE BAND: The Swing Shift (25 minutes) (recorded 4/8/44).
Stealing Apples/My Heart Tells Me v, JD/Nine-Twenty Special/Cow Cow Boogie v, RM/Snafu Jump/The Music Stopped v, JD/The Eyes And Ears Of The World (Paramount On Parade).

12.45 AEFP Broadcast – JACK RUSIN, piano.

14.01 GFP Broadcast – AMERICAN BAND OF SUPREME ALLIED COMMAND (recorded repeat of last Thursday's AEFP broadcast).

18.15 AEFP Broadcast – SWING SEXTET: The Uptown Hall.
'S Wonderful/The Very Thought Of You/How High The Moon/Irresistible You v, JD/Rosetta.

Note – According to Haynes' diary some pre-recordings were made today, but no details survive in the radio archives and none are mentioned in the Activities list.

? evening 'Small dance unit' directed by Phil Cogliano played at the Officers Club at Milton Ernest Hall. (100)

Sunday 6 August

am 'Small string unit' directed by Harry Katzman played at Chapel services at Milton Ernest Hall.

12.45 AEFP Broadcast – SERGEANT JOHNNY DESMOND: A Soldier and a Song. You Are The Rainbow/Stairway To The Stars/I Dreamt I Dwelt In Harlem (*Band*)/I'll Be Seeing You.

pm Concert (full Band) at 8th Air Force bomber base at Halesworth, E. Suffolk. (1,500)

evening Concert (full Band) at 8th Air Force fighter base at Boxted, Essex. (3,000)

Monday 7 August

am According to Haynes' diary some pre-recordings were made but no details survive in the radio archives and none are mentioned in the Activities list.

pm Concert (without Strings) at US General Hospital, Cirencester (3,500): another in evening (4,000)

19.45 AEFP Broadcast – STRINGS WITH WINGS. With A Song In My Heart/Londonderry Air (featuring George Ockner, violin)/Someone to Watch Over Me/Poem, by Harry Hartwick/Trees/There's A Small Hotel.

Tuesday 8 August

am According to Haynes' diary some pre-recordings were made but no details survive in the radio archives and none are mentioned in the Activities list.

18.15 AEFP Broadcast – SWING SEXTET: The Uptown Hall. You're Lucky For Me/Body And Soul/Blue Room/She's Funny That Way V, JD/Oh Lady Be Good.

20.05 AEFP Broadcast – AMERICAN DANCE BAND: The Swing Shift (25 minutes). King Porter Stomp/Rhapsody in Blue/Jeep Jockey Jump/Time Alone Will tell V, JD/Tripargate Gallop 'Glider Rider Jump'/I'll Get By V, JD/I Hear You Screaming.

Wednesday 9 August

11.00 AEFP Pre-recording – SWING SEXTET: The Uptown Hall. Broadcast 18.15 this evening.

pm Concert at SHAEF (Main), Bushey Park, near Teddington, Middlesex. (3,000)

18.15 AEFP Broadcast – SWING SEXTET: The Uptown Hall (Recorded this morning). Making Whooppee/Confessing/Blue Skies/I Surrender Dear V, JD/I'll Remember April.

19.45 AEFP Broadcast – STRINGS WITH WINGS. No broadcast (replaced by pipes and drums from GFP): the Band were at SHAEF.

Thursday 10 August

Note – According to Haynes' diary some pre-recordings were made today but no details survive in the radio archives and none are mentioned in the Activities list.

15.30 BBC Pre-recording – AMERICAN DANCE BAND: American Eagle in Britain, from Rainbow Corner (ARC Club), London, for future broadcast in USA. (500)

17.30 AEFP Broadcast – JACK RUSIN: Keyboard Contrasts.

20.30 AEFP and Home Service Broadcast – AMERICAN BAND OF SUPREME ALLIED COMMAND, from Paris Cinema (BBC studio), Lower Regent Street, London. Guest Artist, Paula Green.
Tail End Charlie/Body and Soul/Tessa's Torch Song V, Paula Green/*Medley*: Danny Boy, All Of My Life V, JD, Cherokee, Blue Danube/Holiday For Strings.

21.14–23.00 Full Band took part in special recordings for use at National Broadcasters Convention in USA; programme also included Colonel Kirby, Sergeant Broderick Crawford and other artists.

Friday 11 August

11.00   AEFP Broadcast – AMERICAN BAND OF SUPREME ALLIED COMMAND: Morning After (recorded repeat of last night's broadcast).

13.30   AEFP Pre-recording – SERGEANT JOHNNY DESMOND: A Soldier and a Song. Broadcast 13/8/44.

18.15   AEFP Broadcast – SWING SEXTET: The Uptown Hall. Guest Artist: Dinah Shore (recorded insert).
China Boy/These Foolish Things/Stomping At The Savoy/Night And Day v, Dinah Shore (recorded 3/8/44)/The Earl.

19.30   AEFP Pre-recording – SWING SEXTET: The Uptown Hall. (Broadcast 12/8/44).

20.30–22.15   Full Band played a public charity concert at the Corn Exchange, Bedford. (1,200)

20.00–23.00   'Small dance unit' directed by Phil Cogliano played at ARC Enlisted Mens Club, Bromham Road, Bedford. (300)

Saturday 12 August

09.35   AEFP Broadcast – AMERICAN DANCE BAND: The Swing Shift (25 minutes). Snafu Jump/My Buddy/Chattanooga Choo Choo v, RM & CC/ Along The Santa Fe Trail v, JD/Sticky Wicket (*Trio*: Mel Powell, piano, Peanuts Hucko, clarinet, Ray McKinley, drums)/My Heart Tells Me v, JD/ Mission to Moscow.

11.12   AEFP Pre-recording – AMERICAN DANCE BAND: The Swing Shift (25 minutes). Broadcast 15/8/44.

12.45   AEFP Broadcast STRINGS WITH WINGS I'll Get By/Maid With The Flaxen Hair/All The Things You Are/Poem: When 'Neath The Melted Snow, by Corporal Peter Alfano/Trees/Stairway To The Stars.

14.01   GFP Broadcast – AMERICAN BAND OF SUPREME ALLIED COMMAND (recorded repeat of last Thursday's AEFP broadcast).

14.15–15.15   AEFP Pre-recordings – SWING SEXTET: The Uptown Hall.
    [Programme 1] broadcast 15/8/44.
    [Programme 2] broadcast 16/8/44.
    [Programme 3] broadcast 18/8/44.

18.15   AEFP Broadcast – SWING SEXTET: The Uptown Hall (recorded 11/8/44). Guest artist, Dinah Shore (recorded insert). I Got Rhythm/ Sweet Lorraine/You're Lucky For Me/Tessa's Torch Song v, Dinah Shore (recorded 3/8/44)/You Took Advantage Of Me.

evening   Mel Powell and a sextet played at a dance at 9th Air Force Service Command Headquarters at Grove, Berkshire. (400)

Sunday 13 August

12.45   AEFP Broadcast – SERGEANT JOHNNY DESMOND: A Soldier and a Song (recorded 11/8/44). I'll Get By/I'll Remember April/Swing Low Sweet Chariot (*Band*)/Amor Amor.

14.00   Dance Band, with Major Glenn Miller, flew from Twinwood Farm to USAAF base at Langford Lodge, Northern Ireland; string section remained at Bedford.

late pm   Concert at ARC Club, Belfast. (1,200)

evening   Concert at Post Theatre, Langford Lodge. (1,000)

late evening   Band flew to USAAF base at Warton, Lancashire.

Monday 14 August

pm   Concert at USAAF base at Warton, Lancs (10,000)

19.00   AEFP Pre-recording STRINGS WITH WINGS. Broadcast 16/8/44.

19.45   AEFP Broadcast – STRINGS WITH WINGS. My Heart Stood Still/ Someday I'll Find You/Love Walked In/Serenade In Blue/Trees/poem 'Flight Aspect' by A/c E. Denyer Cox (RAF).

Tuesday 15 August

am   Band flew from Warton to USAAF base at Burtonwood, Lancs.

14.30   Concert at USAAF base at Burtonwood, Lancs. (8,000)

19.00   Concert at USAAF base at Burtonwood, Lancs. (9,000)

18.14   AEFP Broadcast – SWING SEXTET: The Uptown Hall (recorded 12/8/44) Guest artist, Dinah Shore.

At Sundown/Don't Blame Me/Rose Room/I Couldn't Sleep A Wink Last Night v, Dinah Shore, (recorded 3/8/44)/Between The Devil And The Deep Blue Sea.

20.05   AEFP Broadcast – AMERICAN DANCE BAND: The Swing Shift (25 minutes) (recorded 12/8/44).

Stealing Apples/Irresistible You v, JD & CC/Caribbean Clipper/She's Funny That Way v, JD/Wigan Pier Wiggle (*Trio*)/Going My Way v, JD/ Everybody Loves My Baby.

late evening: Band flew back from Burtonwood to Twinwood Farm.

Wednesday 16 August

pm   Concert at hospital at Bentley Priory, Near Stanmore, Middlesex. (1,000)

18.15   AEFP Broadcast – SWING SEXTET: The Uptown Hall (recorded 12/8/44) Guest Artist, Dinah Shore.

Liza/The Very Thought Of You/Love Is The Sweetest Thing/ Honeysuckle Rose v, Dinah Shore (recorded 3/8/44)/Flying Home.

19.45   AEFP Broadcast – STRINGS WITH WINGS (recorded 14/8/44).

You're My Everything/Habanera/April In Paris/You And The Night And The Music/Trees/Poem, 'Men Of The 9th' by Private First Class W D Diddans (*Stars and Stripes*).

Thursday 17 August

17.30   AEFP Broadcast – JACK RUSIN: Keyboard Contrasts.

20.30   AEFP Broadcast (not carried by Home Service from now onwards) – AMERICAN BAND OF THE AEF. Guest Artist, Beryl Davis.

I Hear You Screaming/Stormy Weather/It's Love, Love, Love v, Beryl Davis/*Medley*: Mother Macree, I Couldn't Sleep A Wink Last Night v, JD, I Can't Give You Anything But Love, Baby v, Peanuts Hucko, trumpet solo Bernie Priven, The Wang Wang Blues/Pearls On Velvet (featuring Mel Powell, piano)/The Caisson Song.

Friday 18 August

09.30 AEFP Pre-recording – AMERICAN DANCE BAND: The Swing Shift (25 minutes) Broadcast 19/8/44.

AEFP Pre-recording – SWING SEXTET: The Uptown Hall. Broadcast 19/8/44.

11.01 AEFP Broadcast – AMERICAN BAND OF THE AEF: Morning After (recorded repeat of last night's broadcast).

15.30–16.30 Concert (full Band) at 8th Air Force fighter base at Steeple Morden, Cambridgeshire. (5,000)

18.15 AEFP Broadcast – SWING SEXTET: The Uptown Hall (recorded 12/8/44). Guest Artist, Dinah Shore.

Blow Top/Where Or When/ How High The Moon/Night And Day v, Dinah Shore (recorded 3/8/44)/Rosetta.

20.30 Concert (full Band) at 8th Air Force bomber base at Attlebridge, Norfolk. (10,000) Band stayed overnight.

Saturday 19 August

09.35 AEFP Broadcast – AMERICAN DANCE BAND: The Swing Shift (25 minutes) (recorded 18/8/44).

Sun Valley Jump/Rhapsody In Blue/Juke Box Saturday Night v, CC/The Music Stopped v, JD/Tinecongle Tinkle (*trio*)/Time Alone Will Tell v, JD/Flying Home.

12.45 AEFP Broadcast – JACK RUSIN: Keyboard Contrasts.

14.01 GFP Broadcast – AMERICAN BAND OF THE AEF (recorded repeat of last Thursday's broadcast).

18.15 AEFP Broadcast – SWING SEXTET: The Uptown Hall (recorded 18/8/44).

Making Whoopee/I'll Be Seeing You v, JD/Jubilee/ I Don't Know Why v, CC/Stomping At The Savoy.

'Small dance unit' directed by Mel Powell played at Officers dance at 8th Air Force fighter base at Boxted. (600)

Sunday 20 August

Band had their first day off since arriving at Bedford.

12.45 AEFP Broadcast – SERGEANT JOHNNY DESMOND: A Soldier And A Song (recorded 28/7/44).

Star Eyes/Now I Know/Tuxedo Junction (*Band*)/The Music Stopped (previously broadcast 30/7/44).

Monday 21 August

17.45   AEFP Pre-recording – STRINGS WITH WINGS. Broadcast 23/8/44.
19.45   AEFP Broadcast – STRINGS WITH WINGS
I'm In The Mood for Love/Loch Lomond (featuring George Ockner, violin)/What Is There To Say (featuring George Ockner, violin)/My Silent Love.

Tuesday 22 August

11.15   AEFP Pre-recording – SWING SEXTET: The Uptown Hall. Broadcast 23/8/44.
14.15   AEFP Pre-recording – STRINGS WITH WINGS. Broadcast 28.8.44.
18.15   AEFP Broadcast – SWING SEXTET: The Uptown Hall
Flying Home/Rose Room/You Took Advantage of Me/Goodnight Wherever You Are v, JD & CC/Blue Skies.
19.00   AEFP Pre-recording – SWING SEXTET: The Uptown Hall. Broadcast 25/8/44.
20.05   AEFP Broadcast – AMERICAN DANCE BAND: The Swing Shift (25 minutes). No broadcast: replaced by 'Here's To Romance' (Ralph Block Orchestra).

Wednesday 23 August

11.00   AEFP Pre-recording – SERGEANT JOHNNY DESMOND: A Soldier And A Song. Broadcast 17/9/44.
14.30   Concert (full Band) at 8th Air Force bomber base at Podington, Beds. (3,000)
18.15   AEFP Broadcast – SWING SEXTET: The Uptown Hall (recorded 22/8/44).
I'll Remember April/Don't Blame Me/On The Sunny Side Of The Street/Irresistible You v, JD & CC/Oh Lady Be Good.
19.45   AEFP Broadcast – STRINGS WITH WINGS (recorded 21/8/44)
More Than You Know (featuring George Ockner, violin)/Dancing In The Dark/Estrellita (featuring George Ockner, violin)/Holiday For Strings.
evening: Concert (full Band) at 8th Air Force bomber base at Framlingham, E. Suffolk. (6,000) Band stayed here overnight.

Thursday 24 August

am   Band flew from Framlingham back to Thurleigh bomber base, thence to Bedford.
17.30   AEFP Broadcast – JACK RUSIN: Keyboard Contrasts.
20.30   AEFP Broadcast – AMERICAN BAND OF THE AEF Guest artist, Doreen Villiers.
Swing Low Sweet Chariot/I'll Be Seeing You v, JD/That's Sabotage v, Doreen Villiers/*Medley*: Long Long Ago, The Music Stopped v, JD, Dipsy Doodle, Blue Is The Night/I'm Heading For California v, RM & CC/American Patrol.

302

Note – According to Haynes' diary, three pre-recordings and three broadcasts were made today, including one at 14.30; according to the radio archives and the Activities list only two broadcasts were made, as listed above, and no pre-recordings.

Friday 25 August

11.01 AEFP Broadcast – AMERICAN BAND OF THE AEF (30 minutes): Morning After (recorded repeat of last night's broadcast).

11.15 AEFP Pre-recording – AMERICAN DANCE BAND: The Swing Shift (25 minutes). Broadcast 26/8/44.

pm Concert (full Band) 8th Air Force bomber base at Wendling, Norfolk (3,000); then flew on to Knettishall, W Suffolk.

18.15 AEFP Broadcast – SWING SEXTET: The Uptown Hall (recorded 22/8/44). Rosetta/Where Or When/Blow Top/What A Difference A Day Made v, JD/S'Wonderful (*Quartet*: Mel Powell, piano, Peanuts Hucko, clarinet, Trigger Alpert, bass, Ray McKinley, drums).

evening Concert (full Band) at 8th Air Force bomber base at Knettishall, W Suffolk. (7,000) Band stayed here overnight.

Saturday 26 August

09.35 AEFP Broadcast – AMERICAN DANCE BAND: The Swing Shift (25 minutes) (recorded 25/8/44).
Mission To Moscow/Stardust/I'm Heading For Californian v, RM & CC/Going My Way v, JD/Ramsbottom Wriggle (*trio*)/Along The Santa Fe Trail v, JD/Eyes And Ears of The World.

am Band flew back from Knettishall to Twinwood Farm, thence to Bedford.

12.45 AEFP Broadcast – JACK RUSIN: Keyboard Contrasts – programme cancelled and replaced by Johnny Dennis Novelty Swing Quartet.

14.01 GFP Broadcast – AMERICAN BAND OF THE AEF (recorded repeat of last Thursday's broadcast).

18.15 AEFP Broadcast – SWING SEXTET: The Uptown Hall (recorded 28/7/44). Liza/Sweet Lorraine/Blue Room/I Couldn't Sleep A Wink Last Night v, CC/The Earl. (previously broadcast 29/7/44).

evening: Zeke Zarchy and a sextet played at a dance at the 8th Air Force fighter base at Steeple Morden. (500)

Sunday 27 August

12.45 AEFP Broadcast – SERGEANT JOHNNY DESMOND SINGS.
My Ideal/Night And Day/My Heart Tells Me/Uncle Tom (*Band*).

15.30 Concert at RAF airfield Twinwood Farm, near Bedford. (1,000)

evening Jack Rusin accompanied Bing Crosby in Variety Bandbox recording at the Queensberry All-Services Club, London.

Monday 28 August

13.15 Full Band flew from Twinwood Farm to RAF Harrowbeer, Devon; thence by trucks to Plymouth.

pm Concert (Dance Band) at US Navy Hospital at Manadon, Nr. Plymouth. (750) Concert (Strings With Wings) at US Navy's Shafter's Field, near Plymouth. (2,000)

late pm Concert (Dance Band) at Shafter's Field. (750)

evening Concert (Strings With Wings) at Manadon Hospital. (600)

evening Concert (full Band) for British and American servicemen at Odeon Theatre, Plymouth. (4,000) Band stayed overnight at Plymouth.

19.45 AEFP Broadcast – STRINGS WITH WINGS (recorded 22/8/44).
Maybe/There's A Small Hotel (featuring George Ockner, violin)/Jeannie With The Light Brown Hair/Lover Come Back To Me.

Tuesday 29 August

Band stranded at Plymouth by bad weather all day and overnight.

15.30 AEFP Pre-recording – JACK RUSIN, with BING CROSBY: Keyboard Contrasts. Broadcast ?2/9/44.

18.15 AEFP Broadcast – SWING SEXTET: The Uptown Hall (recorded 25/7/44).
Love Is The Sweetest Thing/These Foolish Things/Louise/I Don't Know Why v, CC/Blue Skies.

20.05 AEFP Broadcast – AMERICAN DANCE BAND: The Swing Shift (25 minutes). No broadcast (Band stranded at Plymouth): replaced by 'Here's To Romance' (Ray Bloch Orchestra).

23.00 AEFP Pre-recording – JACK RUSIN with BING CROSBY: Keyboard Contrasts. Broadcast ?2/9/44.

Wednesday 30 August

11.25 Band arrived back at Twinwood Farm from Plymouth.

13.30 AEFP Pre-recording – AMERICAN BAND OF THE AEF with BING CROSBY. Broadcast 3/9/44 as 'Bing Crosby Sings' in place of Sergeant Johnny Desmond.
Also, two songs broadcast 9/9/44 in 'Swing Shift' programme.

AEFP Pre-recording – AMERICAN BAND OF THE AEF with BING CROSBY: White Christmas, broadcast 19/12/44.

18.15 AEFP Broadcast – SWING SEXTET: The Uptown Hall.
China Boy/The Very Thought Of You/Don't Be That Way/Embraceable You v, JD/Hallelujah.

19.45 AEFP Broadcast – STRINGS WITH WINGS.
Sure Thing/Claire de Lune/Sweet And Lovely (featuring George Ockner, violin)/September Song.

20.30 AEFP Pre-recordings – JACK RUSIN: Keyboard Contrasts
     [Programme 1] broadcast 9/9/44
     (Programme 2] broadcast 2/9/44.

304

Thursday 31 August

15.30 BBC Pre-recording – AMERICAN DANCE BAND: American Eagle In Britain, from Rainbow Corner (ARC Club), London, for future broadcast in USA (30 minutes).

17.30 AEFP Broadcast – JACK RUSIN: Keyboard Contrasts. No broadcast – replaced by records.

20.30 AEFP Broadcast – AMERICAN BAND OF THE AEF. From Paris Cinema, Lower Regent Street, London. Guest artist, Bing Crosby.

Here We Go Again/Long Ago And Far Away v, Bing Crosby/ *Medley*: My Buddy, Amor Amor v, Bing Crosby, Music Makers, Farewell Blues/Swinging On a Star v, Bing Crosby accompanied by the Swing Sextet/Poinciana v, Bing Crosby and CC.

Friday 1 September

11.01 AEFP Broadcast – AMERICAN BAND OF THE AEF: Morning After (recorded repeat of last night's broadcast).

15.00–16.00 Concert (full Band) at 8th Air Force bomber base at Tibbenham, Norfolk, (3,000) Then by trucks to Thorpe Abbotts, Norfolk.

18.15 AEFP Broadcast – SWING SEXTET: The Uptown Hall. Programme cancelled – replaced by recordings of last night's opening of the Stage Door Canteen, London, including Bing Crosby (18.15–18.59).

19.00–20.00 – Concert (full Band) at 8th Air Force bomber base at Thorpe Abbotts. (3,000) Band stayed here overnight.

Saturday 2 September

09.35 AEFP Broadcast – AMERICAN DANCE BAND: The Swing Shift. No broadcast – Band at Thorpe Abbotts overnight; replaced by Eric Winstone and his Orchestra (Home Service).

12.45 AEFP Broadcast – JACK RUSIN: Keyboard Contrasts (recorded 30/8/44, with Bing Crosby insert, recorded 29/8/44).

14.01 GFP Broadcast – AMERICAN BAND OF THE AEF (recorded repeat of last Thursday's broadcast).

18.15 AEFP Broadcast – SWING SEXTET: The Uptown Hall. No broadcast (replaced by Eric Winstone and his Orchestra) – Band in London for:

18.30 GFP and AEFP Broadcast – AMERICAN BAND OF THE AEF: Atlantic Spotlight (30 minutes) – live broadcast jointly with NBC in New York.

The American Band of the AEF played Flying Home/I'll Be Seeing You v, JD/Juke Box Saturday Night v, Marion Hutton (in Atlantic City) and Modernaires (in NY)/In The Mood.

20.15–21.30 Concert (full Band) at the Queensberry All-Services Club, London. (2,500)

Sunday 3 September

Day off for the Band.

11.01 AEFP Broadcast – ATLANTIC SPOTLIGHT (recorded repeat of yesterday's broadcast).

12.45 AEFP Broadcast – BING CROSBY SINGS, accompanied by the AMERICAN BAND OF THE AEF (replacing Sergeant Johnny Desmond Sings).

Amor Amor/Long Ago And Far Away/White Christmas/I'll Be Seeing You.

Monday 4 September

19.45 AEFP Broadcast – STRINGS WITH WINGS.

It Could Happen To You/Habanera/The Man I Love/None But The Lonely Heart.

20.30 AEFP Pre-recording – STRINGS WITH WINGS. Broadcast 18/9/44.

Tuesday 5 September

18.15 AEFP Broadcast – SWING SEXTET: The Uptown Hall.

You're Lucky For Me/Body And Soul/You Go To My Head/She's Funny That Way v, JD/Oh Lady Be Good.

20.05 AEFP Broadcast – AMERICAN DANCE BAND: The Swing Shift (25 minutes). Breaking In A New Pair Of Shoes/Star Eyes v, JD/One Of Them Things/Sweet And Low/Original composition, title unknown (*Trio*)/Time Alone Will Tell v, JD/Snafu Jump.

Note – According to Haynes' diary some pre-recordings were made today but no details of them survive in the radio archives, and none are mentioned in the Activities list.

Wednesday 6 September

14.30 AEFP Pre-recordings – SWING SEXTET: The Uptown Hall.

  [Programme 1] (with Beryl Davis), broadcast 16/9/44.
  [Programme 2] (with Beryl Davis), broadcast 19/9/44.
  [Programme 3] (with Beryl Davis), broadcast 20/9/44.

18.15 AEFP Broadcast – SWING SEXTET: The Uptown Hall.

Making Whoopee/There's A Small Hotel v, CC/Exactly Like You/I Surrender Dear v, JD/Between The Devil And The Deep Blue Sea.

19.45 AEFP Broadcast – STRINGS WITH WINGS.

With A Song In My Heart/Summertime/Annie Laurie.

21.00 AEFP Pre-recording – STRINGS WITH WINGS. Broadcast 2/10/44.

Thursday 7 September

11.00 AEFP Pre-recording – SWING SEXTET: The Uptown Hall 3/10/44.

20.30 AEFP Broadcast – AMERICAN BAND OF THE AEF. Guest Artist, Gloria Brent.

In The Mood/Body And Soul/Tuxedo Junction/*Medley*: Songs My Mother Taught Me, It's Love, Love, Love v, CC, In An Eighteenth

Century Drawing Room, Blue Orchids v, JD/Time Alone Will Tell v, Gloria Brent/All's Well Mademoiselle v, JD & CC, arranged by Jerry Gray.

'Small dance unit' played for a dance at the ARC Officers' Club, Goldington Road, Bedford. (300)

Friday 8 September

11.01 AEFP Broadcast – AMERICAN BAND OF THE AEF: Morning After (recorded repeat of last night's broadcast).

15.00 AEFP Pre-recording – AMERICAN DANCE BAND: The Swing Shift (25 minutes). Broadcast 16/9/44.

18.15 AEFP Broadcast – SWING SEXTET: The Uptown Hall.
Hallelujah/Confessing/Blue Skies/Where Or When v, JD/I Got Rhythm.

19.30 AEFP Pre-recording – SWING SEXTET: The Uptown Hall. Broadcast 16/11/44.

Saturday 9 September

09.35 AEFP Broadcast – AMERICAN DANCE BAND: The Swing Shift (25 minutes). Guest Artist: Bing Crosby (pre-recorded inserts).
I Hear You Screaming/Ain't Misbehaving/If I Had My Way v, Bing Crosby (recorded 30/8/44)/Shine On Harvest Moon/Early Morning Blues (*trio*)/Amor Amor v, Bing Crosby (recorded 30/8/44)/Stealing Apples.

11.15 AEFP Pre-recording – AMERICAN DANCE BAND: The Swing Shift. Broadcast 19/9/44.

12.45 AEFP Broadcast – JACK RUSIN Keyboard contrasts (recorded 30/8/44)

14.01 GFP Broadcast – AMERICAN BAND OF THE AEF (recorded repeat of last Thursday's AEFP broadcast).

14.30 AEFP Pre-recording – AMERICAN BAND OF THE AEF. Broadcast 19/12/44.

17.00 AEFP Pre-recording – STRINGS WITH WINGS. Broadcast 11/9/44.

18.15 AEFP Broadcast – SWING SEXTET: The Uptown Hall.
At Sundown/Once In A While v, JD/On The Sunny Side Of The Street (*Quartet*)/I Surrender Dear v, JD/Blow Top.

20.00–24.00 Mel Powell and a sextet with Bernie Privin played at 2nd Anniversary dance at 8th Air Force base at Thurleigh, Beds. (1,500)

Sunday 10 September

12.45 AEFP Broadcast – SERGEANT JOHNNY DESMOND: Soldier and a Song.
My Heart Stood Still/It could Happen To You/Breaking In A New Pair Of Shoes (*Band*)/I'll Be Seeing You.

evening Concert (full Band) at 8th Air Force bomber base at Horham, West Suffolk. (6,500) (But *see also* page 146 regarding concert at Knettishall.)

Monday 11 September

09.45 AEFP Pre-recording – SWING SEXTET: The Uptown Hall. Broadcast 12/9/44.

11.15 AEFP Pre-recording – AMERICAN DANCE BAND: The Swing Shift (25 minutes). Broadcast 12/9/44.

pm or evening Concert (full Band) for 82nd Airborne Div. Troops, De Montford Hall, Leicester. (4,000)

19.45 AEFP Broadcast – STRINGS WITH WINGS (recorded 9/9/44).
I'll Get By/Sweet And Low/Indian Summer/Old Man River.

Tuesday 12 September

18.15 AEFP Broadcast – SWING SEXTET: The Uptown Hall (recorded 11/9/44).
Louise/Long Ago And Far Away v, JD/World Is Waiting For The Sunrise (*Quartet*)/Caravan.

20.05 AEFP Broadcast – AMERICAN DANCE BAND: The Swing Shift (25 minutes) (recorded 11/9/44).
Get Happy/Swing Low Sweet Chariot/I'll Walk Alone v, JD/Bubble Bath/Bromham Boogie (*Trio*)/My Heart Tells Me v, JD/Everybody Loves My Baby.

18.30–19.45 Concert (full Band) at 8th Air Force bomber base at Hardwick, Norfolk. (5,800) Band stayed here overnight.

Wednesday 13 September

15.45 AEFP Pre-recording – SWING SEXTET: The Uptown Hall. Broadcast 15/9/44.

18.15 AEFP Broadcast – SWING SEXTET: The Uptown Hall.
Perdido/Love Is Just Around The Corner/When Your Lover Has Gone v, JD/You're Driving Me Crazy.

19.45 AEFP Broadcast – STRINGS WITH WINGS
World Is Waiting For The Sunrise/What Is There To Say/They Didn't Believe Me/Moonlight Serenade.

20.15 AEFP Pre-recording – STRINGS WITH WINGS. Broadcast 8/12/44.

Thursday 14 September

10.00 AEFP Pre-recording – JACK RUSIN: Keyboard Contrasts. Broadcast 16/9/44. – JACK RUSIN: Piano Parade.
    [Programme 1] broadcast 23/9/44.
    [Programme 2] broadcast 30/9/44.
    [Programme 3] broadcast 7/10/44.

15.30 BBC Pre-recording – AMERICAN DANCE BAND: American Eagle In Britain, from Rainbow Corner (ARC Club), London, for future broadcast in USA.

20.30½ AEFP Broadcast – AMERICAN BAND OF THE AEF from Queensberry All-Services Club, London. Guest Artist, Paula Green.
Get Happy/At Last v, Paula Green/I've Got A Heart Filled With Love

For You Dear v, JD/*Medley*: Shubert's Serenade, Irresistible You v, JD & cc, Little Brown Jug, Rhapsody In Blue/Parachute Jump (*Quartet*: Powell, piano, Hucko, clarinet, Alpert, bass, McKinley, drums)/The Victory Polka v, JD, cc & Band.

Note – Major Glenn Miller's interview with Vernon Harris for the 'Wishing Well' broadcast was probably recorded today, not the 15th (*see* page 148).

Friday 15 September

11.00 AEFP Broadcast – AMERICAN BAND OF THE AEF: Morning After (recorded repeat of last night's broadcast).

London – BBC Pre-recording – *Here's Wishing You Well Again*, with Major Glenn Miller interviewed by Vernon Harris for 'The Wishing Well' (but *see also* page 148).

pm Band left Bedford for Rougham.

18.15 AEFP Broadcast – SWING SEXTET: The Uptown Hall (recorded 13/9/44).

Stomping At The Savoy/When A Woman Loves A Man (featuring Mel Powell, piano)/After You've Gone/Swinging On a Star v, JD & cc / Temptation.

evening Concert (full Band) with Dinah Shore, but without Major Miller, at 8th Air Force bomber base at Rougham, near Bury St Edmunds, Suffolk; Band stayed overnight.

Saturday 16 September

09.35 AEFP Broadcast – AMERICAN DANCE BAND: The Swing Shift (25 minutes) (recorded 8/9/44).

It Must Be Jelly/Georgia On My Mind/Peggy The Pin Up Girl v, RM & cc/My Ideal v, JD/Original composition, unknown title (*Trio*)/Now I Know v, JD/Snafu Jump.

am Band travelled from Rougham to London by road.

12.45 AEFP Broadcast – JACK RUSIN: Keyboard Contrasts (recorded 14/9/44)

14.00 GFP Broadcast – AMERICAN BAND OF THE AEF. No repeat broadcast of last Thursday's AEFP broadcast: replaced by Jack Leon Orchestra from Drury Lane 'By Way Of Music'.

14.00 Recording session (full Band) with Dinah Shore at HMV studio, London.

        Stardust v, Dinah Shore.

        All I Do Is Dream Of You v, Dinah Shore.

        I've Got A Heart Filled With Love For You, Dear v, JD & cc.

        Farewell Blues.

(None of these recordings has ever been issued).

Also: Music for US Special Services film.

18.15 AEFP Broadcast – SWING SEXTET: The Uptown Hall (recorded 6/9/44).Guest artist: Beryl Davis.

Flying Home/Rose Room/You Took Advantage Of Me/Confessing v,
Beryl Davis/Stomping At The Savoy.

Sunday 17 September
 Day off for the Band.
12.45 AEFP Broadcast – SERGEANT JOHNNY DESMOND: A Soldier And A
Song. (recorded 23/8/44).
Suddenly It's Spring/Where Or When/Here We Go Again (*Band*)/
Without A Song.

Monday 18 September
 Day off for the band.
19.15½ AEFP Broadcast – STRINGS WITH WINGS. (recorded 4/9/44).
Sure Thing/Claire De Lune/Sweet And Lovely/September Song.

Tuesday 19 September
 Day off for the Band.
18.30 AEFP Broadcast – AMERICAN DANCE BAND: The Swing Shift
(recorded 9/9/44).
Breaking In A New Pair Of Shoes/Sleepy Town Train/Along The Santa
Fe Trail v, JD/I'm Heading For California v, RM & CC/What Is This
Thing Called Love (*Trio*)/Going My Way v, JD/Tail End Charlie.
19.45 AEFP Broadcast – SWING SEXTET: The Uptown Hall (recorded 6/
9/44). Guest artists, Beryl Davis and Bernie Privin (trumpet).
China Boy/You Go To My Head (featuring Bernie Privin, trumpet)/I'm
In The Mood For Love v, Beryl Davis/The Earl.
Note – The above times were the new regular times for these pro-
grammes.

Wednesday 20 September
 Day off for the Band.
18.15 AEFP Broadcast – SWING SEXTET: The Uptown Hall (recorded 6/
9/44). Guest artist Beryl Davis.
I Want To Be Happy/Body And Soul/What Is This Thing Called Love
(*Quartet*)/Sweet Lorraine v, Beryl Davis/Rosetta.
19.45 AEFP Broadcast – STRINGS WITH WINGS. No broadcast: replaced
by live broadcast by Yehudi Menuhin and BBC Symphony Orchestra
from Home Service (19.15–20.00).

Thursday 21 September
18.15 GFP Broadcast – *Here's Wishing You well Again*, including Major
Glenn Miller interviewed by Vernon Harris for the 'Wishing Well'
(recorded 15/9/44, but *see also* page 148).
20.30 AEFP Broadcast – AN AMERICAN BAND OF THE AEF from the
Queensberry All-Services Club, London. Guest artists, United States
Navy Dance Band, directed by Sam Donahue.
Flying Home/I'll Be Seeing You v, JD/Somebody Loves Me (Navy

Band)/*Medley*: I Dream Of Jeannie With The Light Brown Hair, I Couldn't Sleep A Wink Last Night, V, JD & CC, Begin The Beguine, Blue Rain/LST Part (Navy Band)/One O'Clock Jump (combined AEF and Navy Bands).

Friday 22 September
11.00   AEFP Broadcast – AMERICAN BAND OF THE AEF: Morning After (recorded repeat of last night's broadcast).
16.00   AEFP Pre-recording – AMERICAN DANCE BAND: The Swing Shift. Broadcast 7/10/44.
18.15   AEFP Broadcast – SWING SEXTET: The Uptown Hall.
You're Driving Me Crazy/These Foolish Things/Untitled composition by Peanuts Hucko (*Quartet*)/I'll Walk Alone V, JD/I'll Remember April/*Theme* and You're Driving Me Crazy.
20.00–23.00   'Small dance unit' directed by Phil Cogliano played at ARC Enlisted Mens Club, Midland Road, Bedford.

Saturday 23 September
09.30   AEFP Broadcast – AMERICAN DANCE BAND: The Swing Shift.
Sun Valley Jump/Is You Is You Ain't My Baby V, RM/The Day After Forever V, JD/Juke Box Saturday Night V, CC/Giggleswick Gallop (*Trio*)/Time Alone Will Tell V, JD/Spanish Shawl (arranged by Carmen Mastren)/Eyes And Ears Of The World.
10.45   AEFP Pre-recording – SWING SEXTET: The Uptown Hall. Broadcast 23/11/44.
11.45   AEFP Broadcast – JACK RUSIN: Piano Parade (recorded 14/9/44).
13.01   GFP Broadcast – AMERICAN BAND OF THE AEF (recorded repeat of last Thursday's AEFP broadcast).
14.45   AEFP Pre-recording – SERGEANT JOHNNY DESMOND. Broadcast 24/9/44.
18.15   AEFP Broadcast – SWING SEXTET: The Uptown Hall.
How High The Moon/Have A Little Dream On Me (*Quartet*)/She's Funny That Way V, JD/Temptation.
19.30   AEFP Pre-recording – STRINGS WITH WINGS. Broadcast 25/9/44.

Sunday 24 September
12.45   AEFP Broadcast – SERGEANT JOHNNY DESMOND (recorded 23/9/44).
My Prayer/Louise/Caribbean Clipper (*Band*)/I'll Remember April.
13.00–14.00   Concert (full Band) for Airborne Troops in hangar at North Witham, Lincolnshire. (2,500)
15.00–16.00   Public charity concert (full Band) at State Cinema, Grantham, Lincolnshire. (1,500 plus overflow outside)

Monday 25 September
15.30   Concert (full Band) at US Army 91st General Hospital, Oxford.
(1,200)
19.15   AEFP Broadcast – STRINGS WITH WINGS (recorded 23/9/44)
Flamingo/Pavanne/Smoke Gets In Your Eyes/Moonlight Serenade.
19.30   Concert (full Band) at 8th Air Force 7th Photo Reconnaissance
Group, Mount Farm, Oxfordshire. (3,500)

Tuesday 26 September
18.30   AEFP Broadcast – AMERICAN DANCE BAND: The Swing Shift.
King Porter Stomp/Ida v, RM/Somebody's Wrong/How Blue The Night
v, JD/Untitled original composition (*Trio*)/Cherry/I'll Get By v, JD/9.20
Special.
19.45   AEFP Broadcast – SWING SEXTET: The Uptown Hall.
Blue Room/Sophisticated Lady/Sugar (*Quartet*)/When Your Lover Has
Gone v, JD/The Sheik of Araby.
20.45   AEFP Pre-recording – SWING SEXTET: The Uptown Hall.
Broadcast 16/12/44.

Wednesday 27 September
14.45   AEFP Pre-recording – SERGEANT JOHNNY DESMOND: A Soldier
And A Song, Broadcast 20/11/44.
18.16   AEFP Broadcast – SWING SEXTET: The Uptown Hall.
Rosetta/Sweet Lorraine/Poor Butterfly (*Quartet*: Powell, piano, Hucko,
clarinet, Joe Shulman, bass, Frank Ippolito, drums)/Once In A While v,
JD/Don't Be That Way.
19.45   AEFP Broadcast – STRINGS WITH WINGS.
Make Believe/Tico Tico/My Prayer/My Silent Love.
20.45   AEFP Pre-recording – STRINGS WITH WINGS. Broadcast 20/12/44.

Thursday 28 September
15.30   BBC Pre-recording – AMERICAN DANCE BAND: American Eagle In
Britain, from Rainbow Corner (ARC Club), London, for future broadcast
in USA.
20.30   AEFP Broadcast – AMERICAN BAND OF THE AEF from the
Queensberry All-Services Club, London. Guest Artist, Pat Kirkwood.
Get Happy/Long Ago And Far Away v, JD/Is You Is Or Is You Ain't
My Baby v, RM/*Medley*: Flow Gently Sweet Afton, Moondreams v, JD &
CC, Don't Be That Way, Blue Champagne/My Kind Of Music v, Pat
Kirkwood/Anvil Chorus.

Friday 29 September
10.01   AEFP Broadcast – AMERICAN BAND OF THE AEF: Morning After
(recorded repeat of last night's broadcast).
10.30   AEFP Pre-recording – STRINGS WITH WINGS. Broadcast 27/12/44.
14.45   AEFP Pre-recording – AMERICAN DANCE BAND: The Swing Shift.
Broadcast 16/12/44.

18.15   AEFP Broadcast – SWING SEXTET: The Uptown Hall.
Dream A Little Dream Of Me/Get Happy (Carmen Mastren, guitar,
and Phil Cogliano, violin)/Swinging On A Star v, JD & CC/Perdido.
19.15   AEFP Pre-recording – SWING SEXTET: The Uptown Hall.
Broadcast 20/12/44.

Saturday 30 September
09.30   AEFP Broadcast – AMERICAN DANCE BAND: The Swing Shift.
Seven-O-Five/Song Of The Volga Boatmen/The Day After Forever v,
JD/Wham Re Bop Boom Bam v, RM/Perrywinkle Wallop (*Trio*)/Spanish
Shawl/I Dream Of You v, JD/Another One Of Them Things.
11.00   AEFP Pre-recording – SWING SEXTET: The Uptown Hall.
Broadcast 21/12/44.
11.45   AEFP Broadcast JACK RUSIN: Piano Parade (recorded 14/9/44).
13.01   GFP Broadcast AMERICAN BAND OF THE AEF (recorded repeat of
Thursday's broadcast).
14.45   AEFP Pre-recording – AMERICAN DANCE BAND: The Swing Shift.
Broadcast 3/10/44.
18.15   AEFP Broadcast – SWING SEXTET: The Uptown Hall.
At Sundown/Lum De De (*Quartet*)/I'll Walk Alone v, JD/Caravan.
19.30   AEFP Pre-recording – SERGEANT JOHNNY DESMOND: Soldier And
A Song. Broadcast 1/10/44.

Sunday 1 October
12.45   AEFP Broadcast – SERGEANT JOHNNY DESMOND: Soldier And A
Song (recorded 30/9/44).
Star Eyes/I'll Walk Alone/Jeep Jockey Jump (*Band*)/I Only Have Eyes
For You.
15.30   Concert (full Band)without Major Glenn Miller at 8th Air Force
bomber base at Great Ashfield, near Elmswell, Suffolk. (15,000)
16.15   Special broadcast (15 minutes) by full Band and guest stars from
Great Ashfield by shortwave to USA in honour of 200th Mission of 385th
Bomb Group.

Monday 2 October
15.30   Concert (full Band) without Major Miller at 8th Air Force
bomber base at Nuthampstead, Herts. (3,000)
19.05   AEFP Broadcast – STRINGS WITH WINGS (recorded 6/9/44).
It Could Happen To You/Habanera/The Man I Love/None But The
Lonely Heart.

Tuesday 3 October
15.30   Concert (full Band) at 8th Air Force fighter base, Kingscliffe,
Northants. (2,500)
18.30   AEFP Broadcast – AMERICAN DANCE BAND: The Swing Shift
(recorded 30/9/44).

Swanee River/Uncle Tom/Peggy The Pin-Up Girl v, RM & CC/I Dream Of You v, JD/Perrywinkle Wallop (*Trio*)/Is You Is Or Is You Ain't My Baby v, RM/Now I Know v, JD/King Porter Stomp.

19.45   AEFP Broadcast – SWING SEXTET: The Uptown Hall (recorded 7/9/44).

How High The Moon/I Don't Know Why v, CC/At Sundown (*Quartet*)/Once In A While v, JD/Oh Lady Be Good.

Wednesday 4 October

14.00   AEFP Pre-recordings – JACK RUSIN: Piano Parade.

  [Programme 1] broadcast 16/12/44.
  [Programme 2] broadcast 23/12/44.

18.15   AEFP Broadcast – SWING SEXTET: The Uptown Hall.

Emaline/Louise/If Dreams Come True (*Quartet*: Powell, piano, Hucko, clarinet, Shulman, bass, Private First Class Frankie Maine (? actually Ippolito,) drums)/I'll Be Seeing You v, JD/Night In Tunisia (arranged by Addison Collins, Jr).

19.45   AEFP Broadcast – STRINGS WITH WINGS.

Embraceable You/Orchids In The Moonlight/May Night/Sure Thing.

Note – According to Haynes' diary, five pre-recordings were made today, but details of only the two Jack Rusin pre-recordings survive in the radio archives and they are the only ones given in the Activities list.

Thursday 5 October

20.30   AEFP Broadcast – AMERICAN BAND OF THE AEF from the Queensberry All-Services Club, London. Guest artist, RSM George Melachrino.

Great Day (arranged by Jerry Gray)/Goodnight, Good Neighbour v, George Melachrino /String of Pearls/*Medley*: Caprice Viennoise, I'll Walk Alone v, JD, My Isle Of Golden Dreams, Birth Of The Blues/It Could Happen To You v, JD/What Do You Do In The Infantry v, JD, CC & Band.

Friday 6 October

10.00   AEFP Broadcast – AMERICAN BAND OF THE AEF: Morning After (recorded repeat of last night's broadcast).

18.15   AEFP Broadcast – SWING SEXTET: The Uptown Hall.

Hallelujah/You Took Advantage Of Me/Capener Close Clambake (*Quartet*)/I Surrender Dear v, JD/The Earl.

Saturday 7 October

09.30   AEFP Broadcast – AMERICAN DANCE BAND: The Swing Shift (recorded 22/9/44).

I Hear You Screaming/Song Of The Volga Boatmen/Shoo Shoo Baby v, CC/The Day After Forever v, JD/California Here I Come (*Trio*)/I'll Walk Alone v, JD/Bubble Bath/Beat Me Daddy Eight To The Bar v, RM.

11.45 AEFP Broadcast – JACK RUSIN: Piano Parade (recorded 14/9/44).

13.01 GFP Broadcast – AMERICAN BAND OF THE AEF (recorded repeat of Thursday's broadcast).

18.15 AEFP Broadcast – SWING SEXTET: The Uptown Hall.
Flying Home/Don't Blame Me/Portrait Of A Worried Cat (*Quartet*: Powell, piano, Hucko, clarinet, Alpert, bass, McKinley, drums)/What A Difference A Day Made v, JD/Blue Skies.

Sunday 8 October

12.45 AEFP Broadcast – SERGEANT JOHNNY DESMOND: Soldier And A Song.
You're The Rainbow/All The Things You Are/Somebody's Wrong (*Band*)/I'll Be Seeing You.

16.15 AEFP Pre-recording – AMERICAN DANCE BAND: The Swing Shift. Broadcast 21/12/44.

Monday 9 October

Note – From now on until 13 December practically all the broadcasts by the AEF Band and its smaller bands were live, following the orders of 5 October signed by Lieutenant Colonel Niven.

19.15 AEFP Broadcast – STRINGS WITH WINGS. Details unavailable.

Tuesday 10 October

18.30 AEFP Broadcast – AMERICAN DANCE BAND: The Swing Shift.
Mission to Moscow/This I Love Above All v, JD/I Thought I'd Get It But I Guess I've Had It Blues (*Trio*)/Sweet And Low/9.20 Special/Irresistible You v, JD & CC/Swing Low Sweet Chariot/Bubble Bath.

19.45 AEFP Broadcast – SWING SEXTET: The Uptown Hall. No broadcast.
In future there were only three broadcasts a week by the Swing Sextet – on Wednesdays, Fridays and Saturdays, until the new broadcasting schedule began on Monday 13 November.

Wednesday 11 October

18.15 AEFP Broadcast – SWING SEXTET: The Uptown Hall. Details unavailable.

19.45 AEFP Broadcast – STRINGS WITH WINGS. Details unavailable.

Thursday 12 October

20.30 AEFP Broadcast – AMERICAN BAND OF THE AEF from the Queensberry All-Services Club, London. Guest artist, Jack Hylton.
Caribbean Clipper/My Prayer v, JD/Mission To Moscow/*Medley*: Going Home, Star Eyes v, JD, Honeysuckle Rose, My Blue Heaven/She Shall Have Music v, JD, Orchestra conducted by Jack Hylton/Poinciana v, JD & CC.

Friday 13 October

10.01 AEFP Broadcast – AMERICAN BAND OF THE AEF: Morning After (recorded repeat of last night's broadcast).

15.45 AEFP Pre-recording – AMERICAN DANCE BAND: The Swing Shift. Broadcast 14/10/44.

18.15 AEFP Broadcast – SWING SEXTET: The Uptown Hall.
Stomping At The Savoy/Caravan/I'm Through With Love v, JD/Song of The Wanderer.

Saturday 14 October

09.30 AEFP Broadcast – AMERICAN DANCE BAND: The Swing Shift (recorded 13/10/44).
Breaking In A New Pair Of Shoes/Rainbow Rhapsody/I'm Heading For California v, RM & CC/It Could Happen To You v, JD/Ode To Pinetop (*Trio*)/Is You Is Or Is You Ain't My Baby v, RM/The Day After v, JD/Great Day.

11.45 AEFP Broadcast – JACK RUSIN: Piano Parade.

13.01 GFP Broadcast – AMERICAN BAND OF THE AEF (recorded repeat of Thursday's broadcast).

18.15 AEFP Broadcast – SWING SEXTET: The Uptown Hall. Guest Artist, Bernie Privin (trumpet).
Temptation/What Is There To Say/Sweet And Lovely v, JD & CC / Strutting With Some Barbecue (featuring Bernie Privin, trumpet).

Sunday 15 October

12.45 AEFP Broadcast – SERGEANT JOHNNY DESMOND.
Amor Amor/The Lamp Is Low/Begin The Beguine (*Band*)/The Music Stopped.

pm The AEF Band played at the Jazz Jamboree concert at the Stoll Theatre, London. During the evening Major Glenn Miller and some of the men from the AEF Band visited the Feldman Swing Club.

Monday 16 October

19.15 AEFP Broadcast – STRINGS WITH WINGS.
I'm In The Mood For Love/You And The Night And The Music/Serenade/Bess You Is My Woman Now.

Tuesday 17 October

18.30 AEFP Broadcast – AMERICAN DANCE BAND: The Swing Shift.
Seven-O-Five/String Of Pearls/The Big Ones Are Eating The Little Ones/How Blue The Night v, JD/Sensation (*Trio*: Powell, piano, Hucko, tenor sax, McKinley, drums) I'll Get By v, JD/Wham Re Bop Boom Bam v, RM.

Wednesday 18 October
18.15 AEFP Broadcast – SWING SEXTET: The Uptown Hall.
How High The Moon/Sophisticated Lady/Don't Blame Me v,
JD/Perdido.
19.45 AEFP Broadcast – STRINGS WITH WINGS. Details unavailable.

Thursday 19 October
16.00 Rehearsal at Queensberry Club, London.
20.30 AEFP Broadcast – AMERICAN BAND OF THE AEF. No broadcast;
however, the Band played at the Queensberry Club in the evening as
usual and a broadcast was recorded (tunes not known) with Sally
Douglas as guest artist and repeated next morning in the AEFP and on
Saturday in the GFP. A note in the radio archives says 'broadcast
cancelled owing to emergency'. The broadcast was replaced by commercial 78s (15 minutes) and 'Listen At Ease' (AFN recording) (15
minutes).

Friday 20 October
10.01 AEFP Broadcast – AMERICAN BAND OF THE AEF: Morning After
(recorded repeat of last night's programme).
15.45 AEFP Pre-recording – AMERICAN DANCE BAND: The Swing Shift.
Broadcast 21/10/44.
18.45 AEFP Broadcast – SWING SEXTET: The Uptown Hall. No
broadcast: 'cancelled 15 minutes before airtime due to sudden illness'
(Activities list); replaced by Glenn Miller civilian band records.

Saturday 21 October
09.30 AEFP Broadcast – AMERICAN DANCE BAND: The Swing Shift
(recorded 20/10/44.
Somebody's Wrong/Sleepy Town Train/Peggy The Pin-Up Girl v, RM &
CC/Eyes And Ears Of The World (featuring Peanuts Hucko, clarinet)/
This I Love Above All v, JD/Fighting Biting Stomp (*Trio*)/I Dream Of
You v, JD/Get Happy.
11.45 AEFP Broadcast – JACK RUSIN: Piano Parade.
13.01½ GFP Broadcast – AMERICAN BAND OF THE AEF (recorded repeat of Thursday's programme).
18.15 AEFP Broadcast – SWING SEXTET: The Uptown Hall.
You're Lucky For Me/Meet The Band/I'll Walk Alone v, JD/Between
The Devil And The Deep Blue Sea.

Sunday 22 October
12.45 AEFP Broadcast – SERGEANT JOHNNY DESMOND: Soldier And A
Song. How Sweet You Are/Sweet And Lovely/It Could Happen To You.

Monday 23 October
19.05 AEFP Broadcast – STRINGS WITH WINGS. Details unavailable.

Tuesday 24 October
18.30 AEFP Broadcast – AMERICAN DANCE BAND: The Swing Shift.
Flying Home/Rainbow Rhapsody/I've Got A Heart Filled With Love
For You Dear V, JD & CC/Snafu Jump/My Shining Hour V, JD/Biggleswade
Wiggle (*Trio*)/The Day After Forever V, JD/One O'Clock Jump.

Wednesday 25 October
18.15 AEFP Broadcast – SWING SEXTET: The Uptown Hall.
Shandy (composed by Carmen Mastren)/Embraceable You V, JD/
Somebody Loves Me.
19.45 AEFP Broadcast – STRINGS WITH WINGS. Details unavailable.

Thursday 26 October
16.00 Rehearsal at Queensberry Club, London.
20.30 AEFP Broadcast – AMERICAN BAND OF THE AEF, from the
Queensberry All-Service Club, London. Guest artist, Anne Shelton.
American Patrol/Stardust/On Wisconsin/*Medley*: Old Refrain, Same
Old Love, V JD, Smoke Gets In Your Eyes, Blue Again/Spring Will Be A
Little Late This Year V, Anne Shelton/You Are My Sunshine V, JD & CC.

Friday 27 October
10.01 AEFP Broadcast – AMERICAN BAND OF THE AEF. Morning After
(recorded repeat of last night's broadcast).
15.45 AEFP Pre-recording – AMERICAN DANCE BAND: The Swing Shift.
Broadcast 28/10/44.
18.15 AEFP Broadcast – SWING SEXTET: The Uptown Hall.
Somebody Loves Me/East Of The Sun V, JD/(rest unknown).

Saturday 28 October
09.30 AEFP Broadcast – AMERICAN DANCE BAND: The Swing Shift
(recorded 27/10/44).
Sun Valley Jump/Is You Is Or Is You Ain't My Baby V, RM/How Blue
The Night V, JD/Juke Box Saturday Night V, CC/Original composition,
title unknown/(*Trio*)/I Dream Of You V, JD/Spanish Shawl/King Porter
Stomp.
11.45 AEFP Broadcast – JACK RUSIN: Piano Parade.
13.01 GFP Broadcast – AMERICAN BAND OF THE AEF (recorded repeat
of Thursday's broadcast).
18.15 AEFP Broadcast – SWING SEXTET: The Uptown Hall.
I'll Remember April/Love Is Just Around The Corner/After You've
Gone (*Trio* or *Quartet*)/I'll Walk Alone V, JD/Rosetta.

Sunday 29 October
12.45 AEFP Broadcast – SERGEANT JOHNNY DESMOND: Soldier And A
Song.
I'll Remember April/Fellow On A Furlough/The First Few Days/Oh
Lady Be Good (*Band*)/Louise.

'Small dance unit' directed by Phil Cogliano played for a dance at ARC Enlisted Mens Club, Midland Road, Bedford. (300)

Monday 30 October
am and pm   ABSIE recording session – AMERICAN BAND OF THE AEF, HMV studios, London. 'Music For The Wehrmacht'
* Broadcast over ABSIE 8/11/44.
19.15   AEFP Broadcast – STRINGS WITH WINGS.
How Am I To Know/There's a Small Hotel/Sweet And Low/I'll Be Seeing You.

Tuesday 31 October
18.30   AEFP Broadcast – AMERICAN DANCE BAND: The Swing Shift.
Here We Go Again/Cow Cow Boogie v, RM/Oh Lady Be Good/This I Love Above All v, JD/Vamp Till Ready (composed by Ray McKinley) (Septet)/Stealing Apples.
(*Note* – Vamp Till Ready, was recorded by the post-war New Glenn Miller Orchestra directed by Ray McKinley.)

Wednesday 1 November
18.15   AEFP Broadcast – SWING SEXTET: The Uptown Hall. Guest artist, Bernie Privin (trumpet).
Making Whoopee/You Go To My Head (featuring Bernie Privin, trumpet)/She's Funny That Way v, JD/Oh Lady Be Good.
19.45   AEFP Broadcast – STRINGS WITH WINGS. Details unavailable.

Thursday 2 November
16.00   Rehearsal at Queensberry All-Services Club, London.
20.30   AEFP Broadcast – AMERICAN BAND OF THE AEF. From the Queensberry All-Services Club. No guest artists from now on.
Get Happy/I'll Be Seeing You v, JD/Anchors Aweigh/*Medley*: Long Long Ago, The Music Stopped v, JD, The Dipsey Doodle, Blues In My Heart/Have You Got Any Gum, Chum (written by Murray Kane) v, JD & CC/Jerry's Aachen Back (*Quartet*: Mel Powell, piano, Peanuts Hucko, clarinet, Trigger Alpert, bass, Ray McKinley, drums)/Song Of The Volga Boatmen.

Friday 3 November
10.01   AEFP Broadcast – AMERICAN BAND OF THE AEF: Morning After (recorded repeat of last night's broadcast).
18.15   AEFP Broadcast – SWING SEXTET: The Uptown Hall.
Temptation/Emaline/I Must Have That Man (*Quartet*)/I'm Through With Love v, JD/Rose Room.

Saturday 4 November
09.30   AEFP Broadcast – AMERICAN DANCE BAND: The Swing Shift. Transferred to Saturday afternoon, 15.01 from now on.

* Information on some of these programmes is confused and incomplete.

11.45   AEFP Broadcast – JACK RUSIN: Piano Parade.
13.01   GFP Broadcast – AMERICAN BAND OF THE AEF (recorded repeat of last Thursday's broadcast).
15.01   AEFP Broadcast – AMERICAN DANCE BAND: The Swing Shift.
Flying Home/Watcha Know Joe v, RM/Sweet And Lovely v, CC/9.20 Special/Georgia On My Mind/Uptown Flavour (*Trio*)/I'll Walk Alone v, JD/I Hear You Screaming.
18.15   AEFP Broadcast – SWING SEXTET: The Uptown Hall. Guest Artist, Bernie Privin, trumpet.
Caravan/Dream A Little Dream Of Me (*Quartet*)/I'll Be Seeing You v, JD/Strutting With Some Barbecue (featuring Bernie Privin, trumpet).

Sunday 5 November
12.45   AEFP Broadcast – SERGEANT JOHNNY DESMOND.
All The Things You Are/My Heart Stood Still/I Only Have Eyes For You/Deep Summer Music.

Monday 6 November
am and pm   ABSIE recording sessions – AMERICAN BAND OF THE AEF, HMV Studios, London: 'Music For The Wehrmacht' (see footnote to Monday 30 October) Two programmes, broadcast over ABSIE on 15/11/44 and 22/11/44.
19.15   AEFP Broadcast – STRINGS WITH WINGS (From Maida Vale Studios, London). Guest conductor, Sir Adrian Boult.
Seranade For Strings (Elgar)/Clouds Nocturne (Debussy)/Annie Laurie.

Tuesday 7 November
18.30   AEFP Broadcast – AMERICAN DANCE BAND: The Swing Shift.
Breaking In A New Pair Of Shoes/Stardust/Got Any Gum, Chum v, CC/I Dream Of You v, JD/Nobody's Sweetheart Now (*Trio*)/The Day After Forever v, JD/Sweet And Low/Everybody Loves My Baby.

Wednesday 8 November
13.30   ABSIE Broadcast – AMERICAN BAND OF THE AEF: 'Music For The Wehrmacht' (See footnote on page 319.) Compères, 'Isle' and Major Glenn Miller. (recorded 30/10/44).
Theme (Moonlight Serenade)/In The Mood/Stardust/Song Of The Volga Boatmen/Long Ago And Far Away v, JD/Is You Is Or Is You Ain't My Baby v, RM/Great Day/*Theme*.
18.15   AEFP Broadcast – SWING SEXTET: The Uptown Hall.
Song Of The Wanderer/Shandy/One Two Button Your Shoe (*Quartet*)/Limehouse Blues.
19.45   AEFP Broadcast – STRINGS WITH WINGS. Details unavailable.

Thursday 9 November
14.00   Rehearsal at Queensberry Club, London.
20.30   AEFP Broadcast – AMERICAN BAND OF THE AEF, from The
Queensberry All-Services Club, London.
Jeep Jockey Jump/It Could Happen To You v, JD/On Brave Old Army
Team/*Medley*: Londonderry Air, Spring Will Be A Little Late This Year
v, JD, Cherokee, Blue Danube/Is You Is Or Is You Ain't My Baby v,
RM/Flying Home.

Friday 10 November
10.01   AEFP Broadcast – AMERICAN BAND OF THE AEF: Morning After
(recorded repeat of last night's broadcast).
18.15   AEFP Broadcast – SWING SEXTET: The Uptown Hall.
Flying Home/What Is There To Say/I Must Have That Man (*Quartet*).

Saturday 11 November
11.45   AEFP Broadcast – JACK RUSIN: Piano Parade.
13.01   GFP Broadcast – AMERICAN BAND OF THE AEF (recorded repeat
of Thursday's broadcast).
15.01   AEFP Broadcast – AMERICAN DANCE BAND: The Swing Shift.
Here We Go Again/Swing Low Sweet Chariot/The Music Stopped v,
JD/Bubble Bath/My Buddy/Hobba Hobba Hop (*Trio*)/Spring Will Be A
Little Late This Year v, JD/Mission To Moscow.
18.15   AEFP Broadcast – SWING SEXTET: The Uptown Hall.
Little White Lies/Stars Fell On Alabama/Pennies From Heaven
(*Quartet*)/Once In A While v, JD/Blue Room.
evening   Mel Powell and a sextet played for a dance at the Officers
Club, Milton Ernest Hall.

Sunday 12 November
   Day off for the Band.
12.45   AEFP Broadcast – SERGEANT JOHNNY DESMOND. Broadcasts
transferred to Monday evenings from now onwards.

Monday 13 November
am and pm   ABSIE recording session – AMERICAN BAND OF THE AEF,
HMV studios, London: 'Music For The Wehrmacht' (see footnote to
Monday 30 October) Broadcast over ABSIE 29/11/44.
17.40   AEFP Broadcast – CARMEN MASTREN (Guitar) and TRIGGER
ALPERT (Bass) accompanied THE BEVERLEY SISTERS: AEF Extra (15
minutes).
It's Love, Love, Love/Banks Of The Wabash; other items by other
artists.
Note – The American Band of the AEF and its smaller bands began a new
broadcasting schedule today (*see* page 192).
19.00   AEFP Broadcast – SERGEANT JOHNNY DESMOND: Sergeant
Johnny Desmond Sings. From Maida Vale studios, London.

Long Ago And Far Away/Sweet Lorraine/Get Happy (*Band*)/Spring Will Be A Little Late This Year.

19.15   AEFP Broadcast – STRINGS WITH WINGS. From Maida Vale studios, London.
How Deep Is The Ocean/Estrellita/Indian Summer/Sure Thing.

Tuesday 14 November
14.00   Rehearsal at Queensberry Club, London.
20.30   AEFP Broadcast – AMERICAN BAND OF THE AEF, From Queensberry Club, London, conducted by Jerry Gray; compère, Sergeant Keith Jamieson (AEFP announcer).
Here We Go Again/Body And Soul/Beat me Daddy Eight To A Bar v, RM/*Medley*: My Buddy, Now I Know v, JD, Music Makers, Farewell Blues/Deep Summer Music v, JD/I Hear You Screaming.

Wednesday 15 November
   Major Glenn Miller flew to Paris to see General Barker.
10.01   AEFP Broadcast – AMERICAN BAND OF THE AEF: Morning After (recording of last night's broadcast).
13.30   ABSIE Broadcast – AMERICAN BAND OF THE AEF: 'Music For The Wehrmacht' (See footnote on page 319.) Compères, Ilse and Major Glenn Miller. (recorded 6/11/44).
American Patrol/Summertime/Tuxedo Junction/Now I Know v, JD /Begin The Beguine/The Anvil Chorus.
14.01   AFN Broadcast – AMERICAN BAND OF THE AEF: Visiting Hour (59 minutes).
 AEF BAND: Here We Go Again/Stardust/It Could Happen To You v, JD.
SWING SEXTET: I'll Remember April/If Dreams Come True/Caravan.
STRINGS WITH WINGS: I'll Get By/There's A Small Hotel/Indian Summer.
AMERICAN DANCE BAND: King Porter Stomp/Is You Is Or Is You Ain't My Baby v, RM/Everybody Loves My Baby.
AEF BAND: *Medley*: Danny Boy, Spring Will Be A Little Late This Year v, JD, Cherokee, The Blue Danube/Snafu Jump.
18.15   AEFP Broadcast – SWING SEXTET: The Uptown Hall.
At Sundown/Body And Soul/Avalon (*Quartet*)/Embraceable You v, JD/You're Driving Me Crazy.
19.45   AEFP Broadcast – STRINGS WITH WINGS.
Sweet And Lovely/Deep River/Our Waltz.

Thursday 16 November
19.30   AEFP Broadcast – AMERICAN DANCE BAND: The Swing Shift.
Eyes And Ears Of The World/You Go To My Head (featuring Bernie Privin, trumpet)/Beat Me Daddy Eight To The Bar v, RM/How Blue The Night v, Artie Malvin/Popsie's Pooch (*Trio*)/This I Love Above All v, AM/Sleepy Town Train/Somebody's Wrong.

21.15   AEFP Broadcast – SWING SEXTET: The Uptown Hall.
Note – There is conflicting evidence in the radio archives as to whether this programme was live or pre-recorded; in fact, owing to the illness of Mannie Thaler a pre-recording made on September 8th, 1944, was broadcast.
I'll Remember April/These Foolish Things/Exactly Like You (*Quartet*), including Joe Shulman, bass/I'll Be Seeing You v, JD/Caravan.

Friday 17 November
14.00   Rehearsal at Queensberry Club.
20.30   AEFP Broadcast – AMERICAN BAND OF THE AEF: Moonlight Serenade from Queensberry Club, London; conducted by Jerry Gray; compère, Sergeant Keith Jamieson (AEFP announcer).
Seven-O-Five/Sweet Lorraine v, Artie Malvin/Tuxedo Junction/*Medley*: I Dream Of Jeannie With The Light Brown Hair, Amor Amor v, AM, Begin The Beguine, Blue Rain/Down The Road A-piece v, RM and Trigger Alpert/Great Day.

Saturday 18 November
   Major Glenn Miller returned from Paris to Bedford.
11.45   AEFP Broadcast – JACK RUSIN: Piano Parade.
13.01   GFP Broadcast – AMERICAN BAND OF THE AEF: Moonlight Serenade (recorded repeat of last night's broadcast).
15.01   AEFP Broadcast – AMERICAN DANCE BAND: The Swing Shift.
Tail End Charlie/Oh Lady Be Good/She's Funny That Way v, Artie Malvin/Spanish Shawl/Seven-O-Five/It Could Happen To You v, AM/The Big Ones Are Eating The Little Ones.
18.15   AEFP Broadcast – SWING SEXTET: The Uptown Hall.
Broadcast cancelled owing to the illness of Mel Powell and replaced by commercial recordings of classical music (8.10 to 18.30).

Sunday 19 November
   Day off for the band.

Monday 20 November
am and pm   ABSIE recording Session – AMERICAN BAND OF THE AEF, HMV studios, London: 'Music For The Wehrmacht' (see footnote to Monday 30 October.) With songs by Irene Manning. Two programmes recorded, broadcast over ABSIE ?6/12/44 and ?
19.00   AEFP Broadcast SERGEANT JOHNNY DESMOND: A Soldier And A Song.
Note – There is conflicting evidence in the radio archives as to whether this broadcast was live or pre-recorded; however, Sergeant Johnny Desmond was ill with influenza and missed several broadcasts around this time so it seems likely that a reserve recording made on 27/9/44 was broadcast.
That Old Black magic/Where Or When/Seven-O-Five (*Band*)/My Prayer.

19.15   AEFP Broadcast – STRINGS WITH WINGS.
Please/What Is There To Say/Memories Of You/I'll Remember April.

Tuesday 21 November

07.30   AEFP Broadcast – AMERICAN DANCE BAND: The Swing Shift:
Return Engagement (recorded repeat of last Saturday's broadcast).

14.00   Rehearsal at Queensberry All-Services Club, London.

20.30   AEFP Broadcast – AMERICAN BAND OF THE AEF, from the
Queensberry All-Services Club.

Tail End Charlie/Rhapsody In Blue/GI Jive V, RM & CC/*Medley*: Mother
Macree, It Could Happen To You V, JD, I Can't Give You Anything But
Love Baby V, Peanuts Hucko, Wang Wang Blues/Little Brown Jug/You
Are My Sunshine (V, Jerry Gray according to the radio archives but this
is probably a misprint for Johnny Desmond – Jerry Gray probably wrote
the arrangment; V, also CC).

Wednesday 22 November

Agreement reached between SHAEF and BBC for the Band to go to Paris
on 16th December to play for troops for six weeks; programmes to be
pre-recorded for broadcasting while they were away.

10.01   AEFP Broadcast – AMERICAN BAND OF THE AEF: Morning After
(recorded repeat of last night's broadcast).

13.30   ABSIE Broadcast – AMERICAN BAND OF THE AEF: 'Music For The
Wehrmacht' (See footnote on page 319.) Compères: 'Ilse' and Major
Glenn Miller. (recorded 6/11/44).

Here We Go Again/My Heart Tells Me V, JD/String Of Pearls/Stormy
Weather/Poinciana V, AM & CC.

14.00   AFN Broadcast – AMERICAN BAND OF THE AEF, SWING SEXTET,
STRINGS WITH WINGS and AMERICAN DANCE BAND: 'Visiting Hour' (59
minutes).

AEF Band: Caribbean Clipper/Long Ago And Far Away V, AM/Juke Box
Saturday Night V, CC.

SWING SEXTET: Blue Skies/Stomping At The Savoy.

STRINGS WITH WINGS: Sweet And Lovely/These Foolish Things/Tico
Tico.

AMERICAN DANCE BAND: Eyes And Ears Of The World/Peggy The Pin-
Up Girl V, RM & CC/Stealing Apples.

AEF BAND: *Medley*: Long Long Ago, The Music Stopped V, AM, Dipsey
Doodle, Blues In My Heart/Holiday For Strings.

18.15   AEFP Broadcast – SWING SEXTET: The Uptown Hall.

(*Note* – According to the radio archives this broadcast was live – however, as it included Sergeant Johnny Desmond it must have been a pre-
recording, date unknown.)

Somebody Loves Me/The Very Thought Of You/Somebody's Wrong
(*Quartet*)/Don't Blame Me V, JD/Blue Skies.

19.45   AEFP Broadcast – STRINGS WITH WINGS. Details unavailable.

324

Thursday 23 November

19.30 AEFP Broadcast – AMERICAN DANCE BAND: The Swing Shift.
Anchors Aweigh/Rhapsody In Blue/Have You Got Any Gum, Chum V,
CC/Way Down Yonder In New Orleans/I Dream Of You V, AM/Original
composition, title unknown (*Trio*)/Now I Know V, AM/On, Brave Old
Army Team.

21.15 AEFP Broadcast – SWING SEXTET: The Uptown Hall (recorded
23/9/44).

(*Note* – according to the radio archives this broadcast was live; however,
as Sergeant Johnny Desmond was ill with influenza the pre-recording
noted above was broadcast.)

Guest artist, Bernie Privin, trumpet.

Blue Skies/You Go to My Head (featuring Bernie Privin, trumpet)/Long
Ago And Far Away V, JD/Perdido.

evening Dance Band (probably directed by Sergeant Ray McKinley)
played at the Officers Club at Milton Ernest Hall.

Friday 24 November

07.30 AEFP Broadcast – AMERICAN DANCE BAND: The Swing Shift:
Return Engagement (recording of last night's broadcast.

14.00 Rehearsal at the Queensberry All-Services Club, London.

Note – during this afternoon a recording by the American Band of the AEF
was scheduled for 16.45–17.45; however, there is no evidence that it was
actually made or, if so, subsequently broadcast.

20.30 AEFP Broadcast – AMERICAN BAND OF THE AEF: Moonlight
Serenade, from the Queensberry All-Services Club.

Sun Valley Jump/Long Ago And Far Away V, AM/Mission To Moscow/
Medley: Mighty Like A Rose, Amor Amor V, AM, Chattanooga Choo
Choo V, RM & CC, Bye Bye Blues/String Of Pearls/Oranges And Lemons
(concert arrangement by Jerry Gray of the AEFP call sign).

Saturday 25 November

The Band and its smaller bands began pre-recording eight weeks
programmes for broadcasting while they were away in Paris (*see* page
196).

AEFP Pre-recordings – AMERICAN BAND OF THE AEF.

[Programme 1] broadcast 22/12/44 (Moonlight Serenade)
[Programme 2] broadcast 29/12/44 (Moonlight Serenade)
[Programme 3] broadcast 2/1/45.

11.45 AEFP Broadcast – JACK RUSIN: Piano Parade.

13.01 GFP Broadcast – AMERICAN BAND OF THE AEF: Moonlight
Serenade (recorded repeat of last night's broadcast).

15.01 AEFP Broadcast – AMERICAN DANCE BAND: The Swing Shift.
Snafu Jump/Stardust/I'm Heading For California V, RM & CC/Breaking
In a New Pair Of Shoes/I'll Walk Alone V, JD/Cheesecake (*Trio*)/Time
Waits For No-one V, JD/Flying Home.

AEFP Pre-recordings – STRINGS WITH WINGS.

   [Programme 1] broadcast 1/1/45.

   [Programme 2] broadcast 3/1/45.

   [Programme 3] broadcast 8/1/45.

18.15 AEFP Broadcast – SWING SEXTET: The Uptown Hall. Emaline/Charmaine/(rest of tunes not known).

Sunday 26 November

AEFP Pre-recordings – SERGEANT JOHNNY DESMOND.

   [Programme 1] broadcast 18/12/44.

   [Programme 2] broadcast 8/1/45.

   [Programme 3] broadcast 15/1/45.

   [Programme 4] ? not broadcast.

afternoon Major Glenn Miller appeared on the stage at a 'Carnival of Music' charity concert at the Granada Cinema, Bedford, and conducted four USAAF dance bands in the concert finale:

Army Air Corps Song, Star Spangled Banner, God Save The King.

Monday 27 November

AEFP Pre-recordings – AMERICAN BAND OF THE AEF.

   [Programme 1] broadcast 5/1/45 (Moonlight Serenade)

   [Programme 2] broadcast 9/1/45.

—STRINGS WITH WINGS.

   [Programme 1] broadcast 10/1/45.

   [Programme 2] broadcast 15/1/45.

ABSIE recording Session AMERICAN BAND OF THE AEF, HMV studios, London: 'Music For The Wehrmacht' (See footnote on page 319.) Two programmes recorded, broadcast over ABSIE on ? 13/12/44 and ?

19.01 AEFP Broadcast – SERGEANT JOHNNY DESMOND.

I'll Remember April/Indian Summer/For The First Time/Amor Amor.

19.15 AEFP Broadcast – STRINGS WITH WINGS.

Make Believe/Mood Indigo/Lover Come Back To Me/Dancing In The Dark.

Tuesday 28 November

07.30 AEFP Broadcast AMERICAN DANCE BAND: The Swing Shift: Return Engagement (recorded repeat of last Saturday's broadcast).

AEFP Pre-recordings – AMERICAN BAND OF THE AEF. Broadcast 12/1/45 (Moonlight Serenade).

—SERGEANT JOHNNY DESMOND SINGS. Broadcast 1/1/45.

14.00 Rehearsal at the Queensberry All-Services Club, London.

20.30 AEFP Broadcast – AMERICAN BAND OF THE AEF.

In The Mood/Sweet And Lovely v, JD/Juke Box Saturday Night v, CC/ *Medley*: Flow Gently Sweet Afton, Moondreams v, JD & CC, Don't Be That Way, Blue Champagne/Everybody Loves My Baby/Poinciana v, JD & CC.

Wednesday 29 November

AEFP Pre-recordings – SWING SEXTET: The Uptown Hall.

  [Programme 1] broadcast 23/12/44.

  [Programme 2] broadcast 27/12/44.

  [Programme 3] broadcast 28/12/44.

  [Programme 4] broadcast 30/12/44.

  [Programme 5] broadcast 3/1/45.

  [Programme 6] broadcast 4/1/45.

  [Programme 7] broadcast 6/1/45.

10.01 AEFP Broadcast – AMERICAN BAND OF THE AEF: Morning After (recorded repeat of last night's broadcast).

13.30 ABSIE Broadcast – AMERICAN BAND OF THE AEF: 'Music For The Wehrmacht' (See footnote to Monday 30 October) (recorded 13/11/44.) Compères: Ilse and Major Glenn Miller.

Caribbean Clipper/Smoke Gets In Your Eyes/Little Brown Jug/Where Or When v, AM/Cow Cow Boogie v, RM/Holiday For Strings.

18.15 AEFP Broadcast – SWING SEXTET: The Uptown Hall.

Blue Room/Sophisticated Lady/Sugar (*Quartet* including Corporal Joe Shulman, bass)/When Your Lover Has Gone v, JD/The Sheik.

19.45 AEFP Broadcast – STRINGS WITH WINGS. Details unavailable.

AEFP Pre-recordings – STRINGS WITH WINGS.

  [Programme 1] broadcast 17/1/45.

  [Programme 2] broadcast 22/1/45.

Thursday 30 November

AEFP Pre-recordings – AMERICAN DANCE BAND: The Swing Shift.

  [Programme 1] broadcast 23/12/44.

  [Programme 2] broadcast 28/12/44.

19.30 AEFP Broadcast – AMERICAN DANCE BAND: The Swing Shift.

Get Happy/You Go To My Head (featuring Bernie Privin, trumpet)/ Sweet And Lovely v, JD & CC/Is You Is Or Is You Ain't My Baby v, RM/Time Waits For No-one v, JD/Spam What Am (*Trio*)/She's Funny That Way v, AM/9.20 Special.

12.15 AEFP Broadcast – SWING SEXTET: The Uptown Hall.

How High The Moon/Dream A Little Dream Of Me (*Quartet*)/She's Funny That Way v, JD/Temptation.

Friday 1 December

07.30 AEFP Broadcast – AMERICAN DANCE BAND: The Swing Shift: Return Engagement (recorded repeat of last night's broadcast).

AEFP Pre-recordings – AMERICAN BAND OF THE AEF.

  [Programme 1] broadcast 13/2/45.

  [Programme 2] broadcast 26/1/45 (Moonlight Serenade).

  [Programme 3] ? not broadcast.

14.00 Rehearsal at Queensberry All-Services Club, London.

20.30 AEFP Broadcast – AMERICAN BAND OF THE AEF: Moonlight Serenade.
Great Day/White Christmasv, JD/Swing Low Sweet Chariot/*Medley*: All Through The Night, Time Waits For No-one v, JD, Take It Easy, Blue Hawaii/Tea For Two (*Quartet*: Powell, piano, Hucko, clarinet, Alpert, bass, McKinley, drums)/Holiday For Strings.

Saturday 2 December
AEFP Pre-recordings – AMERICAN DANCE BAND: The Swing Shift.
    [Programme 1] broadcast 30/12/44.
    [Programme 2] broadcast 4/1/45.
    [Programme 3] broadcast 6/1/45
    [Programme 4] broadcast 11/1/45.
11.45 AEFP Broadcast – JACK RUSIN: Piano Parade.
13.01 GFP Broadcast – AMERICAN BAND OF THE AEF: Moonlight Serenade (recorded repeat of last night's broadcast).
15.01 AEFP Broadcast – AMERICAN DANCE BAND: The Swing Shift. Details unavailable.
AEFP Pre-recordings – STRINGS WITH WINGS.
    [Programme 1] broadcast 31/1/45.
    [Programme 2] broadcast 5/2/45.
(two more programmes, details unknown)
18.15 AEFP Broadcast – SWING SEXTET: The Uptown Hall.
Hallelujah/Louise/If Dreams Come True (*Quartet*)/I'll Be Seeing You v, JD/Night In Tunisia.

Sunday 3 December
AEFP Pre-recordings – SERGEANT JOHNNY DESMOND.
    [Programme 1] broadcast 22/1/45.
    [Programme 2] broadcast 29/1/45.
    [Programme 3] broadcast 5/2/45.
AEFP Pre-recordings – SWING SEXTET: The Uptown Hall.
    [Programme 1] broadcast 10/1/45.
    [Programme 2] broadcast 11/1/45.
    [Programme 3] broadcast 13/1/45.
    [Programme 4] broadcast 17/1/45.
    [Programme 5] broadcast 18/1/45.
    [Programme 6] broadcast 20/1/45.

Monday 4 December
AEFP Pre-recordings – AMERICAN DANCE BAND: The Swing Shift.
    [Programme 1] broadcast 13/1/45.
    [Programme 2] broadcast 18/1/45.
    [Programme 3] broadcast 20/1/45.
    [Programme 4] ? not broadcast.
AEFP Pre-recordings – STRINGS WITH WINGS.

328

[Programme 1] broadcast 7/2/45.

[Programme 2] ? not broadcast.

19.01   AEFP Broadcast – SERGEANT JOHNNY DESMOND.
Without A Song/It Had To Be You/Sweet And Lovely/Time Waits For No-one.

19.15   AEFP Broadcast – STRINGS WITH WINGS.
You And The Night And The Music/Stardust/Tico Tico/Over The Rainbow.

Tuesday 5 December

07.30   AEFP Broadcast – AMERICAN DANCE BAND: The Swing Shift: Return Engagement (recorded repeat of last Saturday's broadcast).

AEFP Pre-recordings – AMERICAN BAND OF THE AEF.

[Programme 1] ? not broadcast.

[Programme 2] ? not broadcast.

14.00   Rehearsal at Queensberry All-Services Club, London.

20.30   AEFP Broadcast – AMERICAN BAND OF THE AEF. Broadcast cancelled, although the Band played a show at the Club and recorded a programme which was broadcast next morning: tonight's broadcast was replaced by commercial records.

Wednesday 6 December

10.01   AEFP Broadcast – AMERICAN BAND OF THE AEF: Morning After (recording of programme cancelled last night).

13.30   ABSIE Broadcast – AMERICAN BAND OF THE AEF: 'Music For The Wehrmacht' (see footnote to Monday 30 October) Compères, Ilse and Major Glenn Miller; guest artist Irene Manning. (recorded ? 20/11/44).
Tail End Charlie/All The Things You Are v, Irene Manning/Mary Is A Grand Old Name v, IM/Long Ago And Far Away v, IM/Begin The Beguine v, IM/Everybody Loves My Baby.

AEFP Pre-recordings – SWING SEXTET: The Uptown Hall.

[Programme 1] broadcast 9/2/45.

[Programme 2] broadcast 26/1/45.

[Programme 3] broadcast 27/1/45.

[Programme 4] broadcast 31/1/45.

[Programme 5] broadcast 2/2/45.

[Programme 6] broadcast 3/2/45.

[Programme 7] broadcast 7/2/45.

18.15   AEFP Broadcast – SWING SEXTET: The Uptown Hall.
Stars Fell On Alabama/Charmaine/On The Sunny Side Of The Street (*Quartet*)/What A Difference A Day Made v, JD/Somebody Loves Me.

19.45   AEFP Broadcast – STRINGS WITH WINGS.
I Surrender Dear/Sophisticated Lady/Sweet And Low/How Deep is The Ocean.

Thursday 7 December

AEFP Pre-recordings – AMERICAN DANCE BAND: The Swing Shift.

    [Programme 1] broadcast 25/1/45.

    [Programme 2] broadcast 27/1/45.

19.30 AEFP Broadcast – AMERICAN DANCE BAND: The Swing Shift.
Stealing Apples/Rhapsody In Blue/Sweet And Low/Somebody's
Wrong/Going My Way v, JD/Fruit Cake (*Trio*)/I Dream Of You v, JD/
Beat Me Daddy Eight To The Bar v, RM/Sanfu Jump.

21.15 AEFP Broadcast – SWING SEXTET: The Uptown Hall. Guest
artist, Bernie Privin, trumpet.
Rosetta/East Of The Sun v, JD/I'm Going To Sit Right Down And Write
Myself A Letter (*Quartet*)/Please Don't Talk About Me When I'm Gone
(featuring Bernie Privin, trumpet).

Friday 8 December

07.30 AEFP Broadcast – AMERICAN DANCE BAND: The Swing Shift:
Return Engagement (recorded repeat of last night's broadcast).

AEFP Pre-recordings: AMERICAN BAND OF THE AEF ?not broadcast.

SERGEANT JOHNNY DESMOND ? not broadcast.

AMERICAN DANCE BAND: The Swing Shift

    [Programme 1] broadcast 8/2/45.

    [Programme 2] broadcast 1/2/45.

    [Programme 3] broadcast 3/2/45.

    [Programme 4] ? not broadcast.

20.30 AEFP Broadcast – AMERICAN BAND OF THE AEF: Moonlight
Serenade, from Bedford.
Stealing Apples/Going My Way v, JD/Pearls On Velvet (featuring Mel
Powell, piano)/*Medley*: Old Refrain, I'll Get By v, JD, Smoke Gets In
Your Eyes, Blue Again (featuring Bernie Privin, trumpet)/I'm Going To
Sit Right Down And Write Myself A Letter (*Trio*)/Flying Home.

Saturday 9 December

AEFP Pre-recordings – SWING SEXTET: The Uptown Hall.

    [Programme 1] broadcast 13/12/44.

    [Programme 2] broadcast 14/12/44.

STRINGS WITH WINGS.

    [Programme 1] broadcast 13/12/44.

    [Programme 2] (Christmas programme) not broadcast.

11.45 AEFP Broadcast – JACK RUSIN: Piano Parade.

13.01 GFP Broadcast – AMERICAN BAND OF THE AEF: Moonlight
Serenade (recorded repeat of last night's broadcast).

15.01 AEFP Broadcast – AMERICAN DANCE BAND: The Swing Shift.
Sun Valley Jump/Jubilee/I'm Heading For California v, RM & CC/
Mission to Moscow/This I Love Above All v, JD/China Boy (*Trio*)/
Down The Road A-piece v, RM & Trigger Alpert/Anvil Chorus.

18.15 AEFP Broadcast – SWING SEXTET: The Uptown Hall.

Stomping At The Savoy/What Is There To Say/Lum De Do (*Quartet*)/I Surrender Dear v, JD/Lady Be Good.

Sunday 10 December
AEFP Pre-recordings – JACK RUSIN: Piano Parade.
  [Programme 1] broadcast 13/1/45.
  [Programme 2] broadcast 30/12/44.
  [Programme 3] broadcast 20/1/45.
  [Programme 4] broadcast 27/1/45.
  [Programme 5] broadcast probably 6/1/45

Monday 11 December
AEFP Pre-recording – JACK RUSIN: Piano Parade, broadcast 3/2/45.
19.00 AEFP Broadcast – SERGEANT JOHNNY DESMOND: Soldier And A Song.
Now I Know/Louise/Alone.
19.15 AEFP Broadcast – STRINGS WITH WINGS. Details unavailable.

Tuesday 12 December
07.30 AEFP Broadcast – AMERICAN DANCE BAND: The Swing Shift: Return Engagement (recorded repeat of last Saturday's broadcast).
14.00 Rehearsal at the Queensberry All-Services Club, London.
Note – during this rehearsal two pre-recordings were scheduled to be made by the American Dance Band (The Swing Shift) (*see* page 201). It seems probable that the following two pre-recordings were actually made:
Swing Shift – broadcast 14/12/44.
AEF band Moonlight Serenade – Broadcast 15/12/44.
20.30 AEFP Broadcast – AMERICAN BAND OF THE AEF. Guest artist, Morton Downey.
Everybody Loves My Baby/It Had To Be You v, JD/*Medley*: Long Long Ago, The Music Stopped v, JD, The Dipsey Doodle, Blues In My Heart/I'll Get By v, Morton Downey/The Red Cavalry March (arranged by Jerry Gray)/Stomping At The Savoy (instead of usual signature tune Moonlight Serenade).
This was the last live broadcast by the AEF Band or its small bands in England; it was also the last time that Major Glenn Miller conducted the Band.

Wednesday 13 December
10.01 AEFP Broadcast – AMERICAN BAND OF THE AEF: Morning After (recorded repeat of last night's broadcast).
13.30 ABSIE Broadcast – AMERICAN BAND OF THE AEF: 'Music For The Wehrmacht' (See footnote on page 319.) Compères, 'Ilse' and Major Glenn Miller (recorded 27/11/44).
Jeep Jockey Jump/All The Things You Are v, JD/Swing Low Sweet Chariot/ Body And Soul/ Beat Me Daddy Eight To A Bar v, RM/Get Happy.

18.15 AEFP Broadcast – SWING SEXTET: The Uptown Hall (recorded 9/12/44). Guest artist, Bernie Privin, trumpet.
Blue Skies/Don't Blame Me v, JD/One Two Button Your Shoe (*Quartet*)/Way Down Yonder In New Orleans (featuring Bernie Privin, trumpet)/Triple X (with Bernie Privin, trumpet)
19.45 AEFP Broadcast – STRINGS WITH WINGS (recorded 9/12/44). Flamingo/Sweet And Lovely/Stars In Your Eyes/I'll Be Seeing You.

Thursday 14 December
19.30 AEFP Broadcast – AMERICAN DANCE BAND: The Swing Shift (recorded 12/12/44).
Swing Low Sweet Chariot/Sleepy Town Train/Sweet And Low/My Shining Hour v, JD/Fry Me Cookie With A Can Of Lard (*Trio*)/Time Waits For No-one v, JD/Waiting For The Evening Mail v, RM/King Porter Stomp.
21.15 AEFP Broadcast – SWING SEXTET: The Uptown hall (recorded 9/12/44).
I'll Remember April/I'll Be Seeing You v, JD/S'Wonderful (*Quartet*)/Sweet Georgia Brown/Please Don't Talk About Me When I'm Gone.

Friday 15 December
07.30 AEFP Broadcast – AMERICAN DANCE BAND: The Swing Shift: Return Engagement (recorded repeat of last night's broadcast).
13.45 Major Glenn Miller and Lieutenant Colonel Baessell took off in an 8th Air Force UC-64A Norseman aircraft (piloted by Flight Officer John R S Morgan) from Twinwood Farm RAF airfield, near Bedford, to fly to Paris. Lieutenant Haynes and the Band were due to follow in three C-47 aircraft of USAAF Air Transport Command from Bovingdon the next day. Major Miller, the other officers and the plane were never seen again.
20.30 AEFP Broadcast – AMERICAN BAND OF THE AEF: Moonlight Serenade (recorded 12/12/44).
Enlisted Men's Mess/Sweet And Lovely v, JD/Waiting For The Evening Mail v, RM/*Medley*: Sweet And Low, Things Ain't What They Used To Be, A Blues Serenade/Good Enough To Keep (*Quintet*: Powell piano, Privin trumpet, Hucko clarinet, Alpert bass, McKinley drums)/Oranges And Lemons.

Saturday 16 December
Lieutenant Haynes and the band stranded in England by bad weather.
11.45 AEFP Broadcast – JACK RUSIN: Piano Parade (recorded 4/10/44).
13.01 GFP Broadcast – AMERICAN BAND OF THE AEF: Moonlight Serenade (recorded repeat of last night's broadcast).
15.01 AEFP Broadcast – AMERICAN DANCE BAND: The Swing Shift (recorded 29/9/44).

Get Happy/In A Sentimental Mood/I'm Heading for California v, RM & CC/How Blue The Night v, JD/Shine (*Trio*) (Powell, piano, Hucko, tenor saxophone, McKinley, drums)/Stealing apples/The Music Stopped v, JD/Anvil Chorus.

18.15 AEFP Broadcast – SWING SEXTET: The Uptown Hall (recorded 26/9/44).

Rosetta/Love Is The Sweetest Thing (featuring Addison Collins, Jr., French horn)/As Long As I Live (*Quartet*) What A Difference A Day Makes v, JD/The Sheik.

Sunday 17 December
Lieutenant Haynes and the Band still stranded in England by bad weather.

Monday 18 December
am Lieutenant Haynes and the Band flew from Twinwood Farm to Paris and discovered when they arrived that Major Miller had not reached Paris; one officer (Lieutenant Paul Morden) and nine enlisted men of the unit remained at Bedford.

19.00 London – AEFP Broadcast – SERGEANT JOHNNY DESMOND (recorded 26/11/44).

I'll Walk Alone/Blue Is The Night/I'll Be Seeing You.

19.15 London – AEFP Broadcast – STRINGS WITH WINGS (recorded 13/9/44).

All The Things You Are/Waltz For Strings/Indian Summer/Going Home.

Tuesday 19 December
07.30 London – AEFP Broadcast – AMERICAN DANCE BAND: The Swing Shift: Return Engagement (recorded repeat of last Saturday's broadcast).

20.30 London – AEFP Broadcast – AMERICAN BAND OF THE AEF (recorded 9/9/44). Guest artist, Bing Crosby (recorded 30/8/44).

Enlisted Men's Mess/It Could Happen To You v, JD/I'm Heading For California v, RM & CC/*Medley*: I Dream Of Jeannie With The Light Brown Hair, I Couldn't Sleep A Wink Last Night, v, JD, Begin the Beguine, Blue Again/The Army Air Corps Song v, The Band/Sweet Lorraine v, JD/White Christmas v, Bing Crosby.

Wednesday 20 December
10.01 London – AEFP Broadcast – AMERICAN BAND OF THE AEF: Morning After (recorded repeat of last night's broadcast).

13.30 London – ABSIE Broadcast – AMERICAN BAND OF THE AEF: 'Music For The Wehrmacht' (See footnote on page 319.) (recorded ?20/11/44 or ?27/11/44).

Compères: 'Ilse' and Major Glenn Miller.

Spring Will Be A Little Late This Year/(rest of tunes not known).

18.15 London – AEFP Broadcast – SWING SEXTET: The Uptown Hall (recorded 29/9/44). Guest artist: Phil Cogliano, violin.
Dream A Little Dream Of Me/Swinging On A Star v, JD & CC/Get Happy (featuring Phil Cogliano, violin)/Temptation.
19.45 London – AEFP Broadcast – STRINGS WITH WINGS (recorded 27/9/44).
Over The Rainbow/May Night/Tico Tico/Pavanne.

Thursday 21 December
19.30 London – AEFP Broadcast – AMERICAN DANCE BAND: The Swing Shift (recorded 8/10/44).
Everybody Loves My Baby/In A Sentimental Mood/Cow Cow Boogie v, RM/Somebody's Wrong/I Dream Of You v, JD/If Dreams Come True (*Trio*)/My Ideal v, JD/Caribbean Clipper
21.15 London – AEFP Broadcast – SWING SEXTET: The Uptown Hall (recorded 30/9/44).
Making Whoopee/I Don't Know Why v, CC/When Your Lover Has Gone v, JD/You're Driving Me Crazy.
20.00 Paris – Concert by the AEF Band at the Palais de Glace for American troops on leave (4,300).

Friday 22 December
07.30 London – AEFP Broadcast – AMERICAN DANCE BAND: The Swing Shift: Return Engagement (recorded repeat of last night's broadcast).
20.30 London – AEFP Broadcast – AMERICAN BAND OF THE AEF: Moonlight Serenade (recorded 25/11/44).
I Hear You Screaming/Spring Will Be A Little Late This Year v, JD/Have You Any Gum, Chum v, CC/*Medley*: Caprice Viennoise, I'll Walk Alone, v, JD, My Isle Of Golden Dreams, Birth Of The Blues/ETO -What A Horrible Morning Blues (*Trio*)/Holiday For Strings.
Paris – Concert, AEF Club, cancelled owing to military curfew.

Saturday 23 December
11.45 London – AEFP Broadcast – JACK RUSIN: Piano Parade (recorded 4/ 10/44).
13.01 London – GFP Broadcast – AMERICAN BAND OF THE AEF: Moonlight Serenade (recorded repeat of last night's broadcast).
15.01 London – AEFP Broadcast – AMERICAN DANCE BAND: The Swing Shift (recorded 30/11/44).
King Porter Stomp/Oh Lady Be Good/Juke Box Saturday Night v, CC / Spring Will Be A Little Late This Year v, JD/Watcha Know Joe v, RM/Pass Over Lightly (*Trio*)/The Day After Forever v, JD/Way Down Yonder In New Orleans.
18.15 London – AEFP Broadcast – SWING SEXTET: The Uptown Hall (recorded 29/11/44).

Blue Room/Sophisticated Lady/Sugar (*Quartet*, including Joe Shulman, bass)/When Your Lover Has Gone v, JD/The Sheik.
Paris – Concert, Palais de Glace, cancelled owing to military curfew.

Sunday 24 December
14.30   Paris – Concert by the full Band, Olympia Theatre. (1,800)
18.00   (London) SHAEF announced that Major Glenn Miller was missing.
18.08½   London – News flash on AEFP that Major Miller was missing, followed by interlude music from The Messiah on records.
20.00   Paris – Concert by the full Band, Olympia Theatre. (1,800)

Monday 25 December
10.00   Paris – Rehearsal in Olympia Theatre.
14.30   Paris – Concert in Olympia Theatre. (1,500)
15.15   London – AEFP Broadcast – STRINGS WITH WINGS. Christmas programme (recorded 9/12/44) cancelled and replaced by carols by Army Group Choir.
15.30   Paris – Pre-recording – AMERICAN BAND OF THE AEF – Christmas greeting from the Band to the USA for later broadcasting in USA.
18.05   London – AEFP Broadcast – 'AEF Christmas Show' – CANADIAN BAND OF THE AEF (25 minutes) from Queensberry All-Services Club, London.
18.30   BRITISH BAND OF THE AEF (30 minutes) from Queensberry All-Services Club, London.
19.01   AMERICAN BAND OF THE AEF, conducted by Sergeant Jerry Gray (29 minutes) from Olympia Theatre, Paris; compère, Warrant Officer Paul Dudley.
Great Day/I'll Be Seeing You v, JD/It Must Be Jelly/*Medley*: Silent Night, Sweet Lorraine, v, JD, Jingle Bells v, CC, White Christmas/The Red Cavalry March/Oranges And Lemons.
19.30   Grand round-up with all three bands (30 minutes):
CANADIAN BAND: *Medley*: Tipperary, Keep The Home Fires Burning, Pack Up Your Troubles/CYRIL FLETCHER, accompanied by the Canadian Band: Odd Odes, Nellie Quaint, The Blasted Heath.
BRITISH BAND: Lazy Day/JACKIE HUNTER, accompanied by the British Band: The Life Of The Party.
AMERICAN BAND: Oranges And Lemons.
COMBINED BANDS and audiences: Auld Lang Syne.
The entire two-hour broadcast was live and the last hour was also broadcast simultaneously in the Home Service, and via shortwave in Canada over CBC and in the USA over Mutual.

Tuesday 26 December

07.30 London – AEFP Broadcast – AMERICAN DANCE BAND: The Swing Shift: Return Engagement (recorded repeat of last Saturday's broadcast).

10.01 London – AEFP Broadcast – Morning After: Grand round-up from AEF Christmas Show (Recorded repeat of last night's broadcast).

14.30 Paris – Concert in Olympia Theatre. (1,000)

20.30 London – AEFP Broadcast – AMERICAN BAND OF THE AEF. Broadcast cancelled – replaced by 'Ali Sad Sack and the Forty Quartermasters, an unbelievable pantomime for the AEF'. (20.15–21.00).

Wednesday 27 December

15.30 Paris – Concert at American Red Cross Club 'Rainbow Corner'. (400)

18.15 London – AEFP Broadcast – SWING SEXTET: The Uptown Hall (recorded 29/11/44).
How High The Moon/Dream A Little Dream Of Me (*Quartet*, including Joe Shulman, bass)/She's Funny That Way v, JD/Temptation.

19.45 London – AEFP Broadcast – STRINGS WITH WINGS (recorded 29/9/44).
World Is Waiting For The Sunrise/Orchids In The Moonlight/Jeannie With The Light Brown Hair.

20.00 Paris – Concert at Casual Det. Billet (according to Activities list): however, in contrast to the two concerts given here for today, Haynes' diary mentions two afternoon concerts at the Olympia Theatre – one by the full Band and one by the McKinley Dance Band – and an evening concert by the full Band at the Magazin du Fayal for US Army MPS.

Thursday 28 December

11.00 London – Home Service Broadcast – SWING SEXTET: The Up-town Hall (recorded, date unknown). Details unavailable.

14.30 London – GFP Broadcast – AEF Christmas Show – recorded extracts from the broadcast on Monday evening, including the AMERICAN BAND OF THE AEF.

15.30 Paris – Concert (full Band) at ARC 'Rainbow Corner'. (500)

19.30¼ London – AEFP Broadcast – AMERICAN DANCE BAND: The Swing Shift (recorded 30/11/44).
Get Happy/You Go To My Head (featuring Bernie Privin, trumpet)/Sweet And Lovely v, JD & CC/Is You Is Or Is You Ain't My Baby v, RM/Time Waits For No-one v, JD/Spam What Am (*Trio*)/She's Funny That Way v, JD/9.20 Special.

21.15¼ London – AEFP Broadcast – SWING SEXTET: The Uptown Hall (recorded 29/11/44).
Somebody Loves Me/The Very Thought Of You/Somebody's Wrong (*Quartet*, including Joe Shulman, bass)/Don't Blame Me v, JD/Blue Skies.

336

Friday 29 December

07.30   London – AEFP Broadcast – AMERICAN DANCE BAND: The Swing Shift: Return Engagement (recorded repeat of last night's broadcast).

14.30   Paris – Concert by the AEF Band at the US Army 48th General Hospital. (2,200)

20.00   Paris – Concert by the AEF Band at the AEF Club, Grand Hotel. (900)

20.30   London – AEFP Broadcast – AMERICAN BAND OF THE AEF: Moonlight Serenade (recorded 25/11/44). (Major Miller's announcements replaced by ?.)

Jeep Jockey Jump/It Could Happen To You v, JD/On, Brave Old Army Team/*Medley*: Londonderry Air, My Prayer v, JD, Cherokee, Blue Danube/Is You Is Or Is You Ain't My Baby v, RM/Flying Home.

Saturday 30 December

11.45   London – AEFP Broadcast – JACK RUSIN: Piano Parade (recorded 10/12/44).

13.01   London – GFP Broadcast – AMERICAN BAND OF THE AEF: Moonlight Serenade (recorded repeat of last night's broadcast).

15.01   London – AEFP Broadcast – AMERICAN DANCE BAND: The Swing Shift (recorded 2/12/44).

On, Brave Old Army Team/My Buddy (trumpet solo, Zeke Zarchy)/Have You Got Any Gum, Chum v, CC/Down The Road A-piece v, RM & Trigger Alpert/How Blue The Night v, JD/Love Is Just Around The Corner (*Trio*)/This I Love Above all v, JD/Anchors Aweigh.

14.30   Paris – Concert by the AEF Band at the US Army 217th General Hospital. (1,000)

18.15   London – AEFP Broadcast – SWING SEXTET: The Uptown Hall (recorded 29/11/44).

I'll Remember April/These Foolish Things/Exactly Like You (*Quartet*, including Joe Shulman, bass)/I'll Be Seeing You v, JD/Caravan.

20.00   Paris – Concert by the AEF Band at the Palais de Glace. (1,500)

Sunday 31 December

10.30   Paris – Rehearsal in the Olympia Theatre.

14.30   Paris – Concert in the Olympia Theatre. (1,000)

15.30   Paris – Pre-recording from Olympia Theatre for BBC in London (perhaps only a line test in preparation for live relay from Olympia Theatre broadcast in AEF Programme at 23.03 this evening).

22.30   Paris – Concert in Olympia Theatre. (1,800)

23.03–23.39½   London – AEFP Broadcast – AMERICAN BAND OF THE AEF (37 minutes). Special live relay from the Olympia Theatre, Paris. Conducted by Jerry Gray; compère, Paul Dudley. Details unavailable.

Monday 1 January 1945

14.30   Paris – Concert in the Olympia Theatre. (1,200)

19.01   London – AEFP Broadcast – SERGEANT JOHNNY DESMOND SINGS (recorded 28/11/44).

Going My Way/Time Waits For No-one/Cherokee (*Band*)/I'll Remember April.

19.15   London – AEFP Broadcast – STRINGS WITH WINGS (recorded 25/11/44).

My Heart Stood Still/April In Paris/I'll See You Again/September Song.

20.00   Paris – Concert in the Olympia Theatre. (1,500)

Tuesday 2 January

07.30   London – AEFP Broadcast – AMERICAN DANCE BAND: The Swing Shift: Return Engagement (recorded repeat of last Saturday's broadcast).

14.30   Paris – Concert in the Olympia Theatre. (1,000)

20.00   Paris – Concert in the Palais De Glace. (700)

20.30   London – AEFP Broadcast – AMERICAN BAND OF THE AEF (recorded 25/11/44) (Major Miller's announcements replaced by Sergeant Keith Jamieson)

Get Happy/I'll Be Seeing You v, JD/Anchors Aweigh/*Medley*: Long Long Ago, The Music Stopped v, JD, The Dipsey Doodle, Blues In My Heart/The GI Jive v, RM & CC/Jerry's Aachen Back (*Quartet*)/Song Of The Volga Boatmen.

Wednesday 3 January

10.01   London – AEFP Broadcast – AMERICAN BAND OF THE AEF: Morning After (recorded repeat of last night's broadcast).

15.30   Paris – Concert at American Red Cross Club 'Rainbow Corner'. (500)

18.15   London – AEFP Broadcast – SWING SEXTET: The Uptown Hall (recorded 29/11/44).

Little White Lies/Stars Fell On Alabama/Pennies From Heaven/ (*Quartet*, including Joe Shulman)/Spring Will Be A Little Late This Year v, JD/Blue Room.

19.45   London – AEFP Broadcast – STRINGS WITH WINGS (recorded 25/11/44).

Spring Will Be A Little Late This Year/Jeannie With The Light Brown Hair/Lover Come Back To Me/I'm In The Mood For Love.

20.30   Paris – Concert at Olympia Theatre or Marignan Theatre (conflicting evidence as to where the concert took place, but the Marignan became a regular Wednesday date). (1,600)

Thursday 4 January

15.30   Paris – Concert at American Red Cross Club 'Rainbow Corner'. (500)

338

19.30   London – AEFP Broadcast – AMERICAN DANCE BAND: The Swing
Shift (recorded 2/12/44).
Here We Go Again/Peggy The Pin-Up Girl v, RM & CC/Spanish Shawl
(arr. Carmen Mastren)/It Could Happen To You v, JD/I Must Have
That Man (*Quartet*)/I'll Walk Alone v, JD/Eyes And Ears Of The World.
20.00   Paris – Concert at the Palais De Glace. (1,200)
21.15   London – AEFP Broadcast – SWING SEXTET: The Uptown Hall
(recorded 29/11/44).
Song Of The Wanderer/Shandy/One, Two, Button Your Shoe (*Quartet*,
including Joe Shulman, bass)/Limehouse Blues.

Friday 5 January
07.30   London – AEFP Broadcast – AMERICAN DANCE BAND: The Swing
Shift: Return Engagement (recorded repeat of last night's broadcast).
14.30   Paris – Concert at 40th General Hospital. (1,100)
20.00   Paris – Concert at AEF Club, Grand Hotel. (900)
20.30   London – AEFP Broadcast – AMERICAN BAND OF THE AEF:
Moonlight Serenade. (recorded 27/11/44) (Major Miller's announcements replaced by ?).
American Patrol/Stardust/On, Wisconsin/*Medley*: Old Refrain, Same
Old Love v, JD, Smoke Gets In Your Eyes, Blue Again/If Dreams Come
True (*Boogie Woogie Quartet*)/You Are My Sunshine v, probably JD & CC.

Saturday 6 January
11.45   London – AEFP Broadcast – JACK RUSIN: Piano Parade (recorded
probably 10/12/44).
13.01   London – GFP Broadcast – AMERICAN BAND OF THE AEF (recorded repeat of last Tuesday's broadcast).
14.30   Paris – Concert at 203rd General Hospital. (1,000)
15.01   London – AEFP Broadcast – AMERICAN DANCE BAND: The Swing
Shift (recorded 2/12/44).
Somebody's Wrong/String Of Pearls/Juke Box Saturday Night v, CC /
Sweet And Low v, RM/This I Love Above All v, JD/Pass Over Lightly
(*Trio*: Piano, clarinet, drums)/How Blue The Night v, JD/American
Patrol.
18.15   London – AEFP Broadcast – SWING SEXTET: The Uptown Hall
(recorded 29/11/44).
Rosetta/Sweet Lorraine/Poor Butterfly (*Quartet*, including Joe Shulman,
bass)/Once In A While v, JD/Don't Be That Way.
20.00   Paris – Concert at Palais De Glace. (1,000)

Sunday 7 January
   Paris – Day off for the entire unit.

Monday 8 January

14.30   Paris – Concert at Olympia Theatre. (1,100)

19.01   London – AEFP Broadcast – SERGEANT JOHNNY DESMOND SINGS (recorded 26/11/44).

It Could Happen To You/Fellow On A Furlough/All The Things You Are (*Orchestra*)/I'll Get By.

19.15   London – AEFP Broadcast – STRINGS WITH WINGS (recorded 25/11/44).

Make Believe/What Is There To Say/They Didn't Believe Me/I'll Remember April.

20.00   Paris – Concert At Olympia Theatre. (1,800)

20.30   AEFP recording made during the concert; however, there is no trace of this recording having been broadcast in the AEFP.

Tuesday 9 January

07.30   London – AEFP Broadcast – AMERICAN DANCE BAND: The Swing Shift:

Return Engagement (recorded repeat of last Saturday's broadcast).

14.30   Paris – Concert at Olympia Theatre. (800)

20.00   Paris – Concert at Palais De Glace. (700)

20.30   London – AEFP Broadcast – AMERICAN BAND OF THE AEF (recorded 27/11/44) (Major Miller's announcements replaced by ?)

Sun Valley Jump/Long Ago And Far Away V, JD/Mission To Moscow/*Medley*: Mighty Like A Rose, Amor Amor V, JD, Chattanooga Choo Choo V, RM & CC, Bye Bye Blues/String Of Pearls/Oranges And Lemons V, JD & CC.

Wednesday 10 January

10.01   London – AEFP Broadcast – AMERICAN BAND OF THE AEF: Morning After (recorded repeat of last night's broadcast).

15.30   Paris – Concert at American Red Cross Club 'Rainbow Corner'. (500)

18.15   London – AEFP Broadcast – SWING SEXTET: The Uptown Hall (recorded 3/12/44).

How High The Moon/Sophisticated Lady/The Earl (featuring Mel Powell, piano)/Perdido

19.45   London – AEFP Broadcast – STRINGS WITH WINGS (recorded 27/11/44).

Embraceable You/My Romance/Smoke Gets In Your Eyes/All The Things You Are.

20.30   Paris – Concert at Marignan Theatre. (1,800)

Thursday 11 January

15.30   Paris – Concert at American Red Cross Club 'Rainbow Corner'. (500)

19.30   London – AEFP Broadcast – AMERICAN DANCE BAND: The Swing Shift (recorded 2/12/44).

Way Down Yonder In New Orleans/Sleepy Town Train/Sweet And Lovely v, JD & cc/Is You Is Or Is You Ain't My Baby v, RM/I'll Get By v, JD/Downtown Flavour (*Trio*)/She's Funny That Way v, JD/The Anvil Chorus.

20.00   Paris – Concert at Palais De Glace. (500)
21.15   London – AEFP Broadcast – SWING SEXTET: The Uptown Hall (recorded 3/12/44).

Hallelujah/Louise/If Dreams Come True (*Quartet*, including Frank Ippolito, drums)/I'm Through With Love v, JD/Night In Tunisia (arr. Addison Collins, Jr)

Friday 12 January
07.30   London – AEFP Broadcast – AMERICAN DANCE BAND: The Swing Shift: Return Engagement (recorded repeat of last night's broadcast).
14.30   Paris – Concert at 62nd General Hospital. (1,000)
20.00   Paris – Concert at AEF club, Grand Hotel. (250)
20.30   London – AEFP Broadcast – AMERICAN BAND OF THE AEF: Moonlight Serenade (recorded 28/11/44) (Major Miller's announcements replaced by ?)

Snafu Jump/Body And Soul/Tuxedo Junction/*Medley*: Songs My Mother Taught Me, It's Love, Love, Love v, cc, In An Eighteenth Century Drawing Room, Blue Orchids v, JD/I Must Have That Man (*Quartet*)/ What Do You Do In The Infantry v, cc and Ensemble.

Saturday 13 January
11.45   London – AEFP Broadcast – JACK RUSIN: Piano Parade. (recorded probably 10/12/44).
13.01   London – GFP Broadcast – AMERICAN BAND OF THE AEF: Moonlight Serenade (recorded repeat of 17/11/44 broadcast).
14.30   Paris – Concert at 108th General Hospital. (1,200)
15.01   London – AEFP Broadcast – AMERICAN DANCE BAND: The Swing Shift (recorded 4/12/44).

Mission To Moscow/Shine On Harvest Moon/Irresistible You v, JD & cc/Bubble Bath/My Shining Hour v, JD/Bromham Road Blues (*Trio*)/The Day After Forever v, JD/Stealing Apples.

18.15   London – AEFP Broadcast – SWING SEXTET: The Uptown Hall (recorded 3/12/44).

I'm Coming Virginia/Deep Summer Music/Blue Skies/Where Or When v, JD/I Got Rhythm (*Quartet*, including Frank Ippolito, drums).

20.00   Paris – Concert at Palais De Glace. (700)

Sunday 14 January
   Paris – day off for entire unit.

Monday 15 January
13.00   Paris – Rehearsal at Olympia Theatre.
14.30   Paris – Concert at Olympia Theatre. (1,400)

15.30 Paris – AEFP Pre-recording during the Olympia concert – AMERICAN BAND OF THE AEF.? not broadcast (radio archives confused on broadcast dates of today's recordings).

19.01 London – AEFP Broadcast – SERGEANT JOHNNY DESMOND SINGS (recorded 26/11/44).

Now I Know/The Music Stopped/Amor Amor (*Orchestra*)/I Only Have Eyes For You.

19.15 London – AEFP Broadcast – STRINGS WITH WINGS (recorded 27/11/44).

Please/There's A Small Hotel/Memories Of You/Orchids In The Moonlight.

20.00 Paris – Concert at Olympia Theatre. (1,800)

20.30 Paris – AEFP Pre-recording during the Olympia Concert – AMERICAN BAND OF THE AEF (30 minutes): Moonlight Serenade. Broadcast 16/1/45, 17/1/45.

Tuesday 16 January

07.30 London – AEFP Broadcast – AMERICAN DANCE BAND: The Swing Shift:

Return Engagement (recorded repeat of last Saturday's broadcast).

14.30 Paris – Concert at Olympia Theatre. (1,500)

20.00 Paris – Concert at Palais De Glace. (500)

20.30 London – AEFP Broadcast – AMERICAN BAND OF THE AEF (recorded 15/1/45).

Stealing Apples/Rhapsody In Blue/You Are My Sunshine v, JD & CC / *Medley*: In The Gloaming, It Had To Be You v, JD, Stomping At The Savoy, Deep Purple/The Red Cavalry March.

Wednesday 17 January

10.01 London – AEFP Broadcast – AMERICAN BAND OF THE AEF: Morning After (recorded repeat of last night's broadcast).

15.30 Paris – Concert at American Red Cross Club 'Rainbow Corner'. (650)

18.15 London – AEFP Broadcast – SWING SEXTET: The Uptown Hall (recorded 3/12/44).

Flying Home/Rose Room/Jubilee/I'll Walk Alone v, JD/You Took Advantage Of Me.

19.45 London – AEFP Broadcast – STRINGS WITH WINGS (recorded 29/11/44).

You Go To My Head/Serenade In Blue/Clair De Lune/Sure Thing.

20.30 Paris – Concert at Marignan Theatre. (1,600)

Thursday 18 January

15.30 Paris – Concert at American Red Cross Club 'Rainbow Corner'. (650)

19.30 London – AEFP Broadcast – AMERICAN DANCE BAND: The Swing Shift (recorded 4/12/44).

Great Day/Georgia On My Mind/Chattanooga Choo Choo v, RM & CC
/Everybody Loves My Baby/Time Waits For No-one v, JD/Bugle Call
Rag (*Trio*)/I'll Walk Alone v, JD/On, Brave Old Army Team.
20.00   Paris – Concert at Palais De Glace. (800)
21.15   London – AEFP Broadcast – SWING SEXTET: The Uptown Hall
(recorded 3/12/44).
At Sundown/Body And Soul/Avalon (*Quartet*, including Frank Ippolito,
drums)/Embraceable You v, JD/You're Driving Me Crazy.

Friday 19 January
07.30   London – AEFP Broadcast – AMERICAN DANCE BAND: The
Swing Shift:
Return Engagement (recorded repeat of last night's broadcast).
14.30   Paris – Concert at 198th General Hospital. (2,000)
20.00   Paris – Concert at AEF Club, Grand Hotel. (1,000)
20.30   London – AEFP Broadcast – AMERICAN BAND OF THE AEF:
Moonlight Serenade. (recorded possibly on 15/1/45 or 8/1/45).
American Patrol/It Could Happen To You v, JD/Sleepy Town
Train/*Medley*: Going Home, Sweet And Lovely v, JD, Honeysuckle
Rose, My Blue Heaven/Is You Is Or Is You Ain't My Baby v, RM/
Jubilee (*Trio* or *Quartet*)/All's Well, Mademoiselle v, JD & CC.

Saturday 20 January
11.45   London – AEFP Broadcast – JACK RUSIN: Piano Parade (recorded 10.12.44).
13.00   London – GFP Broadcast – AMERICAN BAND OF THE AEF
(recorded repeat of last Tuesday's broadcast).
14.30   Paris – Concert at 1st General Hospital. (1,200)
15.01   London – AEFP Broadcast – AMERICAN DANCE BAND: The
Swing Shift (recorded 4/12/44).
Snafu Jump/Stardust/I'm Heading for California v, RM & CC/Another
One Of Them Things/Now I Know v, JD/Cheesecake (*Trio*)/Time
Alone Will Tell v, JD/Flying Home.
16.00   Paris – Concert at 1st General Hospital. (1,200)
18.15   London – AEFP Broadcast – SWING SEXTET: The Uptown Hall
(recorded 3/12/44).
Making Whoopee/Deep Summer Music/You Turned The Tables On
Me (*Quartet*)/Between The Devil And The Deep Blue Sea.
20.00   Paris – Concert at Palais De Glace. (1,000)

Sunday 21 January
   Paris – Day off for the entire unit.

Monday 22 January
17.00   Paris – Concert at Olympia Theatre. (1,500)

17.30 (or 15.15?) Paris – AEFP Pre-recording during the Olympia concert – AMERICAN BAND OF THE AEF. Broadcast 23/1/45, 24/1/45 and 27/1/45 (GFP).

19.01 London – AEFP Broadcast – SERGEANT JOHNNY DESMOND SINGS (recorded 3/12/44).
Spring Will Be A Little Late This Year/The Lamp Is Low/Deep Summer Music.

19.15 London – AEFP Broadcast – STRINGS WITH WINGS (recorded 29/11/44).
Someone To Watch Over Me/Londonderry Air/Embraceable You.

20.00 Paris – Concert at Olympia Theatre. (2,000)

20.30 (or 22.00?) Paris – AEFP Pre-recording during the Olympia Concert – AMERICAN BAND OF THE AEF. ? not broadcast.

Tuesday 23 January

07.30 London – AEFP Broadcast – AMERICAN DANCE BAND: The Swing Shift:
Return Engagement (recorded repeat of last Saturday's broadcast).

17.00 Paris – Concert at Olympia Theatre. (1,600)

20.00 Paris – Concert at Palais De Glace. (700)

20.30 London – AEFP Broadcast – AMERICAN BAND OF THE AEF (recorded 22/1/45).
I'll Be Seeing You v, JD/Swing Low Sweet Chariot/*Medley*: Sweet And Low, Sweet Lorraine v, JD, Things Ain't What They Used To Be, A Blues Serenade/Waiting For The Evening Mail v, RM/Poinciana v, JD & CC.

Wednesday 24 January

10.30 London – AEFP Broadcast – AMERICAN BAND OF THE AEF: Morning After (recorded repeat of last night's broadcast).

16.30 Paris – Concert at American Red Cross Club 'Rainbow Corner'. (650)

18.15 London – AEFP Broadcast – SWING SEXTET: The Uptown Hall. Broadcast cancelled – replaced by George Formby recording from General Overseas Service.

19.45 London – AEFP Broadcast – STRINGS WITH WINGS. Broadcast cancelled – replaced by 'AEF Encore', with Morton Downey and Sergeant Broderick Crawford.

20.30 Paris – Concert at Marignan Theatre. (1,800)

Thursday 25 January

16.30 Paris – Concert at American Red Cross Club 'Rainbow Corner'. (650)

19.30 London – AEFP Broadcast – AMERICAN DANCE BAND: The Swing Shift (recorded 7/12/44).
Sun Valley Jump/I'm Heading For California v, RM & CC/Jubilee/Anvil

Chorus/This I Love Above All v, JD/China Boy (*Trio*)/Down The Road
A-piece v, RM & Trigger Alpert/Tail End Charlie.
20.00 Paris – Concert at Palais De Glace (400)
21.15 London – AEFP Broadcast – SWING SEXTET: The Uptown Hall.
Broadcast cancelled – series transferred to Fridays at 21.15.

Friday 26 January
07.30 London – AEFP Broadcast – AMERICAN DANCE BAND: The Swing
Shift: Return Engagement (recorded repeat of last night's broadcast).
14.30 Paris – Concert at 7th Cont. Hospital. (1,250)
16.00 Paris – Concert at 7th Cont. Hospital. (1,250)
20.00 Paris – Concert at AEF Club, Grand Hotel. (1,000)
20.30 London – AEFP Broadcast – AMERICAN BAND OF THE AEF:
Moonlight Serenade (recorded 1/12/44). Major Miller's announcements
replaced by Sergeant Dick Dudley.
In The Mood/Sweet And Lovely v, JD/Juke Box Saturday Night v, CC/
Medley: Flow Gently Sweet Afton, Moondreams v, JD & CC, Don't Be
That Way, Blue Champagne/Dealer's Choice (*Quartet*)/Poinciana v, JD
& CC.
21.15 London – AEFP Broadcast – SWING SEXTET: The Uptown Hall
(recorded 6/12/44).
Charmaine/Stars Fell On Alabama/On The Sunny Side Of The Street
(*Quartet*)/What A Difference A Day Made v, JD/Somebody Loves Me.

Saturday 27 January
 Paris – Concerts cancelled owing to cold halls – day off for unit.
11.45 London – AEFP Broadcast – JACK RUSIN: Piano Parade (recorded
10/12/44).
13.01 London – GFP Broadcast – AMERICAN BAND OF THE AEF (recorded repeat of last Tuesday's broadcast).
15.01 London – AEFP Broadcast – AMERICAN DANCE BAND: The Swing
Shift (recorded 7/12/44).
Stealing Apples/Rhapsody In Blue/Got Any Gum, Chum v,
CC/Somebody's Wrong/Going My Way v, JD/Fruit Cake (*Trio*)/I Dream
Of You v, JD/Beat Me Daddy Eight To A Bar v, RM/Snafu Jump.
18.15 London – AEFP Broadcast – SWING SEXTET: The Uptown Hall
(recorded 6/12/44).
Blow Top/What Is There To Say/Pass Over Lightly (*Quartet*)/Spring
Will Be A Little Late This Year v, JD/Triple X (featuring Bernie Privin,
trumpet).

Sunday 28 January
 Paris – Day off for the entire unit.

Monday 29 January

17.00   Paris – Concert at Olympia Theatre. (1,500)

17.30   Paris – AEFP Pre-recording during the Olympia Concert – AMERICAN BAND OF THE AEF. Broadcast 30/1/45, 31/1/45 and 3/2/45 (GFP).

19.01   London – AEFP Broadcast – SERGEANT JOHNNY DESMOND (recorded 3/12/44).

Louise/My Heart Stood Still/Goodnight Wherever You are/All The Things You Are.

19.15   London – AEFP Broadcast – STRINGS WITH WINGS (recorded ?). Details not available.

20.00   Paris – Concert at Olympia Theatre.

20.30   Paris – AEFP Pre-recording during Olympia Concert – AMERICAN BAND OF THE AEF: Moonlight Serenade. Broadcast 2/2/45.

Tuesday 30 January

07.30   London – AEFP Broadcast – AMERICAN DANCE BAND: The Swing Shift.

Return Engagement (recorded repeat of last Saturday's broadcast).

14.00   Paris – Rehearsal at Olympia Theatre.

17.00   Paris – Concert at Olympia Theatre. (1,500)

17.30   Paris – AEFP Pre-recording during Olympia Concert – AMERICAN DANCE BAND: The Swing Shift. Broadcast 10/2/45 and 13/2/45.

20.00   Paris – Concert at AEF Club, Grand Hotel. (1,000)

20.30   London – AEFP Broadcast – AMERICAN BAND OF THE AEF (recorded 29/1/45).

Sun Valley Jump/Long Ago And Far Away v, JD/On, Wisconsin/*Medley*: Annie Laurie, Moondreams v, JD & CC, Alexander's Ragtime Band, Blue Is The Night/After You've Gone (*Quartet*)/Army Air Corps Song v, JD, CC & Ensemble.

Wednesday 31 January

10.01   London – AEFP Broadcast – AMERICAN BAND OF THE AEF: Morning After (recorded repeat of last night's broadcast).

16.30   Paris – Concert at American Red Cross Club 'Rainbow Corner'. (650)

18.15   London – AEFP Broadcast – SWING SEXTET: The Uptown Hall (recorded 6/12/44).

Oh Lady Be Good/You Go To My Head (featuring Bernie Privin, trumpet)/She's Funny That Way v, JD/Emmaline.

19.45   London – AEFP Broadcast – STRINGS WITH WINGS (recorded 2/12/44).

I'll Get By/You're My Everything/Body And Soul/Our Waltz.

20.30   Paris – Concert at the Marignan Theatre. (2,000)

346

Thursday 1 February

16.30 Paris – Concert at American Red Cross Club 'Rainbow Corner'. (650)

19.30 London – AEFP Broadcast – AMERICAN DANCE BAND: The Swing Shift (recorded 8/12/44).

Breaking In A New Pair Of Shoes/Rainbow Rhapsody/Whatcha Know, Joe? V, RM/Bubble Bath/She's Funny That Way V, JD/Love Is Just Around The Corner (*Trio*)/Time Waits For No-one V, JD/The Eyes And Ears Of The World (Paramount On Parade).

22.15 Paris – Concert at Olympia Theatre. (1,000)

23.00 Paris – AEFP Pre-recording during Olympia Concert – AMERICAN DANCE BAND: The Swing Shift. Broadcast 15/2/45 and 16/2/45.

Friday 2 February

07.30 London – AEFP Broadcast – AMERICAN DANCE BAND: The Swing Shift.

Return Engagement (recorded repeat of last night's broadcast).

14.30 Paris – Concert at 194th General Hospital. (1,500).

16.30 Paris – Concert at 194th General Hospital. (1,500)

20.00 Paris – Concert at AEF Club, Grand Hotel. (1,000)

20.30 London – AEFP Broadcast – AMERICAN BAND OF THE AEF: Moonlight Serenade (recorded 29/1/45).

Great Day/The Lamp Is Low V, JD/Little Brown Jug/*Medley*: Long Long Ago, Louise V, JD, The Dipsey Doodle, Blue Is The Night/Whatcha Know, Joe? V, RM/Oranges And Lemons.

21.15 London – AEFP Broadcast – SWING SEXTET: The Uptown Hall (recorded 6/12/44).

You're Driving Me Crazy/Dream A Little Dream Of Me/I'd Do Most Anything For You (*Quartet*)/I Surrender Dear V, JD/Struttin' With Some Barbecue (featuring Bernie Privin, trumpet).

22.15 Paris – Olympia Theatre – AEFP Pre-recordings – STRINGS WITH WINGS.

[Programme 1] broadcast 14/2/45
[Programme 2] broadcast 12.2.45

Saturday 3 February

Paris – Day off for the entire unit.

11.45 London – AEFP Broadcast – JACK RUSIN: Piano Parade (recorded 11/12/44).

13.01 London – GFP Broadcast – AMERICAN BAND OF THE AEF (recorded repeat of last Tuesday's broadcast).

15.01 London – AEFP Broadcast – AMERICAN DANCE BAND: The Swing Shift (recorded 8/12/44).

Everybody Loves My Baby/Beat Me Daddy Eight To The Bar V, RM/The Day After Forever V, JD/Bubble Bath/Many Are Cold But Few Frozen (*Trio*)/Along The Santa Fe Trail V, JD/Shine On Harvest Moon/Get Happy.

18.15   London – AEFP Broadcast – SWING SEXTET: The Uptown Hall (recorded 6/12/44).
Little White Lies/Deep Summer Music/After You've Gone (*Quartet*)/ East Of The Sun v, JD/I'll Remember April.

Sunday 4 February
Paris – Day off for the entire unit.

Monday 5 February
17.00   Paris – Concert at the Olympia Theatre. (1,500)
17.30   Paris – AEFP Pre-recording during the Olympia Concert – AMERICAN BAND OF THE AEF. Broadcast 6/2/45, 7/2/45, 10/2/45 (GFP).
19.01   London – AEFP Broadcast – SERGEANT JOHNNY DESMOND SINGS (recorded 3/12/44).
Where Or When/In The Blue Of Evening/Deep Purple (*Orchestra*)/ Sweet Lorraine.
This was the last Johnny Desmond programme.
19.15   London – AEFP Broadcast – STRINGS WITH WINGS (recorded 2/12/44).
You And The Night And The Music/Stardust/Tico Tico/Over The Rainbow.
20.00   Paris – Concert at the Olympia Theatre. (2,000)
20.30   Paris – AEFP Pre-recording during the Olympia Concert – AMERICAN BAND OF THE AEF. Moonlight Serenade. Broadcast 9/2/45.

Tuesday 6 February
07.30   London – AEFP Broadcast – AMERICAN DANCE BAND: The Swing Shift:
Return Engagement (recorded repeat of last Saturday's broadcast).
17.00   Paris – Concert at the Olympia Theatre. (1,500)
17.30   Paris – AEFP Pre-recording during the Olympia Concert – AMERICAN DANCE BAND: The Swing Shift. Broadcast 17/2/45, 20/2/45.
20.00   Paris – Concert at the AEF Club, Grand Hotel. (1,000)
20.30   London – AEFP Broadcast – AMERICAN BAND OF THE AEF (recorded 5/2/45).
It Must Be Jelly/I Only Have Eyes For You v, JD/*Medley*: Silver Threads Among The Gold, Rainbow Corner v, CC, My Guy's Come Back, St Louis Blues/Waiting For The Evening Mail v, RM/Meadowlands (The Red Cavalry March).
Note – for this broadcast and the repeats on 7/2/45 (AEFP) and 10/2/45 (GFP) the song Accentuate The Positive v, RM, was deleted from the recording and Waiting For The Evening Mail (date unknown) substituted as above.
Note also – the first part of the programme up to the end of My Guy's Come Back was transcribed on to AFRS 16 inch disc Yank Bandstand No. 30.

348

Wednesday 7 February

10.01   London – AEFP Broadcast – AMERICAN BAND OF THE AEF: Morning After (recorded repeat of last night's broadcast).

16.30   Paris – Concert at American Red Cross Club 'Rainbow Corner'. (650)

18.15   London – AEFP Broadcast – SWING SEXTET: The Uptown Hall (recorded 6/12/44).

Shandy/Please Don't Talk About Me When I'm Gone (featuring Bernie Privin, trumpet)/I Must Have That Man (*Trio*)/Triple X (featuring Bernie Privin, trumpet).

19.45   London – AEFP Broadcast – STRINGS WITH WINGS (recorded 4/12/44).

April In Paris/Annie Laurie/Holiday For Strings.

20.30   Paris – Concert at the Marignan Theatre. (2,000)

Thursday 8 February

16.30   Paris – Concert at Grand Central Red Cross Club. (800)

19.30   London – AEFP Broadcast – AMERICAN DANCE BAND: The Swing Shift (recorded 8/12/44).

I Hear You Screaming/In A Sentimental Mood/Ida V, RM/Another One Of Them Things (featuring Bernie Privin, trumpet)/That Old Black Magic V, JD/The Blues (*Trio*)/Waiting For The Evening Mail, V, RM/On, Brave Old Army Team.

Friday 9 February

07.30   London – AEFP Broadcast – AMERICAN DANCE BAND: The Swing Shift:

Return Engagement (recorded repeat of last night's broadcast).

14.30   Paris – Concert at 48th General Hospital. (2,000)

20.00   Paris – Concert at AEF Club, Grand Hotel. (1,000)

20.30   London – AEFP Broadcast – AMERICAN BAND OF THE AEF: Moonlight Serenade. (recorded 5/2/45).

Tail End Charlie/Body And Soul/I've Got A Heart Filled With Love For You Dear V, JD & CC/*Medley*: Mother Macree, I'm Making Believe V, JD, I Can't Give You Anything But Love Baby V, Peanuts Hucko, trumpet solo Bernie Privin, Wang Wang Blues/Holiday For Strings.

21.15   London – AEFP Broadcast – SWING SEXTET: The Uptown Hall (recorded 6/12/44).

I'm Coming Virginia/Louise/What Is This Thing Called Love (*Quartet*)/I'll Walk Alone V, JD/You're Lucky For Me.

This was the last Swing Sextet Uptown Hall programme.

22.45   Paris – Olympia Theatre – AEFP Pre-recordings: AMERICAN DANCE BAND: The Swing Shift. Broadcast 22/2/45, 23/2/45.

23.20   STRINGS WITH WINGS

[Programme 1] broadcast 19/2/45

23.40

[Programme 2] broadcast 21/2/45

Saturday 10 February

13.01 London – GFP Broadcast – AMERICAN BAND OF THE AEF 'Moonlight Serenade' (recorded repeat of last night's broadcast).

15.01 London – AEFP Broadcast – AMERICAN DANCE BAND: The Swing Shift (recorded 30/1/45).

I Hear You Screaming/Sleepy Town Train/How Blue The Night v, JD/ Chattanooga Choo Choo v, RM & CC/Time Waits For No-one v, JD/ Waiting For The Evening Mail v, RM/On, Brave Old Army Team.

20.00 Paris – Concert at Grand Central Red Cross Club. (600)

Sunday 11 February

Paris – Day off for the entire unit.

Monday 12 February

17.00 Paris – Concert at Olympia Theatre. (1,800)

17.30 Paris – AEFP Pre-recording during Olympia concert – band unknown; no trace of this recording ever having been broadcast in the AEFP.

19.15 London – AEFP Broadcast – STRINGS WITH WINGS (recorded 2/2/45).

Stairway To The Stars/There's A Small Hotel/Tico Tico/Body And Soul.

20.00 Paris – Concert at Olympia Theatre. (2,200)

Tuesday 13 February

07.30 London – AEFP Broadcast – AMERICAN DANCE BAND: The Swing Shift:

Return Engagement (recorded repeat of last Saturday's broadcast).

17.00 Paris – Concert at Olympia Theatre. (1,800)

Note – the usual Tuesday pre-recording by the American Dance Band was cancelled owing to faulty recording channels.

20.00 Paris – Concert at the AEF Club, Grand Hotel. (1,000)

20.30 London – AEFP Broadcast – AMERICAN BAND OF THE AEF (recorded 1/12/44) (Major Miller's announcements were replaced by Sergeant Dick Dudley).

Caribbean Clipper/I'll Walk Alone v, JD/I'm Heading For California v, RM & CC/*Medley*: Schubert's Serenade, Irresistible You v, JD & CC, Little Brown Jug, Rhapsody In Blue/Parachute Jump (*Quartet*)/The Victory Polka.

Wednesday 14 February

10.00 London – AEFP Broadcast – AMERICAN BAND OF THE AEF: Morning After (recorded repeat of last night's broadcast).

16.30 Paris – Concert at American Red Cross Club 'Rainbow Corner'. (650)

350

19.45 London – AEFP Broadcast – STRINGS WITH WINGS (recorded 2/2/45).
Over The Rainbow/Sweet And Lovely/Going Home/Sure Thing.
20.30 Paris – Concert at the Marignan Theatre. (2,000)

Thursday 15 February
16.30 Paris – Concert at Grand Central Red Cross Club. (800)
19.30 London – AEFP Broadcast – AMERICAN DANCE BAND: The Swing Shift (recorded 1/2/45).
King Porter Stomp/Swing Low Sweet Chariot/She's Funny That Way v, JD/Spam What Am (*Trio*)/Juke Box Saturday Night v, CC/It Could Happen To You v, JD/Is You Is Or Is You Ain't My Baby v, RM/Flying Home.
22.45 Paris – AEFP Pre-recordings (Olympia Theatre) – AMERICAN DANCE BAND: The Swing Shift:
   [Programme 1] ? not broadcast.
23.20 [Programme 2] broadcast 24/2/45, 27/2/45.

Friday 16 February
07.30 London – AEFP Broadcast – AMERICAN DANCE BAND: The Swing Shift:
Return Engagement (recorded repeat of last night's broadcast).
14.30 Paris – Concert at 40th General Hospital. (1,200)
16.30 Paris – Concert at 40th General Hospital. (1,200)
20.00 Paris – Concert at AEF Club, Grand Hotel. (1,000)
20.30 London – AEFP Broadcast – AMERICAN BAND OF THE AEF:
Moonlight Serenade. (recorded, date unknown – recording made by SHAEF in Paris and brought to London).
Jeep Jockey Jump/Long Ago And Far Away v, JD/On, Wisconsin/*Medley*: Annie Laurie, Moondreams v, JD & CC, Alexander's Ragtime Band, Blue Is The Night/Pearls On Velvet/With My Head In The Clouds v, JD & CC.
22.45 Paris – AEFP Pre-recordings (Olympia Theatre) – STRINGS WITH WINGS
   [Programme 1] broadcast 26/2/45
23.05 [Programme 2] broadcast 28/2/45

Saturday 17 February
13.01 London – GFP Broadcast – AMERICAN BAND OF THE AEF (recorded repeat of last Tuesday's broadcast).
15.01 London – AEFP Broadcast – AMERICAN DANCE BAND: The Swing Shift (recorded 6/2/45).
Anchors Aweigh/Little Brown Jug/I'll Walk Alone v, JD/With Malice And No Thought (*Trio*)/Is You Is Or Is You Ain't My Baby v, RM/My Buddy/Bubble Bath/Eyes And Ears Of The World (Paramount On Parade).

Note – for this broadcast and the repeat on 20/2/45 (AEFP) the song Accentuate The Positive was deleted from the recording and Is You Is Or Is You Ain't My Baby (recorded 1/2/45) was substituted as above.
20.00   Paris – Concert at Grand Central Red Cross Club. (600)

Sunday 18 February
20.30   Paris – Public Concert at Théâtre National de l'Opéra, in aid of French Prisoner of War Relief Funds. (2 hours and a quarter). (2,200)

Monday 19 February
14.30   Paris – Concert at Olympia Theatre. (1,200)
15.15   Paris – AEFP Pre-recordings during Olympia Concert – AMERICAN BAND OF THE AEF.
   [Programme 1] broadcast 20/2/45, 21/2/45, 24/2/45 (GFP).
16.00   [Programme 2] broadcast 27/2/45, 28/2/45, 3/3/45 (GFP).
19.15   London – AEFP Broadcast – STRINGS WITH WINGS (recorded 9/2/45).
My Romance/What Is There To Say/Sweet And Low.
20.00   Paris – AEFP Pre-recording during Olympia Concert – AMERICAN BAND OF THE AEF: Moonlight Serenade. Broadcast 23/2/45.

Tuesday 20 February
07.30   London – AEFP Broadcast – AMERICAN DANCE BAND: The Swing Shift:
Return Engagement (recorded repeat of last Saturday's broadcast).
14.30   Paris – Concert at Olympia Theatre. (1,400)
15.30   Paris – AEFP Pre-recording during Olympia Concert – AMERICAN DANCE BAND: The Swing Shift. Broadcast 3/3/45, 6/3/45.
20.00   Paris – Concert at AEF Club, Grand Hotel. (1,000)
20.30   London – AEFP Broadcast – AMERICAN BAND OF THE AEF (recorded 19/2/45).
Mission To Moscow/Deep Summer Music V, JD/Song Of The Volga Boatmen/*Medley*: Mighty Like A Rose, Amor Amor V, JD, Chattanooga Choo Choo V, RM & CC, Bye Bye Blues/Sweet Georgia Brown (*Quartet*)/Oranges and Lemons.

Wednesday 21 February
10.01   London – AEFP Broadcast – AMERICAN BAND OF THE AEF: Morning After (recorded repeat of last night's broadcast).
16.30   Paris – Concert at American Red Cross Club 'Rainbow Corner'. (650)
19.45   London – AEFP Broadcast – STRINGS WITH WINGS (recorded 9/2/45).
I'll See You Again/Smoke Gets In Your Eyes/Our Waltz/Spring Will Be A Little Late This Year.
20.30   Paris – Concert at the Marignan Theatre. (2,000)

Thursday 22 February

16.30　Paris – Concert at Grand Central Red Cross Club. (800)

19.30¼　London – AEFP Broadcast – AMERICAN DANCE BAND – The Swing Shift (recorded 9/2/45).

On, Wisconsin/Tuxedo Junction/I Dream Of You v, JD/Spanish Shawl/Boogie Bounce (*Trio*)/The Music Stopped v, JD/Whatcha Know, Joe v, RM/Stealing Apples.

22.45　Paris – AEFP Pre-recording (Olympia Theatre) – AMERICAN DANCE BAND: The Swing Shift. Broadcast 8/3/45, 9/3/45.

Friday 23 February

07.30¼　London – AEFP Broadcast – AMERICAN DANCE BAND: The Swing Shift:

Return Engagement (recorded repeat of last night's broadcast).

14.30　Paris – Concert at 97th General Hospital. (1,000)

16.30　Paris – Concert at 97th General Hospital. (1,000)

20.00　Paris – Concert at AEF Club, Grand Hotel. (1,000)

20.30¼　London – AEFP Broadcast – AMERICAN BAND OF THE AEF: Moonlight Serenade. (recorded 19/2/45).

I Hear You Screaming/As Long As There's Music v, JD/Tuxedo Junction/*Medley*: Songs My Mother Taught Me, Dance With A Dolly v, CC, In An Eighteenth Century Drawing Room, Blue Orchids/The Red Cavalry March.

22.45　Paris – AEFP Pre-recordings: STRINGS WITH WINGS
　　[Programme 1] broadcast 5/3/45

23.10　[Programme 2] broadcast 7/3/45

Saturday 24 February

　　Paris – Day off for the entire unit.

13.01　London – GFP Broadcast – AMERICAN BAND OF THE AEF (recorded repeat of last Tuesday's broadcast).

15.01¼　London – AEFP Broadcast – AMERICAN DANCE BAND: The Swing Shift (recorded 15/2/45).

Everybody Loves My Baby/String Of Pearls/How Blue The Night v, JD/Shoo Shoo Baby v, CC/Eyes And Ears Of The World (Paramount On Parade)/The Day After Forever v, JD/Waiting For The Evening Mail v, RM/No Compree (composed by and featuring Mel Powell, piano).

Sunday 25 February

　　Paris – Day off for the entire unit.

Monday 26 February

14.30　Paris – Concert at Olympia Theatre. (1,500)

15.15　Paris – AEFP Pre-recordings during Olympia Concert – AMERICAN BAND OF THE AEF: Moonlight Serenade. Broadcast 2/3/45.

19.15¼　London – AEFP Broadcast – STRINGS WITH WINGS (recorded 16/2/45).

Someone To Watch Over Me/Someday I'll Find You/I've Told Every Little Star/Yesterdays.

20.00   Paris – Concert at Olympia Theatre. (2,000)
20.30   Paris – AEFP Pre-recording during Olympia Concert – AMERICAN BAND OF THE AEF. Broadcast 6/3/45, 7/3/45, 10/3/45 (GFP) 11/3/45 (GFP).

Tuesday 27 February
07.30   London – AEFP Broadcast – AMERICAN DANCE BAND: The Swing Shift:
Return Engagement (recorded repeat of last Saturday's broadcast).
14.30   Paris – Concert at Olympia Theatre. (1,400)
15.15   Paris – AEFP Pre-recording during Olympia Concert – AMERICAN DANCE BAND: The Swing Shift. Broadcast 10/3/45, 13/3/45.
20.00   Paris – Concert at AEF Club, Grand Hotel. (1,000)
20.30¼ London – AEFP Broadcast – AMERICAN BAND OF THE AEF: (recorded 19/2/45).
Everybody Loves My Baby/It Could Happen To You v, JD/*Medley*: Old Refrain, I'm Making Believe v, JD, Smoke Gets In Your Eyes, Blue Again/Waiting For The Evening Mail v, RM/No Compree/The Squadron Song.

Wednesday 28 February
10.01   London – AEFP Broadcast – AMERICAN BAND OF THE AEF: Morning After (recorded repeat of last night's broadcast).
16.30   Paris – Concert at American Red Cross Club 'Rainbow Corner'. (650)
19.45   London – AEFP Broadcast – STRINGS WITH WINGS (recorded 16/2/45).
Love Walked In/Diane/Indian Summer/I'll Be Seeing You.
20.30   Paris – Concert at Marignan Theatre. (2,000)

Thursday 1 March
16.30   Paris – Concert at Grand Central Red Cross Club. (650)
19.30   London – AEFP Broadcast – AMERICAN DANCE BAND: The Swing Shift (recorded 15/2/45).
Mission To Moscow/This I Love Above All v, JD/Little Brown Jug/What A Silly Place To Get Water On The Knee (*Trio*)/I Dream Of You v, JD/Nine Twenty Special/Juke Box Saturday Nightv, CC/On, Brave Old Army Team.
22.45   Paris – AEFP Pre-recording (Olympia Theatre) – AMERICAN DANCE BAND: The Swing Shift Broadcast 15/3/45, 16/3/45.

Friday 2 March
07.30   London – AEFP Broadcast – AMERICAN DANCE BAND: The Swing Shift:

354

Return Engagement (recorded repeat of last night's broadcast).

15.00 Paris – Concert at 104th General Hospital. (1,200)

20.00 Paris – Concert at AEF Club, Grand Hotel. (1,000)

20.30 London – AEFP Broadcast – AMERICAN BAND OF THE AEF: Moonlight Serenade (recorded 26/2/45).

Great Day/All The Things You Are v, JD/Adios/*Medley*: Londonderry Air, It had To Be You v, JD, Cherokee, Blue Danube/Peggy The Pin-Up Girl v, RM & CC/Flying Home.

22.45 Paris – AEFP Pre-recordings (Olympia Theatre) – STRINGS WITH WINGS Broadcast 14/3/45.

23.10 another recording, not subsequently broadcast.

Saturday 3 March

13.01 London – GFP Broadcast – AMERICAN BAND OF THE AEF (recorded repeat of last Tuesday's broadcast).

15.01 London – AEFP Broadcast – AMERICAN DANCE BAND: The Swing Shift (recorded 20/2/45).

Breaking In A New Pair Of Shoes/I'll Walk Alone v, JD/My Guy's Come Back/Oh Lady Be Good (*Trio*: Phil Cogliano, violin, Carmen Mastren, guitar, and Trigger Alpert, bass)/Beat Me Daddy Eight To The Bar v, RM/Shine On Harvest Moon/She's Funny That Way v, JD/King Porter Stomp.

20.00 Paris – Concert at Grand Central Red Cross Club. (650)

Sunday 4 March

Paris – Day off for entire unit.

Monday 5 March

14.30 Paris – Concert at Olympia Theatre. (1,500)

15.15 Paris – AEFP Pre-recording during Olympia Concert – AMERICAN BAND OF THE AEF details not known – recording not subsequently broadcast.

19.15 London – AEFP Broadcast – STRINGS WITH WINGS (recorded 23/2/45).

Claire De Lune/Orchids In The Moonlight/Home On The Range.

20.00 Paris – Concert at Olympia Theatre. (2,000)

20.30 Paris – AEFP Pre-recording during Olympia Concert – AMERICAN BAND OF THE AEF: Moonlight Serenade. Broadcast 9/3/45.

Tuesday 6 March

07.30 London – AEFP Broadcast – AMERICAN DANCE BAND: The Swing Shift:

Return Engagement (recorded repeat of last Saturday's broadcast).

14.30 Paris – Concert at Olympia theatre. (1,400)

15.15 AEFP Pre-recording during Olympia Concert – AMERICAN DANCE BAND: The Swing Shift. Broadcast 17/3/45, 20/3/45.

20.00 Paris – Concert at AEF Club, Grand Hotel. (1,000)

20.30   London – AEFP Broadcast – AMERICAN BAND OF THE AEF (recorded 26/2/45).

Caribbean Clipper/Together v, JD/String Of Pearls/*Medley*: Killarney, Rainbow Corner v, CC, Moonlight Serenade, Wabash Blues/Is You Is Or Is You Ain't My Baby v, RM/S'Wonderful (*Trio*)/The Victory Polka v, JD, CC & Ensemble.

Wednesday 7 March

10.01   London – AEFP Broadcast – AMERICAN BAND OF THE AEF: Morning After (recorded repeat of last night's broadcast).

14.30   Paris – Concert at American Red Cross Club 'Rainbow Corner'. (650)

19.45   London – AEFP Broadcast – STRINGS WITH WINGS (recorded 23/2/45).

It Could Happen To You/Clouds/There's A Small Hotel.

19.00   Paris – Concert at SHAEF (Main), Versailles. (1,000)

20.30   Paris – Concert at SHAEF (Main), Versailles. (1,000)

Thursday 8 March

16.30   Paris – Concert at Grand Central Red Cross. (650)

19.30   London – AEFP Broadcast – AMERICAN DANCE BAND: The Swing Shift (recorded 22/2/45).

Caribbean Clipper/Stardust/Somebody's Wrong/How Blue The Night v, JD/Shoemaker's Apron (*Trio*)/Song Of The Volga Boatmen/Some Other Time v, JD/Snafu Jump.

22.45   Paris – AEFP Pre-recording (Olympia Theatre) – AMERICAN DANCE BAND: The Swing Shift. Broadcast 22/3/45, 23/3/45.

Friday 9 March

07.30   London – AEFP Broadcast – AMERICAN DANCE BAND: The Swing Shift:

Return Engagement (recorded repeat of last night's broadcast).

20.00   Paris – Concert at AEF Club, Grand Hotel. (1,000)

20.30   London – AEFP Broadcast – AMERICAN BAND OF THE AEF: Moonlight Serenade. (recorded 5/3/45).

American Patrol/Embraceable You v, JD/You Are My Sunshine v, JD & CC/*Medley*: Sweet And Low, A Fellow On A Furlough v, JD, Things Ain't What They Seem To Be (*Trio*)/Out Of The Blue (? Army Air Corps Song)/Avalon (? *Trio* or *Quartet*)/On, Brave Old Army Team.

22.45   Paris AEFP Pre-recording (Olympia Theatre) – STRINGS WITH WINGS

   [Programme 1] broadcast 12/3/45

23.10   [Programme 2] broadcast 19/3/45

Saturday 10 March

13.01   London – GFP Broadcast – AMERICAN BAND OF THE AEF (recorded repeat of last Tuesday's broadcast).

356

This was the last Saturday broadcast in the GFP – from March 11 they were transferred to Sundays at 12.30 – 1.00 p.m.

15.01 London – AEFP Broadcast – AMERICAN DANCE BAND: The Swing Shift (recorded 27/2/45).

Get Happy/Sweet And Low/I Dream Of You v, JD/Accentuate The Positive v, RM & CC/Some Other Time v, JD/Stealing Apples.

20.00 Paris – Concert at Grand Central Red Cross Club. (650)

Sunday 11 March

Paris – Day off for the entire unit.

12.30 London – GFP Broadcast – AMERICAN BAND OF THE AEF (recorded repeat of last Tuesday's broadcast).

Monday 12 March

14.30 Paris – Concert at Olympia Theatre. (1,500)

15.15 Paris – AEFP Pre-recording during Olympia Concert – AMERICAN BAND OF THE AEF. Broadcast 13/3/45, 14/3/45 and 18/3/45 (GFP).

19.16¾ London – AEFP Broadcast – STRINGS WITH WINGS (recorded 9/3/45).

Out Of Nowhere/Londonderry Air/They Didn't Believe Me/I Love You Truly.

20.00 Paris – Concert at Olympia Theatre. (2,000)

20.30 Paris – AEFP Pre-recording during Olympia Concert – AMERICAN BAND OF THE AEF. 'Moonlight Serenade'. (Broadcast 16/3/45).

Tuesday 13 March

07.30 London – AEFP Broadcast – AMERICAN DANCE BAND: The Swing Shift:

Return Engagement (recorded repeat of last Saturday's broadcast).

14.30 Paris – Concert at Olympia Theatre. (1,400)

15.15 Paris – AEFP Pre-recording during Olympia Concert – AMERICAN DANCE BAND: The Swing Shift. Broadcast 24/3/45, 27/3/45.

20.00 Paris – Concert at AEF Club, Grand Hotel. (1,000)

20.30 London – AEFP Broadcast – AMERICAN BAND OF THE AEF (recorded 12/3/45).

Sun Valley Jump/Estrellita/Song Of The Volga Boatmen/*Medley*: Annie Laurie, Fascinating You v, JD, Alexander's Ragtime Band, Blue Is The Night/No Compree/The Caisson Song v, Ensemble.

Wednesday 14 March

10.01 London – AEFP Broadcast – AMERICAN BAND OF THE AEF: Morning After (recorded repeat of last night's broadcast).

14.30 Paris – Concert at American Red Cross Club 'Rainbow Corner'. (650)

19.45   London – AEFP Broadcast – STRINGS WITH WINGS (recorded 2/3/45).

The Man I Love/The Maid With The Flaxen Hair/Mood Indigo/As Long As There's Music.

20.00   Paris – Concert at the Hotel Commodore for British Troops. (1,000)

Thursday 15 March

16.30   Paris – Concert at Grand Central Red Cross. (650)

19.30   London – AEFP Broadcast – AMERICAN DANCE BAND: The Swing Shift (recorded 1/3/45).

Breaking In A New Pair Of Shoes/Sleepy Town Train/She's Funny That Way v, JD/Fruitcake (*Trio*)/String Of Pearls/As Long As There's Music v, JD/One O'Clock Jump.

22.00   Paris – Special recordings for US 9th Air Force (Olympia Theatre).

22.40   Paris – AEFP Pre-recordings (Olympia Theatre) – AMERICAN DANCE BAND: The Swing Shift.

   [Programme 1] broadcast 29/3/45, 30/3/45.

23.15   [Programme 2] broadcast 31/3/45, 3/4/45.

Friday 16 March

07.30   London – AEFP Broadcast – AMERICAN DANCE BAND: The Swing Shift:

Return Engagement (recorded repeat of last night's broadcast).

15.00   Paris – Concert at 62nd General Hospital. (2,000)

20.00   Paris – Concert at AEF Club, Grand Hotel. (1,000)

20.30   London – AEFP Broadcast – AMERICAN BAND OF THE AEF: Moonlight Serenade (recorded 12/3/45).

Measure For Measure/As Long As There's Music v, JD/Notre Dame Victory March/*Medley*: Drink To Me Only, The Very Thought Of You, Blue Skies/Swing Low Sweet Chariot/The Trolley Song v, JD, CC & Ensemble.

22.40   Paris – AEFP Pre-recordings (Olympia Theatre) – STRINGS WITH WINGS

   [Programme 1] broadcast 21/3/45

23.00   [Programme 2] broadcast 26/3/45

23.20   [Programme 3] broadcast 28/3/45

Saturday 17 March

   Paris – Day off for the entire unit.

15.01   London – AEFP Broadcast – AMERICAN DANCE BAND: The Swing Shift (recorded 6/3/45).

I Hear You Screaming/Some Other Time v, JD/Tuxedo Junction/Train 88 (*Trio*)/The Day After Forever v, JD/Waiting For The Evening Mail v, RM/The Big Beat (featuring Ray McKinley, drums).

Sunday 18 March
Paris – Day off for the entire unit.
12.30 London – GFP Broadcast – AMERICAN BAND OF THE AEF (recorded repeat of last Tuesday's broadcast).

Monday 19 March
14.30 Paris – Concert at Olympia Theatre. (1,400)
15.15 Paris – AEFP Pre-recording during Olympia Concert – AMERICAN BAND OF THE AEF. Broadcast 20/3/45, 21/3/45, 25/3/45 (GFP).
19.15 London – AEFP Broadcast – STRINGS WITH WINGS (recorded 9/3/45).
Song Is You/Old Man River/To A Wild Rose/When Day Is Done.
20.00 Paris – Concert at Olympia Theatre. (2,000)
20.30 Paris – AEFP Pre-recording during Olympia Concert – AMERICAN BAND OF THE AEF: Moonlight Serenade. Broadcast 23/3/45.

Tuesday 20 March
07.30¼ London – AEFP Broadcast – AMERICAN DANCE BAND: The Swing Shift:
Return Engagement (recorded repeat of last Saturday's broadcast).
14.30 Paris – Concert at Olympia Theatre. (1,600)
14.45 Paris – AEFP Pre-recordings during Olympic Concert – AMERICAN BAND OF THE AEF: Moonlight Serenade. Broadcast 30/3/45.
15.20 AMERICAN DANCE BAND: The Swing Shift. Broadcast 4/4/45, 6/4/45.
20.00 Paris – Concert at AEF Club, Grand Hotel. (1,000)
20.30¼ London – AEFP Broadcast – AMERICAN BAND OF THE AEF (recorded 19/3/45).
Limehouse Blues/Some Other Time v, JD/It Must Be Jelly/*Medley*: Old Refrain, Alone Till The Day v, JD, Smoke Gets In Your Eyes, Blue Again/Pearls On Velvet (featuring Mel Powell, piano)/Guns In The Sky v, JD & CC.

Wednesday 21 March
10.01 London – AEFP Broadcast – AMERICAN BAND OF THE AEF: Morning After (recorded repeat of last night's broadcast).
15.30 Paris – Concert at American Red Cross Club 'Rainbow Corner'. (650)
19.45 London – AEFP Broadcast – STRINGS WITH WINGS (recorded 16/3/45).
Over The Rainbow/Embraceable You/Pavanne/Some Other Time.
20.00 Paris – Concert at Palais De Glace. (2,000)

359

Thursday 22 March

16.30   Paris – Concert at Grand Central Red Cross. (650)

19.30   London – AEFP Broadcast – AMERICAN DANCE BAND: The Swing Shift (recorded 8/3/45).

King Porter Stomp/Oh Lady Be Good/How Blue The Night V, JD/Way Down Yonder In New Orleans/Shoemaker's Apron (*Trio*)/As Long As There's Music V, JD/Accentuate The Positive V, RM/Caribbean Clipper.

22.40   Paris – AEFP Pre-recordings (Olympia Theatre) – AMERICAN DANCE BAND: The Swing Shift.

[Programme 1] broadcast 7/4/45, 10/4/45.

23.15   [Programme 2] broadcast 11/4/45.

Friday 23 March

07.30   London – AEFP Broadcast – AMERICAN DANCE BAND: The Swing Shift:

Return Engagement (recorded repeat of last night's broadcast).

20.00   Paris – Concert at AEF Club, Grand Hotel. (1,000)

20.30   London – AEFP Broadcast – AMERICAN BAND OF THE AEF: Moonlight Serenade (recorded 19/3/45).

Here We Go Again/You're So Sweet To Remember V, JD/Little Brown Jug/*Medley*: Swanee River, Dance With A Dolly V, CC, Smoke Rings, My Blue Heaven/You Are My Sunshine V, JD & CC/I Hear You Screaming.

22.40   Paris – AEFP Pre-recordings (Olympia Theatre) – STRINGS WITH WINGS.

[Programme 1] broadcast 4/4/45.

23.00   [Programme 2] broadcast 6/4/45.

23.20   [Programme 3] broadcast 11/4/45.

Saturday 24 March

15.01   London AEFP Broadcast – AMERICAN DANCE BAND: The Swing Shift (recorded 13/3/45).

Mission To Moscow/Little Brown Jug/I Dream Of You V, JD/Fruit Cake (*Trio*)/Wham, Rebop, Boom Bam V, RM/Time Alone Will Tell V, JD/The GI Jive V, RM & CC/Flying Home.

Note – for this broadcast and the repeat on 27/3/45 (AEFP) the song Time Alone Will Tell originally included in the programme was deleted from the recording and the same song was taken from a recording made on 4/12/44 and substituted as above.

20.00   Paris – Concert by the American Dance Band directed by Sergeant Ray McKinley at the Grand Central Red Cross. (650)

20.00   Paris – Concert by the Strings With Wings at the Théâtre National de l'Opéra, with Andre Kostelanetz and singer Lily Pons. (2,200) (*see* page 236).

Sunday 25 March

12.30   London – GFP Broadcast – AMERICAN BAND OF THE AEF (recorded repeat of last Tuesday's broadcast).

20.00 Paris – Concert by the strings with wings at the Théâtre National de l'Opéra, with Andre Kostelanetz and Lily Pons, (2,200) (*see* page 236).

Monday 26 March
14.30 Paris – Concert at Olympia Theatre. (1,400)
14.40 Paris – AEFP Pre-recordings during Olympia Concert – AMERICAN BAND OF THE AEF.
[Programme 1] broadcast 6/4/45
15.20]Programme 2] broadcast 27/3/45, 28/3/45, 1/4/45 (GFP).
19.15 London – AEFP Broadcast – STRINGS WITH WINGS (recorded 16/3/45).
How Deep Is The Ocean/Sweet And Lovely/Estrellita/You And The Night And The Music.
20.00 Paris – Concert at Olympia Theatre. (2,000)
20.30 Paris – AEFP Pre-recording during Olympia Concert – AMERICAN BAND OF THE AEF. Broadcast 3/4/45, 4/4/45, 8/4/45 (GFP).

Tuesday 27 March
07.30 London – AEFP Broadcast – AMERICAN DANCE BAND: The Swing Shift:
Return Engagement (recorded repeat of last Saturday's broadcast).
14.30 Paris – Concert at Olympia Theatre. (1,400)
14.50 Paris – AEFP Pre-recordings during Olympia Concert – AMERICAN BAND OF THE AEF. Broadcast 10/4/45, 11/4/45, 15/4/45, (GFP).
15.25 AMERICAN DANCE BAND: The Swing Shift. Broadcast 17/4/45.
20.00 Paris – Concert at AEF Club, Grand Hotel. (1,000)
20.30 London – AEFP Broadcast – AMERICAN BAND OF THE AEF (recorded 26/3/45).
Introduction To A Waltz/Fascinating You v, JD/Tuxedo Junction/ *Medley*: Carry Me Back To Old Virginny, Together v, JD, Alouette, Blue Moon/Accentuate The Positive v, RM & CC/Measure For Measure.

Wednesday 28 March
10.01 London – AEFP Broadcast – AMERICAN BAND OF THE AEF: Morning After (recorded repeat of last night's broadcast).
16.00 Paris – Concert at American Red Cross Club 'Rainbow Corner'. (650)
19.45 London – AEFP Broadcast – STRINGS WITH WINGS (recorded 16/3/45).
Please/Memories Of You/None But The Lonely Heart/Serenade In Blue.
20.00 Paris – Concert at Palais De Glace. (2,000)
21.45 Paris – Concert at Hotel Commodore for Air Transport Command Group 27. (600)

22.30   Paris – AEFP Pre-recordings (Olympia Theatre) – STRINGS WITH WINGS.

[Programme 1] broadcast 25/4/45.
22.50   [Programme 2] broadcast 27/4/45.
23.20   [Programme 3] broadcast 2/5/45.

Thursday 29 March
16.00   Paris – Concert at Grand Central Red Cross. (650)
19.30   London – AEFP Broadcast – AMERICAN DANCE BAND: The Swing Shift (recorded 15/3/45).
King Porter Stomp/Sleepy Town Train/Some Other Time v, JD/I've Found A New Baby (*Trio*: Phil Marino (Cogliano), violin, Carmen Mastren, guitar, Trigger Alpert, bass)/Spanish Shawl/It Could Happen To You v, JD/No Compree/Somebody's Wrong.
22.35   Paris – AEFP Pre-recordings (Olympia Theatre) – AMERICAN DANCE BAND: The Swing Shift.

[Programme 1] broadcast 18/4/45, 20/4/45.
23.15   [Programme 2] (not broadcast, perhaps intended for 14/4/45).

Friday 30 March (Good Friday)
07.30   London – AEFP Broadcast – AMERICAN DANCE BAND: The Swing Shift:
Return Engagement (recorded repeat of last night's broadcast).
14.30   Paris – Concert at General Hospital. (1,800)
20.30   London – AEFP Broadcast – AMERICAN BAND OF THE AEF: Moonlight Serenade (recorded 20/3/45).
Tail End Charlie/Rhapsody in Blue/*Medley*: (inserted from recording made on 19/3/45) Old Refrain, Alone, v, JD, Smoke Gets In Your Eyes, Blue Again/Adios/The Trolley Song v, JD, CC & Ensemble.
20.00   Paris – Concert at AEF Club, Grand Hotel. (1,000)
22.35   Paris – AEFP Pre-recordings (Olympia Theatre) – STRINGS WITH WINGS

[Programme1] broadcast 13/4/45.
23.00   [Programme 2] broadcast 18/4/45.
23.20   [Programme 3] broadcast 20/4/45.

Saturday 31 March
Paris – Day off for the entire unit.
15.01   London – AEFP Broadcast – AMERICAN DANCE BAND: The Swing Shift (recorded 15/3/45).
Way Down Yonder In New Orleans/Song Of The Volga Boatmen/This I Love Above All v, JD/There's Going To Be An Inspection (*Trio*)/Bubble Bath/As Long As There's Music v, JD/Juke Box Saturday Night v, CC/Snafu Jump.

Sunday 1 April (Easter Sunday)
Paris – Day off for the entire unit.

12.30   London – GFP Broadcast – AMERICAN BAND OF THE AEF (recorded repeat of last Tuesday's broadcast).

Monday 2 April (Easter Monday)
14.30   Paris – Concert at Olympia Theatre. (1,500)
14.45   AEFP Pre-recordings during Olympia Concert – AMERICAN BAND OF THE AEF.
   [Programme 1] broadcast 13/4/45.
15.20   [Programme 2] broadcast 17/4/45, 18/4/45, 22/4/45 (GFP).
19.15   London – *Note* – AEFP introduced a new broadcasting schedule for the AEF Band's smaller bands: the Strings With Wings formerly heard at this time on Mondays moved to Wednesdays at 12.45.
20.00   Paris – Concert at Olympia Theatre. (2,000)
20.30   AEFP Pre-recording during Olympia concert – AMERICAN BAND OF THE AEF. Broadcast 20/4/45.

Tuesday 3 April
07.30   London – AEFP Broadcast – AMERICAN DANCE BAND: The Swing Shift:
Return Engagement (recorded repeat of last Saturday's broadcast).
14.30   Paris – Concert at Olympia Theatre. (1,400)
14.45   AEFP Pre-recordings during Olympia Concert – AMERICAN BAND OF THE AEF Broadcast 24/4/45, 25/4/45, 29/4/45 (GFP).
15.20   AMERICAN DANCE BAND: The Swing Shift. Broadcast 21/4/45.
20.00   Paris – Concert at AEF Club, Grand Hotel. (1,000)
20.30   London – AEFP Broadcast – AMERICAN BAND OF THE AEF (recorded 26/3/45).
Long Tall Mama/Easter Parade/Sleepy Town Train/*Medley*: Loch Lomond, I'll Be Thinking Of you v, JD, My Guy's Come Back, Mood Indigo/Juke Box Saturday Night v, CC/Don't Try Painting Your Easter Powdered Eggs/The Army Air Corps Song.

Wednesday 4 April
10.01   London – AEFP Broadcast – AMERICAN BAND OF THE AEF: Morning After (recorded repeat of last night's broadcast).
12.45   London – AEFP Broadcast – STRINGS WITH WINGS (recorded 23/3/45).
Love's Old Sweet Song/Someone To Watch Over Me/Claire De Lune/There's A Small Hotel.
16.00   Paris – Concert at American Red Cross Club 'Rainbow Corner'. (650)
20.00   Paris – Concert at Palais de Glace. (2,300)
21.15   London – AEFP Broadcast – AMERICAN DANCE BAND: The Swing Shift (recorded 20/3/45).
Everybody Loves My Baby/String Of Pearls/The Day After Forever v, JD/Doing Things (*Trio*: Phil Cogliano, violin, Carmen Mastren, guitar,

Trigger Alpert, bass))/Nine-Twenty Special/I Dream Of You v, JD /Waiting For The Evening Mail v, RM/On, Brave Old Army Team.

22.30   Paris – AEFP Pre-recordings (Olympia Theatre) – STRINGS WITH WINGS.

[Programme 1] broadcast 4/5/45.

22.55   [Programme 2] broadcast 14/4/45.

23.15   [Programme 3] broadcast 14/4/45.

Thursday 5 April

16.00   Paris – Concert at Grand Central Red Cross. (650)

22.35   Paris – AEFP Pre-recordings (Olympia Theatre) – AMERICAN DANCE BAND: The Swing Shift.

[Programme 1] broadcast 25/4/45, 27/4/45.

23.10   [Programme 2] broadcast 28/4/45.

Friday 6 April

07.30   London – AEFP Broadcast – AMERICAN DANCE BAND: The Swing Shift:

Return Engagement (recorded repeat of last Wednesday's broadcast).

14.30   Paris – Concert at 108th General Hospital. (1,500)

20.00   Paris – Concert at AEF Club, Grand Hotel. (1,000)

20.30   London – AEFP Broadcast – AMERICAN BAND OF THE AEF (recorded 26/3/45).

? /Embraceable You v, JD/When Johnny Comes Marching Home v, CC/Medley: Silver Threads Among The Gold, At The Rainbow Corner v, CC, Snowfall, St Louis Blues/American Patrol/I Only Have Eyes For You v, JD/What Do You Do In The Infantry v, CC & Ensemble.

21.45   London – AEFP Broadcast – STRINGS WITH WINGS (recorded 23/3/45).

I'll See You Again/Going Home/What is There To Say/Home On The Range.

22.35   Paris – AEFP Pre-recordings (Olympia Theatre) – STRINGS WITH WINGS.

[Programme 1] broadcast 9/5/45.

23.00   [Programme 2] broadcast 11/5/45.

23.20   [Programme 3] broadcast 16/5/45.

Saturday 7 April

17.01   London – AEFP Broadcast – AMERICAN DANCE BAND: The Swing Shift (recorded 22/3/45).

Sun Valley Jump/Swing Low Sweet Chariot/As Long As There's Music v, JD/Shoemaker's Apron (*Trio*)/Breaking In A New Pair Of Shoes/She's Funny That Way v, JD/When Johnny Comes Marching Home v, CC / Stealing Apples.

19.00   Paris – Concert by the Strings With Wings at the Ritz Hotel.

Sunday 8 April

Paris – Day off for the entire unit.

13.30 London – GFP Broadcast – AMERICAN BAND OF THE AEF (recorded repeat of last Tuesday's broadcast).

Monday 9 April

14.30 Paris – Concert at Olympia Theatre (1,500)

14.45 Paris – AEFP Pre-recordings during Olympia Concert – AMERICAN BAND OF THE AEF.

[Programme 1] broadcast 27/4/45.

15.20 [Programme 2] broadcast 1/5/45, 2/5/45, 6/5/45 (GFP)

20.00 Paris – Concert at Olympia Theatre. (2,000)

20.30 Paris – AEFP Pre-recording during Olympia Concert – AMERICAN BAND OF THE AEF. Broadcast 4/5/45.

Tuesday 10 April

07.30 London – AEFP Broadcast – AMERICAN DANCE BAND: The Swing Shift:

Return Engagement (recorded repeat of last Saturday's broadcast).

14.30 Paris – Concert at Olympia Theatre. (1,600)

14.45 AEFP Pre-recordings during Olympia Concert – AMERICAN BAND OF THE AEF. Broadcast 29/5/45, 30/5/45, 3/6/45 (GFP).

15.20 AMERICAN DANCE BAND: The Swing Shift. Broadcast 5/5/45.

20.00 Paris – Concert at the AEF Club, Grand Hotel. (1,000)

20.30 London – AEFP Broadcast – AMERICAN BAND OF THE AEF (recorded 27/3/45).

Everybody Loves My Baby/My Prayer V, JD/Oh Lady Be Good (featuring Phil Cogliano, violin)/*Medley*: Mighty Like A Rose, Amor Amor V, JD, Chattanooga Choo Choo V, RM & CC, Bye Bye Blues/ Poinciana V, JD & CC/ The Anvil Chorus.

Wednesday 11 April

10.01 London – AEFP Broadcast – AMERICAN BAND OF THE AEF: Morning After (recorded repeat of last night's broadcast).

12.45 London – AEFP Broadcast – STRINGS WITH WINGS (recorded 23/3/45).

Lover Come Back To Me/April In Paris/Tico Tico/Our Waltz.

15.30 Paris – Concert at American Red Cross Club 'Rainbow Corner'. (650)

20.00 Paris – Concert at Palais De Glace. (2,000)

21.15 London – AEFP Broadcast – AMERICAN DANCE BAND: The Swing Shift (recorded 22/3/45).

Get Happy/It Could Happen To You V, JD/S'Wonderful (*Trio*)/Dance With A Dolly V, CC/One O'Clock Jump/My Buddy/Time Waits For No-one V, JD/Drums Away (featuring Ray McKinley – this was the same number as The Big Beat, broadcast on 17/3/45).

22.20   Paris – AEFP Pre-recording (Olympia Theatre) – AMERICAN DANCE BAND: The Swing Shift. Broadcast 2/5/45.

Thursday 12 April
15.30   Paris – Concert at Grand Central Red Cross. (650)
22.30   Paris – AEFP Pre-recordings (Olympia Theatre) – AMERICAN DANCE BAND: The Swing Shift.
  [Programme 1] broadcast 12/5/45, 15/5/45.
23.00   [Programme 2] broadcast 9/5/45.

Friday 13 April
07.30   London – AEFP Broadcast – AMERICAN DANCE BAND: The Swing Shift:
Return Engagement – programme cancelled owing to death of President Roosevelt on 12/12/45, and replaced by records of marching and waltzing.
20.00   Paris – Concert at AEF Club, Grand Hotel. (1,000)
20.30   London – AEFP Broadcast – AMERICAN BAND OF THE AEF (recorded 2/4/45).
Great Day/Estrellita/Wham Re-bop Boom Bam v, RM & CC/*Medley*: I Dream Of Jeannie With The Light Brown Hair, Easter Sunday v, JD, Begin The Beguine, Blue Rain/Long Ago And Far Away v, JD/All's Well Mademoiselle v, JD & CC.
21.15   London AEFP Broadcast – STRINGS WITH WINGS (recorded 30/3/45).
All The Things You Are/Sweet And Lovely/My Romance/Over The Rainbow.
22.45   Paris – AEFP Pre-recordings (Olympia Theatre) – STRINGS WITH WINGS.
  [Programme 1] broadcast 18/5/45 (*see also* note on 18/4/45).
23.05   [Programme 2] broadcast 23/5/45.

Saturday 14 April
  Paris – Day off for the entire unit.
17.01   London – AEFP Broadcast – STRINGS WITH WINGS (recorded 4/4/45).
My Heart Stood Still/Maid With The Flaxen Hair/Holiday For Strings/Old Man River/Body And Soul/To A Wild Rose/They Wouldn't Believe Me/I Love You Truly.
Note – the above two Strings With Wings recordings were broadcast in place of the usual Swing Shift programme because of the death of President Roosevelt on 12/4/45.

Sunday 15 April
  Paris – Day off for the entire unit.
13.30   London – GFP Broadcast – AMERICAN BAND OF THE AEF (recorded repeat of last Tuesday's broadcast).

Monday 16 April
14.30   Paris – Concert at Olympia Theatre. (1,800)

14.45   AEFP Pre-recordings during Olympia Concert – AMERICAN BAND OF THE AEF.
   [Programme 1] broadcast 11/5/45.
15.20   [Programme 2] broadcast 15/5/45, 16/5/45, 20/5/45 (GFP).
20.00   Paris – Concert at Olympia Theatre. (2,000)
20.30   AEFP Pre-recording during Olympia concert – AMERICAN BAND OF THE AEF.
   [Programme 3] broadcast 18/5/45.

Tuesday 17 April
07.30   London – AEFP Broadcast – AMERICAN DANCE BAND: The Swing Shift:
Return Engagement (30 minutes) (*Note* – this was not a repeat, as last Saturday's broadcast was cancelled owing to the death of President Roosevelt) (recorded 27/3/45).
Snafu Jump/Little Brown Jug/Fascinating You V, JD/Five Packs Of What You Want And Two Packs Of What You Got Blues (*Trio* or *Quartet*)/ Bubble Bath/Peggy The Pin-Up Girl V, RM & CC/Embraceable You V, JD/Eyes And Ears Of The World.
(This was the last Tuesday 'Swing Shift' in the Return Engagement series; it was replaced by 'Top Ten'.)

14.30   Paris – Concert at the Olympia Theatre. (1,700)
14.45   AEFP Pre-recordings during Olympia Concert – AMERICAN BAND OF THE AEF. Broadcast 22/5/45, 23/5/45, 27/5/45 (GFP).
15.20   AMERICAN DANCE BAND: The Swing Shift. Broadcast 9/6/45, 12/6/45.
20.00   Paris – Concert at AEF Club, Grand Hotel. (1,000)
20.30   London – AEFP Broadcast – AMERICAN BAND OF THE AEF (recorded 2/4/45).
Long Tall Mama/Any Moment Now V, JD/Anchors Aweigh/*Medley*: All Through The Night, You're So Sweet To Remember, Take It Easy V, CC, Blue Hawaii/Waiting For The Evening Mail V, RM/After You've Gone (*Trio*: Mel Powell, piano, Peanuts Hucko, clarinet, Ray McKinley, drums)/Oranges And Lemons V, JD & CC.

Wednesday 18 April
10.01   London – AEFP Broadcast – AMERICAN BAND OF THE AEF: Morning After (abbreviated recording of last night's broadcast: 10.01¾–10.07 commercial records/10.07¾–10.26 AEF Band recording/10.26–10.30 Mantovani record! – presumably due to transmission fault or faulty recording).
12.45   London – AEFP Broadcast – STRINGS WITH WINGS (recorded 30/3/45).

Stairway To The Stars/I Have Told Every Little Star/Clouds/Someone
[To Watch Over Me ?].

15.30   Paris – Concert at American Red Cross Club 'Rainbow Corner'.
(650)

20.00   Paris – Concert at Palais De Glace. (2,000)

21.15   London – AEFP Broadcast – AMERICAN DANCE BAND: The Swing
Shift (recorded 29/3/45).

Mission To Moscow/American Patrol/Some Other Time v, JD/Icing On
Cheesecake (*Trio*: Mel Powell, piano, Peanuts Hucko, clarinet, Ray
McKinley, drums)/Shine On Harvest Moon/Embraceable You v, JD /
Waiting For The Evening Mail v, RM/Eyes And Ears Of The World

Note – for this broadcast and the repeat on 20/4/45 Accentuate The
Positive and Somebody's Wrong were deleted from the recording and
Waiting For The Evening Mail and Eyes And Ears Of The World
(recorded on 12/4/45) substituted as above.

22.00   Paris – Concert by the American Dance Band directed by
Sergeant Ray McKinley at the Empire Theatre (Jazz Festival). (2,200)

22.40   Paris – AEFP Pre-recordings (Olympia Theatre) – STRINGS WITH
WINGS.

   [Programme 1] broadcast 18/5/45 (one tune only, see broadcast date).

   [Programme 2] broadcast 25/5/45.

23.00   [Programme 3] broadcast 30/5/45.

Thursday 19 April

16.00   Paris – Concert at Grand Central Red Cross. (650)

22.40   Paris – AEFP Pre-recording (Olympia Theatre) – AMERICAN
DANCE BAND: The Swing Shift.

   [Programme 1] broadcast 26/5/45, 29/5/45.

   [Programme 2] not broadcast (only one pre-recording is mentioned in
the Activities list).

Friday 20 April

07.30   London – AEFP Broadcast – AMERICAN DANCE BAND: The Swing
Shift:

Return Engagement (recorded repeat of last Wednesday's broadcast).

14.00   Paris – Concert at 1st General Hospital. (1,500)

20.00   Paris – Concert at AEF Club, Grand Hotel. (1,000)

20.30   London – AEFP Broadcast – AMERICAN BAND OF THE AEF (recorded 2/4/45).

Mission To Moscow/Body And Soul/When Johnny Comes Marching
Home v, CC/*Medley*: Going Home, Moondreams v, JD & CC, Honeysuckle
Rose, My Blue Heaven/It Could Happen To You v, JD/The Victory
Polka v, CC.

Note – For this broadcast Accentuate The Positive was deleted from the
recording and When Johnny Comes Marching Home (recorded on
16/4/45) substituted as above.

21.45   London – AEFP Broadcast – STRINGS WITH WINGS (recorded 30/3/45).
The Song Is You/Flamingo/Habanera/When Day Is Done.
20.30   Paris – AEFP Pre-recordings (Olympia Theatre) – AMERICAN DANCE BAND: The Swing Shift.
  [Programme 1] broadcast 19/5/45, 22/5/45.
23.10   [Programme 2] (details not known: not broadcast).

Saturday 21 April
17.01   London – AEFP Broadcast – AMERICAN DANCE BAND: The Swing Shift (recorded 3/4/45).
Caribbean Clipper/Oh Lady Be Good/As Long As There's Music V, JD/ Nut Cake (*Trio*)/Dance With A Dolly V, CC/How Blue The Night V, JD/ Eight Beat Ball/On, Brave Old Army Team.
18.00   Paris – Concert by the Strings With Wings at Ritz Hotel. (250)
19.30   Paris – Concert by the American Dance Band directed by Sergeant Ray McKinley. (1,200)

Sunday 22 April
  Paris – Day off for the entire unit.
13.30   London – GFP Broadcast – AMERICAN BAND OF THE AEF (recorded repeat of last Tuesday's broadcast).

Monday 23 April
14.30   Paris – Concert at Olympia Theatre. (1,800)
14.45   AEFP Pre-recordings during Olympia Concert – AMERICAN BAND OF THE AEF.
  [Programme 1] not broadcast.
15.20   [Programme 2] broadcast 8/5/45, 9/5/45.
20.00   Paris – Concert at Olympia Theatre. (2,000)
20.30   AEFP Pre-recording during Olympia Concert – AMERICAN BAND OF THE AEF. Broadcast 24/5/45, 25/5/45.

Tuesday 24 April
14.30   Paris – Concert at Olympia Theatre. (1,900)
14.45   AEFP Pre-recordings during Olympia Concert – AMERICAN BAND OF THE AEF. Broadcast 1/6/45.
15.20   AMERICAN DANCE BAND: The Swing Shift. Broadcast 2/6/45.
Paris – Recordings for AFRS by The American Band of the AEF.
20.30   London – AEFP Broadcast – AMERICAN BAND OF THE AEF (recorded 3/4/45).
Flying Home/I Only Have Eyes For You V, JD/It Must Be Jelly/*Medley*: My Buddy, Same Old Love V, JD, Music Makers, Farewell Blues/The Red Cavalry March.

Wednesday 25 April
10.01   London – AEFP Broadcast – AMERICAN BAND OF THE AEF: Morning After (recorded repeat of last night's broadcast).

08.56 Paris – Band flew in three C-47s to Nice for twelve days – landed at Nice approx. 11.56.

12.45 London – AEFP Broadcast – STRINGS WITH WINGS (recorded 28/3/45).

World Is Waiting For The Sunrise/Sophisticated Lady/I'll Remember April/Make Believe.

20.00 Nice – Concert at American Red Cross Casino Club. (2,700)

21.15 London – AEFP Broadcast – AMERICAN DANCE BAND: The Swing Shift (recorded 5/4/45).

I Hear You Screaming/Sleepy Town Train/Fascinating You V, JD /S'Wonderful (*Trio*)/Nine-Twenty Special/She's Funny That Way V, JD/ Waiting For The Evening Mail V, RM/The Eyes And Ears Of The World (Paramount On Parade).

Thursday 26 April
14.00 Nice – Concert at American Red Cross Casino Club. (2,100)
20.00 Nice – Dance at American Red Cross Casino Club. (2,900)

Friday 27 April
07.30 – AEFP Broadcast – AMERICAN DANCE BAND: The Swing Shift. Return Engagement (recorded repeat of last Wednesday's broadcast).
Note – This was the last Friday Swing Shift programme in the Return Engagement series; it was replaced by 'Top Ten'.

14.00 Nice – Concert at American Red Cross Casino Club. (2,300)
20.00 Nice – Concert at American Red Cross Casino Club. (2,400)
20.30 London – AEFP Broadcast – AMERICAN BAND OF THE AEF (recorded 9/4/45).

In The Mood/More And More V, JD/Get Happy/*Medley*: Old Black Joe, I've Got The Blues V, JD, I've Got Sixpence V, CC, Rhapsody In Blue/ String Of Pearls/The Trolley Song V, JD & CC.

12.45 London – AEFP Broadcast – STRINGS WITH WINGS (recorded 28/3/45).
More Than You Know/Sweet And Low/Yesterdays/I Surrender Dear.

Saturday 28 April
15.00 Cannes – Concert at Miramar Hotel Terrace. (3,000)
17.01 London – AEFP Broadcast – AMERICAN DANCE BAND: The Swing Shift (recorded 5/4/45).
Somebody's Wrong/Whatcha Know Joe? V, RM/I Dream Of You V, JD/ Plain And Fancy Blue (*Trio*)/Shoo Shoo Baby V, CC/Time Alone Will Tell V, JD/My Guy's Back/Everybody Loves My Baby.
21.00 Cannes – Dance at Miramar Hotel Ballroom. (2,000)

Sunday 29 April
13.30 London – GFP Broadcast – AMERICAN BAND OF THE AEF (recorded repeat of last Tuesday's broadcast).
15.00 Cannes – Concert at Miramar Hotel Ballroom. (2,000)

21.30   Cannes – Dance at Martinez Hotel Ballroom. (1,750)

Monday 30 April
   Nice – Seven days' leave in Nice for entire unit.

Tuesday 1 May
20.30   London – AEFP Broadcast – AMERICAN BAND OF THE AEF (recorded 9/4/45).
Here We Go Again/My Prayer v, JD/And Her Tears Flowed Like Wine v, RM/*Medley*: Schubert's Serenade, Some Other Time v, JD, Little Brown Jug, Under A Blanket Of Blue/No Compree/With My Head In The Clouds v, CC & Ensemble.

Wednesday 2 May
10.01   London – AEFP Broadcast – AMERICAN BAND OF THE AEF: Morning After (recorded repeat of last night's broadcast).
12.45   London – AEFP Broadcast – STRINGS WITH WINGS (recorded 28/4/45).
How Am I Tonight/The Touch Of Your Hand/Jeannie With The Light Brown Hair/Sure Thing.
21.15   London – AEFP Broadcast – AMERICAN DANCE BAND: The Swing Shift (recorded 11/4/45).
King Porter Stomp/I Dreamt I Dwelt In Harlem/Embraceable You v, JD/Nut Cake (*Trio*)/Breaking In A New Pair Of Shoes/How Blue The Night v, JD/Oh Lady Be Good/Beat Me Daddy Eight To The Bar v, RM/Flying Home.
Note – for this broadcast Accentuate The Positive was deleted from the recording and Beat Me Daddy Eight To The Bar and Flying Home (from a recording made on 20/2/45) were substituted as above.

Thursday 3 May

Friday 4 May
20.30   London – AEFP Broadcast – AMERICAN BAND OF THE AEF (recorded 9/4/45).
I Hear You Screaming/As Long As There's Music v, JD/I Dreamt I Dwelt In Harlem/*Medley*: In The Gloaming, Alone v, JD, Stomping At The Savoy, Deep Purple/Nutcake (*Trio*: Mel Powell, piano, Peanuts Hucko, clarinet, Ray McKinley, drums)/Candy v, JD & CC/The Caisson Song.
21.45   London – AEFP Broadcast – STRINGS WITH WINGS (recorded 4/4/45) details not available.

Saturday 5 May
17.01   London – AEFP Broadcast – AMERICAN DANCE BAND: The Swing Shift (recorded 10/4/45).
Snafu Jump/Swing Low Sweet Chariot/Embraceable You v, JD/Things Is Tense (*Trio*)/Chattanooga Choo Choo v, RM & CC/Some Other Time

v, JD/Is You Is Or Is You Ain't My Baby v, RM/Drums Away (The Big Beat).

Sunday 6 May
13.30 London – GFP Broadcast – AMERICAN BAND OF THE AEF (recorded repeat of last Tuesday's broadcast).
16.32 Nice – The Band flew in three C-47s back to Paris at the end of their leave, landing at Villacoublay at 20.25.

Monday 7 May
14.30 Paris – Concert at Olympia Theatre. (1,600)
15.15 AEFP Pre-recording during Olympia Concert – AMERICAN BAND OF THE AEF.
  [Programme 1] not broadcast.
20.00 Paris – Concert at Olympia Theatre. (2,100)
20.45 AEFP Pre-recording during Olympia Concert – AMERICAN BAND OF THE AEF.
  [Programme 2] broadcast 5/6/45, 6/6/45, 10/6/45 (GFP).
Note – fighting stopped in the European war early this morning.

Tuesday 8 May (V-E Day)
14.30 Paris – Band played at special V-E celebration at the Palais de Chaillot. (3,200)
20.00 Paris – Concert at the AEF Club, Grand Hotel. (1,000)
22.30 London – AEFP Broadcast – AMERICAN BAND OF THE AEF (postponed from 20.30 as there was a 'Victory Salute From The USA' at that time). (recorded 23/4/45)
Flying Home/Let's Take The Long Way Home v, JD/Kalamazoo v, CC/ *Medley*: Loch Lomond, Any Moment Now v, JD, Smoke Rings, Mood Indigo/Anchors Aweigh/Oranges And Lemons v, JD & CC.

Wednesday 9 May
10.01 London – AEFP Broadcast – AMERICAN BAND OF THE AEF: Morning After (recorded repeat of last night's broadcast).
12.45 London – AEFP Broadcast – STRINGS WITH WINGS (recorded 6/4/45).
Some Other Time/My Silent Love/May Night/I'll Get By.
15.30 Paris Concert at American Red Cross Club 'Rainbow Corner'. (700)
20.00 Paris – Concert at Palais De Glace cancelled – holiday.
21.15 London – AEFP Broadcast – AMERICAN DANCE BAND: Swing Shift (recorded 12/4/45).
I Hear You Screaming/Song Of The Volga Boatmen/As Long As There's Music v, JD/Lots of Blues And A Little Boogie (*Trio*)/My Guy's Come Back/I'll Walk Alone v, JD/Waiting For The Evening Mail v, RM/Eyes And Ears Of The World (Paramount On Parade).
This was the last Wednesday broadcast by the Swing Shift.

Thursday 10 May
15.30   Paris – Concert at Grand Central Red Cross. (650)
22.30   Paris – AEFP Pre-recording (Olympia Theatre) – AMERICAN
DANCE BAND: The Swing Shift.
   [Programme1] broadcast 16/6/45, 19/6/45.
23.10   [Programme 2] broadcast 23/6/45, 26/6/45.

Friday 11 May
20.00   Paris – Concert at AEF Club, Grand Hotel. (1,000)
20.30   London – AEFP Broadcast – AMERICAN BAND OF THE AEF (recorded 16/4/45).
Jeep Jockey Jump/Stardust/When Johnny Comes Marching Home v,
CC/*Medley*: Drink To Me Only, Rainbow Corner, v, CC, The Very
Thought Of You, Blue Skies/Caribbean Clipper/At Last v, JD/The
Squadron Song v, Ensemble.
21.45   London – AEFP Broadcast – STRINGS WITH WINGS (recorded
6/4/45).
As Long As There's Music/Alone Together/Pavanne/The Man I Love.
22.45   Paris – AEFP Pre-recordings (Olympia Theatre) – STRINGS WITH
WINGS.
   [Programme 1] broadcast 1/6/45.
23.10   [Programme 2] broadcast 6/6/45.

Saturday 12 May
   Paris – Day off for the entire unit.
17.01   London – AEFP Broadcast – AMERICAN DANCE BAND: The Swing
Shift (recorded 12/4/45).
Sun Valley Jump/Ida v, RM/Some Other Time v, JD/Confetti For
Clarinet (featuring Peanuts Hucko)/Angel Cake (*Trio*)/Way Down
Yonder In New Orleans/Fascinating You v, JD/Mission To Moscow.

Sunday 13 May
   Paris – Day off for the entire unit.
13.30   London – GFP Broadcast – AMERICAN BAND OF THE AEF
(broadcast cancelled – replaced by feature programme 'And Now
Japan', 13.15–13.54).

Monday 14 May
14.30   Paris – Concert at Olympia Theatre. (1,400)
14.45   AEFP Pre-recordings during Olympia Concert – AMERICAN BAND
OF THE AEF.
   [Programme 1] broadcast 12/6/45, 13/6/45, 17/6/45 (GFP).
15.20   [Programme 2] broadcast 15/6/45.
20.00   Paris – Concert at Olympia Theatre. (2,000)
20.45   AEFP Pre-recording during Olympia Concert – AMERICAN BAND
OF THE AEF. Broadcast 8/6/45.

Tuesday 15 May

08.30   London – AEFP Broadcast – AMERICAN DANCE BAND: The Swing Shift (recorded repeat of last Saturday's broadcast).

14.30   Paris – Concert at Olympia Theatre. (1,500)

14.45   AEFP Pre-recordings during Olympia Concert – AMERICAN BAND OF THE AEF Broadcast 19/6/45, 20/6/45, 24/6/45 (GFP).

15.20   AMERICAN DANCE BAND (details not known – recording not broadcast).

20.00   Paris – Concert at AEF Club, Grand Hotel. (1,000)

20.30   London – AEFP Broadcast – AMERICAN BAND OF THE AEF (recorded 16/4/45).

Measure For Measure/More And More v, JD/Swing Low Sweet Chariot/*Medley*: Mother Macree, Together v, JD, I Can't Give You Anything But Love Baby v, Peanuts Hucko, trumpet solo Bernie Privin, Wang Wang Blues/The Mariners Own Song.

22.40   Paris – AEFP Pre-recordings (Olympia Theatre) – STRINGS WITH WINGS

   [Programme 1] broadcast 8/6/45.

23.00   [Programme 2] broadcast 13/6/45.

Wednesday 16 May

10.01   London – AEFP Broadcast – AMERICAN BAND OF THE AEF: Morning After (recorded repeat of last night's broadcast).

12.40   Paris – Band flew from Orly to Fitzlauer airfield, Germany; thence in buses to Bad Wildungen arriving at 15.00; stayed here overnight.

12.45   London – AEFP Broadcast – STRINGS WITH WINGS (recorded 6/4/45).

How Deep Is The Ocean/Diane/Orchids In The Moonlight/I Surrender Dear.

Thursday 17 May

12.30   Bad Wildungen, Germany – Band played at a luncheon given by General Omar N. Bradley, Commanding General of US 12th Army Group, for USSR Marshall Koniev, Commader of the 1st Ukranian Army Group, and his staff. (250)

19.30   Bad Wildungen – Concert for troops of US 12th Army Group. (2,900)

Friday 18 May

10.50   Bad Wildungen – Band flew from Fitzbauer back to Paris; landed at Orly 13.05.

20.30   London – AEFP Broadcast – AMERICAN BAND OF THE AEF (recorded 16/4/45).

Long Tall Mama/The Lamp Is Low v, JD/Sleepy Town Train/*Medley*: Caprice Viennoise, Candy v, CC, My Isle Of Golden Dreams, Birth Of

The Blues/When Johnny Comes Marching Home Again V, CC/Introduction To A Waltz.

Note – for this broadcast the song Accentuate The Positive was deleted from the recording and When Johnny Comes Marching Home (from a recording made on 16/4/45 [Programme 1] substituted as above).

21.45 London – AEFP Broadcast – STRINGS WITH WINGS (recorded 13/4/45).

You're My Everything/Priere/Indian Summer/September Song.

Note – for this broadcast the tune September Song was deleted from the recording and the same song (from a recording made on 18/4/45 [Programme 1] substituted as above).

Saturday 19 May
Paris – Day off for the unit.

17.01 London – AEFP Broadcast – AMERICAN DANCE BAND: The Swing Shift (recorded 20/4/45).

Tail End Charlie/Bubble Bath/Embraceable You V, JD/Accentuate The Positive V, RM & CC/Somebody's Wrong/She's Funny That Way V, JD/Waiting For The Evening Mail V, RM/Drums Away (The Big Beat).

Sunday 20 May
Paris – Day off for the unit.

13.30 London – GFP Broadcast – AMERICAN BAND OF THE AEF (recorded repeat of last Tuesday's broadcast).

Monday 21 May
14.30 Paris – Concert at Olympia Theatre. (1,900)

14.50 AEFP Pre-recordings during Olympia Concert – AMERICAN BAND OF THE AEF. Broadcast 26/6/45, 27/6/45.

15.25 AMERICAN DANCE BAND: The Swing Shift. Broadcast 30/6/45, 3/7/45.

20.00 Paris – Concert at Olympia Theatre. (2,100)

20.50 AEFP Pre-recording during Olympia Concert – AMERICAN BAND OF THE AEF. Broadcast 22/6/45.

Tuesday 22 May
08.30 London – AEFP Broadcast – AMERICAN DANCE BAND: The Swing Shift (recorded repeat of last Saturday's broadcast).

14.30 Paris – Concert at Olympia Theatre. (1,700)

14.45 AEFP Pre-recordings during Olympia Concert – AMERICAN BAND OF THE AEF. Broadcast 29/6/45.

15.20 AMERICAN DANCE BAND: The Swing Shift. Broadcast 7/7/45, 10/7/45.

20.00 Paris – Concert at AEF Club, Grand Hotel. (1,100)

20.30 London – AEFP Broadcast – AMERICAN BAND OF THE AEF (recorded 17/4/45). Compère: Broderick Crawford.

Tail End Charlie/April In Paris V, JD/Wham Re-bop Boom Bam V, RM &

cc/*Medley*: Schubert's Serenade, You're So Sweet To Remember v, jd, Little Brown Jug, Under A Blanket Of Blue/Some Other Time v, jd/ The Anvil Chorus.

22.40   Paris – AEFP Pre-recordings (Olympia Theatre) – STRINGS WITH WINGS.

[Programme 1] broadcast 15/6/45.

23.00   [Programme 2] broadcast 20/6/45.

Wednesday 23 May

10.01   London – AEFP Broadcast – AMERICAN BAND OF THE AEF: Morning After (recorded repeat of last night's broadcast).

12.45   London – AEFP Broadcast – STRINGS WITH WINGS (recorded 13/4/45).
Love Walked In/Sweet And Low/Starry Night/I Dream Of Jeannie With The Light Brown Hair.

15.30   Paris – Concert at American Red Cross Club 'Rainbow Corner'. (600)

22.40   Paris – AEFP Pre-recordings (Olympia Theatre) – AMERICAN DANCE BAND: The Swing Shift.

[Programme 1] broadcast 14/7/45, 17/7/45.

23.15   [Programme 2] broadcast 19/7/45, 23/7/45.

Thursday 24 May

15.30   Paris – Concert at Grand Central Red Cross Club. (650)

20.30   London – AEFP Broadcast – AMERICAN BAND OF THE AEF (recorded 23/4/45).
I Dreamt I Dwelt In Harlem/April In Paris v, jd/And Her Tears Flowed Like Wine v, rm/*Medley*: Old Black Joe, I've Got The Blues, v, jd, I Got Sixpence v, cc, Rhapsody In Blue/Song Of The Volga Boatmen/The Trolley Song v, jd & cc.
Note – the regular Friday broadcast by the AEF Band was transferred to Thursday for this week only.

22.30   Paris – AEFP Pre-recordings (Olympia Theatre) – AMERICAN DANCE BAND: The Swing Shift

[Programme 1] not broadcast.

23.10   [Programe 2] not broadcast.

Friday 25 May

20.00   Paris – Concert at AEF Club, Grand Hotel. (1,000)

20.30   London – AEFP Broadcast – AMERICAN BAND OF THE AEF (broadcast was transferred to Thursday evening, May 24, and this spot was taken by 'ITMA')

21.45   London – AEFP Broadcast – STRINGS WITH WINGS (recorded 18/4/45).
Stairway To Heaven/Kashmiri Love Song/Body And Soul/It Could Happen To You.

22.30–24.00   Paris AEFP Pre-recordings (Olympia Theatre) – STRINGS
WITH WINGS.

[Programme 1] broadcast 29/6/45.
[Programme 2] broadcast 22/6/45.
[Programme 3] broadcast 27/6/45.
[Programme 4] broadcast 4/7/45.

Saturday 26 May
Paris – Day off for unit.

17.01   London – AEFP Broadcast – AMERICAN DANCE BAND: The Swing
Shift (recorded 19/4/45).
Everybody Loves My Baby/Spanish Shawl/As Long As There's Music
v, JD/Seven-O-Five/My Guy's Come Back/This I Love Above All v, JD/
And Her Tears Flowed Like Wine v, RM/Snafu Jump.

Sunday 27 May
13.30   London – GFP Broadcast – AMERICAN BAND OF THE AEF (recorded repeat of last Tuesday's broadcast).

20.30   Paris – Concert at the Salle Pleyel to civilian audience for benefit
of French ex-prisoners of war (2½ hours). (3,700)

Monday 28 May
14.30   Paris – Concert at Olympia Theatre. (2,000)

14.50   AEFP Pre-recordings during Olympia Concert – AMERICAN BAND
OF THE AEF.

[Programme 1] broadcast 3/7/45, 4/7/45.

15.35   [Programme 2] broadcast 10/7/45, 11/7/45, 15/7/45 (GFP).

20.00   Paris – Concert at Olympia Theatre. (2,150)

20.50   AEFP Pre-recording during Olympia Concert – AMERICAN BAND
OF THE AEF.

[Programme 3] broadcast 6/7/45.

Tuesday 29 May
08.30   London – AEFP Broadcast – AMERICAN DANCE BAND: The Swing
Shift (recorded repeat of last Saturday's broadcast).

14.30   Paris – Concert at Olympia Theatre.

14.45   AEFP Pre-recordings during Olympia Concert – AMERICAN BAND
OF THE AEF.

[Programme 1] broadcast 13/7/45.

15.25   [Programme 2] broadcast 17/7/45, 18/7/45.

20.00   Paris – concert at AEF Club, Grand Hotel. (1,100)

20.30   London – AEFP Broadcast – AMERICAN BAND OF THE AEF (re-
corded 10/4/45).
Sun Valley Jump/Fascinating You v, JD/American Patrol/*Medley*: Old
Refrain, I'm Making Believe v, JD, Smoke Gets In Your Eyes, Blue
Again/Great Day/Poinciana v, JD & CC.

22.30 Paris – AEFP Pre-recordings (Olympia Theatre) – STRINGS WITH WINGS.

[Programme 1] broadcast 11/7/45.

22.50 [Programme 2] broadcast 6/7/45.

Wednesday 30 May

10.01 London – AEFP Broadcast – AMERICAN BAND OF THE AEF: Morning After (recorded repeat of last night's broadcast).

12.45 London – AEFP Broadcast – STRINGS WITH WINGS (recorded 18/4/45).

These Foolish Things/Yesterday/The Moon Is Low/Lover Come Back To Me.

20.00 Paris – Concert at Columbia Red Cross Club. (1,300)

22.35 Paris – AEFP Pre-recordings (Olympia Theatre) – AMERICAN DANCE BAND: The Swing Shift.

[Programme 1] broadcast 26/7/45.

23.15 [Programme 2] not broadcast.

Thursday 31 May

15.30 Paris – Concert at Grand Central Red Cross Club. (700)

22.30 Paris – AEFP Pre-recordings (Olympia theatre) – STRINGS WITH WINGS.

[Programme 1] broadcast 20/7/45.

22.50 [Programme 2] broadcast 18/7/45.

23.15 [Programme 3] broadcast 13/7/45.

Friday 1 June

20.00 Paris – Concert at AEF Club, Grand Hotel. (1,000)

20.30 London – AEFP Broadcast – AMERICAN BAND OF THE AEF (recorded 24/4/45).

Jeep Jockey Jump/Estrellita v, JD/Long Tall Mama/*Medley*: I Dream Of Jeannie With The Light Brown Hair, As Long As There's Music v, JD, Begin The Beguine, Blue Rain/Candy v, CC/The Army Air Corps Song v, JD, CC & Ensemble.

21.45 London – AEFP Broadcast – STRINGS WITH WINGS (recorded 11/5/45).

Say It With Music/Pale Moon/Irresistible You/Evening In Paris.

22.30 Paris – AEFP Pre-recordings (Olympia Theatre) – STRINGS WITH WINGS.

[Programme 1] broadcast 25/7/45.

22.50 [Programme 2] broadcast 27/7/45.

23.15 [Programme 3] not broadcast.

Saturday 2 June

Paris – Day off for the unit.

17.01 London – AEFP Broadcast – AMERICAN DANCE BAND: The Swing Shift (recorded 24/4/45).

I Hear You Screaming/The Big Ones Are Eating The Little Ones/
Fascinating You v, JD/Confetti For Clarinet (featuring Peanuts Hucko,
clarinet)/Peggy The Pin-Up Girl v, RM & CC/The Day After Forever v,
JD/Stealing Apples.

Sunday 3 June
13.30   London – GFP Broadcast – AMERICAN BAND OF THE AEF (recorded repeat of last Tuesday's broadcast).

Monday 4 June
14.30   Paris – Concert at Olympia Theatre. (1,750)
14.50   AEFP Pre-recordings during Olympia concert – AMERICAN BAND
OF THE AEF.
   [Programme 1] not broadcast
15.25   [Programme 2] broadcast 20/7/45.
20.00   Paris – Concert at Olympia Theatre. (2,100)
20.45   AEFP Pre-recording during Olympia Concert – AMERICAN BAND
OF THE AEF.
   [Programme 3] broadcast 24/7/45, 25/7/45.

Tuesday 5 June
08.30   London – AEFP Broadcast – AMERICAN DANCE BAND: The Swing
Shift (recorded repeat of last Saturday's broadcast).
14.30   Paris – Concert at Olympia Theatre (This was the last Concert
by the Band at the Olympia Theatre). (1,600)
15.00   AEFP Pre-recording during Olympia Concert – AMERICAN BAND
OF THE AEF 'The American Band Of The AEF Says Farewell' (compère,
Sergeant Broderick Crawford). Broadcast 28/7/45.
20.00   Paris – Concert at AEF Club, Grand Hotel. (1,100)
20.30   London – AEFP Broadcast – AMERICAN BAND OF THE AEF (re-
corded 5/5/45).
American Patrol/More And More v, JD/Fishing Them Up Gup (Trio)/
Medley: Flow Gently Sweet Afton, Moondreams v, JD & CC, Don't Be
That Way, Blue Champagne/Swing Low Sweet Chariot/Poinciana v, JD
& CC.

Wednesday June 6
10.01   London – AEFP Broadcast – AMERICAN BAND OF THE AEF:
Morning After (recorded repeat of last night's broadcast).
   Paris – Day off for the unit.
12.45   London – AEFP Broadcast – STRINGS WITH WINGS (recorded
11/5/45).
World Is Waiting For The Sunrise/As Long as There's Music/Long Ago
And Far Away v, JD/All The Things You Are/What Is There To Say.

Thursday 7 June
15.30   Paris – Concert at Grand Central Red Cross Club. (700)

Friday 8 June

20.00 Paris – Concert at AEF Club, Grand Hotel. (1,000)

20.30¼ London – AEFP Broadcast – AMERICAN BAND OF THE AEF (recorded 14/5/45).

Sun Valley Jump/Some Other Time v, JD/*Medley*: All Through The Night, You're So Sweet To Remember v, JD, Take It Easy v, CC, Blue Hawaii/Waiting For The Evening Mail v, RM/The Red Cavalry March.

21.45½ London – AEFP Broadcast – STRINGS WITH WINGS (recorded 15/5/45).

I'll See You Again/Londonderry Air/Just The Way You Look Tonight/I'll Be Seeing You.

Saturday 9 June

Paris – The Band prepare to leave on Monday for six-week tour of US Army bases in Germany.

17.01 London – AEFP Broadcast – AMERICAN DANCE BAND: The Swing Shift (recorded 17/4/45).

Nine-Twenty Special/Oh Lady Be Good/I Dream Of You v, JD/Tea For Three (*Trio*)/Mission To Moscow/Embraceable You v, JD/Cow Cow Boogie v, RM/Shine On Harvest Moon/Get Happy.

Note – for this broadcast and the repeat on 12/6/45 Shine On Harvest Moon was taken from a recording probably made on 20/4/45 and inserted into the recording as above.

Sunday 10 June

13.30 London – GFP Broadcast – AMERICAN BAND OF THE AEF (recorded repeat of last Tuesday's broadcast).

Monday 11 June

Paris – The Band's scheduled departure for Germany delayed by bad weather.

Tuesday 12 June

Paris – Band's departure for Germany still delayed by bad weather.

08.30 London – AEFP Broadcast – AMERICAN DANCE BAND: The Swing Shift (recorded repeat of last Saturday's broadcast).

20.30 London – AEFP Broadcast – AMERICAN BAND OF THE AEF (recorded 14/5/45). Compère, Broderick Crawford.

Measure For Measure/Any Moment Now v, JD/Tuxedo Junction/ *Medley*: Old Refrain, I'm Making Believe v, JD, Smoke Gets In Your Eyes, Blue Again/Sleepy Town Train/The Victory Polka v, JD & CC.

Wednesday 13 June

10.01 London – AEFP Broadcast – AMERICAN BAND OF THE AEF: Morning After (recorded repeat of last night's broadcast).

12.45 London – AEFP Broadcast – STRINGS WITH WINGS (recorded 15/5/45).

Some Other Time/Orchids In The Moonlight/Going My Way/Our Waltz.

14.15   Paris – Band flew from Villacoublay to Regensburg, Germany, arriving at 16.50.

Regensburg – Concert for 1137th Engineering Group, us Army.

Thursday 14 June

15.00   Regensburg – Concert at Half Crown Theatre.
19.00   Regensburg – Concert at Half Crown Theatre.

Friday 15 June

Regensburg – Concerts (probably two).

20.30   London – aefp Broadcast – american band of the aef (recorded 14/5/45) Compère: Broderick Crawford.

Here We Go Again/Stormy Weather/When Johnny Comes Marching Home v, cc/*Medley*: In The Gloaming, Together v, jd, Stomping At The Savoy, Deep Purple/Let's Take The Long Way Home v, jd/On, Brave Old Army Team.

21.45   London – aefp Broadcast – strings with wings (recorded 22/5/45).

Just One More Chance/Going Home/A Love Like This/Serenade In Blue.

Saturday 16 June

Regensburg – band in trucks to Weiden: 2 concerts, stayed overnight in German barracks.

17.01   London – aefp Broadcast – american dance band: The Swing Shift (recorded 10/5/45).

King Porter Stomp/Swing Low Sweet Chariot/Some Other Time v, jd/ Spanish Shawl/Candy v, cc/One O'Clock Jump/Anchors Aweigh.

Sunday 17 June

13.30   London – gfp Broadcast – american band of the aef (recorded repeat of last Tuesday's broadcast).

Weiden – Band in trucks to Amberg: 1 concert; then on the Schwartzenfeld: 1 Concert; returned to Regensburg in the evening.

Monday 18 June

Regensburg – Day off for the Band.

Tuesday 19 June

08.30   London – aefp Broadcast – american dance band: The Swing Shift (recorded repeat of last Saturday's broadcast).

Regensburg – Band in trucks to Dingolfing: 3 concerts; stayed overnight.

20.30   London – aefp Broadcast – american band of the aef (recorded 15/5/45). Compère: Broderick Crawford.

Great Day/Stardust/Don't Fence Me In v, jd & cc/*Medley*: Mother

Macree, Fascinating You, v, JD, I Can't Give You Anything But Love Baby, v, Peanuts Hucko, trumpet solo Bernie Privin, Wang Wang Blues/And Her Tears Flowed Like Wine v, RM/The Caisson Song.

Wednesday 20 June
10.01 London – AEFP Broadcast – AMERICAN BAND OF THE AEF. Morning After (recorded repeat of last night's broadcast).
12.45 London – AEFP Broadcast – STRINGS WITH WINGS (recorded 22/5/45).
You're My Everything/Kashmiri Song/Alone Together/I've Told Every Little Star.
Dingolfing – Band in trucks to Landau: 1 concert; then on to Geiselhöring – 2 concerts; returned to Regensburg in the evening.

Thursday 21 June
Regensburg – Day off for the Band.

Friday 22 June
Regensburg – Band in trucks to Passau till June 25th: played 5 concerts and had one day off.
20.30 London – AEFP Broadcast – AMERICAN BAND OF THE AEF (recorded 21/5/45). Compère: Broderick Crawford.
Tail End Charlie/Estrellita/Don't Fence Me In v, JD & CC/*Medley*: Sweet And Low, A Fellow On A Furlough v, JD, Things Ain't What They Used To Be, A Blues Serenade/Uncle Tom/Oranges And Lemons v, JD & CC.
Note – Uncle Tom was played by the pre-war civilian Glenn Miller Band, but not recorded; after the war it was recorded by the Glenn Miller Band directed by Tex Beneke under the title of Texas Tex.
21.45 London – AEFP Broadcast – STRINGS WITH WINGS (recorded 25/5/45).
Someone To Watch Over Me/Sweet And Low/Tico Tico/Memories Of You.

Saturday 23 June
Passau—
17.01 London – AEFP Broadcast – AMERICAN DANCE BAND: The Swing Shift (recorded 10/5/45).
Mission To Moscow/My Buddy/Juke Box Saturday Night v, CC/Stealing Apples/Embraceable You v, JD/I Dreamt I Dwelt In Harlem/Sweet And Low/Flying Home.

Sunday 24 June
Passau—
13.30 London – GFP Broadcast – AMERICAN BAND OF THE AEF (recorded repeat of last Tuesday's broadcast).

Monday 25 June
Passau—

Tuesday 26 June

08.30 London – AEFP Broadcast – AMERICAN DANCE BAND: The Swing Shift (recorded repeat of last Saturday's broadcast).

20.30¼ London – AEFP Broadcast – AMERICAN BAND OF THE AEF (recorded 21/5/45).

I Hear You Screaming/Embraceable You v, JD/Kalamazoo v, cc/*Medley*: My Buddy, As Long As There's Music v, JD, Music Makers, Farewell Blues/It Must Be Jelly/Can't Help Singing v, JD.

Passau – Band in trucks to Straubing: 1 concert; then returned to Regensburg.

Wednesday 27 June

10.01¼ London – AEFP Broadcast – AMERICAN BAND OF THE AEF: Morning After (recorded repeat of last night's broadcast).

12.45 London – AEFP Broadcast – STRINGS WITH WINGS (recorded 25/5/45).

Embraceable You/Clouds/The Song Is You.

Regensburg – Concert.

Thursday 28 June

Landshut – 2 concerts.

Friday 29 June

Kelheim – 1 concert.

Neumarkt – 1 concert.

20.30 London – AEFP Broadcast – AMERICAN BAND OF THE AEF (recorded 22/5/45). Compère: Broderick Crawford.

Get Happy/Body And Soul/I Dreamt I Dwelt In Harlem/*Medley*: Caprice Viennois, More And More v, JD, My Isle Of Golden Dreams, Birth Of The Blues/At Last v, JD/Introduction To A Waltz.

21.45¼ London – AEFP Broadcast – STRINGS WITH WINGS (recorded 25/5/45).

I'll Remember April/Home On The Range/A Love Like This v, JD/When Day Is Done.

Saturday 30 June

Regensburg – Band flew to Erlangen, arrived 12.40; played 1 concert; stayed overnight.

17.01 London – AEFP broadcast – AMERICAN DANCE BAND: The Swing Shift (recorded 21/5/45).

Stealing Apples/Little Brown Jug/Embraceable You v, JD/Crisis (*Trio*?)/Nine-Twenty Special/I'll Walk Alone v, JD/Is You Is Or Is You Ain't My Baby v, RM/Everybody Loves My Baby.

Sunday 1 July

13.30 London – GFP Broadcast – AMERICAN BAND OF THE AEF. Programme cancelled – replaced by recording of The Brains Trust.

383

Erlangen – Band in trucks to Nuremburg; played two-hour concert in former Nazi stadium (40,000); returned in trucks to Regensburg late at night.

Monday 2 July

Tuesday 3 July
08.30   London – AEFP Broadcast – AMERICAN DANCE BAND: The Swing Shift (recorded repeat of last Saturday's broadcast).
    Cham – 1 concert.
20.30   London – AEFP Broadcast – AMERICAN BAND OF THE AEF (recorded 28/5/45). Compère: Broderick Crawford.
Limehouse Blues/Saturday Night is The Loneliest Night Of The Week v, JD/American Patrol/*Medley*: Carry Me Back To Old Virginny, Some Other Time. v, JD, Alouette v, CC, Blue Moon/The Spirit Is Willing/Can't Help Singing v, JD.

Wednesday 4 July
10.01   London – AEFP Broadcast – AMERICAN BAND OF THE AEF: Morning After (recorded repeat of last night's broadcast).
12.45   London – AEFP Broadcast – STRINGS WITH WINGS (recorded 25/5/45).
Sure Thing/Alone Together/The Moon Is Low v, JD/My Romance.
    Regensburg – 1 Concert.

Thursday 5 July

Friday 6 July
20.30   London – AEFP Broadcast – AMERICAN BAND OF THE AEF (recorded 28/5/45). Compère: Broderick Crawford.
Flying Home/Smoke Gets In Your Eyes/You Are My Sunshine v, JD / *Medley*: Annie Laurie, Any Moment Now v, JD, Alexander's Ragtime Band/Caribbean Clipper/Waiting For The Evening Mail v, RM/The Army Air Corps Song v, JD, CC & Ensemble.
21.45   London – AEFP Broadcast – STRINGS WITH WINGS (recorded 29/5/45).
Say It With Music/None But The Lonely/Just The Way You Look Tonight v, JD/I Surrender Dear.

Saturday 7 July
17.01   London – AEFP Broadcast – AMERICAN DANCE BAND: The Swing Shift (recorded 22/5/45).
I Hear You Screaming/String Of Pearls/I Dream Of You v, JD/Accentuate The Positive v, RM & CC/Jeep Jockey Jump/Fascinating You v, JD/Snafu Jump.

Sunday 8 July
13.30 London – GFP Broadcast – AMERICAN BAND OF THE AEF. Programme cancelled – replaced by live broadcast by Ted Heath and his Music (13.09–14.00).

Monday 9 July
Regensburg – Band left Regensburg for good, flew to Schweinfurt, arrived at 20.35, thence in trucks to Bad Neustadt, stayed overnight.

Tuesday 10 July
08.30 London – AEFP Broadcast – AMERICAN DANCE BAND: The Swing Shift (recorded repeat of last Saturday's broadcast).
20.30 London – AEFP Broadcast – AMERICAN BAND OF THE AEF (recorded 28/5/45). Compère: Broderick Crawford.
Long Tall Mama/You're So Sweet To Remember v, JD/Mission To Moscow/*Medley*: Londonderry Air, It Had To be You v, JD, Cherokee, Blue Danube/Candy v, JD & CC/The Anvil Chorus.
Bad Neustadt – 2 concerts; Band stayed overnight.

Wednesday 11 July
10.01 London – AEFP Broadcast – AMERICAN BAND OF THE AEF: Morning After (recorded repeat of last night's broadcast).
12.45 London – AEFP Broadcast – STRINGS WITH WINGS (recorded 29/5/45).
How Deep is The Ocean/Pale Moon/Diane/Yesterdays.
Bad Neustadt – Band in trucks to Schweinfurt – 1 concert.

Thursday 12 July
Erlangen – 1 concert

Friday 13 July
Erlangen – Band in trucks to Bayreuth – 1 concert in Wagner Theatre (Festspielhaus).
20.30 London – AEFP Broadcast – AMERICAN BAND OF THE AEF (recorded 29/5/45). Compère: Broderick Crawford.
Everybody Loves My Baby/My Prayer v, JD/Wham Re-bop Boom Bam v, RM/*Medley*: I'll Take You Home Again Kathleen, There Goes That Song Again v, JD, Rose Room, Blue Room/Seven-O-Five/Alone v, JD / Marines Hymn.
21.45 London – AEFP Broadcast – STRINGS WITH WINGS (recorded 31/5/45).
I'll See You Again/Maid With The Flaxen Hair/Serenade In Blue/Our Waltz.
evening Bayreuth – 1 concert at nearby airfield; Band stayed overnight.

Saturday 14 July

10.38   Bayreuth – Band flew to Schweinfurt, arrived 11.05, thence in trucks to Bad Kissingen – 1 concert; stayed overnight.

17.01   London – AEFP Broadcast – AMERICAN DANCE BAND: The Swing Shift (recorded 23/5/45).

Sun Valley Jump/Rhapsody In Blue/Bubble Bath/I Didn't Know About You v, JD/Time For Refill (*Trio* ?)/Don't Fence Me In v, CC/Waiting For The Evening Mail v, RM/The Eyes And Ears Of The World (Paramount On Parade).

This was the last Saturday broadcast of the Swing Shift.

Sunday 15 July

Bad Kissingen – Band returned to Schweinfurt; 10.30 flew to Venlo, Holland, arrived 11.40.

13.30   London – GFP Broadcast – AMERICAN BAND OF THE AEF (recorded repeat of last Tuesday's broadcast).

This was the last broadcast of the AEF Band in the GFP.

evening   Venlo – 1 concert; Band stayed overnight.

Monday 16 July

10.55   Venlo – Band flew to airfield near Méharicourt en Roye, France, arrived 12.06; played 1 concert; stayed overnight.

Tuesday 17 July

08.30   London – AEFP Broadcast – AMERICAN DANCE BAND: The Swing Shift (recorded repeat of last Saturday's broadcast).

13.54   Méharicourt – Band flew to Anecy, arrived 15.45; thence by trucks to Chamonix – played 1 concert; stayed overnight.

20.30   London – AEFP Broadcast – AMERICAN BAND OF THE AEF (recorded 29/5/45). Compère: Broderick Crawford.

Here We Go Again/April In Paris v, JD/Don't Fence Me In v, JD & CC/*Medley*: Mighty Like A Rose, Amor Amor v, JD, Chattanooga Choo Choo v, RM & CC, Bye Bye Blues/Lady Be Good/The Trolley Song v, JD & CC.

Wednesday 18 July

10.01   London – AEFP Broadcast – AMERICAN BAND OF THE AEF; Morning After (recorded repeat of last night's broadcast).

12.45   London – AEFP Broadcast – STRINGS WITH WINGS (recorded 31/5/45).

Stairway [? To The Stars]/I Dream Of Jeannie With The Light Brown Hair/May Night/It Could Happen To You v, JD.

13.45   Anecy – Band flew to Villacoublay, Paris, arrived 15.28.

Thursday 19 July

18.30   London – AEFP Broadcast – AMERICAN DANCE BAND: The Swing Shift (recorded 23/5/45).

King Porter Stomp/Uncle Tom/How Blue The Night v, JD/Dance With

A Dolly v, cc/My Guy's Come Back/Embraceable You v, jd/One O'Clock Jump.

Friday 20 July
13.00   Paris – Band flew from Villacoublay to Kaufbeuren, Germany; arrived 13.08 – played 1 concert.
18.00   Kaufbeuren – Band flew to Fürstenfeldbruck, arrived 18.20 – 1 concert; stayed overnight.
20.30   London – aefp Broadcast – american band of the aef (recorded 4/6/45).
American Patrol/Saturday Night Is The Loneliest Night Of The Week v, jd & cc/Begin The Beguine/*Medley*: Going Home, More And More v, jd, Honeysuckle Rose, My Blue Heaven/Accentuate The Positive v, rm/On, Brave Old Army Team.
Note – for this broadcast, as the recording was incomplete the *Theme* and American Patrol were inserted from a recording made on 7/5/45 [Programme 2].
21.45   London – aefp Broadcast – strings with wings (recorded 31/5/45).
The Song Is You/Pavanne (Ravel)/Indian Summer v, jd/I Love You Truly.

Saturday 21 July
10.15   Fürstenfeldbruck – Band flew to Frankfurt, arrived 11.30.
   Frankfurt – Concert for staff of shaef (Main); at this concert a special plaque and a citation from General Eisenhower were presented to the Band.
This was the Band's last official concert in their posting to the eto.

Sunday 22 July
09.32   Frankfurt – Band flew to Villacoublay; arrived 11.46; billeted at nearby Camp Price Albert.

Monday 23 July

Tuesday 24 July
08.30   London – aefp Broadcast – american dance band: The Swing Shift (recorded repeat of last Thursday's broadcast).
early evening   Villacoublay – concert at airfield; then to St Lazare Station, Paris, to board 22.00 train to Le Havre; departed 22.54.
20.30   London – aefp Broadcast – american band of the aef (recorded 4/6/45). Compère: Broderick Crawford.
Song Of The Volga Boatmen/Laura v, jd/Get Happy/*Medley*: Drink To Me Only, There Goes That Song Again v, jd, The Very Thought Of You, Blue Skies/How You Going To Keep Them Down On The Farm Now That They've Seen Berlin (with additional lyrics by Artie Malvin and Bill Conway) v, cc/Holiday For Strings.

Wednesday 25 July

06.16 Band arrived at Le Havre; billeted at Camp Herbert Tareyton till 5/8/45.

10.01 London – AEFP Broadcast – AMERICAN BAND OF THE AEF: Morning After (recorded repeat of last night's broadcast).

12.45 London – AEFP Broadcast – STRINGS WITH WINGS (recorded 1/6/45).

Love Walked In/Estrellita/I Don't Know Why V, JD/Mood Indigo.

Thursday 26 July

18.30 London – AEFP Broadcast – AMERICAN DANCE BAND: The Swing Shift (recorded 30/5/45).

Flying Home/Little Brown Jug/I'll Walk Alone V, JD/Whoever You Is (unpublished composition) (*Trio* ?)/My Guy's Come Back/Accentuate The Positive V, RM & CC/On, Brave Old Army Team.

This was the last broadcast by the American Dance Band.

Friday 27 July

20.30 London – AEFP Broadcast – AMERICAN BAND OF THE AEF. Programme transferred to Saturday evening, 28/7/45 at 22.15; this Friday spot was filled by Jack Payne and his Orchestra.

21.45 London – AEFP Broadcast – STRINGS WITH WINGS (recorded 1/6/45).

I'm In The Mood For Love/The Touch Of Your Hand/Long Ago And Far Away V, JD/The World Is Waiting For The Sunrise.

This was the last broadcast by the Strings With Wings.

Saturday 28 July

Le Havre – Open air concert for troops at Camp Herbert Tareyton.

22.15 London – AEFP Broadcast – 'THE AMERICAN BAND OF THE AEF SAYS FAREWELL' (recorded 5/6/45). Compère: Broderick Crawford.

In The Mood/Stardust/Juke Box Saturday Night V, CC/*Medley*: Mighty Like A Rose, Amor Amor, V, JD, Chattanooga Choo Choo V, RM & CC, Rhapsody In Blue/Long Ago And Far Away V, JD/The Anvil Chorus.

This programme was the last to be broadcast on the AEFP (except for a special farewell compilation which followed it) and was introduced by a spoken appreciation of the Band by Captain Franklin Engelman. The AEFP closed down permanently shortly after 23.00.

APPENDICES

Sound recordings by the Band

A Wartime recordings for the US Government not originally available to the public

During the two and a half years the Band existed they made many recordings for various US Government agencies: the Special Services Division of the War Department, the Armed Forces Radio Service and the Overseas Branch of the Office of War Information. The principal series of these recordings are listed below. Although at the time they were not available to the general public, in the years since the Second World War many of them have been issued on commercial long-playing records (*see* pages 394–411).

V-Discs*

These were twelve-inch 78 r.p.m. records pressed on unbreakable vinylite in order to stand up to rough wear on active service, as the ordinary shellac records of the time would soon get broken. They were produced by the Special Services Division of the War Department for free distribution to US Servicemen and their canteens wherever American troops were stationed. They included all kinds of music, including classical, and from 1942 to 1949 a total of 905 V-Discs were produced in large numbers and sent all over the world. At first there were an Army Series and a Navy Series, but from V-Disc 516 onwards there was one combined series; the Army and Navy series contained the same records but were numbered differently. At first, the records were copies of the ordinary commercial issues of the time on vinylite pressings, but from late 1943 onwards many bands and singers made records specially for V-Discs, including Captain Glenn Miller and the Army Air Forces Training Command Orchestra.

---

* A wealth of detail on all V-Discs is given in the definitive work *V-Discs: A History and Discography*, by Richard S. Sears; (Greenwood Press, Westport, Conn.; London, 1980) and *V-Discs: First Supplement* (1986).

A total of 41 tunes by the Miller Army Air Forces Orchestra was made available on V-Discs: some were specially recorded in the RCA Victor studios in New York, but the majority were taken from *I Sustain the Wings* broadcasts or rehearsals.

Captain Glenn Miller and the 418th AAFTC Orchestra:

65A* Stardust. Spoken introduction by Captain Glenn Miller. (29 Oct 1943) **B** St Louis Blues March (Music For Marching Men Series) (29 Oct 1943)

91A Stormy Weather (29 Oct 1943) **B** Buckle Down Winsocki; El Capitan (Music For Marching Men Series) (29 Oct 1943)

Captain Glenn Miller and the AAFTC Orchestra:

123A Going Home; Honeysuckle Rose; My Blue Heaven (Abridged medley, with medley themes but no spoken introductions) (10 Dec 1943) **B** (Civilian Glenn Miller Band: In The Mood)

144A The Squadron Song. v, The Band; Tail End Charlie (Dec. 10th, 1943) **B** Don't Be That Way; Blue Champagne (11 Dec 1943)

183A Embraceable You. String Section Only; The GI Jive. v, Sgt Ray McKinley and the Crew Chiefs. (21 Jan 1944) **B** (Duke Ellington Orchestra)

201A Moondreams. v, Sgt Johnny Desmond and the Crew Chiefs. (21 Jan 1944) **B** (Civilian Glenn Miller Band: Sleepy Town Train)

223A Everybody Loves My Baby; Stomping At The Savoy (20 May, 1944) **B** Stealing Apples (21 Jan 1944)

242A A Fellow On A Furlough. v, Sgt Johnny Desmond; Guns In The Sky. v, Sgt Johnny Desmond and the Crew Chiefs **B** Poinciana. v, Sgt Johnny Desmond and the Crew Chiefs (20 May 1944)

281A Sun Valley Jump; Chattanooga Choo Choo. v, Sgt Ray McKinley and the Crew Chiefs. (3 June 1944) **B** (Artie Shaw and his Orchestra)

302A (Benny Goodman and his All-Star Band and Quartet) **B** In The Gloaming; Deep Purple (20 May 1944)

334A My Buddy; Farewell Blues (10 June 1944) **B** (David Rose and his Orchestra)

381A I've Got A Heart Filled With Love For You. v, Sgt Johnny Desmond, Cpl Artie Malvin and the Crew Chiefs. (13 May 1944) **B** (Dinah Shore)

421A Holiday For Strings (3 June 1944) **B** (Paul Barron and his Orchestra)

466A Bye Bye Blues (3 June 1944); Wang Wang Blues (13 May 1944) **B** (Harry James and his Orchestra)

482A I Can't Give You Anything But Love, Baby. v, Sgt Peanuts Hucko. (13 May 1944); Little Brown Jug. (27 May 1944) **B** (Charlie Barnet and his Orchestra)

---

* Numbers are the Army Series.

504A The Army Air Corps Song. v, Sgt Johnny Desmond and the Band; I Hear You Screaming. (27 May 1944) **B** (Woody Herman and his Orchestra)
522A St Louis Blues [actually, St Louis Blues March, the same recording as on V-Disc 65B] **B** (Mus. First Class Sam Donahue and the Navy Dance Band)
533A Songs My Mother Taught Me; Peggy the Pin-Up Girl. v, Sgt Ray McKinley and the Crew Chiefs. (29 Apr 1944) **B** (Mus. First Class Sam Donahue and the Navy Dance Band).

Major Glenn Miller's AAF Overseas Orchestra:
587A Why Dream. v, Sgt Johnny Desmond. (10 Nov 1945); Passage Interdit (6 Oct 1945) **B** (Jack Teagarden and his Orchestra)
601A Symphony. v, Sgt Johnny Desmond (13 Oct 1945) **B** (Benny Goodman Sextet)
842A (Tony Pastor Orchestra) **B** In The Mood (17 Nov 1945)

A number of other Glenn Miller recordings were put on to V-Discs but they were by the pre-war civilian Glenn Miller Band, not the Army Air Forces Band.

Armed Forces Radio Service Transcriptions

These were 16-inch 33⅓ r.p.m. records produced for broadcasting by American Forces Network radio stations wherever American troops were stationed throughout the world.

Programme No.
P-101 Moonlight Serenade; Rhapsody In Blue; Little Brown Jug; Peggy The Pin-Up Girl. v, Sgt Ray McKinley and the Crew Chiefs.
P-106 Moondreams. v, Sgt Johnny Desmond and the Crew Chiefs; In An Eighteenth Century Drawing Room; Farewell Blues; Don't Be That Way; Blue Champagne.
P-292 Put Your Arms Around Me Honey. v, the Crew Chiefs; The Dipsey Doodle; Sun Valley Jump; In The Mood.
P-293 String Of Pearls; Cherokee; American Patrol; The Anvil Chorus.
P-297 Song Of The Volga Boatmen; Annie Laurie; I Hear You Screaming; Snafu Jump.
P-298 What Do You Do In The Infantry. v, the Crew Chiefs; Juke Box Saturday Night. v, the Crew Chiefs; There Are Yanks. v, Sgt Ray McKinley and the Crew Chiefs; Jeep Jockey Jump.
P-299 Over There. v, the Band; Mission to Moscow; It Must Be Jelly; Enlisted Men's Mess.
P-300 Sleepy Town Train; Speak Low. v, Sgt. Johnny Desmond; Now I Know. v, Sgt Johnny Desmond.
P-301 With My Head In The Clouds. v, Cpl Artie Malvin and the Crew Chiefs; Pearls On Velvet; Oh What A Beautiful Morning. v, Sgt Johnny Desmond and the Crew Chiefs.
P-302 My Ideal. v, Sgt Johnny Desmond; Holiday For Strings; Going Home.

P-501 Tuxedo Junction; Symphony. v, Sgt Johnny Desmond; Rhapsody In Blue; In The Middle of May. v, Sgt Johnny Desmond.

P-502 Passage Interdit; Homesick. v, Sgt Johnny Desmond; Swing Low Sweet Chariot; The More I See You. v, Sgt Johnny Desmond.

P-517 Things Ain't What They Used To Be; Poinciana. v, Sgt Johnny Desmond and the Crew Chiefs; Why Dream. v, Sgt Johnny Desmond; 705.

P-602 Here We Go Again; American Patrol; Oranges And Lemons. v, Sgt Johnny Desmond and the Crew Chiefs.

P-604 Blue Is The Night; I Can't Give You Anything But Love Baby. v, Sgt Peanuts Hucko; I Don't Want To Be Loved. v, Sgt Johnny Desmond; Tail End Charlie.

P-701 The Anvil Chorus; Things Ain't What They Used To Be; Mission To Moscow; Cherokee.

P-713 Bye Bye Blues; Wang Wang Blues; I Can't Give You Anything But Love Baby. v, Sgt Peanuts Hucko; Little Brown Jug.

P-1122 Stardust; Songs My Mother Taught Me; Passage Interdit; Homesick. v, Sgt Johnny Desmond.

Office of War Information – Overseas Branch transcriptions

These were 16-inch 33⅓ r.p.m. records produced by the OWI and sent out to foreign radio stations as part of the American Government's propaganda activities. Each record side lasted about fourteen minutes, each began and ended with the 'I Sustain The Wings' theme and each tune was separated by a short bridge passage which was the first few bars of 'The Army Air Corps Song'. There were no spoken announcements on the records.

Music From America – Unannounced Popular Series
Programme No.

   1 Tuxedo Junction; I Love You. v, Sgt Johnny Desmond; Holiday For Strings.

   2 Caribbean Clipper; I Dream Of Jeannie With The Light Brown Hair; Pearls On Velvet; With My Head In The Clouds.

   3 Mission To Moscow; Honeysuckle Rose; Stardust; The Anvil Chorus.

   4 In The Mood; In The Gloaming; Stormy Weather; Over There. v, the Band.

   5 Sun Valley Jump; Suddenly It's Spring. v, Sgt Johnny Desmond; Cherokee; Here We Go Again.

   6 Stealing Apples; Rhapsody In Blue; The Dipsey Doodle; Oh What A Beautiful Morning. v, Sgt Johnny Desmond and the Crew Chiefs.

   7 Jeep Jockey Jump; Songs My Mother Taught Me; Stomping At The Savoy; Poinciana. v, Sgt Johnny Desmond and the Crew Chiefs.

8 Tail End Charlie; Speak Low. v, Sgt Johnny Desmond; Caprice Viennoise; The Victory Polka.

9 It Must Be Jelly; The Music Stopped. v, Sgt Johnny Desmond; Begin The Beguine; Snafu Jump.

10 American Patrol; Summertime; This Is A Lovely Way To Spend An Evening. v, Sgt Johnny Desmond and the Crew Chiefs; Song Of The Volga Boatmen.

11 Flying Home; Moonlight Serenade ('concert' version); String Of Pearls; Guns In The Sky. v, Sgt Johnny Desmond and the Band.

12 I Hear You Screaming; How Sweet You Are. v, Sgt Johnny Desmond; Going Home; Little Brown Jug.

13 Enlisted Men's Mess; Now I Know. v, Sgt Johnny Desmond; All Through The Night; Don't Be That Way; Put Your Arms Around Me Honey. v, Sgt Johnny Desmond, the Crew Chiefs and the Band.

14 Keep 'Em Flying; Moondreams. v, Sgt Johnny Desmond and the Crew Chiefs; Music Makers; All The Things You Are; The Squadron Song. v, the Crew Chiefs and the Band.

15 705; Along The Santa Fe Trail. v, Sgt Johnny Desmond; Farewell Blues; There'll Be A Hot Time In The Town Of Berlin. v, Sgt Ray McKinley, the Crew Chiefs and the Band.

16 Bubble Bath; The Blue Danube; Blue Is The Night; Everybody Loves My Baby.

17 Nine-Twenty Special; Going My Way. v, Sgt Johnny Desmond; The Way You Look Tonight; Oh Lady Be Good.

18 Long Tall Mama; Our Waltz. (String section only); My Blue Heaven; Swing Low Sweet Chariot.

19 Caribbean Clipper; Time Alone Will Tell. v, Sgt Johnny Desmond; I Dream Of Jeannie With The Light Brown Hair; With My Head In The Clouds. v, the Crew Chiefs.

20 Here We Go Again; Annie Laurie. (String section only); Goodnight Wherever You Are. v, Sgt Johnny Desmond and the Crew Chiefs; Music Makers.

21 Tuxedo Junction; A Fellow On A Furlough. v, Sgt Johnny Desmond; Summertime; I've Got A Heart Filled With Love For You. v, Sgt Johnny Desmond and the Crew Chiefs.

22

23 Mission to Moscow; Irresistible You. v, Sgt Johnny Desmond and the Crew Chiefs; Going Home (string section only); There'll Be A Hot Time In The Town Of Berlin. v, Sgt Ray McKinley and the Crew Chiefs.

B Publicly issued recordings (revised 1994)

Apart from the four tunes recorded in London for His Master's Voice on 16 September 1944, which were never actually issued (*see* page 152), the Band made no records at all during its lifetime for commercial record companies for release to the public. Because of this, any records intended for the public in later years could only be copies of records originally made for other purposes such as radio broadcasting or for various uses by the US Government, and in the years since the Second World War many such recordings have been reprocessed and issued on long-playing records by the commercial record industry in the USA and elsewhere.

The first records of the Band ever issued to the public anywhere appeared in New York in February 1952. They were two ten-inch long-playing records entitled 'Major Glenn Miller and his AEF Orchestra featuring Sgt Ray McKinley', Volumes 1 and 2. They bore no issue numbers nor the name of the issuing company, but were described on the sleeves as 'Major Glenn Miller – A Tribute' and 'An AFN Presentation'. The recordings on the two LPs were originally made in the HMV studios in London in October and November 1944 when the Band pre-recorded some propaganda programmes to be broadcast over the American Broadcasting Station in Europe (ABSIE) in their series 'Music For The Wehrmacht' (*see* page 183).

The LPs contained extracts from the first three ABSIE programmes, not original complete broadcasts – a total of fifteen tunes, most of them with the original announcements in German and English by a girl announcer identified only as 'Ilse' and Major Glenn Miller.

Volume 1:

Side 1 – Introductory announcement by Ilse. *Theme*: Moonlight Serenade; American Patrol [6 Nov 1944]; Great Day [30 Oct 1944]; String Of Pearls [6 Nov 1944].

Side 2 – In The Mood [30 Oct 1944]; Poinciana. v, Artie Malvin and the Crew Chiefs. [6 Nov 1944]; Now I Know. v in German by Johnny Desmond. [6 Nov 1944].

Volume 2:

Side 1 – Begin The Beguine [6 Nov 1944]; Summertime [6 Nov 1944]; Song Of The Volga Boatmen [30 Oct 1944]; My Heart Tells Me. v in German by Johnny Desmond [6 Nov 1944].

Side 2 – Tuxedo Junction [6 Nov 1944]; Is You Is Or Is You Ain't My Baby? v in English by Ray McKinley [30 Oct 1944]; Anvil Chorus. Featuring Ray McKinley, drums [6 Nov 1944]; *Theme*: Moonlight Serenade and closing announcment by Ilse and Major Glenn Miller.

(*Note* – the dates given above, which do not appear on the record sleeves, are the dates the music was recorded; for the dates it was actually broadcast, *see* Part 2).

These two 'AFN LPs' as they have become known (although of course originally they were nothing to do with AFN) were available only for a very short time. Following legal action by the Glenn Miller Estate in New York City they were withdrawn from sale and copies are now extremely rare.

It was another three and a half years before the next records of the Band were issued to the public. This time, RCA Victor, the company for which the civilian Glenn Miller Band had recorded before the war, negotiated contractual agreements with the Glenn Miller Estate, the AAF Band musicians and singers, and the National Broadcasting Company to issue recordings from the 'I Sustain The Wings' radio series dating from 1943 (*see* page 25), and in September 1955 RCA Victor issued in the USA an album of five long-playing records of the Band playing in these programmes. The recordings came from the archives of NBC: some were from actual broadcasts, some from rehearsals, and among them were six complete medleys of 'Something old, something new, something borrowed and something blue' announced by Captain Glenn Miller; apart from these medleys, all the announcements to the music were excluded from the LPs in the album. The sound quality of the recordings was very high and the album remains one of the most notable issues of the LP era.

The album was entitled 'Glenn Miller Army Air Force Band' and was issued as five 12″ LPs, catalogue number Victor LPT-6702, containing the following music:

Side 1 Over There. v, The Band; This Is A Lovely Way To Spend An Evening. v, Johnny Desmond and the Crew Chiefs.; The GI Jive. v, Ray McKinley and the Crew Chiefs.; *Medley* Flow Gently Sweet Afton, Moondreams. v, Johnny Desmond and the Crew Chiefs,Don't Be That Way, Blue Champagne; Holiday For Strings.

Side 2 Peggy The Pin-Up Girl. v, Ray McKinley and the Crew Chiefs.; Going My Way. v, Johnny Desmond; *Medley*: I Dream Of Jeannie With The Light Brown Hair.; I Couldn't Sleep A Wink Last Night. v, Johnny Desmond and the Crew Chiefs.; Alexander's Ragtime Band, Blue Rain; I've Got A heart Filled With Love For You. v, Johnny Desmond, Artie Malvin and the Crew Chiefs.; The Anvil Chorus.

Side 3 There Are Yanks. v, Johnny Desmond, Ray McKinley and the Crew Chiefs; Stardust; Song Of The Volga Boatmen; How Sweet You Are. v, Johnny Desmond; Pearls On Velvet. featuring Mel Powell, *piano*; There'll Be A Hot Time In The Town Of Berlin. v, Ray McKinley and the Crew Chiefs.

Side 4 What Do You Do In The Infantry. v, Artie Malvin and the Crew Chiefs; Farewell Blues; Sun Valley Jump; *Medley*: In The Gloaming, For The First Time. v, Johnny Desmond, Stomping At The Savoy, Deep Purple; Stormy Weather.

Side 5 Mission To Moscow; My Ideal. v, Johnny Desmond; Tuxedo Junction; In An Eighteenth Century Drawing Room; I Hear You

Screaming; I'll Be Around. v, Johnny Desmond and the Crew Chiefs; Poinciana. v, Johnny Desmond and the Crew Chiefs.

Side 6 Flying Home; Long Ago And Far Away. v, Johnny Desmond; It Must Be Jelly; *Medley*: Going Home, Goodnight Wherever You Are. v, Johnny Desmond and the Crew Chiefs, I Can't Give You Anything But Love, Baby. v impersonations of Louis Armstrong by Peanuts Hucko, Louis Armstrong trumpet impersonation by Bernie Privin, The Wang Wang Blues; Here We Go Again.

Side 7 Jeep Jockey Jump; Blues In My Heart; Juke Box Saturday Night. v, Artie Malvin and the Crew Chiefs, Harry James trumpet impersonation by Bobby Nichols; People Will Say We're In Love. v, Johnny Desmond; St Louis Blues March; Time Alone Will Tell. v, Bob Carroll; The Victory Polka. v, Johnny Desmond, the Crew Chiefs and the Band.

Side 8 The Army Air Corps Song. v, the Band; Suddenly It's Spring. v, Johnny Desmond; I Love You. v, Johnny Desmond; *Medley*: Long Long Ago, The Music Stopped. V, Johnny Desmond, The Dipsey Doodle; Wabash Blues; Everybody Loves My Baby.

Side 9 Enlisted Men's Mess; Absent Minded. v, Johnny Desmond; My Blue Heaven; I've Got Sixpence. v, Artie Malvin and the Band; Begin The Beguine; Blue Is The Night; In The Mood; Oh What A Beautiful Morning. v, Johnny Desmond and the Crew Chiefs.

Side 10 Tail End Charlie; Speak Low v, Johnny Desmond *Medley*: Londonderry Air, Shoo Shoo Baby, v, Artie Malvin and the Crew Chiefs, The Way You Look Tonight, The Blue Danube; Pistol Packing Mama. v, Carmen Mastren, Ray McKinley and the Crew Chiefs.

The collection was also issued as an album of fifteen 7″ Extended Play records (minus The Wang Wang Blues and The Blue Danube), catalogue number Victor EPOT-6702.

Late in 1955 RCA Victor in New York produced a special sales promotion package to publicize the Army Air Force Band album and to tie in with their fiftieth anniversary celebrations. This package consisted of a booklet about the Band and a specially produced 7 inch 45 r.p.m. record containing material which was not included in the album. The booklet was entitled 'Where Is The Band Today' and included brief notes on what the men in the Band had been doing since the end of the war and contemporary photographs of most of them. It also contained a large wartime photograph of the whole Band gathered in front of a Flying Fortress 'somewhere in England'. The record contained the following items:

Side 1 – A BBC interview between Major Glenn Miller and Vernon Harris dated 15 September 1944, and lasting approximately two minutes. This interview was in fact the one recorded for 'The Wishing Well' in the weekly BBC programme 'Here's Wishing You Well Again' (*see* page 148) and was actually broadcast on 21 September 1944, in the General Forces Programme and the AEF Programme; the interview was probably recorded on 14 September, not the 15th.

The Band playing 'With My Head In The Clouds', v by Sgt Johnny Desmond and the Crew Chiefs (*part only*).

Side 2 – 'Moonlight Serenade' (*part only*); 'Symphony', v. Johnny Desmond (*part only*); *Theme*: 'I Sustain The Wings' and closing announcment by Captain Glenn Miller from the Band's last broadcast in the USA on 10 June 1944, before leaving for the European Theater of Operations.

The booklet and the record were only available for a short time and are now very rare.

In September 1956 the complete Army Air Force Band album (five LPS, not the Extended Play version) was issued in Great Britain by His Master's Voice and in other 'HMV countries', with the catalogue number HMV Record Library Series No. 637; unfortunately the booklet and the EP were not.

The complete Glenn Miller Army Air Force Band album has not been available in either the USA or Great Britain for many years. However, from time to time single LPS containing selected items from the album have been issued both in the USA and Great Britain. Many of these have also been deleted from the issuing companies' catalogues but at the time of writing (May 1986) the following were available:

'This Is Glenn Miller and the Army Air Force Band' (double album)
Side 1 – Flying Home; Holiday For Strings; Sun Valley Jump; Farewell Blues; Everybody Loves My Baby.
Side 2 – St Louis Blues March; This Is A Lovely Way To Spend An Evening; The Anvil Chorus; I Love You; Begin The Beguine.
Side 3 – Stardust; Tuxedo Junction; Blues In My Heart; Song Of The Volga Boatmen; Stormy Weather.
Side 4 – Juke Box Saturday Night; In The Mood; Poinciana; Mission to Moscow; Tail-End Charlie.
Catalogue number: RCA VPM-6080 (USA); RCA DHY-0004 (Gt Britain).
'Glenn Miller and the Army Air Force Band. A Legendary Performer, Vol 3'*
Side 1 – Over There; Stardust; I've Got A Heart Filled With Love For You; *Medley*: Londonderry Air, Shoo Shoo Baby, The Way You Look Tonight, The Blue Danube; The Victory Polka.
Side 2 – St Louis Blues March; Stormy Weather; Mission To Moscow; Long Ago and Far Away; Pistol Packing Mama; Flying Home.
Catalogue number: RCA CPL1-2495 (USA); RCA PL-12495 (Gt Britain).
'Glenn Miller and the Army Air Force Band'. (Jazz Tribune Series No. 15) (double album).
French LP: RCA Black and White NL-89767(2).
Side 1 – Over There; Anvil Chorus; Stardust; Song of the Volga Boatmen; Farewell Blues; There Are Yanks; My Ideal.
Side 2 – Mission To Moscow; Sun Valley Jump; Tuxedo Junction; I'll

---

* Volumes 1 and 2 contained recordings by the pre-war civilian Miller Band.

397

Be Around; Poinciana; I Hear You Screaming; Juke Box Saturday Night; My Blue Heaven.

Side 3 – St Louis Blues March; It Must Be Jelly; Blues In My Heart; Everybody Loves My Baby; *Medley*: Alexander's Ragtime Band, Stomping At The Savoy, Deep Purple, Don't Be That Way, I Can't Give You Anything But Love, Wang Wang Blues, Shoo Shoo Baby, The Way You Look Tonight.

Side 4 – Victory Polka; There'll Be A Hot Time In The Town Of Berlin; Flying Home; Here We Go Again; Jeep Jockey Jump; Enlisted Men's Mess; Begin The Beguine; In The Mood.

US Air Force Museum Records.

Starting in 1976, the Gift Shop of the US Air Force Museum at the Wright-Patterson Air Force Base near Dayton, Ohio, began to sell long-playing records of the Army Air Forces Band specially made for them by RCA Victor in New York and containing selections from the original five-record album issued by RCA Victor in 1956. To date, two such LPs have been made available by the museum:

'The Glenn Miller Army Air Force Band'

Side 1 – Stardust; *Medley*: Long Long Ago, The Music Stopped, The Dipsey Doodle, Wabash Blues; My Ideal; I Hear You Screaming; This Is A Lovely Way To Spend An Evening; What Do You Do In The Infantry; Speak Low.

Side 2 – Poinciana; Tuxedo Junction; Long Ago And Far Away; Pistol Packing Mama; My Blue Heaven; St. Louis Blues March; The Victory Polka.

Catalogue number: DLP-1-0194 (electronic stereo).

'The Major Glenn Miller Army Air Force Band. Volume II'

Side 1 – Begin The Beguine; *Medley*: Flow Gently Sweet Afton, Moondreams, Don't Be That Way, Blue Champagne; Peggy The Pin-Up Girl; Suddenly It's Spring; Juke Box Saturday Night; Mission To Moscow; There Are Yanks.

Side 2 – Holiday For Strings; In The Mood; I'll Be Around; Pearls On Velvet; Jeep Jockey Jump; Absent Minded; The GI Jive; The Anvil Chorus.

Catalogue number: DLP-1-0314; (electronic stereo).

Starting in July 1980, the Museum Gift Shop made available three more LPs. However, these records consist of new material never before issued by RCA Victor and like the two previous records are available exclusively from the Museum Gift Shop:

'The Glenn Miller Army Air Force Band. Volume III'

Side 1 – *Theme*: I Sustain The Wings *and* Moonlight Serenade.; In The Mood, announced by Captain Glenn Miller [From radio broadcast, USA, 1943]; Irresistible You. V, Johnny Desmond and the Crew Chiefs.; 9.20 Special; Songs My Mother Taught Me; Bubble Bath; *Medley*: A Fellow

On A Furlough. v, Johnny Desmond *and* Guns In The Sky. v, Johnny Desmond and Band, announced by Captain Glenn Miller; Along The Santa Fe Trail. v, Johnny Desmond.

Side 2 – *Theme*: Moonlight Serenade *and* introduction spoken by Captain Glenn Miller. [From radio broadcast, England, 20 July 1944]; Caribbean Clipper; Why Dream? v, Johnny Desmond; 705; *Medley*: I've Got The Blues. v, Johnny Desmond *and* With My Head In The Clouds. v, Artie Malvin, Johnny Desmond and the Crew Chiefs [From radio broadcasts, London, 27 Apr 1945 (pre-recorded Paris, 9 Apr 1945) and 1 May 1945 (pre-recorded Paris, 9 Apr 1945]; Now I Know. v, Johnny Desmond; announced by Captain Glenn Miller [From radio broadcast, New York, 1944]; Cherokee. Announced by Captain Glenn Miller [From radio broadcast, New York, 1944]; More and More. v, Johnny Desmond [From radio broadcast London, 27 Apr 1945 (pre-recorded Paris, 9 Apr 1945)]; The Squadron Song. v, Johnny Desmond and the Band; Closing announcement by Captain Glenn Miller.; BBC announcement of Major Glenn Miller's disappearance on 15 Dec 1944. [This is a 'reconstruction', recorded in December 1954, not the original broadcast in 1944.]

'Major Glenn Miller Army Air Force Band. Volume IV'

Side 1 – 'I Sustain The Wings' radio broadcast excerpts—
Theme: (I Sustain The Wings) and introduction by Captain Glenn Miller (26 Feb 1944); A String Of Pearls. (22 Apr 1944); Symphony. v, Johnny Desmond. (17 Nov 1945); The Dipsey Doodle. (8 Jan 1944); *Theme*: (I Sustain The Wings). German Propaganda Broadcast excerpts—
Theme: (Moonlight Serenade) and introduction by Major Glenn Miller and Ilse. (November 6, 1944); Here We Go Again (6 Nov 1944); All The Things You Are. v, Johnny Desmond (in German) (27 Nov 1944); Beat Me Daddy Eight to The Bar. v, Ray McKinley (27 Nov 1944); Moonlight Serenade (30 Oct 1944).

(*Note* – the dates given above which appear on the record sleeve are the dates the music was recorded: the actual broadcasts were made shortly afterwards (*see* Part 2).)

Side 2 – 'The Swing Shift' broadcast excerpts—
Theme: (Get Along Song). v, Ray McKinley. (4 Dec 1944); Snafu Jump. (4 Dec 1944); You, Fascinating You. v, Johnny Desmond. (5 Apr 1945); Waiting For The Evening Mail. v, Ray McKinley. (20 Apr 1945); How Blue The Night. v, Johnny Desmond. (1st part 11 Apr 1945; 2nd part 8 Mar 1945); *Theme*: (Get Along Song). v, Ray McKinley. (18 Aug 1944). 'Strings With Wings' broadcast excerpts—
Theme: (I Sustain The Wings); The Song Is You. (31 May 1945) *Theme*: (I Sustain The Wings) and dialogue by Paul Dudley [*not* Paul Dubov, as given on the record sleeve]. (15 May 1945).

'The Uptown Hall' broadcast excerpts—
Theme: (My Guy's Come Back) (6 Dec 1944) One, Two, Button Your Shoe. (9 Dec 1944).

Closing dialogue by Paul Dudley [*not* Keith Jamieson, as given on the record sleeve]. (3 Dec 1944).

Tribute by President Eisenhower.

(*Note* – the dates for Side 2 given above which appear on the record sleeve are the dates the music was recorded; for the dates it was actually broadcast, *see* Part 2; the tribute by President Eisenhower comes from a radio tribute to Glenn Miller broadcast in the USA).

Major Glenn Miller Army Air Force Band, Volume V'

Side 1 – German Propaganda Broadcast (announcements by Major Glenn Miller and Ilse); *Theme*: (Moonlight Serenade) (6 Nov 1944); American Patrol (6 Nov 1944); Is You Is Or Is You Ain't My Baby? v, Ray McKinley (30 Oct 1944); My Heart Tells Me. v, Johnny Desmond (6 Nov 1944); Cow Cow Boogie. v, Ray McKinley (20 Nov 1944); *Theme*: (Moonlight Serenade) (20 Oct 1944) [actually, 30 Oct?]; 'The Swing Shift' broadcast—

Theme: (Howdy Friends) v, Ray McKinley (20 Apr 1945); Tail End Charlie (date unknown); And Her Tears Flowed Like Wine. v, Ray McKinley (9 Apr 1945); Speak Low. v, Johnny Desmond (date unknown).

Side 2 – Drums Away (6 Mar 1945); The Red Cavalry March (3 Apr 1945); Chattanooga Choo Choo. v, Ray McKinley and the Crew Chiefs (3 May 1944); The Trolley Song. v, Johnny Desmond and the Crew Chiefs (9 Apr 1945); Long Ago And Far Away. v, Johnny Desmond (date unknown); The Eyes And Ears Of The World (5 Apr 1945); *Theme*: (The Git Along Song) v, Ray McKinley (date unknown).

(*Note* – the dates given above which appear on the record sleeve are the dates the music was recorded; for the dates it was actually broadcast, *see* Part 2).

Other Records

Although the original RCA Victor five-LP album remains the most comprehensive recorded collection of the Band, in recent years numerous LPS have been issued by small specialist companies in Great Britain and other countries. They contain a variety of material from broadcasts and transcription recordings; some of the items are alternative performances of tunes in the Victor album, while others are previously unissued tunes some of which the Band did not play until they were in the ETO.

The following LPS have been issued to date:

'Mostly Swinging! Fifteen Melodies Played by the Army Air Force Training Command [*sic*] Under the Direction of Captain Glenn Miller'
Swedish LP: Phontastic NOPH 1

Side 1 – *Theme*: I Sustain The Wings [From OWI Program No. 15]; 705 [From OWI Program No. 15]; Swing Low Sweet Chariot [From OWI Program No. 18]; There'll Be A Hot Time In The Town Of Berlin. v, Ray McKinley and the Crew Chiefs. [From OWI Programme No. 15];

Lady Be Good [From OWI Program No. 17]; Long Tall Mama [From OWI Program No. 18]; Along The Santa Fe Trail. v, Johnny Desmond [From OWI Program No. 15]; Everybody Loves My Baby [From OWI Program No. 16];

Side 2 – 9.20 Special [From OWI Program No. 17]; Our Waltz [*string section only*) [From OWI Program No. 18]; Bubble Bath [From OWI Program No. 16]; The Way You Look Tonight [From OWI Program No. 17]; Going My Way. v, Johnny Desmond [From OWI Program No. 17]; Here We Go Again [From OWI Program No. 20]; Goodnight Wherever You Are. v, Johnny Desmond and the Crew Chiefs [From OWI Program No. 20].

'Keep On Flying' – Major Glenn Miller and the Army Air Force Band

British LP: Swing world sws 5

Side 1 – *Theme*: I Sustain The Wings and Jeep Jockey Jump. Announced by Captain Glenn Miller [From radio broadcast, USA, 1944]; Now I Know. v, Johnny Desmond. Announced by Captain Glenn Miller [From radio broadcast, USA 1944]; Put Your Arms Around Me, Honey. v, Crew Chiefs and the Band; Keep 'Em flying; Music Makers; The Squadron Song. v, Johnny Desmond and the Band.

Side 2 – 705; Bubble Bath; Guns In The Sky. v, Johnny Desmond and the Crew Chiefs. Announced by Captain Glenn Miller [From radio broadcast, USA 1944]; A Fellow On A Furlough. v, Johnny Desmond; Little Brown Jug; Why Dream? v, Johnny Desmond; Passage Interdit; *Closing theme* I Sustain The Wings and announcement by Captain Glenn Miller; last few bars of My Buddy.

'Glenn Miller Army Air Force Band 1943/44. Rare performances. First Time On Record!'

Rarities No. 63 [*see* also Sandy Hook LP page 404]

Side A – *Radio broadcast*, USA October 1943 [all items announced by Captain Glenn Miller]: *Theme*: I Sustain The Wings; The Anvil Chorus; Stormy Weather; Juke Box Saturday Night. v, the Crew Chiefs; *Theme*: I Sustain The Wings; *Radio broadcast*, USA October 1943 [all items announced by Captain Glenn Miller]: *Theme*: I Sustain The Wings; Jeep Jockey Jump; All The Things You Are; Song Of The Volga Boatmen; With My Head In The Clouds. v, Artie Malvin and the Crew Chiefs; *Theme*: I Sustain The Wings.

Side B – *Radio broadcast*,USA March 1944 [all items announced by Captain Glenn Miller]: *Theme*: I Sustain The Wings; I Hear You Screaming; Long Ago And Far Away. v, Johnny Desmond; Cherokee; Peggy The Pin-Up Girl. v, Ray McKinley and the Crew Chiefs; *Theme*: I Sustain The Wings. *Radio broadcast*, USA February 1944 [all items announced by Captain Glenn Miller]: *Theme*: I Sustain The Wings; In The Mood; Holiday For Strings; String Of Pearls; Don't Be That Way; *Theme*: I Sustain The Wings. (*Note* – this programme seems to be a composite one from different dates).

'American Rhapsody. Major Glenn Miller and the Army Air Force Band'
British LP: Swing World sws 11
Side 1 – Rhapsody In Blue (Recorded New York, 27 May 1944); Symphony. v Johnny Desmond (Recorded New York, 13 Oct 1945); El Capitan. (Recorded New York, 29 Oct 1943); In The Gloaming (Recorded New York, 20 May 1944); Deep Purple (Recorded New York, 20 May 1944); *Medley*: Killarney, I've Got A Heart Filled With Love For You. v, Bob Carroll and the Crew Chiefs, Moonlight Serenade, Wabash Blues; [Medley announced by Captain Glenn Miller] (from a radio broadcast, New York, 8 Apr 1944).
Side 2 – Oranges And Lemons. v, Johnny Desmond and the Crew Chiefs (Recorded New York, 13 Oct 1945); Buckle Down Winsocki (Recorded New York, 29 Oct 1943); Stealing Apples (Recorded New York, 21 Jan 1944); The Red Cavalry March. [Announced by Paul Dudley; from a radio broadcast, London, 24 Apr 1945] (pre-recorded Paris, 3 Apr 1945).
(*Note* – Recording dates and places are as given on the record sleeve)
'Glenn Miller Army Air Force Band 1943/44. Rare Performances. First Time On Record!' Volume 2.
Rarities No. 68
Side A – Flying Home; Sleepy Town Train; Things Ain't What They Used To Be; American Patrol; Homesick, That's All. v, Johnny Desmond; St Louis Blues; The Anvil Chorus.
Side B – Snafu Jump; Serenade In Blue; Coming In On A Wing And A Prayer (v, The Glee Club); Blue Again; The Dipsey Doodle; Annie Laurie; It Must Be Jelly; Moonlight Serenade.
(*Note* – No recording dates or places – or even vocalists! – are given on the sleeve of this LP.)
'Glenn Miller Army Air Force Band 1943/44. Rare Performances. First Time On Record!' Volume 3.
Rarities No. 72
Side A – Blue Skies; The More I See You. v, Johnny Desmond; Here We Go Again; Begin The Beguine. v, Tony Martin; Little Brown Jug; I Don't Want To Be Loved. v, Johnny Desmond; Jingle Bells. v, Artie Malvin and the Crew Chiefs; Swing Low Sweet Chariot.
Side B – Passage Interdit; I've Got A Heart Filled With Love For You. v, Artie Malvin and the Crew Chiefs; Put Your Arms Around Me Honey. v, Crew Chiefs and the Band; Great Day; Embraceable You (*String section only*); Caribbean Clipper; Blue Moon; Tail End Charlie; Bubble Bath.
(*Note* – No vocalists are given on the sleeve of this LP, neither are places or dates of recording except that the last two titles are said to have been recorded in April 1945 with the Band directed by Sgt Ray McKinley: they probably originate from a 'Swing Shift' radio pre-recording made on 17 April 1945, and first broadcast on 19 May 1945.)
'Major Glenn Miller and the Army Air Force Band. Golden Serenade'
British LP: Swing World sws 1

Side 1 – Moonlight Serenade [mistakenly given as Serenade In Blue on the sleeve and the record label]; Take It Easy. v, the Crew Chiefs; Snafu Jump; Later Tonight. v, Johnny Desmond and the Crew Chiefs; Mood Indigo; If That's The Way You Want It Baby. v, the Crew Chiefs; Blue Skies; It's Love, Love, Love. v, the Crew Chiefs; Blue Orchids. v, Johnny Desmond; Smoke Gets In Your Eyes.

Side 2 – If You Please. v, Tony Martin and Glee Club; You'll Never Know. v, Tony Martin; Schubert's Serenade; Loch Lomond; Coming In On A Wing And A Prayer. v, Tony Martin and the Band; Sunday, Monday or Always. v, Tony Martin; Star Eyes. v, Bob Carroll; Drink To Me Only; My Heart Tells Me. v, Johnny Desmond, announced by Captain Glenn Miller; Music Makers; Blue Moon.

(*Note* – No recording dates or places are given on the sleeve of this LP.)

Major Glenn Miller and the Army Air Force Band. 'Silver Serenade'
British LP: Swing World SWS 2

Side 1 – Poinciana. v, Johnny Desmond and the Crew Chiefs; Serenade In Blue; Easter parade. v, Johnny Desmond and the Crew Chiefs; Paper Doll. v, the Crew Chiefs; White Christmas; The Spirit Is Willing; Silent Night; Blue Rain.

Side 2 – Chattanooga Choo Choo. v, Ray McKinley and the Crew Chiefs; St Louis Blues; My Buddy; Body And Soul; Songs My Mother Taught Me; I Never Mention Your Name [wrongly listed as I'll Never Mention Your Name]. v, Tony Martin and the Glee Club; I'll Be Home For Christmas. v, Johnny Desmond; 705 [wrongly listed as Here We Go Again] [incomplete].

(*Note* – No recording dates or places are given on the sleeve of this LP.)

'Glenn Miller On V-Disc. Glenn Miller and AAFTC Orchestra Featuring Ray McKinley and Johnny Desmond.'
Japanese LP: Dan Records VC-5025

Side A – Peggy The Pin-Up Girl. v, Ray McKinley and the Crew Chiefs (V-Disc 533A); Songs My Mother Taught Me (V-Disc 533A); Symphony. v, Johnny Desmond (V-Disc 601A); I've Got A Heart Filled With Love For You Dear. v, Johnny Desmond, Artie Malvin and the Crew Chiefs (V-Disc 381A); Holiday For Strings (V-Disc 421A); Wang Wang Blues (V-Disc 466A);

Side B – Passage Interdit (V-Disc 587A); The Army Air Corps Song. v, Johnny Desmond and the Band (V-Disc 504A); I Hear You Screaming (V-Disc 504A); Why Dream. v, Johnny Desmond (V-Disc 587A); *Medley*: Going Home, Honeysuckle Rose, My Blue Heaven (V-Disc 123A); St Louis Blues [actually St Louis Blues March] (V-Disc 522A).

'Glenn Miller and his Army Air Force Orchestra'
American LP: Soundcraft 1004; British LP: Jasmine JASM 2503.

Side 1 – 10 June 1944 – War Bond Rally, Chicago Theatre ['I Sustain The Wings' broadcast; all items announced by Captain Glenn Miller]: *Theme*: I Sustain The Wings; Flying Home; Long Ago And Far Away. v,

Johnny Desmond; *Medley*: My Buddy, Now I Know. v, Johnny Desmond, Music Makers, Farewell Blues; Poinciana. v, Johnny Desmond and the Crew Chiefs; *Theme*: I Sustain The Wings, and farewell announcement by Captain Glenn Miller before the Band goes overseas.

Side 2 – 'I Sustain The Wings' Broadcast, 15 April 1944 [all items announced by Captain Glenn Miller]: *Theme*: I Sustain The Wings; Caribbean Clipper; The Air Force Song and aerial photo drama; *Medley*: Songs My Mother Taught Me, It's Love, Love, Love. v, The Crew Chiefs, In An Eighteenth Century Drawing Room, Blue Orchids. v, Bob Carroll; WAC Recruit Spot; There Are Yanks. v, Ray McKinley and the Crew Chiefs; *Theme*: I Sustain The Wings and closing announcements.

'Glenn Miller Army Air Force Orchestra'
American LP: Soundcraft 1005; British LP: Jasmine JASM 2504.
Side 1 – November 1944 – Propaganda Broadcasts ['Music For The Wehrmacht']; *Theme*: Moonlight Serenade; In The Mood; Stardust; Now I Know. v, Johnny Desmond; String Of Pearls; BBC Interview between Major Glenn Miller and Vernon Harris for 'The Wishing Well', September 15th 1944 [actually broadcast 21 September and probably recorded on 14 September not 15th – *see* page 148].

Side 2 – Propaganda Broadcasts (*continued*); Poinciana. v, Artie Malvin and the Crew Chiefs; Long Ago And Far Away. v, Johnny Desmond; Is You Is Or Is You Ain't My Baby v, Ray McKinley; Great Day; BBC News announcement, 24 Dec 1944, that Major Miller was reported lost. [This is a 'reconstruction', recorded in December 1954, not the original broadcast in 1944.]

'Uncle Sam Presents The Band of the Army Air Forces Training Command under the Direction of Captain Glenn Miller – Four Complete 1943 and 1944 Broadcasts'
American LP: Sandy Hook SH 2055. Sandy Hook Release No. 55
(*Note* – this LP contains exactly the same recordings as are on Rarities LP No. 63 (*see* page 401.)

'Hallelujah. The Glenn Miller Service Orchestra in the USA and Europe'
British LP: Magic AWE 6
Side 1 – Radio broadcast excerpts: Hallelujah (16 Oct 1943); Now We Know. v, Tony Martin and the Crew Chiefs (7 Aug 1943); *Medley*: Caprice Viennoise, Sunday, Monday or Always. v, Artie Malvin, My Isle Of Golden Dreams, Birth Of The Blues, (6 Nov 1943, announced by Captain Glenn Miller); Irresistible You. v, Bob Carroll (25 Mar 1944); Time Alone Will Tell. v, Johnny Desmond (27 May 1944); In My Arms. v, Ensemble (7 Aug 1943); Alouette. v, Artie Malvin and Glee Club (31 July 1943); Tuxedo Junction (13 Oct 1945).
Side 2 – King Porter Stomp (15 Mar 1945) ['Swing Shift']; Wham. v, Ray McKinley and the Crew Chiefs (24 May 1945) ['Swing Shift']; The Way You Look Tonight. v, Johnny Desmond (15 May 1945) ('Strings With Wings'); In The Middle Of May. v, Johnny Desmond and the

Crew Chiefs [given on the record sleeve as 20 May 1945, but this is incorrect]; Watcha Know Joe. v, Ray McKinley and the Band (5 Apr 1945) ['Swing Shift']; Somebody's Wrong. (7 Dec 1944) ['Swing Shift']; Oh, Lady Be Good. (20 Feb 1945) (Trio: Carmen Mastren guitar, Phil Cogliano (Phil Marino), violin, and Trigger Alpert, bass; from a 'Swing Shift' programme); Spanish Shawl. (15 Mar 1945) ['Swing Shift'].

(*Note* – The dates for Side 2 given above which appear on the record sleeve are the dates the music was recorded; for the dates it was actually broadcast, *see* Part 2).

'Bing Crosby with Glenn Miller and the American Band of the Allied Expeditionary Forces Orchestra' [*sic*]

American LP: Broadway Intermission BR-114

Side 1 – Recording of AEFP broadcast, London (Paris Cinema studio), Thursday, 31 Aug 1944, 8.30–9.00 p.m.; *Theme*: Moonlight Serenade; Here We Go Again; Long Ago And Far Away. v, Bing Crosby; *Medley*: My Buddy, Amor, Amor. v, Bing Crosby, Music Makers; Farewell Blues; Swinging On A Star. v, Bing Crosby and The Crew Chiefs; accompanied by the Swing Sextet; Poinciana. v, Bing Crosby and The Crew Chiefs; *Theme*: Moonlight Serenade.

(*Note* – all the items in the programme are introduced by Major Glenn Miller, who also chats with Bing Crosby.)

Side 2 – Miscellaneous recordings of Bing Crosby – not with the Miller Band.

'Glenn Miller and his AAF Band'

British LP: Spectrum B.92.93

Side 1 – Put Your Arms Around Me Honey. v, The Crew Chiefs; The Dipsey Doodle; Sun Valley Jump; In The Mood – AFRS Transcription P-292.*

String Of Pearls; Cherokee; American Patrol – AFRS Transcription P-293*.

Side 2 – Anvil Chorus – AFRS Transcription P-293;* Song Of The Volga Boatmen; Annie Laurie; I Hear Ya Screamin'; Snafu Jump – AFRS Transcription P-279*

Juke Box Saturday Night. v, The Crew Chiefs; There Are Yanks. v, Ray McKinley and The Crew Chiefs; AFRS Transcription P-298*

'Swingin' With Glenn Miller and his Orchestra "Live"' [Actually Captain Glenn Miller and the Army Air Forces Training Command Orchestra] (*Limited Edition*)

American LP Marshmallow MMLP-103

Side 1 – Pearls On Velvet; *Medley*: Annie Laurie, My Ideal. v, Johnny Desmond, Alexander's Ragtime Band, Blue As The Night Above Me; The Victory Polka. v, Johnny Desmond and the Crew Chiefs, [From 'I Sustain The Wings' radio broadcast, 29 Jan 1944; announcements by

* See page 391

405

Captain Glenn Miller].

It Must Be Jelly; *Medley*: Mother Macree, I Couldn't Sleep A Wink Last Night, v, Johnny Desmond and The Crew Chiefs, I Can't Give You Anything But Love, Baby. v, Peanuts Hucko; Wang Wang Blues, I've Got A Heart Filled With Love. v, Johnny Desmond, Artie Malvin and The Crew Chiefs [From 'I Sustain The Wings' radio broadcast, 13 May 1944].

Side 2 – *Theme*: I Sustain The Wings; Tail End Charlie; My Ideal. v, Johnny Desmond; Sleepy Town Train; *Medley*: Going Home, Paper Doll. v, The Crew Chiefs, Honeysuckle Rose, My Blue Heaven; What Do You do In The Infantry. v, The Crew Chiefs and the Band [From 'I Sustain The Wings' radio broadcast, 4 Dec 1943; announcements by Captain Glenn Miller.]

Symphony To A Lost Love [This isn't actually on the record, although listed on the sleeve]; Pistol Packin' Mama. v, Carmen Mastren, Ray McKinley and The Crew Chiefs.

'The Glenn Miller Service Orchestra in the USA and Europe. Vol 2 Autumn Serenade'

British LP: Magic AWE 9 (also cassette CAWE 9)

Side 1 – Snafu Jump (recorded 26 Feb 1944); I Don't Want To Be Loved. v, Johnny Desmond (recorded 6 Oct 1945); American Patrol (recorded 6 Nov 1943); Summertime (recorded 6 Nov 1944); Have Ya Got Any Gum, Chum?.v, Murray Kane and The Crew Chiefs (recorded 3 Nov 1945); All Through The Night (recorded early 1944); Autumn Serenade. v, Johnny Desmond (recorded 3 Nov 1945).

Side 2 – Caribbean Clipper (recorded 11 Feb 1944); Chattanooga Choo Choo. v, Ray McKinley and The Crew Chiefs (recorded 3 June 1944); Enlisted Men's Mess (recorded 19 May 1944); My Prayer. v, Johnny Desmond (recorded 9 Apr 1945); Moonlight Serenade (recorded 30 Oct 1944); The Trolley Song. v, Johnny Desmond and The Crew Chiefs (Recorded 9 Apr 1945).

(*Note* – Recording dates are as given on the record sleeve. 'Summertime' and 'Moonlight Serenade' are actually from 'Music For The Wehrmacht' programmes; 'My Prayer' and 'The Trolley Song' are from two different AEFP broadcasts pre-recorded on 9 Apr and broadcast respectively on 1 May 1945, and 27 Apr 1945; 'Chattanooga Choo Choo' is the recording used on V-Disc 281A (actually a rehearsal for an 'I Sustain The Wings' programme; most of the other items are from 'I Sustain The Wings' programmes.)

'Glenn Miller and the Army Air Force Band featuring Mel Powell. Swing and Sweet'

Swedish LP: Phontastic NOST-7651

Side 1 – Caribbean Clipper; Song Of The Volga Boatmen; Snafu Jump; Stormy Weather; Over There [v, The Band]; Sun Valley Jump; Here We Go Again; American Patrol.

Side 2 – In The Mood; With My Head In The Clouds. [v, Artie Malvin and the Crew Chiefs]; Stealin' Apples; Jeep Jockey Jump; Songs My Mother Taught Me; Tail End Charlie; Poinciana [v, Johnny Desmond and the Crew Chiefs]; It Must Be Jelly.

(*Note* – No recording dates or places are given on the sleeve of this LP, beyond saying that all recordings were probably made from late autumn 1943 to June 1944.)

'The Glenn Miller Service Orchestra in the USA and Europe. Volume 3. 40th Anniversary Album. Get Happy'

British LP Magic AWE 11 (also Cassette CAWE 11)

Side 1 – Anvil Chorus. Announced by Captain Glenn Miller. (Recorded [*From a live broadcast*], 20 July 1944), [AEF Band]; I Only Have Eyes For You. v, Johnny Desmond (20 Oct 1945); Limehouse Blues (Spring 1945); Parachute Jump (*Boogie Woogie Quartet*) 1 Dec1944* [From an AEF Band broadcast]; Accentuate The Positive. v, Ray McKinley and the Crew Chiefs (6 Oct 1945); Blue Rain (17 Nov 1944), [AEF Band]; Measure For Measure (Spring 1945).

Side 2 – Down The Road A-Piece. v, Ray McKinley and [Trigger Alpert], (17 Nov 1944), [AEF Band]; Annie Laurie (Strings only) (26 May 1944); Get Happy (27 Nov 1944), [AEF Band, from a 'Music For The Wehrmacht' programme]; My Guy's Come Back (5 Apr 1945)* ['Swing Shift']; I Dream Of You. v, Johnny Desmond (5 Apr 1945)* ['Swing Shift']; Train 88 (*Boogie Woogie Trio*) (6 Mar 1945)* [From a 'Swing Shift' broadcast]; Anchors Aweigh [25 Nov 1944)* [AEF Band].

(*Note* – For titles marked * the dates given above which appear on the record sleeve are the dates the music was recorded; for the dates it was actually broadcast *see* Part 2.)

'Piano Forte' Mel Powell and his Uptown Hall Gang

Swedish LP: Phontastic NOST-7649

Side 1 – The Earl. Announced by Paul Dubov. (28 July 1944)*; Sweet Lorraine. Announced by Paul Dubov. (28 July 1944)*; Lady Be Good. Announced by Paul Dubov. [Given on the record sleeve as 26 Sept and 3 December 1944, but both dates are incorrect! Probably pre-recorded on 6 Dec 1944]*; Making Whoopee. Announced by Paul Dubov. (9 Aug 1944); Blue Skies. Announced by Paul Dubov. (9 Aug 1944); Confessing. Announced by Paul Dubov. (9 Aug 1944); As Long As I Live. Announced by Paul Dubov.; I'll Remember April. Announced by Paul Dubov. (9 Aug 1944).

Side 2 – One Two Button Your Shoe (9 Dec 1944)*; Way Down Yonder In New Orleans. Announced by Paul Dudley (9 Dec 1944)*; Shandy. Announced by Paul Dubov. [Given as 3 Dec 1944, but this is incorrect; probably pre-recorded on 6 Dec 1944]*; Triple X. Announced by Paul Dudley and Mel Powell. (9 Dec 1944)*; Please Don't Talk About Me When I'm Gone. Announced by Paul Dubov. [Given as 3 Dec 1944, but this is incorrect; probably pre-recorded on 6 Dec 1944]*; Sweet Georgia

Brown. Announced by Paul Dudley. (9 Dec 1944)*; Night In Tunisia. Announced by Paul Dudley.; *Theme*: My Guy's Come Back, and closing announcement by Paul Dubov. [Given as 3 Dec 1944, but this is incorrect; probably pre-recorded on 6 Dec 1944, and broadcast on 7 Feb 1945]*.

(*Note* – The dates listed above are as given on the record sleeve, with corrections noted where required; dates marked * are dates the music was recorded – for the dates it was broadcast *see* Part 2.)

'A Soldier and a Song' Johnny Desmond (1920–1985) with the Glenn Miller Service Orchestra 1943–45 Memorial Album

British LP: Magic AWE-16 (also cassette CAWE-16)

Side 1 – Long Ago And Far Away. Announced by Captain Glenn Miller. (New York, 20 Apr 1944); Indian Summer (accompanied by the Strings With Wings). (Paris, 31 May 1945)*; I'm Through With Love (accompanied by the Swing Sextet, led by Sgt Mel Powell) (Bedford, 3 Dec 1944)*; In The Blue Of Evening (New York, 23 Oct 1943); Speak Low. (Newark, New Jersey, 19 May 1944); Amor, Amor. ('new' tune from medley). Announced by Captain Glenn Miller. (New York, 3 June 1944); I'll Be Seeing You. (Paris, 22 Jan 1945)*; Moondreams ('new' tune from medley). Announced by Captain Glenn Miller. (Bedford, 3 Aug 1944).

Side 2 – Going My Way. Announced by Captain Glenn Miller. (New York, 3 June 1944); The Music Stopped ('new' tune from medley) Announced by Major Glenn Miller. (Bedford, 24 Aug 1944); There Goes That Song Again ('new' tune from medley). Announced by Sgt Broderick Crawford. (Paris 4 June 1945)*; Laura. (Paris, 4 June 1945)*; Just The Way You Look Tonight (accompanied by the Strings With Wings). Anounced by WO Paul Dudley. (Paris, 15 May 1945)*; Blue Orchids ('blue' tune from medley) Announced by Major Glenn Miller. (Bedford, 7 Sept 1944); Embraceable You (accompanied by the American Dance Band) Announced by Sgt Ray McKinley. (Paris, 20 Apr 1945)*.

(*Note* – For titles marked * the dates given above which appear on the record sleeve are the dates the music was recorded; for the dates it was actually broadcast *see* Part 2.)

'Uncle Sam Presents' The Army Air Forces Training Command Orchestra Directed by Captain Glenn Miller.

British LP: HEP 32

Side 1 – *Theme*: I Sustain The Wings; Moonlight Serenade; American Patrol. Announced by Captain Glenn Miller. [From radio broadcast, New York, 1 Apr 1944]; People Will Say We're In Love. v, Tony Martin. [From 'I Sustain The Wings' broadcast, 24 July 1943]; Stealing Apples. [From OWI Programme 6 (24 Mar 1944)]; Moondreams. v, Johnny Desmond and The Crew Chiefs. (New York, 21 Jan 1944) [V-Disc 201]; Honeysuckle Rose. Announced By Captain Glenn Miller.

(From radio broadcast, New York, 4 Dec 1943); Rhapsody In Blue. Announced by Captain Glenn Miller. (From radio broadcast, New York, 18 Sept 1943). The Anvil Chorus. [from 'I Sustain The Wings' broadcast, 31 July 1943].

Side 2 – Buckle Down, Winsocki. (New York, 29 Oct 1943) [V-Disc 91]; Caribbean Clipper. [From 'Treasury Star Parade' broadcast], (New York, 11 Feb 1944); Speak Low. v, Johnny Desmond. Announced by Captain Glenn Miller [From 'Treasury Star Parade' broadcast], 11 Feb 1944); Sleepy Town Train. [From 'I Sustain the Wings' broadcast] (4 Dec 1943); Embraceable You (String Section Only). (New York, 21 Jan 1944) [V-Disc 183]; Blue Skies, [From 'I Sustain The Wings' broadcast, 24 July 1943]; Annie Laurie. [From radio broadcast, 18 Mar 1944]; Sun Valley Jump. (New York, 3 June 1944) [V-Disc 281: from an 'I Sustain The Wings' broadcast]; Moonlight Serenade ('concert' version). [From 'I Sustain The Wings' broadcast, 8 Apr 1944].

'Glenn Miller and his Army Air Force Orchestra – the 1943 Band in Hi-Fi'

American LP: Soundcraft LP-1015

Side 1 – Complete broadcast, 11 Dec 1943: *Theme*: 'I Sustain The Wings'; Moonlight Serenade; American Patrol; All The Things You Are; Song Of The Volga Boatmen; Holiday For Strings; Poinciana. v, Johnny Desmond and The Crew Chiefs; In The Mood; Sun Valley Jump; *Theme*: and Lady Be Good.

Side 2 – Complete broadcast, 4 Dec 1943: *Theme* 'I Sustain The Wings'; Tail End Charlie; My Ideal. v, Johnny Desmond; Honeysuckle Rose. Featuring Mel Powell, piano; What Do You Do In The Infantry. v, The Crew Chiefs; *Theme*: and Seven O Five.

(*Note* – although the date given on the record sleeve for the first programme is 11 Dec 1943, this is in fact a composite of several programmes.)

'Glenn Miller AEF Orchestra Directed by Ray McKinley on the Continent'

American LP: Soundcraft LP-1016

Side 1 – 'Swing Shift' programme 30 Apr 1945: *Theme*: 'The Git Along Song', v, Ray McKinley; I Hear You Screaming; Sleepy Town Train; You, Fascinating You. v, Johnny Desmond; S'Wonderful (*Trio*: Mel Powell, *piano*, Peanuts Hucko, *clarinet*, and Ray McKinley, *drums*); Nine Twenty Special.

Side 2 – She's Funny That Way. v, Johnny Desmond; Waiting For The Evening Mail. v, Ray McKinley; Eyes And Ears Of The World; *Theme*: 'The Git Along Song', v, Ray McKinley; 'Swing Shift' programme 24 May 1945 (*extracts*): Somebody's Wrong [not listed on the record sleeve]; Wham. v, Ray McKinley; Mission To Moscow; *Theme*: 'Git Along Song', v, Ray McKinley.

(*Note* – the programme dated 30 Apr 1945, was actually pre-recorded in

Paris on 5 Apr 1945, and first broadcast in the AEFP on 25 Apr 1945; the items dated 24 May 1945, are possibly from a pre-recording made on that date but not actually broadcast.)

'Glenn Miller Army Air Force Orchestra – Christmas Programme'
American LP: Soundcraft LP-1017
Side 1 – 'I Sustain The Wings' Christmas Programme, 18 Dec 1943: *Theme*: 'I Sustain The Wings'; I Hear You Screaming; *Medley*: In The Gloaming, For The First Time. v, Johnny Desmond, Stomping At The Savoy, Deep Purple; Air Force drama – 'Johnny The Kid Next Door'; Along The Santa Fe Trail. v, Johnny Desmond; WAC Promotion.
Side 2 – Oh What A Beautiful Morning. v, Johnny Desmond; – *Christmas Medley*: Silent Night; I'll Be Home For Christmas v, Johnny Desmond, Jingle Bells. v, The Crew Chiefs, White Christmas; American Patrol; *Theme*: 'I Sustain The Wings'.
(*Note* – the Christmas Medley and American Patrol were not part of the broadcast on 18 Dec)

'Major Glenn Miller and his Army Air Force Orchestra Present The Wehrmacht Hour' – American Broadcasting Station in Europe Propaganda Broadcasts, November 1944
American LP: Soundcraft LP-1018
Side 1 – *Theme*: 'Moonlight Serenade'; Here We Go Again; My Heart Tells Me. v, Johnny Desmond (sung in German); Anvil Chorus; Begin The Beguine; Song Of The Volga Boatmen; Summertime.
Side 2 – In The Mood; Stormy Weather; Smoke Gets In Your Eyes; Begin The Beguine. v, Irene Manning (sung in German); Little Brown Jug; Cherokee.

'My Guy's Come Back'. Glenn Miller's Uptown Hall Gang led by Mel Powell with Peanuts Hucko and Beryl Davis.
British LP: Esquire s 316
Side 1 – My Guy's Come Back (5 Feb 1945, from an AEF Band programme, broadcast 6 February 1945); S'Wonderful (*Quartet*); Sweet Georgia Brown; Please Don't Talk About Me When I'm Gone (last three, 9 December 1944, broadcast 14 December 1944); With Malice And No Thought (unknown date); Sweet Lorraine. v, Beryl Davis (6 September 1944, broadcast 20 September 1944); The Earl (28 July 1944, broadcast July 29 1944); Jerry's Aachen Back (*Quartet*) (25 November 1944 from an AEF Band programme, broadcast 2 January 1945); Powell Pow Wow (*piano solo*) (unknown date); The Blue Room (28 July 1944, broadcast 29 July 1944).
Side 2 – Way Down Yonder In New Orleans; Triple-X (last two 9 December 1944, broadcast 13 December 1944); Parachute Jump (*Quartet*) (1 December 1944, from an AEF Band programme broadcast 13 February 1945); Shandy (7 December 1944, broadcast 7 February 1945); What Is This Thing Called Love (*Quartet*) (6 September 1944, broadcast 20 September, 1944); I'll Remember April (9 August 1944,

broadcast 9 August 1944); Fruit Cake (*Trio*) (7 December, 1944, from a 'Swing Shift' programme, broadcast 27 February 1945); Left Swings Right (*piano solo*) (unknown date); Blow Top (12 August 1944, broadcast 18 August 1944); My Guy's Come Back (*closing theme*) (7 December 1944, broadcast 7 February 1945).

(*Note* – these recordings, except where stated otherwise, originate from 'Uptown Hall' broadcasts; the piano solos may be by Jack Rusin, not Powell; the announcer on the December 9 recordings is wo Paul Dudley, not Cpl Paul Dubov as stated on the record sleeve; 'Fruit Cake' was broadcast on 27 January, not 27 February.)

Major Glenn Miller, (Big Bands Half-Speed Masters) (double album)

American LP album: Time-Life STBB-17

Side 1 – Over There; GI Jive (last two, 8 January 1944); Peggy The Pin-Up Girl* (25 March5 1944); Speak Low* (12 February 1944); Tail End Charlie* (5 February 1944).

Side 2 – Anvil Chorus (18 March 1944); Oh, What A Beautiful Morning (18 December8 1943); There Are Yanks (19 February 1944); Pistol-Packing Mama (2 October 1943); Everybody Loves My Baby (Autumn, 1943 [or 20 May 1944?]).

Side 3 – Enlisted Men's Mess (22 January 1944); I'll Be Around* (25 December 1943); There'll Be A Hot Time In Berlin (22 April 1944); People Will Say We're In Love (December, 1943); Pearls On Velvet (19 February 1944).

Side 4 – St Louis Blues March (29 October 1943); Poinciana (8 April 1944); It Must Be Jelly* (14 October 1943); Jeep Jockey Jump* (12 February 1944); Victory Polka* (11 December 1943); Farewell Blues* (10 June, 1944).

(*Note* – These recordings were issued in the RCA Victor album Glenn Miller Army Air Force Band (*see* page 395), except that titles marked with * are different performances from those in the Victor album. All titles are followed by audience applause; there are no announcements. The dates above are as given in the Time-Life album.

The album is available only in the USA by mail order from Customer Services, Time-Life Music, 541 North Fairbanks Court, Chicago, Illinois 60611.)

Glenn Miller Army Air Force Orchestra. The Complete V-Disc Sessions. Volume 1.

American LP: Sounds Great SG-8013

Side 1 – Stardust; Buckle Down, Winsocki; El Capitan; St Louis Blues March; Stormy Weather; The Squadron Song.

Side 2 – Tail End Charlie; *Medley*: Going Home, Honeysuckle Rose, My Blue Heaven; Don't Be That Way; Blue Champagne; Embraceable You; GI Jive.

(*Note* – for details of all Miller AAF V-Discs *see* page 389.)

Glenn Miller and his Orchestra go to War [*sic*]

American LP: Radiola MR-1160

Side 1 – The German Wehrmacht Hour (November 1944). BBC Origination: In The Mood (*theme*); Stardust; Tuxedo Junction; Now I Know. v, Johnny Desmond (in German); String Of Pearls; Poinciana. v, Johnny Desmond and The Crew Chiefs; Long Ago And Far Away. v, Johnny Desmond (in German); Is You Is Or Is You Ain't My Baby? v, Ray McKinley.

Side 2 – The German Wehrmacht Hour continued: Great Day; Moonlight Serenade (*theme*); I Sustain The Wings. NBC net, May 6 1944: Caribbean Clipper; Now I Know. v, Johnny Desmond (in English); Salute to the Aerial Reconaissance Photographers, with Broderick Crawford; *Miller medley*: Songs My Mother Taught Me, It's Love, Love, Love. v, The Crew Chiefs, In An Eighteenth-Century Drawing Room, Blue Orchids. v, Bob Carroll; Join The WAC. v, The Crew Chiefs; There Are Yanks. v, Ray McKinley and The Crew Chiefs

(*Note* – despite giving 'BBC Origination' for the Wehrmacht Hour, the programme was not a BBC undertaking, but a production of the US Office of War Information [*see* pages 183–184].)

Glenn Miller and the Army Air Force Band. The Legend

British LP: Dance Band Days DBD 01.

Side 1 – Jeep Jockey Jump; Symphony. v, Johnny Desmond; Rhapsody In Blue; Seven-O-Five; *Medley*: Killarney, I've Got A Heart Filled With Love. v, Bob Carroll and The Crew Chiefs, Moonlight Serenade (concert version), Wabash Blues.

Side 2 – Why Dream. v, Johnny Desmond; Here We Go Again; A Fellow On A Furlough. v, Johnny Desmond; Passage Interdit; Little Brown Jug; Bubble Bath and closing theme (I Sustain The Wings) and announcement by Glenn Miller.

(*Note* – This LP is a mixture of broadcast extracts and transcription recordings.)

Glenn Miller Army Airforce Orchestra Live in 1944 [actually 1944–45]

British LP: Jazz Band Records EB 412.

Side 1 – Radio broadcast 12 February 1944: *Theme*: (I Sustain The Wings); Jeep Jockey Jump; Speak Low. v, Johnny Desmond; Juke Box Saturday Night. v, The Crew Chiefs; With My Head In The Clouds. v, Artie Malvin and The Crew Chiefs; *Theme*: (I Sustain The Wings) and Oh, Lady Be Good (*part only*). Russian Patrol [i.e. Meadowlands or The Red Cavalry March; listed as unknown date 1944, but actually broadcast USA 29 September 1945]. Newscast, New York, 25 December 1944 [NBC] announcing Glenn Miller missing.

Side 2 – Radio broadcast 18 March 1944: *Theme*: (I Sustain The Wings); The Anvil Chorus; A Lovely Way To Spend An Evening. v, Johnny Desmond and The Crew Chiefs; Annie Laurie; There'll Be A Hot Time

In The Town Of Berlin. v, Ray McKinley and The Crew Chiefs; *Theme*: (I Sustain The Wings) and Oh So Good (*part only*). AEF Station Break; She Shall Have Music [wrongly listed as We Shall Have Music]. v, Johnny Desmond. Time Alone Will Tell. v, Gloria Brent; All's Well, Mademoiselle. v, Johnny Desmond and The Crew Chiefs; *Theme*: (Moonlight Serenade). (Last three items from an AEFP broadcast, 7 September 1944.)

The Jazz Club Français Records

While the Band was in Paris from December 1944 to July 1945, some of the jazz musicians made some records for the Jazz Club Français (*see page 237*). After the war these records were issued to the public, first in France and Belgium and in 1948 in Great Britain, all as 78 r.p.m. records. Since that time they have also appeared in various forms on long-playing and extended-play records in Britain and on the Continent.

A total of twenty-five tunes were issued originally by the Jazz Club Français and the band was called 'The Jazz Club Mystery Hot Band'; in Belgium on the Victory label they were called 'The Jazz Club Mystery Jivers'; and in Great Britain on the Esquire label they were called for the first time 'Glenn Miller's Uptown Hall Gang' although the band was not in fact the original 'Uptown Hall' broadcasting band. No exact recording dates are known but from the original master numbers there seem to have been three (or perhaps four) separate recording sessions;

(1) Bernie Privin (*trumpet*), Peanuts Hucko (*clarinet and tenor saxophone*), Mel Powell (*piano*), Joe Shulman (*bass*), Ray McKinley (*drums*), Django Reinhardt (*guitar*) – How High The Moon; If Dreams Come True; Halleluja (or, Beating Those Hallelujah Drums); Stomping At The Savoy.
Same group as above, except that Carmen Mastren (guitar) replaced Django Reinhardt – I Must Have That Man; Please Don't Talk About Me When I'm Gone; S'Wonderful; Someday Sweetheart; Blue Skies.
(2) Bernie Privin (*trumpet*), Peanuts Hucko (*clarinet and tenor saxophone*), Mel Powell (*piano*), Joe Shulman (*bass*), Carmen Mastren (*guitar*), Ray McKinley (*drums*) – Red Light; You're Driving Me Crazy; You're Driving Me Crazy (another take); On The Sunny Side Of the Street.
(3 Mel Powell (*piano solos*) – Homage To Fats Waller; Homage to Debussy; For 'Miss Black'; Don't Blame Me.
Full Personnel – Pennies From Heaven; One, Two, Button Your Shoe; At Sundown; Stealing Apples (or, Stealing Smack's Apples).
Ray McKinley Trio: Peanuts Hucko (*clarinet*), Mel Powell (*piano*), Ray McKinley (*drums*) – Sugar; After You've Gone; Shoemaker's Apron; China Boy.

Over the years these recordings have been issued in various combinations of tunes on 78, EP and LP records. The most complete set, containing twenty-four tunes, was on two French CBS LPs (CBS 63052 and CBS 63130), but these are no longer obtainable. At the time of writing (May 1986) sixteen tunes by

the full personnel and the four Mel Powell solos are available in Great Britain
on the following two Esquire LPs:

'Glenn Miller's Uptown Hall Gang'
British LP: Esquire ESQ 302
Side 1 – How High The Moon; If Dreams Come True; Beating Those
Halleluja Drums; Stomping At The Savoy; I Must Have That Man; Please
Don't Talk About Me When I'm Gone; S'Wonderful; Someday, Sweetheart.
Side 2 – Blue Skies; Red Light; You're Driving Me Crazy; On The Sunny
Side Of The Street; Pennies From Heaven; One, Two, Button Your Shoe; At
Sundown; Stealing Smack's Apples.

'I Love A Piano'
British LP: Esquire ESQ 304
This LP inlcuded the four Mel Powell piano solos recorded in Paris in 1945
(other items on the LP were by a Teddy Wilson Trio and a Mary Lou
Williams Quartet):
Side 2 – Homage To Fats; Homage To Debussy; For Miss Black; Don't
Blame Me.

Compact Discs
Major Glenn Miller and the Army Air Force Band. (RCA **Bluebird**
ND 86360)
1 St Louis Blues March (29 Oct 1943); 2 Peggy The Pin-Up Girl (25
March 1944); 3 Speak Low (12 Feb 1944); 4 Tail End Charlie (5 Feb
1944); 5 Anvil Chorus (18 March 1944); 6 Oh, What A Beautiful Morn-
ing (18 Dec 1943); 7 There Are Yanks (19 Feb 1944); 8 Everybody Loves
My Baby (Autumn 1943); 9 Enlisted Men's Mess (22 Jan 1944); 10 I'll
Be Around (25 Dec 1943); 11 There'll Be A Hot Time In The Town Of
Berlin (22 April 1944); 12 People Will Say We're In Love (Dec 1943); 13
Pearls On Velvet (19 Feb 1944); 14 Poinciana (8 April 1944); 15 It Must
Be Jelly (14 Oct 1943); 16 Jeep Jockey Jump (12 Feb 1944); The Victory
Polka (11 Dec 1943).
(*Note* – This CD was also issued as Volume 1 of a three-CD box set entitled
The Genius of Glenn Miller (RCA Bluebird ND 90572).)
Glenn Miller and the Army Air Force Band. (**French** RCA ND
89767. Black and White Series, Jazz Tribune No 15). (2 CDS)
(*Note* – This CD set contains the same recordings as on Long
Playing Records French RCA Black and White NL 89767 (2) (*see* page
397).)
**Memories of World War II, Featuring the Army Air Force Band
with Johnny Desmond.** (**Compose 9064–2**)
1 These Are The Yank Years [*actually*, There Are Yanks]; 2 The Music
Stopped; 3 Oh, What A Beautiful Morning; 4 Why Dream?; 5 The
Trolley Song; 6 Irresistible You; 7 A Fellow On A Furlough *and* Guns In
The Sky; 8 Along The Santa Fe Trail; 9 I Don't Want To Be Loved; 10
My Heart Tells Me; 11 Speak Low; 12 Long Ago and Far Away; 13 My

Ideal; 14 A Lovely Way To Spend An Evening; 15 The Victory Polka;
16 Suddenly It's Spring; 17 People Will Say We're In Love; 18 I'll Be
Around; 19 What Do They Do In The Infantry?; 20 Johnny Desmond
medley not with the AAF Band: I'll Never Smile Again, Tangerine, At
Last, C'est Si Bon.

(*Note* – no recording dates or places are mentioned in the booklet, but
the recordings are mostly from V-Discs or transcriptions. Major Glenn
Miller is not mentioned in either the booklet or on the record label, but
is heard introducing Johnny Desmond in 'The Music Stopped' and
'Guns In The Sky'.)

Glen Miller and the Army Air Force Orchestra. The Legend. (**Dance Band Days** DBCD 01)

1 Jeep Jockey Jump; 2 Symphony; 3 Rhapsody In Blue; 4 Seven-O-Five;
5 *Medley*: Killarney, I've Got A Heart Filled With Love For You,
Wabash Blues; 6 Everybody Loves My Baby; 7 In The Mood; 8 There'll
Be A Hot Time In The Town Of Berlin; 9 Speak Low; 10 Keep 'Em
Flying; 11 Moonlight Serenade; 12 Why Dream?; 13 Here We Go Again;
14 A Fellow On A Furlough; 15 Passage Interdit; 16 Little Brown Jug;
17 Deep Purple; 18 Juke Box Saturday Night; 19 Now I Know; 20
Bubble Bath and *Closing Theme* ('I Sustain The Wings') and announcement by Glenn Miller.

(*Note* – This CD is an expanded version of Long Playing Record Dance
Band Days DBD 01 [*see* page 412].)

Army Air Forces Overseas Orchestra conducted by Sgt Jerry Gray. Farewell Performances. (**Hindsight** HCD 248)

1 I Sustain The Wings (*opening theme*); 2 Tail End Charlie; 3 In The
Gloaming; 4 Homesick, That's All (v, Johnny Desmond); 5 I Can't Give
You Anything But Love (v, Peanuts Hucko; trumpet solo, Bernie
Privin); 6 Rhapsody In Blue; 7 Tuxedo Junction; 8 Oranges and Lemons
(v, Johnny Desmond and the Crew Chiefs); 9 American Patrol; 10
Swing Low, Sweet Chariot; 11 Sun Valley Jump; 12 Have You Got Any
Gum, Chum? (v, The Crew Chiefs); 13 Autumn Serenade (v, Johnny
Desmond); 14 I Sustain The Wings? (*opening theme*); 15 In The Mood; 16
Stardust; 17–20 *Medley*: My Buddy, In The Middle of May (v, Johnny
Desmond and The Crew Chiefs), Moonlight Serenade, My Blue
Heaven; 21 Symphony (v, Johnny Desmond); 22 The Army Air Corps
Song (v, Johnny Desmond and The Crew Chiefs); 23 Moonlight
Serenade (*closing theme*). (Tracks 1–8 recorded 13 October 1945; Track 9,
October 6 1945; Track 10, 20 October 1945; Tracks 11–13, 3 November
1945; Tracks 14–23, 17 November 1945.) November 17 was the Band's
last broadcast before demobilisation.

Glenn Miller Army Air Force Band Live 1943-44 [**actually** 1943-45]. (**Jazz Band** EBCD 2106-2)

Radio broadcast USA, 9 October 1943; 1 *Theme*: (I Sustain The Wings); 2
Jeep Jockey Jump; 3 All The Things You Are (v, Johnny Desmond); 4

Song Of The Volga Boatmen; 5 With My Head In The Clouds (v, Artie Malvin and The Crew Chiefs); 6 *Closing theme*: (I Sustain The Wings) and Seven-O-Five (*part only*); *Radio broadcast* USA, 12 February 1944; 7 *Theme*: (I Sustain The Wings); 8 Jeep Jockey Jump; 9 Speak Low (v, Johnny Desmond); 10 Juke Box Saturday Night (v, The Crew Chiefs); 11 With My Head In The Clouds (v, Johnny Desmond and The Crew Chiefs); 12 *Theme*: (I Sustain The Wings); 13 Oh, Lady Be Good (*part only*); 14 Russian Patrol [ie, Meadowlands, or The Red Cavalry March; listed as unknown date 1944, but actually broadcast USA 29 September 1945]; 15 Newscast, New York, 25 December 1944 [NBC] announcing Glenn Miller missing. *Radio broadcast* USA, 18 March 1944; 16 *Theme*: (I Sustain The Wings); 17 Anvil Chorus; 18 A Lovely Way To Spend An Evening (v, Johnny Desmond); 19 Annie Laurie; 20 There'll Be A Hot Time In The Town Of Berlin (v, Ray McKinley and The Crew Chiefs); 21 *Theme*: (I Sustain The Wings); 22 Oh, So Good (*part only*); 23 AEF Programme Station Break; 24 She Shall Have Music (v, Johnny Desmond; introduced by Major Glenn Miller and Jack Hylton, from an AEF Programme broadcast, 12 October 1944); 25 Time Alone Will Tell (v, Gloria Brent; introduced by Major Glenn Miller); 26 All's Well, Mademoiselle (v, Johnny Desmond and The Crew Chiefs; introduced by Major Glenn Miller); 27 *Theme*: (Moonlight Serenade) and announcement by Major Glenn Miller. (Tracks 25–27 from an AEF Programme broadcast, 7 September 1944.)

(*Note* – this CD is an expanded version of the LP Jazz Band Records, EB 412 (*see* page 412).)

A Swinging Big Band Christmas. (Laserlight 15 464)
7 Christmas Medley: Silent Night; I'll Be Home For Christmas (v, Johnny Desmond); Jingle Bells (v, The Crew Chiefs); White Christmas. (USA, 1943). (Remaining items by other artists.)

Glen Miller and The Army Air Force Band. Rare Broadcast Performances From 1943–1944. (Laserlight 15 712)
1 Sun Valley Jump; 2 I Got Rhythm; 3 Rhapsody In Blue; 4 My Blue Heaven; 5 Long Ago And Far Away (v, Johnny Desmond); 6 Oh, What A Beautiful Morning (v, Johnny Desmond and The Crew Chiefs); 7 A Tisket A Tasket (v, Marion Hutton); 8 What Do You Do In The Infantry? (v, Artie Malvin and The Crew Chiefs); 9 Solitude; 10 I'll Be Around (v, Johnny Desmond and The Crew Chiefs); 11 Here We Go Again; 12 Jeep Jockey Jump; 13 Over There (v, The Band); 14 Peggy The Pin-Up Girl (v, Ray McKinley and The Crew Chiefs); 15 There'll Be A Hot Time In The Town Of Berlin (v, Ray McKinley and The Crew Chiefs); 16 *Medley*: In The Gloaming, For The First Time (v, Johnny Desmond), Stomping At The Savoy, Deep Purple.

(*Note* – despite the title of the CD, tracks 2, 3, 7 and 9 are by the Glenn Miller civilian band, not the AAF Band.)

Autumn Serenade. The Glenn Miller Service Orchestra in the USA and Europe. Volume II. (**Magic** DAWE 9)

(*Note* – this CD contains the same recordings as on Long Playing Record Magic AWE 9 [*see* page 406]; in the CD listing the date of 'Summertime' is incorrect; it was actually recorded on 6 November 1944.)

American Patrol. Major Glenn Miller's Army Air Force Overseas Orchestra. (**Magic** DAWE 47)

1 *Theme*: (I Sustain The Wings); 2 Flying Home; 3 Long Ago And Far Away (v, Johnny Desmond); 4 *Medley*: Long, Long Ago, Laura (v, Johnny Desmond), Cherokee, Blue Rain; 5 Russian Patrol; 6 *Theme*: (Moonlight Serenade); 7 *Theme*: (I Sustain The Wings); 8 Passage Interdit; 9 The More I See You (v, Johnny Desmond); 10 *Medley*: Danny Boy, I Don't Want To Be Loved (v, Johnny Desmond), Stomping At The Savoy, Deep Purple; 11 American Patrol; 12 '*Swing Shift*' *theme*: (Song And Dance) (v, Ray McKinley); 13 Accentuate The Positive (v, Ray McKinley and The Crew Chiefs); 14 *Theme*: (Moonlight Serenade); 15 *Theme*: (I Sustain The Wings); 16 Tail End Charlie; 17 Symphony (v, Johnny Desmond); 18 *Medley*; In The Gloaming, Homesick (v, Johnny Desmond), I Can't Give You Anything But Love (v, Peanuts Hucko), Rhapsody In Blue; 19 Tuxedo Junction; 20 Oranges And Lemons (v, Johnny Desmond and The Crew Chiefs); 21 *Theme*: (Moonlight Serenade).

(*Note* – No dates are given in the CD listing, but the recordings are from radio broadcasts in the USA in 1945: Tracks 1–6, 29 September; Tracks 7–14, 6 October; Tracks 15–21, 13 October.)

American Patrol. Volume II. Major Glenn Miller's Army Air Forces Overseas Orchestra. (**Magic** DAWE 55)

1 *Theme*: (I Sustain The Wings); 2 Here We Go Again; 3 *Medley*: Going Home, In The Middle Of May (v, Johnny Desmond and The Crew Chiefs), Little Brown Jug, Blue Is The Night; 4 Swing Low Sweet Chariot; 5 The Trolley Song (v, Johnny Desmond and The Crew Chiefs); 6 How Ya Gonna Keep 'Em Down On The Farm? (v, Carmen Mastren and The Crew Chiefs); 7 Seven-O-Five; 8 *Medley*: Flow Gently Sweet Afton, Why Dream? (v, Johnny Desmond), Things Ain't What They Used To Be, A Blues Serenade; 9 Song Of The Volga Boatmen; 10 Poinciana (v, Johnny Desmond and The Crew Chiefs); 11 On, Brave Old Army Team; 12 *Theme*: (Moonlight Serenade); 13 *Theme*: (I Sustain The Wings); 14 In The Mood; 15 Stardust; 16 *Medley*: My Buddy, In The Middle Of May (v, Johnny Desmond and The Crew Chiefs), Moonlight Serenade, My Blue Heaven; 17 The Army Air Corps Song; 18 *Theme*: (Moonlight Serenade.)

(From radio broadcasts USA: Tracks 1–5, 20 October; Track 6, 3 November; Tracks 7–12, 10 November; tracks 13–18, 17 November (the Band's last broadcast).

The Glenn Miller Army Air Force Orchestra. I Sustain The Wings, USA, 1944. (**Magic** DAWE 62)

1 *Theme*: (I Sustain The Wings); 2 I Hear You Screaming; 3 Long Ago And Far Away (v, Johnny Desmond); 4 *Medley*: Schubert's Serenade, Irresistible You (v, Bob Carroll and The Crew Chiefs), Little Brown Jug, Rhapsody In Blue; 5 Peggy The Pin-Up Girl (v, Ray McKinley and The Crew Chiefs); 6 *Theme*: (I Sustain The Wings); 7 American Patrol; 8 Goodnight Wherever You Are (v, Johnny Desmond); 9 *Medley*: All Through The Night, I Love You (v, Johnny Desmond), Take It Easy (v, The Crew Chiefs), Blue Hawaii; 10 Holiday For Strings; 11 *Theme*: (I Sustain The Wings); 12 *Theme*: (I Sustain The Wings); 13 Everybody Loves My Baby; 14 Poinciana (v, Johnny Desmond and The Crew Chiefs); 15 *Medley*: In The Gloaming, A Fellow On A Furlough (v, Johnny Desmond), Stomping At The Savoy, Deep Purple; 16 Join The WAAC (v, The Crew Chiefs); 17 Guns In The Sky (v, Johnny Desmond and The Crew Chiefs); 18 *Theme*: (I Sustain The Wings).

(From radio broadcasts, USA: Tracks 1–5, 25 March 1944; Tracks 6–11, 1 April 1944; Tracks 12–18, 20 May 1944.)

The Glenn Miller Army Air Force Orchestra. I Sustain The Wings, Volume II USA 1943. (**Magic** DAWE 67)

1 *Theme*: (I Sustain The Wings); 2 Here We Go Again; 3 *Medley*: The End Of A Perfect Day, Do You Know (v, Johnny Desmond), Moonlight Sonata, The Blue Room; 4 Star Eyes (v, Johnny Desmond); 5 The Squadron Song (v, Johnny Desmond, The Crew Chiefs and Glee Club); 6 Halleluja; 7 *Medley*: The Old Refrain, Blue Rain (v, Johnny Desmond), Smoke Gets In Your Eyes, Blue Again; 8 *Theme*: (I Sustain The Wings); 9 Sun Valley Jump; 10 How Sweet You Are (v, Johnny Desmond); 11 *Medley*: Silver Threads Among The Gold, Absent Minded (v, Johnny Desmond), String Of Pearls, St Louis Blues; 12 Put Your Arms Around Me Honey (v, The Crew Chiefs); 13 *Theme*: (I Sustain The Wings); 14 *Theme:* (I Sustain The Wings); 15 Snafu Jump; 16 *Medley*: Flow Gently Sweet Afton, Later Tonight (v, Johnny Desmond and The Crew Chiefs), Don't Be That Way, Blue Champagne; 17 Along The Santa Fe Trail (v, Johnny Desmond); 18 Oh, What A Beautiful Morning (v, Johnny Desmond and The Crew Chiefs); 19 *Theme*: (I Sustain The Wings).

(From radio broadcasts, USA: Tracks 1–5, 20 November 1943; Tracks 6–7, 16 October 1943; Tracks 8–13, 27 November 1943; Tracks 14–16, 11 December 1943; Tracks 17–19, 18 December 1943.)

Glenn Miller and his Orchestra Go To War! [*sic*] (**Radiola** CDMR-1160)

(*Note* – this CD contains the same recordings as on Long Playing Record Radiola MR-1160 [*see* page 412].)

II. Glenn Miller. The Essential V-Discs. (Suisa JZCD 302)

1 I've Got A Heart Filled With Love For You Dear (V-Disc 381A); 2

Holiday For Strings (V-Disc 421A); 3 Wang Wang Blues (V-Disc 466A); 4 The Army Air Corps Song (V-Disc 504A); 5 I Hear You Screaming (V-Disc 504A); 6 St Louis Blues [actually, St Louis Blues March] (V-Disc 522A); 7 Peggy The Pin-Up Girl (V-Disc 533A); 8 Songs My Mother Taught Me (V-Disc 533A); 9 Passage Interdit (V-Disc 587A); 10 Why Dream? (V-Disc 587A); 11 Symphony (V-Disc 601A).

(*Note* – for details of Glenn Miller AAF V-Discs, [*see* pages 389–391].)

A small number of performances by the Glenn Miller Army Air Forces Orchestra may be found on other CDs of collections of various artists. All are to be found on the CDs listed above.

C Recordings preserved in the Sound Archives of the BBC

1. American Band of the AEF (Announcements by Major Glenn Miller): *Theme*: 'Moonlight Serenade'; Great Day; Goodnight, Good Neighbour. Sung by RSM George Melachrino accompanied by the full orchestra; String Of Pearls. (This is a recording of the first twelve minutes of a live broadcast from the Queensbury Club on Thursday 5 Oct 1944, at 8.30 p.m. in the Allied Expeditionary Forces Programme.)

2. The American Dance Band – 'The Swing Shift' (Announcements by Ray McKinley): *Theme*: 'The Git Along Song', sung by Ray McKinley, and introductory announcements; Tail End Charlie; Bubble Bath; Embraceable You. Sung by Johnny Desmond, accompanied by the Band.
(This is the first twelve minutes of a programme recorded on 20 April 1945, from the Olympia Theatre in Paris, and first broadcast on Saturday 19 May 1945, at 5.01 p.m. in the Allied Expeditionary Forces Programme.)

3. The Swing Sextet – 'The Uptown Hall' (announcements by Paul Dudley): *Theme*: 'My Guy's Come Back'; Halleluja; Louise; If Dreams Come True played by a quartet consisting of Mel Powell (*piano*), Peanuts Hucko (*clarinet*), Trigger Alpert (*bass*) and Frank Ippolito (*drums*); I'm Through With Love. Sung by Johnny Desmond, accompanied by the Sextet; Night In Tunisia (arranged by Addison Collins, Jr).
(This is a programme recorded from Bedford on 3 Dec 1944, and first broadcast on Thursday 11 Jan 1945, at 9.15 p.m. in the Allied Expeditionary Forces Programme).

4. Strings With Wings (Announcements by Paul Dubov): *Theme*: 'I Sustain The Wings'; The Song Is You; Pavanne (Ravel); Indian Summer. Sung by Johnny Desmond, accompanied by the orchestra; I Love You Truly.
(This is a programme recorded from the Olympia Theatre in Paris on 31 May 1945, and first broadcast on Friday 20 July 1945, at 9.45 p.m. in the Allied Expeditionary Forces Programme.)

Note – These four recordings are strictly for use within the Corporation, but researchers may be able to listen to them (by appointment only) at the National Sound Archives, 29 Exhibition Road, London, SW7.

Index

Arnold, Lt.-Gen. H. H., 47, 217, 257–8.
Atlantic Spotlight, 133, 256.
Attlebridge airfield concert, 124–5.

Bad Neustadt, 249.
Bad Wildungen, 242–4.
Baessell, Norman F., 106, 199, 204, 205–8, 210, 267, 268, 269, 284.
Barker, Major-Gen. R. W., 55, 69–70, 118, 155–6, 175–6, 193–6,
    210–12, 215, 216, 226, 227, 228, 242, 244, 245, 246, 253.
Battle of the Bulge, 209, 210, 211, 213, 214, 220, 272, 280, 281.
Bayreuth, 249, 250.
BBC, 53, 65, 69–70, 167, 212–3, 220–1, 245.
Bedell Smith, Lt.-Gen. W., 55, 173, 174, 248.
Bedford, 62, 63, 65–6, 72, 105, 107–9, 121, 187, 189, 198, 284.
Belfast concert, 122.
Beneke-Miller Orchestra, *see* Miller, Glenn, Orchestra, directed by Tex
    Beneke.
Beneke, Tex, 247, 262.
Bentley Priory concert, 123.
Bergen, Eugene (Gene), 28, 30, 36, 84, 158, 188, 261, 265.
Best, John, 163.
Beverley Sisters, 193.
Bialkin, Morris, 29, 158, 224, 265, 266.
Bluestone, Harry, 48, 256.
Bolling Field, 256.
Boogie Woogie Trio, 79.
Boult, Sir Adrian, 187, 188–9.
Bovingdon airfield, 173, 208, 268, 271, 273.
Boxted airfield concert, 120–1.
Bradley, General Omar N., 242–4, 248.
Breen, Bobby, 246.
Brent, Gloria, 87, 146.
Briggs, Donald, 28.
Brisson, Fred, 248.
British Band of the Allied Expeditionary Force, 131, 218.
British Band of the Supreme Allied Command, 70.
Browne, Sam, 87.
Brynan, Henry, 23, 158, 255, 264.
Burgett, Perry, 18, 23, 27.
Burman, Maurice, 147.
Burtonwood airfield concert, 122.

Caen, Herb, 247.
Camp Herbert Tareyton, 252, 254.
Camp Kilmer, 51.

Camp Prince Albert, 251.

Camp Shanks, 255.

Canadian Band of the Allied Expeditionary Force, 218.

Canadian Band of the Supreme Allied Command, 70.

Cannes, 240, 241.

Canvin, Alderman J., 66, 122.

Carbone, Vince, 99, 261, 264.

Carless, Dorothy, 71, 87, 90, 104, 117.

Carroll, Bob, 27, 41.

Chamonix, 250.

Cheltenham, 121.

Chiltern Hills, 272, 275.

Cirencester, 121.

Cochrane, Tommy, 63.

Cogliano, Phil (Phil Marino), 32, 158, 235, 261, 265.

Collins, Addison Jr. ('Junior' Collins), 33, 41, 80, 261, 264.

Conway, Bill, 216.

Co-Partners Hall, Bedford, 62, 66–7, 87, 160, 197.

Corn Exchange, Bedford, 65–6, 71, 106, 121.

Cornwell, Earl, 158, 261, 265.

Crawford, Broderick, 27, 60, 61, 71, 121, 246.

Crew Chiefs, 41, 79, 262, 264.

Crosby, Bing, 58, 130–3, 167, 168.

Davis, Beryl, 118, 123, 146.

Dean, Basil, 193.

Desmond, Johnny (Johnny Desmond), 37, 41–2, 63, 78, 79, 83–4, 85, 134, 156, 159, 172, 189, 235, 238, 257, 261, 264.

Dingolfing, 249.

Donahue, Sam, 134, 164, 168.

Doolittle, Lt.-Gen. James H., 114–5, 170.

Douglas, Sally, 183.

Down Beat, 247.

Downey, Morton, 185, 201, 211.

Dubov, Paul, 86.

Dudley, Paul, 46, 47, 52–3, 58, 61, 62, 63, 64, 68, 69, 86, 104, 110, 130, 158, 175, 202, 203, 204, 210–11, 218, 221, 227, 228, 231, 233–4, 251, 257, 264, 267, 284–5.

Earlywine, Neal, 205.

Edelson, Milton, 158.

Eighth US Air Force, 100–1, 268–9.

Eisenhower, Gen. Dwight D., 54, 56, 57, 119, 245, 251, 253, 257.

Elmswell (Great Ashfield) airfield concert, 170.

Engelman, Franklin, 56, 74, 87, 141, 252, 253.

Erlangen, 249

ETO (European Theater of Operations (US Army)), 47.

418th Army Air Forces Technical Training Command Band [Miller's],
  see Miller Army Air Forces Band.

Feldman, Victor, 137, 156, 181–2.

Feldman Swing Club, 136–7, 156, 182.

Ferrier, Jack, 99, 265.

Flying Bombs (V-1), 58, 60–4, 68, 123, 171, 176, 185.

Framlingham airfield concert, 127–8.

Frankfurt, 245, 250.

Frankfurt concert, 250, 251.

Freeman, Hank, 18, 99, 260, 265.

Frey, Royal D., 274, 281–3.

Geraldo, 167, 169.

Gentry, Chuck, 18, 50, 265.

GFP (General Forces Programme)(BBC), 56, 88, 93, 168–9, 192, 231,
  238.

Glee Club, 27, 41.

Glenn Miller Day (USA), 247.

Glenn Miller Story, 104, 284.

Goodrich, Brig.-Gen. Donald R., 106, 118, 206, 210.

Gool, Danny, 23, 27.

Gorham, Maurice, 55, 56, 71, 72–3, 91–2, 144–5, 176, 188–9, 190–1,
  194–6, 203, 212, 221, 253.

Gower, Teddy, 64, 162, 195.

Grantham concert, 166.

Gray (Graziano), Jerry, 18, 23, 27, 39, 40, 78, 84, 97, 98,149, 153–4,
  156–8, 171, 201, 203, 212, 218, 220, 227, 229, 231, 232–3, 243, 255,
  261, 262, 263, 264.

Great Ashfield (Elmswell) airfield concert, 170.

Green, Paula, 87, 104, 121, 148.

Grove dance, 122

Guerra, Freddy, 41, 159, 261, 265.

Halesworth airfield concert, 120.

Hall, Larry, 81, 265.

Halliburton, John, 20, 63, 81, 103, 119, 159, 256, 261, 265.

HMV (His Master's Voice), 88, 152–6.

HM Queen Elizabeth, 107–9.

Harding, John, 116, 165, 169, 185, 219, 227.

Hardwick airfield concert, 147.

Harris, Stanley, 28, 29, 35, 158, 188, 215–6, 261, 264.

Harris, Vernon, 148–9.

overseas, 50; flies to Britain, 53; arrival in London, 58; meets Band
at Gourock, 60; meetings at SHAEF, 61, 64, 69; visit to Bedford, 62;
relations with BBC, 74–5; co-composer of 'Git Along Song', 80, and
'My Guy's Come Back', 81–2; meeting with Gorham, 91–2; at
Thurleigh airfield concert, 93–4; meetings at SHAEF, 110; at
Rainbow Corner, 111; at Plaza concert, 111–4; at High
Wycombe, 114–5; at SHAEF (Forward) concert, 118–9; at Boxted
concert, 120–1; at Cirencester concerts and troop hospitals, 121;
Bedford charity concert, 121; in flying 'near-miss', 123; promoted
Major, 123; at Framlingham briefing, 128; composes 'I'm Heading
for California', 128; at Plymouth, 129–30; with Bing Crosby, 131; at
Queensberry Club, 135–6; at Feldman Club, 136–7; memo on pre-
recording, 143; 'Wishing Well' interview and recording, 148–9;
illness, 148; recordings with Dinah Shore, 152–4; relations with
musicians, 159–62; personality, 160, 202; reprimands the
musicians, 160–2; plays dice with musicians, 160; tribute by British
bandleaders, 167–8; interview with Bedell Smith, 174; orders from
Niven, 175; and Jazz Jamboree, 178–82; at Feldman Club, 182;
premonitions, 185–6; programme suggestions, 190–2; flies to Paris to
see Barker, 193; arranges transfer to Paris with Gorham and
Hayes, 195–6; at 'Carnival of Music' concert, 198; last time
conducting Band, 201; thanks Band for pre-recordings, 202;
organises sound truck to take to France, 202; says goodbye to
Gorham, 203; flies from Twinwood Farm to Paris and
disappears, 207; on 8th Air Force casualty report, 215; posted
'Missing', 217; rumours about fate of, 227; court of enquiry into
disappearance, 228; awarded Bronze Star, 229; no clues to fate, 247;
post-war plans, 259–60; disappearance, 266–9; theories as to
fate, 266, 271–2, 273–81; name on Wall Of Missing, 284;
valediction, 285.
Miller, Glenn, Civilian Band, 14, 88.
Miller, Glenn, Orchestra, directed by Tex Beneke, 262–3.
Miller, Helen, 211, 216–7, 229, 255.
Miller, Herb, 204.
Miller, Jimmy, 87, 106.
Milton Ernest Hall, 71, 106, 205, 206.
Modernaires, 133, 134.
Morden, Paul, 203, 226, 229.
Morgan, John R. S., 200, 205–7, 210, 268, 270, 277–80, 281, 284.
Morning After, 86, 191, 238.
Motylinski, Dick, 28, 30, 158, 261, 264.
Mount Farm concert, 166.
Music For The Wehrmacht, 184, 189.

Newbury concert, 110.